THEORY AND PRACTICE OF
GROUP COUNSELING

T H I R D   E D I T I O N

Other books by Gerald Corey:

- *I Never Knew I Had a Choice,* 4th Edition (1990, with Marianne Schneider Corey)
- *Becoming a Helper* (1989, with Marianne Schneider Corey)
- *Group Techniques,* Revised Edition (1988, with Marianne Schneider Corey, Patrick Callanan, and J. Michael Russell)
- *Issues and Ethics in the Helping Professions,* 3rd Edition (1988, with Marianne Schneider Corey and Patrick Callanan)
- *Groups: Process and Practice,* 3rd Edition (1987, with Marianne Schneider Corey)
- *Case Approach to Counseling and Psychotherapy,* 2nd Edition (1986)
- *Theory and Practice of Counseling and Psychotherapy,* 3rd Edition (and *Manual*) (1986)
- *Casebook of Ethical Guidelines for Group Leaders* (1982, with Marianne Schneider Corey and Patrick Callanan)

THEORY AND PRACTICE OF
GROUP COUNSELING

T H I R D   E D I T I O N

Gerald Corey

California State University, Fullerton

*Diplomate in Counseling Psychology,
American Board of Professional Psychology*

Brooks/Cole Publishing Company
Pacific Grove, California

Brooks/Cole Publishing Company
A Division of Wadsworth, Inc.

Printed in the United States of America

10   9   8   7   6

Library of Congress Cataloging-in-Publication Data

Corey, Gerald.
    Theory and practice of group counseling.

    Bibliography: p.
    Includes indexes.
    1. Group counseling.   2. Small groups.   I. Title.
BF637.C6C576   1989   616.89'152   89-7123
ISBN 0-534-10284-0

Sponsoring Editor: *Claire Verduin*
Editorial Assistant: *Gay C. Bond*
Production Editor: *Fiorella Ljunggren*
Production Assistant: *Dorothy Bell*
Manuscript Editor: *William Waller*
Permissions Editor: *Carline Haga*
Interior and Cover Design: *Kelly Shoemaker*
Typesetting: *Kachina Typesetting, Inc.*
Cover Printing: *Phoenix Color Corporation*
Printing and Binding: *The Maple-Vail Book Manufacturing Group*

To the special groups in my life:

- *my family*
- *my friends*
- *my professional colleagues*
- *the human-services students*
- *the members of our weeklong residential groups*
- *the people at Brooks/Cole who work on our books*

GERALD COREY, Professor and Coordinator of the Human Services Program at California State University at Fullerton and a licensed psychologist, received his doctorate in counseling psychology from the University of Southern California. He is a Diplomate in Counseling Psychology, American Board of Professional Psychology; is registered as a National Health Service Provider in Psychology; is a National Certified Counselor; and is a licensed marriage, family, and child counselor. He is a Fellow of the American Psychological Association (Counseling Psychology).

In addition to coordinating an undergraduate program in human services, each semester Jerry teaches both undergraduate and graduate courses in group counseling, as well as courses in experiential groups, the theory and practice of counseling, and professional ethics. With his colleagues he has conducted workshops in the United States, Germany, Belgium, Mexico, and China, with a special focus on training in group counseling. He often presents workshops for professional organizations and at various universities. Along with his wife, Marianne Schneider Corey, and other colleagues, Jerry offers weeklong residential personal-growth groups and residential training and supervision workshops each summer in Idyllwild, California.

Preface

Group counseling is an increasingly popular form of therapeutic intervention in a variety of settings. Although many textbooks deal with groups, very few of them present an overview of various theoretical models and describe how these models apply to group counseling. This book outlines the basic elements of group process, deals with ethical and professional issues special to group work, and presents an overview of the key concepts and techniques of ten approaches to group counseling. The book also attempts an integration of these approaches and encourages students to develop a framework that leads to their own synthesis.

Theory and Practice of Group Counseling is written in a clear and simple style, so that students will have no difficulty understanding the theoretical concepts and their relationship to group practice. The book focuses on the *practical applications* of the theoretical models to group work. This updated and considerably expanded third edition devotes more space to helping readers develop their own syntheses of various aspects of these approaches. It also has two detailed chapters on the stages of a group's development, providing a guide for group leaders in the practice of counseling.

Part I presents an overview of the various types of groups and discusses some general principles that can be applied in working with the reality of cultural diversity in groups. It also covers ethical and professional issues in group work; the stages in the evolution of a group, from its formation to its termination and follow-up; and some basic issues in group membership and group leadership. In this third edition, Part I has the following new elements:

- increased coverage of structured groups
- increased coverage of self-help groups and a comparison between self-help groups and therapy groups
- general principles that group leaders can apply in working with ethnic and minority clients and guidelines for building a sense of multi-cultural awareness into one's group practice
- updated coverage of ethical and legal issues for group practitioners
- practical guidelines for developing an ethical and professional orientation to group work
- a critique of the gap between research and practice in group work and a discussion of ways in which group workers can combine the two
- a summary and discussion of research findings that are helpful in designing and conducting groups
- increased coverage of the therapeutic factors in a group

Part II examines ten theoretical approaches to group counseling. Here the chapters follow a common organizational pattern, so that students can easily compare and contrast the various models. A typical chapter introduces the rationale for the model and its unique characteristics; discusses the model's key concepts and their implications for group process, as well as the model's basic procedures and techniques; defines the role and functions of the group leader; and, when applicable, describes the stages of development of that particular group process. The models' implications for working in a multicultural society are stressed throughout: both the strengths and the limitations of each approach are reviewed in terms of working with ethnic and minority clients in groups. The necessity for flexibility and a willingness to adapt techniques to fit the client's cultural background is emphasized in each chapter. Near the end of each of these theory chapters is an updated and expanded evaluation section, which is primarily devoted to my personal assessment of the approach under discussion. When relevant, however, I have balanced my personal critique with commentaries from other sources. End-of-chapter material also contains recommendations for where to look for further training in each of the theoretical approaches; Questions for Reflection and Discussion, which help students review basic issues; and updated annotated lists of reading suggestions and extensive references to encourage students to expand on the material and broaden their learning through further reading. Some of the theory chapters have been largely rewritten to reflect recent trends; others have only minor revisions. Some of the changes are as follows:

- Coverage of psychoanalytic groups has been expanded to include contemporary trends such as object-relations theory, working with borderline and narcissistic clients, integration of the psychosocial and the psychosexual phases of development, and the role of anxiety and ego-defense mechanisms.

- The chapter on Adlerian group counseling has been largely rewritten and includes more material on lifestyle assessment and more on practical applications of Adlerian concepts to group work.
- The key concepts of psychodrama are discussed more fully, and there are suggestions on how to facilitate a psychodrama at various phases.
- The chapter on the existential approach to groups has been restructured and tightened.
- There is much new material on the person-centered approach to group work, with more emphasis on its historical development and applications. There is also increased coverage of research efforts, the significant contributions of Carl Rogers, and the core therapeutic conditions for growth as applied to groups.
- The chapters on Gestalt therapy and transactional analysis have been updated.
- There is more extensive coverage of behavioral group therapy, including added attention to the stages of behavioral groups; the need for assessment as a basic part of the group process; social-skills and assertiveness-training groups; stress-management training; multimodal group therapy; and research findings.
- The material on rational-emotive therapy in groups has been expanded, especially with regard to therapeutic techniques and procedures.
- The chapter on reality therapy in groups has been largely rewritten to convey some of the major changes in control theory and implications for practice as applied to groups. There is new coverage on special procedures such as the use of paradoxical techniques, the use of humor, and skillful questioning.

In the two chapters in Part III, I have applied the ten models to a group in action in order to illustrate how practitioners of different orientations would view a particular group and how they might deal with certain typical themes that emerge in groups. The aim of these illustrative samples is to make the theoretical perspectives come alive and provide some flavor of the differences and similarities among the approaches. The final chapter compares and contrasts the various group approaches with respect to the goals of group counseling, the role and functions of the group leader, the degree of structuring and division of responsibility in groups, the use of techniques, and the contributions and limitations of the various approaches to group work in a multicultural society. The chapter concludes with a description of an "integrated eclectic model of group counseling," which combines concepts and techniques from all the approaches that have been examined and which should help students attempt their own personal integration. My purpose is to show what aspects of each theory I draw on at the various stages of the group, as well as to offer a basis for blending what may look like diverse approaches to the practice of group work. In this third edition I have expanded the coverage of my own integrated perspective and have provided guidelines for developing one's own synthesis. I recommend that students read Chapters 16 and 17 early in the course, because they provide a useful overview and synthesis. Of course, these two chapters will also be most helpful as integrating tools after readers have studied the contemporary approaches in Part II.

This book is for graduate and undergraduate students in any field involving human service. It is especially suitable for students enrolled in any of the courses under the general designation of Theory and Practice of Group Counseling. The book is also for practitioners who are involved in group work or who are training paraprofessionals to lead various types of groups. Those who may find this book useful are psychiatric nurses, ministers, social workers, psychologists, marriage and family counselors, rehabilitation counselors, community-agency counselors, school counselors, and mental-health professionals who lead groups as a part of their work.

A third edition of *Manual for Theory and Practice of Group Counseling* is available to help students gain maximum benefit from this book and actually experience group process and group techniques. The manual includes questions, suggested activities for the whole class and for small groups, ideas for supervised training groups, summary charts, self-inventories, study guides, group techniques, examples of cases with open-ended alternatives for group-counseling practice, and a comprehensive test on the textbook for review purposes. The manual has also been updated and includes new supplementary materials for the ten theories. Also available is an *Instructor's Resource Manual,* which has been revised to reflect the changes in both the textbook and the student manual.

Acknowledgments

Many of the revisions in this textbook since its original edition in 1981 have come about after discussions with students, colleagues, and professors who use this book. Those students and professionals whom I teach continue to teach me in return, and most of my ideas are stimulated by interactions with them. The supportive challenge of my friends and colleagues (with whom I offer classes and workshops and with whom I co-lead groups) continues to keep my learning fresh and provides me with encouragement to continue practicing, teaching, and writing. These people are J. Michael Russell of California State University at Fullerton; Patrick Callanan, in private practice in Santa Ana, California; Mary Moline of Loma Linda University; Helga Kennedy, in private practice in Auburn, California; and George Williams of California State University at Fullerton. I especially want to recognize the influence on my life and my books of my wife and colleague, Marianne Schneider Corey, with whom I regularly work professionally. Her critiques have been especially valuable in preparing these revisions, and many of the ideas in the book are the product of our many hours of discussions about the practice of group work.

The comments of those who provided reviews have been most helpful in shaping the final product. Those who reviewed the entire manuscript and offered both supportive and critical feedback are Marguerite Carroll, University of Southern Maine; Margaret Cooney, California State University, San Bernardino; Lee Gillis, Georgia College; Barbara Herlihy, University of Houston, Clear Lake; Michael Safko, a Human Services major at California State University, Fullerton, and an undergraduate student reviewer; James V. Wigtil, Ohio State University; and JoAnne Wigtil, a Ph.D. student in Family Relations and Human Development at Ohio State University. The prerevision reviewers, who read and sent evaluations of the prior edition, are Dennis B. Anderson, Southern Illinois University; Mary Ballou, Northeastern University; Arleen C. Lewis, University of Arkansas, Fayetteville; and Carol F. Sisson, Oregon State University and Western Oregon State College.

I value the detailed commentaries I received from reviewers of single chapters. Many people contributed by sharing their expertise in certain areas, and I am very grateful for their assistance. They are:

- Noreen Mokuau, University of Hawaii, and Paul Pedersen, Syracuse University, in the area of multicultural implications for group work
- Chapter 6, psychoanalytic: William Blau, Patton State Hospital, Patton, California; and J. Michael Russell, California State University, Fullerton
- Chapter 7, Adlerian: James Bitter, California State University, Fullerton; Don Dinkmeyer, Communication and Motivation Training Institute, Inc., Coral Springs, Florida; and Monford Sonstegard, California State University, Fullerton
- Chapter 8, psychodrama: Leon Fine, clinical psychologist (and psychodramatist) in private practice in Portland, Oregon
- Chapter 9, existential: James L. Jarrett, University of California, Berkeley; and J. Michael Russell
- Chapter 10, person-centered: David J. Cain, Editor of the *Person-Centered Review*
- Chapter 11, Gestalt therapy: Irma Shepherd, Georgia State University
- Chapter 12, transactional analysis: Joan Fleming, graduate assistant at Youngstown State University
- Chapter 13, behavior therapy: Sheldon Rose, University of Wisconsin–Madison
- Chapter 14, rational-emotive therapy: Albert Ellis, Executive Director of the Institute for Rational-Emotive Therapy, New York
- Chapter 15, reality therapy: Robert E. Wubbolding, Director of the Center for Reality Therapy in Cincinnati
- Chapter 16, case examples of a group in action: Christopher Faiver, Youngstown State University

I appreciate the careful job that Joanna Quintrell did in preparing the indexes. I also want to thank Debbie DeBue, who provided clerical assistance in typing, organizing bibliographies, and performing the many technical tasks necessary to produce a final draft.

This book is the result of a team effort, which includes the combined talents of several people in the Brooks/Cole family. I appreciate the opportunity to work with Claire Verduin, managing editor and psychology editor; with Fiorella Ljunggren, production services manager; and with William Waller, manuscript editor, who gives careful attention to making sure that our books are concise and readable. Their efforts, dedication, and extra time certainly have contributed to the quality of this book. With the professional assistance of these people, the ongoing task of revising this book continues to bring more joy than pain.

Gerald Corey

Contents

P A R T   III

APPLICATION AND INTEGRATION   483

17   *Comparisons, Contrasts, and Integration*   *514*

P A R T

I

BASIC ELEMENTS OF GROUP PROCESS: AN OVERVIEW

1

Introduction

My colleagues and I, as we conduct workshops around the United States, are finding a resurgence of interest in group work. Professional counselors are creating an increasing variety of groups to fit the special needs of a diverse clientele. In fact, the types of groups that can be designed are limited only by one's imagination. This expanded interest underscores the need for broad education and training in both the theory and the practice of group counseling. This book attempts to provide you with a fundamental base of knowledge that you can apply to the many kinds of groups you will be leading.

Groups can be utilized for therapeutic or educational purposes or a combination of the two. Some groups deal primarily with helping people make fundamental changes in their ways of feeling, thinking, and behaving. Other groups, with an educational focus, teach members specific coping skills. This chapter provides a brief overview of some of the types of groups and the differences among them.

You will be expected in the human-services field to be prepared to use group approaches in working with a variety of clients for a variety of purposes. In a state mental hospital, for example, you may be asked to design and lead groups for different kinds of patients, for those who are about to leave the hospital and be reintegrated into the community, or for the patients' families. Groups commonly found in mental hospitals include insight groups, remotivation groups, assertion-training groups, and recreational/vocational-therapy groups. The theoretical approach may be reality therapy or one of the many forms of behavior modification done in a group setting.

3

If you work in a community mental-health center, a college counseling center, or a day-treatment clinic, you will be expected to provide therapeutic services in a wide range of group settings. A sample of groups commonly offered in these community facilities includes consciousness-raising groups for women or men, groups for alcoholics and for adult children of alcoholics, groups for adolescents with a drug habit, crisis-oriented groups for people in some immediate difficulty, groups for senior citizens, groups for people with eating disorders, and groups for parents who are trying to communicate more effectively with their children.

The school is the setting for special groups designed to deal with students' educational, vocational, personal, or social problems. If you work in a school, you may be asked to form a test-anxiety-reduction group, a career-exploration group, a group aimed at teaching interpersonal skills, or some type of self-awareness or personal-growth group.

In sum, for almost any need you can think of, a group approach has been designed to help people meet that need. One of the main reasons for the popularity of the group as a primary therapeutic tool in many agencies and institutions is that it is frequently more effective than the individual approach. This effectiveness stems from the fact that group members can practice their new skills both within the group and in their everyday interactions outside of it. There are practical considerations, too, such as lower cost and broader distribution of the available counselors and therapists.

One problem, however, is that even practitioners with an advanced degree in one of the helping professions often have had very little exposure to the theory and techniques of group work. Many of these professionals find themselves thrust into the role of group leader without adequate preparation and training. It is not surprising that some of them panic and don't know where to begin. Although this book is not intended as an exclusive means of preparing competent group leaders, it is aimed at providing some preparation for coping with the demands of group leadership.

About This Book

Theory and Practice of Group Counseling will introduce you to some basic issues of group leadership and group membership, and it will show you how groups function. The text is also designed to provide you with a good overview of a variety of theoretical models underlying group counseling, so that you can see the connection between theory and practice. The ten chapters that describe these models have a common format, which should enable you to make comparisons among the various approaches.

From this text you will learn only some of the essentials of the therapies explored. The book is *not* designed to make you an expert in any one group approach. Its aim is to provide you with an understanding of some of the significant commonalities and differences among these theoretical models. My hope is that you will become sufficiently motivated to select some approaches and learn more about them by doing additional reading (there are suggestions after each chapter) and by actually experiencing some of these group approaches as a participant. The ultimate goal is for you to develop a sufficient basis to be able to achieve your own theoretical perspective and personal style of group leadership.

This is basically a survey book. Instead of merely focusing on the theoretical aspects of the models selected, the book presents key concepts and deals with how these concepts are applied to group work. The goals of group process, the role and functions of the group leader, and specific techniques and procedures applicable to the group in action are some of the areas of focus. In brief, the book aims at a synthesis between theory and practice and at a balanced view of how group leaders can draw on various theoretical models in their actual practice of group work.

The remainder of Part I treats the basic elements of group process and practice that you'll need to know regardless of the types of groups you may lead or the theoretical orientation you may hold. In Chapter 2 you are introduced to important *ethical and professional issues* that you will inevitably encounter as you lead groups. The emphasis is on the rights of group members and the responsibilities of group leaders. Chapter 3 deals with basic concerns of *group leadership,* such as the personal characteristics of effective leaders, the problems they face, the different styles of group leadership, and the range of specific skills required for effective leading. In Chapters 4 and 5 you are introduced to the major developmental tasks confronting a group as it goes through its various *stages,* from its formation to its termination, evaluation, and follow-up. The central characteristics of the stages that make up the life history of a group are examined, with special attention paid to the major functions of the group leader at each stage. These chapters also focus on the functions of the members of a group and the possible problems that are associated with each stage in the group's evolution.

Part II offers my overview of ten major theoretical approaches to group counseling. These models have been selected to present a balanced perspective of the theories that underlie group practice. More specifically, the *psychoanalytic* model was selected because it is the theory from which most other approaches have developed. Even though you may find some of the psychoanalytic techniques limited, you can still draw on psychoanalytic concepts in your work. The *Adlerian* approach to groups is included because there appears to be a resurgence of interest in Adlerian concepts and procedures in group counseling. The inclusion of *psychodrama* is based on my belief that the action-oriented methods of role playing can be integrated into most forms of group work. The relationship-oriented therapies—which include the *existential* approach, the *person-centered* approach, and the *Gestalt* approach—are important because they stress the experiencing of feelings and interpersonal relationships in group practice. *Transactional analysis* is included because it provides a cognitive structure for group work and can be integrated into a variety of other group approaches. The behavioral-cognitive therapies—*behavior therapy, rational-emotive therapy,* and *reality therapy*—stress action methods and behavior change and have been selected to present the cognitive and behavioral methods of group work.

To provide a framework that will help you integrate the theoretical models, these ten chapters follow a common outline. They present the key concepts of each theory and their implications for group practice; outline the role and functions of the group leader according to the particular theory; discuss how each theory is applied to group practice, including working with family groups; and describe the major techniques employed under each theory. Illustrative examples make the use of these techniques more concrete. Each chapter contains my evaluation of the approach under discussion—an evaluation based on what I consider to be its major strengths and weaknesses—and a brief description of how I incorporate aspects of that approach into my own style of group leadership. Near the end of these chapters are questions for reflection and discussion. Throughout the book I encourage you to look for ways of selectively borrowing from each approach, so that you'll be able to develop a personal style of group leadership that fits the person you are.

Part III focuses on the practical application of the theories and principles covered in Parts I and II. To make such applications more vivid and concrete, Chapter 16 follows a group in action and discusses how the various therapeutic approaches apply to the case. In this way you'll get some idea of how practitioners with differing orientations work with the same group and with the same themes. This comparative view will also demonstrate some of the techniques of group leadership in action. Chapter 17 is designed to help you pull together the various methods and approaches and look for commonalities and differences among them. This chapter also presents my own eclectic approach, which integrates concepts and techniques from the various theories.

I invite you to keep an open mind, yet to read critically. By being an active learner and by raising questions, you'll gain the necessary foundation for becoming an effective group leader. A *Manual for Theory and Practice of Group Counseling* has been designed as a supplement to the textbook, so that you can actually experience the techniques that you are studying. Your active involvement in the manual's exercises and activities will make what you read in this textbook come alive for you.

Overview of the Counseling Group

This book focuses on *counseling* groups. There are other types of therapeutic groups, and most of them share some of the goals, procedures, techniques, and processes of counseling groups. They differ, however, with respect to specific aims, the role of the leader, the kind of people in the group, and the emphasis given to issues such as prevention, remediation, treatment, and development. To make these similarities and differences clear, the discussion of group counseling in this section is followed by brief descriptions of group psychotherapy, structured groups, and self-help groups.

Group counseling has preventive as well as remedial aims. Generally, the counseling group has a specific focus, which may be educational, vocational, social, or personal. The group involves an interpersonal process that stresses conscious thoughts, feelings, and behavior. Often counseling groups are problem oriented; their content and focus are determined largely by the members, who are basically well-functioning individuals who don't require extensive personality reconstruction and whose concerns relate to the developmental tasks of the life span. Group counseling tends to be growth oriented in that its focus is on discovering internal resources of strength. The participants may be facing situational crises and temporary conflicts, or they may be trying to change self-defeating behaviors. The group provides the empathy and support necessary to create the atmosphere of trust that leads to the sharing and exploration of these concerns. Group counseling is often carried out in institutional settings, such as schools, university counseling centers, community mental-health clinics, and other human-services agencies.

The group counselor uses verbal and nonverbal techniques as well as structured exercises. Common techniques include reflection (mirroring the verbal and nonverbal messages of a group member), clarification (helping members understand more clearly what they are saying or feeling), role playing, and interpretation (connecting present behaviors with past decisions). Other common techniques used in group counseling are described in more detail in Chapter 3. Basically, the role of the group counselor is to facilitate interaction among the members, help them learn from one another, assist them in establishing personal goals, and encourage them to translate their insights into concrete plans that involve taking action outside of the group. Counselors perform this role largely by teaching the members to focus on the here and now and to identify the concerns they wish to explore in the group.

Goals

Ideally, the members decide for themselves the specific goals of the group experience. Some of the general goals shared by members of counseling groups are these:

- to learn to trust oneself and others
- to achieve self-knowledge and the development of a unique sense of identity
- to recognize the commonality of the participants' needs and problems and to develop a sense of universality
- to increase self-acceptance, self-confidence, and self-respect in order to achieve a new view of oneself
- to find alternative ways of dealing with normal developmental issues and of resolving certain conflicts

- to increase self-direction, autonomy, and responsibility toward oneself and others
- to become aware of one's choices and to make choices wisely
- to make specific plans for changing certain behaviors and to commit oneself to follow through with these plans
- to learn more effective social skills
- to become more sensitive to the needs and feelings of others
- to learn how to confront others with care, concern, honesty, and directness
- to move away from merely meeting others' expectations and to learn to live by one's own expectations
- to clarify one's values and decide whether and how to modify them

Advantages

There are a number of advantages to group counseling as a vehicle for helping people make changes in their attitudes, beliefs about themselves and others, feelings, and behaviors. One advantage is that participants can explore their styles of relating with others and learn more effective social skills. Another is that members can discuss their perceptions of one another and receive valuable feedback on how they are being perceived in the group.

In many ways the counseling group provides a re-creation of the participants' everyday world, especially if the membership is diverse with respect to age, interest, background, socioeconomic status, and type of problem. As a microcosm of society the group provides a sample of reality, for members' struggles and conflicts in the group are no different from those they experience outside of it. The diversity that characterizes most groups also results in unusually rich feedback for the participants, who can see themselves through the eyes of a wide range of people.

The group offers understanding and support, which foster the members' willingness to explore the problems they have brought with them to the group. The participants achieve a sense of belonging, and through the cohesion that develops they learn ways of being intimate, of caring, and of challenging. In this supportive atmosphere members can experiment with alternative behaviors. They can practice these behaviors in the group, where they receive encouragement as well as suggestions on how to apply what they are learning in the outside world.

Ultimately, it is up to the members themselves to decide what changes they want to make. They can compare the perceptions they have of themselves with the perceptions others have of them and then decide what to do with this information. In essence, the members get a clearer glimpse of the kind of person they would like to become, and they come to understand what is preventing them from becoming that person.

Value for Special Populations

Group counseling can be designed to meet the needs of special populations such as children, adolescents, college students, or the elderly. Special counseling groups with these and other populations are described in the book *Groups: Process and Practice* (M. Corey & Corey, 1987), which offers suggestions on how to set up these groups and on what techniques to use for dealing with the unique problems of each of them. Here I'd like to discuss in brief the value of counseling groups for these special populations.

Counseling Groups for Children. Counseling groups for children can serve preventive or remedial purposes. In schools, group counseling is often suggested for children who display behaviors or attributes such as excessive fighting, inability to get along with peers, violent outbursts, chronic tiredness, lack of supervision at home, and neglected appearance. Small groups can provide children with the opportunity to express their feelings about these and related problems. Identifying children who are developing serious emotional and behavioral problems is extremely important. If these children can receive psychological assistance at an early age, they stand a better chance of coping effectively with the developmental tasks they must face later in life.

Counseling Groups for Adolescents. The adolescent years can be extremely lonely ones, and it is not unusual for an adolescent to feel that there is no one there to help. Adolescence is also a time of deep concerns and key decisions that can affect the course of one's life. Dependence/independence struggles, acceptance/rejection conflicts, identity crises, the search for security, pressures to conform, and the need for approval are all part of this period. Many adolescents are pressured to perform and succeed, and they frequently experience severe stress in meeting these external expectations.

Group counseling is especially suited for adolescents because it gives them a place to express conflicting feelings, explore self-doubts, and come to the realization that they share these concerns with their peers. A group allows adolescents to openly question their values and to modify those that need to be changed. In the group, adolescents can learn to communicate with their peers, can benefit from the modeling provided by the leader, and can safely experiment with reality and test their limits. Another, unique value of group counseling for adolescents is that it offers them a chance to be instrumental in one another's growth. Because of the opportunities for interaction available in the group situation, the participants can express their concerns and be heard, and they can help one another on the road toward self-understanding and self-acceptance.

Counseling Groups for College Students. Counseling groups are a valuable vehicle for meeting the developmental needs of the many students who feel that their college or university is preoccupied with their intellectual development to the exclusion of their emotional and social growth. It was during the years I spent working in the counseling centers at two universities that I became aware of the need for groups on campus. At those universities the existing groups were designed for the relatively healthy students who were experiencing developmental crises. The main purpose of these groups was to offer the participants an opportunity for growth and a situation in which they could deal with issues concerning career decisions, male/female relationships, identity problems, educational plans, isolation feelings on an impersonal campus, and other concerns related to becoming an autonomous person.

Many university and college counseling centers now offer a wide range of structured groups to meet the diverse needs of the students, a few of which are assertion groups, consciousness-raising groups for women and men, groups for minorities, groups for the physically handicapped, stress-reduction groups, groups for middle-aged returning students who are considering career and lifestyle changes, and test-anxiety-reduction groups. These structured groups will be examined briefly in the next section.

Counseling Groups for the Elderly.   Counseling groups can be valuable for the elderly in many of the same ways that they are of value to adolescents. As people grow older, they often experience isolation, and many of them, seeing no hope of meaning—let alone excitement—in their future, may resign themselves to a useless life. Like adolescents, the elderly often feel unproductive, unneeded, and unwanted by society. Another problem is that many older people accept myths about aging, which then become self-fulfilling prophecies. An example is the misconception that old people can't change or that once they retire, they will be doomed to depression. Counseling groups can do a lot to help older people challenge these myths and deal with the developmental tasks that they, like any other age group, must face in such a way that they can retain their integrity and self-respect. The group situation can assist people in breaking out of their isolation and offer the elderly the encouragement necessary to seek for and find meaning in their lives so that they can live fully and not merely exist.

Other Types of Groups

Group Psychotherapy

A major difference between group *therapy* and group *counseling* lies in their goals. Whereas counseling groups focus on growth, development, enhancement, prevention, self-awareness, and releasing blocks to growth, therapy groups typically focus on remediation, treatment, and personality reconstruction. Group psychotherapy is a process of reeducation that includes both conscious and unconscious awareness and both the present and the past. Some therapy groups are primarily designed to correct emotional and behavioral disorders that impede one's functioning. The goal may be a minor or a major transformation of personality structure, depending on the theoretical orientation of the group therapist. Because of this goal, therapy groups tend to be of relatively long duration. The people who make up the group may be suffering from severe emotional problems, deep neurotic conflicts, or psychotic states, and some may exhibit socially deviant behavior. Therefore, many of these individuals are in need of remedial treatment rather than developmental and preventive work. In general, the goal of a therapy group is the achievement of interpersonal and intrapsychic adequacy (Shapiro, 1978).

Group therapists are typically clinical or counseling psychologists, psychiatrists, and clinical social workers. They use a wide range of verbal modalities (which group counselors also use), and some employ techniques to induce regression to earlier experiences, to tap unconscious dynamics, and to help members reexperience traumatic situations so that catharsis can occur. As these experiences are relived in the group, members become aware of and gain insight into past decisions that interfere with current functioning. The group therapist assists members in developing a corrective emotional experience and in making new decisions about the world, others, and themselves. Working through unfinished business from the past that has roots in the unconscious is a primary characteristic of group therapy. This focus on past material, unconscious dynamics, personality reconstruction, and development of new patterns of behavior based on insight also accounts for the longer duration of group therapy.

Group psychotherapy, like group counseling, may be based on one of several therapeutic models. Many therapy groups employ psychoanalytic concepts and procedures, such as working with dreams, focusing on past experiences, trying to uncover the unconscious, and symbolically reliving unfinished significant relationships. Others—for example, behavior-therapy groups and rational-emotive-therapy groups—use techniques aimed at cognitive and behavioral changes. Many therapy groups are characterized by an eclectic approach; that is, concepts and techniques from several theoretical perspectives are incorporated into the practice of the group.

Structured Groups

Structured groups, or groups characterized by some central theme, seem to be gaining in popularity. When my colleagues and I conduct group-process workshops, the practitioners we meet are often very creative in designing short-term groups that deal with a specific theme or particular population. These group workers perceive needs in the community and address these needs by creating groups. Such groups serve a number of purposes: imparting information, sharing common experiences, teaching people how to solve problems, offering support, and helping people learn how to create their own support systems outside of the group setting. Consider just a few examples:

• S. R. Rose (1987) describes a time-limited, structured, small-group treatment program aimed at promoting the social competence of youngsters in middle childhood. This kind of peer group has been found to appeal to children, and it is a natural place for training them in social skills, because it provides opportunities for them to demonstrate and teach as well as observe and learn.

• McWhirter and Liebman (1988) designed an anger-control group to help Vietnam veterans suffering from posttraumatic stress. The six-session program lasts 3 weeks. The authors employ behavioral approaches such as cognitive preparation, skill acquisition and rehearsal, and application and practice. They suggest that this type of structured group has applications for other populations. The anger program has been used with nonpsychotic general psychiatric inpatients.

• Lee (1987) describes a structured group experience promoting the development of manhood identity among Black, male adolescents in grades 7–12. The model represents an innovative approach to group work that aims at increasing awareness and promoting skills associated with a positive Black masculine identity. It is designed to strengthen the body, mind, and soul. This strengthening is accomplished by assisting the members to understand and appreciate the role of the Black man in history, developing their motivation to achieve, fostering positive behavior, and providing positive role models of Black men. The group is led by a skilled counselor.

• Decker and Hall (1987) designed a four-session structured group for college freshmen who are academic underachievers. The total program lasts 10 hours. According to the authors, it has also been used successfully for training graduate students in group leadership. Since its inception in 1983, more than 100 underachieving freshmen have volunteered to participate, and 36 graduate students have received supervision and training in co-leading these groups.

• Gillis and Bonney (1986) present a rationale for using adventurous activities in group counseling. They describe the therapeutic use of structured activities that include arts, crafts, dance, drama, music, writing, storytelling, running, exercise, physical challenge, and board games. They maintain that an advantage of using a physically challenging activity is that several therapeutic issues can be dealt with at once. For example, a single physical activity can simultaneously provide the group with issues such as mastery, empowerment, challenge, cooperativeness, competitiveness, trust, and success or failure.

On a recent trip to Hong Kong I found that structured groups were being used in community mental-health agencies, technical institutes, community colleges, and private colleges and universities. The counselors I spoke with said that the people they were working with favored a short-term, structured, education-oriented group experience. These counselors have more difficulty organizing unstructured groups, with a loosely defined agenda aimed at "personal growth," than they do groups that provide specific help in a specific area of concern. Some of these problem areas are learning interpersonal skills, coping with stress, preparing for job interviews, and learning effective methods of study.

It is clear that structured groups—as opposed to counseling groups or ongoing personal-growth groups—are finding a place in many settings. They appear to be increasingly used in community agencies and in schools. Many college and university counseling centers offer a variety of special groups for particular populations in addition to their unstructured personal-growth groups and counseling groups. For example, some of the structured groups offered by the Counseling-Psychological Services Center at the University of Texas at Austin include the following: Mid-Life Transitions: Values and Life Decisions; Gaining Control of Your Lifestyle and "Workstyle"; Stress Management; Depression-Management Training; Managing Relationships/Ending Relationships; Strategies for Building Self-Confidence for Graduate Women; Learning to Cope with Speech Anxiety; Developing Assertive Behavior; Women in Transition: Shifting Gears; Perfectionism: The Double-Edged Sword; The Aftermath of Suicide: A Special Kind of Grief; Jealousy: Taming the Green-Eyed Monster; and Students with an Alcoholic Parent.

For another example, consider the group-counseling programs available for students at Colorado State University. There are both therapy groups for adult children of alcoholics and also education and support groups for these clients. This counseling center also offers an anxiety-management group, an eating-disorders group, a family-issues group, a group for students of nontraditional age, a relationship-concerns group, a self-esteem group, a group for adult female survivors of childhood sexual abuse, and a personal-identity group for women.

The above list gives you some idea of the scope of topics for structured groups. These groups help people develop specific skills, understand certain themes, or go through difficult life transitions. Although the topics obviously vary according to the interests of the group leader and the clientele, such groups have a common denominator of providing members with increased awareness of some life problem and tools to better cope with it. Typically, the sessions are two hours each week, and the groups tend to be relatively short term. They may last for only four or five weeks, up to a maximum of one semester.

Members are generally asked to complete a questionnaire at the beginning of the group that pertains to how well they are coping with the particular area of concern. Structured exercises and homework assignments are typically introduced as ways of teaching new skills to group members. Another questionnaire is often used at the final session to assess the members' progress. A contract is frequently drawn up as a way of helping members pinpoint specific goals that will guide their participation in the group and stimulate them to practice new skills outside of the group.

Many structured groups are based on a learning-theory model and use behavioral procedures. Chapter 13 provides a detailed description of various such groups, including social-skills-training and assertiveness-training groups, stress-management groups, self-directed groups, and multimodal-therapy groups.

Self-Help Groups

In the past decade there has been a burgeoning of self-help groups that allow people with a common interest to create a support system that protects them from psychological stress and gives them the incentive to begin changing their lives. Both the number and kind of self-help groups have expanded, to the point that there are half a million such groups with a total membership exceeding 15 million people (Katz, 1981). These groups serve a critical need for certain populations that is not being met by professional mental-health workers or by other educational, religious, or community institutions (Cole, 1983; Lieberman, 1980; Lieberman & Borman, 1979). Riordan and Beggs (1987) reviewed the growth of self-help groups and made recommendations on ways in which counselors could use these groups as adjuncts to their practices. From their review of the literature, it is clear that self-help groups now play a significant role in complementing professional assistance.

In his comparison of contemporary healing groups, Lieberman (1980) categorizes them along a continuum. On one end of the continuum is *group psychotherapy,* which involves professionally led groups that often employ the medical model of treating a psychological disorder. On the other end is the *self-help movement,* which consists of organizations of people with similar emotional, physical, or behavioral problems or a common concern or affliction. Examples of these groups are Weight Watchers, Mended Hearts, Recovery, Inc., and Alcoholics Anonymous. The self-help movement's focus is limited to group members who have a common problem or life predicament. Typically, they meet in a community setting such as a school or a church. The members share their experiences, learn from one another, offer suggestions for new members, and provide support and encouragement for people who sometimes do not see any hope for their future.

The two terms *self-help group* and *support group* are often used interchangeably. Self-help groups tend to emphasize their autonomy and internal group resources (Katz, 1981). In many self-help groups the original intent was to use the leader as a model to demonstrate the universality of the need for members to help themselves (Riordan & Beggs, 1988). In support groups, however, the group is often begun by a professional helping organization or individual. Examples of support groups are those aimed at helping widows, widowers, and parents who have lost a child cope with their emotional problems (Lakin, 1985). The entire May 1986 *Journal for Specialists in Group Work* is devoted to support groups. Articles deal with groups for Vietnam veterans experiencing posttraumatic stress, groups for spouses whose partners are employed in stressful occupations, groups for survivors of incest, groups for the bereaved, groups for elderly victims of crime and violence, and groups for relocated adolescents.

Differences between the Self-Help Group and the Therapy Group. Self-help groups and therapy groups have some common denominators. Lakin (1985) notes that both emphasize expressing and sharing emotions. This emphasis is grounded on the assumption that people suffer from unexpressed feelings and thoughts and that maladaptive attitudes and behaviors toward others also result from bottled-up feelings. Both types of groups encourage support, stress the value of affiliation, and aim for behavioral change.

Despite these commonalities between self-help and therapy groups, there are some critical differences (see Riordan & Beggs, 1988). One basic difference involves the goals of the group. Self-help groups have as their central issue a single topic such as addiction, cancer, or obesity, whereas therapy groups have more global goals such as improving general mental health or one's interpersonal functioning (Riordan & Beggs, 1987). Moreover, self-help groups emphasize inspiration, persuasion, and support, whereas therapy groups employ self-understanding, behavioral reinforcement, and member feedback (Lakin, 1985).

A further difference between the two types of groups involves the leadership employed. Self-help groups are led by individuals who are struggling with the same issues as the members of the group, and by intention these leaders are not professionals (Riordan & Beggs, 1987). In most self-help groups the leadership emerges rather than being designated.

With counseling groups and therapy groups, as we have seen, a basic assumption is that the group represents a *social microcosm*. These groups attempt to reflect in some ways all of the dimensions of the members' real social environment. The therapeutic factor that accounts for change in the participants is the group process as a sample of the interpersonal conflicts that members confront in their daily lives. In contrast, self-help groups are not a social microcosm. The interactions of members within the group are not viewed as the primary catalyst for change. Instead, attention is placed on providing an accepting and supportive climate in the group itself. The group becomes a means of helping people modify their beliefs, attitudes, and feelings about themselves. Self-help groups stress a common identity based on a common life situation to a far greater extent than do most other groups.

Another difference between self-help groups and therapy groups involves the issue of politics. In recent decades self-help groups have become increasingly political, as evidenced by those organized within the women's movement. This same politicalization has been adopted by other populations such as ethnic minorities, gay men and lesbians, and other groups that feel they are being subjected to social and political oppression (Lakin, 1985). Thus, self-help groups focus on discussing the external causes of their problems and developing strategies to deal with environmental pressures and barriers. In therapy groups, however, the focus is on ways in which the individual can change even if certain environmental factors do not change. Therapy and counseling groups tend to be an apolitical process, at least with regard to external issues (Riordan & Beggs, 1988).

Riordan and Beggs (1987, 1988) maintain that practitioners must be aware of these differences between self-help and therapy groups so that they can assess the potential benefits of each type for different clients. They suggest that although self-help groups have been a source of valuable help for thousands of people, they are not appropriate for everyone. Thus, in recommending such a group to a client it is important to explore the client's expectations and the possible benefits and risks. Riordan and Beggs also write that even though self-help groups are often therapeutic, they should not be thought of as a replacement for therapy or counseling.

The Future of Self-Help Groups.   People seem to have an increasing interest in banding together to help themselves. Although professionally led counseling and therapy groups still serve a vital role, perhaps it is a healthy sign that people are seeking other methods. It seems to me that many self-help groups serve a unique function, one that cannot always be met in professionally led counseling and psychotherapy groups.

Group Counseling in a Multicultural Context

In this new edition I have added an emphasis on the role of social and cultural factors in the group-counseling process. This change is based on the assumption that for group counseling to be effective, it must take into consideration the cultural backgrounds of both the members and the leader. In Chapters 6–15 I will discuss some of the major strengths and limitations of the ten major theories from a multicultural perspective. This section deals with general principles of effective multicultural group counseling.

Some Definitions

In *multicultural counseling* two or more persons with different ways of perceiving their social environment attempt to work together in a helping relationship (Pedersen, 1988). Other terms that are used in discussing group practice in a multicultural context include *race, ethnicity,* and *minority.* Pedersen defines these terms as follows: *Race* pertains to a shared genetic history or physical characteristics. *Ethnicity* involves a shared sociocultural heritage of religion, history, or common ancestry. *Minority* identifies a group that has received differential and unequal treatment because of collective discrimination. Examples of such minority groups are Blacks, Asian Americans, Hispanics, Native Americans, White ethnics, women, gay men and lesbians, and the handicapped.

The Trend toward Multicultural Awareness

Pedersen (1988) makes the assumption that all counseling can be considered multicultural in the sense that cultural influences are always present. He emphasizes the importance of understanding group differences, as well as individual differences, in making accurate interpretations of behavior. For example, different cultures may interpret the same behavior either differently or in the same way. It is essential that all counselors understand the range of cultural similarities and differences. Culture does influence a client's behavior, whether or not the counselor is aware of it. According to

Pedersen, the current trend toward multicultural awareness among counselors will have an increasing impact on the helping professions in the next decade.

The Challenges and Rewards of Group Work with Various Cultures

The literature dealing with multicultural counseling indicates that ethnic and minority clients underuse mental-health services and social services (Chu & Sue, 1984; Ho, 1984; Lee, Juan, & Hom, 1984; Mokuau, 1985, 1987; Pedersen, 1985, 1988). There are a number of reasons for this failure to make full and appropriate use of existing counseling services. Helpers may be insensitive. Cultural values may inhibit the utilization of services, for in some cultures informal helping processes are used more than professional resources. Some clients hold values that call for them to work out their problems by themselves, and doing so indicates greater maturity than seeking help from others (Ho, 1984). Other explanations for the underuse of services include a lack of knowledge of existing mental-health services, language difficulties, stigma and shame, geographic or community inaccessibility, and conflicts between the client's value system and values underlying contemporary Western therapeutic approaches (Mokuau, 1985).

Practitioners writing about multicultural counseling often assert that many counseling approaches fail to meet the complex needs of various ethnic and minority clients because of stereotyped narrow perceptions of those needs. Asian Americans, Blacks, Hispanics, Native Americans, and members of other minority groups terminate counseling significantly earlier than do Anglo clients. This tendency is often caused by cultural barriers such as language difficulties, class-bound values, and culture-bound values that hinder the formation of a good counseling relationship (Mokuau, 1987; Pedersen, 1988).

If you will be involved in group work with culturally diverse populations (as most populations are), it will be important for you to modify your strategies to meet the unique needs of the members. Various professional organizations have emphasized the ethical responsibility of counselors to know their clients' cultural values before delivering a mental-health service. Although it is unrealistic to expect to have an in-depth knowledge of all cultural backgrounds, it is not unrealistic to have a comprehensive grasp of general principles that you can apply in working effectively with cultural diversity. While upholding a belief in your own values, you must avoid assuming a stance of superiority that leads you to unthinkingly impose your values on others. Your own willingness to put yourself in situations where you can learn about different cultures will be most useful. Your genuine respect of the differences among members of your groups and your openness to learn from them will go a long way in building the trust that is necessary for bridging differences.

Transcending Cultural Encapsulation.   In multicultural group counseling it is important to avoid making rigid and stereotyped generalizations
about individuals within a particular social or cultural group. For example,
Asian Americans comprise many different ethnic groups with diverse cultural experiences (Chu & Sue, 1984). Thus, practitioners who approach all
Asian-American clients as if they were emotionally reserved or nonverbal
are guilty of cultural stereotyping (Mokuau, 1987). Effective group work
from a multicultural perspective involves challenging stereotypes about a
particular group, or an individual within a given group, and modifying
them to fit reality.

Practitioners may encounter resistance from some ethnic or minority
clients because they are using traditional White, middle-class values to
interpret these clients' experiences. Such culturally encapsulated practitioners are not able to view the world through the eyes of all of their
clients. Wrenn (1985) defines the "culturally encapsulated counselor" as one
who has substituted stereotypes for the real world, who disregards cultural
variations among clients, and who dogmatizes technique-oriented def-
initions of counseling and therapy. Culturally encapsulated individuals
maintain a cocoon by evading reality and depending entirely on their own
internalized value assumptions about what is good for society. These encapsulated people tend to be trapped in one way of thinking, believing that
their way is the universal way. They cling to an inflexible structure that
resists adaptation to alternative ways of thinking (Pedersen, 1988).
Pedersen (1981) has outlined three basic propositions of encapsulation: (1)
reality is defined by using a monocultural set of assumptions and
stereotypes; (2) there is a tendency toward insensitivity to cultural variations among individuals; and (3) culturally derived assumptions are
accepted without proof. Culturally encapsulated group counselors tend to
impose their world view on their clients. By doing so, they are demonstrating a lack of respect for the complexity of the human struggles that grow
out of varying cultural backgrounds.

Western models need to be adapted to serve the members of certain
ethnic groups, especially those clients who live by a different value system.
For example, in the Western orientation there are frequently three core
cultural values—freedom, responsibility, and achievement—each of which
has implications for the practice of counseling (Sampson, 1988). As Sampson
has noted, self-contained individualism helps sustain the core values and
institutions that represent the United States today. Freedom, responsibility, and achievement are all assumed to require this individualism for their
realization. Yet many clients from non-Western cultures value interdependence more than independence, social consciousness more than
individual freedom, the welfare of the group more than their own welfare,
and the following of certain traditions more than the defying of tradition. As
Chu and Sue (1984) have written, Western psychological thought emphasizes self-sufficiency, independence from family, and self-growth. However,

many Asian Americans emphasize the collective good and make plans with the family in mind. Also, family roles tend to be highly structured, and "filial piety" exerts a powerful influence; that is, obligations to parents are respected throughout one's life.

If the group experience is largely the product of values that are alien to certain group members, it is easy to see that such members will not embrace the group. Thus, the interventions that leaders make are grounded on some theoretical notions and are also associated with at least implicit values. It is essential that these values be congruent with the client's cultural frame of reference. As you study the ten theories explored in this book, give careful consideration to the underlying value issues that are likely to have a clear impact on your practice. It is apparent that the direct application of many contemporary models of therapy is inappropriate when applied to some clients. However, there also appears to be cultural relevance for certain concepts and techniques drawn from the various therapeutic schools. As a group practitioner, you will use a range of concepts and techniques. It is important to develop selection criteria that will enable you to systematically integrate concepts and techniques that best accommodate the needs of the targeted clientele. Thus, in working with diverse populations, there is a case for effective eclectic strategies (Mokuau, 1985).

Advantages of Group Work with Multicultural Populations.   There appear to be some advantages in using group approaches with ethnic clients (Chu & Sue, 1984). In a group context members can gain much from the power and strength of collective feedback. They can be supportive of one another in patterns that are familiar. Modeling also operates in groups. As members see their peers challenging themselves and making desired changes in their lives, it gives them hope that change is possible for them. Another factor that makes group work valuable is cross-cultural universality. In groups people learn that they are not alone in their struggles. All people experience psychological pain and struggle in various ways. Regardless of cultural variations, people who seek professional help are concerned with alleviating or interpreting their suffering. Because of these underlying human commonalities, it is a mistake to fashion highly specialized groups to accommodate every possible cultural mix.

Some Limitations of Group Work in a Multicultural Context.   Along with the advantages of group counseling in multicultural settings, there are certain cautions. Some individuals may be reluctant to readily disclose personal material or to share family conflicts (Ho, 1984). They may see it as shameful even to have personal problems and all the more shameful to talk about them in front of strangers. In some cultures, in fact, people rely primarily on members of their extended family for help. Rather than seeking professional services, these individuals may be more likely to turn to their own support groups. As a group worker, you need to find ways to reach clients who may want help but do not know where to find it or are reluctant to seek it from a professional. It will be essential to accept the difficulties that clients experience in talking to you about themselves in personal ways, so that the foundation of a therapeutic relationship can be formed.

A related problem in group work with culturally diverse populations pertains to conflicts between members' values and what goes on in a group. In some groups, for example, there is a free exchange of touching and physical contact. Some cultures do not take physical contact so lightly, however, especially heterosexual contact. Clients may make a distinction between displaying physical affection in private and doing so in public (Chu & Sue, 1984). It is easy to see that some clients would be both offended and intimidated by the spontaneous touching that often occurs in groups.

General Guidelines for Group Work with Multicultural Populations

Part of the group process involves confrontation. Although confrontation is frequently misunderstood, it does have therapeutic aspects. It is therapeutic when it invites clients to more deeply explore a particular issue in their lives. It benefits group members when it is appropriate and well timed. On the other hand, confrontation that is harsh, attacking, hostile, and uncaring does not have a beneficial impact. In working with clients from certain cultures, even therapeutic confrontation may not always be appropriate, especially if it is done too soon. In fact, confronting client resistance too quickly and too directly can often be counterproductive with certain cultural groups. These clients may perceive the directness associated with confrontation as a personal criticism and as a personal attack (Ho, 1984). If they feel insulted, the chances are that they will also feel rejected or angry, and such feelings may cement their resistance to becoming involved in the group.

Ethnic and minority clients may display behavior that group leaders interpret as resistance. Often, these clients are not so much *resistant* as they are *reluctant* or, in some cases, simply politely respectful. For example, silence in a group should not always be interpreted as a refusal to participate. Quiet clients may be listening and not speaking because of their cultural conditioning. They may be waiting to be called on. Some clients may be very hesitant to talk about members of their family. This hesitation should not necessarily be interpreted as a stubborn refusal to be open and transparent. Instead, such clients may be influenced by taboos against openly discussing family matters. Group leaders who are able to understand the worlds of their clients are in a better position to patiently help these clients begin to speak. If such clients feel that they are respected, there is a greater chance that they will begin to challenge their hesitation.

Preparing Clients for a Group Experience. Multicultural group counseling demands adequate preparation by members. Screening and selecting members and orienting them to group procedures are especially critical in working with clients from some cultural groups. This preparation is so critical because many of the behaviors expected in a group are foreign to what people do in their everyday lives. For example, their culture may value indirect communication. When they are in a group, they are told to be direct as they speak to one another. In daily life people are often encouraged to mask their real feelings so that they will not offend people. They probably are not encouraged to express their feelings, to talk about their personal problems, or to tell others what or how they think about them. Yet in a group situation they are expected to abide by norms of openness, honesty, and directness, and they are expected to make themselves emotionally vulnerable. Depending on one's cultural background, some of the expected group behaviors may be most demanding and may certainly go against the grain of one's cultural conditioning.

It is important for group leaders to help members clearly identify why they are in a group. Clients need to identify what they want to get for themselves from this process. Group leaders can help by focusing them on where they are now and where they want to go. It is important that members know that group counseling involves change. They should be made aware of the possible consequences of change, not only for themselves but also for others in their lives. Some clients may be shunned by members of their family if they become too outspoken or if they move toward becoming highly individualistic.

Becoming a Culturally Effective Group Counselor.   As you study the ten contemporary theories and apply them to group counseling, think about the cultural implications of the techniques that grow out of them. Perhaps most important of all, give consideration to ways in which you might acquire the personal characteristics required for becoming a culturally effective group counselor. Sue (1978, 1981) has identified the following characteristics as essential for working effectively in a multicultural context:

1. Culturally effective counselors recognize their own values and assumptions in contrast with alternative assumptions.
2. They are aware of basic characteristics of counseling that cut across classes and cultures.
3. They understand the sociopolitical forces that influence the attitudes of minorities or otherwise oppressed groups.
4. They have the capacity to share a client's world view without critically judging this view.
5. They are eclectic in their own counseling style, in that they are able to utilize a wide range of interventions from various theoretical orientations.
6. They possess a range of beliefs, attitudes, ideas, and skills that enable them to develop therapeutic relationships with diverse clients.

Although group practitioners can acquire general knowledge and skills that will enable them to function effectively with groups composed of diverse client populations, they will obviously not know everything about the cultural background of their clients. Thus, there is much to be said for letting clients teach the group leader about relevant aspects of their culture. It is a good idea for leaders to ask members to provide them with the information they will need to effectively work with them. In working with culturally diverse groups, it helps to assess the degree of acculturation that has taken place. This is especially true for clients who have the experience of living in more than one culture. They often have allegiance to their culture of origin, and yet they may also find certain characteristics of their new culture attractive. They often experience conflicts in integrating the two cultures. These core struggles can be very productively explored in the context of an accepting group.

Multicultural counseling is by its very nature diverse. Because there may be many different types of clients within a given group, it is easy to see that there are no ideal therapeutic approaches. Instead, different theories have distinct features that have appeal for different cultural groups. Effective multicultural practice demands an open stance on the part of the practitioner, a flexibility, and a willingness to modify strategies to fit the needs and situations of the individuals within the group. It is clear that no one "right" technique can be utilized across the board with all clients, irrespective of their cultural backgrounds.

Practitioners who truly respect the members in their group will demonstrate a willingness to learn from them. They will be aware of hesitation on the clients' part and will not be too quick to misinterpret these behaviors. Instead, they will patiently attempt to enter the world of their clients as much as they can. It is not necessary for practitioners to have had the same experiences as their clients; what is more important is that they attempt to be open to a similar set of feelings and struggles. If this respect exists, all of the members benefit from cultural diversity within a group. It is not always by similarity, but rather by differences, that we are challenged to look at what we are doing.

2

Ethical and Professional Issues in Group Practice

In my view those who seek to be professional group leaders must be willing to question both their ethical standards and their level of competence. Some of the ethical issues treated in this chapter are the rights of group members, including informed consent and confidentiality; the psychological risks of groups; the uses and misuses of group techniques; the impact of the group leader's values; personal relationships with clients; and community and legal standards. The chapter also deals with standards of education and training for group leaders and the maintaining of competence through continued education.

As a responsible group practitioner, you must clarify your thinking about the ethical and professional issues that are discussed in this chapter. Ethical guidelines for group leaders, as well as professional training standards, have been established by the Association for Specialists in Group Work (ASGW, 1980, 1983). Other organizations have ethical standards that can provide guidance for group counselors. These groups include the American Group Psychotherapy Association (AGPA, 1978), the American Association for Counseling and Development (AACD, 1988), the American Psychological Association (APA, 1973, 1981), the American Association for Marriage and Family Therapy (AAMFT, 1988), the National Association of Social Workers (NASW, 1979), the National Federation of Societies for Clinical Social Work (1985), the American Psychiatric Association (1986), the National Board for Certified Counselors (1987), the National Rehabilitation Counseling Association (1988), and the National Training Laboratory Institute (1969). Many of the state licensure laws for counselors also contain specific ethical standards.

Although you are obligated to be familiar with, and bound by, the ethical code of your professional organization, many of these codes offer only general guidelines. Thus, you will be challenged to learn ways of making ethical decisions in practical situations. The guidelines will give you a general framework to operate from, but you will need to apply principles to concrete cases. It is a good idea to develop an ethical awareness and reflect on ethical issues *before* you actually begin to lead groups.

As I mentioned earlier, the ASGW developed a set of *Ethical Guidelines for Group Leaders* (1980), which were revised and updated in 1989. I am one of seven members of the ASGW's Professional Ethics Committee, which is charged with revising these guidelines. As you will see if you study them, the guidelines are neither completely clear nor all-inclusive. Some are controversial, some are rather general, and some are in need of updating. Nevertheless, they do provide a starting point for practitioners of group work, and they offer a focal point for discussion in group-counseling classes. Much of this chapter deals with specific ethical issues that group workers typically face and examines the present and proposed ASGW guidelines. I will focus on controversial guidelines that are in particular need of revision.

The Rights of Group Participants

My experience has taught me that those who enter groups are frequently unaware of their basic rights as participants, as well as their responsibilities. I believe that it is your function as a group leader to help prospective group members learn what these rights and responsibilities are. Therefore, this section offers a detailed list of group participants' rights.

Keep in mind, however, that there are exceptions to these rights, for there are many variables that determine their range. For example, group members who voluntarily join a counseling group have a right to leave the group if they decide that the group doesn't offer what they need. But this right does not apply to members of involuntary groups in correctional institutions. In that case, participation in a group is an integral part of the rehabilitation program, and it is mandatory. The eventual release of these individuals may be partially contingent on their cooperation and progress in the group. Although the rights listed below primarily concern members of voluntary groups, many of them also apply to involuntary participants. Even when group participation is mandatory, participants do have certain rights, and they should be clearly aware of these rights. For example, if full confidentiality cannot be guaranteed, group members have a right to know what the limits of confidentiality are.

A Basic Right: Informed Consent

If the matter of member rights is discussed at the initial session, the participants are likely to be far more cooperative and active. A leader who provides such a discussion as a matter of policy demonstrates honesty and respect for the members and fosters the trust necessary if group members are to be open and active. Such a leader has obtained the *informed consent* of the participants.

The ASGW's (1980) ethical guidelines clarify the group leader's responsibility for providing information about services to prospective clients. Two of the guidelines that are relevant here are (1) "Group leaders shall fully inform group members, in advance and preferably in writing, of the goals in the group, qualifications of the leader, and procedures to be employed." (2) "Group leaders shall explain, as realistically as possible, exactly what services can and cannot be provided within the particular group structure offered."

Clients have a right to know what they are getting into before they make a commitment. It is the group leader's responsibility to make prospective members aware of their rights and their responsibilities and to demystify the process of a group. Following is a consideration of basic information that members have a right to receive before joining a group. I then list the rights that clients can expect during the course of the group.

Information Clients Deserve before Joining a Group. The following is a list of what group participants have a right to expect before they make the decision to join a group:

- a clear statement regarding the purpose of the group
- a description of the group format, procedures, and ground rules
- a pregroup interview to determine whether this particular group with this particular leader is at this time appropriate to one's needs
- an opportunity to seek information about the group, to pose questions, and to explore concerns
- a statement describing the education, training, and qualifications of the group leader
- information concerning fees and expenses and whether the fee includes a follow-up session; also, information about length of group, frequency and duration of meetings, group goals, and types of technique being employed
- information about the psychological risks involved in group participation
- knowledge of the limitations of the confidential character of the group—that is, of circumstances in which confidentiality must be broken because of legal, ethical, or professional reasons
- clarification of what services can and cannot be provided within the group
- help from the group leader in developing personal goals
- a clear understanding of the division of responsibility between leader and participants
- a discussion of the rights and responsibilities of group members

Clients' Rights during the Group. Following is a list of what members have a right to expect during the course of the group:

- instructions concerning what is expected of the participants
- the freedom to leave the group if it doesn't appear to be what one expected or what one wants or needs at this time
- notice of any research involving the group and of any tape recording or videotaping of group sessions
- if recording does take place, the right to stop it if it restricts member participation
- assistance from the group leader in translating group learning into action in everyday life
- opportunities to discuss what one has learned in the group and to bring some closure to the group experience, so that the participant is not left with unnecessary unfinished business
- a consultation with the group leader should a crisis arise as a direct result of participation in the group, or a referral to other sources of help if further help is not available from the group leader
- the exercise of reasonable safeguards on the leader's part to minimize the potential risks of the group
- respect for member privacy with regard to what the person will reveal as well as to the degree of disclosure
- freedom from undue group pressure concerning participation in group exercises, decision making, disclosure of private matters, or acceptance of suggestions from other group members
- observance of confidentiality on the part of the leader and other group members
- freedom from having values imposed by the leader or other members
- the opportunity to use group resources for growth
- the right to be treated as an individual

The leader should stress that participation in groups carries certain responsibilities as well as rights. Some of these responsibilities are attending regularly, being prompt, taking risks, being willing to talk about oneself, giving others feedback, maintaining confidentiality, and asking for what one needs.

Voluntary Participation and Freedom of Exit

One of the ethical guidelines of the ASGW states: "Group leaders shall inform members that participation is voluntary and that they may exit from the group at any time." This guideline is one that I have difficulty with on several counts. Does it mean that practitioners who are leading groups composed of involuntary members are being unethical? If so, then many are guilty on this score, because groups are often made up of clients who are "sent," and these members cannot be said to be truly voluntary participants. It may be a question of either accepting a heavy fine or a jail sentence or going to group!

When participation is mandatory, informed consent is particularly important. Much effort needs to be directed toward fully informing involuntary members of the nature and goals of the group, the procedures to be used, their rights and responsibilities, the limits of confidentiality, and what effect their level of participation in the group will have on critical decisions about them outside of the group. When groups are involuntary, every attempt should be made to enlist the cooperation of the members and encourage them to continue the group on a voluntary basis. An alternative would be for the group leader to accept involuntary group members only for an initial, limited period. There is something to be said for giving reluctant members a chance to see for themselves what a group is about and then eventually (say, after three sessions) letting them decide if they will return. Of course, there may be consequences for clients who elect not to continue treatment. It seems to me that an ethical question arises when practitioners merely certify that a given client has bodily "shown up" for so many group sessions. Ethical practice would seem to require that group leaders fully explore the issues surrounding voluntary or involuntary group participation with clients who are sent to them. Another problem arises when practitioners conduct groups in prison. The institution is charged with taking steps toward rehabilitation, and groups are often the primary method of treatment. It is interesting to consider the ethical aspects of mandatory group participation in these situations.

The other part of this guideline that troubles me is the "freedom of exit" clause. Leaders should be clear about their policies on attendance, commitment to remaining in a group for a predetermined number of sessions, and leaving a particular session if they do not like what is going on in the group. If members simply drop out of the group, it is extremely difficult to develop a working level of trust or to establish group cohesion. The topic of terminating the group should be discussed during the initial session, and the leader's attitudes and policies should be clarified from the outset. Corey, Corey, Callanan, and Russell (1988) take the position that clients have a responsibility to the leader and other members to explain why they want to leave. There are a number of reasons for such a policy. For one thing, it can be deleterious to members if they leave without having been able to discuss what they considered threatening or negative in the experience. If they simply leave when they become uncomfortable, they are likely to be left with unfinished business, and so are the remaining members. It can surely damage the cohesion and trust in a group, for the remaining members may think that they in some way "caused" the departure. It is a good practice to tell members that if they are even thinking of withdrawing, they should bring the matter up for exploration in a session. Although it is unethical to use *undue* pressure to keep a person in a group, it is critical that members be encouraged to discuss their departure, at least with the group leader.

Although members ultimately have the right to leave a group, they should be taught the importance of informing the leader and the group before deciding. Ideally, the group leader and the members will work cooperatively to determine the degree to which a group experience is productive or counterproductive. My position is that if, at a mutually agreed-on time, members still choose not to participate in a group, they should be allowed to withdraw.

Freedom from Coercion and Undue Pressure

Members can reasonably expect to be respected by the group and not to be subjected to coercion and undue group pressure. On this matter the ASGW's guideline is "Group leaders shall protect member rights against physical threats, intimidation, coercion, and undue peer pressure insofar as it is reasonably possible."

On the one hand, some degree of group pressure is inevitable, and it is even therapeutic in many instances. People in a group are confronted with some of their self-defeating beliefs and behaviors and are challenged to admit what they are doing and determine whether they want to remain the way they are. Further, there is pressure in sessions to speak up, to make personal disclosures, to take certain risks, to share one's reactions to the here-and-now events within the group, and to be honest with the group. It is essential for group leaders to differentiate between destructive pressure and therapeutic pressure. People may need a certain degree of pressure to aid them in breaking through their usual forms of resistance. It is well to keep in mind that the purpose of a group is to help participants find their own answers, not to pressure them into doing what the group thinks is the appropriate course.

On the other hand, members can easily be subjected to needless anxiety if they are badgered to behave in a certain way. Members may also be pressured to take part in communication exercises or nonverbal exercises designed to promote interaction. It is essential that leaders be sensitive to the values of members who decline to participate in certain group exercises. Leaders must make it genuinely acceptable for members to abstain by mentioning this option periodically whenever it is appropriate. It is a good practice for group leaders to teach members how to resist undue group pressure and how to decline gracefully and forcefully to participate in activities they dislike. Finally, for members who may be considering leaving the group, it is unwise for leaders to allow peers to pressure members to remain in the group at all costs.

Experimentation and Research

Group members should be informed of any research involving the group, and their consent should be obtained in writing (Gazda & Mack, 1982). The ASGW's guideline here is "Group leaders shall provide prospective clients with specific information about any specialized or experimental activities in which they may be expected to participate." In addition to providing for informed consent, it is essential that participation in any research associated with a group be voluntary. On this issue the AACD's (1988) standard is clear: "Participation in research must be voluntary. Involuntary participation is appropriate only when it can be demonstrated that participation will have no harmful effects on subjects and is essential to the investigation." Respecting the rights of members does not necessarily imply an inadequate research design. Group leaders who are conducting research or who are experimenting with a group can provide members with the information they need to make an informed choice without delving into every detail about the experiment. Furthermore, leaders can take every step possible to enlist voluntary participation in any research project that involves the group. It is important that members do have the option to decline, however.

If leaders intend to write journal articles or books, it is essential that they take measures to adequately safeguard the confidentiality of the material explored in the group. The same care to disguise identities should be taken if the leaders talk with colleagues about the progress of their groups. Those who conduct group work in community mental-health clinics and schools will probably face the issue of preparing written reports for these institutions. The members have a right to know what kinds of information will appear in an institutional report.

The Use of Group Resources

Members have a right to expect that they will be able to make optimum use of the resources within a group. At times certain members may display problematic behaviors such as monopolizing time, storytelling, asking many questions, making interpretations for others, chronically jumping in, or giving advice or reassurance when it is not appropriate. This type of behavior leaves little time for those members who want time to work on their concerns. The ASGW's guideline is "Group leaders shall insure to the extent that it is reasonably possible that each member has the opportunity to utilize group resources and interact within the group by minimizing barriers such as rambling and monopolizing time." This guideline might be more appropriately written as "Group leaders shall ensure equitable use of group time by each member." Some examples of how the leader might accomplish this are as follows: invite silent members to become involved, acknowledge nonverbal attempts to communicate, discourage rambling and monopolizing of time by members, and avoid placement in a group of individuals who are experiencing a crisis.

Although the group leader does not have to assume complete responsibility for intervening to stop members who are disrupting the group, he or she should notice the situation and work with the group in such a way that one member does not sap the energy of the group and make it difficult for others to do productive work. I see it as the leader's function to teach rambling members to become aware of the ways in which they are presenting themselves to others in the group. Without being sharp or overly critical, a leader can help members learn how to be specific and to avoid getting lost in the details of a story. Members can learn how to share the responsibility so that they are able to maximize the resources in the group. This includes teaching members how to ask for what they want, developing a sense of the time limitations of the sessions, and confronting others decently if they see them disrupting the group process.

The Right to Confidentiality

Confidentiality is a central ethical issue in group counseling. Not only are you as a leader required to keep the confidences of group members; you have the added responsibility of impressing on the members the necessity of maintaining the confidential nature of whatever is revealed in a group. This matter bears reinforcement, from the initial screening interview to the final group session. Confidentiality, as one of the key norms of behavior in a group, is best arrived at through negotiation rather than by a dictate from the leader (Lakin, 1985). If the rationale for confidentiality is clearly presented to each individual during the preliminary interview and again to the group as a whole at the initial session, there is less chance that members will treat this matter lightly. Confidentiality is often on the minds of people when they initially join a group, so it is timely to fully explore this issue.

A good practice is to remind participants from time to time of the danger of inadvertently revealing confidences. My experience continues to teach me that members rarely gossip maliciously about others in their group. However, people do tend to talk more than they should outside the group and can unwittingly offer information about fellow members that should not be revealed. If the maintenance of confidentiality seems to be a matter of concern, the subject should be discussed fully in a group session. Clearly there is no way to ensure that group members will respect the confidences of others. Therefore, practitioners are reckless in making promises to that effect (Lakin, 1985). As a group leader, you can discuss the matter, express your feelings about the importance of maintaining confidentiality, have members sign contracts agreeing to it, and even impose some form of sanction on those who break it. Realize that your own modeling and the importance that you place on maintaining confidentiality will be crucial in setting norms for members to follow. If the members sense that you take confidentiality seriously, there is a greater likelihood that they will also be concerned about the matter. The AACD's (1988) guideline is "The counseling relationship and information resulting therefrom must be kept confidential, consistent with the obligations of the member [counselor] as a professional person. In a group counseling setting, the counselor must set a norm of confidentiality regarding all group participants' disclosures." As Lakin (1985) observes, the group develops a norm of confidentiality because it becomes a matter of mutual interest and mutual protection. Ultimately, it is up to the members to respect the need for confidentiality and to maintain it.

The ASGW's *Ethical Guidelines for Group Leaders* has two principles related to confidentiality: "Group leaders shall protect members by defining clearly what confidentiality means, why it is important, and the difficulties involved in enforcement" and "Group leaders shall inform members about recording of sessions and how tapes will be used."

With respect to the use of audio and videotapes of group sessions, certain steps are necessary to protect the rights of group members and to ensure confidentiality. Members have the right to know of any recordings that might be made and what they will be used for, and their written permission should be secured. If the tapes will be used for research or will be critiqued by a supervisor or other students in a group-supervision session, the members have the right to be informed; they also have the right to deny permission.

Exceptions to Confidentiality.   The AACD specifies exceptions to the general norm of confidentiality regarding all group members' disclosures: "When the client's condition indicates that there is a clear and imminent danger to the client or others, the counselor must take reasonable personal action or inform responsible authorities. Consultation with other professionals must be used where possible."

The *AAMFT Code of Ethical Principles for Marriage and Family Therapists* (1988) spells out specific limitations of confidentiality:

> Marriage and family therapists cannot disclose client confidences to anyone, except: (1) as mandated by law; (2) to prevent a clear and immediate danger to a person or persons; (3) where the marriage and family therapist is a defendant in a civil, criminal, or disciplinary action arising from the therapy (in which case client confidence may only be disclosed in the course of that action); or (4) if there is a waiver previously obtained in writing, and then such information may only be revealed in accordance with the terms of the waiver.

Group workers might do well to give a written statement to each member setting forth the limitations of confidentiality and spelling out specific situations that would demand the breaching of confidences. It seems that such straightforwardness with members from the outset does a great deal to create trust, for at least members know where they stand.

Of course, it is imperative that those who lead groups become familiar with the state laws that have an impact on their practice. Counselors are legally required to report clients' threats to harm themselves or others. This requirement also covers cases of child abuse or neglect, incest, or child molestation. Taking an extreme case, if one of your group members convincingly threatens to seriously injure another person, you may have to consult your supervisor or other colleagues, warn the intended victim, and even notify the appropriate authorities. The threat need not involve others; clients may exhibit bizarre behavior, such as having "visions" or "hearing voices" telling them to maim themselves, that requires you to take steps to have them temporarily hospitalized.

If you lead a group at a correctional institution, you may be required to act as more than a counselor; for instance, you may have to record in a member's file certain behaviors that he or she exhibits in the group. At the same time, your responsibility to your clients requires you to inform them that you are recording and passing on certain information. Generally speaking, you will find that, if you are candid about your actions, you have a better chance of gaining the cooperation of group members than if you hide your disclosures and thereby put yourself in the position of violating their confidences.

Confidentiality with Minors. Another delicate problem related to confidentiality involves group counseling with children and adolescents. Do parents have a right to information that is disclosed by their children in a group? The answer to that question depends on whether you are looking at it from a legal, ethical, or professional viewpoint. Before any minor enters a group, it is a good practice to routinely require written permission from the parents. It is useful to have this permission include a brief statement concerning the purpose of the group, along with comments regarding the importance of confidentiality as a prerequisite to accomplishing such purposes and your intention not to violate any confidences. Clearly, it may be useful to give the parents information about their child, but this can be done without violating confidences. One useful practice to protect the privacy of what goes on in the group is to provide feedback to parents in a session with the child and one or both parents. In this way the child will have less cause to doubt the group leader's integrity in keeping his or her disclosures private.

The APA (1981) has a general guideline for leaders of groups composed of minors: "When working with minors or other persons who are unable to give voluntary, informed consent, psychologists take special care to protect these persons' best interest." On this same issue, the AACD standard suggests: "When working with minors or persons who are unable to give consent, the member protects these clients' best interests." Thus, group leaders have a responsibility in groups that involve children and adolescents to take measures to increase the chances that confidentiality is taken seriously. It is important to work cooperatively with parents and guardians as well as to enlist the trust of the young people. It is also useful to teach minors, in terms that they are capable of understanding, about the nature, purposes, and limitations of confidentiality. In summary, group leaders would do well to continue to remind members to bring up their concerns about confidentiality for discussion whenever the issue is on their minds.

The Issue of Psychological Risks in Groups

Since groups can act as powerful catalysts for personal change, they can also pose definite risks for group members. The nature of these risks—which include life changes that cause disruption, hostile and destructive confrontations, scapegoating, and harmful socializing among members—and what the leader can do about them are the subject of this section. It is unrealistic to expect that a group will not involve risk, for all meaningful learning in life involves taking risks. However, it is the ethical responsibility of the group leader to ensure that prospective group members are aware of the potential risks and to take every precaution against them.

The ASGW's ethical guideline specifies that "group leaders shall stress the personal risks involved in any group, especially regarding potential life-changes, and help group members explore their readiness to face these risks." A minimal expectation is that group leaders discuss with members the advantages and disadvantages of a given group, that they prepare the members to deal with any problems that might grow out of the group experience, and that they be alert to the fears and reservations that members might have.

It is also incumbent on group leaders to have a broad and deep understanding of the forces that operate in groups and how to mobilize those forces for ethical ends. To act ethically, leaders must know what is occurring in the group and how to formulate it in terms that are meaningful and beneficial to the members (Lakin, 1985). Unless leaders exert caution, members may not only miss the benefits of a group but also could be harmed by it psychologically. Ways of reducing these risks include knowing members' limits, respecting their limits and requests, developing an invitational style as opposed to a pushy or dictatorial style, avoiding assaultive confrontations, describing behavior rather than making judgments, and presenting hunches in a tentative way rather than forcing interpretations on members. The next chapter describes group-leadership skills that provide a basis for dealing with some of the issues that have been mentioned here.

Following are a few of the problems that group leaders must warn members about and must work to minimize:

1. Members should be made aware of the possibility that participating in a group (or any other therapeutic endeavor) may disrupt their lives. As members become increasingly self-aware, they may make changes in their lives that, although constructive in the long run, create crisis and turmoil along the way. For example, changes that a wife makes as a result of what she gains in a group may evoke resistance, even hostility, in her husband, with a resulting strain on their marriage. Furthermore, the rest of her family may not appreciate her changes and may prefer the person she was before getting involved in counseling.

2. Occasionally an individual member may be singled out as the scapegoat of the group. Other group members may "gang up" on this person, making him or her the object of hostility or other forms of negativity. Clearly, the group leader can and should take firm steps to eliminate such occurrences.

3. Confrontation, a valuable and powerful tool in any group, can be misused, especially when it is employed to destructively attack another. Intrusive interventions, overly confrontive leader tactics, and pushing of members beyond their limits have been associated with casualties in groups (Lieberman, Yalom, & Miles, 1973). Here, again, leaders (and members as well) must be on guard against behavior that can pose a serious psychological risk for group participants. To lessen the risks of nonconstructive confrontation, leaders can model the type of confrontation that focuses on

specific behaviors and can avoid making judgments about members. They can teach members how to talk about themselves and the reactions they are having to a certain behavior pattern of a given member.

Socializing among Group Members

A related issue is whether socializing among group members hinders or facilitates the group process. This concern can become an ethical issue if members are forming cliques and gossiping about others in the group or if they are banding together and talking about matters that are best explored in the group sessions. If hidden agendas develop through various splinter groups within the group, it is likely that the progress of the group will come to an abrupt halt. Unless the hidden agenda is surfaced and dealt with, it seems very likely that many members will not be able to use the group therapeutically or meet their personal goals.

Yalom (1985) writes that a therapy group teaches people *how* to form intimate relationships but does not *provide* these relationships. He also points out that members meeting outside of the group have a responsibility to bring information about their meeting into the group. The type of out-of-group socialization that interferes with the functioning of the group is counterproductive and should be discouraged. This is especially true in those situations in which participants discuss issues relevant to the group and avoid bringing up the same issues in the group itself.

One of the best ways for the group leader to prevent inappropriate and counterproductive socialization among group members is to bring this issue up for discussion. It is especially timely to explore the negative impact of forming cliques when the group seems stuck and getting nowhere or when it appears that members are not talking about their reactions to one another. The members can be taught that what they do not say in the group itself might very well prevent their group from attaining any level of cohesion.

Reducing Psychological Risks

As indicated earlier, one cannot eliminate psychological risks in groups, but one can minimize them. One way is to use a contract, in which the leader specifies his or her responsibilities and the members specify their commitment by stating what they are willing to explore and do in the group. Such a contract reduces the chances that members will be exploited or will leave the group feeling that they have had a negative experience.

Another safeguard against unnecessary risk is the ability of leaders to sincerely recognize the boundaries of their competence and to restrict themselves to working only with those groups for which their training and experience have properly prepared them. Even if they have a license or certification that *legally* permits them to conduct any kind of therapy group with any population, responsible group leaders realize that they are *ethically* and *professionally* restricted to working within the limits of their background of training. For example, a group leader may be experienced and very skilled in working with children and adolescents in groups yet be unprepared to lead a group of adult psychotics, regardless of what his or her credentials may say.

Ultimately, it is the group leader who is responsible for minimizing the inevitable psychological risks associated with group activity. To best assume this responsibility, the leader must be willing to undergo the supervised practice and course work that will be described later in this chapter.

The Ethics of Group Leaders' Actions

Being a group practitioner demands sensitivity to the needs of the members of your group and to the impact that your values and techniques can have on them. It also demands an awareness of community standards of practice, the policies of the agency where you work, and the state laws that govern group counseling. In the mental-health professions in general there is a trend toward accountability and responsible practice. Graduate programs in counseling and social work are increasingly requiring course work in ethics and the law. In part, these trends may have something to do with the increased vulnerability of mental-health practitioners to malpractice suits.

Almost all of the professional organizations have gone on record as affirming that their members should be aware of prevailing community standards and of the impact that conformity to or deviation from these standards will have on their practice. These organizations state explicitly that professionals will avoid exploitation of the therapeutic relationship, will not damage the trust that is necessary for a relationship to be therapeutic, and will avoid dual relationships if they would interfere with the primary therapeutic aims. Typically, the ethical codes caution against attempting to blend social or personal relationships with professional ones.

Personal Relationships between Leaders and Members

What criteria can a group leader use to determine the appropriateness of personal and social relationships with group members? A key question that leaders need to ask themselves is whether a social relationship is interfering with the therapeutic relationship. They have an ASGW guideline on this issue: "Group leaders shall abstain from inappropriate personal relationships with members throughout the duration of the group and any subsequent professional involvement." What constitutes "inappropriate personal relationships" is not always clear. Making this determination demands honesty in examining one's own motivations and needs. The crux of the matter is to avoid abusing one's power and misusing one's professional role to make personal or social contacts. Unless leaders know themselves and have a sense of self-restraint, it is possible for them to exploit members to meet their own needs. It has been proposed that this guideline be revised as follows: "Group leaders shall avoid misusing the professional role and related power of group leader to make personal or social contacts with members throughout the duration of the group and/or subsequent professional involvement."

Lakin (1985) observes that leaders may find themselves vulnerable at times, in that they will be positively attracted to some members and will react negatively to others. He considers it unethical for leaders to misuse their professional power to satisfy their needs by fostering dependence and by maintaining extragroup social contacts with members. He puts this matter bluntly: "Unfortunately, some of the most noxious leader behaviors may be less the product of ethical insensitivity or misunderstanding than outright psychopathy. Such persons do not and will not practice rigorous self-scrutiny. Such individuals must simply be prevented from assuming group leadership functions" (p. 244).

Three other guidelines explicitly state that dual relationships and sexual intimacies with clients are unethical:

• "Dual relationships with clients that might impair the member's objectivity and professional judgment (e.g., as with close friends or relatives) must be avoided and/or the counseling relationship terminated through referral to another competent professional" (AACD, 1988).

• "The member (counselor) will avoid any type of sexual intimacies with clients. Sexual relationships with clients are unethical" (AACD, 1988).

• "Marriage and family therapists are cognizant of their potentially influential position with respect to clients, and they avoid exploiting the trust and dependency of such persons. Marriage and family therapists therefore make every effort to avoid dual relationships with clients that could impair their professional judgment or increase the risks of exploitation. Examples of such dual relationships include, but are not limited to, business or close personal relationships with clients. Sexual intimacy with clients is prohibited. Sexual intimacy with former clients for two years following the termination of therapy is prohibited" (AAMFT, 1988).

The Impact of the Leader's Values on the Group

In all controversial issues related to the group process, the leader's values play a central role. Your awareness of how your values influence your leadership style is in itself a central ethical issue. Sometimes group counselors are taught to be neutral and are urged to attempt to keep their values separate from their leadership function. My position is that it is neither possible nor desirable for counselors to be scrupulously neutral with respect to values in the therapeutic relationship. Although it is not the proper function of counselors to persuade clients to accept a certain value system, it is critical that counselors be clear about their own values and express them openly when it is relevant and appropriate to the work of the group. But leaders must keep in mind how these values influence their therapeutic work and, ultimately, the directions taken by their clients.

I am inclined to expose my values when they conflict with a member's values. It does not seem therapeutic to feign acceptance or to pretend that no difference of opinion exists. Expressed values are less likely to interfere with the process of a group than values that are concealed.

In my view the crux of the ethical concern in this area is leaders' use of their groups as a forum for advancing their personal agenda or as a way to meet their own needs at the expense of the welfare of the members. The ASGW's guideline here is "Group leaders shall refrain from imposing their own agendas, needs, and values on group members." The critical word is *imposing*. There is a real difference between *imposing* and *exposing* one's values. In the case of imposing a leader's values, the members' integrity is not respected, for they are not seen as capable of discovering a meaningful set of values and acting on them by themselves. In the case of exposition of leader values, in contrast, the members are free to challenge their own thinking against the background of the leader's beliefs, but they can still make their own choices without being burdened with guilt that they are not meeting the leader's expectations. In summary, it is the group leader's function to challenge members to find their own values, not to do the deciding for them. Ethical practice requires that leaders help the participants clarify and define their own values.

Uses and Misuses of Group Techniques

It is important for leaders to have a clear rationale for each technique they use in their groups. This is an area in which theory is a useful guide for practice. As you will see, the ten theories at the core of this book have many therapeutic strategies and techniques flowing from them. Such techniques are a means to accomplish change or to promote exploration and interaction. They can certainly be used ethically and therapeutically, yet they also have the capacity for misuse. Some of the ways in which leaders can practice unprofessionally are using techniques with which they are unfamiliar, using them merely as gimmicks, using them to serve their own hidden agendas or to enhance their power, and using them to pressure members. Lakin (1985) considers the core ethical issue to be whether the leader can use the emotional arousal stimulated by the group without exploiting it. Many techniques that are used in a group do facilitate an intense expression of emotion. For example, guided fantasies into times of loneliness as a child can lead to deep psychological experiences. If leaders use such techniques, they must be ready to deal with any emotional release. What is crucial is to use these techniques properly for the benefit of the members and to avoid the exploitation that occurs when members are pushed to "get into their emotions." Some group leaders measure the efficacy of their group by the level of catharsis, and members can be exploited by a leader who has a need to see them experience intense emotions. This expression of emotion can sometimes be more important in meeting the leader's needs than in meeting the member's. If members do not have a "good catharsis," some leaders (and members) feel that the group is "not getting anywhere."

A definite risk in some groups is physical injury as a result of useful group activities, such as certain "encounter games" that involve releasing pent-up feelings of anger and aggression. Because some of these games entail shoving, pushing, holding down, or wrestling, they can lead to violent outbursts and physical violence. Clearly, group leaders should instigate exercises with great care and only when they are quite sure that the participants will not get out of control. Although it is unrealistic to expect that leaders will always know exactly what will result from an intervention, they should be able to cope with unexpected outcomes.

On this issue of the risks involved in using physical techniques, several guidelines for preventing negative consequences are described by Corey, Corey, Callanan, and Russell (1988):

- If leaders introduce physical techniques, they should protect the person and the other members from harm; they should also be prepared to deal with unforeseen directions that the exercise might take.
- For safety reasons it is generally best not to introduce physical techniques that involve the whole group, especially if these techniques are designed to elicit powerful emotions such as anger.
- Such techniques should not be used unless the leader knows the members quite well and has established a relationship based on trust.
- Leaders who introduce such techniques should have the experience and training to deal with the intense reactions that can follow.
- Beginning group leaders should either avoid using physical techniques or do so only when direct supervision is available or when they are co-leading with an experienced therapist.
- It is unwise to goad or push members into participating in physical exercises. Members can be invited to participate, but they should have the clear option to decline.

The above guidelines do not imply that all physical activities are inappropriate in a group context. Activities that involve physical challenge or adventure through leader-designed, structured exercises can be used productively in a variety of settings, including groups with couples and families. For example, Project Adventure, Inc., has translated many Outward Bound wilderness concepts into viable activities for educational and counseling programs. According to Gillis and Bonney (1986), such adventure activities foster cohesion during the initial stage of a group. Furthermore, a sequence of adventure activities that gradually increases the risk and need for problem solving also seems to raise the level of interpersonal trust within the group.

Techniques have a better chance of being used appropriately when there is a rationale underlying their use. Be sure that a technique fosters the client's self-exploration and self-understanding. At their best, techniques are invented in each unique client situation, and they assist the group member in experimenting with some form of new behavior. It is critical that techniques be introduced in a timely and sensitive manner, with respect for the client, and that they be abandoned if they are not working.

Legal Liability and Malpractice

Group leaders are expected to practice within the code of ethics of their particular profession and to abide by legal standards. Practitioners are subject to civil penalties if they fail to do right or if they actively do wrong to another. If group members can prove that personal injury or psychological harm was caused by a leader's failure to render proper service, either through negligence or ignorance, the leader is open to a malpractice suit. Negligence consists of departing from the standard and commonly accepted practices of others in the profession. Practitioners who are involved in a malpractice action may need to justify the techniques they use. If their therapeutic interventions are consistent with those of other members of their profession in their community, they are on much firmer ground than if they employ uncommon techniques.

Gillis and Bonney (1986) warn about using physically challenging exercises and games without a rationale or without proper administration. They mention that practitioners who use risky physical activities are taking the chance of malpractice action if they are negligent and if group members are physically or psychologically injured by participating.

In providing psychological or counseling services, professionals in two organizations are enjoined against violating or diminishing the legal and civil rights of their clients (American Mental Health Counselors Association, 1980; APA, 1981). This guideline implies that professionals who work with groups must be familiar with the legal aspects of group work. Leaders need to keep up to date with the laws of their state as they affect their professional practice. Those leaders who work with groups of children and adolescents, especially, must know the law as it pertains to matters of confidentiality, parental consent, the right to treatment or to refuse treatment, informed consent, and other legal rights of clients. Such awareness not only protects the group members but also protects group leaders from malpractice suits arising from negligence or ignorance.

Reducing the Chances of Being Sued. The key to a group leader's avoiding a malpractice suit is maintaining *reasonable, ordinary,* and *prudent* practices. The best way to protect yourself from getting involved in a malpractice suit is to take preventive measures, which means not practicing outside the boundaries of your competence. Knowing and following the spirit of the ethical standards of your professional organization and the ethical guidelines for group leaders such as those developed by the ASGW will reduce your chances of being sued for malpractice. Below are some guidelines for group leaders that are useful in translating the terms *reasonable, ordinary,* and *prudent* into concrete actions:

- Give the potential members of your groups enough information that they can make informed choices about group participation.
- Know the legal limitations and state laws that govern group counseling, and practice within these boundaries. Inform members about

legal limitations (such as exemptions to confidentiality, mandatory reporting, and the like).

- Don't promise the members of your group anything that you can't deliver. Help them realize that their degree of effort and commitment will be key factors in determining the outcomes of the group experience.
- In working with minors, secure the written permission of their parents.
- Always consult with colleagues when you are in doubt. Realize that the willingness to consult and to seek supervision implies a high level of professionalism.
- Learn how to assess and intervene in cases in which clients pose a threat to themselves or others.
- Be willing to devote the time it takes to adequately screen, select, and prepare the members of your group.
- Avoid mixing professional relationships with social ones.
- Be able to explain the techniques that you regularly use in your groups. Have a rationale that is tied to some theoretical perspective.

Later in this chapter specific ethical guidelines are presented for leaders to consider throughout the various stages of a group. They provide practical suggestions for reducing the chances of being the target of a malpractice suit.

The Issue of the Group Leader's Competence

Determining One's Own Level of Competence

The ASGW's basic principle is that "group leaders shall not attempt any technique unless thoroughly trained in its use or under supervision by an expert familiar with the intervention." How can leaders determine whether they have the competence to use a certain technique? Although some leaders who have received training in the use of a technique may hesitate to use it (out of fear of making a mistake), other overly confident leaders without training may not have any reservations about trying out new techniques. It is a good policy for leaders to have a clear rationale for any technique they use. Further, it is useful if leaders have experienced these techniques as members of a group. The issue of whether one is competent to lead a specific group or type of group continually faces all professional group leaders. Questions that you are likely to struggle with include these:

- Am I qualified through education to lead this specific group?
- What criteria can I use to determine my degree of competence?
- Perhaps I am "technically qualified," but do I have the practical training or experience necessary to conduct this group?
- How can I recognize my limits?
- If I am not as competent as I'd like to be, what specifically can I do?

There are no simple answers to these questions. Different groups require different leader qualities. For example, you may be fully competent to lead a group of relatively well-adjusted adults or of adults in crisis situations yet not be competent to lead a group of seriously disturbed clients. You may be well trained for, and work well with, adolescent groups, yet you may not have the skills or training to do group work with younger children. You may be successful leading groups with alcoholics or drug addicts yet find yourself ill prepared to work successfully with family groups. In short, you need specific training and supervised experience for each type of group you intend to lead; competence in *some* areas of group work does not imply competence in *all* areas.

Degrees, licenses, and credentials may be necessary but are not sufficient in themselves; all they indicate is a certain background of content and experience, which usually means that you have completed a *minimum* number of years of training and work. Obviously, the quality of training and experience indicated by credentials varies greatly.

Numerous paths can lead one to become a qualified group leader. Professional certification or licensure is an avenue for determining minimal levels of competence. Depending on one's state, it is possible to obtain a counselor license or certificate or a license as a social worker, psychologist, or marriage and family therapist. Yet this type of professional certification alone does not imply competence as a group practitioner.

Most practitioners have had their formal training in one of the branches of the mental-health field, including counseling psychology, clinical psychology, educational psychology, marriage and family counseling, nursing, pastoral psychology, clinical social work, and psychiatry. Generally, however, those who seek to become group practitioners find that formal education, even at the master's or doctoral level, doesn't give them the practical grounding they require to effectively lead groups. Thus, they find it necessary to take a variety of specialized group-therapy-training workshops.

Standards of Professional Preparation for Group Counselors

Effective group-leadership programs are not developed by legislative mandates and professional codes alone. For proficient leaders to emerge, a training program must make group work a priority. Unfortunately, in some master's programs in counseling not even one group course is required. In those programs that do require work in group counseling, there is typically one course that covers both the didactic and experiential aspects of group process. It is a major undertaking to adequately train group counselors in a single course!

In a survey of programs of professional preparation for group counseling, Huhn, Zimpfer, Waltman, and Williamson (1985) found that of the 76 programs in their study, 18% offered group courses at the undergraduate level, 97% at the master's level, and 34% at the doctoral level. Of these 76 programs, 27% offered only one course in group counseling, 37% offered two courses, 15% offered three courses, 11% offered four courses, and 10% offered five or more courses in group counseling.

In its *Professional Standards for Training of Group Counselors,* the ASGW (1983) sets out *knowledge competencies, skill competencies,* and suggested supervised clinical group *experience* for leaders.* In the area of *knowledge competencies,* the ASGW takes the position that the qualified group leader has demonstrated specialized knowledge in the following aspects of group work:

- the major theories of group counseling, including their differences and common concepts
- the basic principles of group dynamics and the key ingredients of group process
- one's own strengths and weaknesses, values, and other personal characteristics that have an impact on one's ability to function as a group leader
- ethical and professional issues special to group work
- updated information on research in group work
- the facilitative and debilitative roles and behaviors that group members may assume
- the advantages and disadvantages of group work and the situations in which it is appropriate or inappropriate as a form of therapeutic intervention
- the characteristics of group interaction and counselor roles involved in the stages of a group's development

In the area of *skill competencies,* the ASGW contends that qualified group leaders should be able to demonstrate a mastery of the following skills:

- being able to screen and assess the readiness of clients to participate in a group
- having a clear definition of group counseling and being able to explain its purpose and procedures to group members
- diagnosing self-defeating behaviors in group members and being able to intervene in constructive ways with members who display such behaviors
- modeling appropriate behavior for group members
- interpreting nonverbal behavior in an accurate and appropriate manner
- using skills in a timely and effective fashion
- intervening at critical times in the group process
- being able to make use of major techniques, strategies, and procedures of group counseling

*Adapted from *Professional Standards for Training of Group Counselors* (ASGW, 1983) and reproduced by permission of the ASGW, a division of the American Association for Counseling and Development, 5999 Stevenson Avenue, Alexandria, VA 22304.

- promoting therapeutic factors that lead to change both in a group and within an individual
- being able to use adjunct group procedures such as homework
- being able to work effectively with a co-leader
- knowing how to effectively bring a group session to a close and how to terminate a group
- using follow-up procedures to maintain and support group members
- using assessment procedures to evaluate the outcomes of a group

In the area of *clinical practice,* the ASGW specifies the following types of supervised experience in group work:

- critiquing group tapes
- observing group-counseling sessions
- participating as a member in a group
- co-leading groups with supervision
- practicum experience: leading a group alone, with critical self-analysis of one's performance as well as a supervisor's feedback
- internship: practice as a group leader with on-the-job supervision

Another professional organization that sets training standards for counselors is the Council for Accreditation of Counseling and Related Educational Programs (CACREP). This body is responsible for accreditation standards for counselor-education programs. In its recent update of standards (1988) it specifies course work in group counseling as a requirement for accreditation. CACREP (1988) expects instruction in the following areas:

- principles of group dynamics, including group-process components, stages of group development, and group members' roles and behaviors
- group-leadership styles and approaches, including characteristics of various types of group leaders
- theories of group counseling, including commonalities, distinguishing characteristics, and pertinent research and literature
- group-counseling methods, including group-counselor orientations and behaviors, ethical considerations, appropriate selection criteria and methods, and methods of evaluating effectiveness
- other types of small-group approaches, theories, and methods

Perspectives on Training Group Counselors

In my view effective training in group leadership includes both didactic and experiential components. Such training should present the typical dilemmas that students are likely to face in their practice. This can best be done through formal course work along with extensive supervised practice in leading and co-leading groups. Ideally, trainees will get experience in leading groups with their peers on campus as a part of their program, and they will have supervised group experience in various community and agency settings with different client populations.

In a training program for group counselors, the ASGW's (1983) professional standards provide a general framework. In addition to formal course work in group process and group counseling and supervised practice in leading or co-leading groups, I recommend at least three experiences: (1) personal counseling, (2) experience as a member of a therapeutic group, and (3) participation in a supervision and training group for group leaders. Following is a discussion of these adjuncts to the professional preparation of group counselors.

Personal Psychotherapy for Group Leaders.   I agree with Yalom's (1985) recommendation that extensive self-exploration is necessary if trainees are to perceive countertransference feelings, recognize blind spots and biases, and use their personal attributes effectively in groups. Although videotapes, work with a co-leader, and supervision all are excellent sources of feedback that can help student group leaders discover some of their blind spots, Yalom maintains that some type of personal therapy is usually necessary for fuller understanding and correction. Group leaders should demonstrate the courage and willingness to do for themselves what they expect members in their groups to do: expand their awareness of self and the effect of that self on others.

Ohlsen, Horne, and Lawe (1988) make the point that practitioners who are not aware of their own psychological needs or who are closed to their own experience of life are not likely to be open to others. Increasing self-awareness is a major reason to seek out personal counseling. In any group there will be many instances of transferences among members and toward the leader. Transference refers to the unconscious process whereby clients project onto someone else past feelings or attitudes toward significant people in their lives. Of course, group leaders can easily become entangled in their own feelings of countertransference, or their own unconscious emotional responses to group members. Leaders also have their unresolved personal problems, and as a result they can project these personal issues onto the members of their group. Through personal counseling, trainees can work through some of their unfinished business that could easily interfere with their effective functioning as a group leader.

Self-Exploration Groups for Group Leaders.   As an adjunct to a group leader's formal course work and internship training, participation in some kind of therapeutic group is extremely valuable. Being a member in a variety of groups can prove to be an indispensable part of training for group leaders. By experiencing their own resistances, fears, and uncomfortable moments in a group; by being confronted; and by struggling with their problems in a group context, practitioners can experience what is needed to build a trusting and cohesive group.

In addition to helping interns resolve personal conflicts and increase self-understanding, a personal-growth group can be a powerful teaching tool. One of the best ways to learn how to assist group members in their struggles is to work yourself as a member of a group. Yalom (1985) strongly recommends a group experience for trainees. Some of the benefits that he suggests are experiencing the power of a group, learning what self-disclosure is about, coming to appreciate the difficulties involved in self-sharing, learning on an emotional level what one knows intellectually, and becoming aware of one's dependency on the leader's power and knowledge. Yalom cites surveys that indicate that 60% to 70% of group-therapy-training programs offer some type of personal group experience.

Training programs differ on whether participating in a group is optional or required, with about half of the programs offering a mandatory group. The ASGW (1983) and the AGPA (1978) recommend personal-group experiences as a part of a comprehensive training program for group counselors. The ASGW calls for 15 hours as the minimum participation in a group experience, and the AGPA suggests 60 hours.

Requiring participation in a therapeutic group as a part of a training program can present some practical and ethical problems of its own. One of the ethical standards of the AACD (1988) is that learning that focuses on self-understanding or personal growth should be voluntary or, if it is required as a part of the educational program, should be made known to prospective students before they enter. A related AACD guideline deals with accommodating students who do not wish to take part in personal-growth experiences: "The member [counseling educator] will at all times provide students with clear and equally acceptable alternatives for self-understanding or growth experiences. The member will assure students that they have a right to accept these alternatives without prejudice or penalty." I have difficulty with this recently added guideline. If an educational program requires a therapeutic group and if students know of this requirement before they enter, I do not see why an "equally acceptable alternative" should be provided. Although some will complain that group participation causes them anxiety, because they are expected to disclose personal issues, candidates who are not willing to deal with this anxiety should probably ask themselves why they are choosing this profession. After all, most programs require a course in statistics and research methods, and for many (including myself) this obstacle is far more anxiety-provoking than being a member of a group.

One potential ethical problem relates to who will conduct the personal group for the trainees. Ideally, the group leader could be an adjunct faculty member who does not teach courses in the program and is not in the position of evaluating students. This arrangement still does not eliminate the reality that students will be talking about themselves in personal ways. However, the problems do not seem insurmountable. This very issue of dealing with one's peers could be a focal point for group exploration. When these students graduate and work in a community agency, they will be expected to cooperate effectively with their colleagues. This means that they will need to be able to handle conflict, power struggles, and personal issues that spill over into professional exchanges.

In many group courses the class is structured to include a combination of didactic and experiential components. With such a structure, the first half of the class typically deals with counseling theories and group-process issues. The content of the discussions may be very similar to the material in this textbook. During the second half of the session many instructors conduct a group in which the students have an opportunity to be a member. Sometimes students co-lead a small group with a peer and are supervised by the instructor. Of course, this arrangement is not without problems either. Students may fear that their grade will be influenced by their participation (or lack of it) in the experiential part of the class. Clear guidelines need to be established so that students know what their rights and responsibilities are. This arrangement does put a bit more pressure on both the instructor and the students. It calls for honesty, maturity, and professionalism. For example, instructors can spell out very clearly the criteria for grading. The criteria may include the results of written reports, oral reports and presentations, essay tests, and objective examinations. The experiential group does not have to be graded, but the students know that they are expected to attend regularly and to participate. One other safeguard is that students can decide for themselves what personal issues they will bring up for exploration. In such a group a productive focus is on here-and-now interactions. Even if members choose not to bring up matters such as their childhood, there is plenty to talk about if they deal with their feelings and reactions to other people in the group. If they openly and honestly learn to deal with one another, they are making great strides in learning how to facilitate a group.

Participation in a Training and Supervision Group. I have found workshops most useful in helping group trainees develop the skills necessary for effective intervention. Also, the trainees can learn a great deal about their response to criticism, their competitiveness, their need for approval, their concerns over being competent, and their power struggles. In working both with university students learning about group approaches and with professionals who want to upgrade their group skills, I have found an intensive weekend workshop effective. In these workshops the participants have ample opportunity to lead their small group for a designated period. After a segment in which the participants lead their group, my colleagues and I intervene by giving feedback and by promoting a discussion by the entire group. By the end of the weekend each participant has led the group at least twice (for an hour each time) under direct supervision. M. Corey and Corey (1986) describe a framework for such a weekend or week-long residential workshop for training and supervision using experiential and didactic methods to help participants refine their skills as group leaders. This type of workshop is a regular part of my own group-counseling courses on both the undergraduate and graduate levels. It is an example of combining personal-growth goals with educational goals. One of the best ways to learn how to facilitate groups is to get extensive experience as both a group member and a group leader, with supervised feedback and teaching. The training workshop provides for this type of learning.

The Role of Continuing Education in Maintaining Competence

The education and training of a group leader are an ongoing process, one that does not terminate when the diploma or license is granted. I believe that continuing education is mandatory for anyone who seeks to develop both as a person and as a group leader. Corey, Corey, and Callanan (1988) suggest several ways of maintaining a high level of competence:

- Develop or upgrade your skills by working with colleagues who have specialized or more advanced knowledge and experience in areas where you need further training.
- Learn new skills by attending conferences and conventions, especially those workshops that are designed for the in-service training of group leaders.
- Take advanced courses in areas you don't know too well, as well as special-interest courses offered through continuing education at various colleges, to keep abreast of current developments in your field.
- Attend workshops that combine didactic and experiential learning, along with some supervised practice.

Most professional organizations are currently attempting to make continuing education a requirement for relicensure. It is my hope, however, that you will take the initiative in updating, developing, and refining your knowledge and techniques rather than relying on mandates to motivate you.

To summarize, as a group leader you need to struggle continually and sincerely with the issue of your competence. Ask yourself, for example:

- What techniques can I skillfully employ?
- What kinds of clients do I work best with in groups?
- With whom do I work least well?
- How far can I go with clients?
- When and how should I refer clients?
- When do I need to consult with other professionals?
- How can I continue to upgrade my professional leadership abilities?

Suggestions for Developing an Ethical and Professional Orientation to Group Work

Group leaders soon learn that the task of developing and maintaining a sense of professional and ethical responsibility is unending. As you gain practical experience, you will find yourself delving even more deeply into basic ethical issues. Thus, I cannot provide you with ready-made answers concerning ethical practice; rather, my aim is to offer some general ethical guidelines, with the hope that they will stimulate you to design your own code of ethical and professional conduct. Such a code will require much honest thinking and evaluating on your part.

What follows are suggestions for responsible group leadership throughout the course of a group's life. These issues will be discussed in greater detail in Chapters 4 and 5.

Considerations before the group begins:

1. Take responsibility for getting the training and supervision you need to do a competent job of leading groups. Avoid undertaking a project that is clearly beyond your scope.
2. Take steps to maintain and upgrade your knowledge and skills. Take courses and professional workshops, and meet regularly with colleagues to discuss your work.
3. Learn what state laws govern the practice of group work. Be aware of ways to lessen the chances that you will be embroiled in a malpractice suit.
4. Develop screening skills that allow you to differentiate between suitable and unsuitable applicants. Also, be able to explain to prospective participants the expectations you have of them, the techniques that are likely to be employed, and the ground rules that will govern the group. Informed consent ensures that members will be partners in the group process.
5. In working with minors in a group, first secure the written permission of parents or guardians. Strive to bring the parents into the process.
6. Discuss the importance of confidentiality with members before they enter a group. Make them aware that confidentiality in the group cannot be guaranteed.
7. Explore the psychological risks of participating in a group with prospective group members. A function of the group leader is to help potential members assess these risks.
8. Articulate a theoretical orientation that guides your practice and provides a rationale for your interventions. Consider which theories are most congruent with the person you are, and give thought to which techniques are most suited to the groups you lead and the nature of your clientele.

Considerations during the early stages of a group's development:

1. Clarify and, if necessary, redefine the purpose of your group. Ensure that your techniques and methods are appropriate for these purposes.

2. Be aware of the impact of your personal values on group members. Make sure that you understand your basic values and how they affect you as a leader and your choice of interventions. Although it is not realistic to keep your values separate from your group leadership, you can expose your values rather than imposing them.

3. Be open to learning about the values of clients who come from a different cultural background from yours. Consider ways to modify your techniques to fit the unique needs of various cultural and ethnic groups.

4. Monitor your behavior, and be conscious of what you are modeling in the group. Are you teaching members by your example? Are you willing to reveal your personal reactions to what you are experiencing in the group? Are you demonstrating patience and respect? Recognize that your behavior is critical in creating a beneficial climate.

5. Remain alert to ways in which your personal reactions to members might inhibit the group process, and monitor your countertransference. Although your personal needs may be met through your professional work, be careful of meeting these needs at the expense of the members of your group. Avoid using the group for your own therapy.

6. Pay attention to how resistance affects you. Ask yourself whether your behavior as a group leader is encouraging the members to talk about their resistance and to explore it. Do you become defensive yourself as you encounter member resistance? Do you respect the resistance of members by attempting to understand the meaning behind it?

7. Be alert for symptoms of psychological debilitation in group members, which may indicate that their participation should be discontinued. Be able to put such clients in contact with appropriate referral resources.

8. Protect the rights of individual group members. By blocking group pressure, ensure that members reveal in the group only what they choose to share. Stop any scapegoating that would deprive individual members of their dignity.

9. Develop and manifest a genuine respect for group members and their capacity to direct their own lives.

10. Keep yourself informed about research findings, and be able to apply this information to increase the effectiveness of your groups.

11. If you are co-leading a group, make the time to meet with your co-leader regularly to talk about the experience of leading together as well to share your perspectives on what is going on in your group.

12. Recognize the importance of ongoing assessment of a group, and assist members in evaluating their own progress after each session.

Considerations during the later stages of a group's development:

1. Continue to question yourself about the modeling you are providing for your group members. Are you demonstrating honest and direct behavior in the group? Are you willing to do in your own life what you are encouraging your members to do in their lives?

2. Be concerned about promoting members' independence from the group. Are your interventions designed to empower the members? Are you structuring the group in such a way as to encourage them to assume an increasing degree of responsibility for the direction the group takes?

3. Do not attempt a technique unless you are trained in its use or under supervision by an expert familiar with the intervention. Consider the benefits of being a member in a group yourself, and experience as a member the techniques that you introduce as a group leader.

4. Consider setting aside time at the end of each group session to encourage members to express their thoughts and feelings about the session. Part of your task as a leader is to help members develop self-evaluation skills.

5. Help participants deal with potentially negative reactions from others in their attempts to apply their group learning to daily life. Help them deal with any regression, and encourage them to develop a support system outside of the group that will increase their chances of maintaining behavioral changes.

6. As problems or concerns arise in the course of leading a group, be open to seeking consultation. Find sources for ongoing supervision. Seeking guidance is a mark of being a professional.

7. Step up your assistance to members in translating what they have learned in the group to daily life. Consider helping them develop contracts that they will put into action once the group ends.

8. Think about ways in which you can combine the functions of practitioner and researcher. Your research efforts can provide you with critical information to improve your groups.

Considerations after the termination of a group:

1. Consider arranging for a follow-up session with the group, so that the members can check their progress and so that you can evaluate the effectiveness of the group as an agent for change.

2. If a group postsession is impractical, think of alternatives so that you can keep track of the members. Consider strategies such as follow-ups by telephone or mail.

3. Consider private postgroup interviews with members to discuss the progress they have made in reaching their personal goals. Such a practice is a preventive measure against the tendency of some members to discount the value of a group experience. Be prepared to make appropriate referrals for further growth experiences.

4. Develop methods of evaluation to determine the effectiveness of a group. Accountability is a way to refine your leadership techniques and to develop your style of leadership. In the student manual of this text are examples of instruments that can be used by both group members and leaders to assess the process and outcomes of sessions. You can also develop your own assessment devices.

5. If you are co-leading, arrange for adequate time to thoroughly discuss the major turning points in your group, from the first group meeting to the final session. Knowing what you know now, what might you have done differently?

Further Reading on the Ethics of Group Work

After completing this chapter you may want a more detailed treatment of ethical, legal, and professional issues in the practice of group work. Two articles of interest are "Training Group Leaders in Ethical Decision Making" (Gumaer & Scott, 1985) and "Group Workers' Perceptions of Ethical and Unethical Behavior of Group Leaders" (Gumaer & Scott, 1986). Another excellent article, "Ethics of Practice: The Beliefs and Behaviors of Psychologists as Therapists" (Pope, Tabachnick, & Keith-Spiegel, 1987), presents the results of a survey questionnaire of APA members regarding the degree to which they engaged in each of 83 behaviors and the degree to which they considered each behavior to be ethical.

If you are interested in more far-ranging reviews of ethical and legal issues in counseling practice, the following are useful sources: *The Law and the Practice of Human Services* (Woody, 1984); *Legal Liability in Psychotherapy* (B. M. Schutz, 1982); *The Counselor and the Law* (Hopkins & Anderson, 1985); *Ethical and Legal Issues in Counseling and Psychotherapy* (Van Hoose & Kottler, 1985); *Issues and Ethics in the Helping Professions* (Corey, Corey, & Callanan, 1988); *Law and Ethics in Counseling* (Hummel, Talbutt, & Alexander, 1985); *Ethics in Psychology* (Keith-Spiegel & Koocher, 1985); *Ethical, Legal and Professional Issues* (Huber & Baruth, 1987); *Ethical Decisions for Social Work Practice* (Loewenberg & Dolgoff, 1988); and *Becoming a Helper* (M. Corey & Corey, 1989).

3

Group Leadership

This chapter focuses on the influence of the group leader, as a person and as a professional, on group process. After discussing the personal characteristics of effective leaders, I analyze the skills and techniques that are necessary for successful leadership and the specific functions and roles of group leaders. This chapter will give you enough information about these crucial topics to allow you to fully benefit from the discussion in the next two chapters of the stages in a group's development. The topics covered in this chapter also represent an important prelude to the theory chapters in Part II.

The Group Leader as a Person

Group-counseling techniques cannot be divorced from the leader's personal characteristics and behaviors. Thus, I don't agree with those who attribute the success or failure of a group mainly to the characteristics of the participants or to the specific techniques being used to get the group moving. These are no doubt important variables, but I don't see them, by themselves, as determining the outcome of a group.

Group leaders can acquire extensive theoretical and practical knowledge of group dynamics and be skilled in diagnostic and technical procedures yet be ineffective in stimulating growth and change in the members of their groups. Leaders bring to every group their personal qualities, values, and life experiences. In order to promote growth in the members' lives, leaders need to live growth-oriented lives themselves. In order to foster honest self-investigation in others, leaders need to have the courage to engage in self-appraisal themselves. In order to inspire others to break away from deadening ways of being, leaders need to be willing to seek new experiences themselves. In short, the most effective group direction is found in the kind of life the group members see the leader demonstrating and not in the words they hear the leader saying.

I am not implying that group leaders must be self-actualized beings who have successfully worked through all of their problems. The issue is not whether leaders have personal problems but whether they are willing to make serious attempts to live the way they encourage members to live. More important than being a finished product is the willingness to continually look at oneself to see whether one's life reflects life-giving values. The key to success as a group leader is the commitment to the never-ending struggle to become more effective as a human being.

Personality and Character

The following personal characteristics are vitally related to effective group leadership, since their presence or absence can facilitate or inhibit the group process. Keep these descriptions in mind as you evaluate your own characteristics in terms of effective group leadership.

Presence. Being emotionally present means being moved by the joy and pain that others experience. If leaders recognize and give expression to their own emotions, they can become more emotionally involved with others. Although this emotional presence doesn't necessarily entail talking about the life experiences associated with these feelings, leaders' ability to draw on these experiences makes it easier for them to empathize with and be compassionate toward the group members. Presence also has to do with "being there" for the group members, which involves genuine caring and a willingness to enter their psychological world. Being present implies that leaders are not fragmented when they come to a group session, that they are not preoccupied with other matters, and that they are open to their reactions in the group.

Personal Power. Personal power involves self-confidence and an awareness of one's influence on others. If group leaders do not feel a sense of power in their own lives (or if they do not feel in control of their destiny), it is difficult for them to facilitate members' movement toward empowerment. In short, it is not possible to give to others what one does not possess. It should be stressed that power does *not* mean domination and exploitation of others, which are abuses of power. Truly powerful leaders use the effect they have on group participants to encourage them to get in contact with their own unused power, not to foster their dependency. Personal power is accompanied by the recognition that one does not need to keep others in an inferior position to maintain one's own power. A part of the group that group leaders may experience stems from sharing in the growth and change of the members. True, if members take the risks to change, the bulk of the credit belongs to them. Yet group leaders are at times a key source of inspiration for members who are struggling to become the powerful people that they are capable of being.

Courage. Effective group leaders are aware that they need to exhibit courage in their interactions with group members and that they cannot hide behind their special role as counselor. They show courage by taking risks in the group and admitting mistakes, by being occasionally vulnerable, by confronting others and revealing their own reactions to those they confront, by acting on intuitions and beliefs, by discussing with the group their thoughts and feelings about the group process, and by being willing to share their power with the group members. They can model important lessons to members by taking a stance toward life and acting in spite of the fact that they are imperfect. When members push themselves to leave familiar and secure patterns, they often report being anxious and scared. Group leaders can demonstrate, through their own behavior, the willingness to move ahead in spite of being afraid.

Willingness to Confront Oneself. One of leaders' central tasks is to promote self-investigation in their clients. Since group counselors cannot expect participants to do something that they themselves are not prepared to do, they must show that they are willing to question themselves. Self-confrontation can take the form of posing and answering questions such as the following:

- Why am I leading groups? What am I getting from this activity?
- Why do I behave as I do in a group? What impact do my attitudes, values, biases, feelings, and behaviors have on the people in the group?
- What needs of mine are served by being a group leader?
- Do I ever use the groups I lead to satisfy my personal needs at the expense of the members' needs?

Self-confrontation is an ongoing process, and there are no simple answers to these questions. The main issue is the *willingness* to continually raise questions in order to determine how honest you are with yourself about your motivations for being a group leader.

Self-awareness is a concomitant of the willingness to confront oneself. This essential characteristic of effective leadership includes awareness not only of one's needs and motivations but also of personal conflicts and problems, of defenses and weak spots, of areas of unfinished business, and of the potential influence of all of these on the group process. Leaders who are self-aware are able to work therapeutically with the transferences that emerge within the group setting, both toward themselves and toward other members. Furthermore, they are aware of their own vulnerabilities, especially their potential countertransference. They do not make the members responsible for their reactions, nor do they use the group as a place to seek their own therapy. Group leaders have the power to control the sessions so that their needs for external confirmation can continually be reinforced through the group. They can create the dangerous situation of a group whose members devote more of their efforts to pleasing the leader than to working on themselves.

Sincerity and Authenticity.   One of the leader's most important qualities is a sincere interest in the well-being and growth of others. Since sincerity involves being direct, it can also involve telling members what they don't want to hear. For a group leader, caring means challenging the members to look at parts of their lives that they are denying and discouraging any form of dishonest behavior in the group.

Authenticity is a close cousin to sincerity. Authentic group leaders do not live by pretenses and do not hide behind masks, defenses, sterile roles, and facades. Authenticity entails the willingness to appropriately disclose oneself and share feelings and reactions to what is going on in the group. But, as we will examine in more detail, authenticity does not imply indiscriminately "letting it all hang out." It is surely possible to be authentic without sharing every fleeting thought, perception, fantasy, and reaction. For instance, even though a leader might initially be sexually attracted to a member, it would not be wise to disclose this reality at the initial session. Such "holding back" does not imply inauthenticity.

Sense of Identity.   If group leaders are to help others discover who they are, they need to have a clear sense of their own identity. This means knowing what one values and living by internally derived standards, not by what others expect. It means being aware of one's own strengths, limitations, needs, fears, motivations, and goals. It means knowing what one is capable of becoming, what one wants from life, and how one is going to get what one wants.

A major part of the group-counseling experience involves members' sorting out for themselves who they are and what identities they have assumed without conscious thought. When people live by outworn identities, their lives become meaningless. An effective group can be instrumental in providing a challenge to members to create projects that will bring a new level of meaning to their lives. Through the group experience members see that their identity is not cast in stone but that they can reshape the purpose of their life. Group leaders who themselves continue to reshape their personal meanings can be an encouragement to the members.

Belief in Group Process and Enthusiasm.   The leader's deep belief in the value of group process is essential to the success of the group. Why should group members believe that the group experience will be of value to them if the leader is without enthusiasm for it? Too often practitioners lead groups in an agency simply because they are expected to, without being convinced that group interventions make a difference.

The enthusiasm that group leaders bring to their groups can have an infectious quality. If leaders radiate life, the chances are slim that they will be consistently leading "dead groups." If group leaders lack enthusiasm for what they are doing, however, it is unlikely that they will inspire group members and provide them with an incentive to work. This is not to say that practitioners should adopt a "cheerleading" style. What I am suggesting is that leaders need to show that they enjoy their work and like being with their groups. A leader's lack of enthusiasm is generally reflected in members' lack of excitement about coming to group sessions and in their resistance to doing significant work.

Inventiveness and Creativity. The capacity to be spontaneously creative and to approach a group with fresh ideas says a lot about the potential effectiveness of a leader. Leaders need to avoid getting trapped in ritualized techniques and programmed presentations that are void of life. It may not be easy to approach each group with new ideas. Inventive and creative leaders are open to new experiences and to lifestyles and values that differ from their own.

One of the main advantages of group work is that it offers so many avenues for being inventive. Many groups with a special focus grow out of a leader's willingness to brainstorm. In fact, group leaders often develop an idea for a special group because of a concern in their life. For instance, group leaders who are struggling with stress in their personal and professional lives might create a support group for professionals with similar concerns. In addition, the very structure of groups encourages creativity in devising a wide range of approaches.

Other Views and a Concluding Comment

A number of authors have addressed the issue of the personal characteristics associated with effective group leadership. Shapiro (1978), for example, describes the "ideal personality for a group therapist" in terms of honesty, integrity, patience, courage, flexibility, warmth, empathy, intelligence, timing, and self-knowledge. Research on the leader characteristics necessary for establishing a therapeutic relationship was done by Carkhuff (1969a, 1969b). His research identified empathy, genuineness, respect, and concreteness as the "primary core of the facilitative dimension." In summarizing the research on characteristics of group leaders, Bednar and Kaul (1978) observe that relatively little research has been done in the area. They conclude: "Despite the nearly universal agreement that leader characteristics are important determinants of the group process and outcomes, the literature does not reflect much empirical interest in the topic" (p. 786).

As you review the list of characteristics of effective group leaders, do not burden yourself with thinking that you have to possess all of these qualities to the utmost. Consider such qualities on a continuum. For instance, it is not a matter that either you have traits such as courage, self-awareness, and a clear sense of identity or you don't. It is likely that the greater your self-awareness, the more likely you will be to facilitate members' self-exploration that will expand their awareness. The challenge is for you to take an honest look at your personal qualities and make an assessment of your ability as a person to inspire others. Your own commitment to living up to your potential is a key tool. Your best way of leading others is by demonstrating what you believe in through your own life. Experiencing your own therapy (either individually or in groups) is one way to remain open to looking at the direction of your life. It is certainly not a matter of being the perfectly integrated group leader who has "arrived." Once you have arrived, after all, there is no place to go!

From my perspective the personal dimensions described in the preceding pages are essential. Yet they are not sufficient for successful leadership. Specialized knowledge and skills, as identified by the ASGW's (1983) *Professional Standards for Training of Group Counselors* and described in the previous chapter, are central to effective group leadership. Later in this chapter we will examine these skills and competencies in greater detail.

Special Problems and Issues for Beginning Group Leaders

Through my work in training and supervising group leaders and providing in-service workshops, I have come across a number of issues with special relevance for beginning leaders. Although these issues must be faced by all group leaders regardless of their experience, they are especially significant for those who are relatively inexperienced.

You may wonder whether you have what it takes to be an effective leader. My advice is to be patient with yourself and not to demand that you immediately become the "perfect group leader." Most practitioners I know (including myself) struggled over their competence when they began leading groups and still have difficult times even after considerable experience. Such self-doubts are less of a problem if you are willing to continue to seek training and to work under supervision.

Initial Anxiety

Before you lead your first group, you will no doubt be anxious about getting the group started and about keeping it moving. In other words, you will probably be asking yourself questions like these with a certain degree of trepidation:

- Do I know enough to lead a group yet?
- What do the participants really expect of me?
- Will I be able to get the group started? How?
- Will I run out of things to say or do well before the end of the session?
- Should I take an active role, or should I wait for the group to start on its own?

- Should I have an agenda, or should I let the group members decide what they want to talk about?
- What techniques shall I use during the early stages of the group?
- What if nobody wants to participate? And what if too many people want to participate? How will I be able to take care of those who want to get involved?
- Will the group members want to come back?

In supervising and training beginning leaders, I encourage them to recognize that these doubts and concerns are perfectly normal and that moderate anxiety can be beneficial, because it can lead to honest self-appraisal. Anxiety can be counterproductive, however, if it begins to feed on itself and is allowed to freeze one into inactivity. Therefore, I encourage beginning leaders to voice their questions and concerns and to explore them in the course of the training sessions. Their very willingness to do this can allay some unnecessary anxiety, for the trainees discover that their peers share their same concerns. Students frequently say that their peers appear to be so much more knowledgeable, skilled, talented, and self-confident than they themselves are. When they hear their peers express anxieties and feelings of inadequacy, these students realize that those who appear to be extremely self-confident are also struggling with self-doubts. The interchanges that occur when trainees are willing to openly discuss their anxieties offer invaluable opportunities for personal and professional growth. Exploring these feelings with peers and a supervisor can help the beginning leader distinguish between realistic and unrealistic anxiety and thus defuse unwarranted and counterproductive anxiety.

Self-Disclosure

Regardless of their years of experience, many group leaders struggle with the problem of self-disclosure. For beginning leaders the issue is of even greater concern. Although *what* to reveal and *when* are factors in determining the appropriateness of self-disclosure, the issue centers on *how much*. It is not uncommon to err on either extreme, disclosing too little or disclosing too much.

Too Little Self-Disclosure.   If you try very hard to maintain stereotyped role expectations and keep yourself mysterious by hiding behind your professional facade, you can lose your personal identity in the group and allow very little of yourself to be known. The reasons for functioning in a role (rather than as a person who has certain functions to perform) are many. One may be the fear of appearing unprofessional or of losing the respect of the members. Another may be the need to keep a distance or to maintain a "doctor/patient" relationship.

In addition to being unwilling to share your personal life, you may also be hesitant to disclose how you feel in the group or how you feel toward certain members. As a way of avoiding sharing your own reactions to what is occurring within the group, you might limit your interventions to detached observations. Such "professional" aloofness may be expressed by making interpretations and suggestions, asking questions rather than making personal statements, acting as a mere coordinator, providing one structured exercise after another to keep the group moving, and clarifying issues. Although these functions are important, they can be carried out without keeping you from revealing what you are presently experiencing in the group.

In my opinion, the most productive form of sharing is disclosure that is related to what is going on in the group. For instance, if you have a persistent feeling that most members are not very motivated and are not investing themselves in the session, you are likely to feel burdened by the constant need to keep the meetings alive all by yourself, with little or no support from the participants. Disclosing how you are affected by this lack of motivation is generally very useful and appropriate.

Too Much Self-Disclosure. At the other end of the continuum are the problems associated with excessive self-disclosure. Most beginning group leaders (and many experienced ones) have a strong need to be approved of and accepted by the group members. It's easy to make the mistake of "paying membership dues" by sharing intimate details to prove that you are just as human as the members. There is a fine line between appropriate and inappropriate self-disclosure. It is a mistake to assume that "the more disclosure, the better." It is also inappropriate to "let it all hang out" without evaluating the reasons for your disclosures, the readiness of the members, the impact that your sharing of intimate details is likely to have on them, and the degree to which your disclosures are relevant to the here-and-now process of the group.

You may be tempted to submit to group pressure to share more of yourself. Members often say to leaders: "We don't know much about you. Why don't you say more about yourself? For example, tell us about your hang-ups. *We* talk about ourselves, and now we'd like to see you come down to our level and open up too!" The members can exert more subtle, but no less strong, pressures for you to "become a member" of the group you are leading. Out of your attempt to avoid getting lost in a professionally aloof role, you may try too hard to be perceived as a friend and a fellow group member. If you decide to share personal concerns, it should be for the benefit of your clients. The place to *explore* these concerns (and thus serve your own needs) is a group in which you are a participant yourself. Group leading is demanding work, and you can make this work even more difficult by confusing your role and functions with those of the participants.

Research Findings on Leader Self-Disclosure. The empirical research on self-disclosure in group counseling is somewhat limited, but it suggests a complex, multidimensional interaction between frequency of disclosure and other factors such as type of group and population, level of disclosure, and timing (Morran, 1982; Stockton & Morran, 1982). After surveying the literature, Dies (1983b) suggests that disclosure can have either a constructive or a detrimental effect on group process and outcome, depending on specific factors such as the type of group, the stage of group development, and the content of disclosure. Group leaders who are open about their own reactions are more likely to facilitate the development of positive interpersonal relationships. But Dies adds the cautionary note that clients tend to expect the group leader to possess confidence and competence and to provide some initial structuring and direction. They may not want leaders to be too revealing of their own feelings, experiences, or conflicts early in the course of a group. Leaders who disclose in a manipulative way can cause members to question their capabilities. But leaders can facilitate interaction within the group by disclosing some of their personal reactions related to the here and now, because such information generally pertains directly to members' opportunities for interpersonal learning (Morran, 1982).

Yalom (1983, 1985) stresses that leader self-disclosure must be instrumental in helping the *members* attain their goals. He calls for selective disclosure that provides members with acceptance, support, and encouragement. For Yalom, group leaders who disclose here-and-now reactions, rather than detailed personal events from their past, facilitate the movement of the group.

Facilitative and appropriate self-disclosure is an essential aspect of the art of group leading. It is not necessary to disclose details of your past or of your personal life in order to make yourself known as a person or to empathize with the participants. A few words can convey a great deal, and nonverbal messages—a touch, a look, a gesture—can express feelings of identification and understanding. Appropriate disclosure does not take the focus away from the client and is never a contrived technique to get the group members to open up. Your sensitivity to how people respond to your disclosures can teach you a lot about their timeliness and value. Timeliness is a truly critical factor, for what might be inappropriate to disclose during the early stages of a group could be very useful at a later stage.

Learning what constitutes valuable self-disclosure does require experience. Experience is essential in learning how to be yourself and how to effectively express feelings of identification and understanding. It can teach you how to overcome the need to prove your humanness at the risk of failing to be authentic or serving your own needs instead of those of the group members.

I think that Kottler (1983) makes an excellent point about the abuse of self-disclosure: "Group leaders who like to hear themselves talk, who, because of ego deficiencies, attempt to impress clients with their prowess, or who use group time to meet their own needs are acting unethically" (p. 10). He suggests that leaders ask themselves: Whom will I help by my sharing? How will it help them? This kind of self-monitoring can ensure that leaders use disclosure to promote client change.

Dealing with Difficult Group Members

Many students in group-counseling classes want to talk about the "difficult" members in the groups they are leading. Learning how to deal therapeutically with resistance and the many forms it takes is a central challenge for group leaders. When beginning counselors encounter members who are highly resistant, they often take the matter personally. They seem to view themselves as not being competent enough to adequately cope with certain problematic members. If they were able to "break through" the layers of defenses of some of these difficult members, they believe, they would then feel competent. When I encounter such attitudes, I encourage my students to look at how they are being personally affected by the wide variety of problem behaviors. I suggest that they avoid categorizing people in their groups as "problem types" and instead attempt to understand the meaning of certain forms of resistance. A few of these forms are intellectualizing, emotionalizing, questioning, giving advice, being overly silent, monopolizing, storytelling, demanding answers and direction from others, dependency, hostility, aggression, and haughtiness. The fact is that many of us would display a variety of avoidance strategies if we were in a group. As old patterns are challenged and as we experience the anxiety that accompanies personal change, we are likely to be very creative in devising a pattern of resistive strategies. Remember, resistance does make sense and emerges from members for a purpose. My way of working with students is to teach them to take into account their own reactions to resistant members rather than focusing entirely on strategies for dealing with "problem members."

Dealing with Your Own Reactions to Member Resistance

When group members exhibit what you consider to be problematic behavior, as a group leader you need to be aware of the tendency to respond with strong feelings. In the previous chapter we saw the importance of becoming aware of your own countertransference and learning how to deal effectively with your feelings. You may be threatened by those members who dominate and attempt to control the group; you may be angered over members who display resistive behavior; you may blame certain clients or the group as a whole for the slow pace or lack of productivity of the group; and you may take personally any signs of resistance.

If you ignore your own reactions, you are in essence leaving yourself out of the interactions that occur in the group. Your own responses—be they feelings, thoughts, reactions, or observations—are often the most powerful resource at your disposal in effectively handling resisting behaviors. As we've seen, a rationale for group leaders to experience their own group therapy is that this kind of self-exploration increases the chances that they will gain awareness of their own blind spots and potential vulnerabilities. Frequently, the "difficult" members who affect us the most are those who remind us of aspects of ourselves that we would just as soon deny.

In dealing with countertransference, supervision is most helpful. As a trainee, you have the opportunity to explore with your supervisor and fellow group leaders your feelings of attraction or dislike toward certain members and learn a lot about yourself in the process. If you are leading a group alone and no longer have supervision, it is important that you be willing to consult with a qualified professional so that you can work through unresolved problems that may lie behind your feelings of countertransference. One of the advantages of working with a co-leader is that the partner can offer valuable feedback from an objective point of view and thus help you see things that may be blocked from your awareness. The topic of handling countertransference is discussed further in Chapter 6.

The Group Leader as a Professional

Group-Leadership Skills

It is a mistake to assume that anyone with certain personal qualities and a desire to help will be an effective group leader. Successful leadership requires specific group-leadership skills and the appropriate performance of certain functions. Like most skills, leadership skills need to be learned and practiced.

Active Listening. Active listening involves paying total attention to the speaker and being sensitive to what is being communicated at the verbal and nonverbal levels. Active listening also involves being attuned to underlying messages—that is, to what is *not* being directly expressed.

Like any skill, active listening can be developed to varying levels. Thus, your ability to hear what is being communicated improves as your expertise improves. Many leaders make the mistake of focusing too intently on the *content* and, in doing so, don't pay enough attention to the *way* in which group members express themselves. Being a skilled group leader entails picking up the rich cues provided by members through their style of speech, body posture, gestures, voice quality, and mannerisms. (The topic of active listening will be dealt with in greater detail in Chapter 10, since attending and listening are key concepts of the person-centered approach to group work.)

Restating. In a sense, restating is an extension of listening. It means recasting what someone said into different words so that the meaning is clearer to both the speaker and the group. Effective restating zeroes in on the core of a person's message, brings into sharper focus the meaning of what was said, and thus eliminates ambiguity. By capturing the essence of a member's message and reflecting it back, the leader helps the person continue the self-exploration process on a deeper level.

Restating is not an easy skill to master. Some group leaders, for example, confine themselves to simply repeating what was said, adding little new meaning and not really clarifying the message. Others overuse the technique, with the result of sounding mechanical and repetitive. The value of accurate and concise restating is twofold: it tells the participants that they are being understood, and it helps them see more clearly the issues they are struggling with and their own feelings and thoughts about these issues.

Clarifying. Clarifying, too, is an extension of active listening. It involves responding to confusing and unclear aspects of a message by focusing on underlying issues and helping the person sort out conflicting feelings. Often members say that they have ambivalent feelings or are feeling many things at once. Clarification can help the participants sort out their feelings so that they can focus more sharply on what they are actually experiencing. The same procedure applies to thinking. At one time or another group participants will say that their thoughts are muddled and they are not sure what they are really thinking. Clarification can help sort out these thoughts. In clarifying, the group leader stays within the individual's frame of reference but, at the same time, helps the client put things into perspective; this, in turn, may lead to a slightly deeper level of self-exploration on the part of the client.

Summarizing. The skill of pulling together the important elements of a group interaction or part of a session is known as summarizing. This ability is particularly useful when making a transition from one topic to another. Rather than merely proceeding from issue to issue, it is valuable to identify common elements in order to increase learning and maintain continuity.

Summarizing is especially needed at the end of a session. It is a mistake for a group leader to end a session abruptly, with little attempt to pull the session together. One of the leader's functions is to help members reflect on and make sense of what has occurred in their group. Summarizing encourages participants to think about what they have learned and experienced in a session and about ways of applying what they have gained to their everyday lives. At the end of the session group leaders may offer their own brief summary or ask each member in turn to summarize what has taken place, what the highlights of the session were, and how each responded to the interaction.

Questioning. Questioning is probably the technique that novice group leaders tend to overuse most. Bombarding members with question after question does not lead to productive outcomes and may even have a negative impact on the group interaction. There are several problems with the ineffective use of questioning. Members feel violated, as if they had been subjected to the "third degree." The questioner probes for personal information while remaining safe and anonymous behind the interrogation. Also, a low-level questioning style on the leader's part provides a poor model for the members, who soon begin to imitate the leader's ineffective questioning style when they deal with one another.

Not all questioning is inappropriate. It is closed questions, which require a mere "yes" or "no" response, that are generally fruitless. And so are "why" questions, because they usually lead to intellectual ruminating. Instead, open questions—questions that open up alternatives and new areas of self-investigation—can be of real value. "*What* are you experiencing right now?" "*What* is happening with your body at this moment?" and "*How* are you dealing with your fear in this group?" are questions that can help the participants become more focused and feel their emotions more deeply. Therefore, it is important that leaders ask questions that, instead of merely probing endlessly, are meant to explore issues in greater depth. (The topic of questioning will be dealt with in greater detail in Chapter 15 as a special procedure used in reality group therapy.)

Interpreting. The leader interprets when he or she offers possible explanations for a participant's behavior, feelings, or thoughts. By offering tentative hypotheses concerning certain patterns of behavior, interpreting helps the individual see new perspectives and alternatives. Interpreting requires a great deal of skill. Interpreting too soon, presenting an interpretation in a dogmatic way, and encouraging the members to become dependent on the leader to provide meanings and answers are some of the common mistakes. Timing is especially important. Interpretations not only have to be made at a time when the person is likely to be willing to consider them but also need to be expressed in a tentative way that gives the person a chance to assess their validity. Although an interpretation may be technically correct, it may be rejected if the leader is not sensitive to the client's willingness or unwillingness to accept it. (I will return to the topic of interpreting in Chapters 6 and 7.)

Confronting. Confrontation can be a powerful way of challenging members to take an honest look at themselves. If it is handled poorly, it also has the potential of being detrimental both to the person being confronted and to the group process. Many beginning leaders shy away from confrontation, because they fear its possible repercussions: blocking the group interaction, hurting someone, or becoming the target of retaliation. The problem with confrontation is that it can easily be seen as an uncaring attack. That's why skilled group counselors confront only when they care about the person, and they do so in a way that gives the person ample opportunity to consider what is being said. Skillful confrontation specifies the behavior or the discrepancies between verbal and nonverbal messages that are being challenged, so that no labeling can possibly occur.

It is useful for leaders to bring their own reactions into the act of confrontation. Thus, skilled counselors would not say "George, you are a boring person." Instead, they might say: "George, I find it difficult to pay attention to what you say. I'm aware that I get impatient and that I tend to tune you out. I really don't like this, and I'd like to be able to attend to what you are saying." (Confrontation is a skill I will discuss in more detail in Chapters 11, 14, and 15.)

Reflecting Feelings. Reflecting feelings is the skill of responding to the essence of what a person has communicated. The purpose is to let members know that they are being heard and understood. Although reflection entails mirroring certain feelings that the person has expressed, it is not merely a bouncing-back process. Reflection is dependent on attention, interest, understanding, and respect for the person. When reflection is done well, it fosters further contact and involvement; feeling understood and achieving a clearer grasp of one's feelings are very reinforcing and stimulate the person to seek greater self-awareness.

Supporting. Supporting means providing group members with encouragement and reinforcement, especially when they are disclosing personal information, when they are exploring painful feelings, and when they are taking risks. A leader can provide support by being fully present at the appropriate time. This full presence is what Ivey (1988) refers to as *attending behavior,* and it requires a combination of skills: listening actively to what is being said, being psychologically present with the client, and responding in a way that encourages the client to continue working and to move forward. Full attention can be communicated in a variety of ways— through eye contact, posture, or gestures and by staying with a client on a single theme.

The essence of this skill is knowing when it will be facilitative and when it will be counterproductive. Some group leaders make the mistake of being overly supportive, of supporting without challenging, or of supporting too soon. I like Egan's (1973) caution about the blending of support and confrontation: "Confrontation without support is disastrous; support without confrontation is anemic" (p. 132). If leaders limit themselves to a style that is almost exclusively supportive, they deprive the members of potentially valuable challenges. Leaders who offer support too quickly when someone is exploring painful material tend to defuse the intensity of the experience and pull group members away from their feelings.

Support is particularly appropriate when people are faced with a crisis, when they are venturing into new territory, when they are trying to rid themselves of unconstructive behavior and establish new behaviors, and when they are attempting to implement what they are learning in the group to situations in their daily lives. (I will return to this topic in Chapter 10.)

Empathizing. The core of the skill of empathy lies in the leader's ability to sensitively grasp the subjective world of the participant and yet retain his or her own separateness. In order to empathize effectively, a leader must care for and respect the group members. A background that includes a wide range of experiences can help the leader identify with others. (Empathy, too, is discussed in more detail in Chapter 10.)

Facilitating. Facilitating is aimed at enhancing the group experience and enabling the members to reach their goals. Facilitation skills involve opening up clear and direct communication among the participants and helping them assume increasing responsibility for the direction of the group. Since facilitating is a vital tool in the person-centered approach, it will be explored in more depth in Chapter 10. Here we briefly consider some specific ways in which group leaders can facilitate group process:

- focusing on resistances within the group and helping members realize when they are holding back and why
- encouraging members to openly express their feelings and expectations
- teaching members to focus on themselves and their feelings
- teaching members to talk directly and plainly to one another
- actively working to create a climate of safety that will encourage members to take risks
- providing support for members as they try new behaviors
- fostering a member-to-member, rather than member-to-leader, interactional style
- encouraging open expression of conflict
- assisting members in overcoming barriers to direct communication
- helping members integrate what they are learning in the group and find ways to apply it to their everyday lives
- helping members achieve closure by taking care of any unfinished business in the group

Initiating.   Dyer and Vriend (1977) use the term *initiating* to refer to the leader's ability to bring about group participation and to introduce worthwhile focal material. They describe two kinds of initiating: (1) getting a group started and (2) exploring new terrain after concluding a phase of work with a group member. Good initiating skills on the leader's part keep the group from floundering without direction. These skills include using catalysts to get members to focus on meaningful work, knowing how to employ various techniques that promote deeper self-exploration, and providing links among the various themes being explored in the group. Whereas appropriate leader direction can give the group a focus and keep it moving, too much direction can lead to passivity on the part of members.

Goal Setting.   Productive goal setting is at the core of group counseling. Note that group leaders do not set goals for the clients; they help group members select and clarify their own specific goals. Although goal setting is especially important during the initial stages of a group, throughout the group's life leaders need to encourage the participants to take another look at their goals, to modify them if necessary, and to determine how effectively they are accomplishing them. Leaders who don't develop the intervention skills of challenging members to formulate concrete goals often find that their groups are characterized by aimless and unproductive sessions. (This topic is dealt with in more detail in Chapters 13 and 15.)

Evaluating. Evaluating is an ongoing process that continues for the duration of a group. After each session the leader needs to assess what is happening in the group as a whole and within individual members. Leaders must also teach participants how to evaluate themselves and how to appraise the movement and direction of their group. For example, if at the end of a session most participants agree that the session was superficial, they can be challenged to find the reasons for the unsatisfactory outcome and to decide what they are willing to do to change the situation. (This topic is also explored in more depth in Chapters 13 and 15.)

Giving Feedback. A skilled group leader gives specific and honest feedback based on his or her observation of and reaction to the members' behaviors and encourages the members to give feedback to one another. One of the great advantages of groups is that the participants can tell other members their reactions to what they observe. The purpose of feedback is to provide a realistic assessment of how a person appears to others. The skill involved in productive feedback relates to the ability to present the feedback so that it is acceptable and worthy of serious consideration. Feedback that is specific and descriptive rather than global and judgmental is the most helpful.

Suggesting. Suggestion is a form of intervention designed to help participants develop an alternative course of thinking or action. It can take many forms, a few of which are giving information and advice, giving "homework assignments," asking members to think of experiments they might try inside and outside of the group, and encouraging members to look at a situation from a different perspective. Giving information and providing appropriate suggestions for alternative plans of action can hasten the progress members make in a group. Suggestions need not always come from the leader; members can make suggestions for others to consider.

The overuse of persuasion, suggestions, and advice entails some dangers. One is that members can be led to falsely believe that simple and neat solutions exist for complex problems. Another is that members may remain dependent on other people to suggest what they should do in the face of future problems, instead of growing toward autonomy. There is a fine line between suggesting and prescribing, and the skill consists in knowing when and how suggestions enhance an individual's movement toward independence.

Protecting. Without assuming a parental attitude toward the group, leaders need to be able to safeguard members from *unnecessary* psychological or physical risks associated with being in a group. Although the very fact of participating in a group does entail certain risks, leaders can step in when they sense that psychological harm may result from a series of group interactions. For example, intervention is called for when a member is being treated unfairly or when an avalanche of feelings from the group is directed toward one person.

It takes skill for a leader to warn members of the possible dangers inherent in group participation without "setting them up" by implanting unnecessary fears about these risks. If leaders are overprotective, the members' freedom to experiment and learn for themselves is unduly restricted. If leaders fail to be protective enough, members may suffer from negative outcomes of the group experience.

Disclosing Oneself. When leaders reveal personal information, as we have seen, they usually have an impact on the group. The skill consists of knowing what, when, how, and how much to reveal. If the leader shares appropriately, the effects on the group are likely to be positive, because the members may imitate his or her willingness and try to make themselves known. If the leader shares too much too soon, the effects are likely to be adverse, because the members may not be able yet to handle such openness comfortably. The most productive disclosure is related to what is taking place within the group. The skill involved in appropriate self-disclosure lies in the ability to present the information in such a way that the members are encouraged to share more of themselves.

Modeling. Group members learn by observing the leader's behavior. If leaders value honesty, respect, openness, risk taking, and assertiveness, they can foster these qualities in the members by demonstrating them in the group. From a leader who shows respect by really listening and empathizing, members learn a direct and powerful lesson in how respect is shown behaviorally. In short, one of the best ways to teach more effective skills of interpersonal relating is by direct example. (Modeling is discussed more fully in Chapter 13.)

Linking. One way of promoting interaction among the members is to look for themes that emerge in a group and then to connect the work that members do to these themes. Group leaders with an interactional bias—that is, those who develop the norm of member-to-member rather than leader-to-member communication—rely a great deal on linking. They encourage members to address others in the group directly, rather than looking at the leader and talking about others who are present. Members often have shared concerns, and through effective linking they can be helped to work through their problems by talking to others with similar concerns. By being alert for common concerns, the leader can promote interaction and increase the level of group cohesion. Through linking several members together, the leader is also teaching them how to take responsibility for involving themselves in the work of others. If the members learn how to bring themselves into group interactions, they become more independent of the leader and are also likely to feel a greater sense of belongingness by being connected to others.

Blocking.   Blocking refers to the leader's intervention to stop counterproductive behaviors within the group. It is a skill that requires sensitivity, directness, and the ability to stop the activity without attacking the person. The focus should be on the specific behavior and not on the person as a whole, and labeling should be avoided. For example, if a member is invading another member's privacy by asking probing and highly personal questions, the leader will point to this behavior as unhelpful, without referring to the person as a "peeping Tom" or an "interrogator." Some of the behaviors that need to be blocked are:

- *Scapegoating.* If several people gang up on an individual and begin dumping their feelings on the person in an accusatory manner, the leader may intervene and ask the members involved to turn their attention to what is going on inside them.
- *Group pressure.* Group leaders need to be aware of subtle or not-so-subtle attempts on the part of some members to pressure others to take a specific course of action or to make certain changes. It is one thing to offer feedback and another to *demand* that others change and accept standards imposed by the group.
- *Questioning.* Members who habitually interrogate others or ask too many closed questions can be invited to try to make direct statements instead of asking questions.
- *Storytelling.* If lengthy storytelling occurs, the leader may intervene and ask the person how the story relates to present feelings and events.
- *Gossiping.* If a member talks *about* another member in the room, the leader can ask the member to speak directly to the person being spoken about.

Other behaviors that group leaders need to watch for and block when necessary include making excuses to justify failure to make changes, breaking confidences, invading a member's privacy, perpetually giving advice, offering support inappropriately, and making inaccurate or inappropriate interpretations. Whatever the behavior, blocking must be carried out gently and sensitively.

Terminating.   Group leaders must learn when and how to terminate their work with individuals as well as groups. The skills required in closing a group session or ending a group successfully include providing members with suggestions for applying what they've learned in the group to their daily lives, preparing the participants to deal with the problems they may encounter outside of the group, providing for some type of evaluation and follow-up, suggesting sources of further help, and being available for individual consultation should the need arise.

Terminating work with an individual takes skill. The person should not be left hanging, and premature closure should be avoided, since it would result in no further self-investigation on the part of the member. Some leaders end up working too long with a given member, simply because they don't know how to wrap up a piece of work comfortably.

An Integrated View of Group-Leadership Skills

It is not unusual for beginning group counselors to feel somewhat over-whelmed when they consider all the skills that are necessary for effective group leadership. If you, too, feel overwhelmed and somewhat discouraged, think about what it was like when you were learning to drive a car. If you had tried to think of all the rules and all the do's and don'ts simultaneously, you would have become frustrated and incapable of responding appropriate-ly. The same applies to developing specific leadership skills. By systemati-cally learning certain principles and practicing certain skills, you can ex-pect to gradually refine your leadership style and gain the confidence you need to use these skills effectively. Participating in a group as a member is one way of developing these skills, for you can learn a lot through observing experienced people. Of course, you also need to practice these skills by leading groups under supervision. Feedback from group members, your co-leader, and your supervisor is essential to the refinement of your leader-ship skills. Seeing yourself in action on a videotape playback can be a powerful source of feedback that allows you to note the specific areas that are most in need of strengthening.

Like all skills, group-leadership skills exist in degrees, not on an all-or-nothing basis. They may be developed only minimally, or they may be highly refined and used appropriately. But through training and supervised experience these skills can be constantly improved. Table 3-1 presents an overview of the group-leading skills discussed in the preceding pages.

Special Skills for Opening and Closing Group Sessions

In training and supervising group leaders, I have found that many of them lack the necessary skills to open and close a group session effectively. For example, some simply select one member and focus on that person while the rest of the group sits passively back. Because of the leader's anxiety to "get things going," any member who raises a question is likely to receive atten-tion, without any attempt to involve the other participants in the interac-tion. The problem is that when a group session begins poorly, it may be difficult to accomplish any sustained work during the rest of the meeting.

The way each session is closed is as important as the way it is initiated. I have observed group leaders who simply allow the time to elapse and then abruptly announce, "Our time is up; we'll see you all next week." Because of the leader's failure to summarize and offer some evaluation of the session, much of the potential value of the meeting is lost. The effective opening and closing of each session ensure continuity from meeting to meeting. Continu-ity makes it more likely that participants will think about what occurred in the group when they are outside of it and that they will try to apply what

Table 3-1. Overview of Group-Leadership Skills

SKILLS	DESCRIPTION	AIMS AND DESIRED OUTCOMES
Active listening	Attending to verbal and nonverbal aspects of communication without judging or evaluating.	To encourage trust and client self-disclosure and exploration.
Restating	Saying in slightly different words what a participant has said to clarify its meaning.	To determine if the leader has understood correctly the client's statement; to provide support and clarification.
Clarifying	Grasping the essence of a message at both the feeling and the thinking levels; simplifying client statements by focusing on the core of the message.	To help clients sort out conflicting and confused feelings and thoughts; to arrive at a meaningful understanding of what is being communicated.
Summarizing	Pulling together the important elements of an interaction or session.	To avoid fragmentation and give direction to a session; to provide for continuity and meaning.
Questioning	Asking open-ended questions that lead to self-exploration of the "what" and "how" of behavior.	To elicit further discussion; to get information; to stimulate thinking; to increase clarity and focus; to provide for further self-exploration.
Interpreting	Offering possible explanations for certain behaviors, feelings, and thoughts.	To encourage deeper self-exploration; to provide a new perspective for considering and understanding one's behavior.
Confronting	Challenging members to look at discrepancies between their words and actions or body and verbal messages; pointing to conflicting information or messages.	To encourage honest self-investigation; to promote full use of potentials; to bring about awareness of self-contradictions.
Reflecting feelings	Communicating understanding of the content of feelings.	To let members know that they are heard and understood beyond the level of words.
Supporting	Providing encouragement and reinforcement.	To create an atmosphere that encourages members to continue desired behaviors; to provide help when clients are facing difficult struggles; to create trust.
Empathizing	Identifying with clients by assuming their frames of reference.	To foster trust in the therapeutic relationship; to communicate understanding; to encourage deeper levels of self-exploration.

Table 3-1 *(continued)*

Skills	Description	Aims and Desired Outcomes
Facilitating	Opening up clear and direct communication within the group, helping members assume increasing responsibility for the group's direction.	To promote effective communication among members; to help members reach their own goals in the group.
Initiating	Promoting group participation and introducing new directions in the group.	To prevent needless group floundering; to increase the pace of group process.
Goal setting	Planning specific goals for the group process and helping participants define concrete and meaningful goals.	To give direction to the group's activities; to help members select and clarify their goals.
Evaluating	Appraising the ongoing group process and the individual and group dynamics.	To promote better self-awareness and understanding of group movement and direction.
Giving feedback	Expressing concrete and honest reactions based on observation of members' behaviors.	To offer an external view of how the person appears to others; to increase the client's self-awareness.
Suggesting	Offering advice and information, direction, and ideas for new behavior.	To help members develop alternative courses of thinking and action.
Protecting	Safeguarding members from unnecessary psychological risks in the group.	To warn members of possible risks in group participation; to reduce these risks.
Disclosing oneself	Revealing one's reactions to here-and-now events in the group.	To facilitate deeper levels of group interaction; to create trust; to model ways of revealing oneself to others.
Modeling	Demonstrating desired behavior through actions.	To provide examples of desirable behavior; to inspire members to fully develop their potential.
Linking	Connecting the work that members do to common themes in the group.	To promote member-to-member interactions; to encourage the development of cohesion.
Blocking	Intervening to stop counterproductive group behavior.	To protect members; to enhance the flow of group process.
Terminating	Preparing the group to close a session or end its existence.	To help members assimilate, integrate, and apply in-group learning to everyday life.

Note: The format of this chart is based on Edwin J. Nolan's article "Leadership Interventions for Promoting Personal Mastery," *Journal for Specialists in Group Work,* 1978, 3(3), 132–138.

they have learned to their everyday lives. Together with encouragement and direction from the leader, it also facilitates the members' task of assessing their own level of participation at each session.

Procedures for Opening a Group Session. With groups that meet on a weekly or other regular basis, group leaders can follow a number of procedures to open the session.

1. Participants can be asked to briefly state what they want to get from the session. I prefer a quick "go around" in which each group member identifies issues or concerns that could be explored during the session. Before focusing on one person, it is a good procedure to give all members a chance to at least say what they want to bring up during the meeting. In this way a loose agenda can be developed, and if a number of people are concerned with similar issues, the agenda will allow the repeated involvement of several members.

2. It is useful to give people a chance to express any thoughts that they might have had about the previous session or to bring up for consideration any unresolved issues from an earlier meeting. Unresolved issues among members themselves or between members and the leader can make progressing with the current agenda most difficult, since the hidden agenda will interfere with productive work until it has surfaced and been dealt with effectively.

3. Participants can be asked to report on the progress or difficulties they experienced during the week. Ideally, they have been experimenting with other ways of behaving outside of the group, they are getting involved in carrying out "homework assignments," and they are working on concrete plans that are action oriented. Even if not all of these desirable activities have taken place, time can be profitably used at the beginning of a session to share successes or to bring up specific problems.

4. The group leader may want to make some observations about the previous meeting or relate some thoughts that have occurred to him or her since the group last met.

Procedures for Closing a Group Session. Before closing a session, allow time for integrating what has occurred, for reflecting on what has been experienced, for talking about what the participants may do between now and the next session, and for discussing other summary matters. The leader may also find it useful to check with the group around the midpoint of the session and say something like "I'm aware that we still have an hour left before we close today. So I want to check with you to see if there are any matters you want to bring up before we close" or "I'd like each of you to give me an idea of how you feel about this session. So far, have you gotten what you wanted from it?" Although these assessments in the middle of a session don't have to be made routinely, doing so from time to time can encourage members to evaluate their progress. If they are not satisfied with either their own participation or what is going on in the session, there is still time to change the course of the group before it ends.

In a similar fashion, group members can be encouraged to assess their direction after they have been together for about half of the group's lifetime. A comment along the following lines may motivate the participants to think about what they can do now to enhance the value of their group experience: "We have been working together for 15 weeks, and in 15 more weeks we'll have our final session. I'd like to go around and have each of you say something about how you'd feel if *this* were the last meeting. What have you gotten from the group? What do you want to be able to say about your experience when the group terminates? In what ways would you like to see the next 15 weeks be the same as, or different from, the past 15?"

Generally members do not automatically evaluate the degree of their investment in the group or the extent of the gains they have made. The leader can do a great deal to guide participants into reflecting on the time limitations of their group and on whether they are satisfied with their participation. Members also need guidance in appraising how fully their goals are being achieved and how effectively the group is operating. If this periodic appraisal is done well, members have a chance of formulating plans for changes in the group's direction before it is too late. Consequently, it is less likely that they will leave the group feeling that they didn't get what they had hoped for when they joined.

In sum, the leader's closing skills bring unity to the group experience and help consolidate the learning that has occurred during a session. The following is a list of steps that group leaders can take toward the end of each weekly session to assist members in evaluating their participation and in bridging the gap between the group and their daily existences.

1. Group leaders should strive to close the session without closing the issues raised during the session. Although the anxiety that results from "leaving people hanging" may be counterproductive, it is not therapeutic to wrap up an issue too quickly. Many leaders make the mistake of forcing resolution of problems prematurely. Being task oriented, they feel uncomfortable about allowing members the time they need to explore and struggle with personal problems. In such instances, the leader's intervention has the effect of resolving quite superficially what may be complex matters that need to be fully explored. It is good for people to leave a session with unanswered questions, so that they will be motivated to think more about their concerns and come up with some tentative solutions on their own. Leaders need to learn the delicate balance between bringing temporary closure to an issue at the end of a session and closing the issue completely. The following comment, for example, indicates that the leader knows how to achieve such a balance: "I'm aware that the matter you worked on today has not been fully resolved. I hope, however, that you'll give further thought to what we did explore and to what you did learn about

yourself today. I look forward to working further with you on this issue in future sessions."

2. Summarizing can be effective at the end of each session. It is helpful to ask members to summarize both the group process and their own progress toward their goals. Comments can be made about common themes and issues that have emerged. The group leader can add summary comments, especially as they pertain to group process, but it is even better to teach members how to integrate what they have learned for themselves.

3. Participants can be asked to tell the group how they perceived the session, to offer comments and feedback to other members, and to make a statement about their level of investment in the session. By doing this regularly, members share in the responsibility of deciding what they will do to change the group's direction if they are not satisfied with it. For example, if participants report week after week that they are bored, they can be asked what they are willing to do to relieve their boredom.

4. It is helpful to focus on positive feedback, too. Individuals who got involved should be recognized and supported for their efforts by both the leader and other participants.

5. Members can report on their homework assignments, in which they tried to put into practice some of their new insights; they can briefly discuss what they are learning about themselves through their relationships in the group context; and they can make plans about applying what they have learned to problem situations outside the group.

6. Participants can be asked whether there are any topics or problems that they would like to put on the agenda for the next session. Besides linking sessions, this procedure prompts the participants to think about ways of exploring these concerns in the next meeting—that is, to work between sessions.

7. Group leaders may want to express their own reactions to the session and make some observations. These reactions and comments about the direction of the group can be very useful in stimulating thought and action on the part of the members.

In summary, the leader interventions that I have described illustrate that careful attention to the opening and closing of group sessions enhances and facilitates learning during a particular session. It has the effect of challenging members to recognize their role in determining the outcomes of the group, and it reminds them of their responsibility for taking active steps to maintain an effective group.

Procedures for Keeping a Session Moving

As you will see in the chapters on the various theories of group counseling, some approaches make extensive use of exercises and structured techniques to keep group sessions moving, whereas other approaches (such as person-centered therapy) reject any reliance on such exercises to promote interaction within the group. Depending on how, when, and why they are used, structured exercises can enhance interaction and provide a focus for work, or they can promote member dependence on the leader for continuing to provide direction. In their eagerness to get a group moving and keep it moving, some leaders try one exercise after another in a hit-or-miss fashion. In my view exercises that relate to the overall plan of the group and are appropriately applied in a timely manner can be a useful tool for promoting change; lacking proper application, they can be counterproductive to the enhancement of group process and of an individual's growth. A more detailed review of this subject is found in *Group Techniques* (Corey, Corey, Callanan, & Russell, 1988).

Group leaders should be careful not to overuse structured exercises. It is the nature of these exercises to foster interaction among group members, and members can quickly become overly dependent on them. If each time members encounter an impasse they are rescued with some kind of exercise, they will not learn to struggle on their own and draw on their own responses to get through the impasse. A typical misuse of structured exercise occurs when the group energy level is low and the members seem to have little investment in the group. If the leader continually plugs in an exercise as a kind of psychological pep pill, the group members will never make the effort to take a look at what is producing this boredom and apathy. Indeed, in this case, the exercise can encourage avoidance behaviors in the members.

I think that structured exercises can be very useful, especially during the initial and the final stages of a group. At the beginning of a group I use certain structured exercises designed to assist members in focusing on their personal goals, in dealing with their expectations and fears, and in building trust. These exercises consist of asking members to work in dyads, triads, and small groups on some selected topic—for example, what they hope to get from the group. During the closing phase of a group, I rely on some behavior-rehearsal exercises, use contracts, suggest homework assignments, and use a variety of other procedures designed to help consolidate learning and facilitate its generalization.

Generally, I don't use techniques to actually stir up the members' desire to work. But once participants commit themselves to work—particularly when they have clearly identified issues to explore and have shown a willingness to penetrate their problems more deeply—I have found that a technique or an exercise can help them deepen their explorations and lead to new awareness and action.

Co-Leading Groups

There are pluses for both you and your group if you are able to arrange to be a co-leader. Leading a group alone can be a lonely experience at times, and the value of meeting with a co-leader for planning and processing should not be underestimated. The co-leadership style has many advantages and a few disadvantages. Here are some of the advantages:

- Group members can benefit from the life experience and insights of two therapists; the leaders may have different perspectives on any given situation.
- Two leaders can complement each other; a group can benefit from the combined strengths of the co-leading team.
- If one of the leaders is female and the other is male, they can re-create some of the original dynamics involved in the members' relationships with their parents; the opportunities for role playing are various.
- Co-leaders can serve as models for the participants with respect to how they relate to each other and to the group.
- The co-leaders can provide each other with valuable feedback; they can discuss what happened in the session and how to improve their skills.
- Each leader can grow from observing, working with, and learning from the other.
- Co-leaders provide more opportunities to facilitate linking among the work of members. While one leader is working with a particular member, the other leader can scan the group to get a sense of how other members are involved.
- The participants have the opportunity of getting feedback from two leaders instead of one; occasional differing reactions may inject vitality into the group and offer opportunities for reflection and further discussion.

Most of the disadvantages of the co-leading model arise when the two leaders fail to create and maintain an effective working relationship. A central factor in determining the quality of this relationship is *respect*. The two leaders are likely to have their differences in leadership style, and they may not always agree or share the same perceptions or interpretations. But if there is mutual respect, they will be open and direct with each other, will trust each other, will work cooperatively instead of competitively, and will be secure enough not to need to "prove" themselves. If this trust is lacking, the members are bound to sense the absence of harmony, and the group will be negatively affected.

The choice of a co-leader, therefore, is an important one. A power struggle between incompatible co-leaders can have the effect of dividing the group. If the co-leaders do not work as a harmonious team, the group may follow their example and become fragmented. If the co-leaders evidence even subtle ongoing friction, they are providing a poor model of interpersonal relating. This friction can lead to unexpressed hostility among the members, which interferes with effective group work. If there are conflicts between leaders, it might be helpful to explore them openly in the group session, but ideally the two leaders have talked about any emerging differences between them in their private meetings. It is not helpful to a group for the co-leaders to pretend that everything is fine when, in fact, there is a strained relationship between them.

Although co-leaders do not necessarily have to work from the same theoretical approach, there are bound to be problems if they have vastly different perceptions about what the purpose of a group is or about their own role and function. For example, consider the situation in which one leader is intent on intervening with a great deal of advice aimed at providing answers for every problem a member raises, whereas the other leader is not interested in quick problem solving but, rather, encourages the members to struggle and to find their own direction. It is likely that they will be working at cross-purposes and that their clients will get different messages about the purpose of the group.

It is important that co-leaders get together regularly to discuss any matters that may affect their work—for example, how they feel about working together, how they see their group, and how they can enhance each other's contribution. Ideally, they will spend time together before and after each session, so that they can plan for the upcoming session, share their perceptions, and iron out any difficulties that arise between them. In the two chapters that follow, I suggest specific issues that co-leaders might talk about in their meetings at each of the various stages of a group.

I prefer the co-leadership model both for leading groups and for training and supervising leaders. Co-leading offers a certain safety, especially when practitioners are leading a group for the first time. It is typical for beginning group leaders to experience self-doubt and anxiety. Facing a group for the first time with a co-leader whom you trust and respect can make what might seem like an onerous task a delightful learning experience.

Styles of Group Leadership

I said at the beginning of this book that my goal was to help you develop a leadership style that is your own and that expresses your uniqueness as a person. I believe that if you attempt to copy someone else's style, you can lose much of your potential effectiveness as a group leader. Surely you will be influenced by supervisors, co-leaders, and leaders of groups and workshops that you attend as a participant. But it is one thing to be influenced by others—most leaders borrow from many resources in developing their style of group leadership—and another to deny your own uniqueness by copying others' therapeutic styles, which may work well for them but may not be suited to you.

In essence, there are as many methods of group counseling as there are leaders; and even those leaders who subscribe to a primary therapeutic model, such as behavior therapy or transactional analysis, show considerable variance in the way they lead groups. As a group leader, you bring your background of experiences and your personality, value systems, biases, and unique talents and skills to the group you lead. You also bring to it your theoretical preferences. You may advocate an approach that emphasizes thinking, one that stresses experiencing and expressing feelings, or one that focuses on action-oriented methods. On the other hand, your approach may be an eclectic one that integrates the thinking/feeling/acting dimensions. Regardless of the kind of approach you favor, your theoretical preferences will no doubt influence your style, especially with regard to the aspects of the group interaction on which you choose to focus. As you study in Part II the ten chapters on theoretical models of group counseling, you will become aware of the commonalities and differences among these models and of the ways in which the various perspectives can shape your style as a group leader.

Two Poles of a Continuum

Shapiro (1978) describes two types of group-leadership styles: the intrapersonally oriented and the interpersonally oriented. These two leadership styles can be best understood as ranging on a continuum from strictly intrapersonal to strictly interpersonal. Those group leaders who are *intrapersonally oriented* tend to deal with group members in a one-to-one manner. This style has often been referred to as individual counseling (or therapy) in a group situation. The focus is on intrapsychic concerns, or the conflicts and dynamics that exist within the individual. There is an interest in one's past, in the development of insight, and on the resolution of internal conflicts. In sum, the style of the intrapersonal leader focuses on the individual rather than on the group's dynamics or on the process of interaction among members.

At the other end of the continuum are those group leaders with an *interpersonal orientation*. They focus on the interactions among the members and on the relationships that are formed in the group. They are less interested than their intrapersonal counterparts in the individual's past, unconscious processes, and intrapsychic conflicts. This style of leadership emphasizes the here and now, the interactions among members, the group as a whole, the ongoing group dynamics, and the obstacles to the development of effective interpersonal relationships within the group.

I agree with Shapiro's contention that successful group leaders are able to incorporate both approaches into their style of leadership. Shapiro also stresses that effective group leaders have an orientation that fits their own personality, regardless of whether it leans toward the interpersonal or the intrapersonal pole. A crucial aspect of a leader's style is knowing when and to what degree each of these two orientations is appropriate with certain members or with a particular group. Learning how to integrate the best features of each orientation into a style that is personally your own is an ongoing process that depends heavily on your actual experience in the practice of leading groups.

Guidelines for Developing a Personal Leadership Style

One way to build a foundation for a personal leadership style, as I have mentioned, is to know the diverse range of theories of group counseling and their implications for styles of leading. Of course, practice in leading groups under supervision, with the benefits of feedback, is one of the best ways to gradually develop a style that can be somewhat distinctive for you. Below are some suggestions of other ways to create a leadership style that will fit for you. The following list is a modification of guidelines for practice based on research summaries done by Dies (1983b), Stockton and Morran (1982), and Bednar and Kaul (1978):

- Strive for positive involvement in the group through genuine, empathic, and caring interactions with members. Be aware that impersonal and judgmental leadership styles can create resistance and thwart the development of trust and cohesion. Your ability to create a climate in which change can occur is far more important than any technique that you can employ.
- Try to attain a reasonably open therapeutic style characterized by appropriate and facilitative self-disclosure. Be willing to share your own reactions and emotional experiences, especially as they relate to events and relationships within the group. On the other hand, exercise caution in disclosing merely to prove that you are human or to win the favor of the members of your group.
- Avoid burdening members with highly personalized or detailed self-disclosures. Become aware of the impact your disclosures have on the group process. If you find that you are consistently bringing the focus to your own pressing concerns, consider finding therapy for yourself.
- Be aware that leader self-disclosure can have either a constructive or a detrimental effect on group process and outcome, depending on specific factors such as the type of group, the stage of the group's development, and the content and manner of the disclosure.
- Help members make maximum use of effective role models, especially from among those fellow members who demonstrate desirable behavior. Reinforce appropriate and risk-taking behavior when it occurs in the sessions. Strive to create a climate in which the members value learning from one another.
- Teach members how to give one another feedback. Realize that positive feedback tends to have a greater impact than does negative feedback.
- Assist members in providing support and understanding for one another. Foster a climate that emphasizes positive, yet honest, intermember interactions. As members develop a genuine sense of caring for one another, they also earn the right to be more challenging.
- Provide a therapeutic balance between support and challenge. Avoid harsh and overly critical confrontations. Model for the members a style of confrontation that is sensitive, caring, respectful, and timely. Confrontation is more likely to be received nondefensively once a foundation of trust has been established. Reflect on the differences between inviting members to examine their behavior and commanding them to be honest.

• If you are working with a co-leader, model openness within this relationship, and display the behaviors that you hope to teach. Maintain a working relationship with your co-leader by meeting before and after sessions and by continuing to communicate with each other during the sessions.

Working within a System

Most groups that you lead will be under the auspices of some type of institution—a school system, a community mental-health organization, a state mental hospital, a clinic or hospital, or a local or state rehabilitation agency. When conducting groups in an institutional setting, one quickly discovers that mastering group-leadership theory and practice doesn't guarantee successful groups. Being able to deal effectively with institutional demands and policies may at times be as important as being professionally competent. On the basis of my experience and of discussions with other professionals who have worked within a variety of systems, I offer some information on what I consider to be important dynamics within institutions that you need to be aware of if you hope to survive in a system.

A common problem among those who regularly do group work in an institutional setting is the constant struggle to retain dignity and integrity in a system where the administrators are primarily concerned with custodial care or with putting out "crisis fires" and are relatively indifferent to the pursuit of genuine group therapy or counseling. Another common problem besetting counselors in an institution relates to demands that they function as leaders of groups that they are unequipped or ill equipped to handle. This problem is intensified by the fact that few institutions provide the training needed for the type of group leadership they demand and burden the counselors they employ with such a work load that these counselors don't have the time to attend any sort of in-service continuing education during their regular working hours. Thus, many institutional counselors are forced to take courses or attend workshops on their own time and at their own expense.

I have touched on a couple of problems of working within an institutional system, and there are more. The point I wish to make is that the problems exist and it is up to you to deal with them and to work within the system while, at the same time, maintaining your professional standards and integrity. Ultimately, the responsibility for conducting successful groups is yours. Beware of blaming external factors for failures in your group-counseling programs. Watch out for statements that absolve you of responsibility and lead you to a sense of personal powerlessness:

• "My administrator is not sympathetic toward my attempts to develop groups."
• "The bureaucratic structure hampers my development of innovative and meaningful programs."

- "I'm prevented from doing any *real* counseling because of office policies."
- "The system doesn't reward us for our efforts."
- "We don't have the funds to do what is necessary."
- "The people in this community are not receptive to the idea of any type of group therapy; they won't come for help even when they need it."

I'm not implying that these complaints don't reflect real obstacles. I know from personal experience how taxing and draining any battle with a bureaucracy can be. There are times when the hassle of merely trying to get a group started in some institutions may overwhelm us to the point of questioning whether the effort is worth it. My point is that, whatever the external obstacles, it is our responsibility to face them and not allow them to render us powerless.

Professional impotency of any kind is a condition that feeds on itself. When counselors abdicate their own power, they assume the role of victims, or they develop the cynical attitude that all their proposals and efforts are doomed—that nothing they do matters or makes any difference. So, by way of summary and restatement, when we surrender our power by placing *all* the responsibility for the failure of our programs outside of ourselves, we are in jeopardy of having our work devitalize us when it should be having the opposite effect.

Group Workers as Practitioners and Researchers

This section examines a knowledge gap between researchers and practitioners, identifies some obstacles to conducting research on groups, and suggests some practical ways to evaluate the process and outcomes of groups. (For a more in-depth treatment of this topic, see Bednar et al., 1987.)

The Gap between Research and Practice

Group workers are under increasing pressures from consumers to demonstrate the value of their therapeutic strategies and to be accountable for programs that receive both public and private funding. In spite of this press toward documenting the efficacy of group counseling, practitioners often view researchers as a "strange breed, preoccupied with rigorous experimental design and methodological control" (Dies, 1983b, p. 27). Further, empirical findings are seldom reported in a way that encourages clinicians to translate research into practice. Only a small percentage of group practitioners utilize research findings in any consistent manner, and very few counselors engage in research of their own. Because of these attitudes, a knowledge gap has been created. If this gap is to be bridged, those leading groups and those conducting research must work cooperatively and see the advantages of accepting the dual role of practitioner/researcher (Morran & Stockton, 1985).

Many group practitioners report that research has only a moderate effect on what they actually do in groups. They often dismiss research without weighing its potential contributions. Because of this lack of interest most group workers have not been willing to devote time to devising evaluative instruments as a part of their clinical practice. It is possible, however, to make systematic observation and assessment a basic part of the practice of group work. Instead of thinking exclusively in terms of rigorous empirical research, group practitioners can begin to consider alternatives to traditional scientific methodology. One such alternative is evaluative research, which is aimed at gathering and assessing data that can be of value in making decisions about programs and in improving the quality of professional service. As Dies (1983a) writes: "Effective clinicians in a sense must be clever researchers, and skillful researchers must be sensitive clinicians. The two roles are not inherently incompatible" (pp. 24–25).

Dealing with Obstacles to Research on Groups

Although I am not engaged in empirical research on groups, as a group practitioner and trainer/supervisor of group workers I do make serious attempts to evaluate group work. For example, for over 17 years my colleagues and I have co-led at least two weeklong residential personal-growth groups each summer. When we began these groups, we administered both pretests and posttests to assess outcomes, as well as conducting both individual and group follow-up sessions. We used several instruments to measure self-concept, levels of self-actualization, and changes in attitudes and values. A shortcoming of small-group research has been the reliance on inadequate or limited measurement instruments (Stockton & Morran, 1982). We found that the instruments we used were too crude to measure the subtle nature of the learning in these small groups. As a result, we came to rely more on self-reporting questionnaires designed to assess the process and outcomes of a group experience. We have continued the practice of evaluating our groups, primarily by reading the participants' written evaluations. We also schedule a follow-up group session to assess the values of the group experience. We are in good company with this practice, for Carl Rogers (1970) has utilized self-reporting instruments in conducting followup studies. Rogers contends that this approach is the best method for understanding what goes on in groups.

Stockton and Morran write that the "group is a highly complicated interactional and multidimensional system, which does not neatly fit the parameters of rigorous experimental control" (1982, p. 38). In my view it is extremely difficult to control most of the variables associated with outcomes in small groups. Unfortunately for the researcher, participants in these groups also live in the real world, which introduces many variables that pollute pure research. If we want to study specific group phenomena, we encounter a range of complexities. Leading groups is a skillful art that can, however, be enhanced by a knowledge of current theory and research.

Combining the Roles of Practitioner and Researcher

Morran and Stockton (1985) offer some specific suggestions for designing applied research to evaluate the process and outcomes of groups:

- Plan to develop a continuing program of study that can be modified to provide increasingly relevant data. This kind of evolving program offers the advantage that each round of data collection can serve as a pilot study for the next.
- Consider your research findings as merely a contribution to a cumulative knowledge base. Single studies need not yield final answers to research questions.
- Select a number of evaluative measures for data collection that are realistic in terms of time, expense, and logistics but that relate to the major process and outcome variables specific to your group.
- Consider selecting (or developing) instruments that are sufficiently sensitive to differences in group outcomes.

Morran and Stockton suggest that specific treatment goals can be used as a focus of study. Once goals have been identified, it is then possible to further define them as cognitive, affective, or behavioral. Delayed effects of treatment need to be taken into consideration so that the long-term results of group participation can be assessed. Group members may make many changes in the ways in which they think, feel, and behave after a group ends. The impact of the growth process may not be evident for some time. Thus, instruments should be developed for evaluating, at appropriate follow-up periods, whether goals have been attained.

Another way of bridging the gap between research and practice is for group workers to seek out their research-oriented colleagues and collaborate with them in devising these instruments. There is real promise in working toward this type of collaboration between colleagues with differing, but mutually complementary, perspectives (Dies, 1983a). This direction seems to offer hope that research findings can be translated into the actual practice of group work.

4

Early Stages in the Development of a Group

This chapter and the next one are meant to be a road map of the stages through which a group progresses. This map is based on my own experience, as well as on the experience and writings of others, and describes the essential issues that characterize the development of a group.

A point that needs to be clarified right away is that the stages described in this chapter don't correspond to discrete and neatly separated phases in the life of a real group. There is considerable overlap between the stages, and groups don't conform precisely to some preordained time sequence that theoretically separates one phase from the next. Also, the content of the group process varies from group to group, and different aspects of that process may be stressed depending on the theoretical orientation of the leader, the purpose of the group, and the population that makes up the group. In spite of these differences, however, there does seem to be some generalized pattern in the evolution of a group.

A clear grasp of the stages of group development, including an awareness of the factors that facilitate group process and of those that interfere with it, will maximize your ability to help the members of your group reach their goals. By learning about the problems and potential crises of each stage, you learn *when* and *how* to intervene. As you gain a picture of the systematic evolution of groups, you become aware of the developmental tasks that must be successfully met if a group is to move forward, and you can predict problems and intervene therapeutically. Finally, knowledge of the developmental sequence of groups will give you the perspective you need to lead group members in constructive directions by reducing unnecessary confusion and anxiety.

Several authors have discussed the stages of group-process development, and from these descriptions it is clear that, whereas the specific *content* of groups varies considerably, the trends and *process* are very similar. In other words, regardless of the nature of the group and the leader's theoretical orientation, there are some generalized trends that become apparent in most groups that meet over a period of time. Gazda (1989) observes that the stages through which counseling groups progress are most clearly visible in closed groups—those that maintain the same membership for the duration of the group. W. Schutz (1973b) writes about three stages: inclusion, control, and affection. Mahler (1969) describes in detail five stages: the formation, involvement, transition, working, and ending stages. Gazda's four stages are similar to Mahler's: exploration, transition, action, and termination. Hansen, Warner, and Smith (1980) write about five stages: initiation of the group, conflict and confrontation, development of cohesiveness, productivity, and termination. Yalom (1985) identifies three stages. The initial stage is characterized by orientation, hesitant participation, and the search for meaning; the second, by conflict, dominance, and rebellion; and the third, the stage of cohesion, by an increase of morale, trust, and self-disclosure.

This chapter begins with an examination of the leader's concerns in forming a group: getting prepared, announcing the group, screening and selecting the members, and preparing them for a successful experience. *Stage 1* of a group, under my four-stage breakdown, is the *orientation phase,* a time of exploration during the initial sessions. *Stage 2,* the *transition stage,* is characterized by dealing with conflict, defensiveness, and resistance. In the following chapter we will continue with *stage 3,* called the *working stage.* This phase is marked by action—dealing with significant personal issues and translating insight into action both in the group and outside of it. In *stage 4,* the *consolidation stage,* the focus is on applying what has been learned in the group and putting it to use in everyday life. I will conclude with an examination of postgroup concerns, including follow-up and evaluation. The description of these stages is based on models presented by various writers as well as on my own observations of the ways groups evolve.

Pregroup Issues: Formation of the Group

If you want a group to be successful, you need to devote considerable time to planning. In my view planning should begin with the drafting of a written proposal. The issues that need to be dealt with in the proposal include the basic purposes of the group; the population to be served; a clear rationale for the group—namely, the need for and justification of that particular group; ways to announce the group and recruit members; the screening and selection of members; the size and duration of the group; the frequency and time of meetings; the group structure and format; the methods of preparing members; whether the group will be open or closed; whether membership will be voluntary or involuntary; and the follow-up and evaluation procedures.

Leader Preparation

It cannot be overstressed that leader preparation at this formative phase is crucial to the outcome of a group. Thus, leaders will spend time wisely by thinking about what kind of group they want and by getting themselves psychologically ready. If your expectations are unclear and if the purposes and structure of the group are vague, the members will surely engage in unnecessary floundering.

Group leaders need to decide the basis for the homogeneity of their groups. By *homogeneous* I mean composed of people who, for example, are similar in ages, such as a group for children, for adolescents, or for the elderly. Other homogeneous groups are those based on a common interest or problem. Thus, there are groups designed for people with a weight problem or for those who are overdependent on drugs or alcohol, as well as consciousness-raising groups for women or for men. Some groups taking place in a school setting are especially designed for children and adolescents with learning difficulties or for those who have serious problems adjusting to the school environment.

For a given population with certain needs, a group composed of homogeneous members is more functional than one composed of people from different populations. Consider, for example, a group for adolescents. Such a group can focus exclusively on the unique developmental problems adolescents face, such as those related to interpersonal relationships, sexual development and identity, and the struggle toward autonomy. In a group designed for and composed exclusively of adolescents, the participants are encouraged to express many feelings that they have kept to themselves; through interaction with others of their same age, they can share their concerns and receive support and understanding.

While homogeneous membership can be more appropriate for certain target populations with definite needs, heterogeneous membership has some definite advantages for many types of personal-growth groups. A heterogeneous group, by representing a microcosm of the social structure that exists in the everyday world, offers the participants the opportunity to experiment with new behavior, develop social skills, and get feedback from many diverse sources. If a simulation of everyday life is desired, it is well to have a range of ages, backgrounds, and interests and concerns.

Announcing a Group and Recruiting Members

How a group is announced influences the way it will be received by potential members and the kind of people who will be attracted to it. It is imperative that you say enough to give prospective members a clear idea about the group's rationale and goals. The written announcement of the formation of a group could include these points:

• the type of group
• the purpose of the group
• the time and place of meetings
• the procedure for joining
• a statement of what the members can expect from the leader(s)
• a statement of the group leader's qualifications and background
• guidelines for determining who is suitable for the group
• fees being charged

Although printed announcements have their value if they can reach the population they are intended for, they have their limitations. Regardless of how specific you are in these announcements, people—at least some of them—are likely to misunderstand them. Because of this risk, I am in favor of making direct contact with the population that is most likely to benefit from the group. For example, if you are planning a group at a school, it is a good idea to make personal visits to several classes to introduce yourself and tell the students about the group. You could also distribute a brief application form to anyone who wanted to find out more about the group.

Screening and Selecting Group Members

Both the AACD (1988) and the ASGW (1980) have guidelines on screening group members. The AACD's ethical standard is as follows: "The member [counselor] must screen prospective group participants, especially when the emphasis is on self-understanding and growth through self-disclosure. The member must maintain an awareness of the group participants' compatibility throughout the life of the group." The ASGW's guideline states:

> The group leader shall conduct a pre-group interview with each prospective member for the purposes of screening [and] orientation, and, insofar as possible, shall select group members whose needs and goals are compatible with the established goals of the group; who will not impede the group process; and whose well-being will not be jeopardized by the group leader.

In keeping with the spirit of this guideline the leader, after recruiting potential members, must next determine whether anyone should be excluded. Careful screening will lessen the psychological risks of inappropriate participation in a group (which were discussed in Chapter 2). During the screening session the leader can spend some time exploring with potential members any fears or concerns they have about participating in a group. The leader can help them make an assessment of their readiness for a group and discuss the potential life changes that might come about. Members should know that there is a price for remaining the way they are as well as for making substantive changes. If members go into a group unaware of the potential impact that their personal changes will have on others in their lives, their motivation for continuing is likely to decrease in the event that they encounter problems with their family. The efforts that the leader devotes to member selection and orientation can result in a group that is motivated and ready to work and contribute.

The following questions will also help you screen and select group members: "How can I decide who is most likely to benefit from the group I plan to create?" "Who is likely to be disturbed by group participation or become a negative influence for the other members?"

Screening should be a two-way process. Therefore, the potential members should have an opportunity at the private screening interview to ask questions to determine whether the group is right for them. Group leaders should encourage prospective members to be involved in the decision concerning the appropriateness of their participation in the group.

Of course, there is always the possibility that the leader has real reservations about including some people who are quite determined to join the group. Ultimately it is the group leader's task to make the decision. It is a difficult decision, and I recognize that screening and selection procedures are subjective. Yet certain guidelines can help a leader make this and other decisions wisely. I find that it is often difficult to determine which candidates will benefit from a group. During the private interview people are often vague about what they hope to get from the group. They may be frightened, tense, and defensive, and they may approach the personal interview as they would a job interview, especially if they are anxious about being admitted to the group. It is not uncommon in my experience to find people actually trying to be vague in their answers and attempting to say what they think I expect of them, much as they might in a job interview.

The basic criterion for the selection of group members is whether they will contribute to the group or whether they will be counterproductive. Some people can quite literally drain the energy of the group so that little is left for productive work. Also, the presence of certain people can make group cohesion difficult to attain. This is especially true of individuals who have a need to monopolize and dominate, of hostile people or aggressive people with a need to act out, and of people who are extremely self-centered and who seek a group as an audience. Others who should generally be excluded from most groups are people who are in a state of extreme crisis, who are suicidal, who have sociopathic personalities, who are highly suspicious, or who are lacking in ego strength and are prone to fragmented and bizarre behavior. It is difficult to say categorically that a certain kind of person should be excluded from all types of groups, for a guiding principle is that the type of group should determine who is accepted. Thus, an alcoholic might be excluded from a personal-growth group but be an appropriate candidate for a homogeneous group of individuals who suffer from addiction problems, be it addiction to alcohol, to other drugs, or to food.

If the private screening session is an opportunity for the leader to evaluate the candidates and determine what they want from the group experience, it is also a chance for the prospective members to get to know the leader and develop a feeling of confidence. The manner in which this initial interview is conducted has a lot to do with establishing the trust level of the group. This is why during the interview I stress the two-way exchange, hoping that members will feel free to ask questions that will help them determine whether they want to join this group at this particular time. Some questions I consider are: Does this person appear to want to do what is necessary to be a productive group member? Has the decision to join the group been made by the person, or has it been influenced by someone else's opinion? Does the candidate have clear goals and an understanding of how a group might help him or her attain them? Is the individual open and willing to share something personal?

The selection of members to ensure optimum group balance often seems an impossible task. Yalom (1985) proposes that cohesiveness be the main criterion in the selection of participants. Thus, the most important thing is to choose people who are likely to be compatible, even though the group may be a heterogeneous one.

In the context of *group psychotherapy,* Yalom argues that unless careful selection criteria are employed, clients may end up discouraged and un-helped. He maintains that it is easier to identify the people who should be excluded from a therapy group than it is to identify those who should be included. Citing clinical studies, he lists the following as poor candidates for a heterogeneous, outpatient intensive-therapy group: brain-damaged people, paranoid clients, hypochondriacs, those who are addicted to drugs or alcohol, acutely psychotic individuals, and sociopathic personalities. In terms of criteria for inclusion, Yalom contends that the client's level of motivation to work is the most important variable. From his perspective groups are useful for people who have interpersonal problems such as loneliness, an inability to make or maintain intimate contacts, feelings of unlovability, fears of being assertive, and dependency. Clients who lack meaning in life, who suffer from diffuse anxiety, who are searching for an identity, who fear success, and who are compulsive workers might also profit from a group experience.

The key point is that screening needs to be done within the context of the type of group that a practitioner is offering. Whether a client is to be included or excluded has much to do with the purposes of the group.

Practical Concerns in the Formation of a Group

Open versus Closed Groups.   Whether the group will be open or closed may in part be determined by the population and the setting. But the issue needs to be discussed and decided at the initial session. There are some distinct advantages to both kinds of groups. In the closed group no new members are added once the group gets under way for the predetermined duration of its life. This practice offers a stability of membership that makes continuity possible and fosters cohesion. A problem with closed groups is that if too many members drop out, the group process is drastically affected.

In an open group new members replace those who are leaving, and this can provide for new stimulation. A disadvantage of the open group is that new members may have a difficult time becoming a part of the group, because they are not aware of what has been discussed before they joined.

Another disadvantage is that the changing of group membership can have adverse effects on the cohesion of the group. Therefore, if the flow of the group is to be maintained, the leader needs to devote time and attention to preparing new members and helping them become integrated.

Voluntary versus Involuntary Membership.   Should groups be composed only of members who are there by their own choice, or can groups function even when they include involuntary members? Obviously, there are a number of advantages to working with a group of clients who are willing to invest themselves in the group process. The most important criterion for inclusion in a group, according to Yalom (1985), is motivation. He maintains that in order to benefit from the group experience, a person must be highly motivated, especially in the case of group therapy. Attending a group because one has been "sent" there by someone greatly curtails the chances for success. Yalom believes that people with a deeply entrenched unwillingness to enter a group should not be accepted. However, he thinks that many of the negative attitudes that involuntary candidates have about groups can be changed by adequately preparing members for a group.

In line with Yalom's view, I have found that many involuntary members learn that a group-counseling experience can help them make some of the changes they want to achieve. In many agencies and institutions, practitioners are expected to lead groups with an involuntary clientele. It is therefore important for these counselors to learn how to work within such a structure rather than holding on to the position that they can be effective only with a voluntary population. If by presenting the group experience in a favorable light the leader can help involuntary members to see the potential benefits of the experience, the chances of productive work taking place will be increased. The key to successful participation lies in thorough member orientation and preparation, as well as in the leader's belief that group process has something to offer to these prospective members.

Group Size.   The desirable size for a group depends on factors such as the age of the clients, the type of group, the experience of the group counselors, and the type of problems explored. Another element to be taken into consideration is whether the group has one leader or more. For ongoing groups with adults, about eight members with one leader seems to be a good size. Groups with children may be as small as three or four. In general, the group should have enough people to afford ample interaction so that it doesn't drag and yet be small enough to give everyone a chance to participate frequently without, however, losing the sense of "group."

Frequency and Length of Meetings.   How often should groups meet? And for how long? These issues, too, depend on the type of group and, to some extent, on the experience of the leader. One a week is a typical format for most counseling groups. With children and adolescents it is usually better to meet for more frequent and shorter sessions. For adults who are relatively well functioning a 2-hour group each week is long enough to allow for some intensive work.

Group Duration.   In my opinion it is wise to set a termination date at the outset of a closed group, so that members have a clear idea of the time limits within which the group operates. In private practice groups can run for 30 to 50 weeks. Many college and high school groups typically run for the length of a semester (about 15 weeks). The duration varies from group to group, depending on the type of group and the population. The group should be long enough to allow for cohesion and productive work yet not so long that the group seems to drag on interminably.

Meeting Place.   Another pregroup concern is the setting. Privacy, a certain degree of attractiveness, and a place that allows for face-to-face interaction are crucial. Since a poor setting can set a negative tone that will adversely affect the cohesion of the group, an effort should be made to secure a meeting place that will make it possible to do in-depth work.

For more detailed information on these practical concerns I suggest Gazda's *Group Counseling: A Developmental Approach* (1989); Shapiro's *Methods of Group Psychotherapy and Encounter: A Tradition of Innovation* (1978); Yalom's *The Theory and Practice of Group Psychotherapy* (1985); Ohlsen, Horne, and Lawe's *Group Counseling* (1988); and Jacobs, Harvill, and Masson's *Group Counseling: Strategies and Skills* (1988).

The Uses of a Pregroup Meeting or the Initial Session

After the group membership has been established, another question needs to be raised: What is the group leader's responsibility in preparing members to get the maximum benefit from their group experience? My bias is that systematic preparation is essential and that it begins at the private screening interview and continues during the first few sessions. Preparation consists essentially of exploring with members their expectations, fears, goals, and misconceptions; the basics of group process; the psychological risks associated with group membership and ways of minimizing them; the values and limitations of groups; guidelines for getting the most from the group experience; and the necessity of confidentiality. This preparation can be done through a preliminary meeting of all those who will be joining a group.

In addition to the private interview with each person before the group is formed, I also use the initial session as a group-screening device. The initial session is a good place to talk about the purposes of the group, to let members know how they will be using group time, to explore many of the possible issues that might be considered in the group, to discuss the ground rules and policies, and to begin the getting-acquainted process. Because I prefer to have people decide early if they are ready for a group and willing to become active members, I encourage the participants to consider the first session as an opportunity to help them make such a decision.

The structuring of the group, including the specification of norms and procedures, should be accomplished early in the group's history. Although some of this structuring will have been accomplished or at least begun at the private intake session, it will be necessary to continue this process the first time the group actually meets. In fact, structuring is an ongoing process, one that will be a vital part of the early phases of your group.

Other writers endorse the idea of systematic preparation for group participation. Egan (1976) uses a skills-contract approach in his human-relations-training groups. He describes research that suggests that lack of structure during the initial phase of a group intensifies the members' fears and unrealistic expectations. Egan's approach to group work is based on the assumption that participants will learn more from a group experience if they have a clear understanding of what the group's goals are and how the group functions. Thus, in his approach to group work, members learn the basics of human-relations training. They learn that the group is a laboratory where experimentation and new behavior are encouraged, that the focus is on the here and now, that sharing of oneself is expected, that giving and receiving feedback are a basic part of the process, and that members are encouraged to apply the skills they acquire in their group to action programs designed for change outside of the group. Egan's view of systematic preparation is summed up in his words to his readers: "The more clearly you understand the experience before you embark upon it, the more intelligently you will be able to give yourself to it and the more valuable it will be to you" (1976, p. 3).

Another advocate of systematic preparation for group members is Yalom (1985). His preparation includes explaining his theory of group work, exploring misconceptions and expectations, predicting early problems and stumbling blocks, discussing how the participants can best help themselves, talking about trust and self-disclosure, and exploring the risks associated with experimenting with new behavior. Yalom also discusses matters such as the goals of group therapy, confidentiality, and extragroup socialization.

While I strongly believe in the value of systematic and complete preparation of group members, I also see the danger of overpreparation. For example, I typically ask members to talk early in the group about any fears or reservations they might have. I also explore a few common risks of participating in a group. In this particular area, however, if the leader becomes overspecific, the members may end up developing concerns or even fears that they never had before and that may become self-fulfilling prophecies. Also, too much structure imposed by the leader can stifle any initiative on the part of the members. The risks inherent in overpreparation should be balanced against those that accompany insufficient preparation. Excessive floundering and useless conflict during the group's later stages are often the result of the fact that some basic skills and understanding of group process have never really been acquired.

My Guidelines for Orientation and Preparation of Members

I begin my preparation program at the time of screening each potential member, and I devote most of the first group meeting (what I call the pregroup meeting) to orientation about group process. This orientation continues during the initial phase of the group. As group-process issues emerge naturally while the group is taking shape, these concerns are dealt with.

I start by discussing with the participants the importance of their own preparation for group work. I stress that what they get from their group will depend largely on their level of investment. During the pregroup meeting and continuing into the initial group sessions, I view my role as helping members examine and decide on their level of commitment. We focus on what they want to get from participating in a group, and I assist them in defining clear, specific, and meaningful personal goals. After they have decided on some personal goals that will guide their work in the group, they are asked to refine these goals by developing a contract. (For details on ways of helping members define personal goals and formulate contracts, see the discussions of transactional analysis, behavioral group therapy, rational-emotive therapy, and reality therapy in Chapters 12–15.)

At the pregroup meeting I ask members to talk about their expectations, their reasons for being in the group, their fears about participating, and their hopes. I also provide them with some pointers on what they can do to maximize the benefit of the group in enabling them to make the changes they desire in their lives. I talk with them about appropriate self-disclosure. They hear that it is their decision to select the life issues that they want to explore in the group. They are also told that it is critical that they be willing to share persistent reactions they are having to here-and-now group interactions. My purpose is to teach them that the group will function only if they are willing to express what they are thinking and feeling about being in the group. In fact, their reactions provide the direction in which we typically proceed during the first few sessions. I also encourage them to bring up any questions or concerns they have about group process.

I ask the members to give some thought before they come to each session about personal issues that they are willing to bring up for exploration. Although they may have a specific agenda when they come to a group meeting, I also encourage them to remain flexible by being willing to work on other issues that may emerge spontaneously as others are interacting in the group. Because I continue to find that reading, reflecting, and writing do help members focus on themes for themselves, I attempt to get them to read selected books. They are typically asked to keep a journal, which allows them to spontaneously write about a range of reactions they have while they are in the group as well as reactions to what they experience in between the sessions. They are encouraged to bring into the group the gist of what they have been writing in their journals. In this way they are taught about the value of continuing work that was begun during a session. Members hear over and over about the importance of using the group to practice new behaviors. I continually remind them that the group is not an end in itself but only a means to helping them acquire new ways of thinking, feeling, and behaving. Thus, they are continually invited to try out new styles of behavior during the sessions to see if they might want to make certain changes.

Implications of Research on Pregroup Preparation

The Value of Preparation. Research indicates that members who receive pregroup preparation generally benefit more from a group experience than do those who are unprepared (Borgers & Tyndall, 1982; LeCluyse, 1983; Muller & Scott, 1984). Members who understand what behaviors are expected of them tend to be more successful (Stockton & Morran, 1982). Members who have been oriented have an increased faith in the group, more awareness of appropriate group behavior and roles, and lower levels of anxiety. They show increased openness and have a greater willingness to disclose themselves and to give and receive feedback (Bednar, Melnick, & Kaul, 1974; LeCluyse, 1983; Yalom, 1983).

Some research indicates that pregroup preparation can be effective in controlling the anxiety that can inhibit members from fully participating in the group process. Although a certain degree of anxiety can be therapeutically productive in most groups, too much anxiety tends to immobilize the group member. Yalom (1983) maintains that the group leader can do a great deal to prevent the unnecessary anxiety that results when a client is thrown into an ambiguous therapy situation. He cites research evidence indicating that a lack of clarity about group goals, methods of achieving these goals, and expected behavior increases the members' frustration with the group. He also cites research showing that members of inpatient therapy groups who had received systematic preparation used the group process better than those who had not been prepared. The prepared clients volunteered more, communicated more often, took more initiative in bringing up personal issues, and engaged in more self-disclosure. Other research suggests that the structured learning experiences of pretraining increase the chance of successful outcomes because they lessen the intense anxiety of the initial sessions while not hindering or obstructing necessary group stages of development (Bednar et al., 1974).

Preparation is particularly important for ethnic and minority clients, for many of them hold values that make it difficult for them to participate fully in a group experience. For example, the free participation and exchange of views in therapy groups appear to be in conflict with Asian values of humility and modesty. Furthermore many Asians do not share Western values of independence, individualism, directness of communication, expressiveness of feelings, and assertiveness (Lee, Juan, & Hom, 1984). Such clients may be threatened in a group experience, especially if they are expected to make deeply personal disclosures too quickly. Therefore, adequate preparation will be essential for Asian-American clients who have had no prior therapeutic experience in a group setting. Careful preparation will reduce the dropout rate of these clients and will help them maximize their gains (Ho, 1984). For individuals of other ethnic groups, preparation is no less important. It is essential that they know the purpose of the group as well as how the group experience can be of personal value to them. Group workers need to be aware that reluctance or resistance may be more the result of cultural background than of an uncooperative attitude.

Objectives and Methods of Pregroup Preparation. Research indicates that the pretraining of group members may be the single most important positive variable influencing group-interaction patterns and member outcome (Bednar & Kaul, 1978). Such preparation has three important objectives: the clarification of expectations, the presentation of guidelines for group participation, and the provision of models for effective behavior. Thus, it is generally aimed at dealing with misconceptions about a group experience, providing information about ways to get the most from a group, predicting stumbling blocks, and helping members establish specific personal goals. After pregroup preparation members tend to engage more readily in interpersonal discussions and to develop a greater degree of cohesiveness than do participants who have not received such training (Bednar et al., 1974).

Pregroup preparation can be used to help establish desired norms early in the life of a group. Borgers and Tyndall (1982) describe three approaches for preparing members: cognitive methods, vicarious experiencing, and behavioral methods. With cognitive methods members acquire information about group process and what is expected of them. Vicarious experiencing includes the use of audio and videotapes and films to model desired group behavior. Behavioral practice involves engaging in structured activities. Borgers and Tyndall conclude: "Perhaps the most valuable pregroup preparation consists of a combination of these approaches and would ideally be fitted to the individual client after considering such factors as risk-taking propensity, interpersonal sensitivity, and level of cognitive functioning" (1982, p. 111). Their conclusions are supported by a review of the research. Studies have consistently shown that groups receiving both cognitive instructions and behavioral modeling do better than those receiving only one treatment or neither (Stockton & Morran, 1982).

Pregroup Issues for Co-Leaders

Teamwork Is Essential. If you are co-leading a group, the central issue at this early stage is that you and your co-leader have equal responsibility in forming the group and getting it going. Both of you need to be clear as to the purpose of the group, what you hope to accomplish with the time you have, and how you will meet your objectives. Cooperation and basic agreement will be essential in getting your group off to a good start.

This cooperative effort might well start with a meeting to develop a proposal, after which both of you present your joint proposal to whoever has the authority to accept it. You and your co-leader will be a team when it comes to matters such as announcing and recruiting for membership; conducting screening interviews and agreeing on whom to include and exclude; agreeing on basic ground rules, policies, and procedures and presenting them to the members as a co-leading team; and sharing in the practical matters that must be handled to implement a group.

It may not always be possible to share equally in all the responsibilities of planning and implementing a group. While it is *ideal* that both leaders interview the applicants, time constraints may make this impractical. Tasks may have to be divided, but as much as possible both co-leaders should be involved in what is necessary to make a group a reality. If one leader does a disproportionate share of the work, the other leader can easily develop a passive role in the leadership of the group once it begins.

Getting Together with Your Co-Leader.   If co-leaders do not know each other or don't have much sense of how the other works professionally, they are likely to get off to a poor start. Simply walking into a group cold, without any initial planning or getting acquainted with your co-leader, is to invite future problems. I have a few suggestions that co-leaders can consider before the initial session:

1. Make the time to at least get to know something about each other personally and professionally.
2. Talk about your theoretical orientation and how each of you perceives groups. What kind of group work has each of you had? In what ways will your theory and leadership style influence the direction the group takes?
3. Does either of you have any concerns or reservations about leading with the other? What might get in the way of your teamwork? How can you use your separate talents productively as a team? How can your differences in leadership style have a complementary effect and actually enhance the group?
4. For the two of you to work together well as a team, you should be in agreement on the ethical aspects of group work. What does each of you consider to be unethical practice, and are you together on actions that are unethical?

Summary of Pregroup Concerns

Member Functions and Possible Problems.   Before joining a group, members must possess the knowledge necessary for making an informed decision concerning their participation. Members should be active in the process of deciding if a group is right for them. Following are some issues that pertain to the role of members at this stage:

- Members should know all the specifics about a group that might have an impact on them.
- Members need to learn how to screen the group leader to determine if this group with this particular leader is appropriate for them at this time.
- Members need to be involved in the decision to include or exclude them from the group.
- Members need to prepare themselves for the upcoming group by thinking about what they want from the experience and how they can attain their goals.

Problems can arise if members

- are coerced into a group
- do not have adequate information about the nature of the group
- are passive and give no thought to what they want or expect from the group

Leader Functions.   The main tasks of group leaders during the formation of a group include these:

- developing a clearly written proposal for the formation of a group
- presenting the proposal to the proper authorities and getting the idea accepted
- announcing the group so as to provide as much information as possible to prospective participants
- conducting pregroup interviews for screening and orientation purposes
- making decisions concerning selection of members
- organizing the practical details necessary to launch a successful group
- getting parental permission, if appropriate
- preparing psychologically for leadership tasks and meeting with co-leader (if appropriate)
- arranging for a preliminary group session for the purposes of getting acquainted, presenting ground rules, and preparing the members for a successful group experience
- making provisions for informed consent and exploring with participants the potential risks involved in a group experience

Final Comments.   Many groups that get stuck at an early developmental stage do so because the foundations were poorly laid at the outset. What is labeled as "resistance" on the part of group members is often the result of the leader's failure to give them adequate orientation. The nature and scope of pregroup preparation are determined largely by the type of group, yet there are common elements that can be addressed in most groups: member and leader expectations, basic procedures of the group, misconceptions about groups, and the advantages and limitations of group participation. This preparation can begin at the individual screening and can be continued during the initial session. Although building pregroup preparation into the design of a group takes considerable effort, the time involved pays dividends as the group evolves. Many potential barriers to a group's progress can be avoided by careful planning and preparation.

Stage 1: Initial Stage—Orientation and Exploration

Characteristics of the Initial Stage

The initial stage of a group is a time of orientation and exploration: determining the structure of the group, getting acquainted, and exploring the members' expectations. During this phase members learn how the group functions, define their own goals, clarify their expectations, and look for their place in the group. At the initial sessions members tend to keep a "public image"; that is, they present the dimensions of themselves they consider socially acceptable. This phase is generally characterized by a certain degree of anxiety and insecurity about the structure of the group. Members are tentative, because they are discovering and testing limits and are wondering whether they will be accepted.

Typically, members bring to the group certain expectations, concerns, and anxieties, and it is vital that they be allowed to express them openly. At this time the leader needs to clear up the participants' misconceptions and, if necessary, demystify groups. I see this initial phase as akin to the first few days one spends in a foreign land, having to learn the rudiments of a new language and different ways of expressing oneself.

Primary Tasks of the Initial Stage: Inclusion and Identity

Finding an identity in the group and determining the degree to which one will become an active group member are the major tasks of the initial stage. W. Schutz (1973a) says that this phase involves deciding whether to be in or out of the group, maintaining one's individuality within the group, and making commitments. The following questions are the kind members often ask themselves at the initial sessions:

- "Will I be in or out of this group?"
- "How much do I want to reveal of myself?"
- "How much do I want to risk?"
- "How safe is it to take risks?"
- "Can I really trust these people?"
- "Do I fit and belong in here?"
- "Whom do I like, and whom do I dislike?"
- "Will I be accepted, or rejected?"
- "Can I be myself and, at the same time, be a part of the group?"

Fried (1972) calls attention to the need for members to resist group pressure that could lead them to relinquish their uniqueness. She stresses the importance of remaining an autonomous and separate human being and not getting lost by fusion in the group. Fried's caution relates to the members' right to maintain their own rhythm and to the need for the members to achieve and maintain a sense of individuation.

The Foundation of the Group: Trust

Most writers agree that establishing trust is vital to the continued development of the group. Without trust, group interaction will be superficial, little self-exploration will take place, constructive challenging of one another will not occur, and the group will operate under the handicap of hidden feelings.

It is a mistake to assume that people will "naturally" trust one another as soon as they enter a group. And why should they trust without question? How do they know that the group will offer a more accepting and safer climate than society at large? My view is that people make a decision whether to trust a group. Such a decision depends in part on the leader's ability to demonstrate that the group can be a safe place in which to be oneself and reveal who and what one is. Also, by encouraging members to talk about any factors that inhibit their trust, the leader supports the therapeutic atmosphere necessary for openness and risk taking on the part of the members.

Ways of Establishing Trust.   The manner in which leaders introduce themselves can have a profound effect on the group's atmosphere. Is the leader enthusiastic, personable, psychologically present, and open? To what degree does the leader trust himself or herself? To what degree does the leader show trust and faith in the group? I have often heard members comment that it felt good to be trusted by their leaders.

The leader's success in establishing a basic sense of trust and security depends in large part on how well he or she has prepared for the group. Careful selection of members and efforts to make sure that the group is appropriate for them are very important, and so is the way in which the leader presents the ground rules of the group. Leaders who show that they are interested in the welfare of individual members and of the group as a whole engender trust. Talking about matters such as the rights of participants, the necessity of confidentiality, and the need for respecting others demonstrates that the leader has a serious attitude toward the group. If leaders care, chances are that the members will also care enough to invest themselves in the group to make it successful.

These comments, however, should not be interpreted to mean that trust building is the exclusive province of group leaders. True, leaders can engender trust by their attitudes and actions, but the level of trust also depends in large part on the members—individually and collectively.

Members usually bring to the group some fears as well as hopes. Participants will trust the group more if they are encouraged to expose their fears, because talking about them is likely to reveal that the fears are shared by others. If one member, for example, is concerned about not being able to express herself effectively and someone else expresses the same concern, almost invariably a bond is established between the two.

Silences and awkwardness are characteristically part of the beginning session. The more unstructured the group, the greater the anxiety and ambiguity about how one is to behave in a group. The members are floundering somewhat as they seek to discover how to participate. As the sessions progress, the members generally find it easier to raise issues and participate in the discussion. More often than not, these issues tend to be safe ones (at the beginning), and there is some talking about other people and there-and-then material. This is one way that the members go about testing the waters. It is as though they were saying "I'll show a part of myself—not a deep and sensitive one—and I'll see how others treat me."

Ways of Maintaining Trust. Another characteristic aspect of this initial phase is the tendency for some participants to jump in and try to give helpful advice as problems are brought up. It is the leader's task to make sure that these "problem-solving interventions" do not become a pattern, since they will cause enough irritation in other members to precipitate a confrontation with those who are quick to offer remedies for everyone's troubles.

The group's atmosphere of trust is also affected by the negative feelings that members often experience at the initial stage toward certain other members or toward the leader and over the fact that the group is not proceeding the way they would like to see it proceed. This is an important turning point in a group, and trust can be lost or enhanced depending on the manner in which negative feelings are dealt with. If conflict is brought out into the open and negative feelings are listened to nondefensively, there's a good chance that the situation producing these feelings can be changed. Members need to know and feel that *it is OK* to have and express negative feelings. Only then can the group move ahead to a deeper level of work. The members feel secure enough to take greater risks and are able to focus on struggles that are personally significant and to express here-and-now feelings.

As members reveal more of themselves to one another, the group becomes cohesive; in turn, this emerging cohesion strengthens the trust that exists in the group and creates the right atmosphere for members to try new ways of behaving in the group. When the members trust one another, they also trust the feedback they receive, which they can use as they try to carry these newly acquired behaviors into their daily lives.

Role of the Group Leader at the Initial Stage

Modeling. When you lead a group, you set the tone and shape the norms as a model-setting participant as well as a technical expert (Yalom, 1985). It is important that you state your own expectations for the group openly during the first session and that you model interpersonal honesty and spontaneity. You need to be aware of your own behavior and of the impact you have on the group and to practice the skills that create a therapeutic milieu.

To be effective, a leader must be able and willing to be psychologically present in the group and to be genuine. A genuine leader is one who is congruent, who does not resort to various roles to maintain artificial distance, and who is willing to do what he or she expects the members to do. Genuineness implies a level of enthusiasm and involvement in one's work as a leader. How can you expect the participants to get involved and believe in the potential of your group if you don't believe in what you are doing or if you are apathetic?

With regard to empathy—both cognitive and affective—you can create a therapeutic situation by being able to see and understand the world from the internal vantage point of the members. Another key characteristic is your sensitivity in attending and responding not only to what is said but also to the subtle messages conveyed beyond words. This applies to individual members as well as to the group as a whole. Finally, the people who make up your group need to sense that you have respect and positive regard for them.

All of these comments acquire special meaning if you keep in mind that, at the initial stage, the participants depend very much on you. They turn to you for direction and structure and often focus so much on you that they neglect their own resources. This situation, which exists in most groups, requires that you be constantly aware of your own need to be seen as an authority figure and to keep tight control on the group. If you are not aware of these needs in yourself, you may keep the members of your group from becoming autonomous.

Helping Identify Goals.   Another of your main tasks as a group leader is to help the participants get involved. You can do a lot to motivate, inspire, and challenge people to *want* to get the most from their group. At this stage you do it mostly by helping them to identify, clarify, and develop meaningful goals. There are *general group goals,* which vary from group to group because they depend on the purpose of the group, and there are *group-process goals,* which apply to most groups. Egan (1976) has described several of them: self-exploration, experimentation, staying in the here and now, making oneself known to others, challenging oneself and others, taking risks, giving and receiving feedback, listening to others, responding to others honestly and concretely, dealing with conflict, dealing with feelings that arise in the group, deciding what to work on, acting on new insights, and applying new behavior in and out of the group.

In addition to establishing these group-process goals, you need to help members establish their own goals. Typically, people in the early stages of a group have vague ideas about what they want from a group experience. These vague ideas need to be translated into specific and concrete goals with regard to the desired changes and to the efforts the person is actually willing to make to bring about these changes. It is during the initial phase that this process needs to take place if the members are to derive the maximum benefit from the group. As I said earlier, you can do much to promote this process by assuming the responsibility of practicing and modeling the skills and attitudes that are necessary for effective group interaction.

One of the leader's basic tasks, and a most challenging one, is to bring hidden agendas out into the open. For example, some members may have hidden goals that are at cross-purposes with group goals. They may have an inordinate need to be the center of attention, or they may sabotage intimacy in a group because of their uncomfortableness in getting close to others. A leader's function is to do what is needed to make these hidden agendas explicit. If such personal goals remain hidden, they are bound to undermine the effectiveness of the group.

The Division of Responsibility.   A basic issue that group leaders must consider is responsibility for the direction and outcome of the group. If a group proves to be nonproductive, is this due to a lack of leader skill, or does the responsibility rest with the group members?

One way of conceptualizing the issue of leader responsibility is to think of it in terms of a continuum. At one end is the leader who assumes a great share of the responsibility for the direction and outcomes of the group. Such leaders tend to have the outlook that unless they are highly directive, the group will flounder. They see their role as that of the expert, and they actively intervene to keep the group moving in ways that they deem productive. A disadvantage of this extreme form of responsible leadership is that it robs the members of the responsibility that is rightfully theirs; if members are perceived by the leader as not having the capacity to take care of themselves, they soon begin to live up to this expectation by being irresponsible, at least in the group.

At the other end of the responsibility continuum is the leader who proclaims: "I am responsible for me, and you are responsible for you. If you want to leave this group with anything of value, it is strictly up to you. I can't do anything for you—make you feel something or take away any of your defenses—unless you allow me to."

Ideally, each leader will discover a balance, accepting a rightful share of the responsibility but not usurping the members' responsibility. This issue is central because a leader's approach to other issues (such as structuring and self-disclosure) hinges on his or her approach to the responsibility issue. The leader's personality is involved in the determination of how much responsibility to assume and what, specifically, this responsibility will include.

Structuring.   Like responsibility, structuring exists on a continuum. The leader's theoretical orientation, the type of group, and the membership population are some factors that determine the amount and type of structuring employed. Providing therapeutic structuring is particularly important during the initial stage, when members are typically confused about what behavior is expected in the group and are therefore anxious. Structure can be either useful or inhibiting in a group's development. Too little structure results in members' becoming unduly anxious, inhibiting their spontaneity. Too much structuring and direction, on the other hand, can foster dependent attitudes and behavior. The members may wait for the leader to "make something happen" instead of taking the responsibility for finding their own direction.

In my own groups the type of structure provided in the initial stage is aimed at assisting members to identify and express their fears, expectations, and personal goals. For example, members participate in dyads, go-arounds, and structured questions as ways of making it easier for them to talk to one another about their life issues. After talking to several people on a one-to-one basis, they feel more comfortable talking openly to the entire group. From the outset I try to help them become aware of what they are thinking and feeling in the here and now and encourage them to directly express their reactions. My interventions are aimed at promoting a high degree of interaction within the group, as opposed to creating the norm of having a few individuals do prolonged work while other members merely observe. This type of structuring is designed to let members assume increased responsibility for getting the most out of the group. As they learn basic norms, they tend to take the initiative rather than waiting for my direction.

What does research teach us about the value of providing structure during the initial stages of a group? Yalom (1983, 1985) cites a body of research evidence indicating that ambiguity with respect to the goals and procedures of the group and to the behavior expected of members increases members' anxiety, frustration, and disengagement. Yalom found that either too much or too little leader activity or leader management was detrimental to the members' growth as well as to the autonomy of the group. Too much leader direction tends to limit the growth of members, and too little results in aimless groups. Yalom sees the basic task of the group leader as providing enough structure to give a general direction to the members while avoiding the pitfall of fostering dependency on the leader. His message to leaders is to structure the group in a way that promotes each member's autonomous functioning. Instead of inviting or calling on members to speak, for example, leaders can show them how to bring themselves into the interactions without being called on.

Research has shown the value of an initial structure that builds supportive group norms and highlights positive interactions among members. The leader must carefully monitor and assess this therapeutic structure throughout the life of a group, rather than waiting to evaluate it during the final stage. Structuring that offers a coherent framework for understanding the experiences of individuals and the group process will be of the most value. When therapeutic goals are clear, when appropriate member behaviors are identified, and when the therapeutic process is structured to provide a framework for change, members tend to engage in therapeutic work more quickly (Dies, 1983b). In agreement with the findings of Dies, another summary of the research indicates that leader direction during the early phases of a group tends to facilitate the development of cohesion and the willingness of members to take risks by revealing themselves to others and giving others feedback (Stockton & Morran, 1982).

Bednar, Melnick, and Kaul (1974) developed a model that shows the value of some type of group structure. In their formulation, as the group's cohesion increases, members gradually begin to feel safer in sharing themselves in meaningful ways, in giving feedback, and in providing support and challenge to others. The authors' general model specifies the following sequence: initial ambiguity and anxiety, increased structure through specific instructions, increased risk taking, increased group cohesion, and increased personal responsibility.

In summary, although many variables are related to the creation of norms and trust during the early phase of a group, providing the optimum balance between too much and too little leader direction is one of the most important. The art is to provide structuring that is not so tight that it robs the group members of the responsibility of finding their own structure. Involving the members in a continual process of evaluating their own progress and that of the group as a whole is one effective way of checking for the appropriate degree of structure. Members need to be taught specific skills of monitoring group process if they are to assume this responsibility.

Co-Leader Issues at the Initial Stage

If you are working with a co-leader, discussing the issues of division of responsibility and structuring is essential for group unity. If you and your co-leader don't agree on the balance of responsibility, your disagreement is bound to have a negative effect on the group.

If you assume the majority of the responsibility to ensure that the group continues to move, for example, while your co-leader assumes almost no responsibility on the ground that the members must decide for themselves what to do with group time, the members will sense this division and be confused by it. Similarly, if you function best with a high degree of structure and your co-leader believes that any structuring should come from the members, this difference of opinion might have a detrimental effect on the group.

For these reasons, it is wise to select a co-leader who has a philosophy of leadership that is compatible with yours, though this does not mean that both of you need to have the same style of leading. You can have differences that complement each other; it is when these differences lead to fragmenting the group that problems occur.

Summary of the Initial Stage

Stage Characteristics. The early phase of a group is a time for orientation and determining the structure of the group. Some of the distinguishing events of this stage are as follows:

- Participants test the atmosphere and get acquainted.
- Members learn the norms and what is expected, learn how the group functions, and learn how to participate in a group.
- Members display socially acceptable behavior; risk taking is relatively low, and exploration is tentative.
- Group cohesion and trust are gradually established if members are willing to express what they are thinking and feeling.
- Members are concerned with whether they are included or excluded, and they are beginning to define their place in the group.
- Negative feelings may initially surface as a testing to determine if all feelings are acceptable.
- A central issue is trust versus mistrust.
- There are periods of silence and awkwardness; members may look for direction and wonder what the group is about.
- Members are deciding whom they can trust, how much they will disclose, how safe the group is, whom they like and dislike, and how much to get involved.
- Members are learning the basic attitudes of respect, empathy, acceptance, caring, and responding—all attitudes that facilitate trust building.

Member Functions and Possible Problems. Early in the course of the group, some specific member roles and tasks are critical to the shaping of the group:

- taking active steps to create a trusting climate
- learning to express one's feelings and thoughts, especially as they pertain to interactions in the group
- being willing to express fears, hopes, concerns, reservations, and expectations concerning the group
- being willing to make oneself known to others in the group
- being involved in the creation of group norms
- establishing personal and specific goals that will govern group participation
- learning the basics of group process, especially how to be involved in group interactions

Some of the problems that can arise are these:

- Members may wait passively for "something to happen."
- Members may keep to themselves feelings of distrust or fears pertaining to the group and thus entrench their own resistance.

- Members may keep themselves vague and unknown, making meaningful interaction difficult.
- Members may slip into a problem-solving and advice-giving stance with other members.

Leader Functions.* The major tasks of group leaders during the orientation and exploration phase of a group are these:

- teaching participants some general guidelines and ways to participate actively that will increase their chances of having a productive group
- developing ground rules and setting norms
- teaching the basics of group process
- assisting members in expressing their fears and expectations and working toward the development of trust
- modeling the facilitative dimensions of therapeutic behavior
- being open with the members and being psychologically present for them
- clarifying the division of responsibility
- helping members establish concrete personal goals
- dealing openly with members' concerns and questions
- providing a degree of structuring that will neither increase member dependence nor promote excessive floundering
- assisting members to share what they are thinking and feeling about what is occurring within the group
- teaching members basic interpersonal skills such as active listening and responding
- assessing the needs of the group and facilitating in such a way that these needs are met
- sharing your expectations and hopes for the group
- showing members that they have a responsibility for the direction and outcome of the group
- making sure that all the members participate in the group's interaction, so that nobody feels excluded

Stage 2: Transition Stage—Dealing with Resistance

Before a group can begin doing productive work, it must typically go through a somewhat difficult transition phase. During this stage members deal with their anxiety, resistance, and conflict, and the leader helps them learn how to begin working on their problems.

Characteristics of the Transition Stage

Anxiety. The transition stage is generally characterized by increased anxiety and defensiveness. These feelings normally give way to genuine openness and trust in the stages that follow. Often the participants articu-

---

*Exercises and activities designed to help students develop specific skills for each of the stages of a group are found in the student manual accompanying this book.

late their anxieties in the form of statements or questions to themselves or to the group, such as these:

- "I wonder whether these people really understand me and whether they care."
- "What good will it do to open myself up in here? Even if it works, what will it be like when I attempt to do the same outside of this group? What if I lose control?"
- "I see myself standing before a door but unwilling to open it for fear of what I'll find behind it. I'm afraid to open the door into myself, because, once I open it a crack, I'm not sure I'll be able to shut it again. I don't know whether I'll like what I see or how you'll respond if I show you what is locked within me."
- "How close can I get to others in here? How much can I trust these people with my inner feelings?"

Anxiety grows out of the fear of letting others see oneself on a level beyond the public image. Anxiety also results from the fear of being judged and misunderstood, from the need for more structure, and from a lack of clarity about goals, norms, and expected behavior in the group situation. As the participants come to trust more fully the other members and the leader, they become increasingly able to share of themselves, and this openness lessens their anxiety about letting others see them as they are.

Conflict and Struggle for Control.   Many writers point out the central role that conflict plays during the transition stage of a group. Yalom (1985) sees this stage as characterized by negative comments and criticism. People may be quite judgmental of others and yet unwilling to open up to the perceptions that others have of them. In Yalom's eyes the transition stage is a time of struggling for power—among the members and with the leader—and establishing a social pecking order. The struggle for control is an integral part of every group: "It is always present, sometimes quiescent, sometimes smoldering, sometimes in full conflagration" (Yalom, 1985, p. 304).

W. Schutz (1973a), too, sees control as the central issue in the second stage of a group. Characteristic group behaviors include competition, rivalry, a jockeying for position, a struggle for leadership, and frequent discussions about the procedure for decision making and division of responsibility. Schutz contends that at this point the primary anxieties of participants relate to having too much or too little responsibility and too much or too little influence.

Before conflict can be dealt with and constructively worked through, it must be recognized. Too often both the members and the leader want to bypass conflict, out of the mistaken assumption that it is negative and indicates a poor relationship. If conflicts are ignored in a group, what originally produced the conflicts festers and destroys the chance for genuine contact. When conflict is recognized and dealt with in such a way that those who are involved can retain their integrity, the foundations of trust between the parties are established. Recognizing that conflict is inevitable and that it can strengthen trust is likely to reduce the probability that members and leader will try to dodge the conflicts that are a natural part of a group's development.

Ignoring conflicts and negative feelings requires energy, and that energy can be better employed to develop an honest style of facing and working through inevitable conflicts. Rogers (1970) observes that the first expression of significant here-and-now feelings is frequently related to negative attitudes toward other group members or toward the leader. According to Rogers, expressing negative feelings is one way to test the freedom and trustworthiness of the group. Members are discovering whether the group is a safe place to disagree, to have and express negative feelings, and to experience interpersonal conflict. They are testing the degree to which they can be accepted when they are not "being nice." The way conflict is recognized, accepted, and worked with has critical effects on the progress of the group. If it is poorly handled, the group may retreat and never reach a productive working stage. If it is dealt with openly and with concern, the members discover that their relationships are strong enough to withstand an honest level of challenge.

Certain group behaviors tend to elicit negative feelings that reflect conflict:

- remaining aloof and hiding behind the stance of observer
- talking too much and actively interfering with the group process through questioning, giving abundant advice, or in other ways distracting people from their work
- dominating the group, using sarcasm, belittling the efforts that are being made, and demanding attention

When intermember conflict is the result of transference, it can be detected in statements such as these:

- "You seem so self-righteous. Every time you begin to talk, I want to leave the room. You remind me of my ex-husband."
- "You bother me so because you look like a well-functioning computer. I don't sense any feeling from you. My father and you would have made a great team!"
- "Your attempts to take care of everyone in here really bother me. You rarely ask anything for yourself, but you are always ready to offer something. Just like my mother—I felt that I could never do anything for her, because she needed nothing."

Challenging the Group Leader.   Often conflicts also involve the group leader. As a group leader, you may be challenged on professional as well as personal grounds. You may be criticized for being "too standoffish" and not revealing enough of yourself, or you may be criticized for being "one of the group" and revealing too much of your private life. Here are some of the comments you may hear from your group:

- "You're judgmental, cold, and stern."
- "No matter what I do, I have the feeling that it'll never be enough to please you. You expect too much from us."
- "You really don't care about us personally. I sense that you're just doing a job and that we don't count."
- "You don't give us enough freedom. You control everything."
- "You push people too much. I feel you aren't willing to accept a no."

It is helpful to distinguish between a *challenge* and an *attack*. An attack can take the form of "dumping" or "hit-and-run" behavior. Members who attack group leaders with statements like "This is how you are" don't give the leaders much chance to respond, since the leaders have already been judged, categorized, and dismissed. It is quite another matter to openly confront leaders with how the members perceive and experience them. A member leaves room for dialogue when she says: "I'm aware that I'm not opening up in here. One reason is that if I do, I feel that you'll push me beyond where I want to go." This member openly states her fears but leaves enough room for the leader to respond and to explore the issue further. This is a challenge, not an attack.

Challenging the leader is often a participant's first significant step toward autonomy. Most members experience the struggle of dependence versus independence. If the members are to become free of their dependency on the leader that is characteristic of the initial group stage, the leader must allow and deal directly with these revealing challenges to his or her authority. Fried (1972) indicates that groups are initially focused on the leader and held together partly by identification with the leader. But if the group is led appropriately, the members become more autonomous and eventually achieve a peer feeling with one another and with the leader. Fried says, "After considerable anxieties have been understood and shed, and after conflicts between submission and angry protest have been settled, a good feeling arises; the group members become cooperative with one another and feel fond of the leader, though they become familiar with his shortcomings" (1972, p. 67).

The way in which you accept and deal with challenges to you personally and to your leadership style greatly determines your effectiveness in leading the group into more advanced levels of development. Because I value the opportunities that challenges from group members offer, I attempt to deal with these challenges directly and honestly, to share how I am affected by the confrontation, to ask members to check out their assumptions, and to tell them how I see myself in regard to their criticism. I believe in keeping the lines of communication open, and I consistently try to avoid slipping into a "leader role" that entails diluting the challenge as a means of self-defense.

Resistance. Resistance is behavior that keeps oneself or others from exploring personal issues or painful feelings in depth. It is an inevitable phenomenon in groups, and unless it is recognized and explored, it can seriously interfere with the group process. Resistance, however, is not merely something to be overcome. Since it is an integral part of one's typical defensive approach to life, it must be recognized as a way of protecting oneself from the anxieties I just examined. For group leaders not to respect the members' resistances is akin to their not respecting the members themselves. An effective way of dealing with resistances is to treat them as an inevitable aspect of the group process; that is, the leader acknowledges that resistance is a member's natural response to getting personally involved in a risk-taking course. An open atmosphere that encourages people to acknowledge and work through whatever hesitations and anxieties they may be experiencing is essential. The participants must be willing to recognize their resistance and to talk about what might be keeping them from full participation.

Before we proceed with our discussion, two points need to be made. One is that the members' unwillingness to cooperate is not always a form of resistance in the proper sense of the term. There are times when member "resistance" is the result of factors such as an unqualified leader, conflict between co-leaders, a dogmatic or authoritarian leadership style, a leader's failure to prepare the participants for the group experience, and a lack of trust engendered by the leader. In other words, group members may be unwilling to share their feelings because they don't trust the group leader or because the group is simply not a safe place in which to open up. It is imperative that those who lead groups look honestly at the sources of resistance, keeping in mind that not all resistance stems from the members' lack of willingness to face unconscious and threatening sides of themselves.

The second point is a warning against the danger of categorizing people and reducing them to labels such as "the monopolist," "the intellectualizer," "the dependent one," or "the quiet seducer." Although it is understandable that prospective leaders will be interested in learning how to handle "problem members" and the disruption of the group that they can cause, the emphasis should be on actual *behaviors* rather than on labels. Regardless of the type of behavior a member exhibits as a characteristic style, he or she is more than that particular behavior. If you see and treat a person just as a "monopolizer" or an "advice giver" or a "help-rejecting complainer," you contribute to cementing that particular behavior instead of helping the person work on the problems behind the behavior.

For example, if Maria is treated as a "monopolizer" and is not encouraged to explore the impact she has on the group, she will continue to see herself as others see her and respond to her. You can help Maria, as well as the entire group, by investigating the reasons for her need to keep the spotlight on herself and the effects of her behavior on the group. People need to become aware of the defenses that may prevent them from getting involved in the group and of the effects of these defenses on the other members. However, they should be confronted with care and in such a way that they are *challenged* to recognize their defensive behaviors and *invited* to go beyond them.

Another limitation of identifying "problem members" rather than problem behaviors is that most of those who participate in groups exhibit, at one time or another, some form of resistance. Occasional advice giving, questioning, or intellectualizing is not in itself a problem behavior. As a matter of fact, the group leader needs to be aware of the danger of letting participants become overly self-conscious of how they behave in the group. If clients become too concerned about being identified as "problem group members," they won't be able to behave spontaneously and openly.

Creating a Supportive and Challenging Climate

For a group to be effective, an appropriate balance must be struck between support and challenge. The research reviews that describe negative outcomes in groups cite aggressively confronting group leaders as presenting the highest risk (Lieberman, Yalom, & Miles, 1973; Yalom, 1985). Based on research findings, Dies (1983b) suggests that leaders should not engage in highly confrontive interventions until they have earned the right to be confrontive, which is achieved primarily by building a trusting relationship with the members. Once the foundation of interpersonal trust has been established, group members tend to be more open to being challenged. Dies recommends that since it takes time to create a supportive atmosphere in a group, confrontive interactions are probably most appropriate at a later stage.

Destructive confrontations, with an attacking quality, can lead to an entrenchment of resistance and breed hostility and mistrust. But confrontation is appropriate even during the early stages of a group if it is done with sensitivity and respect. In fact, trust is often facilitated by caring confrontations on the leader's part. To avoid challenging a group in its early phases is to treat the members as though they were fragile. How leaders deal with conflict, resistance, anxiety, and defensiveness does much to set the tone of the group. In my view members have a tendency to follow the leader's manner of confronting.

Co-Leader Issues at the Transition Stage

As you can see, the transition stage is a critical period in the history of the group, for, depending on how conflict and resistance are handled, the group can take a turn for the better or for the worse. If you are working with a co-leader, a few particular problems can easily develop at this time:

1. *Negative reactions toward one leader.* If members direct a challenge or express negative feelings toward your co-leader, it is as important to avoid taking sides with your co-leader in attacking members as it is to

avoid taking sides with the members in ganging up against the co-leader. What is called for in such an instance is for you to nondefensively (and as objectively as possible) continue your leadership by facilitating a constructive exploration of the situation.

2. *Challenge to both co-leaders.* Assume that several members direct negative feelings to both you and your co-leader, saying: "You leaders expect us to be personal in here, yet we don't know anything about you that is personal. You should be willing to talk about your problems if that is what you expect us to do!" In such a case, difficulties can develop if one of you responds defensively while the other is willing to deal with this confrontation from the members. Ideally, both co-leaders would be willing to talk about the confrontation objectively; if not, this would surely be a vital topic to discuss in the co-leaders' meeting outside of group or during a supervision session. I don't want to convey the impression that all difficulties should be reserved for a private discussion between the co-leaders. As much as possible, matters that pertain to what is happening during sessions should be discussed with the entire group. The failure to do this can easily lead to a *you* versus *them* split within the group.

3. *Dealing with problem behaviors.* In Chapter 3 I emphasized the importance of dealing with your own reactions to members who are "difficult." I want to caution against the tendency of co-leaders to chronically discuss what such members are doing or not doing and never explore how such behavior affects them as leaders. It is a mistake to dwell almost exclusively on strategies for curing problem members while ignoring the leaders' personal reactions to such problematic behaviors.

4. *Dealing with countertransference.* It is not realistic to expect a leader to work equally effectively with every member. At times, this is due to countertransference reactions on the part of one of the leaders. For example, a male leader could have strong and irrational negative reactions to one of the women in the group. It may be that he is seeing his ex-wife in this member and responding to her in cutting ways because of his own unresolved issues over the divorce. When this occurs, the co-leader can be therapeutic for both the member and the leader who is being nontherapeutic. The co-leader can intervene during the session itself as well as explore these inappropriate reactions with the other leader outside the session. Co-leaders who are willing to be objective and honest with each other can have a positive impact through this process of mutual confrontation.

Summary of the Transition Stage

Stage Characteristics.   The transitional phase of a group's development is marked by feelings of anxiety and defenses in the form of various resistances. At this time members are

- wondering what they will think of themselves if they increase their self-awareness and wondering about others' acceptance or rejection of them

- testing the leader and other members to determine how safe the environment is
- struggling with whether to remain aloof or to risk getting involved
- experiencing some struggle for control and power and some conflict with other members or the leader
- learning how to work through conflict and confrontation
- feeling reluctant to get fully involved in working on their personal concerns because they are not sure others in the group will care about them
- observing the leader to determine if he or she is trustworthy and learning from this person how to resolve conflict
- learning how to express themselves so that others will listen to them

Member Functions and Possible Problems.   A central role of members at this time is to recognize and deal with the many forms of resistance. Tasks include

- recognizing and expressing any negative feelings
- respecting one's own resistances but working with them
- moving from dependence to independence
- learning how to confront others in a constructive manner
- recognizing unresolved feelings from the past as they are being acted out in relation to the group leader
- being willing to face and deal with reactions toward what is occurring in the group
- being willing to work through conflicts, rather than avoiding them

Some problems can arise with members at this time:

- Members can be categorized as a "problem type," or they can limit themselves with a self-imposed label.
- Members may refuse to express persistent negative feelings, thus contributing to the climate of distrust.
- If confrontations are poorly handled, members may retreat into defensive postures, and issues will remain hidden.
- Members may collude with one another by forming subgroups and cliques, expressing negative reactions in these cliques outside of the group but remaining silent in the group.

Leader Functions.   Perhaps the central challenge that leaders face during the transition phase is the need to intervene in the group in a sensitive manner and at the right time. The basic task is to provide both the encouragement and the challenge necessary for the members to face and resolve the conflicts that exist within the group and their own resistances and defenses against anxiety. As I indicated earlier, the genuine cohesion that allows for productive work to develop demands that this difficult phase of defensiveness and conflict be experienced and dealt with successfully.

The following are some of the major tasks that you need to perform during this critical period in a group's development:

- teaching group members the importance of recognizing and expressing their anxieties
- helping participants recognize the ways in which they react defensively and creating a climate in which they can deal with their resistances openly
- noticing signs of resistance and communicating to the participants that some of these resistances are both natural and healthy
- teaching the members the value of recognizing and dealing openly with conflicts that occur in the group
- pointing out behavior that is a manifestation of the struggle for control and teaching the members how to accept their share of responsibility for the direction of the group
- providing a model for the members by dealing directly and honestly with any challenges to you as a person or as a professional
- assisting the group members in dealing with any matters that will influence their ability to become autonomous and independent

Leaders need to be especially active during the first and second stages of a group. During the transition stage, active intervention and structuring are important, because generally the participants have not yet learned to work effectively on their own. If a conflict arises, for example, some members may attempt to move on to more pleasant topics or in some other way ignore the conflict. Group leaders need to teach members the value of expressing their feelings, no matter how negative.

Concluding Comments

This chapter has addressed various issues of group membership and group process that are central to your effectiveness as a group leader. I have focused on key concerns as the group is being formed, at its initial phase, and at the transitional period in a group's history. Emphasis has been placed on the central characteristics of the group at each phase, the member functions and possible problems, group-process concepts, and the leader's key tasks. Attention has also been given to co-leader issues during each period of development. It has been mentioned several times that your approach to leadership functions and skills hinges on your understanding of the roles that members play at the various stages in the group. Only if you are clear in your own mind about the various aspects of productive and unproductive member behaviors can you help group participants acquire the skills necessary for a successful group experience and correct behaviors that hinder self-exploration and involvement in the group. The next chapter continues this account of the unfolding of a group.

5

Later Stages in the Development of a Group

Continuing the discussion of the evolutionary process of a group in action, this chapter focuses on the working stage, the final stage, and the postgroup issues of follow-up and evaluation. We will look at the major characteristics of the group at each phase, the member functions and possible problems that are likely to occur, and the group leader's key functions.

Stage 3: Working Stage—Cohesion and Productivity

The working stage is characterized by exploration of significant problems and by effective action to bring about the desired behavioral changes. This is the time when participants need to realize that they are responsible for their lives. Thus, they must be encouraged to decide what issues they want to explore in the group, they need to learn how to become an integral part of the group and yet retain their individuality, and they must filter the feedback they receive and make their own decisions concerning what they will do about it. Consequently, it is very important at this stage that neither the group leader nor the other members attempt to decide on a course of action or make prescriptions for the individual.

Development of Group Cohesion

Nature of Group Cohesion. Cohesion involves the group's attractiveness to the participants and a sense of belonging, inclusion, and solidarity. Although it may begin to develop in the early stages of a group, at this stage it becomes a key element of the group process. If trust has been established and if conflict and negative feelings have been expressed and worked through, the group becomes a cohesive unit. It is, in a sense, as if the group had gone through a testing period and the members had said to themselves "If it's OK to express negative feelings and conflict, then maybe it's OK to get close."

I have found that cohesion occurs when people open up and take risks. The honest sharing of deeply significant personal experiences and struggles binds the group together, because the process of sharing allows members to identify with others by seeing themselves in them. Since cohesion provides the group with the impetus to move forward, it is a prerequisite for the group's success. Without a sense of "groupness" the group remains fragmented, the members become frozen behind their defenses, and their work is of necessity superficial. Groups do not become cohesive automatically. Cohesion is the result of a commitment by the participants and the leader to take the steps that lead to a group-as-a-whole feeling.

Although group cohesion is not in itself a sufficient condition for effective group work, in a sense all the characteristics of a well-functioning group are contingent on it. Cohesion fosters action-oriented behaviors such as self-disclosure, immediacy, mutuality, confrontation, risk taking, and translation of insight into action. Also, without group cohesion the participants don't feel secure enough to maintain a high level of self-disclosure.

Research on Group Cohesion.   What does the research say about the role of cohesion in the successful outcome of a group? As Bednar and Kaul (1978) note, group cohesion is assumed to be a prime therapeutic factor in groups, and successes and failures are frequently attributed to it. But there is relatively little clear and systematic research on the specific factors that are thought to affect cohesion. Bednar and Kaul add: "The research that has been published has led to less consistency of results and interpretation than one would wish. In short, there is little cohesion in the cohesion research" (p. 800). These conflicting conclusions are not surprising, because group cohesion, rather than being a stable factor, is a complex process (Bednar & Kaul, 1985; Stockton & Hulse, 1981).

Yalom (1985) maintains that research evidence shows cohesion to be a strong determinant of a positive group outcome. If members experience little sense of belongingness or attraction to the group, there is little likelihood that they will benefit, and they may well experience negative outcomes. According to Yalom, groups with a here-and-now focus are almost invariably vital and cohesive. By contrast, groups in which members merely talk about issues with a "there-and-then" focus rarely develop much cohesiveness.

Cohesion as a Unifying Force.   Although cohesiveness is necessary for effective group work, it can also actually hinder the group's development. When cohesiveness is not accompanied by a challenge to move forward by both the members and the leader, the group can reach a plateau. The group enjoys the comfort and security of the unity it has earned, but no progress is made.

In many of the adult groups that I lead there are common human themes that most of the members can relate to personally, regardless of their age, sociocultural background, and occupation. Whereas members are likely to be aware in the earlier stages of the group of the differences that separate them, it is quite common as the group reaches a level of cohesion for members to comment on how alike they are in the feelings that connect them. Some of these responses are as follows:

- "I'm not alone in my pain and with my problems."
- "I'm more lovable than I thought I was."
- "I used to think that I was too old to change and that I'd just have to settle for what I have in life. Now I see that what I feel is no different from what the younger people in here feel."
- "I'm hopeful about my future, even though I know that I have a long way to go and that the road will be rough."
- "There are a lot of people in here I feel close to, and I see that we earned this closeness by letting others know who we are."
- "Intimacy is frightening, but it's also rewarding."
- "People can be beautiful once they shed their masks."
- "I learned that the loneliness I felt was shared by most people in this group."

As a group becomes cohesive, it is not uncommon for a woman in her early 20s to discover that she is very much like a man in his late 50s. Both of them may still be searching for parental approval, and they may both be learning how futile it is to look outside of themselves for confirmation of their worth. A man learns that his struggles with masculinity are not too different from a woman's struggles with her femininity. A woman learns that she is not alone when she discovers that she feels resentment over the many demands her family makes on her. An older man sees in a younger male member "his son" and allows himself to feel tenderness and compassion that he did not let himself experience earlier.

Other common themes evolving in this stage lead to an increase of cohesion: remembering painful experiences of childhood and adolescence, becoming aware of the need for and fear of love, becoming able to express feelings that have been repressed, discovering that one's worst enemy lives within oneself, struggling to find a meaning in life, feeling guilt over what one has done or failed to do, longing for meaningful connections with significant people, and beginning a process of finding one's identity. The leader can foster the development of cohesion by pointing out the common themes that link members of the group.

Characteristics of an Effective Working Group

Stage 3 is characterized by productiveness. Now that the members have truly become a group and have developed relationship skills that allow them a greater degree of autonomy, they are less dependent on the leader. Mutuality and self-exploration increase, and the group is focused on producing lasting results. Although the specific characteristics of a cohesive and productive group do vary somewhat with the type of group, there are some general trends that identify a group in its working stage:

• There is a here-and-now focus. People have learned to talk directly about what they are feeling and doing in the group sessions, and they are generally willing to have meaningful interactions. They are talking *to* one another, not *about* one another. They focus more on what is going on in the group than on stories about people outside of the group. When outside issues are brought up, they are often related to the group process. If Henry explores his fears of intimacy, for example, he will typically be asked to talk about being frightened of intimacy in the group as well as in his relationships in the real world.

• Members more readily identify their goals and concerns, and they have learned to take responsibility for them. They are less confused about what the group and the leader expect of them.

• Members are willing to work and practice outside the group to achieve behavioral changes. They are carrying out "homework assignments," and they bring into the sessions any difficulties they have had in practicing new ways of thinking, behaving, and feeling. They are willing to try to integrate emotions, thoughts, and behaviors in their everyday situations. They are better able to catch themselves when they are thinking and acting in old patterns.

• Most of the members feel included in the group. Those who are not active know that they are welcome to participate, and their lack of participation does not discourage others from doing meaningful work. Members who are having a difficult time feeling a sense of connection or belonging are free to bring this problem up in the sessions, and ideally it becomes a focal point for productive work.

• The group has almost become an orchestra, in that individuals listen to one another and do productive work together. Although the participants may still look to the leader for direction, as musicians look to the conductor for cues, they also tend to initiate a direction in which they want to move.

• Members continually assess their level of satisfaction with the group, and they take active steps to change matters if they see that the sessions need changing. In a productive group, members realize that they have a part in the outcomes. If they are not getting what they want, they generally say so.

Therapeutic Factors of a Group

The following brief overview offers a summary of the specific factors that ensure that a group will move beyond the security of cohesiveness into productive work. Three major aspects of the working stage, self-disclosure, confrontation, and feedback, are addressed in some detail.

Trust and Acceptance.   Group members at the working stage trust one another and the leader, or at least they openly express any lack of trust. Trust is manifested in the participants' attitude of acceptance and in their willingness to take risks by sharing meaningful here-and-now reactions. Feeling that they are accepted, the members recognize that in the group they can be who they are without risking rejection. They dare to assert themselves, for example, because they know that they don't have to please everybody. At the working stage trust is generally high, because members have been willing to deal with any barriers to its establishment and mainte-nance. As is the case with other interpersonal relations, however, trust is not a static entity. Even during the advanced stages of a group, trust may ebb and flow, and there is an ongoing challenge for members to talk about how safe they feel in their group.

Empathy and Caring.   Empathy involves a deep capacity to recall, relive, and tap one's feelings through the intense experiences of others. By un-derstanding the feelings of others—such as the need for love and acceptance, hurt about past experiences, loneliness, joy, and enthusiasm—members come to see themselves more clearly. Empathy means caring, and caring is expressed in a group, by genuine and active involvement with the other members. It is also expressed by compassion, support, tenderness, and even confrontation. As people open themselves to others by showing their pain, struggles, joy, excitement, and fears, they make it possible for others to care for them. It is empathy that bridges the gap between peoples of different ethnic and cultural groups and allows them to share in universal human themes. Although clients' specific life circumstances may differ depending on their cultural background, groups allow a diverse range of people to come to realize what they have in common (Yalom, 1985).

Hope.   If change is to occur, members must believe that change is possible, that they need not remain trapped in their past, and that they can take active steps to make their lives richer. Hope is therapeutic in itself, for it gives members the confidence to commit themselves to the demanding work that a group requires and motivates them to explore alternatives. Hope is characteristic of effective group leaders and underlies their beliefs about their clients, themselves, and the basic purposes to be achieved through group counseling (Couch & Childers, 1987).

As Yalom (1985) has indicated, the instillation and maintenance of hope are crucial in group therapy, so that members will remain in the group and other therapeutic factors can take effect. He cites research demonstrating that high levels of client expectation of help before therapy are significantly correlated with positive outcomes. Research also substantiates that the therapist's belief in the group process is critical to motivating clients.

A number of leadership strategies for fostering hope have been proposed (Couch & Childers, 1987). Some of these are using the pregroup interview as an opportunity to instill hope in members by creating positive (but realistic) expectations, acknowledging and validating concerns common to many of the participants, calling attention to improvements that members make, encouraging any signs of subtle and positive movement, letting members acknowledge one another's progress, and helping them assume responsibility for their own progress.

Freedom to Experiment.   Experimentation with different modes of behavior is a significant aspect of the working stage. The group is a safe place in which to try out novel behavior. After such experiments members can decide what behaviors they want to change. In everyday transactions people often behave in rigid and unimaginative ways, for they don't dare deviate from familiar and predictable ways of behaving. With group support participants can practice more functional ways of being. Role playing is often an effective way to practice new skills in interpersonal situations; then these skills can be applied to out-of-group situations. This topic is explored more fully in the discussions of psychodrama (Chapter 8) and Gestalt groups (Chapter 11).

Commitment to Change.   I said earlier that, for change to occur, a person must believe that change is possible. But hope alone is not enough. Constructive change requires a firm resolve to actually do whatever is necessary in order to change. This means deciding *what* to change as well as *how* to change it. Participants need to formulate a plan of action, commit themselves to it, and use the tools offered by the group process to explore ways of carrying it out. The support offered by the group is invaluable in encouraging the members to stick with their commitments even when they experience temporary setbacks. An inherent advantage of groups is that members can use one another to help themselves maintain their commitments. They can agree to call another member when they encounter difficulties in carrying out their plans, or they can call when they have made a successful breakthrough. A "buddy system" can be instrumental in teaching members how to ask for help and how to give this help to others, valuable social skills that they can also apply to relationships outside of the group. The topic of commitment in group counseling is discussed in more detail as it applies to reality group therapy (Chapter 15).

Intimacy.   As W. Schutz (1973a) has suggested, the issue of intimacy becomes very relevant in the third stage of a group. The questions of being liked or disliked and of not being close enough or being too intimate are often a source of great anxiety. According to Schutz, after problems of control are resolved, affection becomes a predominant issue. Therefore, expressions of positive and negative feelings and heightened emotionality between pairs of people are quite common at this stage.

Genuine intimacy develops in a group after people have revealed enough of themselves for others to identify with them. I've found that intimacy increases as people work through their struggles together. Members see that regardless of their differences, they all share certain needs, wants, anxieties, and problems. When members learn that others have similar problems, they no longer feel isolated; identification with others eventually brings about closeness, which allows the members to help one another work through fears related to intimacy. The ultimate goal is to understand how one has avoided intimacy outside of the group and how one can accept intimacy in life without fear.

The group setting provides an ideal arena for members to discover their fears of intimacy and the resistances to getting close to others that they are using. Ormont (1988) describes both the verbal and attitudinal resistances to intimacy that come into play in group therapy. Common *verbal* resistances are displayed by members who seek information as a way of fending off meaningful contact with others; fault-finding members, who focus on the flaws of others as a way of keeping distance; members who pick fights as a way of warding off contact; members who place stipulations on closeness; and members who divert the discussion, especially when others get close to them. Ormont lists the following *attitudinal* resistances to intimacy in groups: self-absorption, detachment, dissatisfaction, distrust, and compliance.

During the working phase members ideally not only recognize their resistances to interpersonal intimacy but also demonstrate a willingness to work through the fears associated with getting close to others, both in their group and in their daily life. Such members tend to fear that if they do get close, they will not be able to control their impulses; if they care, they may suffer abandonment again; if they allow intimacy, they will merge with others and lose a sense of their own identity; and if they experience intimacy, they are opening themselves up to being emotionally wounded in various ways by others. A productive group offers many opportunities for members to face and challenge these fears. They are able to use the here-and-now group experience as a way of working through past hurts and early decisions that block intimacy. Old and unfinished issues are relived in the group context, and new decisions are made possible. Members are able to see connections between ways in which they are avoiding interpersonal intimacy both in the group and with significant others. What occurs within a group as the members develop mature forms of intimacy is detailed as follows by Ormont (1988): members make emotional space for one another; talk is simple and direct; there are no hidden agendas in the group; members are openly taking risks with one another; powerful feelings are present; members regard one another with a freshness that they have not shown before; and they are able to live in the moment, for the lingering remnants of their past hurts have been worked through successfully.

Catharsis.   The expression of pent-up feelings can be therapeutic, because it releases energy that has been tied up in withholding certain threatening feelings. This emotional release, which often occurs in an explosive way, leaves the person feeling freer. Also, keeping a lid on anger, pain, frustration, hatred, and fear means preventing spontaneous feelings such as joy, affection, delight, and enthusiasm from emerging. This emotional release plays an important part in many kinds of groups, but both group leaders and members sometimes make the mistake of concluding that mere catharsis implies "real work." Some disappointed members who do not have emotional releases are convinced that they are not really getting involved. It is not uncommon to witness members who experience "problem envy," or who are convinced that they are not getting as much from the group as others who have had more catharses than they have. Although it is often healing, catharsis by itself is limited in producing long-lasting changes.

Yalom (1985) notes that catharsis is an interpersonal process, for people do not get enduring benefits from ventilating feelings in an empty closet. He stresses that although catharsis is related to a positive outcome and that it is often necessary for change, it is certainly not enough. He puts the impact of catharsis into perspective: "The open expression of affect is without question vital to the group therapeutic process; in its absence a group would degenerate into a sterile academic exercise. Yet it is only a part of the process and must be complemented by other factors" (p. 85).

My experience has taught me that catharsis *may* be a vital part of a person's work in a group, especially if the client has a reservoir of unrecognized and unexpressed feelings. I have also learned that it is a mistake to assume that no real work occurs without a strong ventilation of feelings, since many people appear to benefit in the absence of catharsis. After catharsis has occurred, it is extremely important to work through the feelings that emerged, to gain some understanding of the meaning of the experience, and to make new decisions based on such understanding.

Cognitive Restructuring. A central part of the work done in a group consists of challenging and exploring beliefs about situations. It has been shown that emotionality is related to successful outcomes when it is accompanied by some form of cognitive learning (Lieberman et al., 1973). In other words, understanding the *meaning* of intense emotional experiences is essential to further self-exploration. This cognitive component includes explaining, clarifying, interpreting, providing the cognitive framework needed for change, formulating ideas, and making new decisions. Groups offer members many opportunities to evaluate their thinking and to adopt constructive beliefs in place of self-limiting ones. This process of cognitive restructuring forms a central role in several therapeutic approaches, including Adlerian groups (Chapter 7), transactional analysis (Chapter 12), cognitive-behavioral groups (Chapter 13), and rational-emotive group therapy (Chapter 14). In summary, catharsis can be a very useful tool for change, if the person attempts to conceptualize the emotional experience and put it into words.

Self-Disclosure. Disclosure is not an end in itself; it is the means by which open communication can occur within a group. If disclosure is limited to safe topics or if it is mistaken for exposing secrets, the group cannot move beyond a superficial level. There are many barriers within us that keep us from self-disclosure—for example, fear of the intimacy that accompanies self-revelation, avoidance of responsibility and change, feelings of guilt and shame, fear of rejection, and cultural taboos. The willingness to overcome these barriers and make oneself known to others is a basic requirement at every stage of a group. During the working stage most members have developed enough trust to risk disclosing threatening material.

Since self-disclosure is the principal vehicle of group interaction, it is critical that group participants have a clear understanding of what self-disclosure is and is not. One level of self-disclosure involves sharing one's persistent reactions to what is happening in the group. Another level of self-disclosure entails revealing current struggles, unresolved personal issues, goals and aspirations, joys and hurts, and strengths and weaknesses. If people are unwilling to share of themselves, they make it very hard for others to care for them. In the process of talking about concerns that occurred outside of the group or in the past, it is important for members to relate these issues to the here and now. By focusing on the here and now, participants make direct contact with one another and generally express quite accurately what they are experiencing in the present. The interactions become increasingly honest and spontaneous, because members are more willing to risk revealing their reactions to one another.

On the other hand, self-disclosure does *not* mean revealing one's innermost secrets and digging into one's past. Nor does it mean "letting everything hang out" or expressing every fleeting reaction toward others. Self-disclosure should not be confused with telling stories about oneself or with letting group pressure dictate the limits of one's privacy. At times, in striving to be "open and honest" or in perceiving pressure from others in the group, some members say more than is necessary for others to understand them. They disclose so much that nothing remains private, and as a result they may feel deprived of their dignity.

In working with culturally diverse populations, keep in mind that self-disclosure is highly valued in most of the traditional counseling approaches that are covered in this book. However, self-disclosure is foreign to the values of some cultural groups. This premium that is placed on self-disclosure by most therapeutic approaches is often in conflict with the values of some European ethnic groups that stress that problems should be kept "in the family." As Sue (1981) has pointed out, culturally different clients are likely to experience considerable anxiety about these differences. They may be slow to self-disclose until they are fairly certain that it is safe to do so, which usually involves some testing of the leader and of other group members.

Unless clients challenge the obstacles to disclosure, their participation in a group will be very limited. As a group leader, you can recognize that some individuals with certain ethnic and cultural backgrounds will have difficulties in readily sharing their feelings and reactions, let alone revealing their deeper struggles. You can help such clients by demonstrating respect for their cultural values and at the same time encouraging them to express what they want from you and from the group. With your support and the understanding of other members, they are in a position to clarify their values pertaining to self-disclosure and can decide the degree to which they are willing to make themselves known to others. A good starting point is for them to talk about their difficulty in revealing themselves in a group setting.

Confrontation.   Like self-disclosure, confrontation is a basic ingredient of the working stage; if it is absent, stagnation results. Constructive confrontation is an invitation to examine discrepancies between what one says and what one does, to become aware of unused potential, and to carry insights into action. When confrontation takes place in the supportive environment of a group, it can be a true act of caring.

In a successful group, confrontation occurs in such a way that the confronters share their reactions to the person being confronted rather than their judgments of the person. A negative style of confrontation—that is, confrontation done in a hostile, indirect, or attacking way—is avoided, because it may leave people feeling judged and rejected. Done with care and sensitivity, confrontation by others ultimately helps members develop the capacity for the self-confrontation necessary to work through the problems they need to resolve.

Confrontation is an issue that group members, as well as group leaders, frequently misunderstand; it is often feared, misused, and seen as a negative act to be avoided at all costs. In my opinion, although support and empathy are certainly essential to group process, they can become counterproductive if carried to an excess. In other words, a group can cease to be effective if its members have colluded to interact only on a supportive level and agreed to focus almost exclusively on strengths and positive feedback. Unwillingness to challenge the others to take a deeper look at themselves results in overly polite and supportive exchanges that bear little resemblance to everyday interactions and that provide no incentive to extend oneself.

Group leaders can productively devote time to helping the participants clear up their misconceptions regarding confrontation and learn *what* to confront and *how* to confront in a constructive way. One of the most powerful ways of teaching constructive and caring confrontation is for leaders to model this behavior in their interactions in the group. By being direct, honest, sensitive, respectful, and timely in their confrontations, leaders provide the members with valuable opportunities to learn these skills through observing the leader's behavior.

Egan (1977) sees confrontation as an invitation to examine some aspect of one's interpersonal style. Challenging others to look at themselves with greater depth and awareness can motivate them to take action to make changes in their lives. The absence of this challenge can lead to complacency and to unwillingness to make full contact with others.

Here are some practical guidelines for effective confrontation. The first five are offered by Egan (1977, pp. 218–221).

1. Confront in a spirit of accurate understanding.
2. Be tentative, as opposed to dogmatic, but avoid being apologetic.
3. Be concrete by describing specific behavior; avoid judging and categorizing the person.
4. Confront only those people you care for and with whom you want to reach deeper closeness.
5. Confront only when you have earned the right to do so.

In addition to Egan's guidelines, I typically emphasize the following points about effective confrontation:

• Remember that confrontation must be based on respect for others and that it is aimed at challenging others to look at unrecognized and un-explored aspects of themselves.

• Use confrontation only if you want to get closer to a client and only if you are willing to stay with the person after the confrontation.

• Learn to discriminate between what may be a judgmental attack and a caring challenge. For example, instead of saying "All you do is take from the group; you never give anything of yourself," you may say: "I'm aware that you rarely speak in the group, and I miss hearing from you. I'm wondering whether your silence is OK with you or whether you'd like to be saying more. Are you aware of anything that's preventing you from express-ing your feelings and thoughts?"

• When you confront a person, address his or her specific behaviors that affect others in the group and explain exactly what the effect is.

• Take responsibility for your behaviors instead of making others responsible for how you respond. Thus, instead of saying "You make me angry when you go off on your tangents," say "I get impatient and angry when you digress." Instead of saying "You're boring," say "I'm aware that I have a hard time staying with you when you speak, and I find that I'm becoming bored."

In sum, confrontation should be done in such a manner as to preserve the dignity of the one confronted, without prejudice to the person, and with the purpose of helping the person identify and see the consequences of his or her behavior. Most important, confrontation should open up the channels of communication and not close them.

Benefiting from Feedback.   Although I treat the topics of self-disclosure, confrontation, and feedback separately for the purpose of discussion, these therapeutic factors have some degree of overlap in actual practice. Most feedback entails self-disclosure, and sometimes feedback can be confrontational. Take, for example, the group member who says to another member: "I was very affected by the way you role-played talking to your father. It reminded me of my own father and the way I struggle with getting close to him." This is an example of both giving feedback and self-disclosing. Now consider the group member who says: "When you talked about your father, your fists were clenched, yet you were smiling. I don't know which to believe—your fists or your smile." This type of feedback illustrates a confrontation, as well as some degree of self-disclosure. The person giving feedback disclosed some here-and-now reactions to another member.

If members give one another their reactions and perceptions honestly and with care, all participants are able to hear what impact they have had on others and can then decide what, if anything, they want to change. Such feedback is one of the most important ways in which learning takes place in a group. It can be of great help to the person who is exploring a problem, attempting to resolve a difficult situation, or trying different ways of behaving. Following are some points that can help members learn how to give and receive feedback:

- Global feedback is of little value. Reactions to specific behavior in the group provide a person with an immediate, independent assessment that can be compared with the person's own view.
- Concise feedback given in a clear and straightforward manner is more helpful than statements with qualifiers or interpretive or mixed feedback (Stockton & Morran, 1980).
- Difficult feedback must be timed well and given in a nonjudgmental way, or else the person receiving it is likely to become defensive and reject it.
- Positive feedback is almost invariably rated as being more desirable, having greater impact, and leading to greater intention to change than negative feedback. Focus on the person's strengths as well as behaviors that might be a source of difficulty (Dies, 1983b; Morran, Robison, & Stockton, 1985; Morran & Stockton, 1980).
- Negative feedback seems to be more credible and helpful if it comes at a later phase of the group; it is more likely to be accepted when it has been preceded by positive feedback (Stockton & Morran, 1981).
- Negative feedback is easier to take if the member who is giving it talks about how he or she has been affected by the other member's behavior. This practice lessens the chances that members will be judged, for those who give feedback are focusing on themselves at the same time that they are talking to others about their behavior.
- Feedback with a quality of immediacy—that is, feedback given as a here-and-now reaction—is especially valuable and is far better than "stored-up" reactions.
- Leader feedback is generally of higher quality than member feedback, but it is not more readily accepted (Morran et al., 1985).

Members sometimes make a global declaration such as "I'd like feedback!" If such clients have said very little, it is difficult to give them many reactions. Members need to learn how to ask for specific feedback and how to receive it. There is value in listening nondefensively to feedback, in really hearing what others want to say to us, and then in considering what we are willing to do with this information. As the group progresses to a working stage, members are typically more willing to freely give one another their reactions.

Commentary.   As my colleagues and I have written elsewhere (Corey, Corey, Callanan, & Russell, 1988), not all groups reach the working stage that is being described here. This does not necessarily mean that the leader is ineffective. Changing membership in a group can block its progress. Some populations simply may not be ready for the level of intensity that is often part of a working phase. If the tasks of the initial and transition stages were never mastered, then the group can be expected to be stuck. For instance, some groups don't get beyond the hidden agendas and unspoken conflicts that were typical of earlier sessions. Or the members may simply not be willing to give much of themselves beyond safe and superficial encounters. They may have made a decision to stop at a safe level characterized by mutual support, rather than also challenging one another to move into unknown territory. Early interchanges between members and the leader or among members may have been abrasive, thus creating a climate of hesitancy and unwillingness to trust others. The group may be oriented toward solving problems or patching up differences. This orientation can discourage self-exploration, for as soon as a member raises a problem, some members may rush in with advice on how to remedy the situation. For reasons such as these and others, some groups never progress beyond the initial stage or the transition stage.

My colleagues and I have also observed that when a group does get to the working stage, it doesn't necessarily progress as tidily as the above characterization may suggest. Earlier themes of trust, unconstructive conflict, and the reluctance to participate surface time and again in a group's history. As one member put it, "There is no trust heaven in groups!" Trust is not a matter that is dealt with once and for all during the early stages of development. As the group faces new challenges, deeper levels of trust have to be earned. Also, considerable conflict may be resolved during the initial stage or transition stage, but new conflicts emerge in the advanced phases and must be faced and worked through. As is true with any intimate relationship, the relationships in the group are not static. Utopia is never reached, for the smooth waters may well turn into stormy seas for a time. Commitment to functioning as a group is necessary to do the difficult yet rewarding work of progressing.

Co-Leader Issues at the Working Stage

The importance of meeting with one's co-leader throughout the duration of the group cannot be overemphasized. Many of the issues I suggested earlier for discussion at these co-leader meetings also apply to the working stage. A few other issues are particularly relevant to this stage:

Ongoing Evaluation of the Group.   Co-leaders can make it a practice to devote some time to appraising the direction the group is taking and its level of productivity. If the group is a closed one with a predetermined duration (say, 20 weeks), the co-leaders would do well to evaluate the group's progress around the 10th week. This evaluation can be a topic of discussion privately and in the group itself. For example, if both leaders feel that the group is bogging down and that members seem to be losing interest in the sessions, they should surely bring these perceptions into the group. Then members will have the opportunity to look at their degree of satisfaction with the group's direction and progress. It is a good idea to use a written evaluation or checklist such as that found in the accompanying student manual.

Discussion of Techniques.   It is useful for co-leaders to discuss techniques and leadership styles. One of the leaders may be hesitant to try a technique because of fearing to make a mistake, because of not knowing where to go next, or because of passively waiting for permission from the co-leader to introduce techniques. Such issues, along with any stylistic differences between leaders, are topics for exploration.

Theoretical Orientations.   It is not essential that co-leaders share the same theory of group work, for differing theoretical preferences can sometimes blend nicely. However, it is important that the two leaders be working toward the same general purposes. If they have conflicting aims, both they and the group members become confused, and there is little chance for cohesion to develop. Co-leaders can learn a lot from discussing theory as it applies to practice. Therefore, I encourage leaders to read, attend workshops and special seminars, and then discuss what they are learning. Doing so can result in bringing to the group sessions some new and interesting variations.

Self-Disclosure Issues.   Self-disclosure was discussed earlier in this chapter, but I want to add here the value of co-leaders' exploring their sense of appropriate and therapeutic leader self-disclosure. For example, if you are willing to share with members your reactions that pertain to group issues yet are reserved in disclosing personal outside issues, whereas your co-leader freely and fully talks about his or her marital situation in the group, then members may perceive you as holding back. This is another issue that can be discussed both in the group and privately.

Confrontation Issues.   What I have said about self-disclosure also applies to confrontation. You can imagine the problems that could ensue if one leader used harsh and unrelenting confrontations to get members to open up while the other leader was providing support to the exclusion of any confrontation. One leader can easily be labeled as the "good guy" while the confronting one is seen as the "bad guy." If such differences in style exist, they surely need to be talked about at length between the co-leaders if the group is not to suffer.

Summary of the Working Stage

Stage Characteristics. When a group reaches the working stage, the central characteristics include the following:

- The level of trust and cohesion is high.
- Communication within the group is open and involves an accurate expression of what is being experienced.
- Leadership functions are likely to be shared by the group, in that members interact with one another freely and directly.
- There is a willingness to risk threatening material and to make oneself known to others; members bring to the group personal topics they want to discuss and understand better.
- Conflict among members is recognized and dealt with directly and effectively.
- Feedback is given freely and accepted and considered nondefensively.
- Confrontation occurs in a way in which those doing the challenging avoid slapping judgmental labels on others.
- Members are willing to work outside the group to achieve behavioral changes.
- Participants feel supported in their attempts to change and are willing to risk new behavior.
- Members feel hopeful that they can change if they are willing to take action; they do not feel helpless.

Member Functions and Possible Problems. The working stage is characterized by the exploration of personally meaningful material. To reach this stage, members have certain tasks and roles:

- bringing into group sessions issues that they are willing to discuss
- giving others feedback and being open to receiving it
- assuming some leadership functions, especially by sharing how they are affected by others' presence and work in the group
- practicing new skills and behaviors in daily life and bringing the results to the sessions
- offering both challenge and support to others and engaging in self-confrontation
- continually assessing their satisfaction with the group and actively taking steps to change their level of involvement in the sessions if necessary

Some problems may arise at this time:

- Members may collude to relax and enjoy the comfort of familiar relationships and avoid challenging one another.

- Members may gain insights in the sessions but not see the necessity of action outside of the group to bring about change.
- Members may withdraw because of anxiety over others' intensity.

Leader Functions. Some of the central leadership functions at this stage are these:

- providing systematic reinforcement of desired group behaviors that foster cohesion and productive work
- looking for common themes among members' work that provide for some universality
- continuing to model appropriate behavior, especially caring confrontation, and disclosing ongoing reactions to the group
- supporting the members' willingness to take risks and assisting them in carrying this behavior into their daily living
- interpreting the meaning of behavior patterns at appropriate times so that members will be able to reach a deeper level of self-exploration and consider alternative behaviors
- being aware of the therapeutic factors that operate to produce change and intervening in such a way as to help members make desired changes in feelings, thoughts, and actions
- focusing on the importance of translating insight into action; encouraging members to practice new skills
- encouraging members to keep in mind what they want from the group and to ask for it

Stage 4: Final Stage— Consolidation and Termination

Of all the group-leadership skills perhaps none is more important than the capacity to assist members in transferring what they have learned in the group to their outside environments. It is during the termination phase that consolidation of learning occurs; this is a time for summarizing, pulling together loose ends, and integrating and interpreting the group experience.

I see the initial and final stages as the most decisive times in the group's life history. If the initial phase is effective, the participants get to know one another and establish their own identity in the group. An atmosphere of trust develops, and the groundwork is laid for later intensive work. The final stage of a group's development is critical because it is at this time that members engage in the cognitive work necessary to make decisions regarding what they have learned about themselves. If this phase is poorly handled by the group leader, the chances that the members will be able to use what they have learned are greatly reduced. Worse yet, members can be left with unresolved issues and without any direction on how to bring these issues to closure.

It is essential that termination issues be brought up early in the course of a group's history. In every beginning the end is always a reality, and members need periodic reminders from the leader that their group will eventually end. Unless leaders recognize their own feelings about termination and are able to deal with them constructively, however, they are in no position to help members deal with separation issues. Some group leaders find endings difficult, for a variety of reasons, and they tend to ignore feelings of sadness or grief that some will experience as a group comes to an end.

I agree with Shapiro's (1978) view that termination is often the phase of group work that leaders handle most ineptly. He gives as reasons the leader's own needs for reassurance and resistance to terminating the group, as well as his or her lack of training for this especially difficult stage. There is a danger that as group members become aware that the end of the group is nearing, they will isolate themselves so that they do not have to deal with the anxiety that accompanies separation. Work generally tapers off, and new issues are rarely raised. If members are allowed to distance themselves too much, they will fail to examine the possible effects of their group experience on their out-of-group behavior. Thus, it is crucial that leaders help the participants put into meaningful perspective what has occurred in the group.

Effective Ways of Terminating a Group

This section deals with ways of terminating the group experience by exploring questions such as these: How can members best complete any unfinished business? How can members be taught, as they leave the group, to carry what they have learned with them and to use it to deal more effectively with the demands of their daily existence? What are the relevant issues and activities in the closing phases of a group? Because of space limitations, most of my discussion focuses on the termination of a closed group—that is, a group that consists of the same members throughout its life and whose termination date has been decided in advance.

Dealing with Feelings.   During the final stages of the group it is a good practice for the leader to remind members that there are only a few sessions remaining, so that they can prepare themselves for termination and achieve successful closure of the group experience. Members need help in facing the reality that their group will soon end. Feelings about separation, which often take the form of avoidance or denial, need to be fully brought out and explored. It is the leader's job to facilitate an open discussion of the feelings of loss and sadness that accompany the eventual termination of an intense and highly meaningful experience. As Yalom (1985) says, the counselor has the responsibility to keep group members focused on the reality and meaning of the ending of their group. The members can be helped to face separation by the leader's disclosure of his or her own feelings about terminating the group.

During the initial phase, members are often asked to express their fears of *entering* fully into the group. Now, they should be encouraged to share their fears or concerns about *leaving* the group and having to face day-to-day realities without the group's support. It is not uncommon for members to say that they have developed genuine bonds of intimacy and have found a trusting and safe place where they can be themselves without fear of rejection. They may dread the prospect of being deprived of this intimacy and support. Also common are concerns of not being able to be as trusting and open with people outside the group. The leader's task is to remind the participants that if their group is special—close, caring, and supportive—it is because the members made the choice and the commitment to work together. Therefore, they can make similar choices and commitments, and be equally successful, in their relationships outside the group. This "boost of confidence" is not intended to deny the sense of loss and the sadness that may accompany the ending of a group. On the contrary, mourning the separation can be an enriching experience if the members of the group are encouraged to fully express their grief and anxiety.

Preparing for the Outside World.   During the consolidation stage group leaders need to prepare the participants to deal with those with whom they live and work. Role playing can be extremely helpful for practicing different ways of responding to the people who are significant in one's life. By trying out new ways of dealing with significant others in a symbolic way through role playing, members can get valuable feedback from others and consider new alternatives.

As Libo (1977) remarks, participants who are leaving a group tend to focus on how they can change others. The focus should instead be on changing oneself. Libo believes that when you change, others in your life are likely to change as well. Thus, if you want more affection, you need to be more affectionate. The feedback from the group can help members concentrate on changing themselves rather than making plans to change others.

Examining the Effects of the Group on Oneself.   Toward the end of the group it is useful to give all members an opportunity to put into words what they have learned from the entire group experience and how they intend to apply their increased self-understanding. To be fruitful, this examination must be concrete and specific. Statements such as "This group has been great. I really grew a lot, and I learned a lot about people as well as myself" are so general that the person who made the comments will soon forget what specifically was meaningful about the group experience. When someone makes this kind of sweeping statement, the leader can help the person express his or her thoughts and feelings more concretely by asking questions: "How has the group been good for you? In what sense have you grown a lot? What do you mean by 'great'? What are some of the things you actually learned about others and yourself?" I believe that focusing on the specific, conceptualizing, and sharing feelings and impressions increase the chances that members will retain and use what they have learned.

Giving and Receiving Feedback.   The giving and receiving of feedback are crucial during the final phases. Although members of an effective group have been sharing their perceptions and feelings at each session, the opportunity to give and receive summary feedback has a value of its own. To help participants take advantage of this opportunity, during one of the last few sessions I generally ask the members to give a brief summary of how they have perceived themselves in the group, what conflicts have become clearer, what the turning points were, what they expect to do with what they have learned, and what the group has meant to them. Then the others in the group say how they have perceived and felt about that person. I have found that concise and concrete feedback that also relates to the hopes and fears that the person has expressed is most valuable. Vague comments such as "I think you're a neat person" are of scarce long-term value. I've found that it is useful to ask members to write down specific feedback in their journals. If they do not record some of the things that people say to them, they tend to forget quickly. If they make a record, they can look months later at what others told them to determine if they are progressing toward their goals.

Completing Unfinished Business.   Some time needs to be allotted to working through any unfinished business relating to transactions between members or to the group process and goals. Even if some issues cannot be resolved, members should be encouraged to talk about them. For example, a member who has been silent throughout most of the group may say that she never felt safe enough to talk about her real concerns. Although it may be too late to work through this issue to everyone's satisfaction, it is still important to look at it and not leave it dangling.

Carrying the Learning Further.   I routinely discuss the various ways in which participants can go further with what they've learned in the group. These ways may include participation in other groups, individual counseling, or some other kind of growth experience. Mahler (1969) calls the ending stage of the group a "commencement," for now members can apply what they've learned to future problems and thus give their lives new directions. Also, participation in a successful group generally results in awareness of a number of specific issues. Members are not always able to work through these issues thoroughly; thus, they need to continue the process of exploration by finding other avenues of personal growth.

Co-Leader Issues at the Final Stage

It is critical that co-leaders agree on termination. They need to be in tune with each other about not bringing up new material that can't be dealt with adequately before the end of the group. At times, certain members may have saved up some topics until the very end, almost hoping that there would be no time to explore them; it could be tempting for one of the co-leaders to initiate new work with such a member while the other co-leader is set on bringing the group to an end.

There are some other specific areas that you and your co-leader can talk about during the final stage to ensure that you are working together to effectively wrap up the group experience:

- Are there any members that either of you is concerned about and any things you might want to say to certain members?
- Are there perceptions and reactions either of you has about the group that would be useful to share with the members before the final session?
- Are both of you able to deal with your own feelings of separation and ending? If not, you may collude with the members by avoiding talking about feelings pertaining to the termination of the group.
- Have both of you given thought to how you can best help members review what they've learned from the group and translate this learning to everyday situations?

Summary of the Final Stage

Stage Characteristics.   During the final phase of a group the following characteristics are typically evident:

- There may be some sadness and anxiety over the reality of separation.
- Members are likely to pull back and participate in less intense ways, in anticipation of the ending of the group.
- Members are deciding what courses of action they are likely to take.
- There may be some fears of separation as well as fears about being able to implement in daily life some of what was experienced in the group.
- Members may express their fears, hopes, and concerns for one another and tell one another how they were experienced.
- Group sessions may be devoted partly to preparing members to meet significant others in everyday life. Role playing and behavioral rehearsal for relating more effectively to others are common.
- Members may evaluate the group experience.
- There may be talk about follow-up meetings or some plan for accountability so that members will be encouraged to carry out their plans for change.

Member Functions and Possible Problems.   The major task facing members during the final stage of a group is consolidating their learning and transferring what they have learned to their outside environment. This is the time for them to review and put into some cognitive framework the meaning of the group experience. Some tasks for members at this time are

- to deal with their feelings about separation and termination
- to prepare for generalizing their learning to everyday situations
- to give others a better picture of how they are perceived

- to complete any unfinished business, either issues they have brought into the group or issues that pertain to people in the group
- to evaluate the impact of the group
- to make decisions and plans concerning what changes they want to make and how they will go about making them

Some problems can occur at this time:

- Members may avoid reviewing their experience and fail to put it into some cognitive framework, thus limiting the generalization of their learning.
- Due to separation anxiety, members may distance themselves.
- Members may consider the group an end in itself and not use it as a way of continuing to grow.

Leader Functions.   The group leader's central tasks in the consolidation phase are to provide a structure that allows participants to clarify the meaning of their experiences in the group and to assist members in generalizing their learnings from the group to everyday situations. Tasks at this period include these:

- assisting members in dealing with any feelings they may have about termination
- giving members an opportunity to express and deal with any unfinished business within the group
- reinforcing changes that members have made and ensuring that members have information about resources to enable them to make further changes
- assisting members in determining how they will apply specific skills in a variety of situations in daily life
- working with members to develop specific contracts and homework assignments as practical ways of making changes
- assisting participants to develop a conceptual framework that will help them understand, integrate, consolidate, and remember what they have learned in the group
- providing opportunities for members to give one another constructive feedback
- reemphasizing the importance of maintaining confidentiality after the group is over

Postgroup Issues: Follow-Up and Evaluation

Just as the formation of a group and the leader's preparatory activities greatly affect the group's progress through its various stages, the work that confronts the leader once the group has come to an end is also highly important. Two issues are dynamically related to the successful completion of a group's development: follow-up and evaluation. The questions that need to be raised are: What kind of follow-up should be provided after the termination of a group? What is the group leader's responsibility in evaluating the outcomes of a group? How can the leader help members evaluate the effectiveness of their group experience?

The Follow-Up Session

It is wise at the final session of a group to decide on a time for a follow-up session to discuss the group experience and put it in perspective. I routinely schedule a follow-up meeting 3 months after the conclusion of a short-term intensive group. I think that a follow-up session is also of great value for groups that meet over a period of time on a weekly basis. These sessions are valuable not only because they offer the group leader an opportunity to assess the outcomes of the group but also because they give the members the chance to gain a more realistic picture of the impact that the group has had on them and their peers.

At the follow-up session members can discuss the efforts they have made since the termination of the group to implement their learning in the real world. They can report on the difficulties they have encountered, share the joys and successes they have experienced in life, and recall some of the things that occurred in the group. A follow-up session also provides people with the opportunity to express and work through any afterthoughts or feelings connected with the group experience. At this time the mutual giving of feedback and support is extremely valuable.

I believe that the element of accountability that a follow-up session encourages maximizes the chances of long-lasting benefits from the group experience. Many people have reported that simply knowing that they would be coming together as a group 1, 2, or 3 months after the group's termination and that they would be giving a self-report provided the stimulus they needed to stick with their commitments. Finally, the follow-up session offers leaders another opportunity to remind participants that they are responsible for what they become and that, if they hope to change their situation, they must take active steps to do so.

After the termination of a group, some of the participants may seek other avenues to further the process of growth begun in their group. Having been away from the group for some time, the former members may be more amenable to the idea of joining another group or seeking individual counseling to work through certain areas that they believe need further exploration. Thus, the follow-up session is an ideal place to discuss other avenues for continued growth.

Individual Follow-Up Sessions

Besides the group follow-up, I endorse the idea of leaders' arranging for a one-to-one follow-up session with each member. These postgroup individual interviews, which may last only 20 minutes, help the leader determine the degree to which members have accomplished their goals, because in the individual session members may reveal reactions that they would not share with the entire group. Also, this one-to-one contact tells the participants that the leader is concerned and does care. The individual interview provides ideal opportunities to discuss referral sources and the possible need for further professional involvement—matters that are probably best handled individually. Furthermore, the combination of individual postgroup interviews and a group follow-up session gives leaders much valuable information about the level of effectiveness of the group and provides the opportunity to discuss how future groups could be improved.

Although it is ideal to conduct individual follow-up sessions, I realize that this may not be practical in some settings. In a community mental-health clinic, for example, it might be difficult to arrange for this kind of follow-up. One option is a telephone call.

Evaluating Results

I have referred several times to the need for the leader to evaluate the results of a group. Personally, I find it difficult to objectively assess outcomes by using empirical procedures. I have made attempts at objective assessment by administering a variety of tests and inventories both before and after a group experience to determine the nature and degree of change in participants. But in my experience none of these measures is adequate to detect subtle changes in attitudes, beliefs, feelings, and behavior. Consequently, I have come to rely on subjective measures that include a variety of self-reports.

According to Rogers, a naturalistic study that concentrates on the personal and subjective views of the participants provides the deepest insights into the meaning of the group experience. These self-reports give a picture of both the process and the outcomes from the points of view of the participants. Rogers maintains that this phenomenological type of study "may well be the most fruitful way of advancing our knowledge in these subtle and unknown fields" (1970, p. 133). Some of the subjective procedures I typically rely on to evaluate a group and decide ways to improve future groups involve the use of "reaction papers," individual postgroup interviews, group follow-up meetings, and questionnaires that I mail to participants.

Generally I ask people *before* they enter a group to put down in writing what their concerns are and what they expect from the group. I strongly encourage members to keep an ongoing journal of their experiences in the group and in their everyday lives between sessions. This writing process helps participants focus on relevant trends and on the key things they are discovering about themselves and others through group interaction. After the group ends, I ask members to write a couple of reaction papers before our follow-up group meeting. These postgroup papers give participants a chance to recall significant occurrences in the group and provide them with an opportunity to discuss what specifically they liked most and least about the group. Now that the group has ended, participants can evaluate its impact differently. Many people have told me that these postgroup reaction papers are very useful, because they provide the impetus necessary to continue on their own the work initiated in the group situation. The writing process is a useful tool for self-evaluation and is in itself therapeutic.

Finally, I often give a brief questionnaire that members fill out when we come together for the postgroup meeting. The members evaluate the techniques used, the group leader, the impact of the group on them, and the degree to which they think they have changed because of their participation in the group. The following questions are designed to get information on key matters:

- Did the group have any negative effects on you?
- How has the group influenced you in relation to others?
- Have your changes been lasting so far?

The questionnaire is a good way to get members focused right before the exchange of reactions that occurs in the follow-up session. It, too, provides useful data for evaluating the group.

Postgroup Issues for Co-Leaders

After the group has ended, co-leaders should discuss their experience in leading with each other and attempt to put the entire history of the group into perspective. What follows are some ideas that you might explore with your co-leader as a way to integrate your experiences and learning:

- Discuss the balance of responsibility between the co-leaders. Did one co-leader assume primary responsibility for directing while the other followed? Did one leader overshadow the other?
- Was one co-leader overly supportive and the other overly confrontive?
- How did your styles of leadership blend, and what effect did this have on the group?
- Did you agree on basic matters such as which direction the group was taking and what was needed to keep it progressing?
- Talk about what each liked and did not like about leading with the other. You can benefit by a frank discussion of what each of you learned from the other personally and professionally, including weaknesses and strengths, skills, and styles of leading.
- Compare your self-evaluation as a leader with your co-leader's evaluation of you. Be aware of certain areas needing further work; in this way, each of you can grow in your capacity to lead effectively.*
- You both can learn much from talking about and reviewing the turning points in the group. How did the group begin? How did it end? What happened in the group to account for its success or failure? This global assessment helps you understand group process, which can be essential in leading future groups.

*Group-leader evaluation forms and self-evaluation scales are given in the student manual that accompanies this text.

Summary of Postgroup Issues

Member Functions and Possible Problems. After their group has ended, the members' main functions are applying what they have learned to an action program in their daily lives, evaluating the group, and attending a follow-up session (if appropriate). Some key postgroup tasks for members are

- finding ways of reinforcing themselves so that they will continue to grow
- keeping some record of their changes, including progress and problems
- attending an individual session to discuss how well their goals were met or a follow-up group session to share with fellow members what they have done with their group experience

Some problems can occur at this time:

- If members have difficulty applying what they learned in the group to everyday situations, they may become discouraged and discount the value of the group.
- Members may have problems in continuing with new behaviors without the supportive environment of the group.
- Members may forget that change demands time, effort, and practice, and thus they may not use what they've learned.

Leader Functions. The last session of the group is not a signal that the leader's job is finished, for there are important considerations after termination. Follow-up and evaluation procedures should be implemented. Leaders have the following tasks after a group ends:

- offering private consultations if any member should need this service, at least on a limited basis to discuss a member's reactions to the group experience
- if applicable, providing for a follow-up group session or individual interviews to assess the impact of the group
- finding out about specific referral resources for members who want or need further consultation
- encouraging members to find some avenues of continued support and challenge so that the ending of the group can mark the beginning of a search for self-understanding
- developing an organized approach for evaluating the results of the group
- assisting members to develop contracts that will enable them to make use of support systems among the group members and outside the group
- if applicable, meeting with the co-leader to assess the overall effectiveness of the group

Concluding Comments

I have mentioned more than once that the stages in the life of a group do not generally flow neatly and predictably in the order described in the last two chapters. In actuality there is considerable overlap between stages, and once a group moves to an advanced stage of development, there may be temporary regressions to earlier developmental stages.

Knowledge of the major tasks that confront participants and leader during the different phases of the group's evolution allows you to intervene at the right time and with a clear purpose. Knowledge of the group's critical turning points enables you to assist the members in mobilizing their resources, so that they can successfully meet the demands facing them as their group progresses. Knowledge of the typical pattern of groups gives you an overall perspective that enables you to determine which interventions are useful and which ones are not. Also, this perspective allows you to predict certain crises in the life of the group and find ways of resolving these crises successfully.

REFERENCES AND SUGGESTED READINGS FOR PART I

American Association for Counseling and Development. (1988). *Ethical standards* (rev. ed.). Alexandria, VA: Author.

American Association for Marriage and Family Therapy. (1988). *AAMFT code of ethical principles for marriage and family therapists.* Washington, DC: Author.

American Group Psychotherapy Association. (1978). *Guidelines for the training of group psychotherapists.* New York: Author.

American Mental Health Counselors Association. (1980). *Code of ethics for certified clinical mental health counselors.* Alexandria, VA: Author.

American Psychiatric Association. (1986). *Principles of medical ethics, with annotations especially applicable to psychiatry.* Washington, DC: Author.

American Psychological Association. (1973). Guidelines for psychologists conducting growth groups. *American Psychologist, 28*(10), 933.

American Psychological Association. (1981). Ethical principles of psychologists. *American Psychologist, 36*(6), 633–651.

Association for Specialists in Group Work. (1980). *Ethical guidelines for group leaders.* Alexandria, VA: Author.

Association for Specialists in Group Work. (1983). *Professional standards for training of group counselors.* Alexandria, VA: Author.

Bass, S., & Dole, A. (1977). Ethical leader practices in sensitivity training for prospective professional psychologists. *Journal Supplement Abstract Series, 7*(2), 47–66.

Bednar, R. L., Corey, G., Evans, N. J., Gazda, G. M., Pistole, M. C., Stockton, R., & Robison, F. F. (1987). Overcoming obstacles to the future development of research on group work. *Journal for Specialists in Group Work, 12*(3), 98–111.

Bednar, R. L., & Kaul, T. J. (1978). Experiential group research: Current perspectives. In S. L. Garfield & A. E. Bergin (Eds.), *Handbook of psychotherapy and behavior change* (2nd ed.). New York: Wiley.

Bednar, R. L., & Kaul, T. J. (1985). Experiential group research: Results, questions, and suggestions. In S. L. Garfield & A. Bergin (Eds.), *Handbook of psychotherapy and behavior change* (3rd ed.). New York: Wiley.

Bednar, R. L., Melnick, J., & Kaul, T. J. (1974). Risk, responsibility, and structure: A conceptual framework for initiating group counseling and psychotherapy. *Journal of Counseling Psychology, 21,* 31–37.

Bloch, S., Browning, S., & McGrath, G. (1983). Humour in group psychotherapy. *British Journal of Medical Psychology, 56,* 89–97.

Blustein, D. L. (1982). Using informal groups in cross-cultural counseling. *Journal for Specialists in Group Work, 7*(4), 260–265.

Borgers, S. B., & Tyndall, L. W. (1982). Setting expectations for groups. *Journal for Specialists in Group Work, 7*(2), 109–111.

Burke, M. J., & Hayes, R. L. (1986). Peer counseling for elderly victims of crime and violence. *Journal for Specialists in Group Work, 11*(2), 107–113.

Carkhuff, R. R. (1969a). *Helping and human relations: Vol. 1. Selection and training.* New York: Holt, Rinehart & Winston.

Carkhuff, R. R. (1969b). *Helping and human relations: Vol. 2. Practice and research.* New York: Holt, Rinehart & Winston.

Childers, J. H., Jr. (1986). Group leadership training and supervision: A graduate course. *Journal for Specialists in Group Work, 11*(1), 48–52.

Childers, J. H., Jr., & Saltmarsh, R. E. (1986). Neurolinguistic programming in the context of group counseling. *Journal for Specialists in Group Work, 11*(4), 221–227.

Chu, J., & Sue, S. (1984). Asian/Pacific-Americans and group practice. In L. E. Davis (Ed.), *Ethnicity in social group work practice* (pp. 23–35). New York: Haworth Press.

Cole, S. A. (1983). Self-help groups. In H. I. Kaplan & B. J. Sadock (Eds.), *Comprehensive group psychotherapy* (2nd ed.). Baltimore: Williams & Wilkins.

Colson, D. B., & Horwitz, L. (1983). Research in group psychotherapy. In H. I. Kaplan & B. J. Sadock (Eds.), *Comprehensive group psychotherapy* (2nd ed.) (pp. 304–311). Baltimore: Williams & Wilkins.

Corey, G. (1981). Description of a practicum course in group leadership. *Journal for Specialists in Group Work, 6*(2), 100–108.

Corey, G. (1982). Practical strategies for planning therapy groups. In P. Keller (Ed.), *Innovations in clinical practice: A sourcebook: Vol. 1.* Sarasota, FL: Professional Resource Exchange.

Corey, G. (1983). Group counseling. In J. A. Brown & R. H. Pate (Eds.), *Being a counselor: Directions and challenges.* Pacific Grove, CA: Brooks/Cole.

Corey, G. (1984). Ethical issues in group therapy. In P. Keller (Ed.), *Innovations in clinical practice: A sourcebook: Vol. 3.* Sarasota, FL: Professional Resource Exchange.

Corey, G. (1986a). *Case approach to counseling and psychotherapy* (2nd ed.). Pacific Grove, CA: Brooks/Cole.

Corey, G. (1986b). *Theory and practice of counseling and psychotherapy* (3rd ed.) and *Manual.* Pacific Grove, CA: Brooks/Cole.

Corey, G., & Corey, M. (1990). *I never knew I had a choice* (4th ed.). Pacific Grove, CA: Brooks/Cole.

Corey, G., Corey, M., & Callanan, P. (1981). In-service training for group leaders in a prison hospital: Problems and prospects. *Journal for Specialists in Group Work, 6*(3), 130–135.

Corey, G., Corey, M., & Callanan, P. (1982). A *casebook of ethical guidelines for group leaders.* Pacific Grove, CA: Brooks/Cole.

Corey, G., Corey, M., & Callanan, P. (1988). *Issues and ethics in the helping professions* (3rd ed.). Pacific Grove, CA: Brooks/Cole.

Corey, G., Corey, M., Callanan, P., & Russell, J. M. (1980). A residential workshop for personal growth. *Journal for Specialists in Group Work, 5*(4), 205–215.

Corey, G., Corey, M., Callanan, P., & Russell, J. M. (1982). Ethical considerations in using group techniques. *Journal for Specialists in Group Work, 7*(3), 140–148.

Corey, G., Corey, M., Callanan, P., & Russell, J. M. (1988). *Group techniques* (rev. ed.). Pacific Grove, CA: Brooks/Cole.

Corey, M., & Corey, G. (1986). Experiential/didactic training and supervision workshop for group leaders. *Journal of Counseling and Human Service Professions, 1*(1), 18–26.

Corey, M., & Corey, G. (1987). *Groups: Process and practice* (3rd ed.). Pacific Grove, CA: Brooks/Cole.

Corey, M., & Corey, G. (1989). *Becoming a helper.* Pacific Grove, CA: Brooks/Cole.

Couch, R. D., & Childers, J. H. (1987). Leadership strategies for instilling and maintaining hope in group counseling. *Journal for Specialists in Group Work, 12*(4), 138–143.

Council for Accreditation of Counseling and Related Educational Programs. (1988, July). *Accreditation procedures manual and application.* Alexandria, VA: Author.

Davis, L. E. (Ed.). (1984) *Ethnicity in social group work practice.* New York: Haworth Press.

Decker, T. W., & Hall, D. W. (1987). Multicomponent group interventions for academic underachievers. *Journal for Specialists in Group Work, 12*(4), 150–155.

Dies, R. R. (1980). Current practice in the training of group psychotherapists. *International Journal of Group Psychotherapy, 30*(2), 169–185.

Dies, R. R. (1983a). Bridging the gap between research and practice in group psychotherapy. In R. R. Dies & K. R. MacKenzie (Eds.), *Advances in group psychotherapy: Integrating research and practice* (pp. 1–16). New York: International Universities Press.

Dies, R. R. (1983b). Clinical implications of research on leadership in short-term group psychotherapy. In R. R. Dies & K. R. MacKenzie (Eds.), *Advances in group psychotherapy: Integrating research and practice* (pp. 27–78). New York: International Universities Press.

Dies, R. R. (1985). Research foundations for the future of group work. *Journal for Specialists in Group Work, 10*(2), 68–73.

Dies, R. R., & MacKenzie, K. R. (Eds.). (1983). *Advances in group psychotherapy: Integrating research and practice.* New York: International Universities Press.

Donigian, J., & Malnati, R. (1987). *Critical incidents in group therapy.* Pacific Grove, CA: Brooks/Cole.

Dyer, W., & Vriend, J. (1977). *Counseling techniques that work.* New York: Funk & Wagnalls.

Egan, G. (1973). *Face to face: The small-group experience and interpersonal growth.* Pacific Grove, CA: Brooks/Cole.

Egan, G. (1976). *Interpersonal living: A skills/contract approach to human-relations training in groups.* Pacific Grove, CA: Brooks/Cole.

Egan, G. (1977). *You and me: The skills of communicating and relating to others.* Pacific Grove, CA: Brooks/Cole.

Fried, E. (1972). Individuation through group psychotherapy. In C. J. Sage & H. S. Kaplan (Eds.), *Progress in group and family therapy.* New York: Brunner/Mazel.

Gazda, G. M. (1982). *Basic approaches to group psychotherapy and group counseling* (3rd ed.). Springfield, IL: Charles C Thomas.

Gazda, G. M. (1989). *Group counseling: A developmental approach* (4th ed.). Boston: Allyn & Bacon.

Gazda, G. M., & Mack, S. (1982). Ethical practice guidelines for group work. In G. M. Gazda (Ed.), *Basic approaches to group psychotherapy and group counseling* (3rd ed.). Springfield, IL: Charles C Thomas.

George, R. L., & Dustin, D. (1988). *Group counseling: Theory and practice.* Englewood Cliffs, NJ: Prentice-Hall.

Gillis, H. L., & Bonney, W. C. (1986). Group counseling with couples or families: Adding adventure activities. *Journal for Specialists in Group Work, 11*(4), 213–220.

Gumaer, J., & Scott, L. (1985). Training group leaders in ethical decision making. *Journal for Specialists in Group Work, 10*(4), 198–204.

Gumaer, J., & Scott, L. (1986). Group workers' perceptions of ethical and unethical behavior of group leaders. *Journal for Specialists in Group Work, 11*(3), 139–150.

Hansen, J. C., Warner, R. W., & Smith, E. M. (1980). *Group counseling: Theory and process* (2nd ed.). Chicago: Rand McNally.

Ho, M. K. (1984). Social group work with Asian/Pacific-Americans. In L. E. Davis (Ed.), *Ethnicity in social group work practice* (pp. 49–61). New York: Haworth Press.

Hopkins, B. R., & Anderson, B. S. (1985). *The counselor and the law* (2nd ed.). Alexandria, VA: American Association for Counseling and Development.

Huber, C. H., & Baruth, L. G. (1987). *Ethical, legal and professional issues in the practice of marriage and family therapy.* Columbus, OH: Charles E. Merrill.

Huhn, R. P., Zimpfer, D. G., Waltman, D. E., & Williamson, S. K. (1985). A survey of programs of professional preparation for group counseling. *Journal for Specialists in Group Work, 10*(3), 124–133.

Hummel, D., Talbutt, L., & Alexander, D. (1985). *Law and ethics in counseling.* New York: Van Nostrand Reinhold.

Ivey, A. E. (1988). *Intentional interviewing and counseling: Facilitating client development* (2nd ed.). Pacific Grove, CA: Brooks/Cole.

Ivey, A. E., & Authier, J. (1978). *Microcounseling: Innovations in interviewing, counseling, psychotherapy, and psychoeducation* (2nd ed.). Springfield, IL: Charles C Thomas.

Jacobs, E. E., Harvill, R. L., & Masson, R. L. (1988). *Group counseling: Strategies and skills.* Pacific Grove, CA: Brooks/Cole.

Kaplan, H. I., & Sadock, B. J. (Eds.). (1983). *Comprehensive group psychotherapy* (2nd ed.). Baltimore: Williams & Wilkins.

Katz, A. H. (1981). Self-help and mutual aid: An emerging social movement? *American Review of Sociology, 7,* 129–155.

Kaul, T. J., & Bednar, R. L. (1985). Experiential group research: Results, questions, and suggestions. In S. L. Garfield & A. Bergin (Eds.), *Handbook of psychotherapy and behavior change* (3rd ed.). New York: Wiley.

Keith-Spiegel, P., & Koocher, G. (1985). *Ethics in psychology.* New York: Random House.

Kottler, J. A. (1983). *Pragmatic group leadership.* Pacific Grove, CA: Brooks/Cole.

Kottler, J. A. (1986). *On being a therapist.* San Francisco: Jossey-Bass.

Kutash, I. L., & Wolf, A. (Eds.). (1986). *Psychotherapist's casebook.* San Francisco: Jossey-Bass.

Lakin, M. (1985). *The helping group: Therapeutic principles and issues.* Reading, MA: Addison-Wesley.

Lakin, M. (1986). Ethical challenges of group and dyadic psychotherapies: A comparative approach. *Professional Psychology: Research and Practice, 17*(5), 454–461.

LeCluyse, E. E. (1983). Pretherapy preparation for group members. *Journal for Specialists in Group Work, 8*(4), 170–174.

Lee, C. C. (1987). Black manhood training: Group counseling for male Blacks in grades 7–12. *Journal for Specialists in Group Work, 12*(1), 18–25.

Lee, P. C., Juan, G., & Hom, A. B. (1984). Group work practice with Asian clients: A sociocultural approach. In L. E. Davis (Ed.), *Ethnicity in social group work practice* (pp. 37–47). New York: Haworth Press.

Libo, L. (1977). *Is there a life after group?* New York: Anchor Books.

Lieberman, M. A. (1980). Group methods. In F. H. Kanfer & A. P. Goldstein (Eds.), *Helping people change* (2nd ed.). New York: Pergamon Press.

Lieberman, M. A., & Borman, L. D. (1979). *Self-help groups for coping with crisis.* San Francisco: Jossey-Bass.

Lieberman, M., Yalom, I., & Miles, M. (1973). *Encounter groups: First facts.* New York: Basic Books.

Loewenberg, F., & Dolgoff, R. (1988). *Ethical decisions for social work practice* (3rd ed.). Itasca, IL: F. E. Peacock.

Luft, J. (1984). *Group processes: An introduction to group dynamics* (3rd ed.). Palo Alto, CA: Mayfield.

MacDevitt, J. W. (1987). Conceptualizing therapeutic components of group counseling. *Journal for Specialists in Group Work, 12*(2), 76–84.

Mahler, C. A. (1969). *Group counseling in the schools.* Boston: Houghton Mifflin.

McWhirter, J. J., & Liebman, P. C. (1988). A description of anger-control therapy groups to help Vietnam veterans with posttraumatic stress disorder. *Journal for Specialists in Group Work, 13*(1), 9–16.

Miller, M. J. (1986). On the perfectionistic thoughts of beginning group leaders. *Journal for Specialists in Group Work, 11*(1), 53–56.

Mokuau, N. (1985). Counseling Pacific Islander–Americans. In P. Pedersen (Ed.), *Handbook of cross-cultural counseling and therapy* (pp. 147–155). Westport, CT: Greenwood Press.

Mokuau, N. (1987). Social workers' perceptions of counseling effectiveness for Asian-American clients. *Journal of the National Association of Social Workers, 32*(4), 331–335.

Morran, D. K. (1982). Leader and member self-disclosing behavior in counseling groups. *Journal for Specialists in Group Work, 7*(4), 218–223.

Morran, D. K., Robison, F. F., & Stockton, R. (1985). Feedback exchange in counseling groups: An analysis of message content and receiver acceptance as a function of leader versus member delivery, session, and valance. *Journal of Counseling Psychology, 32,* 57–67.

Morran, D. K., & Stockton, R. (1980). Effect of self-concept on group member reception of positive and negative feedback. *Journal of Counseling Psychology, 27,* 260–267.

Morran, D. K., & Stockton, R. (1985). Perspectives on group research programs. *Journal of Specialists for Group Work, 10*(4), 186–191.

Muller, E. J., & Scott, T. B. (1984). A comparison of film and written presentations used for pregroup training experiences. *Journal for Specialists in Group Work, 9*(3), 122–126.

Napier, R. W., & Gershenfeld, M. K. (1988). *Groups: Theory and experience* (3rd. ed.). Boston: Houghton Mifflin.

National Association of Social Workers. (1979). *Code of ethics.* Washington, DC: Author.

National Board for Certified Counselors. (1987). *Code of ethics.* Alexandria, VA: Author.

National Federation of Societies for Clinical Social Work. (1985). *Code of ethics.* Silver Spring, MD: Author.

National Rehabilitation Counseling Association. (1988). *Ethical standards for rehabilitation counselors.* Alexandria, VA: Author.

National Training Laboratory Institute. (1969). *Standards for the use of laboratory methods.* Washington, DC: Author.

Nishio, K., & Bilmes, M. (1987). Psychotherapy with Southeast Asian American clients. *Professional Psychology: Research and Practice, 18*(4), 342–346.

Nolan, E. (1978). Leadership interventions for promoting personal mastery. *Journal for Specialists in Group Work, 3*(3), 132–138.

Ohlsen, M. M., Horne, A. M., & Lawe, C. F. (1988). *Group counseling* (3rd ed.). New York: Holt, Rinehart & Winston.

Ormont, L. R. (1988). The leader's role in resolving resistances to intimacy in the group setting. *International Journal of Group Psychotherapy, 38*(1), 29–46.

Pedersen, P. (1981). Triad counseling. In R. Cornisi (Ed.), *Innovative psychotherapies* (pp. 840–855). New York: Wiley.

Pedersen, P. (Ed.). (1985). *Handbook of cross-cultural counseling and therapy.* Westport, CT: Greenwood Press.

Pedersen, P. (1988). *A handbook for developing multicultural awareness.* Alexandria, VA: American Association for Counseling and Development.

Pope, K. S., Tabachnick, B. G., & Keith-Spiegel, P. (1987). Ethics of practice: The beliefs and behaviors of psychologists as therapists. *American Psychologist, 42*(11), 993–1006.

Priddy, J. M. (1987). Outcome research on self-help groups: A humanistic perspective. *Journal for Specialists in Group Work, 12*(1), 2–9.

Riordan, R. J., & Beggs, M. S. (1987). Counselors and self-help groups. *Journal of Counseling and Development, 65*(8), 427–429.

Riordan, R. J., & Beggs, M. S. (1988). Some critical differences between self-help and therapy groups. *Journal for Specialists in Group Work, 3*(1), 24–29.

Rogers, C. R. (1970). *Carl Rogers on encounter groups.* New York: Harper & Row.

Rose, S. R. (1987). Social skills training in middle childhood: A structured group approach. *Journal for Specialists in Group Work, 12*(4), 144–149.

Rosenbaum, M. (1982). Ethical problems of group psychotherapy. In M. Rosenbaum (Ed.), *Ethics and values in psychotherapy: A guidebook.* New York: Free Press.

Sampson, E. E. (1988). The debate on individualism: Indigenous psychologies of the individual and their role in personal and societal functioning. *American Psychologist, 43*(1), 15–22.

Schutz, B. M. (1982). *Legal liability in psychotherapy*. San Francisco: Jossey-Bass.

Schutz, W. (1973a). *Elements of encounter*. Big Sur, CA: Joy Press.

Schutz, W. (1973b). Encounter. In R. Corsini (Ed.), *Current psychotherapies*. Itasca, IL: F. E. Peacock.

Schwab, R. (1986). Support groups for the bereaved. *Journal for Specialists in Group Work, 11*(2), 100–106.

Shaffer, J., & Galinsky, M. D. (1989). *Models of group therapy* (2nd ed.). Englewood Cliffs, NJ: Prentice-Hall.

Shapiro, J. L. (1978). *Methods of group psychotherapy and encounter: A tradition of innovation*. Itasca, IL: F. E. Peacock.

Stockton, R., & Hulse, D. (1981). Developing cohesion in small groups: Theory and research. *Journal for Specialists in Group Work, 6*(4), 188–194.

Stockton, R., & Morran, D. K. (1980). The use of verbal feedback in counseling groups: Toward an effective system. *Journal for Specialists in Group Work, 5*, 10–14.

Stockton, R., & Morran, D. K. (1981). Feedback exchange in personal growth groups: Receiver acceptance as a function of valence, session, and order of delivery. *Journal of Counseling Psychology, 28*, 490–497.

Stockton, R., & Morran, D. K. (1982). Review and perspective of critical dimensions in therapeutic small group research. In G. M. Gazda (Ed.), *Basic approaches to group psychotherapy and group counseling* (3rd ed.) (pp. 37–85). Springfield, IL: Charles C Thomas.

Sue, D. W. (1978). Eliminating cultural oppression in counseling: Toward a general theory. *Journal of Counseling Psychology, 25*, 419–428.

Sue, D. W. (1981). *Counseling the culturally different: Theory and practice*. New York: Wiley.

Sue, S. (1988). Psychotherapeutic services for ethnic minorities: Two decades of research findings. *American Psychologist, 43*(4), 301–308.

Van Hoose, W., & Kottler, J. (1985). *Ethical and legal issues in counseling and psychotherapy* (2nd ed.). San Francisco: Jossey-Bass.

Woody, R. H. (1984). *The law and the practice of human services*. San Francisco: Jossey-Bass.

Wrenn, C. G. (1985). Afterward: The culturally encapsulated counselor revisited. In P. Pedersen (Ed.), *Handbook of cross-cultural counseling and therapy* (pp. 323–329). Westport, CT: Greenwood Press.

Yalom, I. D. (1983). *Inpatient group psychotherapy*. New York: Basic Books.

Yalom, I. D. (1985). *The theory and practice of group psychotherapy* (3rd ed.). New York: Basic Books.

Zimpfer, D. G. (1984a). *Group work in the helping professions: A bibliography*. Muncie, IN: Accelerated Development.

Zimpfer, D. G. (1984b). Pattern and trends in group work. *Journal for Specialists in Group Work, 9*(4), 204–208.

Zimpfer, D. G. (1985a). Demystifying and clarifying small-group work. *Journal for Specialists in Group Work, 10*(3), 175–181.

Zimpfer, D. G. (1985b). Texts used most widely in preparation for group counseling. *Journal for Specialists in Group Work, 10*(1), 51–56.

Zimpfer, D. G. (1987a). Groups for the aging: Do they work? *Journal for Specialists in Group Work, 12*(2), 85–92.

Zimpfer, D. G. (1987b). Group treatment for those involved with incest. *Journal for Specialists in Group Work, 12*(4), 166–177.

Zimpfer, D. G., Waldman, D. E., Williamson, S. K., & Huhn, R. P. (1985). Professional training standards in group counseling: Idealistic or realistic? *Journal for Specialists in Group Work, 10*(3), 134–143.

P A R T

II

THEORETICAL APPROACHES TO GROUP COUNSELING

Leading a group without an explicit theoretical rationale is somewhat like flying a plane without a map and instruments. Techniques and procedures must be based on a theoretical model, although group leaders need to formulate their own conception of the group process and develop a personal approach to group work. Some students think of a theoretical model as a rigid structure that prescribes step by step what to do in specific situations. That's not my understanding of theory. I see theory as a set of general guidelines that you can use in your practice. A theory is a map that provides direction and guidance in examining your basic assumptions about human beings, in determining your goals for the group, in clarifying your role and functions as a leader, in explaining the group interactions, and in evaluating the outcomes of the group.

Developing a theoretical stance involves more than merely accepting the tenets of any one theory. It is an ongoing process in which group leaders keep questioning the what, how, and why of their practice. I encourage my students to take a critical look at the key concepts of the various theories and to also consider the theorists behind them, since a theory is generally a personal expression of the person who developed it. I further encourage my students not to blindly follow any theory in totality, so that they will remain open and seriously consider the unique contributions as well as the limitations of the different approaches. If someone swallows a theory whole, the theory never gets properly digested and integrated. The theoretical stance that each therapist needs to develop must be closely related to the therapist's values, beliefs, and personal characteristics. Thus, the first step in developing one's own approach is to come to an increased awareness of self.

I also warn my students of the danger of discarding a theory in its entirety because of their objections to some aspects of it. For example, some students initially see little practical relevance in the psychoanalytic approach. They object to the lengthy period of time required by analysis, they consider the analysis of unconscious material as being beyond their scope of competence, and they typically don't appreciate the anonymous role of the therapist. I encourage these students to examine the model to see what concepts they *can* incorporate. Being critical of certain dimensions doesn't imply rejecting prematurely potentially valuable ideas.

When practitioners settle on one theory and don't recognize its limitations, they are likely to misuse it and to assume that it is an axiom and a set of proven facts rather than a tool for inquiry. If your theoretical perspective causes you to ignore all others, you may force your clients to fit its confines instead of using it to understand them. The problem with adopting a theory in full is that one can become a "true believer." And the problem with true believers is that they severely limit their vision by screening out anything that doesn't fit their preconceived structures. Also, since they assume that their approach contains the whole truth, they are likely to try to impose it on others and to expect the same complete acceptance from them.

In Part I we looked at the elements that are required for effective group leadership. In Part II we'll explore ten approaches to group counseling and see how these views influence a leader's actual practice.

6

The Psychoanalytic Approach to Groups

Introduction

Psychoanalytic theory has influenced most of the other models of group work presented in this textbook. Some of these other approaches are basically extensions of the analytic model, some are modifications of analytic concepts and procedures, and some have emerged as a reaction against psychoanalysis. It is fair to say that most theories of group counseling have borrowed concepts and techniques from psychoanalysis. As a group counselor you may have neither the training nor the motivation to conduct analytic groups. Even if you do not have command of the techniques required for uncovering unconscious material and reconstructing personality, however, the basic psychoanalytic concepts can become an integral part of your own theoretical approach.

This chapter is devoted to an overview of the psychoanalytic and psychosocial perspectives and to a brief introduction to contemporary trends in psychoanalytic thinking. I also outline the stages of development in an individual's life. Although Sigmund Freud made significant contributions to our understanding of *psychosexual development* of the individual during early childhood, he wrote little about the *psychosocial* influences on human development beyond childhood. Because of this gap, I have given special emphasis to Erik Erikson's (1963, 1982) psychosocial perspective, which provides a comprehensive framework for understanding the individual's basic concerns at each stage of life from infancy through old age. Erikson can be considered a psychoanalyst as well as an ego psychologist, who built on Freudian concepts by continuing the story of human development where Freud left off.

Historical Background

In discussing the key concepts and basic techniques that characterize a psychoanalytic group, this chapter draws on some of Freud's major themes. Although he focused on individual psychodynamics and on the dyadic relationship between a patient and an analyst, his ideas and contributions do have implications for the practice of analytic group therapy.

The person credited with first applying psychoanalytic principles and techniques to groups is Alexander Wolf, a psychiatrist and psychoanalyst. He began working with groups in 1938 because he did not want to turn away patients who needed but could not afford intensive individual therapy. His experiences increased his interest in this approach, and he made it his primary mode of therapy. Wolf stresses psychoanalysis *in* groups (as opposed to psychoanalysis *of* groups), since he has consistently maintained that he does not treat a group. Rather, his focus is on each individual in interaction with other individuals.

In an examination of the evolution of psychoanalytic group therapy in the United States, Tuttman (1986) writes that its theoretical and technical elements make up a mosaic of "homegrown" and "imported" themes. He maintains that psychoanalytic theory and practice have been influenced by the fact that the United States is a pluralistic society. Because there are many isolated schools of thought, it has been difficult to move toward the integration and advancement of psychoanalytic group theory. Tuttman notes that among the central current psychoanalytic concepts are the contributions of British psychoanalysts, including Bion (1959), Ezriel (1950), Foulkes (1965), and Pines (1981, 1983). Other contributions include the psychoanalytic theories of Balint (1968), Fairbairn (1954), A. Freud (1936, 1969), Guntrip (1969), Klein (1975), and Winnicott (1957, 1965). Tuttman also recognizes the contributions of the American practitioners of psychoanalytic developmental and ego psychology, object-relations theory, and self psychology. Some of these practitioners are Hartmann, Kris, and Lowenstein (1946); Kernberg (1975, 1976); Kohut (1971, 1977); Mahler (1968, 1971); and Spitz (1957, 1965).

Goal of the Analytic Group

The goal of the analytic process is the restructuring of the client's character and personality system. This goal is achieved by making unconscious conflicts conscious and examining them. Specifically, psychoanalytic groups reenact the family of origin in a symbolic way via the group, so that the historical past of each group member is repeated in the group's presence. Wolf (1963, 1975) developed group applications of basic psychoanalytic techniques such as working with transference, free association, dreams, and the historical determinants of present behavior. He stresses the re-creation of the original family, so that members can work through their unresolved problems. Their reactions to fellow members and to the leader are assumed to reveal symbolic clues to the dynamics of their relationships with significant figures from their family of origin. Although these reactions are taken from the here and now, there is a constant focus on tracing them back to the early history of the members (Tuttman, 1986). Wolf's approach is aimed at a controlled and systematic regression of the personality in the service of strengthening the ego.

Mullan and Rosenbaum (1978) speak of the process of re-creating one's family as the *regressive-reconstructive* approach to psychoanalytic group therapy. This term refers to a regression into each member's past in order to achieve the therapeutic goal of a reconstructed personality that is characterized by social awareness and the ability to be creatively involved in life. Mullan and Rosenbaum view the group as a "slice of life" that in many respects duplicates the original family. The group leader applies understanding to the familylike connections that arise among the members and between the members and the therapist. The leader imposes a minimum of structure, and the group is heterogeneous, representing various segments of everyday life. This heterogeneity increases the chances of the group's being a microcosm of society, so that members can reexperience conflicts that originated in the family context.

The thrust of analytic groups, according to Wolf and Kutash (1986), rests with the creative growth of the individual ego or self. The authors see the term *group therapy* as a misnomer, for the focus is on the treatment of ailing individuals rather than ailing groups. Further, Wolf (1983) asserts that a group's preoccupation with group dynamics, with here-and-now interactions, and with cohesion can distract from the central core of analytic work. However, he believes that the group atmosphere allows for a deeper analytic searching than is possible in individual analysis because the group ego supports and facilitates deeper exploration. He believes that the exploration of intrapsychic processes enables the members to develop a detailed understanding of the nature of their submission to the significant people in their nuclear family and to the other members in their analytic group.

The Therapeutic Process

The therapeutic process focuses on re-creating, analyzing, discussing, and interpreting past experiences and on working through defenses and resistances that operate at the unconscious level. (*Working through* is a psychoanalytic concept that refers to repetition of interpretations and overcoming of resistance, thus allowing the client to resolve dysfunctional patterns that originated in childhood and to make choices based on new insights.) Insight and intellectual understanding are important, but the feelings and memories associated with self-understanding are crucial. Because clients need to relive and reconstruct their past and work through repressed conflicts in order to understand how the unconscious affects them in the present, psychoanalytic group therapy is usually a long-term and intensive process.

Most practitioners with a traditional analytic orientation value the anonymous role of the leader, because they believe that such a role encourages members to project toward the leader the feelings they had for significant people in their lives. Many analytically oriented group therapists, however, place less value on the nondisclosing role of the leader and tend to share their personal reactions with the group's members. All analytic and analytically oriented therapists consider the process of analyzing and interpreting transference feelings as the core of the therapeutic process, since it is aimed at achieving insight and personality change.

A group format that utilizes psychoanalytic concepts and techniques has some specific advantages over individual analysis:

- Members are able to establish relationships that are similar to those that existed in their own families; this time, however, the relationships occur in a group setting that is safe and conducive to favorable outcomes.
- Group participants have many opportunities to experience transference feelings toward other members and the leader; they can work through these feelings and thus increase their self-understanding.
- Participants can gain more dramatic insight into the ways their defenses and resistances work.
- Dependency on the authority of the therapist is not as great as in individual therapy, for group members also get feedback from other members.
- Group members learn that it is acceptable to have and express intense feelings that they may have kept out of awareness.
- In the group setting members have many opportunities to learn about themselves and others, in fact and in fantasy, through interactions with peers as well as with the leader. The material for analysis is available not only in terms of historical recollection but also on the basis of interaction with fellow members.
- The group setting encourages members to examine their projections. It is difficult for them to cling to some of their resistances and distortions when others in the group confront them on the ways in which they are misrepresenting reality. Furthermore, observing similar conflicts in others can help ease defensiveness and show them they are not alone. Resistance melts away in the atmosphere of mutual revelation and exploration in a group to a greater extent than is typically true of one-to-one therapy.
- Analysis in groups immediately confronts a member's idealistic expectation of having an exclusive relationship with the therapist. The experience of supporting others and the discovery of universal struggles encourage a fuller range of responses than does individual therapy.

Key Concepts

Influence of the Past

Psychoanalytic work focuses on the influence of the past on current personality functioning. Experiences during the first 6 years of life are seen as the roots of one's conflicts in the present. When I consider typical problems and conflicts of group members, the following come to mind: an inability to freely give and accept love; a difficulty in recognizing and dealing with feelings such as anger, resentment, rage, hatred, and aggression; an inability to direct one's own life and resolve dependence/independence conflicts; a difficulty in separating from one's parents and becoming a unique person; a need for and a fear of intimacy; a difficulty in accepting one's own sexual identity; and guilt over sexual feelings. According to the psychoanalytic view, these problems of adult living have their origin in early development. Early learning is not irreversible; but to change its effects, one must become aware of how certain early experiences have contributed to one's present personality structure.

Although practitioners with a psychoanalytic orientation focus on the historical antecedents of current behavior, it is a mistake to assume that they dwell on the past to the exclusion of present concerns. A common misconception about psychoanalytic work is that it resembles an archaeological digging out of relics from the past. As Locke (1961) points out, psychoanalytic group work consists of "weaving back and forth between past and present, between present and past" (p. 30). "It is essential that the therapist move back and forth in time, trying always to recapture the past or to see the repetition in the present and to become aware of the early traumatic event which made for the neurotic pattern of the individual today" (p. 31).

Thus, it is essential that participants understand and use historical data in their group work. At the same time, they also need to be aware of the pitfalls of getting lost in their past by recounting endless and irrelevant details of their early experiences. In the view of Wolf and Kutash (1986), the recital of yesterday's events can be uselessly time consuming and can inhibit progress. They see this use of history as essentially a form of resistance, and they suggest that talking about events in one's childhood is not as useful as dealing with the past in relation to here-and-now interactions within the group:

> History has the greatest significance when evoked and recalled by the discovery and analysis of resistance and transference in the moment of their occurrence—that is, when history has a bearing on the present which is meaningful to both the patient and the analyst. The present neurotic behavior is envisioned as a multidimensional photograph of the significant past. Careful scrutiny of the immediate moment will recall pertinent traumatic events. Personal flashbacks may be vividly illuminating, and the exploration and understanding of the past in terms of its influence on the present are essential to creation of a wholesome present and future [1986, p. 340].

The Unconscious

The concept of the unconscious is one of Freud's most significant contributions and is the key to understanding his view of behavior and the problems of personality. The unconscious consists of those thoughts, feelings, motives, impulses, and events that are kept out of awareness of the conscious ego. From the Freudian perspective, most of human behavior is motivated by forces outside conscious experience. What we do in everyday life is frequently determined by these unconscious motives and needs. Painful experiences during early childhood and the feelings associated with them are buried in the unconscious. The early traumas are such that conscious awareness would cause intolerable anxiety to the child. The child's repression of them does not automatically lift with time, and the client reacts to threats to the repression as if the anxiety associated with the early events would still be intolerable if these were recalled. Thus, the "shadow of the past" haunts the present. But the trauma was intolerable only to the *child;* with an adult perspective on the world the client can handle the memory with relative ease. Therefore, the therapist helps make the unconscious conscious, and the anxiety is *not* intolerable; hence, the client is helped to be free of the tyranny of the past repressions.

Unconscious experiences have a powerful impact on our daily functioning. Indeed, Freud's theory holds that most of our "choices" are not freely made; rather, they are determined by forces within us of which we are not aware. Thus, we select mates to meet certain needs that may have never been satisfied; we select a job because of some unconscious motive; and we continually experience personal and interpersonal conflicts whose roots lie in unfinished experiences that are outside the realm of our awareness.

According to the psychoanalytic theory, consciousness is only a small part of the human experience. Like the greater part of the iceberg that lies below the surface of the water, the larger part of human experience exists below the surface of awareness. The aim of psychoanalysis is to make the unconscious material conscious, for it is only when we become conscious of the motivations underlying our behavior that we can choose and become autonomous. The unconscious can be made more accessible to awareness by working with dreams, by using free-association methods, by learning about transference, by understanding the meaning of resistances, and by employing the process of interpretation. Analytic therapists move back and forth between reality and fantasy, the conscious and the unconscious, the rational and the nonlogical, and thought and feeling.

The concept of the unconscious has deep significance for analytic group therapy. The focus on unconscious motives deemphasizes the here and now and interpersonal interactions per se. The emphasis is, instead, on dealing with one's own dynamics. This includes focusing on the historical determinants of current behavior, exploring the meaning of dreams and fantasies, dealing with resistances, and working through transference distortions. In the psychoanalytic view a group that ignores the role of the unconscious and focuses exclusively on conscious here-and-now interactions among participants is more an encounter group than a therapy group. Also, denial of the manifestations of the unconscious as it operates in a group makes in-depth work with individual members almost impossible.

Although it is true that exhaustive work with the unconscious determinants of behavior and personality reconstruction is beyond the scope of group counseling as it is generally practiced, I believe that group counselors need to have an understanding of how unconscious processes operate. This understanding provides counselors with a conceptual framework that helps them make sense of the group interactions, even if the unconscious is not directly dealt with by the members.

Anxiety

In order to appreciate the psychoanalytic model, one must understand the dynamics of anxiety. Anxiety is a feeling of dread and impending doom that results when repressed feelings, memories, desires, and experiences bubble to the surface of awareness. It is a fearful feeling in response to something in the environment or within the individual. We experience anxiety when we sense that we are dealing with feelings that threaten to get out of our control. Often anxiety is "free-floating"; that is, it is vague and general, not yet having crystallized into specific form.

Anxiety in the Group Situation.   Wolf (1983) points out that anxiety emerges when defenses or resistances are attacked. He writes that many members experience anxiety over the idea of joining an analytic group. During the course of the group, anxiety is revealed in many ways in the members' interactions. Mullan and Rosenbaum (1978) view it as a necessary part of regressive-reconstructive group therapy. As the members dissolve their defenses, they experience anxiety. This anxiety is seen as a necessary by-product of taking risks in the group, a process that eventually leads to constructive changes.

Wolf and Kutash (1986) conceptualize anxiety as it is manifested in a group from the perspective of the equilibrium/disequilibrium theory. In their model individuals feel anxiety, or a state of disequilibrium, when they are not experiencing the optimal level of stress for their needs. The interpersonal environment of the group can be characterized by three patterns of interaction: (1) a generally destructive balance ("group disequilibrium"), (2) a generally constructive balance ("group equilibrium"), or (3) a generally comfortable but stultifying balance ("group malequilibrium").

Group disequilibrium exists when members experience too little intimacy (isolation) or too much intimacy (engulfment). In either case, they feel anxiety as the result of the imbalance. This anxiety has its roots in the family of origin, but in the group situation members participate unconsciously in re-creating their anxiety-arousing patterns. Kutash and Wolf (1983) point out that there is a danger that the group itself can become as pathogenic as their original family. Without skillful management by the group therapist, dependency can bind members together as neurotically as was the case in their original family.

Group equilibrium is achieved when the members constructively re-create their family, but with a new look. The group members provide familial surrogates for bringing out transference reactions. The members of an analytic group eventually realize the extent to which they are re-creating their own childhood family in every social setting and inappro-priately investing others with qualities that characterized their earlier family relationships.

Group malequilibrium exists when group members become so comfort-able with one another that they avoid challenging one another's defenses. Members attempt to control and reduce their anxiety by avoiding conflict, and they unconsciously negotiate to bypass anxiety-arousing topics and ignore stressful but potentially growth-inducing material.

Ego-Defense Mechanisms

The ego-defense mechanisms were first formulated by psychoanalytic theory as a way of explaining behavior. These defense mechanisms protect the ego from threatening thoughts and feelings. Conceptually, the ego is that part of the personality that performs various conscious functions, including keeping in contact with reality. When there is a threat to the ego, anxiety is experienced. Although we may be interested in the growth that comes from facing reality directly, we attempt to protect ourselves from experiencing anxiety. The ego defenses enable us to soften the blows that come with emotional wounding, and they are one way of maintaining a sense of personal adequacy. Although the ego defenses do involve self-deception and distortion of reality, they are not considered essentially pathological. It is only to the degree that they impair a person's ability to deal effectively with the tasks of life that their use becomes problematic. Even though these mechanisms are learned and become a habitual mode of defense against anxiety, they do operate outside one's consciousness.

In a group situation there are many opportunities to observe a variety of defensive behaviors. In many cases the defenses that were used in childhood when we were threatened continue to be the pattern when we feel threatened in the group. A main therapeutic value of a group is that, through feedback from the leader and the other members, clients can be-come increasingly aware of their defensive styles of interaction. With awareness, members are eventually able to choose direct forms of dealing with anxiety-producing situations as they emerge in a group.

Several common ego defenses are typically manifested in the pattern of interactions in the therapeutic group:

• *Repression* involves excluding from consciousness threatening or painful thoughts and desires. By pushing thoughts or feelings that are distressing or painful into the unconscious, people sometimes manage the anxiety that grows out of situations involving guilt and conflict. In groups, adults often have no recollection of the details of incestuous events that may have occurred in early childhood. If adults were physically or emotionally abused in childhood, they might well have blocked out the pain and anxiety associated with these events by pushing the memories into the unconscious. As other members experience a catharsis and work through the pain associated with incest, however, a member who has repressed the experience may find that she is also emotionally triggered, and unconscious material may surface to awareness.

• *Denial* plays a defensive role similar to that of repression, yet it generally operates at the preconscious or conscious level. In denial there is an effort to suppress unpleasant reality. It consists of coping with anxiety by "closing our eyes" to the existence of anxiety-producing reality. In a therapy group, members sometimes stubbornly refuse to accept that they have any problems. They may attempt to fool both themselves and others by saying that they have "worked on" certain problems and that they therefore no longer have any concerns to deal with in the group. A common form of denial can be heard in this member's statement: "I really don't have any more issues with my father, who died when I was 7 years old, because I worked on the pain over this event a couple of times in prior groups."

• *Regression* involves returning to a less mature developmental level. In the face of severe stress or crisis we sometimes revert to old patterns that worked for us earlier. For instance, a man in a therapy group may retreat to childlike behaviors and become extremely frightened and dependent as he faces a crisis precipitated by his wife's decision to leave him for another man.

• *Projection* involves attributing our own unacceptable thoughts, feelings, behaviors, and motives to others. In a group setting members may be very able to see the faults of others. They may also attribute to other members certain feelings and motives that would lead them to feel guilty if they owned these feelings and motives. Of course, groups offer many opportunities to view projection in action. Members often reexperience old feelings that were common in their family of origin. They typically project feelings onto the group leaders that they had toward their parents, and they "see" their siblings in certain group members. Projection is the basis of transference, which is a useful process to explore within the group context. Chronic advice giving can be a form of projection.

• *Displacement* entails a redirection of some emotion (such as anger) from a real source to a substitute person or object. Group members who are frustrated are likely to feel angry. If members are not allowed to get away with pouting or employing some other attention-seeking behaviors, for example, they may lash out in a hostile way toward some member who is relatively nonthreatening. Although their anger may be a result of a group leader's confrontation, they may pick a safer target on whom to vent their hostility.

• *Reaction formation* involves behaving in a manner that is opposite to one's real feelings. It serves as a defense against anxiety that would result from accepting feelings that one is striving to disown. This defense is exhibited in a group by the woman who is "sugary sweet" yet really harbors many hostile feelings that she dares not express. It is also displayed by the man who tries to convince himself and others in his group that he does not care if others reject him, either in this group or at home (yet who underneath very much wants the acceptance of others). These behaviors cover up one's real feelings, for dealing with hostility or rejection would be very painful. In these cases there is an exaggeration of being sweet or of being emotionally indifferent to rejection. The excessive quality of these behaviors is what makes them a form of defense.

• *Rationalization* is a defense mechanism whereby we try to justify our behavior by imputing logical and admirable motives to it. Some people manufacture "good" reasons to explain away a bruised ego. This defense involves an attempt to minimize the severity of disappointment over losses or failures. In groups there are many opportunities to observe this behavioral pattern in action. Members may devote a great deal of energy to focusing on "others out there" as the source of their problems. Some men may be quick to blame their mother's coldness as the reason that they avoid getting close to the women in the group. Or such members may have a well-developed rationale for how their problems would be nonexistent if only their daughter or wife would change.

Although the ego-defense mechanisms have some adaptive value, their overuse can become problematic. It is true that self-deception can soften harsh reality, but the fact is that reality does not change through the process of distorting those aspects of it that produce anxiety. In the long run, when these defensive strategies do not work, the result is even greater anxiety. The group situation is ideal for enabling individuals to learn to recognize the indirect methods that they resort to when they feel emotionally threatened. To avoid judging such behavior, it is possible to work with members in therapeutic ways so that they can increase their tolerance for coping with anxiety and can learn direct ways of dealing with difficult interpersonal situations.

Resistance

In psychoanalytic therapy resistance is defined as the individual's reluctance to bring into conscious awareness threatening unconscious material that has been previously repressed or denied. It can also be viewed as anything that prevents members from dealing with unconscious material, thus keeping the group from making progress. Resistance is the unconscious attempt to defend the self against the high degree of anxiety that the client fears would result if the material in the unconscious were uncovered. As Locke (1961) put it, group members need to protect themselves against the "flooding of the conscious by the forbidden feeling, fantasy, or memory" (p. 72). Resistance is the "fight to maintain the defense"; thus, it is "the defense of the defense."

One method of therapeutically dealing with resistance is through free association; this includes an uncensored and uninhibited flow of ideas produced by the client that offers clues about the person's unconscious conflicts. According to Wolf (1983) and Wolf and Schwartz (1962), resistances emerge with clarity as members continue to free-associate with one another and as old feelings recur in the present. When these defenses surface, they are observed, analyzed, and interpreted. Support offered by the group helps the person break through his or her defenses. Durkin (1964) stresses that resistance is a basic part of the analytic group, and she warns group leaders not to be surprised by or impatient with it. She also warns leaders not to interpret resistance, which is a natural phenomenon of all groups, as a sign of their own ineptness, because such an interpretation would seriously interfere with their task of helping the members break through the resistance so that therapeutic progress can continue.

There are many kinds of resistances, some relating to apprehension about joining a group, some to participation in the group process, and some to the desire to leave the group (Locke, 1961). One common resistance stems from the belief that one cannot benefit from the group situation, because help cannot come from people who are themselves in trouble. Wolf (1963) lists other sources of resistance in group members: fear that one's privacy will be invaded; need to "own" the therapist exclusively; fear of "meeting" again one's original family in the group—namely, recognizing one's parents or siblings in some of the participants—and having to deal with the anxiety produced by these encounters; unconscious fear of giving up neurotic trends; and anxiety about the freedom that a group offers—including the freedom to discuss anxiety.

Wolf (1963) also explores other forms of resistance, which surface during the advanced stages of group analysis. Members may "go blank" when they are asked to free-associate about other group members, or they may escape personal exploration by simply watching others and refusing to participate. Some members hide behind the analysis of other members, and some engage in lengthy recitations of their life histories, thus avoiding the challenge of facing the present. Additional manifestations of resistance include these:

- always arriving late or not showing up at all
- maintaining an attitude of complacency or indifference
- hiding behind a wall of silence or talking incessantly
- intellectualizing
- exhibiting an exaggerated need to help others in the group
- showing distrust
- behaving uncooperatively
- acting out
- using the group for mere socializing

These are by no means the only manifestations of resistive behavior; what they all have in common is the fear of recognizing and dealing with that part of oneself that is locked in the unconscious.

How do group analysts deal with resistance? Durkin (1964) maintains that in order to penetrate and work through resistances, the therapist needs to enlist the cooperation of members. Therefore, he or she must start with the client's immediate problems as they are manifested through resistive behaviors. Durkin stresses the importance of dealing with disappointments and resentments, because members will otherwise become increasingly angry, less desirous of opening up, and more resistant. Thus, resistances are not just something to be overcome. Because they are valuable indications of the client's defenses against anxiety, they should be acknowledged and worked through by therapist and client together, with the clear understanding that they are both working toward the same ends. Generally, it is best to call attention to those manifestations of resistance that are most readily observable and to work with these behaviors first. In doing so, leaders should take care not to label or censure group members, because unacceptable criticism will only increase resistive behaviors. It can also be useful to bring other group members into the analysis of individual members' resistances.

Transference

Transference is a basic concept of the psychoanalytic approach. It refers to the client's unconscious shifting to the therapist of feelings, attitudes, and fantasies (both positive and negative) that stem from reactions to significant persons from the client's past. The key issue of transference is the distortion imposed on the therapeutic relationship by prior relationships, usually childhood ones. Analytic technique is designed to foster the client's transference. But the therapeutic setting, unlike the original situation, does not punish the person for experiencing or expressing these feelings. If a client perceives the therapist as a stern and rejecting father, he or she does not receive from the therapist the expected negative responses. Instead, the therapist accepts the client's feelings and helps the client understand them.

By reliving their past through the transference process, clients gain insight into the ways in which the past is obstructing present functioning. Insight is achieved by working through unresolved conflicts that keep the person fixated and that make full emotional growth impossible. Basically, the negative effects of painful early experiences are counteracted by working through similar conflicts in the therapeutic setting.

Since transference also manifests itself in groups through the members' attempts to win the approval of the leader, these attempts can be explored to find out whether they reflect the client's need for universal approval and how such a need governs the person's life. Remember that groups can provide a dynamic understanding of how people function in out-of-group situations.

If the transference relationship is poorly handled by the therapist, the client may become resistive to the point that therapeutic progress is arrested. There are therapists who encourage client dependency in order to derive a feeling of power from the extreme need that clients develop for them. The result is often regression to a childlike situation in which the therapist is cast in a parental role. One of the advantages of group therapy is that, because of the presence of other group members, this dependency and concomitant regression are not as likely to occur as in individual therapy.

Group therapy also offers the possibility of multiple transferences. In individual therapy the client's projections are directed toward the therapist alone; in group therapy they are also directed toward other members. The group constellation provides rich possibilities for reenacting past unfinished events, especially when other members stimulate such intense feelings in an individual that he or she "sees" in them a father, mother, spouse, ex-lover, boss, and so on.

The element of rivalry that often exists in a group can also be valuable therapeutic material to explore. Group participants tend to compete for the attention of the leader—a situation reminiscent of earlier times, when they had to vie for their parents' attention with their brothers and sisters. Thus, sibling rivalry can be explored in group as a way of gaining increased awareness of how the participants dealt with competition as children and how their past success or lack of it affects their present interactions with others.

The opportunity that psychoanalytic groups offer for multiple transferences is stressed by several authors. The group is a conducive milieu in which to relive significant past events because "the group of today becomes the family of yesterday" says Locke (1961, p. 102). Wolf (1963) and Wolf and Schwartz (1962) observe that the group members serve as transference figures for other members and that the main work of the analytic group consists of identifying, analyzing, and resolving these projections onto family surrogates in the group. The leader has the task of helping members discover the degree to which they respond to others in the group as if they were their parents or siblings. By interpreting and working through their transferences, participants become increasingly aware of their fixations and deprivations and of the ways in which past events interfere with their ability to appraise and deal with reality.

Mullan and Rosenbaum (1978) call the focusing on and using of transference reactions the "hallmarks of psychoanalysis." These authors also discuss the value of using a male and a female as co-therapists. This arrangement replicates faithfully the original nuclear family, and it enables members to reenact early expectations of their father and mother.

Countertransference

From time to time the therapist's own feelings become entangled in the therapeutic relationship, obstructing or even destroying objectivity. According to psychoanalytic theory, countertransference consists of a therapist's unconscious emotional responses to a client, resulting in a distorted perception of the client's behavior. Wolf (1983) makes it clear that no analytic leader is totally free of involvement in transference or countertransference. Kutash and Wolf (1983) describe countertransference as the leader's "unconscious, involuntary, inappropriate, and temporarily gratifying response to the patient's transference demands" (p. 135).

To the degree that countertransference is present, group therapists react to members as if they were significant figures of their own original family. Group leaders need to be alert to signs of unresolved conflicts within themselves that could interfere with the effective functioning of a group and create a situation in which members are used to satisfy their own unfulfilled needs. If, for example, group leaders have an extreme need to be respected, valued, and confirmed, they can become overdependent on the members' approval and reinforcement. The result is that much of what they do is designed to please the group members in order to ensure their continued support. It is important to differentiate between appropriate emotional reactions and countertransference. For example, if a member typically shows up late for the group and finds all sorts of reasons to justify his lateness, the group leader may become angry with him. Her anger toward his behavior is not necessarily unrealistic. However, if her father had a trait of justifying his behavior and if a common thread exists between the group member and her father, her emotional reactions are likely to represent countertransference.

There are a number of manifestations of countertransference:

- seeing oneself in certain clients and overidentifying with them to the point of becoming unable to work effectively with them
- projecting onto clients some traits that one despises in oneself and regarding such clients as not amenable to treatment or impossible to work with
- engaging in seductive behavior and taking advantage of the leader's role to win the special affection of certain group members
- becoming overprotective by being a benign substitute parent

With inpatient groups, countertransference reactions take on a heightened degree of intensity. The therapist's reactions are a powerful instrument for understanding the dynamics of the group. The therapist's countertransference provides a new perspective on the affective issues underlying the rapidly shifting events typical of inpatient groups. Without understanding their own reactions, therapists are likely to blindly misuse the common techniques of providing support and confronting defenses in inpatient groups (Brabender, 1987).

The unresolved conflicts and repressed needs of group therapists can seriously interfere with the group process and can lead therapists to abuse their position of leadership. The difficulty in recognizing one's own countertransference and the necessity that such reactions be acknowledged and therapeutically dealt with provide a rationale for group leaders to experience their own therapy. The analytic approach requires that therapists undergo psychoanalysis to become conscious of their own dynamics and of the ways in which these dynamics can obstruct therapeutic tasks.

As noted by Brabender (1987), countertransference can be an avenue for understanding the dynamics of a group. She reminds us that group therapists are not immune to feelings such as hate, envy, guilt, admiration, and love. Her position is that "the full experience and tolerance of all of these therapist feelings within the inpatient group enables group members to realize the richness of their humanity in relation to one another" (p. 566). But it is essential that the therapist's feelings be conscious and self-acknowledged if they are to be used in therapeutic ways. It is also crucial to use good judgment and timing in expressing certain feelings.

Basic Techniques

Free Association

The basic tool for uncovering repressed or unconscious material is free association: communicating whatever comes to mind, regardless of how painful, illogical, or irrelevant it may seem. Group members are expected to report feelings immediately, without trying to exercise censorship, and the group discussion is left open to whatever the participants may bring up, instead of revolving around an established theme. Foulkes (1965) refers to this process as "free-floating discussion," or "free group association."

One adaptation of free association to groups is the so-called "go-around technique," which uses free association to stimulate member interaction (Wolf, 1963). After a good rapport has developed in the conducive atmosphere fostered by sharing dreams and fantasies, members are encouraged to free-associate about each person in the group. Each participant goes around to each of the other members and says the first thing that comes to mind about that person. According to Wolf, the go-around method makes all the members adjunct therapists; that is, instead of remaining passive recipients of the leader's insights, the participants actively contribute to the interpretation of key meanings. Wolf contends that if group members say whatever comes into their heads about another, "they will intuitively penetrate a resistive facade and identify underlying attitudes" (1963, p. 289). As a result, the participants reveal inner feelings, become less guarded, and often develop the ability to see underlying psychic conflicts. Also, all group members have an opportunity to know how the other participants view them.

Wolf and Kutash (1986) suggest that it is useful when a client reports a dream to ask other members to free-associate with it. In this way they are being active and do not feel excluded as they listen to the details of another member's dream. The group can explore not only the dreamer's but also the other members' associations.

In summary, free association encourages members to become more spontaneous and to uncover unconscious processes, so that they can achieve keener insights into their psychodynamics. This procedure also promotes unity and active participation in the group process.

Interpretation

Interpretation is a therapeutic technique used in the analysis of free associations, dreams, resistances, and transference feelings. In making interpretations, the group therapist points out and explains the underlying meaning of behavior. Interpretations are designed to accelerate the therapeutic process of uncovering unconscious material. The assumption is that well-timed and accurate interpretations can be used by the client to integrate new data that will lead to new insights. Interpretation requires considerable skill. If therapists force their interpretations on clients in a dogmatic fashion, clients are likely to close off and become increasingly defensive. If clients are presented with an accurate interpretation at an inappropriate time, they may fight the therapeutic process and resist other therapeutic interventions.

Scheidlinger (1987) maintains that an interpretation is simply a hypothesis and that no matter how elegantly conceived, it is still subject to confirmation or refutation. He suggests that when group members reject a therapist's interpretation, it might mean that the interpretation is inaccurate, not that they are being resistant. He writes that the correct timing of an interpretation in group therapy involves both a given member's readiness to understand and accept it and also the readiness of other group members. He adds that premature interpretations are likely to promote undue anxiety and lead to considerable resistance. The way interpretations are phrased and their manner of presentation, according to Scheidlinger, will certainly affect the degree to which they are considered by members. He formulates his interpretations in the form of questions, a practice that conveys the notion that they are merely hypotheses.

Interpretations that are presented as hypotheses and not as facts are more likely to be considered by clients. For example, Sam keeps making inappropriate interventions when other members express intense feelings and thus causes the others to lose contact with their feelings. The leader finally intervenes and says: "Sam, you seem to want to reassure Julie by trying to convince her that everything will work out for her. I have a hunch that you become uncomfortable when you see a person in pain; so you rush in, trying to take that person's pain away. Could it be that you're trying to avoid painful experiences yourself?" This comment alerts Sam to a possible reason for his ingroup behavior. If Sam thinks about the leader's interpretation, he may discover other meanings that he is not now conscious of. Whether he will respond nondefensively has a lot to do with the manner in which the interpretation is made. In this case, the leader's tentative approach doesn't pose a threat and doesn't push Sam into accepting something that he may not be ready to accept.

In making interpretations, a few other general rules are useful:

- Interpretation should deal with material that is close to the client's awareness. In other words, the therapist needs to interpret material that clients have not yet seen for themselves but that they are ready and able to incorporate.
- Interpretation should begin from the surface and go as deep as the client can emotionally tolerate.
- It is best to point out a form of defense or resistance before interpreting the feeling or conflict that lies underneath the defense or resistance.

Sharing of Insights by Members.   One of the advantages of the psychoanalytic method in groups is that members are encouraged to share their insights about other participants. This process can be very supportive and can accelerate progress. Even though the members do not systematically make interpretations, leaving that function to the therapist, they can have a deep effect on other members by being direct, unrehearsed, and confrontive. As members become more familiar with one another, they become increasingly able to recognize defensive strategies and offer very perceptive observations. Fellow members' reactions may elicit more consideration and thought than those coming from an expert, but they may also be resisted with more tenacity. Some group therapists are concerned that a member may make inappropriate comments—that is, insights that the person in question is not ready to handle. This concern is somewhat lessened by what typically happens when someone is presented with an insight that is timed poorly or inaccurately: generally the person rejects the insight or in some way discounts it on the ground that it comes from a peer rather than from an expert.

Wolf, Schwartz, McCarty, and Goldberg (1972) observe that the therapist's interpretation of dreams, fantasies, transference, resistance, defensiveness, slips of tongue, and free associations allows the group members to become aware of these phenomena both in themselves and in others. Here too, as in free association, the group members are adjunct therapists as well as patients, for they interpret the manifestations of the unconscious in themselves and in others in the group. Elsewhere, Wolf (1963) writes that successful analysts learn to value the useful contribution of the group to mutual insight. The group can greatly benefit from the sharing of interpretations, because "patients sometimes show themselves to be closer to the unconscious truth than their physician" (p. 313).

Bion's Method of Interpretation of Group Process.   Interpretations can be directed to the group as a whole as well as to individual participants. For example, group members may be operating under the unspoken agreement that they will be polite and supportive and that they will not challenge one another. By observing the group process and sharing his or her observations with the group, the therapist can be instrumental in helping the members see their hidden motives and reach a deeper level of interaction. Here, too, *how* the leader presents the observations is crucial. The interpretation of the group as a whole was developed by W. R. Bion (1959), a British psychiatrist. Bion provided the group with no direction or structure. As a result of this style of leadership (or lack of it), group members typically grew confused and angry and displayed many other reactions. Bion became more interested in the group's dynamics than in the individual's dynamics; thus, he formulated interpretations of the group as a whole rather than of individual members' reactions.

As he continued to work with groups, Bion observed three basic assumptions that groups develop on their way to becoming a "work group": *dependency, fight/flight,* and *pairing.* The dependency-oriented group attempts to coax the professional leader to do for it what it feels it cannot do for itself. The fight/flight group resists structure by the leader or another member by rebelling against or ignoring the person. Members of the pairing group form dyads and hope that these pairings will do the work that they need to do as individuals. It was Bion's goal to help the participants achieve the ability to function effectively in work groups. Toward this goal, all of his interpretations were group interpretations. He would confront the group members with their behaviors that reflected one of the three basic assumptions. His hope was that as the members became aware of their unrealistic demands on the group leader and on one another, they would develop more realistic and effective methods of functioning as individuals within the group.

Yalom (1985) gives Bion credit for his contributions to viewing the group as a whole, for his focus on the here-and-now interactions and events within the group, and for his attempt to understand unconscious forces that influence the activity within the group. Although Yalom acknowledges the innovative aspects of Bion's group psychology of the unconscious, he takes a critical view of what he considers to be a highly restricted role of the group leader. In his opinion, there is limited therapeutic effectiveness in groups in which the leader remains impersonal, hidden, and passive and restricts his or her behavior to impersonal group interpretation. Yalom says that a powerful body of research demonstrates the critical role of the relationship in the therapeutic process. Surely this relationship variable was lacking in Bion's approach. Although Yalom does not quarrel with the importance of the group-as-a-whole phenomenon and group-process interpretation, he does contend that the curative factors operating in a group are mediated by other leader activities, including norm-shaping activities. He writes: "I strenuously disagree with a restriction of the therapist role. Interpretation, as I have indicated, does play an important role in therapy, but it is by no means the only ingredient in successful therapy" (p. 198).

Dream Analysis

Analysis of dreams is an essential procedure for uncovering unconscious material. Freud saw dreams as "the royal road to the unconscious," because they express unconscious needs, conflicts, wishes, fears, and repressed experiences. When a dream is shared in a group and worked through, the participant gains new insight into the motivations and unresolved problems behind it. Some motivations are so unacceptable to the person that they can be expressed only in disguised or symbolic form. Thus, an advantage of working with dreams in a group is that it allows members to deal in a concrete way with feelings and motivations that otherwise they couldn't face. After exploring the various facets and possible meanings of a dream in a supportive group, members may be more willing to accept themselves and explore other unresolved problems that elicit feelings of guilt and shame.

It should be noted that dreams have both a *manifest* (or conscious) content and a *latent* (or hidden) content. The manifest content is the dream as it appears to the dreamer; the latent content consists of the disguised, unconscious motives that represent the hidden meaning of the dream. A psychoanalytic group works at both levels. Since dreams are viewed as the key that unlocks what is buried in the unconscious, the goal is to search for the latent beneath the manifest and to gradually uncover repressed conflicts.

In her article "The Dream in Psychoanalytic Group Therapy," Kolb (1983) takes the position that dreams can be viewed from both an intrapersonal and an interpersonal perspective. She contends that the dream experience itself, often without interpretation, taps unconscious mental activity in a manner unequaled by most other clinical experiences. She adds: "The contributions of the group members provide additional material not only to understand the dream and the dreamer but also to work on and to work out the dynamics of the other contributors from their own associations" (p. 51).

In the first session, group members are told that the sharing of their dreams, fantasies, and free associations is essential to the analysis and understanding of the dynamics behind confused thinking, feeling, and behaving. Even though therapists may have a great deal of insight into clients' dreams, they generally give little analysis during the early stages of a group. Instead, the members are encouraged to offer their own analyses (Mullan & Rosenbaum, 1978).

According to Wolf (1963), the interpretation of dreams is an essential aspect of the analytic process and should continue throughout the various stages of a group. It is an essential technique because the unconscious material that dreams reveal has a liberating effect on the participants. Members are encouraged to interpret and free-associate with one another's dreams in order to reach the deepest levels of interaction. Wolf reports that the entire group becomes "engrossed in dream analysis with its attendant associations, catharsis, sense of liberation and mutuality, all of which contribute toward the group unity which is so important in the first stages of treatment" (p. 287). He stresses the importance of a nonjudgmental attitude on the part of the leader toward the emerging unconscious material. The leader's tolerant approach encourages a similar attitude in the members, and the group soon becomes a compassionate and supportive family.

Besides their value for unblocking unconscious material from the client's past, dreams also contain a wealth of meaningful material concerning what is going on in the group, since the members' dreams reveal their reactions to the therapist and to the other members (Locke, 1961). The dreamer reports the dream and tells the group what meanings and associations it has for him or her. Then the group as a whole responds; other group members give their reactions to the dream and suggest cross-associations. The result is stimulation within the group.

The exploring of dreams in a group has another valuable aspect. As members analyze the dreams of others and offer their own associations, they also project significant dimensions of themselves. In other words, the group members are both interpreting *and* projecting, a process that often leads to extremely valuable insights. Wishes, fears, and attitudes are revealed as members associate with one another's dreams. One person's dream becomes the dream of the whole group, a process that is the "true essence of dream work in group psychoanalysis" (Locke, 1961, p. 133). Readers interested in a more detailed discussion of dream work in an analytic group are referred to Wolf and Schwartz (1962, pp. 135–161) and to Kolb (1983).

Insight and Working Through

Insight means awareness of the causes of one's present difficulties. In the psychoanalytic model insight is also an awareness, intellectual as well as emotional, of the relationship between past experiences and present problems. As clients develop keener insight, they become increasingly able to recognize the many ways in which these core conflicts are manifested, both in the group and in their daily lives. New connections are formed, and dominant themes begin to emerge. For example, if in the course of group work some members discover that they need to please everyone at all costs, they come to see the effects of their need for approval on their lives.

But the analytic process doesn't stop at the insight level; working through core problems and conflicts is an essential aspect of analytically oriented group and individual therapy. Thus, if group members hope to change some aspect of their personality, they must *work through* resistances and old patterns—typically, a long and difficult process. Working through is one of the most complex aspects of analysis, and it requires deep commitment. The working-through process involves reexperiencing the unfinished business in the context of transference (multiple transference, in group analysis).

Working through represents the final phase of the analytic group and results in increased consciousness and integration of the self. According to Wolf and Schwartz (1962), the leader, after discovering the dynamics of an individual's problems and symptoms, carefully maps a course of action to deal with them. These authors maintain that participants make progress and change as a result of a cooperative effort between the group leader and the client within the context of a thoughtful and flexible treatment plan.

It should be mentioned that early conflicts are rarely *completely* worked through. Most individuals may, from time to time, have to deal again with these deeply rooted issues. Thus, it is a mistake to think of working through as a technique that frees the individual from any vestige of old patterns.

The Alternate Session

Wolf and his colleagues (1972) write about two goals of psychoanalytic groups that are characteristic of the final stages of a group's development: helping members find more effective ways of relating to other people and encouraging them to grow as persons so that they can think independently and stand by themselves. The technique of the *alternative session* has proven quite successful in the pursuit of both these goals. The alternate session takes place, without the group leader, at the home of one of the members. These leaderless sessions are aimed at contributing to an intimate atmosphere that stimulates uninhibited participation.

In enumerating the advantages of the alternative session, Mullan and Rosenbaum (1978) mention developing group cohesion, increasing the creative potential of each member, enhancing the group's therapeutic function, and heightening a sense of belonging in the group. Mullan and Rosenbaum see the leader's absence as requiring a shift of responsibility, a search for new goals and values, different relationship patterns, and mutual efforts to cope with problems, all factors that contribute to greater autonomy in the members. The alternate session also provides ways of testing this newly acquired autonomy, since the participants' ability to function without the leader may be an indication of their readiness to separate from the therapist. Finally, the alternate session can enhance the regular sessions because it attests to the leader's faith in the members' ability to use their own resources within the group to work toward personal action and social integration.

Role and Functions of the Group Leader

The leaders of psychoanalytic groups have as a primary function helping participants gradually uncover the unconscious determinants of their present behavior. They do this by paying attention to unconscious conflicts, using free association, analyzing the hidden meanings of dreams, interpreting resistance and transference, and assisting members to identify and work through unfinished business that has led to their present conflicts. When skillfully handled, this role provides a useful model for the members to emulate when responding to one another. Thus, members are expected to share their insights concerning behavior in the group, suggest interpretations, deal confrontively with the resistances they observe, encourage silent members to speak, deal assertively with disruptive behavior, and offer support as others are working through difficult material. In sum, members learn to play a therapeutic role for one another.

In spite of the great variations found among psychoanalytically oriented group therapists, most of them have a leadership style characterized by objectivity, warm detachment, and relative anonymity. The goal is to foster transference. Some leaders believe that the more therapists can remain anonymous, the more members can project onto them their own images of what they expect leaders to be, images that are seen as expressions of the members' unconscious needs. A central task of the leader is to work out and work through these transference distortions—toward the leader and toward other members—as they are manifested in the group. As the group interaction increases, the leader pursues participants' unconscious motivations and investigates the historical roots of these motivations through analysis and interpretation. Other functions of the leader include

- creating a climate that encourages members to express themselves freely
- setting limits to in-group and out-of-group behavior
- giving support when support is therapeutic and the group is not providing it
- helping members face and deal with resistances within themselves and in the group as a whole
- fostering members' independence by gradually relinquishing some leadership functions and by encouraging interaction
- attracting members' attention to the subtle aspects of behavior and, through questions, helping them explore themselves in greater depth

According to Wolf (1983), the most significant function of the group therapist is to promote members' interpersonal relationships beyond the one with the therapist. Wolf suggests that an exclusive involvement with the therapist can insulate the client and lead to a symbiotic relationship. The promoting of interaction with others in the group expands the member's choices and fosters growth.

Other functions and tasks of the leader are identified by Wolf (1963) and Wolf and Schwartz (1962):

- making efforts to acknowledge errors and being secure enough to transfer some leadership functions to the group
- avoiding a dictatorial style of leadership aimed at converting members to the leader's point of view
- welcoming manifestations of transference in the group as opportunities for fruitful work
- guiding members toward full awareness and social integration
- seeing the group as a potentially powerful catalytic agent
- recognizing the participants' potential ability to assist in the interpretation and integration of material produced by other members and their capacity to be close to the unconscious truth of one another
- being alert to the individual differences within the group
- employing the skills necessary to resolve intragroup conflict
- maintaining an optimistic attitude when the group falters
- modeling simplicity, honesty, and directness

- setting the tone of emotional freedom by being open about one's own feelings
- watching for destructive alliances within the group

To be able to effectively carry out these many functions, group leaders have the paramount obligation to understand their own dynamics throughout the therapeutic process. To do so, they may need consultation and occasional supervision. Their own personal therapy can be most valuable in helping them recognize signs of countertransference and ways in which their own needs and motivations influence their group work.

As noted earlier, most psychoanalytic therapists strive for objectivity and relative anonymity. Foulkes (1965) refers to the therapist as a "conductor," a participant member who is nondirective yet active. The leader's main function, Foulkes says, "is that of analyst, catalyst, and interpreter" (p. 79). In a similar vein Mullan and Rosenbaum (1978) state that the group leader "maintains an anonymity and privacy about himself and his extragroup life" (p. 129), without, however, hiding his affective and human side. Leaders do not use the group for their own therapy.

Wolf and his associates (1972) are representative of those psychoanalytic practitioners who do focus on the therapist/client relationship and on the importance of the group leader's personal characteristics. After working within the framework of analytic group therapy for many years, they have come to the conclusion that success depends not only on the theoretical and technical constructs of psychoanalysis but also on the therapist as a person. They assert that the focus of psychoanalysis has gradually shifted from the patient's psychodynamics to the *relationship* between therapist and client.

Developmental Stages and Their Implications for Group Work

Introduction

This section describes a developmental model that has significant implications for group work. The model is based on Erikson's eight stages of human development and on the Freudian stages of psychosexual development. Such a combination provides group leaders with the conceptual framework required for understanding trends in development, major developmental tasks at each stage of life, critical needs and their satisfaction or frustration, potentials for choice at each stage of life, critical turning points or developmental crises, and the origins of faulty personality development that can lead to later personality conflicts.

Erikson (1963, 1982) built on and extended Freud's ideas by stressing the psychosocial aspects of development. Although he was intellectually indebted to Freud, he did not accept all of Freud's views. He viewed human development in a more positive light than Freud had and emphasized growth and the rational side of human nature, whereas Freud had stressed the irrational aspects of development. Moreover, psychosocial theory maintains that the ego, not the id, is the life force of human development (Erikson, 1963). The ego is viewed as the component of the self that is in contact with the outside world through cognitive processes such as thinking, perceiving, remembering, reasoning, and attending.

Erikson's theory of development holds that psychosexual and psychosocial growth occur together and that at each stage of life we face the task of establishing an equilibrium between ourselves and our social world. Psychosocial theory stresses the integration of the biological, psychological, and social aspects of development. Erikson describes development in terms of the entire life span, which he divides into eight stages, each of which is characterized by a specific crisis to be resolved. According to Erikson, each *crisis* represents a *turning point* in life. At these turning points, either we can achieve successful resolution of our conflicts and move forward, or we can fail to resolve the conflicts and regress. To a large extent, our lives are the result of the choices we make at each stage.

This conceptual framework is useful for all group leaders, regardless of their theoretical orientation. Irrespective of the model underlying one's group practice, the following questions need to be raised as group work proceeds:

- What are some of the themes that give continuity to a person's life?
- What are the client's ongoing concerns and unresolved conflicts?
- What is the relationship between this individual's current problems and significant events in earlier years?
- What influential factors have shaped the person's character?
- What were the major turning points and crises in the client's life?
- What choices did the individual make at these critical periods, and how did he or she deal with these various crises?
- In what direction does the person seem to be moving now?

Stage 1: Infancy— Trust versus Mistrust (Birth to 12 Months)

According to Erikson (1963), an infant's basic task is to develop a sense of trust in self, others, and the world. Infants need to count on others and to feel wanted and secure. By being held, caressed, and cared for, they learn basic trust.

Freud labeled the first year of life the *oral stage;* sucking the mother's breast satisfies the infant's need for food and pleasure. According to the psychoanalytic view, the events of this period are extremely important for later development. Infants who don't get enough love and food may later develop greediness and acquisitiveness, because material things become substitutes for what they really wanted and didn't get. Later personality problems that stem from the oral stage include a mistrustful view of the world, a tendency to reject love, a fear of loving and trusting, and an inability to establish intimate relationships.

Erikson sees the first year of life in terms of *trust* versus *mistrust*. If the significant others (especially the parents) in an infant's life provide the necessary love and satisfy its physical needs, it develops a sense of trust. If, on the other hand, the parents are not responsive to its needs, it develops an attitude of mistrust toward the world, especially toward interpersonal relationships. Clearly, infants who feel accepted are in a more favorable position to successfully meet future developmental crises than are those who don't receive adequate nurturing. Children who receive love generally accept themselves, whereas children who feel unwanted and unloved tend to experience difficulties in doing so.

Some of the behavioral characteristics of people who have a sense of basic trust are an ability to ask others for emotional support, a focus on the positive aspects of others' behavior, an ability to balance giving and receiving, a willingness to self-disclose, and a generally optimistic world view (Hamachek, 1988).

Implications for Group Work. The connection between these ideas and the practice of group psychotherapy seems quite clear. A common theme explored in groups is the feeling of being unloved and uncared for and the concomitant acute need for someone who will deeply care and love. Time after time, group members recall early feelings of abandonment, fear, and rejection, and many of them have become fixated on the goal of finding a symbolic "parent" who will accept them. Thus, much of their energy is directed toward seeking approval and acceptance. The problem is compounded by the fact that, being unable to trust themselves and others, they are afraid of loving and of forming close relationships.

Group leaders can help these clients express the pain they feel and work through some of the barriers that are preventing them from trusting others and fully accepting themselves. Erikson (1968) observes that these clients tend to express their basic mistrust by withdrawing into themselves every time they are at odds with themselves, others, or the world.

It should be noted that each stage builds on the psychological outcomes of the previous stage(s). In this regard, establishing a sense of basic trust is a foundation for later personality development. As you will see with the stages to come, when a foundation of trust, autonomy, initiative, and industry is laid, young people are ready for the challenges facing them during adolescence: establishing a clear sense of who they are as individuals and developing a positive self-concept (see Hamachek, 1988).

Stage 2: Early Childhood—
Autonomy versus Shame and Doubt (12 Months to 3 Years)

Freud called the next 2 years of life the *anal stage,* because the anal zone comes to be of major significance in the formation of personality. The main tasks that children must master during this stage include learning independence, accepting personal power, and learning how to express negative feelings such as jealousy, rage, aggression, and destructiveness. Thus, it is at this stage that children begin their journey toward autonomy. They play an increasingly active role in taking care of their own needs and begin to communicate what they want from others. This is also the time when they continually encounter parental demands; they are restricted from fully exploring their environment, and toilet training is being imposed on them. The Freudian view is that parental feelings and attitudes during this stage have significant consequences for later personality development.

During the anal stage children experience feelings of hostility, rage, and aggression. If they are taught, directly or indirectly, that they are bad merely for having these feelings, they soon learn to bottle up these emotions. Having learned that parental love is conditional and that love is going to be withheld if they express "negative" feelings, they repress anger and hostility. Thus, the process of disowning feelings is set in motion, and it often leads to an inability later in life to accept many of one's own real feelings.

From Erikson's viewpoint the years between 1 and 3 are a time for developing a sense of *autonomy*. Children who don't master the task of gaining some measure of self-control and the ability to cope with the world develop a sense of *shame* and *doubt* about themselves and their adequacy. At this age children need to explore the world, to experiment and test their limits, and to be allowed to learn from their mistakes. If parents do too much for their children and try to keep them dependent, they are likely to inhibit the children's autonomy and hamper their capacity to deal with the world successfully.

What are some of the characteristics of people who have a sense of autonomy? They can make their own decisions about significant matters, they can deny requests without feeling guilty, they resist being dominated by those who want to control them, they can work well by themselves or with others, they can pay attention to their own inner senses when deciding on a course of action, they have a basic belief in their capabilities, and they feel relatively at ease in group situations (Hamachek, 1988).

Implications for Group Work.   By understanding the dynamics of this stage of life, the group leader can gain access to a wealth of useful material. Many of those who seek help in a group have not learned to accept their anger and hatred toward those they love and need to get in touch with the disowned parts of themselves that are at the bottom of these conflicting feelings. In order to do this, they may need to relive and reexperience situations in their distant past in which they began to repress intense feelings. In the safe environment of the group they can gradually learn ways of expressing their locked-up feelings, and they can work through the guilt associated with some of these emotions. Groups offer many opportunities for catharsis (expressing pent-up feelings) and for relearning.

Group participants who have a limited degree of autonomy and many self-doubts have developed a lifestyle characterized by leaning on others. These people join a group to reacquire their potential for power and to develop the ability to define who they are and what they are capable of doing—in brief, to gain psychological control of their lives. Here, too, the group offers the opportunity to investigate how one's emotionally dependent style originally developed and to learn concrete ways of becoming more self-reliant.

Stage 3: The Preschool Age— Initiative versus Guilt (3 to 6 Years)

In Freud's *phallic stage* sexual activity becomes more intense. The focus of attention is on the genitals, and sexual identity takes form. Preschool children become curious about their bodies. They explore them and experience pleasure from genital stimulation. And they show increased interest in the differences between the sexes and ask questions about reproduction. The way in which parents respond, verbally and nonverbally, to their children's emerging sexuality and sexual interest is truly crucial in determining the kinds of attitudes, sexual and otherwise, that their children develop.

According to the Freudian view, the basic conflict of the phallic stage centers on the unconscious incestuous desires that children develop for the parent of the opposite sex. These feelings are highly threatening, so they are repressed, yet they remain as powerful determinants of later personality development. Along with the wish to possess the parent of the opposite sex comes the unconscious wish to displace the parent of the same sex.

The boy desires the mother's attention, develops feelings of resentment toward the father, yet also fears that the father will retaliate for his incestuous feelings toward the mother. This psychosexual developmental process is known as the *Oedipus complex*. The process is unconscious, of course, since repression is operating to keep the anxiety in check.

The boy typically develops fears related to his penis, which Freud termed *castration anxiety*. This fear plays a major role in the boy's life at this time. His fear is that his father will punish him by cutting off the offending organ. Because of his fear, the boy is said to repress his sexual desire for his mother. If the Oedipal conflict is adequately resolved, the boy replaces his sexual longings for his mother with more socially acceptable forms of affection. He develops a strong identification with his father, deciding that if he cannot beat his father, he will join him.

Although the *female phallic phase* is not so clearly described by Freud as is the male stage, there is a female counterpart to the Oedipus complex known as the *Electra complex*. The girl's first love object is her mother, but this love is transferred to her father during this stage. She develops negative feelings toward her mother but eventually, when she realizes that she cannot successfully compete for her father's attention, identifies with her mother by assuming some of her behavioral characteristics.

This period sees the development of the *superego*, which is the construct that refers to inner controls or ideals that guide the individual's behavior. During the phallic stage there is a conflict between the impulses of the *id* and the *superego*. The *id* is the part of the personality, present at birth, that is blind, demanding, and insistent. Its function is to discharge tension and return to homeostasis. The *superego* is that part of the personality that represents one's moral training. It strives for perfection, not pleasure. The *ego* has the task of mediating between external reality and inner demands. The ego consists of all modes of thought used by individuals to reach their goals and to defend their self-concepts.

Since this is a time of conscience formation, one critical danger is the parental indoctrination of rigid and unrealistic moral attitudes. Also, if the parents manifest a negative attitude toward their children's increased sexual awareness, the children learn that their sexual feelings are evil and that their curiosity about sexual matters is unacceptable. As a consequence, they become guilty about their natural impulses, afraid of asking questions and thinking for themselves, and prone to blindly accepting parental teachings. Sexual feelings and interest in sexual matters become anxiety provoking and are thus repressed. The denial of one's sexuality established at this age is then carried over into adult life and typically leads to conflicts, guilt, remorse, and self-condemnation. Another critical danger is that parents may be extremely lax in teaching any sense of values or that their modeling may be very poor. Such parents can teach children to act strictly on their own behalf and ignore any sense of concern for others. So, on one side are those individuals whose consciences are harshly punitive, and on the other side are people whose consciences are woefully absent. The latter are sociopathic individuals, whose main personality characteristics include a marked lack of ethical or moral development and an inability to behave in accordance with a framework of social values. Psychoanalytic theory provides a perspective for understanding the differences between these two extremes of conscience development.

Erikson, in contrast, contends that the basic task of the preschool years is to establish a sense of *competence* and *initiative*. This is the time for becoming psychologically ready to pursue activities of one's own choosing. If children are allowed the freedom to select meaningful activities, they tend to develop a positive outlook characterized by the ability to initiate and follow through. But if they are not allowed to make at least some of their own decisions or if their choices are ridiculed, they are likely to develop a sense of *guilt* over taking initiative. Typically, they will refrain from taking an active stance and will increasingly let others make decisions for them.

What are some of the characteristics of people who have a sense of initiative? They like accepting new challenges, they tend to set goals and then do what is necessary to accomplish them, they are self-starters, they have high energy levels, they have a clear sense of personal adequacy, and they have a balanced sense of ethics without being overly moralistic (Hamachek, 1988).

Implications for Group Work. In our therapy groups my colleagues and I see manifestations of Oedipal and Electra struggles. It is a mistake to conceive of these struggles literally. We observe the general theme of symbolically wanting to replace the parent of the same sex, so that the parent of the opposite sex can be the object of attention. Other themes include wanting to be noticed and valued by the parent of the opposite sex, feelings of attraction to the parent of the opposite sex, and struggles with the parent of the same sex.

In most therapy and counseling groups, participants struggle with issues related to sex-role identity. Many men and women have incorporated stereotypical notions of what it means to be a man or a woman, and they have consequently repressed many of their feelings that don't fit these stereotypes. A group can be the place where these women and men challenge such restricting views and become more whole.

Because concerns about sexual feelings, attitudes, values, and behavior are often kept private, people feel very much alone with their sexual concerns. Groups offer the chance to openly express these concerns, to correct faulty learning, to work through repressed feelings and events, and to begin to formulate a different view of oneself as a female or male sexual being. Perhaps the most important function of a group is that it gives members permission to have feelings and to talk honestly about them.

Stage 4: The School Age—
Industry versus Inferiority (6 to 12 Years)

Freudians call middle childhood the *latency stage*. After the torrent of sexual impulses of the preceding years, this period is relatively quiescent. There is a decline in sexual interests, which are replaced by interests in school, playmates, sports, and a whole range of new activities. Around 6, children begin to reach out for new relationships with others in the environment.

Erikson stresses the active, rather than the latent, aspect of this stage and the unique psychosocial tasks that must be met at this time if healthy development is to take place. Children need to expand their understanding of the physical and social worlds and continue to develop appropriate sex-role identities. They must also form personal values, engage in social tasks, learn to accept people who are different from them, and acquire the basic skills needed for schooling. According to Erikson, the central task of middle childhood is the achievement of a sense of *industry,* and the failure to do so results in a sense of *inadequacy* and *inferiority.* Industry refers to setting and achieving goals that are personally meaningful. If children fail at this task, they are unlikely to feel adequate as adults, and the subsequent developmental stages will be negatively influenced.

People who have a sense of industry enjoy learning, have a sense of curiosity, experiment with new ideas and arrive at a new synthesis, feel excitement over being productive, take a sense of pride in doing at least one thing well, accept criticism nondefensively, and have a strong sense of persistence (Hamachek, 1988).

Implications for Group Work.   The following are some of the problems originating at this stage that group leaders should expect to encounter in their group work: a negative self-concept, feelings of inadequacy relating to learning, defensiveness in response to criticism, feelings of inferiority in establishing social relationships, conflicts about values, a confused sex-role identity, unwillingness to face new challenges, dependency, and lack of initiative.

To see how the leader's knowledge of the problems and promises of this period of life can promote the therapeutic process, let's look at a participant who suffers from feelings of inferiority. Rachel fears failure so much that she shies away from college because she is convinced that she could never make it. In a group Rachel can be helped to see possible connections between her feelings of inadequacy and events that occurred when she was in elementary school. Perhaps she had a series of negative learning experiences, such as being told, openly or not, by her teachers that she was stupid and couldn't learn. Before Rachel can overcome her inadequacy feelings with regard to the demands of college, she may have to go back to the traumatic events of her childhood, relive them, and express the pain she felt then. Through the support of the group she can experience again many of her buried feelings and begin to put the events of her past in a different perspective. Eventually, she may also realize that she doesn't have to wreck her academic career now because of something that happened in grade school.

Stage 5: Adolescence— Identity versus Identity Confusion (12 to 20 Years)

Adolescence is a stage of transition between childhood and adulthood. It is a time for continually testing limits, rejecting ties of dependency, and establishing a new identity. It is most of all a time of conflict, especially between the desire to break away from parental control and the fear of making independent decisions and living with the consequences.

In Freudian theory the final psychosexual stage of development, called the *genital stage,* is the longest and extends far beyond adolescence; it begins at the time of puberty and lasts until senility sets in, at which time the individual tends to regress to earlier stages. In essence, Freud saw the developmental period from birth to age 5 as the foundation on which later personality development was built. Thus, he focused on that period and didn't devote much attention to the events of later childhood or to those of adulthood. Erikson picked up where Freud left off and devoted a great deal of attention to the later stages, especially adolescence. He saw the crisis that characterizes adolescence—the identity crisis—as the most important of life. The task of this period is to establish an identity, or a sense of oneself as a unique person.

What does Erikson mean by *identity crisis?* He means that most conflicts of the adolescent years are related to the development of a personal identity. Adolescents struggle to define who they are, where they are going, and how they will get there. Because all kinds of changes—physical as well as social—are taking place and because society applies diverse pressures, many adolescents have difficulty finding a stable identity. They experience pressure from school, from their parents, from their peer group, from members of the other sex, and from society at large, and these demands are often conflicting. In the midst of this turmoil the adolescent has the task of ultimately deciding where he or she stands in the face of these varying expectations. If the adolescent fails, *identity confusion* results, and the person will lack purpose and direction in later years.

What are some of the characteristic behaviors of people who have a sense of identity? They have a stable self-concept, they have a clear sense of goals; they are less susceptible to peer pressure, they generally accept themselves, they are able to make decisions without vacillating, they assume a sense of responsibility for what happens to them, and they are able to be physically and emotionally close to selected individuals without losing themselves (Hamachek, 1988).

During adolescence there is a refocusing of the issues of separating from one's parents and becoming an independent person. Also, conflicts over sex roles and sexual identity run high during these years. Adolescents may be uncertain about how to deal with their sexual impulses. They are often not sure whether they want to be heterosexual, homosexual, or bisexual, and they may experience a homosexual panic. Clarifying their sexual identity, which is simply a part of the broader picture of their general identity, is a major task during these years, and it often extends into young adulthood.

Clarifying and integrating one's values into an organic system that is personally meaningful is another difficult and anxiety-filled task of adolescence. In order to develop a personal philosophy of life, adolescents must make key decisions in a broad spectrum of areas: ethics and sexual morals, religious beliefs, life expectations, values in intimate relationships, education, and career. In meeting these challenges, young people need adequate models, for most values are learned not by direct instruction but by contact with people who provide inspiration through example. Often the models are inadequate or even nonexistent. Adolescents are especially aware of duplicity in adults, and they have a low tolerance for phoniness. They are influenced more by what they observe than by what they are told they *ought* to be.

Implications for Group Work. In my groups a good deal of time is devoted to exploring and resolving the dependence/independence conflicts that are so prevalent in adolescence. A central struggle involves the process of separation and individuation. In a therapy group adolescents may sometimes need to explore a missed period of early development and connection with a significant other. The group therapist could serve as this object for a time by offering a corrective relationship.

Some group members relive their adolescence in the group, and they often go through experiences that they sealed off during that time. For example, they may have allowed others to make all the major decisions for them. In the group they become conscious of how they have let themselves give up self-direction for the comfort of direction from others. Through a relearning process they take active steps that gradually lead to taking charge of their own lives.

Group counseling is especially suited for adolescents. It provides a forum in which they can express and explore conflicting feelings and discover that they are not alone in these conflicts. A group context allows open questioning of and modification of values and an opportunity to practice communication skills with peers and adults. In a group setting adolescents can safely experiment with reality, test their limits, express themselves, and be heard.

The unresolved issues of adolescence are manifest in many of the problems that adults bring to a group. In most of the groups I've led, one of the most persistent themes is the search for identity: "Who am I? How did I get this way? What do I really stand for? Where am I going, and how will I get there? If I get there, what will it ultimately mean?" Adults continue to wrestle with identity issues. If they failed to achieve a sense of personal identity when they were adolescents, they have difficulties in most areas of their adult lives. Until they recognize the unfinished business from those early years, they cannot effectively meet the challenges presented by the other stages of life.

Stage 6: Young Adulthood— Intimacy versus Isolation (20 to 35 Years)

In Erikson's view we enter adulthood after we have mastered the conflicts of adolescence and established a firm personal identity. During the sixth stage, young adulthood (ages 20–35), our sense of identity is tested again by the challenge of *intimacy* versus *isolation.*

An essential characteristic of the psychologically mature person is the ability to form intimate relationships. In order to achieve true intimacy with others, we need to have confidence in our own identity, because intimacy involves commitment and the ability to share and to give from our own centeredness. The failure to achieve intimacy leads to alienation and isolation. Young adulthood is also a time for focusing on one's interests, for becoming established in an occupation, and for carving out a satisfying lifestyle. It is a time for dreams and life plans but also a time for productivity.

Implications for Group Work.   In many adult groups considerable time is devoted to exploring the members' priorities. Participants struggle with concerns of interpersonal intimacy, talk about their unfulfilled dreams, question the meaningfulness of their work, wonder about the future, and reevaluate the patterns of their lives to determine what changes they need to make. Perhaps the greatest value of a group for people engaged in these struggles is the opportunity to take another look at their dreams and life

plans and determine the degree to which their lives reflect these aspirations. If the gap is great, the participants are encouraged to find ways of
changing the situation.

Typically, young adults bring to a group the problems related to living
with another person and establishing a family. The central struggle of this
period is the intimacy crisis, a conflict between the need to maintain a sense
of one's own separateness and the need to establish close relationships. The
successful resolution of the intimacy crisis involves achieving a balance
between taking care of oneself and actively caring for others. Those who fail
to strike this balance either focus exclusively on the needs of others, thus
neglecting their own needs, or are so self-centered that they have little room
for concern about others. Of course, the quality of the young adult's ability
to form interpersonal relationships is greatly influenced by what took place
during early development.

Stage 7: Middle Age— Generativity versus Stagnation (35 to 60 Years)

The seventh stage is characterized by a need to go beyond ourselves and our
immediate families and be actually involved with helping and guiding the
next generation. The mature years can be one of the most productive periods
of our lives, but they can also entail the painful experience of facing the
discrepancy between what we set out to accomplish in young adulthood and
what we have actually accomplished.

Erikson sees the stimulus for continued growth during this stage in the
conflict between *generativity* and *stagnation.* Generativity is a broad concept
that is manifested in the ability to love well, work well, and play well. If
people fail to achieve a sense of productivity, they begin to stagnate and to
die psychologically. When we reach middle age, we become more sharply
aware of the inevitability of our own eventual death. This awareness of
mortality is one of the central features of the mid-life crisis and colors our
evaluations of what we are doing with our lives. For the first time we must
deal with the fact that we will not achieve what we believed we would, that
we have not lived up to our earlier expectations.

Implications for Group Work.   The changes that occur during this life
stage and the crises and conflicts that accompany them represent valuable
opportunities for group work. Participants are often challenged to make
new assessments, adjustments, and choices in order to open up new
possibilities and reach new levels of meaning. For example, most parents
have to adjust to the departure of their children. If they focused much of
their effort on their children, they now need to look elsewhere for a sense of
purpose and self-fulfillment. Group participants can explore ways of finding
productive new pursuits. Knowledge of adult development allows the group
leader to watch for the hopelessness that so many people experience during
middle age and to help them go beyond the destructive view that "that's all

there is to life." It takes caring and skilled leadership to inspire people to look for new meanings and to "invent themselves" in novel ways.

Stage 8: Later Life—
Integrity versus Despair (above 60 Years)

The eighth, and last, stage of life confronts the individual with crucial developmental tasks, such as adjusting to the death of a spouse or friends, maintaining outside interests, adjusting to retirement, and accepting losses in physical and sensory capacities. But the central task of the final stage is reviewing the past and drawing conclusions.

According to Erikson, the successful resolution of the core crisis of this stage—the conflict between *integrity* and *despair*—depends on how the person looks back on the past. *Ego integrity* is achieved by those who feel few regrets; they see themselves as having lived productive and worthwhile lives, and they feel that they have coped with their failures as well as their successes. They are not obsessed with what might have been and are able to derive satisfaction from what has been. They see death as a part of the life process and can still find meaning and satisfaction in the time left.

Failure to achieve ego integrity leads to feelings of despair, hopelessness, guilt, resentment, and self-rejection. People with this perspective are constantly aware of unfinished business; they yearn for another chance at life that they know they will never have, and they cannot accept the thought of dying, because they have wasted their lives. Thus, they are desperate.

Implications for Group Work.   Groups for the elderly are becoming increasingly popular, as Burnside's (1984) excellent book *Working with the Elderly: Group Processes and Techniques* indicates. She describes a range of special groups created to meet the unique needs of the elderly. For example, *reality-oriented groups* are designed for regressed older people who have been diagnosed as suffering from chronic brain syndrome. *Remotivation-therapy groups* focus on simple matters of daily living and emphasize discussion of specific issues of interest to the participants. *Reminiscing groups* are designed to help the elderly remember and reconstruct the past. *Counseling groups* are intended to explore the problems that are common among older people, provide a supportive milieu, enhance a sense of belonging, and offer opportunities for testing reality.

To work successfully with the elderly in a group situation, the leader must take into account the basic limitations in their resources for change without adopting a fatalistic attitude that would only reinforce their sense of hopelessness. Those who lead groups for the elderly need to have realistic expectations. Although dramatic personality changes are quite unlikely, change—no matter how small and subtle—does occur and has a meaningful and beneficial impact on the participants (Corey & Corey, 1987).

Burnside (1984) notes that group work with the elderly requires more structure and direction than work with other age groups. Because of older people's special physical and psychological problems, group leaders are challenged to devise methods that provide support and encouragement. One of the most important elements of group work with the elderly is, in Burnside's opinion, careful and effective communication between leader and members. (For further reading on the topic of group work with older people, see Burnside, 1984.)

The salient issues of this stage of life have implications not only for group leaders working with older adults but also for those who work with young or middle-aged adults. Often these younger people express the fear of getting older. As they begin to see the years slip by, they feel the increasing pressure of making something of their lives. Some worry about being all alone when they are old, and some are afraid of financial or physical dependency on others. Group leaders can help these people realize that perhaps the only way to deal constructively with these fears is to prepare now for a satisfying life as they grow old. Asking the question "What would you like to be able to say about your life when you reach old age?" is a good way to start. What the members say in answer to this question (to themselves and in the group) can dictate the decisions they need to make now and the specific steps they must take in order to achieve a sense of integrity at a later age.

Contemporary Trends in Psychoanalytic Group Theory

Psychoanalytic theory, rather than being closed or static, is continually evolving. Freud's ideas were based on an id psychology, characterized by conflicts over the gratification of basic needs. Later, writers in the social-psychological school moved away from Freud's orthodox position and contributed to the growth and expansion of the psychoanalytic movement by incorporating the cultural and social influences on personality. Then *ego psychology,* with its stress on psychosocial development throughout the life span, was developed by Erikson, among others.

Object-Relations Theory

The evolution of psychoanalytic theory and practice did not cease with these developments. A new trend in psychoanalytic thinking characterized the 1970s and the 1980s. These newer approaches are often classified in terms of *self-psychology* or *object-relations theory.* Object relations are interpersonal relationships as they are represented intrapsychically. The term *object* was used by Freud to refer to that which satisfies a need, or to the significant person or thing that is the object or target of one's feelings or drives. It is used interchangeably with the term *other* to refer to an important person to whom the child or, later, the adult becomes attached. Rather than being individuals with a separate identity, others are perceived as objects for gratifying needs. Thus, object relations are interpersonal relationships that shape the individual's current interactions with people. Object-relations theories depart from orthodox psychoanalysis, although some theorists attempt to integrate the increasingly divergent trends that characterize this school of thought (St. Clair, 1986).

These contemporary theoretical trends in psychoanalytic thinking center on predictable developmental sequences in which the early experiences of the self shift in relation to an expanding awareness of others. Once self/other patterns are established, it is assumed, they influence later interpersonal relationships. This influence occurs through a process of searching for a type of experience that comes closest to the patterning established by the early experiences. For example, people who are either overly dependent or overly detached can be repeating patterns of relating that they established with their mother when they were toddlers. In short, current behavior in the world largely repeats early internal patterning (Hedges, 1983). These newer theories provide insight into how an individual's inner world can cause difficulties in living in the actual world of people and relationships (St. Clair, 1986).

Mahler's Perspective on Early Development

Mahler (1968) is a key figure in the evolution of the object-relations approach. She focused her studies on the interactions between the child and the mother in the first 3 years of life and formulated theories about the intrapsychic events of these early years. Mahler believes that the individual begins in a state of psychological fusion with the mother and progresses gradually to separation. The unfinished crises and residues of the earlier state of fusion, as well as the process of separating and individuating, have a profound influence on later relationships. Object relations of later life build on the early relationship between mother and child and the child's search for a reconnection with the mother (St. Clair, 1986). Psychological development can be thought of as the evolution of the way in which individuals separate from and differentiate themselves from others. In group work participants can become aware of how they are bringing very early patterns into their present interactions, which can be experienced within the group itself.

Dealing with Borderline and Narcissistic Personalities

Perhaps the most significant developments of recent psychoanalytic theory have focused on borderline and narcissistic personality disorders. According to the *Diagnostic and Statistical Manual of Mental Disorders* (American Psychiatric Association, 1987), the essential features of the *borderline* personality are an unstable view of one's self and instability in relating to others. Such people occupy a border area between neurosis and psychosis. The essential features of the *narcissistic* personality are a pervasive pattern of grandiosity, hypersensitivity to the evaluations of others, and a lack of empathy. Both of these personality patterns begin by early adulthood. Among the most significant theorists in this area are Kernberg (1975, 1976) and Kohut (1971, 1977, 1984). Kohut maintains that people are their healthiest and best when they can feel both independence and attachment, taking joy in themselves and also idealizing others.

From the perspective of object-relations theory, new light is shed on the understanding of personality disorders. According to St. Clair (1986), borderline and narcissistic disorders seem to result from traumas and developmental disturbances during the separation/individuation phase. However, the full manifestations of the personality and behavioral symptoms tend to develop in early adulthood. Narcissistic and borderline symptoms such as omnipotence, splitting (a defensive process of keeping incompatible feelings separate), and grandiosity are behavioral manifestations of developmental tasks that were disturbed or not completed earlier (St. Clair, 1986).

Implications for Group Work with the Borderline Personality. A borderline personality disorder is characterized by instability, periods of irritability, self-destructive acts, impulsive anger, and extreme mood shifts. Borderline people typically experience extended periods of disillusionment, punctuated by occasions of euphoria. Interpersonal relations are often intense and unstable, with marked changes of attitude over time, mood shifts, and intense anger. There is frequently impulsive and unpredictable behavior that can cause physical harm. A marked identity disturbance is generally manifested by uncertainty about life issues pertaining to self-image, sexual orientation, career choice, and long-term goals. Kernberg (1975) describes the syndrome as including a lack of clear identity, a lack of deep understanding of other people, poor impulse control, and the inability to tolerate anxiety. In recent years a great deal more clarity about borderline individuals has emerged, especially due to Kernberg's work. They are more disorganized than neurotics but more integrated than psychotics (Kernberg, 1975). They have a chaotic, primitive personality structure. Under stress they are highly unstable, and they resort to a variety of self-destructive behaviors.

In working with borderline clients from ethnic minorities, Comas-Diaz and Minrath (1985) have found that integrating a psychoanalytic theoretical model with a sociocultural context is essential for effective psychotherapy. Sociocultural factors tend to complicate the borderline dynamics, which revolve around the dimension of identity. Many of these clients experience pervasive feelings of loneliness, and there is an underlying theme of "Where do I belong?" Because socioeconomic and political factors permeate the lives of these clients, Comas-Diaz and Minrath contend, therapy cannot rely exclusively on an insight orientation. The authors maintain that it is essential for therapists to enter the client's life as a real person and to attempt to fully understand the client's life circumstances. It appears that these identity issues could appropriately be dealt with in group therapy.

Kretsch, Goren, and Wasserman (1987) found that borderline individuals showed a consistent and significant improvement through their involvement in group therapy, especially in the area of improved ego functioning: "The group is either a stronger stimulant or a more appropriate setting for eliciting pronounced changes in ego functioning" (p. 110). Yalom's (1985) view of group therapy with borderline clients is consistent with the study just cited. For him, their core problem lies in the area of intimacy. The group offers the therapeutic factors of cohesiveness and of reality testing. Yalom contends that if these individuals can accept feedback and observations provided by other members and if their behavior is not highly disruptive, the group can offer them supportive refuge from daily stresses. The regression of these individuals is far less pronounced in a group. Although borderline individuals may distort reality and express primitive, chaotic needs and fears, they are continually confronted with reality through the group process, which helps to keep these feelings somewhat under control. If the group begins to ignore borderline members, they assume deviant roles and act out in the group, and therapy fails.

Implications for Group Work with the Narcissistic Personality.
Children who lack the opportunity either to differentiate or to idealize others while also taking pride in themselves may later suffer from narcissistic personality disorders. This syndrome is characterized by an exaggerated sense of self-importance and an exploitive attitude toward others, which serves the function of masking a frail self-concept. Such individuals tend to be exhibitionistic, they seek attention and admiration from others, and they have a tendency toward extreme self-absorption.

Kernberg (1975) characterizes narcissistic people as focusing on themselves in their interactions with others, having a great need to be admired, possessing shallow affect, and being exploitive and at times establishing parasitic relationships with others. He writes that narcissistic individuals have a shallow emotional life, derive little enjoyment from life other than tributes received from others, and tend to depreciate those from whom they expect few narcissistic pleasures.

Kohut (1971) characterizes narcissistic people as being highly threatened in maintaining their self-esteem and as having feelings of emptiness and deadness. These individuals are typically searching for someone who will serve as an object to feed the famished self. (Kohut uses the term "selfobject" to refer to a person used to foster self-esteem and a sense of well-being.) They look for people whom they can admire for their power, because they see themselves as worthwhile only if they are associated with such selfobjects. Yet their inner void cannot be filled, so their search for confirmation by others is never-ending. These people attempt to merge with powerful or beautiful selfobjects. Because of their impoverished sense of self and their unclear boundaries between self and others, they have difficulty in differentiating between their own thoughts and feelings and those of the selfobject.

Yalom (1985) discusses the problems involved when narcissistic individuals are in group therapy. They have difficulty in sharing group time, in understanding and empathizing with others, and in forming relationships with others in the group. These clients have a constant need for center stage. They often assess a group's usefulness to them in terms of how much time is devoted to them and, especially, how much attention they receive from the therapist. They are likely to be bored and impatient while other members are working, and they also tend to divert the discussion back to themselves. These individuals have unrealistic expectations of the other members, for they feel that they are special and deserve the group's attention, yet they are not willing to give to others. According to Yalom, a major task of the group is to manage such highly vulnerable members in the group. The leader must focus on the nature of the current forces, both conscious and unconscious, that are influencing the way narcissistic members relate to others in the group.

Evaluation of the Psychoanalytic Model

There is much in the psychoanalytic approach that I consider of great value. The analytic model provides a conceptual framework for understanding an individual's history, and in this regard group practitioners can learn to think psychoanalytically even if they do not practice psychoanalytically. Although some psychoanalytic techniques may have limited utility for the group counselor, many analytic concepts help explain the dynamics operating both in individuals and in the group as a whole.

It is important to consider one's past in order to fully understand one's present behavior. Many of the conflicts brought to a group are rooted in early childhood experiences. Although I am not advocating that one become preoccupied with the past by digging it up and then dwelling on it, I contend that ignoring the influence of the past leads to superficial group work. Understanding this influence gives people more control over their present behavior.

Another psychoanalytic concept I find of particular importance is resistance. Even when members are in a group by their own choice, I observe stubborn resistances, especially during the early development of a group. These resistances are manifestations of various fears; unless they are dealt with, they are not going to go away. Therefore, I find it necessary to face them by exploring them fully. In fact, I typically ask members to share with the group the ways in which they expect their own resistance to interfere with their group work. Some members seem to know quite well that they will sabotage themselves and resist change by intellectualizing, by being overly nurturing to fellow members, or by convincing themselves that their problems are not really very pressing. If members recognize their resisting behaviors when they occur, they have a chance to do something about them.

The psychoanalytic concepts of anxiety and the ego-defense mechanisms that emerge as a way to cope with this anxiety are most useful for group practitioners. Although in some groups the leader may not focus on confronting and working through these defensive structures, it is essential to learn to respect defenses and to recognize how they develop and how they manifest themselves in the group interactions. Dealing with the defenses against anxiety provides a useful framework for intense group work. Members have the opportunity to challenge some of their defensive strategies, and in the process of learning how to communicate in nondefensive ways, they can also learn new ways of responding.

Transference and countertransference have deep implications for group work. Although not all feelings between members and leader are the result of these processes, a leader must be able to understand their value and role. I find the analytic concept of projection quite useful in exploring certain feelings within the group, because projections toward the leader and toward other members are valuable clues to unresolved conflicts within the person that can be fruitfully worked through in the group.

The group can also be used to re-create early life situations that are continuing to have an impact on the person. In most groups there are individuals who elicit feelings of attraction, anger, competition, avoidance, aggression, and so forth. These feelings may be similar to those that members experienced toward significant people in the past. Thus, members will most likely find symbolic mothers, fathers, siblings, and lovers in their group. These transferences within the group and the intense feelings that often characterize them are fruitful avenues to explore.

Modifications of Classical Analytic Practice

An approach that integrates Freud's psychosexual stages of development with Erikson's psychosocial stages is, in my view, most useful for understanding key themes in the development of personality. I do not think that working solely on an insight level will result in changes; it is essential to explore sociocultural factors as they pertain to the struggles of individuals at the various phases of their development. Unless group practitioners have a good grasp of the major tasks and crises of each stage of development, they have little basis for determining whether developmental patterns are normal or abnormal. Also, a synthesis of Freud's and Erikson's theories offers a general framework for recognizing conflicts that participants often explore in groups. According to Hamachek (1988), the major strength of psychosocial theory is that it acknowledges that humans are biological, psychological, and social beings and that an interactive mix of these inner and outer forces shapes them. Hamachek considers a weakness of the psychosocial theory to be the ambiguity surrounding what behaviors to look for during any particular growth stage that allow a more specific evaluation of a person's psychosocial growth.

The newer developments, object-relations theories and self psychology, offer valuable conceptions for group therapists. There have been a number of breakthroughs in working with borderline and narcissistic individuals in group therapy. As we have seen, the group offers some unique advantages over the one-to-one relationship in working with borderline personalities. Many practitioners who were trained in classical psychoanalysis have modified analytic concepts and techniques to fit group situations. I have encountered a number of therapists who think in psychoanalytic terms but draw on other therapeutic models. They work with analytic concepts such as the unconscious, defenses, resistances, transference and countertransference, and the significance of the past, but they also borrow techniques from other approaches.

Applying the Psychoanalytic Approach in Multicultural Settings

Psychoanalytically oriented therapy in groups, if modified, can be appropriate for culturally diverse populations. In his article "Toward a Sociocultural Psychotherapy for Low-Income Ethnic Minorities," De La Cancela (1985) mentions specifically the value of preparing clients during the preliminary phase of therapy. He also suggests that therapists reduce the social distance between themselves and their clients, that they work toward establishing rapport, and that they educate and motivate clients to reflect on feelings and to reveal themselves. Comas-Diaz and Minrath (1985) recommend that the diffused sense of identity prevalent among borderline clients from ethnic minorities be examined from both a sociocultural and a developmental perspective. They also suggest that exploring the meaning of ethnicity and race within the therapeutic relationship is essential for the working through of the clients' diffused sense of identity. Erikson's psychosocial approach seems to have particular relevance here. Comas-Diaz and Minrath suggest that one aid to helping clients rebuild their identity is to emphasize strengths rather than deficiencies.

Many cultural groups stress family history. A review of a client's past and of how this past is having an important bearing on current functioning may be appropriate as a conceptual framework. Working in symbolic ways can also be powerful, especially with clients who are reluctant to talk about their personal problems. The use of play therapy with children is an example. Another vehicle is the use of pictures of the family at different periods of the client's childhood. The leader might say: "Select a picture that has particular meaning for you. Tell me what you remember during these times. As you look at the picture, what thoughts and feelings come to you?" Once group members begin talking to one another about their memories based on pictures, they are likely to be more open in dealing with emotional material.

The role that the psychoanalytic practitioner assumes may fit in with the values and expectations of ethnic clients. Many clients approach group therapy with the expectation that the leader should assume this position of authority and should be an expert in helping them deal effectively with their problems. Typically the psychoanalytic leader assumes these roles, so this style of relationship may be conducive to helping ethnic clients begin to trust and believe that they can be helped.

There may also be some difficulties in applying a psychoanalytic approach with minority clients. This is especially true in working within the framework of long-term, in-depth, intrapsychic analysis, which may be in direct conflict with some clients' social framework and interpersonal and environmental perspective. A systems perspective, including the role of the family, one's network of friends and extended family, and social and environmental factors, is more compatible to ethnic clients.

A major problem is the length of time that psychoanalytic therapy takes. Many minority clients come to a group to solve immediate and pressing problems. Psychoanalytic therapy is less concerned with short-term problem solving than it is with long-term personality reconstruction. Thus, clients may be very impatient with this form of therapy.

As Comas-Diaz and Minrath (1985) point out, issues of prejudice and discrimination and feelings of guilt occur in cross-cultural counseling (a situation in which the counselor has a different cultural, ethnic, or racial background than the client). Thus, therapists of all ethnic and racial backgrounds need to recognize and confront their own biases and prejudices. Comas-Diaz and Minrath emphasize that the conflicts of minority clients result from the interplay of intrapsychic and sociocultural forces and that therapists may at times feel overwhelmed with the myriad of problems presented by these clients. These authors suggest that it is the therapist's role to address the pervasiveness of these factors in the client's daily life. If these sociocultural forces are not acknowledged, many ethnic minorities are likely to feel alienated from both the therapist and the therapy process.

Questions for Reflection and Discussion

1. To what extent are psychoanalytic groups appropriate for all sociocultural and socioeconomic groups? For what populations do you think they are best suited? In what cases do you think they are not suitable?

2. Compare and contrast psychoanalysis in groups with one-to-one therapy. What are some advantages of group analysis over the dyadic situation? What are some limitations and disadvantages?

3. What are your thoughts about alternate sessions as a supplement to regular sessions with the leader? What is the rationale for a group meeting without the leader? What values do you see in this method? What are some possible problems involved in alternate sessions?

4. In general, psychoanalytic groups focus on the intrapsychic dynamics of the individual and emphasize relating everything that occurs in the group to historical determinants. What do you think of this focus on the individual's dynamics? What are some advantages and disadvantages of such a focus?

5. The psychoanalytic group in some ways replicates the original family of the members. Emphasis is put on recognizing and exploring multiple transferences in a group as a way of dealing with early familial issues. What are the possibilities of such a focus? To what degree do you think doing this can be an emotionally corrective experience?

6. Review the psychosexual and psychosocial stages of human development, which consist of an integration of Freud's and Erikson's ideas.

How do these stages apply to you? Were there any critical turning points in your life that had an impact on who you are today? What applications of this developmental framework do you see for group counseling?

7. What do you imagine it would be like for you to be a member of a psychoanalytic group? Knowing what you do of yourself, what resistances might you experience? How would you manifest your resistance? How do you think you would deal in a group with your resistance?

8. What concepts and techniques from the psychoanalytic approach would you be most interested in incorporating into your style of group leadership?

9. From an analytic perspective, therapists are not totally free of countertransference reactions. What kind of members do you think you'd have the greatest difficulty in working with therapeutically? How do you see your reactions to certain types of members as related to your own unresolved personal issues?

10. Psychoanalytic group leaders tend to maintain a stance characterized by objectivity, warm detachment, and relative anonymity. What do you think of this style?

Where to Go from Here

If you would like to learn more about psychoanalytic groups, you would do well to join the American Group Psychotherapy Association. Membership includes a subscription to an excellent journal, the *International Journal of Group Psychotherapy,* which is published four times a year. The journal contains a variety of articles dealing with both the theory and practice of group therapy, and many of the articles relate to psychoanalytic groups. The AGPA has a training program for group therapists and graduate students; successful completion results in a certificate. The program entails taking 90 hours of didactic instruction about group therapy, leading therapy groups for at least 60 hours, having at least 25 hours of qualified supervision in group leadership, and participating as a member of a group or groups for at least 60 hours. Each year in February the AGPA sponsors a 5-day annual meeting that features a variety of institutes, seminars, open sessions, and workshops. Although psychodynamic groups are featured, other group orientations are offered as well. Many of these full-day and half-day workshops are directed toward issues of interest to psychodynamic practitioners. The AGPA does have a student-member category. For further information about journal subscriptions and membership requirements, contact

American Group Psychotherapy Association, Inc.
25 East 21st Street, 6th Floor
New York, NY 10010
Phone: (212) 477-2677

RECOMMENDED SUPPLEMENTARY READINGS

Object relations and self psychology: An introduction (St. Clair, 1986) provides an overview and critical assessment of two streams of psychoanalytic theory and practice: object-relations theory and self psychology. An introductory chapter describes the basic concepts and deals with some core issues. Especially useful are the chapters discussing the approaches of Margaret Mahler, Otto Kernberg, and Heinz Kohut. There are also chapters devoted to the models of Klein, Fairbairn, Winnicott, and Jacobson. The issues and concepts of these models are presented relatively clearly (considering that the primary sources are difficult to read). The book looks at how these different theorists vary from one another and how they depart from the classical Freudian model. This is a good place to start if you want an update on the contemporary trends in psychoanalysis.

Psychoanalysis in groups (Wolf & Schwartz, 1962) offers an excellent overview of the stages of development of an analytic group, the role of the group analyst, and the practical aspects of the analytic group process. This book also discusses the alternate session, acting out, dreams, working through, and the misuse of the group.

Beyond the couch: Dialogues in teaching and learning psychoanalysis in groups (Wolf, Schwartz, McCarty, & Goldberg, 1970) presents basic psychoanalytic concepts that apply to the theory and technique of analytic groups. Specific issues such as the training experience, the alternate session, extragroup socialization, transferences in the group, the nature of supervision, transference theory, and termination are explored.

Group psychotherapy: Theory and practice (Mullan & Rosenbaum, 1978) is written mainly from a psychoanalytic perspective. Part II deals with the psychoanalytic method and innovations. Stages of group development, the alternate session, conceptual foundations of the analytic group, transference and countertransference, and the group organization are a few of the topics covered. I highly recommend this book for both beginning and advanced group practitioners.

REFERENCES AND SUGGESTED READINGS*

American Psychiatric Association. (1987). *Diagnostic and statistical manual of mental disorders* (4th ed.). Washington, DC: Author.

Arlow, J. A. (1984). Psychoanalysis. In R. J. Corsini (Ed.), *Current psychotherapies* (3rd ed.). Itasca, IL: F. E. Peacock.

Arlow, J. A. (1989). Psychoanalysis. In R. J. Corsini & D. Wedding (Eds.), *Current psychotherapies* (4th ed.). Itasca, IL: F. E. Peacock.

Bacal, H. A. (1985). Object relations in the group from the perspective of self-psychology. *International Journal of Group Psychotherapy, 35*(4), 483–501.

Balint, M. (1968). *The basic fault.* London: Tavistock.

Baruch, D. (1964). *One little boy.* New York: Dell (Delta).

Bion, W. R. (1959). *Experience in groups and other papers.* New York: Basic Books.

Blum, H. P. (1986). Psychoanalysis. In I. L. Kutash & A. Wolf (Eds.), *Psychotherapist's casebook.* San Francisco: Jossey-Bass.

*Brabender, V. M. (1987). Vicissitudes of countertransference in inpatient group psychotherapy. *International Journal of Group Psychotherapy, 37*(4), 549–567.

*Brenner, C. (1974). *An elementary textbook of psychoanalysis* (rev. ed.). Garden City, NY: Anchor Press.

Burnside, I. M. (Ed.). (1984). *Working with the elderly: Group processes and techniques* (2nd ed.). Boston: Jones & Bartlett.

*Books and articles marked with an asterisk are suggested for further study.

Colson, D. B. (1985). Transference-countertransference patterns in psychoanalytic group therapy: A family systems view. *International Journal of Group Psychotherapy, 35*(4), 503–517.

*Comas-Diaz, L., & Minrath, M. (1985). Psychotherapy with ethnic minority borderline clients. *Psychotherapy, 22*(25), 418–426.

Corey, G., & Corey, M. S. (1987). *Groups: Process and practice* (3rd ed.). Pacific Grove, CA: Brooks/Cole.

Corey, G., & Corey, M. S. (1990). *I never knew I had a choice* (4th ed.). Pacific Grove, CA: Brooks/Cole.

Day, M. (1981). Process in classical psychodynamic groups. *International Journal of Group Psychotherapy, 31*(2), 153–174.

Debbane, E. G., de Carufel, F. L., Bienvenu, J. P., & Piper, W. E. (1986). Structures in interpretations: A group psychoanalytic perspective. *International Journal of Group Psychotherapy, 36*(4), 517–532.

De La Cancela, V. (1985). Toward a sociocultural psychotherapy for low-income ethnic minorities. *Psychotherapy, 22*(25), 427–435.

*Durkin, H. (1964). *The group in depth.* New York: International Universities Press.

*Erikson, E. H. (1963). *Childhood and society* (2nd ed.). New York: Norton.

Erikson, E. H. (1964). *Insight and responsibility: Lectures on the ethical implications of psychoanalytic insight.* New York: Norton.

Erikson, E. H. (1968). *Identity: Youth and crisis.* New York: Norton.

Erikson, E. H. (1982). *The life cycle completed.* New York: Norton.

Ezriel, H. (1950). A psychoanalytic approach to group treatment. *British Journal of Medical Psychology, 23,* 59–74.

Fairbairn, W. R. D. (1954). *An object-relations theory of the personality.* New York: Basic Books.

Foulkes, S. H. (1965). *Therapeutic group analysis.* New York: International Universities Press.

Foulkes, S. H., & Anthony, E. J. (1965). *Group psychotherapy: The psychoanalytic approach* (2nd ed.). London: Penguin.

Freud, A. (1936). The ego and the mechanisms of defense. In *The writings of Anna Freud: Vol. 2.* New York: International Universities Press.

Freud, A. (1969). Difficulties in the path of psychoanalysis. In *The writings of Anna Freud: Vol. 7* (pp. 124–156). New York: International Universities Press.

*Freud, S. (1949). *An outline of psychoanalysis.* New York: Norton.

*Freud, S. (1955). *The interpretation of dreams.* New York: Basic Books.

*Glatzer, H. T. (1978). The working alliance in analytic group psychotherapy. *International Journal of Group Psychotherapy, 28*(2), 147–161.

Goldman, G. D., & Milman, D. S. (1978). *Psychoanalytic psychotherapy.* Reading, MA: Addison-Wesley.

Grotjahn, M. (1984). The narcissistic person in analytic group therapy. *International Journal of Group Psychotherapy, 34*(2), 243–256.

Guntrip, H. (1969). *Schizoid phenomena, object-relations and the self.* New York: International Universities Press.

*Hall, C. S. (1954). *A primer of Freudian psychology.* New York: New American Library.

*Hamachek, D. F. (1988). Evaluating self-concept and ego development within Erikson's psychosocial framework: A formulation. *Journal of Counseling and Development, 66*(8), 354–360.

Hannah, S. (1984). Countertransference in in-patient group psychotherapy: Implications for technique. *International Journal of Group Psychotherapy, 34*(2), 257–272.

Hartmann, H., Kris, F., & Lowenstein, R. M. (1946). Comments on the formation of psychic structure. In *The psychoanalytic study of the child: Vol. 2* (pp. 11–38). New York: International Universities Press.

Hedges, L. E. (1983). *Listening perspectives in psychotherapy.* New York: Aronson.

Kaplan, S. R. (1967). Therapy groups and training groups: Similarities and differences. *International Journal of Group Psychotherapy, 17,* 473–504.

*Kernberg, O. F. (1975). *Borderline conditions and pathological narcissism.* New York: Aronson.

Kernberg, O. F. (1976). *Object-relations theory and clinical psychoanalysis.* New York: Aronson.

Klein, M. (1975). *The psycho-analysis of children.* New York: Dell.

Kohut, H. (1971). *The analysis of the self.* New York: International Universities Press.

Kohut, H. (1977). *The restoration of the self.* New York: International Universities Press.

Kohut, H. (1984). *How does psychoanalysis cure?* Chicago: University of Chicago Press.

*Kolb, G. E. (1983). The dream in psychoanalytic group therapy. *International Journal of Group Psychotherapy, 33*(1), 41–52.

Kretsch, R., Goren, Y., & Wasserman, A. (1987). Change patterns of borderline patients in individual and group therapy. *International Journal of Group Psychotherapy, 37*(1), 95–112.

*Kutash, I. L., & Greenberg, J. C. (1986). Psychoanalytic psychotherapy. In I. L. Kutash & A. Wolf (Eds.), *Psychotherapist's casebook.* San Francisco: Jossey-Bass.

*Kutash, I. L., & Wolf, A. (1983). Recent advances in psychoanalysis in groups. In H. I. Kaplan & B. J. Sadock (Eds.), *Comprehensive group psychotherapy* (2nd ed.). Baltimore: Williams & Wilkins.

Locke, N. (1961). *Group psychoanalysis: Theory and technique.* New York: University Press.

Mahler, M. S. (1968). *On human symbiosis and the vicissitudes of individuation.* New York: International Universities Press.

Mahler, M. S. (1971). A study of the separation and individuation process. In *The psychoanalytic study of the child: Vol. 26* (pp. 403–422). New York: Quadrangle.

Mullan, H., & Rosenbaum, M. (1978). *Group psychotherapy: Theory and practice* (2nd ed.). New York: Free Press.

Nadelson, C. C. (1978). Marital therapy from a psychoanalytic perspective. In T. J. Paulino & B. S. McCrady (Eds.), *Marriage and marital therapy: Psychoanalytic, behavioral and systems theory perspectives.* New York: Brunner/Mazel.

Ormont, L. R. (1988). The leader's role in resolving resistances to intimacy in the group setting. *International Journal of Group Psychotherapy, 38*(1), 29–46.

Pines, M. (1981). The frame of reference of group psychotherapy. *International Journal of Group Psychotherapy, 31,* 275–285.

Pines, M. (1983). Psychoanalysis and group analysis. *International Journal of Group Psychotherapy, 33*(2), 155–170.

Poey, K. (1985). Guidelines for the practice of brief, dynamic group therapy. *International Journal of Group Psychotherapy, 35*(3), 331–354.

Rutan, J. F. L. S., Alson, A., & Molin, R. (1984). Handling the absence of group leaders: To meet or not to meet. *International Journal of Group Psychotherapy, 34*(2), 257–287.

*St. Clair, M. (1986). *Object relations and self psychology: An introduction.* Pacific Grove, CA: Brooks/Cole.

*Saravay, S. M. (1978). A psychoanalytic theory of group development. *International Journal of Group Psychotherapy, 28*(4), 481–507.

Scheidlinger, S. (1987). On interpretation in group psychotherapy: The need for refinement. *International Journal of Group Psychotherapy, 37*(3), 339–352.

Shaffer, J., & Galinsky, M. D. (1989). *Models of group therapy* (2nd ed.). Englewood Cliffs, NJ: Prentice-Hall.

Spitz, R. (1957). *No and yes: On the genesis of human communication.* New York: International Universities Press.

Spitz, R. (1965). *The first year of life.* New York: International Universities Press.

Tuttman, S. (1986). Theoretical and technical elements which characterize the American approaches to psychoanalytic group psychotherapy. *International Journal of Group Psychotherapy, 36*(4), 499–515.

Whitaker, D. S., & Lieberman, M. A. (1964). *Psychotherapy through the group process.* New York: Atherton.

Winnicott, D. W. (1957). *Collected papers.* New York: Basic Books.

Winnicott, D. W. (1965). *The maturational process and the facilitating environment.* New York: International Universities Press.

*Wolf, A. (1963). The psychoanalysis of groups. In M. Rosenbaum & M. Berger (Eds.), *Group psychotherapy and group function.* New York: Basic Books.

Wolf, A. (1975). Psychoanalysis in groups. In G. M. Gazda (Ed.), *Basic approaches to group psychotherapy and group counseling* (2nd ed.). Springfield, IL: Charles C Thomas.

*Wolf, A. (1983). Psychoanalysis in groups. In H. I. Kaplan & B. J. Sadock (Eds.), *Comprehensive group psychotherapy* (2nd ed.). Baltimore: Williams & Wilkins.

Wolf, A., & Kutash, I. L. (1985). Di-egophrenia and its treatment through psychoanalysis in groups. *International Journal of Group Psychotherapy, 35*(4), 519–530.

*Wolf, A., & Kutash, I. L. (1986). Psychoanalysis in groups. In I. L. Kutash & A. Wolf (Eds.), *Psychotherapist's casebook* (pp. 332–352). San Francisco: Jossey-Bass.

*Wolf, A., & Schwartz, E. K. (1962). *Psychoanalysis in groups.* New York: Grune & Stratton.

*Wolf, A., Schwartz, E. K., McCarty, G. J., & Goldberg, I. A. (1970). *Beyond the couch: Dialogues in teaching and learning psychoanalysis in groups.* New York: Science House.

*Wolf, A., Schwartz, E. K., McCarty, G. J., & Goldberg, I. A. (1972). Psychoanalysis in groups: Contrasts with other group therapies. In C. J. Sager & H. S. Kaplan (Eds.), *Progress in group and family therapy.* New York: Brunner/Mazel.

Wong, N. (1983). Fundamental psychoanalytic concepts: Past and present understanding of their applicability to group psychotherapy. *International Journal of Group Psychotherapy, 33*(2), 171–191.

*Yalom, I. D. (1983). *Inpatient group psychotherapy.* New York: Basic Books.

*Yalom, I. D. (1985). *The theory and practice of group psychotherapy* (3rd ed.). New York: Basic Books.

Adlerian
Group Counseling

Introduction

While Sigmund Freud was developing his system of psychoanalysis, a number of other psychiatrists also interested in the psychoanalytic approach were independently studying the human personality. Two of these were Alfred Adler and Carl Jung. These three thinkers attempted to collaborate, but it became evident that Freud's basic concepts of sexuality and biological determinism were unacceptable to Adler and Jung. Whereas Freud believed that sexual repression caused neurotic disorders, Adler contended that the basic problem pertained to the struggle of individuals to become all that they might become. Adler emphasized a psychology of growth, rather than a psychology of the abnormal personality. After about nine years of association, the three parted company, with Freud taking the position that the others had deserted him.

Later, a number of psychoanalysts deviated from Freud's position. Some of them, notably Karen Horney, Harry Stack Sullivan, and Erich Fromm, essentially followed Adler's concepts; their system, like Adler's, was strongly social in nature in contrast to Freud's biological (instinctual) emphasis. Even though the positions of Sullivan, Horney, and Fromm are usually called neo-analytic, it would be more logical, as Heinz Ansbacher has suggested, to call them neo-Adlerian, since they moved away from Freud's deterministic point of view and toward Adler's sociopsychological view of human nature.

Another major difference between Freud and Adler involves the populations with which they worked. Freud focused on the individual psychodynamics of a neurotic population, and Freudian psychoanalysis was largely confined to more affluent clients. By contrast, Adler was a politically and socially oriented psychiatrist who showed a great deal of concern for the common person; part of his mission was to bring psychotherapy to the working class and to translate psychological concepts into practical methods for helping a varied population meet the challenges of life.

Because of Adler's basic assumption of the all-important social nature of human beings, he was interested in working with clients in a group context. He combined his social interests and his concern with the personality by becoming an educator and establishing family-education and child-guidance clinics. He devoted much time to lecturing on and demonstrating to both parents and professional groups the application of his principles to treating children. He pioneered live demonstrations by interviewing children, adults, teachers, and parents in front of a group.

To fully appreciate the development of the practice of Adlerian psychology, one must recognize the contributions of Rudolf Dreikurs, who was largely responsible for transplanting Adler's ideas to the United States. It was Dreikurs who developed and refined Adler's concepts into a clear-cut, teachable system with practical applications for family life, education, preventive mental health, and, especially, group psychotherapy (Terner & Pew, 1978). Dreikurs was a key figure in developing the Adlerian child-guidance clinics in the United States. Work with children and their parents in a group setting paved the way for Dreikurs's pioneering group psychotherapy. He introduced groups into his busy psychiatry practice in 1928 as a time-saving measure, yet he soon found that they were a more effective way of reaching people than individual therapy. He was perhaps the first to employ group therapy as a way of facilitating insights into each participant's life-style (Terner & Pew, 1978).

Adler's contributions to counseling, especially group counseling, are discussed in this separate chapter because of the far-reaching implications of his work and because of the renewed interest in Adlerian theory and practice. This resurgence of interest is attested to by the increasing number of national and international institutes and societies that offer training in Adlerian techniques, including Adlerian group counseling. Dinkmeyer, Dinkmeyer, and Sperry (1987) discuss the applications of Adlerian principles to group work with a wide population: very young children, older children, adolescents, college students, and adults. They also describe Adlerian group counseling for teachers, parent- and family-education groups, family-therapy groups, and marriage counseling.

Key Concepts

Overview of the Adlerian View of the Person

Adler's system emphasizes the social determinants, rather than the biological aspects, of behavior, its goal directedness, and its purposeful nature.

This "socioteleological" approach implies that people are primarily motivated by social forces and are striving to achieve certain goals. Paramount is the striving for significance, "a movement toward the fulfillment of the goal to achieve unique identity and to belong" (Dinkmeyer et al., 1987, p. 16). The search for significance is related to our basic feelings of inferiority with regard to others, which motivate us to strive for mastery, superiority, power, and, ultimately, perfection. Inferiority feelings can thus be the wellspring of creativity; perfection, not pleasure, is the goal of life.

Freud's historical/causal approach sees behavior as governed by forces within us that are beyond our control. Adler's system, instead, stresses self-determination and consciousness (rather than the unconscious) as the center of personality. We are not the victims of fate but creative, active, choice-making beings whose every action has purpose and meaning. Movement toward goals and our anticipation of the future are far more important than what has happened to us in the past. Behavior can be understood only if one takes a holistic approach and looks at all actions from the perspective of the individual's chosen style of life. Each of us has a unique lifestyle, or personality, which starts to develop in early childhood to compensate for and overcome some perceived inferiority. Our lifestyle influences our experience of life and interactions with others. It consists of our views about ourselves and the world and of the distinctive behaviors we use to pursue our goals.

Because of its stress on responsibility, on the striving for superiority, and on the search for value and meaning in life, Adler's approach is basically a growth model. The striving for superiority is best conceived of as a "moving from a perceived minus to a perceived plus" (Ansbacher & Ansbacher, 1956). Adlerians reject the idea that some individuals are psychologically "sick" and in need of a "cure." Instead, they view their work as teaching people better ways to meet the challenges of life tasks, providing direction, helping people change their mistaken notions, and offering encouragement to those who are discouraged.

Holism

The Adlerian approach, also known as *individual psychology,* is based on a holistic view of the person. (The word *individual* does not imply a focus on the individual client as opposed to people in groups.) In individual psychology, holism refers to viewing the person as a unified whole. Holism also refers to the unity of personality, which occurs after an individual has selected a life goal (Ansbacher & Ansbacher, 1956, p. 189). Individuals are always more than the sum of their parts. Thoughts, feelings, beliefs, convictions, attitudes, and actions are all expressions of the uniqueness of the person. One implication of this view is that the client is seen as an integral part of a social system. There is more focus on *inter*personal factors than on *intra*personal ones. The therapist is oriented toward understanding the client's social situation and the attitudes he or she has about it. Viewing people in relationship to social systems is basic to group and family therapy.

Creativity and Choice

From the Adlerian perspective humans are not merely determined by heredity and environment. Instead, they have the capacity to influence and create events. Adler believed that *what* we are born with is not as crucial as the *use* we make of our natural endowment. Adlerians do recognize the fact that biological and environmental conditions limit our capacity to choose and to create. Although they reject the deterministic stance of Freud, they do not go to the other extreme by maintaining that individuals can become whatever they want. The Adlerian position is one of "soft determinism," which holds that humans are, in fact, limited by heredity and environment. As Corsini (1987) notes, however, Adlerians stress the creativity of the individual in moving beyond the limits set by biology and by society. The Adlerian position is that within the framework of limitations we have a wide range of choices open to us.

From the Adlerian viewpoint healthy people strive to become the master of their fate. Adlerians base their practice on the assumption that people are creative, active, and self-determining. They have little sympathy with perspectives that cast a client in the role of a passive victim. As an illustration of the implications of this view, consider the confrontive quality of Dreikurs's (1967) typical remark to a man who complained about his wife's behavior and who tried to play a helpless role: "And what did you do?" Dreikurs developed a style of challenging clients to become aware of the ways in which they were active participants in situations that they perceived as problematic. His therapy was aimed at showing clients that, although they could not directly change the behavior of others, they did have power to change their own reactions and attitudes toward others.

Phenomenology

Adler was perhaps the first major theorist to stress a phenomenological orientation toward therapy. His psychology is phenomenological in that it pays attention to the subjective fashion through which people perceive their world. This subjective reality includes the individual's views, beliefs, perceptions, and conclusions. People give their experiences meaning. Furthermore, each individual writes the script, produces it, directs it, and acts out the roles. Humans are creative beings who decide on their actions based on their subjective perceptions (Sherman & Dinkmeyer, 1987, p. 8).

As you will see in chapters that follow, many contemporary theories have incorporated this notion of the client's subjective perception of reality, or personal world view, as a basic factor explaining behavior. Some of the other group approaches that have a phenomenological perspective are psychodrama, existential therapy, person-centered therapy, Gestalt therapy, the cognitive therapies, and reality therapy.

Teleology

According to Adler, all forms of life are characterized by a trend toward growth and expansion. Adler replaces deterministic explanations with a teleological explanation: humans live by goals and purposes, they are moved by the anticipation of the future, and they create meaning.

Individual psychology contends that we can be understood best by looking at where we are going and what we are striving to accomplish (Corsini, 1987). Thus, in contrast to the Freudian psychoanalytic emphasis on the past, Adlerians are interested in the future without playing down the importance of past influences. The three aspects of time are dynamically interrelated. Our decisions are based on what we have experienced in the past, on our present situation, and on what we are moving toward in our lives. In short, Adlerians look for a continuity, or pattern, in a client's life, but always with the emphasis on the goal-directed nature of all behavior.

Social Interest

According to Manaster and Corsini (1982), social interest, known as *Gemeinschaftsgefühl*, is possibly the single most distinctive and valuable concept in individual psychology. The term *social interest* refers to an individual's attitudes in dealing with other people in the world, and it includes striving for a better future for humanity. Adler equates social interest with a sense of identification and empathy with others. Quoting a phrase from an unidentified English author, he says that social interest means "to see with the eyes of another, to hear with the ears of another, to feel with the heart of another" (Ansbacher & Ansbacher, 1956, p. 135).

Individual psychology rests on a central belief that our happiness and success are largely related to a social connectedness. As social beings we have a need to be of use to others and to establish meaningful relationships in a community. Since we are embedded in a society, we cannot be understood in isolation from the social context. We are primarily motivated by a desire to belong. Only within the group can we actualize our potentialities.

Adler (1964) writes that we have strong needs to feel united with others and that only when this is the case will we be able to act with courage in facing and dealing with life's problems. He contends that we must successfully master three main tasks: our relationships with friends, our work, and our family (including love). Dreikurs and Mosak (1966, 1967) discuss two additional life tasks: the self-task (getting along with ourselves) and the spiritual task. Adler maintains that the degree to which we successfully share with others and are concerned with the welfare of others is an index of our overall personality and level of maturity. In other words, social interest is the measure of mental health, insofar as it is reflected in our capacity to give and receive and in our willingness to cooperate for the common benefit of others (Sherman & Dinkmeyer, 1987, p. 12).

This key concept of social interest has significant implications for group counseling: the general goals of the group are to increase self-esteem and to develop social interest. The group focuses on discovering the members' mistaken assumptions that are keeping them from feeling adequate and from being interested in others. Dinkmeyer (1975) uses a procedure in which group members introduce themselves by addressing Adler's original three life tasks. The members present how they function (1) socially with friends and acquaintances—how they get along with others and what sense of belonging and acceptance they experience; (2) in work, including their degree of involvement, the meaning they derive from work, and what they are able to do for others through their work; and (3) with their family and others they love. Are they able to receive love and give it to others? How comfortable are they with their sexual identification? What is the quality of intimacy in their lives?

From what has been said about social interest, it is clear that humans have a strong need to belong and to find a significant place in society. Manaster and Corsini (1982) contend that the absence of this feeling of belonging and of being wanted is one of the most devastating of all emotions: "Individual Psychology asserts that humans not only need other humans, but they also need to be needed, to have a feeling of belonging" (p. 47). "Adlerians generally equate social interest and mental health. Persons without social interest cannot be healthy, whereas persons with social interest may be healthy" (p. 50).

This concept is applied to group counseling by structuring the group so that members can meet some of their needs for affiliation with others. Alienation, which is the opposite of social interest, is seen as a major problem of contemporary society. It is hoped that one of the outcomes of a group experience will be that members grow to increasingly accept themselves, even though they are imperfect. Out of their greater ability to accept themselves, they will be more capable of establishing meaningful relations with others and of being productive members of society.

Inferiority/Superiority

In his earlier writings Adler speaks about feelings of inferiority, which are typically associated with children's early recognition of their dependent position vis-à-vis adults and nature. From the very beginning our recognition of helplessness is characterized by feelings of inferiority. Adler does not view this inferiority as a negative force. On the contrary, out of our basic inferiority comes the motivation to master our environment. We attempt to compensate for feelings of inferiority by finding ways in which to control the forces in our lives, as opposed to being controlled by them. As Bitter (1987) has noted, when inferiority feelings become so exaggerated that they constrict our movement and our sense of self-worth, they become an inferiority complex. Such a complex can be a reaction to perceived negative influence or can result from mistaken notions and faulty interpretations.

Our goal striving involves moving from a feeling of inferiority to one of superiority. According to Ansbacher (1974), inferiority feelings and compensation lost their primary importance for Adler over the years. In his later writings Adler speaks more of the goal of success and the urge toward perfection and self-mastery, or becoming what we are able to become.

Role of the Family

Adlerians place a great deal of emphasis on family processes, which play a significant role in the development of the personality during childhood. The climate of relationships among family members is known as the *family atmosphere*. The term *family constellation* describes the psychological and social configuration of the family group. It is the system of relationships in which self-awareness develops. This system includes and is maintained by oneself, by one's parents and siblings, and by any others living in the household (Powers & Griffith, 1987).

Dreikurs takes the position that sibling relationships are more influential in personality development than relationships between the child and the parents. In addition, children incorporate many of the personal characteristics of their parents, and they learn a great deal about life by observing and interacting with their parents (Sherman & Dinkmeyer, 1987).

According to Adlerians, the meaning that people give to their own position in the family constellation and the positions of their siblings is more important than the actual chronological ages of the siblings. The personality characteristics of each person in the family, the emotional bonds between family members, the size of the family, and the sex of the siblings are all factors in the family constellation. The child's position and role in the family influence later personality development (Powers & Griffith, 1987).

Powers and Griffith (1987) write that the family members rehearse a way of relating to others that will become a vital part of their style of life. They add that the family is not an encapsulated system apart from the community. Once material is gathered about the client's family constellation, a summary is drawn up so that interpretations can be made. The summary contains the person's strengths and weaknesses, and it is used in helping clients gain a fuller understanding of the influence their family still has on them. In developing a summary of the client's family constellation, it is important to consider factors such as the person's extended family, role models outside the family, and experiences in the neighborhood and school. It is also important to take into account the ethnic, religious, social, and economic milieu reported by the client.

Specifically, Powers and Griffith mention the following as crucial topics to include in the summary of the family constellation: birth order, family atmosphere, family values, masculine guiding line (the characteristics, attitudes, interests, and competencies ascribed to the father, and not shared by the mother), feminine guiding line (the characteristics, attitudes, interests, and competencies ascribed to the mother, and not shared by the father), the role of the client in the family, the role of the siblings in the family, role models and alliances, the experience of neighborhood and school in childhood and adolescence, the experience of the sexual challenge in adolescence, and major unresolved issues remaining from childhood and adolescence. These factors serve to reinforce one's self-perception and one's view of the world, rather than to formulate them.

Lifestyle

Lifestyle refers to an individual's basic orientation to life and the themes that characterize the person's existence. It is influenced first by one's family constellation and family atmosphere. The formative experiences within the family, particularly among siblings, contribute to establishing a set of guidelines for understanding life that eventually make up the lifestyle (Sherman & Dinkmeyer, 1987). Adler sees us as actor, creator, and artist of our life. In striving for goals that are meaningful to us, we develop a unique style of life (Ansbacher, 1974). This concept helps explain how all our behavior fits together so that there is some consistency to our actions. Everything we do is related to the final goal of our life.

No two persons develop exactly the same style. In striving for the goal of superiority, some people develop their intellect, others develop their physical being, and so on. Our style of life is learned primarily during the first 5 years of life. Adler believes, along with Freud, that our earliest impressions lay the foundation of our lifestyle. But he stresses that these childhood experiences in themselves are not crucial; rather, it is our *interpretation* of these events that is significant. Adler emphasizes that our interpretations of early influences may lead to the developing of a faulty lifestyle. Although we are not determined by our past, we are significantly influenced by our perceptions and interpretations of these past events. But we are not doomed to remain the victims of unfortunate experiences. Once we become aware of the patterns and continuity of our life, especially of certain mistaken notions that we have developed, we are then in a position to modify those faulty assumptions and thus make basic changes. We can use childhood experiences to *consciously* create our own lifestyle.

Behavioral Disorders

Adler sees emotional disorders as "failures in life." Psychological and behavioral disorders can be considered erroneous ways of living, or mistaken assumptions. They can include a faulty lifestyle, a mistaken goal of success, and an underdeveloped social interest. Since Adlerians maintain that clients do not suffer from a disease but from discouragement and a failure to solve the problems and tasks set by life, therapy is based on an educational model, not a medical model. Applied to group counseling, this emphasis means that much of what goes on in a group is a process of encouraging clients and teaching them a better approach so that they can succeed.

Application of Adlerian Principles to Group Work

Adler and his co-workers used a group approach in their child-guidance centers in Vienna as early as 1921 (Dreikurs, 1969). As noted earlier, Dreikurs extended and popularized Adler's work, especially with regard to group applications, and used group psychotherapy in his private practice for over 40 years. His rationale for groups is the following: "Since man's problems and conflicts are recognized in their social nature, the group is ideally suited not only to highlight and reveal the nature of a person's conflicts and maladjustments but to offer corrective influences" (1969, p. 43). Inferiority feelings can be challenged and counteracted effectively in groups, and the mistaken concepts and values that are at the root of social and emotional problems can be deeply influenced by the group, since it is a value-forming agent.

The group provides the social context in which members can develop a sense of belonging and a sense of community. Dinkmeyer (1975) writes that group participants come to see that many of their problems are interpersonal in nature, that their behavior has social meaning, and that their goals can best be understood in the framework of social purposes. Some of the specific therapeutic factors that Dinkmeyer finds operating in Adlerian groups are these:

- The group provides a mirror of the person's behavior.
- Members benefit from feedback from other members and the leaders.
- Members both receive help from others and give help.
- The group provides opportunities for testing reality and for trying new behavior.
- The group context encourages members to take action to change their life.
- Transactions in the group help members understand how they function at work and at home and also reveal how they seek to find their place in society.
- The group is structured in such a way that members can meet their need for belonging.

According to Dinkmeyer and his colleagues (1987), Adlerian counseling has four major objectives, which correspond to four phases of the therapeutic process:

1. establishing an empathic relationship
2. understanding beliefs, feelings, motives, and goals
3. developing insight into mistaken goals and self-defeating behaviors
4. seeing alternatives and making new choices

Phases of the Adlerian Group

Like the psychoanalytic approach to groups, Adlerian group counseling involves the investigation and interpretation of one's early past. As the following discussion indicates, however, there are some fundamental differences between Adlerians and Freudians.

In writing about the characteristics of the Adlerian approach to group work, Dreikurs (1969) and Sonstegard, Dreikurs, and Bitter (1982) outline four phases of group counseling, which correspond to the four goals of counseling just listed and which overlap to some extent:

1. establishing and maintaining the proper therapeutic relationship
2. exploring the dynamics operating in the individual (assessment)
3. communicating to the individual an understanding of self (insight)
4. seeing new alternatives and making new choices (reorientation)

Phase 1: Establishing and Maintaining the Relationship

In the initial phase the emphasis is on establishing a good therapeutic relationship based on cooperation and mutual respect. Group participants are encouraged to be active in the process, for they are responsible for their own participation in the group. It is not always easy to create an active atmosphere, because even those clients who are most eager to make progress may be unwilling to do the work required for effective group participation and may be determined to prove that they are helpless (Dreikurs, 1969). Dreikurs sees the group as conducive to a good client/counselor relationship. In the group situation there is ample opportunity to work on trust issues and to strengthen the relationship between member and leader. Also, by witnessing positive changes in peers, participants can see how well the group works.

The Adlerian therapeutic relationship is one between equals. A democratic atmosphere prevails, and the effective group-counseling relationship is based on mutual respect. This does not imply that members do anything they please, however, for firmness in a spirit of kindness is necessary in all group counseling (Sonstegard et al., 1982). Sonstegard and his colleagues point out that winning the client's cooperation is essential for effective group counseling. Therapist and client work together toward mutually agreed-on goals. A contract may be a part of this shared therapeutic venture. In groups, the contract indicates what clients want and expect from the group and specifies the responsibilities of the leader and participants. Adlerians believe that counseling, individual or group, progresses only when the therapeutic process focuses on what *clients* see as personally significant and on areas that *they* want to explore and change. This is what Dreikurs (1967) says of the collaborative nature of the Adlerian therapeutic relationship and of the necessity for aligning the client's and the therapist's goals:

> Therapeutic cooperation requires an alignment of goals. When the goals and interests of the patient and therapist clash, no satisfactory relationship can be established. Winning the patient's cooperation for the common task is a prerequisite for any therapy; maintaining it requires constant vigilance. What appears as "resistance" constitutes a discrepancy between the goals of the therapist and those of the patient [p. 65].

Phase 2: Analysis and Assessment—Exploring the Individual's Dynamics

The aim of the second phase is twofold: understanding one's lifestyle and seeing how it is affecting one's current functioning in all the tasks of life (H. Mosak, 1989). The leader may begin by exploring how the participants are functioning at work and in social situations and how they feel about themselves and their sex-role identities.

According to Dreikurs (1969), the individual's goals and current lifestyle become much more obvious in interactions with others in the group. Also, clients may respond differently when they are confronted by fellow participants than when they are confronted by the counselor alone.

Adlerian group counselors use a number of assessment techniques. Process assessments of the members' family constellation, relationship difficulties, early recollections, dreams, and art work produce clues to each person's life goal and lifestyle (Sonstegard et al., 1982). Analysis and assessment rely heavily on the exploration of the client's family constellation, which includes evaluating the conditions that prevailed in the family when the person was a young child in the process of forming lifestyle convictions and basic assumptions. Dinkmeyer and his associates (1987) describe a family-constellation questionnaire that provides insight into clients' self-perception, sibling relationships, significant forces in their life, and key decisions they have made.

Another assessment procedure is asking clients to report their early recollections along with the feelings and thoughts that accompanied these childhood incidents. These early recollections are more than a report; they reveal beliefs, "basic mistakes," self-defeating perceptions, and unique laws of psychological movement (Dinkmeyer et al., 1987). Adlerians contend that people remember only those past events that are consistent with their current views of themselves (Adler, 1958). Dreikurs (1969) adds that, once people develop such views, they perceive only that which fits their views. This self-perception strengthens the person's "private logic," which in turn helps the individual maintain his or her basic convictions. Early recollections provide an understanding of how we view and feel about ourselves, how we see the world, what our life goals are, what motivates us, what we believe in, and what we value.

The lifestyle investigation, which includes exploration of one's family background and life story, reveals a pattern of *basic mistakes*. H. Mosak (1989) writes that the lifestyle can be conceived of as a personal mythology; people behave as if the myths were true, because, for them, they are true. Mosak lists five basic mistakes: (1) overgeneralizations, (2) impossible goals, (3) misperceptions of life and its demands, (4) denial of one's basic worth, and (5) faulty values.

During the assessment phase the counselor's main task is to integrate and summarize data from the lifestyle investigation and to interpret how the mistaken notions and personal mythology are influencing the client. This is done in a clear and concise way so that clients can recognize their own dynamics and pinpoint their assets. The analysis of the lifestyle is an ongoing process and helps client and counselor develop a plan for counseling. According to Dreikurs (1969), analysis of the lifestyle and of its psychodynamic forces can be carried out in both individual and group settings, but the group format offers certain definite advantages:

> The patient's goals and movements become much more obvious in the interaction with his fellow group members than in the limited interaction between him and the therapist. Furthermore, the therapist no longer depends entirely on the verbal reports by the patient about his interaction with others outside of the therapeutic session; he sees him in action during the session. Not infrequently, the patient appears in a quite different light

when confronted by other members of the group, than when he is alone with the therapist. Certain facades of his personality may become more pronounced, or visible [pp. 44–45].

Phase 3: Insight

Whereas the classical analytic position is that personality cannot change unless there is insight, the Adlerian view is that insight is only a step toward change and not a necessary prerequisite for it (Dreikurs, 1969). Insight, then, is not an end in itself, but a means to an end. People can make abrupt and significant changes without much insight. Mosak (1989) defines insight as "understanding translated into constructive action." He contends that the Freudian notion that insight must precede behavioral change frequently results in extended treatment and encourages clients to postpone taking action to change. Mere intellectual insight can lead to the endless "Yes, but" game of "I know I should stop, but . . ."

According to Sonstegard and his colleagues (1982), groups are more effective than individual counseling in helping people gain insight and redirect their mistaken goals and mistaken notions. These authors write that the interaction within a group provides an ideal setting for learning about oneself. Furthermore, the sense of social connectedness that develops in groups enables members to see parts of themselves in others. The writers contend that the personal disclosures and interpretations during the group sessions are of value both for the person to whom they are directed and for the others in the group, who learn from these disclosures. One of the advantages of a group is that the insights and statements of other members often carry more weight than observations and interpretations provided by the leader.

In a group context the insight phase is concerned with helping participants understand *why* they are functioning as they are. Members learn about themselves by exploring their own goals, personal mythology, and lifestyle. Dreikurs (1969) contends that it is during this and the next phase that clients receive the greatest benefit from a group. The group facilitates the process of gaining insight, because as members experience resistance in themselves, they can also observe resistance in other members. There is enough similarity in basic mistaken attitudes and faulty motivations among all participants to allow the members to observe themselves in others and to help one another.

Interpretation is a technique that facilitates the process of gaining insight into one's lifestyle. Interpretation deals with the reasons why members are behaving the way they are in the here and now. By offering an outside frame of reference, the counselor helps participants see their behaviors from a different perspective and thus gain access to a wider range of alternatives (Dinkmeyer et al., 1987). Interpretations are never forced on the client; they are presented tentatively in the form of hypotheses: "Could it be . . . ?" "I have a hunch that I'd like to share with you . . ." "It seems to me that . . ." Therefore, interpretations are open-ended sharings that can be explored in group sessions. The ultimate goal of this process is that clients will come to understand their own role in creating a problem, the ways in which they are maintaining the problem, and what *they* can do to improve the situation.

Phase 4: Reorientation

The end product of the group process is reorientation. The reorientation phase involves considering alternative attitudes, beliefs, goals, and behaviors. Members are helped to redirect their mistaken goals and mistaken notions. One of the aims is teaching participants how to become more effective in dealing with the tasks of life. Another aim is challenging and encouraging clients to take risks and make changes.

Dreikurs (1969) believes that groups are especially useful during the reorientation phase, because they stimulate action and new orientations. The group becomes an agent in bringing about change because of the improved interpersonal relationships among members. The group process allows members to see themselves as others do and to recognize faulty self-concepts or mistaken goals that they are pursuing (Sonstegard et al., 1982).

Encouragement is a basic aspect of this phase. Through encouragement, clients begin to experience their own inner resources and the power to choose for themselves and direct their own lives. The encouragement so necessary at this stage is found in the support of the group and in its equalitarian nature, which removes social distance and reduces the risk of self-disclosure. In Dreikurs's words, "It is this social atmosphere of equality which characterizes a therapy group and which exerts one of the most effective therapeutic influences on each one of its members" (1969, p. 47).

Reorientation is the action phase of a group, during which new decisions are made and goals are modified. To challenge self-limiting assumptions, members are encouraged to act *as if* they were the persons they wanted to be. They are asked to "catch themselves" in the process of repeating old patterns that have led to ineffective behavior. Commitment is an essential ingredient of the reorientation phase; if clients hope to change, they must be willing to set tasks for themselves and do something specific about their problems. Commitment is also needed to translate new insights into concrete action.

Role and Functions of the Adlerian Counselor

The concept of the anonymous counselor is not part of the Adlerian view. An anonymous counselor would increase the distance from the client and interfere with the equalitarian, person-to-person relationship basic to the Adlerian approach. As Mosak (1989) writes, the Adlerian counselor has feelings and opinions and is free to express them.

Other Adlerian writers stress the active role of the counselor as a participant in a collaborative therapeutic effort. Dinkmeyer and his colleagues (1987) view the role of the group leader as establishing and maintaining the group process. They write that the members expect the leader to assume responsibility for the group's movement: "The leader must participate actively in the development of norms that facilitate growth and interpersonal learning. He intentionally establishes a structure for the group and indicates guidelines for behavior, such as congruence, open interaction, involvement, nonjudgmental acceptance, confrontation, and commitment" (p. 198). The leader assumes the functions of a facilitator who both creates and encourages the development of therapeutic conditions, such as universality, support, opportunities to experiment with new behavior, and feedback. These processes promote interpersonal learning, individual growth, and a sense of group cohesiveness.

Another evidence of the Adlerian counselor's strong role is the commitment to active procedures such as confrontation, self-disclosure, interpretation, and analysis of prevailing patterns. The counselor challenges the clients' beliefs and goals and helps them translate what they have learned in the group process into new beliefs and behaviors. Dinkmeyer and his associates (1987) point out that counselors serve as models for their clients, who often learn more from what counselors do, in the group as well as in their personal lives, than from what they say. This implies that counselors need to have a clear sense of their own identity, beliefs, and feelings. They must also be aware of the basic conditions that are essential for the growth of clients: empathy, respect, care, genuineness, openness, sincerity, positive regard, understanding of the dynamics of behavior, and the ability to use action-oriented techniques that stimulate changes in clients.

Adlerian Family Counseling

Adlerians have a long history of working with families and studying family dynamics. Adler presented demonstrations with family groups in the child-guidance clinics of Vienna. The Adlerian approach is unique in giving special attention to the relationships between siblings and the position a person occupies in his or her family. Additionally, because Adlerians view most human problems as social in nature, they may give greater importance to the relationships among people than they do to the psychodynamics of the individual, as is usually the case in family counseling.

Goals of Adlerian Family Counseling

The basic goal of this approach is to improve parent/child and other family relationships. Teaching family members how to better deal with one another and how to live together as social equals is part of this goal. Dinkmeyer and his associates (1987) write: "This aim is accomplished by sharing with the family group the principles of democratic conflict resolution, by reorienting the family members away from destructive modes of communication, and, most importantly, by teaching all members of the family to be agents of encouragement" (p. 238).

Responsibility of Family Members in the Counseling Process

One assumption is that family counseling is undertaken voluntarily. Family members are expected to attend a series of sessions and also to become involved in seriously carrying out homework assignments. Parents may be asked to join a study group in which they are given information for improving family life. In this process the family counselor functions as a teacher. Counselors assume the role of helping parents better understand the factors that are contributing to the difficulties at home, and they suggest ways in which to deal with these problems. Ultimately, it is hoped, family members will learn effective strategies for resolving their own conflicts and the problems in their family by showing respect for one another. They learn how to focus on issues that are dividing the family and how to reach new agreements or make compromises, and they actively participate in responsible decision making.

Techniques of Family Counseling

Many of the techniques used in family counseling were pioneered by Adler, although some of them have been discovered independently of his influence. However, most of the techniques practiced in the United States today are the work of Dreikurs. A brief summary of these basic techniques, as described by Lowe (1982), follows.

The *initial interview* begins the process of counseling family groups. Its purpose is to help the counselor assess the child's behavior, evaluate the parents' methods of child rearing, understand the climate in the home, and be able to recommend specific changes in the family situation. This process focuses on encouragement and on the strengths of all family members. It is essential that rapport be established so that productive work can be done. The family constellation is given special attention in this initial interview. Family members may be asked how they spend a typical day. A certain view of life begins to emerge, based on the pattern of interaction among siblings and their position in the family. The parents are also asked how they view their family situation. For example, they are asked to talk about what concerns them about their children. The family counselor also makes an appraisal, but a more objective one, of the goals of the children, the family atmosphere, methods of training, and the strengths of the family members. The interview ends with a series of recommendations for homework for the parents and significant others.

In their description of family group counseling, Sonstegard and his colleagues (1982) mention that they always insist on the participation of all the children in the family. The problems of the children are viewed as an expression of the interpersonal problems within the family.

Role playing and other action-oriented methods are often a part of the sessions. Interpretation is a basic part of Adlerian counseling and continues during all of the sessions. In each family the interpersonal dynamics are exposed and explained to all participants, which forms the basis for creating new relationships. Counseling consists of interpretations and suggestions for handling the problems within the family. The main objective of all these suggestions is to change existing relationships and mistaken notions of the child (Sonstegard et al., 1982). The purpose of interpretation is to provide some insight for family members, but more important than having them merely see and understand what they are doing is encouraging them to translate what they are learning into behavioral terms. In other words, insights that do not result in an action program and behavioral changes are of little real value.

Evaluation of the Adlerian Approach to Groups

My group practice has been influenced by several Adlerian concepts, some of which I have incorporated in my work. Emphasis on the social forces that motivate behavior and the search for mastery, superiority, and power are two of them. Another is an interest in the patterns that people develop out of their relationships with their parents and siblings. Also, the notion that we develop a unique lifestyle as a response to our perceived inferiority is quite intriguing to me.

The Adlerian approach deviates in many ways from the psychoanalytic model. Most Adlerians consider themselves very separate from the Freudians and maintain that much of Adler's work was done independently of Freud. There are, however, some important commonalities between the two approaches, including a focus on critical periods of development, an interest in early recollections, and an emphasis on interpretation. As we have seen, there are also a number of areas of difference.

In my opinion one of the strengths of the Adlerian approach is its integrative nature. It is a holistic approach that encompasses the full spectrum of human experience, and practitioners have a great deal of freedom in working with clients in ways that are uniquely suited to their own therapeutic style. Even though Adlerians accept the same theoretical concepts, they do not have a monolithic view of the therapeutic process. Corsini (1987) writes that although the philosophy and theory are well-established and are held by all Adlerians, the methods of assessment and treatment differ substantially. Some Adlerians are very directive, and others are more nondirective. Some are willing to disclose themselves, and others rarely make personal disclosures to their clients. Adlerians who were trained by Adler tend to ask for one early recollection, whereas those who were trained by Dreikurs might routinely ask for as many as six to ten recollections as a part of the lifestyle interview. Dreikurs asked for the number of early recollections that permitted the forming of a pattern. Adlerian practitioners are not bound to follow a specific procedure, nor are they limited to using certain techniques. There can be almost as many methods as there are Adlerian therapists. The basic criterion is that therapeutic techniques fit the theory and the client. Thus, therapists are encouraged to grow both personally and professionally by being inventive.

Applying the Adlerian Approach in Multicultural Settings

Adlerian theory is well suited to working with culturally diverse clients. Most Adlerian principles are consistent with the values of a number of cultural groups. One Eastern value, for example, pertains to fostering a spirit of interdependence and striving for collective goals, an emphasis that is one of the aims of group counseling. The mechanisms of a group can thus be employed in helping people help themselves in ways that are consistent with their cultural values. Although the Adlerian approach is called individual psychology, the focus is on the person in a social context. As Corsini (1987) notes, Adlerian uses of groups are more varied than those in any other system. Adlerians' interest in helping others, in social interest, in belonging, and in the collective spirit fits well with the group process. Those cultures that stress the group welfare over the individual's welfare and that emphasize the role of the family will find the Adlerian focus on social interest to be congruent with their values.

The Adlerian emphasis on the subjective fashion in which people view and interpret their world leads to a respect for clients' unique values and perceptions. Adlerians do not decide for clients what they should change or what their goals should be; rather, they work cooperatively with their clients in ways that enable them to reach their self-defined goals.

Adlerian practitioners are not wedded to any particular set of techniques. Instead, they are conscious of the value of fitting their techniques to the needs of their clients. Although they utilize a diverse range of techniques, most of them do conduct an assessment of each member's lifestyle. This analysis is heavily focused on the structure and dynamics within the family. Many ethnic clients have been conditioned to respect their family heritage and to appreciate the impact of their family on their own personal development. Thus, these clients are likely to be receptive to an exploration of their lifestyle, since it involves a detailed discussion of their own place within their family.

The Contributions of Adlerian Psychology to Other Approaches

In several important respects, Adler seems to have paved the way for the current developments in the cognitive therapies. Adlerians' basic premise is that if they can change clients' thinking, they can change their behavior and feelings, as explained in the following passage.

In dealing with anyone in therapy our first concern is the intellect: to try to understand the person's thinking. We are not so concerned with the feelings or with the behavior, seeing these other two aspects as dependent on thinking. Consequently, Adlerian psychology is a personality theory. We say, putting it simply, that as one thinks, one feels and acts [Corsini, 1987, p. 23].

One of the strengths of the Adlerian approach is that its concepts have group applications in both clinical and educational settings (Sonstegard et al., 1982). As we have seen, its emphasis on social factors makes it suitable for working with individuals in groups, including parent-education groups, teacher groups, and family counseling.

It is difficult to overestimate the contributions of Adler to contemporary therapeutic practice. His influence went beyond group counseling, extending into the community mental-health movement. According to Ansbacher (1974), the trend toward community mental health, including the use of paraprofessionals, is in line with Adler's early efforts. Abraham Maslow, Viktor Frankl, and Rollo May have acknowledged their debt to Adler. Both Frankl and May see Adler as a forerunner of the existential movement because of his position that human beings are free to choose and are entirely responsible for what they make of themselves. This view makes Adler also a forerunner of the subjective approach to psychology, which focuses on the internal determinants of behavior: values, beliefs, attitudes, goals, interests, personal meanings, subjective perceptions of reality, and strivings toward self-realization. Furthermore, the Adlerian view is congruent with many of the other current psychological schools, such as Gestalt therapy, learning theory, transactional analysis, reality therapy, person-centered therapy, and logotherapy. All these approaches are based on a similar concept of the person as purposive and self-determining and as ever striving for growth, value, and meaning in this world (Terner & Pew, 1978).

The following brief overview lists the areas in which Adler's views are recognizable in the other models to be discussed in this book:

- *Psychodrama:* focus on the here and now, on the universality of human struggles, and on early experiences and family relationships; use of ventilation and spectator therapy
- *Existential approach:* emphasis on the need to face the realities of life, on the importance of finding meaning and purpose in one's existence, on accepting personal responsibility, on seeing alternatives and making new choices, and on striving for mastery and self-actualization; use of confrontation
- *Person-centered approach:* holistic view of behavior, focus on growth, subjective perspective, and view that humans are always in the process of becoming and striving toward goals; stress on the importance of empathy and support, active listening, and acceptance
- *Gestalt:* focus on the here and now, on nonverbal communication, on learning to take risks to live fully, and on dealing with impasses

- *Transactional analysis:* attention to the individual's life plan, focus on reevaluating old decisions and making new and more appropriate ones, equalitarian relationship between client and therapist, and goal alignment; use of therapeutic contracts as a way of providing direction for sessions
- *Behavior therapy:* emphasis on encouragement and positive reinforcement and on concreteness, problem solving, and decision making; use of contracts, analysis, and assessment
- *Rational-emotive therapy:* attention to mistaken attitudes and faulty beliefs and to the need to learn new orientations; clients' confrontation of self-defeating internalized sentences; use of analysis and action methods
- *Reality therapy:* focus on commitment as a prerequisite for change, on responsibility and strengths; use of reorientation and reality testing; similarity between the concept of success and failure identity in reality therapy and the concept of encouragement and discouragement in the Adlerian model

As you proceed with your study of the other therapeutic models, I encourage you to continue to pay attention to the similarities and differences among these approaches. Such a comparative perspective will deepen your understanding of the group process, help you formulate your own approach to group work, and increase the number of practical applications that these systems offer to your work as a group leader.

Questions for Reflection and Discussion

1. What are your thoughts about Adler's idea that inferiority can actually be the basis for success? Can you relate the striving for superiority to your own life?
2. Adler talks about the family constellation and birth order as important factors in shaping one's personality. What implications do these concepts have for group counseling? How can a group replicate a family? How do these ideas relate to your own life?
3. Social interest is a key Adlerian concept. How can a group increase social interest, and how is the group an appropriate form of intervention in the light of Adlerian principles?
4. What major contrasts do you see between Freud and Adler? Do you see a basis for integrating some psychoanalytic concepts with Adlerian ones?
5. How might you work with the concept of style of life in a group setting?
6. What is your evaluation of Adler's view that we can be understood only by looking at our goals and our future strivings? Again, how might you integrate this idea into actual practice in a group?

7. Adlerians see group counseling as a form of teaching and learning, and because of this they make use of advice and information. What possible advantages and disadvantages do you see in this focus?
8. What are some key Adlerian principles that you could use to understand your own life better?
9. What are your reactions to the four phases of the Adlerian group? How could they apply to groups you might want to lead?
10. For what kind of clients do you think Adlerian groups would be best suited? Do you think they would be appropriate for all populations? Explain.

Where to Go from Here

If you find that your thinking is allied with the Adlerian approach, you might consider seeking training in individual psychology or becoming a member of the North American Society of Adlerian Psychology. To obtain current information on the society, contact

Neva Hefner, Executive Director
North American Society of Adlerian Psychology
202 S. State Street, Suite 1212
Chicago, IL 60604-1905
Phone: (312) 939-0834

NASAP publishes a newsletter and maintains a list of current institutes, training programs, and workshops in Adlerian psychology. The quarterly *Individual Psychology: The Journal of Adlerian Theory, Research, and Practice* can be obtained by contacting

Guy J. Manaster and Jon Carlson, Editors
Individual Psychology
Department of Educational Psychology
University of Texas
Austin, TX 78712

Recommended Supplementary Readings

Individual Psychology: The Journal of Adlerian Theory, Research, and Practice features current developments dealing with aspects of the social, psychological, and personality theory founded by Adler. Articles relate to theoretical and research issues as well as practical concerns and methods.

Adlerian counseling and psychotherapy (Dinkmeyer et al., 1987) gives a good basic presentation of the theoretical foundations of Adlerian counseling and applies basic concepts to the practice of group counseling. There are excellent chapters dealing with the phases and techniques of the counseling process. There are also chapters on family and marital therapy, consultation with teachers, and parent education.

Understanding life-style: The psycho-clarity process (Powers & Griffith, 1987) is one of the best sources of information for doing a lifestyle analysis. This book comes alive with many good clinical examples. Separate chapters deal with interview techniques, lifestyle assessment, early recollections, the family constellation, and methods of summarizing and interpreting information.

Systems of family therapy: An Adlerian integration (Sherman & Dinkmeyer, 1987) explains family organization and dynamics from an Adlerian perspective. The structure of Adlerian family therapy and the basics of change are discussed within the framework of an integrative theory. There is a useful chapter on Adlerian family therapy techniques.

Individual psychology: Theory and practice (Manaster & Corsini, 1982) is a very readable overview of Adlerian psychology. The authors trace the approach's history, describe its current status, present a clear summary of key Adlerian concepts, including the dynamics of personality, and discuss the application of these concepts to the practice of both individual and group counseling. Several excellent chapters are devoted to the theory and practice of counseling, including descriptions of Adlerian techniques that can be applied to working with individuals, groups, and families.

The Individual psychology of Alfred Adler (Ansbacher & Ansbacher, 1956) is a comprehensive collection of Adler's writings that shows the development and refinement of his thinking. This is one of the definitive sources on the Adlerian approach.

Superiority and social interest: A collection of later writings (Adler, 1973), edited by H. L. Ansbacher and R. R. Ansbacher, contains various writings by Adler on topics such as his basic assumptions, his theory of the neuroses, case studies, and his views of religion and mental health. It also has a biographical essay on Adler and a chapter on the increasing recognition of his influence on current practice.

REFERENCES AND SUGGESTED READINGS*

Adler, A. (1958). *What life should mean to you.* New York: Capricorn.

Adler, A. (1964). *Social interest: A challenge to mankind.* New York: Capricorn.

Adler, A. (1969). *The practice and theory of individual psychology.* Paterson, NJ: Littlefield.

*Adler, A. (1973). *Superiority and social interest: A collection of later writings* (3rd rev. ed.) (H. L. Ansbacher & R. R. Ansbacher, Eds.). New York: Viking Press.

Ansbacher, H. L. (1974). Goal-oriented individual psychology: Alfred Adler's theory. In A. Burton (Ed.), *Operational theories of personality.* New York: Brunner/Mazel.

*Ansbacher, H. L., & Ansbacher, R. R. (Eds.). (1956). *The individual psychology of Alfred Adler.* New York: Basic Books.

Bitter, J. (1979). An interview with Heinz Ansbacher. *Journal of Individual Psychology, 35*(1), 95–110.

Bitter, J. (1987). Communication and meaning: Satir in Adlerian context. In R. Sherman & D. Dinkmeyer (Eds.), *Systems of family therapy: An Adlerian integration* (pp. 109–142). New York: Brunner/Mazel.

*Corsini, R. J. (1987). Adlerian groups. In S. Long (Ed.), *Six group therapies.* New York: Plenum.

Dinkmeyer, D. (1975). Adlerian group psychotherapy. *International Journal of Group Psychotherapy, 25*(2), 219–226.

Dinkmeyer, D. (1986). Adlerian family therapy: An integrative therapy. *Individual Psychology: The Journal of Adlerian Theory, Research, and Practice, 42*(4), 471–479.

*Books and articles marked with an asterisk are suggested for further study.

*Dinkmeyer, D. C., Dinkmeyer, D. C., & Sperry, L. (1987). *Adlerian counseling and psychotherapy* (2nd ed.). Columbus, OH: Charles E. Merrill.

Donigian, J., & Malnati, R. (1987). *Critical incidents in group therapy.* Pacific Grove, CA: Brooks/Cole.

*Dreikurs, R. (1960). *Group psychotherapy and group approaches: The collected papers of Rudolf Dreikurs.* Chicago: Alfred Adler Institute.

Dreikurs, R. (1967). *Psychodynamics, psychotherapy, and counseling: Collected papers.* Chicago: Alfred Adler Institute.

Dreikurs, R. (1969). Group psychotherapy from the point of view of Adlerian psychology. In H. M. Ruitenbeek (Ed.), *Group therapy today: Styles, methods, and techniques.* Chicago: Aldine-Atherton.

Dreikurs, R., & Mosak, H. H. (1966). The tasks of life: 1. Adler's three tasks. *The Individual Psychologist, 4,* 18–22.

Dreikurs, R., & Mosak, H. H. (1967). The tasks of life: 2. The fourth task. *The Individual Psychologist, 4,* 51–55.

Lowe, R. N. (1982). Adlerian/Dreikursian family counseling. In A. M. Horne & M. M. Ohlsen (Eds.), *Family counseling and therapy.* Itasca, IL: F. E. Peacock.

*Manaster, G. J., & Corsini, R. J. (1982). *Individual psychology: Theory and practice.* Itasca, IL: F. E. Peacock.

Mosak, B., & Mosak, H. (1985). *A bibliography for Adlerian psychology: Vol. 2.* New York: McGraw-Hill.

Mosak, H. (1979). Adlerian psychotherapy. In R. J. Corsini (Ed.), *Current psychotherapies* (2nd ed.). Itasca, IL: F. E. Peacock.

Mosak, H. (1989). Adlerian psychotherapy. In R. J. Corsini & D. Wedding (Eds.), *Current psychotherapies* (4th ed.). Itasca, IL: F. E. Peacock.

Mozdzierz, G. J., Lisiecki, J., Bitter, J. R., & Williams, A. L. (1984). *Role-functions for Adlerian therapists.* Unpublished manuscript.

*Powers, R. L., & Griffith, J. (1987). *Understanding life-style: The psycho-clarity process.* Chicago, IL: The Americas Institute of Adlerian Studies.

*Sherman, R., & Dinkmeyer, D. (1987). *Systems of family therapy: An Adlerian integration.* New York: Brunner/Mazel.

*Sonstegard, M., Dreikurs, R., & Bitter, J. (1982). The teleoanalytic group counseling approach. In G. M. Gazda (Ed.), *Basic approaches to group psychotherapy and counseling* (3rd ed.). Springfield, IL: Charles C Thomas.

Terner, J., & Pew, W. L. (1978). *The courage to be imperfect: The life and work of Rudolf Dreikurs.* New York: Hawthorn Books.

8

Psychodrama

Introduction

Psychodrama, created and developed by J. L. Moreno, is a primarily group-therapy approach in which the client acts out or dramatizes past, present, or anticipated life situations and roles in an attempt to gain deeper understanding, achieve catharsis, and develop behavioral skills. Significant events are enacted to help the client get in contact with unrecognized and unexpressed feelings, to provide a channel for the full expression of these feelings and attitudes, and to encourage new behavior. The methods of psychodrama are best thought of as tools for helping people relate to one another more effectively. Blatner and Blatner (1988) say that the term *drama* does not refer to theatrics; rather, it pertains to reworking our lives as if they were dramatic situations and we were the playwrights.

Psychodrama had its origins in the Theater of Spontaneity, which Moreno started in Vienna in 1921. People who participated in the Theater were not professional actors, and they didn't have any scripts. Instead, they played out in a spontaneous manner events from the daily newspaper or topics suggested by the audience. After the act people in the audience were invited to discuss the experiences they had had while observing the performance. Moreno found that the personal problems, and thus the reactions, of the audience influenced not only the choice of the topic but also the way in which the participants played their parts. He also found that both the people involved in the play and the people in the audience experienced a psychological release of pent-up feelings (catharsis). The Theater of Spontaneity led

221

him to develop the group methods and specialized therapeutic techniques that he later incorporated into psychodrama.

Psychodrama is designed to facilitate the expression of feelings in a spontaneous and dramatic way through the use of role playing. One of its values in group work is that it allows a maximum number of people to play various roles and receive feedback about the impact of these roles (Orcutt, 1977). The techniques of psychodrama lend themselves very well to producing lively group interaction, exploring interpersonal problems, experimenting with novel ways of approaching significant others in one's life, and reducing one's feelings of isolation. (Although psychodramatic therapy is interpersonally oriented, *intra*personal aspects of group members' lives are often explored.) Zerka Moreno (1983) writes that "psychodrama represents a major turning point away from the treatment of the individual in isolation and toward the treatment of the individual in groups, from treatment by verbal methods toward treatment by action methods" (p. 158).

In many ways psychodrama was the precursor of many other group approaches, including Gestalt, encounter, and some applications of behavior-therapy groups. These orientations often use techniques that were originally developed by J. L. Moreno, and many of the role-playing and action-oriented methods used in these groups are adaptations of the specialized techniques that he pioneered.

Psychodrama and its development cannot be understood apart from its founder. In many ways, this approach is an extension of Moreno's personality. His dramatic interests can be traced to what he called the healthy megalomania of his childhood play. Later, when he was about 20, children's play caught his interest as he observed it in Vienna's parks. He began telling the children stories, which they would then enact. He observed that when they had no scripts, their portrayals were highly spontaneous and creative (Blatner & Blatner, 1988).

Of all the approaches discussed in this book, psychodrama is the system most ideally suited for group work. However, its methods can be used effectively in individual counseling and in family therapy.

Key Concepts

View of Human Nature

Moreno stresses that individuals are fully responsible for their actions and for the persons they are and will be. Thus, we see in Moreno a precursor of existentialists such as Albert Camus and Jean-Paul Sartre. Moreno rejects Freud's position that only through a lengthy process of psychoanalysis can humans become free of the irrational forces that rule them. He also rejects the medical model, which views people as psychologically sick. Instead, he sees clients as having been damaged through social acculturation (Fine, 1979). For Moreno, freedom from the bondage of irrational forces can be achieved using psychodramatic methods, with breakthroughs often occurring suddenly and spontaneously. It is to be noted, however, that these breakthroughs do not necessarily free the client from the bondage of ruling unconscious forces. Working through and integration still take time.

The philosophy of psychodrama is based on the assumption that spontaneity and creativity are the central forces of human experience. On the human, social level people have the capacity and skills for encountering one another openly, honestly, and in the here and now. Psychodrama represents a holistic approach that considers people in their physical, psychological, and social roles (Fine, 1979). Moreno's approach is predicated on the assumption that humans in society are continually evolving. People who are open to their internal strengths have the capability of meeting external demands in creative ways.

Action

Moreno's action-oriented methods represent an extension of the psychoanalytic approach, which he views as passive. Moreno sees the psychoanalytic method as constricting, rather than freeing, the individual. He is convinced of the therapeutic value of acting out one's problems rather than merely talking about them. In psychodrama, members enact their conflicts by bringing either past or anticipated events into the present. They are generally encouraged to maximize all expression, action, and verbal communication rather than to reduce it. However, some clients who act out their feelings need to learn some degree of emotional control. They may be stuck in emoting and even use it as a defense. Thus, psychodrama can be used to teach people both effective expression of their feelings and effective control of them. In contrast to psychoanalysis, it emphasizes personal interaction and encounter, focus on here and now, spontaneity and creativity, full expression of feelings, and reality testing.

Although Moreno repudiates psychoanalytic therapy, his methods are grounded in psychoanalytic concepts. Psychodrama and psychoanalysis differ substantially in their techniques but not in their goals. A special characteristic of the psychodramatic method is that it is applicable to almost any theoretical framework.

Encounter and Tele

The *encounter* is defined by Greenberg (1974) as that which occurs when individuals immediately and meaningfully confront themselves or significant others on the psychodramatic stage. The encounter always occurs in the context of the here and now, regardless of whether the enactment relates to a past event or to an anticipated one. Effective classical psychodrama consists of taking a moment or a particular situation in one's life and expanding it in various dimensions. Through this process individuals have the opportunity to reexperience the event or to experience it in a novel way, and thus they gain insight into themselves and practice behavioral change.

In 1917 Moreno edited a literary journal, *Daimon,* the leading existentialist publication of that period (Treadwell & Treadwell, 1972). He also wrote a small book entitled *Invitation to Encounter,* from which he often quoted this particular passage:

> A meeting of two: eye to eye, face to face.
> And when you are near I will tear your eyes out
> And place them instead of mine,
> And you will tear my eyes out
> And will place them instead of yours,
> And I will look at you with your eyes
> And you will look at me with mine.

Encountering is at the very core of psychodrama, for through this process people not only meet but also understand one another on a deep and significant level. By their very nature encounters entail an element of surprise, because they are not rehearsed or forced. The encounter entails dimensions of both transference and empathy, yet it goes beyond them. It fosters a sense of community in a group, which builds the trust that is necessary for productive work.

Related to encounter is the concept Moreno terms *tele,* the two-way flow of feelings between members of a psychodramatic group. Tele is an interpersonal exchange. Moreno calls it a "feeling of individuals into one another, the cement which holds groups together" (1964, p. xi). Tele accounts for a person's ability to penetrate and understand another person. Moreno considers it "therapeutic love." Through tele there is a strengthening of bonds, a promotion of continuity and stability, and a sense of group cohesion. Tele is the sum total of the feeling aspects of empathy, transference, and countertransference; it is the factor responsible for the increased interaction among participants of a group. Through it, they can find creative alternatives for working out interpersonal conflicts. In this sense, tele is a therapeutic factor related to change. Healing of individuals occurs through a reciprocal empathic feeling.

Spontaneity and Creativity

Moreno considers spontaneity and creativity to be characteristics of the self-realized person. He sees them as the central ingredients in both psychodrama and healthy living. From his perspective spontaneity is an adequate response to a new situation and a novel response to an old situation. The essential qualities of spontaneity include openness, a freshness of approach, a willingness to take initiative and risk, and an integration of external realities with one's internal world of thinking and feeling. Spontaneity is not to be confused with impulsivity, for it includes an intention to achieve a constructive result (Blatner & Blatner, 1988). It influences the present situation and the reporting of past situations. From this viewpoint the present determines the past, rather than the past determining the present.

Most of us can be highly creative if we allow ourselves to be spontaneous. Moreno observed that children in Vienna, in contrast to adults, were able to enter into role-playing and fantasy situations without any difficulty and to freely express their feelings. As people grow older, they tend to become less and less spontaneous. To remedy this tendency, Moreno and his associates developed methods of spontaneity training aimed at freeing people from limiting scripts and rigid and stereotyped responses. They adopted techniques that encouraged the uninhibited participation of the audience, and they stressed the need to get in touch with one's fantasies and feelings by enacting situations that trigger certain emotions. Moreno assigned so much importance to spontaneity that he considered spontaneity training as the way of enabling people to take dramatic steps in the future and to meet new situations from a fresh perspective.

Although the development of spontaneity is valued in psychodramatic groups, Nicholas (1984) cautions against pushing members too quickly to allow their spontaneity to be expressed. She suggests that group members be treated gently and respectfully and that they be allowed to get involved in the group action in ways of their choosing when they feel ready to do so. She believes that the most important teaching tool for enhancing spontaneity is the leader's ability to model spontaneous behavior. For this reason she recommends that group leaders obtain their own training in psychodrama and that they experience other creative and expressive group approaches. To be able to create a climate that fosters the development of spontaneity, it is essential that leaders be aware of their own feelings and express and draw on their feelings in intuitive ways.

Dealing with the Present

Psychodrama emphasizes enacting conflicts or crisis situations in the present, as opposed to merely verbalizing about them in a detached way. A basic tenet is that everything occurs in the here and now, whether the person is dealing with an event that occurred in the past or is concerned about a future event. The theory is that reliving a scene from the past gives the participants the opportunity to examine how that event affected them at the time it occurred and a chance to deal differently with the event *now*. By replaying a past event in the present, individuals are able to assign new meaning to it. Through this process they work through unfinished business and put a new and different ending to that earlier situation. Through the enactment and the subsequent catharsis, insight often occurs.

In practical terms, psychodrama offers encouragement to members to speak in the present tense and to use action words. The placing of members in the present, regardless of when the scenes actually happened, has a tendency to reduce verbal reporting and turns members into actors (Z. T. Moreno, 1987). Elsewhere, Zerka Moreno (1983) contends that the future has typically been neglected in therapeutic practice. When participants in psychodrama enact anticipated events as though they were taking place in the here and now, they achieve an increased awareness of their available options. In this sense psychodrama can be considered a rehearsal for life.

Catharsis

Catharsis occurs when stored-up feelings are finally expressed. In psychodrama a client experiences catharsis by verbally and physically acting out an emotion-laden situation. This release of pent-up feelings is more meaningful when participants deal with real-life situations and spontaneously express what they are feeling. Anger, sadness, hatred, rage, and despair, as well as joy and ecstasy, are tapped and released. Although catharsis is often a natural part of the psychodramatic process, it is not accurate to assume that catharsis is an end in itself. After this experience of letting go of stored-up feelings, members often gain a new perspective on an old problem and begin to feel and think differently about it. Thus, they open themselves to the possibility of behaving in new and appropriate ways in a variety of situations.

Insight

Insight, or an increased awareness of a problem situation, often follows an emotional purging. Although catharsis typically occurs during the intensity of a psychodramatic session, insight does not always follow immediately. It can occur during the enactment or at its end, when members are sharing their feelings and reactions to what happened on the stage; but it is often achieved a day or even weeks later (Greenberg, 1986). Both the participants in a psychodrama and members of the audience can experience catharsis and thus achieve insight. Once people allow themselves the freedom to release intense emotions that have in many instances been controlling them, they begin the critical process of gaining control over these feelings that they have been avoiding. This allows them to develop alternative frames of reference and see events in a new light. Members quite often then develop a dawning awareness of how they are sometimes keeping old scenes alive because they have not dealt with threatening feelings. They gradually come to an emotional and cognitive understanding that they do not have to continue living as they did in the past.

Reality Testing

The psychodramatic group provides its members with an opportunity to test reality, because it consists of real people and real-life situations. The assumptions and fantasies of an individual can be checked out for validation with other members. Also, others in the group can suggest alternatives for action, many of which the client may not have considered.

Consider the following example of how a psychodramatic group offers members ways in which to test reality. A young woman is in great emotional pain over what she sees as her father's indifference to her. After concluding a psychodramatic enactment in which the young woman tells her father of her feelings of missing his love, she may still be angry with him and expect him to make the first move to change matters. During the discussion phase others in the group can point out that she is making the assumption that *he* must be the person to initiate a closer relationship. In reality, the father may well be fearful of showing her affection and attention, thinking that she is not interested in such a relationship with him. The group can be instrumental in helping her see that, if she wants to change her relationship with her father, she may have to make the initial move.

Role Playing

Role playing entails acting a part in an impromptu production. The enactment of a role does not have to be some kind of artificial performance. It can be an expression of what a person genuinely feels, fears, or would like to become. In a sense, we play multiple roles in everyday life; some of them are an extension of our unique identity, and others are stultifying and restrict our identity. Moreno's basic idea is that we have the capacity to become more conscious and creative in how we play our roles. We can examine the roles we play, renegotiate them, and choose different ways to play the ones we choose to keep. In psychodrama, members are given the freedom to try out a diversity of roles, thereby sharpening their focus on parts of themselves that they would like to present to others. Playing roles also enables participants to get in contact with aspects of themselves that they were not aware of. They can challenge stereotyped ways of responding to people and break out of behaving within a rigid pattern, creating new dimensions of themselves. Even if they fail in a new role, they know that they will have many opportunities to try again until they learn new behavioral approaches to the situations that bring them anxiety.

Role playing is a key technique, yet it should not be concluded that it is synonymous with psychodrama. It can be used by therapists of various theoretical orientations, including psychoanalysts, Adlerians, Rogerians, and eclectic therapists (Corsini, 1966). As you will see, different forms of role playing are often used in Gestalt groups, in transactional analysis, in rational-emotive therapy, and in behavioral groups. For example, in a behavioral group the focus is typically on rehearsing specific interpersonal skills. Members are likely to role-play situations such as a job interview, asking someone for a date, or dealing assertively with a pushy salesperson. Yet in a behavioral group the members work on developing and practicing concrete social skills that will help them deal effectively with a range of interpersonal situations. In psychodrama, role playing is typically characterized by a high degree of emotional intensity and often leads to a catharsis and some degree of insight. The various members of a psychodramatic group are used to portray various characters so that scenes from an individual's life can be replayed. In Gestalt groups the focus is also on getting into contact with and expressing feelings, but the one particular member who is working assumes all the roles in a given scene and interchangeably acts out the multiple characters. In behavioral groups, as you will see later, role playing is a central procedure in helping members unlearn old and ineffective behavior patterns and acquire new and effective ways of behaving. In contrast to the psychodramatic group, however, the behavioral group is not concerned with ventilation of feelings so much as with practicing specific skills and rehearsing concrete behaviors for given situations that are problematic for members. So, although role playing is a basic part of many therapeutic approaches to group work, it is practiced in different ways with different purposes.

As it is used in psychodramatic groups, role playing can serve three primary functions, as Corsini (1966) has noted. First, it can be used as a method of *diagnosis*. As members role-play various situations, the group leader has ample opportunities to learn more about how they think and feel (as well as what they do). Role playing can also be used as a means of *instruction*. Through a modeling process members learn more effective interpersonal skills by observing a variety of ways to deal with problems. Finally, it can be used as a method of *training,* for by getting involved in the active process of playing roles, members often develop new insights and new coping skills.

Basic Components of the Psychodramatic Method

The psychodramatic method consists of the following components: a director (the person who produces a psychodrama out of the many components that make up the finished product), a protagonist (the person who is presenting a problem to be explored), the auxiliary egos (the people portraying significant others in the protagonist's life as a way of helping him or her explore an enactment), the audience (the others in the group, before whom the problem is actually explored and who typically participate in the enactment), and the stage. The stage represents an extension of the life space of the protagonist, and as such it should be large enough to allow for movement of the protagonist, the auxiliary egos, and the director. The stage area should simulate, at least symbolically, each scene that the protagonist recalls. If an actual stage is not available, a section of the room can be designated as the area where all the action will take place. Props can be placed in the action area, and when a protagonist emerges from the group, he or she moves to this area to create the psychodrama.

The Director

According to Zerka Moreno (1987), the director's function is complicated and involves a combination of art and science. She asserts that it takes approximately 2 years to train a director. She contends that the more fully the director lives, the better he or she will be able to fulfill the functions demanded in a psychodrama.

According to J. L. Moreno (1964), the director has the role of producer, catalyst/facilitator, and observer/analyzer. Directors help in the selection of the protagonist and then decide which of the special psychodramatic techniques are best suited for the exploration of the person's problem. They organize the psychodrama, play a key role in warming up the group, and pay careful attention to what emerges in the drama. Directors function as catalysts/facilitators in that they assist the protagonist in developing a scene and facilitate the free expression of feelings. At times they make therapeutic interpretations to help the protagonist gain a new understanding of a problem. Haskell (1973) describes specific functions of psychodramatic directors:

- planning the session so that various group members have an opportunity to be the protagonist and so that the problems presented are relevant to the needs and interests of the group
- providing an accepting and tolerant atmosphere that lends itself to spontaneous expressions of feelings associated with meaningful events
- warming up the group so that the participants will be psychologically ready to freely and fully explore personal issues and identify their goals
- providing support and direction for the protagonist; this includes suggesting appropriate techniques designed to enhance the enactments
- encouraging spontaneity and catharsis and helping the protagonist interpret what he or she experiences during the psychodrama
- suggesting relationships that might be explored, scenes that might be enacted, and experiments that might be tried
- stopping the action for clarification whenever necessary, and making sure that the roles are being properly enacted
- paying careful attention to the reactions of the group members and, if it seems appropriate, trying to bring other participants into the psychodrama; also, assisting other members in deriving therapeutic benefits from the experience
- protecting the protagonist from being verbally attacked by other members of the group or from being subjected to simplistic directives and advice
- leading a group discussion after the action is over—a function that entails encouraging members to give the protagonist feedback and share what they experienced during the psychodrama, what they learned from it, and what experiences and feelings they think they have in common with the protagonist
- summarizing the experience on the basis of the feedback obtained in the discussion and the enactments, thus providing a good closure for one experience and a direct lead into another area of exploration

Corsini (1966) concludes that effective directors possess both creativity and courage. Asserting that directing role playing involves not only technical skills but also *creativity,* Corsini makes it clear how many variables directors must attend to. They must not only depend on their own resources for being inventive but also find ways of tapping the creativity within the group. They must make decisions about what aspects of a psychodrama to focus on and quickly arrange for reenactment of certain scenes. In addition, they must be able to function as a guide by using their clinical expertise and technical knowledge to help individuals bring to the surface, explore, and work through their personal concerns. Directors must also find ways of involving as many members as possible in the protagonist's work. Effective directors are able to invent techniques that will highlight a member's struggles. They must be able to improvise, and their improvisations must have structure and meaning.

Directors must also have *courage,* for many of the techniques they use involve some degree of risk and of the unknown. It takes courage for directors to run the risk of being found wanting before the public eye as they work with protagonists who are exposing themselves (Greenberg, 1986). Although they are not impulsive, good psychodramatic leaders trust their clinical hunches enough to try techniques that can have a powerful effect on the members.

In addition to the characteristics of courage and creativity, qualities such as self-confidence, self-knowledge, and clinical expertise are essential. Nevertheless, group leaders who are interested in incorporating psychodrama into their style of leadership should realize that they do not have to be perfect in their first attempts to apply its methods. I have found that some beginning leaders become needlessly intimidated when they think about the personal qualities and skills needed for effectively using psychodrama. With supervised practice, experience as a member of a psychodramatic group, and specialized training, they can acquire competence in this powerful approach.

The Protagonist

The protagonist either volunteers or is selected by the group and the director. It is the protagonist who selects the event to be explored. In the case of a past event the protagonist is asked to reenact the substance of the event without attempting to recall the exact transaction or words. Spontaneity is encouraged. As soon as possible the director encourages the protagonist to move into action rather than merely talking about the event. Protagonists are asked to deal with the significant people in their past as though these symbolic figures were present. This here-and-now focus intensifies the feelings that are experienced and provides a new understanding of the relationships between protagonists and significant people in their past. In the enactment of the psychodrama the protagonist's fears and fantasies come to life and enable him or her to modify intrapsychic and interpersonal processes.

Fine (1979) describes the protagonist as the composer of an opera. It is the protagonist who writes the score and the lyrics. The director, like the conductor of the opera, follows the script and facilitates the interpretation of the drama. Others in the group who function as auxiliaries are much like musicians following scores.

The protagonist generally selects the group members who will serve as auxiliary egos. These choices are made for both conscious and unconscious reasons. Some choices are made on the basis of characteristics of group members that are similar to those of the actual significant others. When a choice is made on this basis, the interaction between the protagonist and auxiliary egos is likely to be more spontaneous, real, and effective. Directors may take exception to this rule if they want a group member to assume a role with particular therapeutic potential.

It is the protagonist's job to teach the auxiliary egos how to play their roles. This sometimes entails giving an auxiliary ego some background on the person he or she is to play and a feeling for the style of that person. Protagonists teach an auxiliary ego the behavioral style of a significant other by acting out that part.

It is important that, as protagonists act out a situation, they have the freedom to explore any aspect of the situation (and related relationships) that seems significant to them. It is the protagonists, not the director, who examine and explore, and it is crucial that their decisions be respected. Although the director may encourage protagonists to reenact a situation or deal with an anticipated event, they decide whether they are willing to follow the director's suggestions. Also, the director may employ a particular technique, but they always have the right to say that they don't want to move in that direction. Effective psychodrama requires sensitivity, on the part of both the director and the group members, to what the protagonist is ready and willing to explore. Protagonists should never be coerced or pressured; the auxiliary egos and the director are there to serve them.

At the end of a scene the protagonist or the director may suggest that the protagonist assume a different role in the same scene to determine whether he or she can respond more effectively. Another suggestion is that the protagonist fantasize about the future by acting out how things might be a year afterward, thus sharing private thoughts with the audience.

A basic Morenean concept is that the protagonist is viewed as an instrument of the group. When the protagonist is selected by the group, he or she is the person in whom the group's problems are most clearly crystallized. Psychodrama thus becomes a group process, rather than individual therapy within a group.

The Auxiliary Egos

An auxiliary ego is anyone in the group who assists the director and protagonist in the psychodramatic production. Auxiliary egos often portray the roles of significant others in the life of the protagonist. These persons may be living or dead, real or imagined. Auxiliaries may also play the roles of inanimate objects, pets, or any emotionally charged object or being that is relevant to the protagonist's psychodrama. The auxiliary egos have other functions: (1) to play out the perceptions held by the protagonist, at least in the beginning; (2) to investigate the interaction between the protagonist and their own roles; (3) to interpret this interaction and relationship; and (4) to act as a therapeutic guide in helping the protagonist develop an improved relationship (Z. T. Moreno, 1987). Effective auxiliary egos can give a psychodrama greater power and intensity. A few ways in which they do this are by helping the protagonist warm up, by intensifying the action, and by mirroring the protagonist. They encourage the protagonist to become more deeply involved in the here and now of the drama.

Auxiliary egos use information about significant others that is conveyed to them by the protagonist through role reversal. It is the director's responsibility to assess whether their role playing is working more for the protagonist's benefit or for their own. In the latter case the auxiliaries may be redirected by the director. The director should be sure to discuss this development during the sharing phase of the group, because it usually has significant therapeutic implications for the auxiliaries. It should be underscored that psychodrama is a *group process* and that auxiliary work has great therapeutic potential. It is a good idea to permit auxiliaries some freedom of expression in their role portrayals. Playing someone else's role often serves as a vehicle for getting in touch with parts of the self not uncovered while playing one's own role. However, Zerka Moreno (1987) warns about possible dangers when there is an enmeshment between the protagonist's psychodrama and the auxiliary ego's drama. She cautions both the auxiliary ego and the director to avoid doing their own psychodrama, thus taking the focus away from the protagonist's drama. It is the director's task to make sure that the spontaneity of the total group involvement is tempered with some degree of purpose and structure so that the psychodrama does not lose its sense of focus.

The Audience

Even when people in the group are not protagonists or auxiliary egos in a psychodrama, they can still benefit in vicarious ways. They can identify with the protagonist, they can experience a release of their own feelings through their empathy, and they can gain insight into some of their own interpersonal conflicts. These other group members—the audience—provide valuable support and feedback to the protagonist. An action scene is generally followed by a discussion that involves the entire group. Other members are asked to share some experiences of their own that are related to the scene they have just observed, and they provide the protagonist with feedback concerning alternative ways of dealing with the situation. Spontaneous reactions and personal sharing are encouraged; members are typically asked to refrain from analyzing the protagonist, offering pat solutions, criticizing, and offering impersonal interpretations. Because of the variety in group membership, the audience's reactions can help the protagonist understand the impact he or she has on others.

Phases of the Psychodramatic Process

Psychodrama consists of three phases: (1) the warm-up (or preaction) phase, (2) the action phase, and (3) the discussion, or sharing, phase. In some groups there is a "postsession rapping" process (Greenberg, 1986, p. 396), although this fourth phase is not essential in psychodrama.

The Warm-Up Phase

J. L. Moreno emphasizes the necessity of a warm-up period designed to get the participants ready for the experience. Such readiness involves being motivated enough to formulate one's goals and feeling secure enough to trust the others in the group. There are many ways to conduct a productive warm-up phase. For example:

- The director gives a brief talk about the nature and purpose of psychodrama, and participants are invited to ask questions.
- Each member is briefly interviewed by the director. A lead question may be "Is there a present or past relationship that you'd like to understand better?" If each person in the group responds to this question, a basis for group cohesion is being established.
- Members can form several sets of dyads and spend a few minutes sharing a conflict that they are experiencing and that they'd like to explore in the session.
- The "going around" technique can facilitate group interaction. Each member is asked to make some brief comments about what he or she is experiencing in the moment. This making the rounds can also focus the members on some aspect of personal work that they would like to do during this particular session.
- In a long-term group with functional people, a nondirective warm-up is often used as a way to get members ready for a session. Members may be simply asked to briefly state what they were aware of as they were coming to the session or to make any comments about their readiness to work.

In addition to structured techniques aimed at warming up a group for action, there are unstructured warm-ups, including the process by which a protagonist emerges from the spontaneous interaction at the beginning of a group session. It is critical that the leader pay close attention to verbal and nonverbal cues as the protagonist describes the issue to be explored. For example, a member may describe himself as reserved and distant from others. He may use some metaphoric or symbolic language that has rich implications. In talking about letting others get close to him, he may allude to "shields" that he has carefully built to protect himself from the pain of rejection. Early in the course of a psychodrama, the director guides the protagonist in establishing the scene in which some significant event took place. In doing this, the leader can draw upon important cues the protagonist gave in presenting his situation, including facial expressions, figures of speech, and body posture. The process of warming up occurs as the protagonist is establishing the scene.

Whatever techniques are used in this getting-acquainted process, it is essential that members know that they will not be coerced to work on issues they choose not to explore. During the warm-up phase, members need to be reassured that the working environment is a safe one, that they are the ones to decide *what* they will reveal and *when* they will reveal it, and that they can stop whenever they want to. If participants have the impression that they will be pressured to "perform" and badgered to go further than they feel ready or willing to, the morale of the group will suffer, and the members will resist participation. The techniques are less important than the spirit and purpose of the warm-up: anything that facilitates the cohesion of the group and the establishing of trust is a useful tool for this phase.

According to Blatner (1973), the most important issue in the warm-up phase is creating an atmosphere that fosters *spontaneity*. In his view the necessary conditions for spontaneous behavior to occur include

- a sense of trust and a climate of psychological safety
- group norms that allow for the expression of emotions and for the inclusion of intuitive dimensions
- an element of playfulness
- a willingness to explore and engage in novel behavior

Blatner emphasizes the importance of the director's own warm-up as a key factor in creating a climate that encourages spontaneous behavior on the part of the group. It is during the warm-up period that directors are developing their own spontaneity. By communicating a sense of authenticity and warmth, they foster a sense of confidence and trust in the group. Similarly, modeling risk taking, self-disclosure, humor, spontaneity, creativity, empathy, and the acceptability of expressing emotions and acting them out contributes to the group's cohesion. A theme may begin to emerge, and a protagonist may be selected and move onto the stage for action.

The Action Phase

The action phase includes the acting out and working through of a past or present situation or of an anticipated event. The enactment begins when the protagonist enters the stage area. It is important to facilitate the process so that the protagonist can move into action as soon as possible. The director can assist the protagonist in getting a clear focus on a particular concern. Rather than having the protagonist tell lengthy details and risk losing the energy of the psychodrama, the director can ask the protagonist questions such as "Who in your life are you having the most trouble with at this time?" "What few words or phrases would best describe your father [mother]?" "What is the main message that you get from your mother [father]?" "When do you feel most criticized by your wife?" "What are the things your husband tells you that upset you the most?" "What are a few lines you'd like to say to your son?" "What would you most like to hear from your daughter?" The point of these questions is to avoid lengthy commentaries on content and instead to focus the protagonist on the process of his or her struggle.

Once the protagonist has a clear sense of what he or she would like to explore, it is possible to create the scene and coach the auxiliary egos. After this focusing process, protagonists act out their problems and relationships on the stage. A single action phase may consist of one to several scenes. Scenes are constructed and enacted as they relate to the protagonist's issues. They may be interpersonal or intrapersonal in nature and usually progress from peripheral issues (presenting problems) to more central issues (the real or deeper problems). The duration of the action phase varies, depending on the director's evaluation of the protagonist's involvement and on the level of involvement of the group.

Fine (1979) observes that sometimes an entire session may be devoted to the group as a whole working through interpersonal issues among members or identifying and modifying norms that have been developing in the group. At other times a common theme such as loneliness, fear of intimacy, and feelings of rejection seems to touch everyone in the group. With skillful facilitation by the group leader each person can become involved with others in here-and-now encounters.

Haskell (1973) offers some guidelines for directors during the action phase of psychodrama:

- The protagonist should be encouraged as soon as possible to enact scenes involving conflicts in relationships.
- All the action should be geared to the here and now. Thus, if a person is dealing with a past situation and says "Then I told him," the director intervenes and says "You are telling him *now*."
- The protagonist needs the freedom to select the event, time, place, and people involved in the situation.
- Generally it is wise to deal first with less significant events and leave the reenacting of more traumatic experiences for later on.
- Protagonists should be asked to reconstruct a situation as faithfully as possible without, however, being overly concerned with recalling the exact words exchanged, so that the flow of action is not inhibited. Instead, they need to know that the essence of an interaction, *as they recall it,* is what's important.
- Protagonists should be encouraged to express themselves as fully as possible, both verbally and nonverbally. However, the director needs to exert caution so that rage is expressed symbolically—for example, by hitting a pillow—and people are not injured.

- Protagonists can be given the opportunity to play the role of each person in their scene (role reversal); this can help them develop an understanding of how others perceived and felt about an event.

The Sharing and Discussion Phase

In the third phase of psychodrama the members share and discuss the action. (For some therapists who use psychodrama, sharing and discussion are separate.) Sharing comes first, consisting of nonjudgmental statements about oneself; the discussion of the group process follows this personal sharing. The participants are asked to share with the protagonist their observations of and reactions to the psychodrama in a constructive and supportive way. The director's task is to initiate and lead a discussion that includes as many participants as possible, so that feedback can be maximized. The director needs to watch for attempts by members to analyze the protagonist or confront the person harshly at a time when, having just revealed intimate life experiences, he or she can be most vulnerable. It is important that protagonists be given an opportunity for some form of closure of their experience. If they have opened themselves up and expressed deep feelings, they need to be able to count on the support of the group in order to integrate psychologically what they have just experienced. If no such opportunity is available through sharing and exploring the meaning of the experience, protagonists may leave the session feeling rejected and lost instead of feeling freer and more purposeful.

It is crucial that the sharing from the audience be personal and nonjudgmental rather than analytical or interpretive. The director must reinforce the kind of sharing that entails self-disclosure, support, and emotional involvement on the part of the members. When members discuss how they were affected by the session, they are fostering their own involvement, transparency, and growth. This is not a time for giving advice to the protagonist or, worse yet, attempting to "cure" the protagonist by providing insightful interpretations into his or her psychodynamics. If participants attempt to analyze or to provide solutions, the director needs to intervene— for example, by asking questions such as these:,

- "How has Jane's experience affected you?"
- "What feelings were stirred up in you as you were participating in Jane's drama?"
- "What experiences in your life relate to Jane's situation?"
- "Are there any feelings you had toward Jane that you'd like to share with her?"

Zerka Moreno (1987) has some excellent guidelines for making the sharing session a therapeutic experience:

- Group members should speak for themselves and not analyze the protagonist.

- Since the protagonist has engaged in open sharing, he or she deserves more than a cold analysis or critique.
- Sharing has healing effects. Healing comes from the disclosure of others' experiences.
- Insight by itself rarely has a healing impact.
- Interpretation and evaluation come later, when the protagonist is not so vulnerable.

During the sharing time, group cohesion typically increases, for members are able to see commonalities. The participation in universal struggles is a way to bond members. Thus, after an effective sharing of experiences, protagonists are not left feeling as though they are alone in an unfriendly universe. They have a basis for feeling accepted, and the personal feedback from other members acts as a reinforcement for them to continue revealing personal concerns.

Closure is an option and depends on the client, the situation, and the group. If the group will not meet again, closure is essential. If the group meets on a regular basis, however, there are times when the leader may defer closure to a later session. A period of discussion can be useful for "winding down" the emotional pitch to a more cognitive level and for helping the protagonist and the audience integrate key aspects of the session. Although the emotional aspects of an enactment are of great therapeutic value, a degree of cognitive integration will maximize the utility of these emotional components. Protagonists can be asked to express what they have learned and the insights they have acquired. It is also a good practice to encourage them to talk about the personal meaning of reliving a situation. They can be stimulated to think of how to cope with their repressed feelings and of how to deal more effectively with similar problem situations in the future.

One useful way to facilitate closure is to arrange for behavioral practice. This allows the protagonist to transfer in-group learning to everyday life. After experimentation with a variety of new behaviors, the person can use some of them with significant others outside the group and cope with situations more effectively. To facilitate behavioral practice, the protagonist presents the situation as it was originally presented in the action phase. Various techniques, such as role reversal, future projection, mirroring, and feedback, are often used to help the protagonist get a clearer idea of the impact of his or her new behavior. (These techniques are described later in the chapter.)

A word of caution concerning closure is in order. Several writers (Blatner, 1973; Goldman & Morrison, 1984; Greenberg, 1986; Leveton, 1977; Z. T. Moreno, 1987) discuss the importance of dealing with unfinished business during the final phase of a psychodrama. Before closing a session, the director may ask members to verbalize any unspoken feelings that have developed. Although it is not always necessary to work things out, it is important that the existence of such unfinished business be mentioned before the session closes. Realistically, although some problems will be opened up and fruitfully explored, the protagonist may be far from having resolved the issue. After a successful sharing session, new work is likely to be shaping up as other members of the group identify with what they have just experienced. Of course, it is not wise to undertake new work in a given session if there is not ample time to address the issue adequately.

Protagonists can gain a good deal of insight and take some significant steps in coping with difficult personal conflicts and yet still not finish with their business. Further exploration and work are generally necessary, and members need to be warned of the danger of attempting premature and forced closure of an issue.

Leveton (1977) points out that some practitioners expect perfection. Unless everything is settled, these leaders feel that they have failed. In order to avoid such feelings, they may try to force closure in situations in which participants are better off continuing to think about what has occurred. One of the most challenging tasks for any director is learning to bring closure to a session without keeping members from further self-exploration, which is necessary for an in-depth resolution of their problems.

An optional part of psychodrama is the "postsession rapping" period, which provides opportunities for some social sharing among the participants. Greenberg (1986) typically invites those who attend a psychodrama to stay for a while and have coffee or tea. This is a time when participants can talk with one another in more informal ways and can say something to another person that they did not have a chance to say during the session. This period also provides further opportunities for people to wind down from an experience.

Techniques of Psychodrama

Psychodrama uses a number of specific techniques to intensify feelings, lead to catharsis, and bring about increased self-understanding. Such understanding is achieved by working through and integrating material that has surfaced in a psychodrama. These techniques, while instrumental to the success of the psychodramatic process, are not ends in themselves but means to the spontaneous expression of feelings by the participants. Thus, J. L. Moreno (1978) warns against the misuse of techniques simply to stir up a dramatic performance.

Directors have the latitude to invent their own techniques or modify standard ones. Because psychodrama can be very powerful, practitioners need to bring caution and commitment to the practice of their technical skills, and they need to know when and how to apply these methods. Effective psychodrama consists of far more than the mere use of certain techniques. Practitioners must learn to know, and work with, the members' psychological world in an educated, trained, sensitive, caring, and creative manner.

I suggest that you keep these cautions in mind as you read the following overview of some standard psychodramatic techniques. These techniques are described in detail in the following sources: Blatner (1973, 1989), Blatner and Blatner (1988), Leveton (1977), J. L. Moreno (1958, 1964), Zerka Moreno (1959, 1965, 1983, 1987), Greenberg (1986), Goldman and Morrison (1984), and Starr (1977).

Blatner and Blatner (1988) present some useful guidelines for selecting appropriate techniques to explore a particular theme:

- Whenever possible, use physical action rather than talking about a situation.
- Use direct address, talking *to* the people most involved (or auxiliaries playing their roles) rather than about them.
- Look for ways to promote the active behavior of other members by involving them in an enactment.
- Make abstract situations more concrete by working with specific scenes.
- Encourage participants to make affirmative statements about themselves by using sentences beginning with "I."
- Continue to encourage members to deal with situations in the past or future as if they were happening in the present moment.
- Recognize and tap the potential for redecisions, renegotiations, and corrective experiences in the present.
- Pay attention to the nonverbal aspects of communication.
- Have participants directly exercise empathic skills through role reversal.
- Include a degree of playfulness, humor, and spontaneity in a situation.
- Utilize symbols and metaphors, personifying them and making them more vivid.
- Include other artistic principles and vehicles, such as movement, staging, props, poetry, art, and music.
- Exaggerate or amplify behavior to explore a wider range of responses.
- Use the warm-up process as a precursor to creative behavior.

Self-Presentation

The protagonist gives a self-portrayal in order to introduce the actor. Let's assume that Jack, the protagonist, wants to explore his relationship with his daughter, Laura. He may do so by demonstrating how he typically approaches her. His self-presentation gives the audience a sense of how he experiences himself in the father/daughter relationship. In the course of the self-presentation he may state the problem as he sees it and may say something about his daughter.

Role Reversal

One form of role reversal consists of the "presentation of the other." In addition to presenting himself or herself, a protagonist may present another significant person (such as mother, father, sibling, lover, close friend, teacher, or relative). The protagonist presents a completely subjective perspective of this significant person by demonstrating how he or she behaves. In this way the protagonist is giving cues to the auxiliary ego so that the scene can be played in a way that is relatively close to the protagonist's experience. Role reversal is indicated when it is appropriate for the protagonist to empathize with the viewpoint of another person. It is also useful during the warm-up phase and in the casting of the scene (Blatner & Blatner, 1988).

Zerka Moreno (1983) makes the point that protagonists must act out the truth as they feel it and from their own subjective stance, regardless of how distorted their presentation may appear to the other members or the leader. For example, Jack, the protagonist, presents his daughter. Preferably, he plays the role of Laura and demonstrates how she typically responds. As a variation, the director can interview Jack as he plays the role of his daughter. This technique will give the director and the group a clearer picture of how Jack perceives Laura and how he thinks she perceives him.

Through role reversal, protagonists are encouraged to empathize with a significant person in their lives. Since they must assume the role of that person within the psychodramatic setting, they begin to develop a deeper appreciation for the world of that person. The auxiliary is instructed to keep the drama true to the protagonist's perception of events. The leader needs to intervene to reduce the chances that the auxiliary will contaminate the process with his or her own dynamics.

Typically, the director suggests a role reversal when it appears that the protagonist would benefit by attempting to "walk in the shoes" of the person with whom he or she is experiencing conflict. In the case of Jack, he can "become" his daughter while another member assumes his role as a father. By playing the role of Laura as he experiences her, Jack may begin to come to a clearer understanding of how *she* feels.

Role reversal is considered to be one of the most powerful tools of psychodrama, and it serves many purposes (Fine, 1979):

- It allows a perceptual shift so that the protagonist can see the situation in a fresh way.
- It gives the protagonist a chance to experience the world from the point of view of the other.
- It allows expansion of the client's awareness and behavior.
- It encourages participants to take responsibility for their behavior and decisions.
- It helps protagonists confront the impact of their immediate interpersonal behavior.

Writing that role reversal is at the heart of role-playing theory as demonstrated in psychodramatic groups, Zerka Moreno (1983) maintains that this technique encourages maximum expression in conflict situations. Protagonists' distortions of these relationships can be brought to the surface, explored, and corrected in action. By reversing roles, protagonists can reintegrate, redigest, and grow beyond situations that are keeping them unfree. Role reversal allows members to fully express their perceptions of reality, to get feedback from others in the group about their subjective views, and to make modifications of their perceptions to the extent that they discover distortions. It can be used throughout the drama to correct or modify the principal auxiliary's role portrayal and to present additional information to the auxiliary. More importantly, it is used throughout the action phase to increase the protagonist's depth of perception of the significant other.

Soliloquy

At times, protagonists are asked to imagine themselves in a place alone where they can daydream out loud (soliloquize). The director may ask a protagonist to stop the action at some point, turn aside, and express her feelings at the moment. Or the director, on sensing ambivalence on the part of another protagonist, may stop the action and ask him to walk around the stage and say what he is thinking and feeling. The protagonist may be engaged in a solitary activity, such as walking home. As a variation, the protagonist may soliloquize with a double as the two walk together. The double can facilitate the protagonist's expression of feelings and thoughts that would typically be kept hidden.

The soliloquy is valuable in helping protagonists clarify their thinking and experience their feelings more intensely (Greenberg, 1986). This technique facilitates an open expression of what they may be thinking and feeling but not verbally expressing. For example, Jack may be asked to verbalize his thoughts during the course of a role reversal. This soliloquy gives him the chance to get a sense of what he believes Laura is thinking and feeling but perhaps not expressing directly. He can also be asked to soliloquize after he has portrayed himself. He does this by summarizing his uncensored thoughts, expressing his feelings, and examining them more closely.

Double Technique

An auxiliary ego stands behind the protagonist and acts with or even speaks *for* him or her. The double can mirror the inner thoughts and feelings of the protagonist, often expressing unconscious material. Doubling facilitates the client's awareness of internal processes and often leads to an expression of unvoiced thoughts and feelings. The double supports the protagonist and also serves as a link between the director and the protagonist. The double may serve an integrative function and also intensify the interaction between the protagonist and the auxiliary ego. It is useful for doubles to assume both the posture and the attitude of protagonists. However, these are merely tools that doubles use to help them fulfill their purpose. This purpose is to help protagonists increase their awareness of inner conflicts and repressed feelings and even express them. According to Leon Fine (personal communication, June 1988), the double is the agent of the protagonist. The double attends to process events and the immediate moment and is available to the protagonist in role reversals and in other roles. In Jack's case, the double technique might be used if he felt stuck or felt overwhelmed by his daughter. The double would then help Jack stay in contact with and express his feelings. Effective doubling often results in the escalation of an interaction, and it is likely to provide the protagonist with the needed catalyst to say things that until now have remained unexpressed.

Multiple doubles may be used to represent and embody the various sides of the protagonist. They can represent the protagonist's internal conflicts, desires, assets, liabilities, or various roles he or she plays in life (Goldman & Morrison, 1984). With Jack, one double may represent the side of him that misses his daughter and wants to express love, and the other double can be the "cold father," who really wants to have nothing to do with her. The doubles may speak at the same time, or they may take turns. If the doubles are effective, the father's ambivalent feelings toward his daughter can be successfully portrayed on the stage, and Jack may come to see which side within him is stronger. Also, he may get a clearer picture of the feelings and attitudes he'd like to express to Laura.

Mirror Technique

An auxiliary ego assumes the role of the protagonist by mirroring the protagonist's postures, gestures, and words as they appeared in the enactment. During the auxiliary ego's mirroring, the protagonist is not on the stage, so that by observing his own behavior reflected by another person, he can see himself as others do. The protagonist stands back and watches a very live form of videotape playback. This process may help the protagonist develop a more accurate and objective self-assessment. Mirroring is basically a feedback process, because the technique sensitizes protagonists to the reality of how others perceive them. This feedback may help clarify any discrepancies between their self-perception and what they communicate of themselves to others (Goldman & Morrison, 1984). Consider the illustration of Jack. If he is mirrored as demanding, critical, aloof, and cold, he is likely to wonder whether that's the way his daughter perceives him. This technique may be particularly useful if others in the group see Jack differently from the way he sees himself or if he has difficulty presenting himself verbally or in action. Blatner and Blatner (1988) caution that mirroring can be a powerful confrontation technique and must be used with discretion. It must be given in the spirit of concern and empathy, rather than making the protagonist the object of ridicule.

The Magic Shop

The "magic shop" is often used as a warm-up technique and may also be elaborated on throughout the action phase. This technique is frequently used with protagonists who are unclear about what they value, who are confused about their goals, or who have difficulty assigning priorities to their values. One at a time, the group members bargain with the "storekeeper," who has the power to grant each member his or her most pressing wish. An auxiliary ego or the director is the storekeeper in a magic shop filled with imaginary qualities. These qualities are not for sale, but they can be bartered for. Thus, clients exchange qualities they possess for qualities they desire. Jack, for example, may want to exchange his competitive style for the ability to open up to his daughter in a loving way. This technique can help him assess his priorities and see what is keeping him from getting what he wants from his relationship with Laura.

Future Projection

The technique of future projection is designed to help group members express and clarify concerns that they have about the future. These concerns are not merely discussed and talked about; rather, the anticipated event is brought into the present moment and acted out. These concerns could include wishes and hopes, dreaded fears of tomorrow, or goals that provide some direction to life. Members create a future time and place with selected people, bring a future event into the present, and get a new perspective on a problem situation. A member who has anxiety over an upcoming interview, for example, is asked to act out a future scene so that she can deal with her fears. Not only can she come into contact with her feelings, but she can also gain insight into behaviors that are likely to impede an effective interview. She can get feedback on the way she presents herself in the interview, and she can practice various behavioral styles to prepare herself psychologically for what she sees as a stressful experience. She may act out either a version of the way she hopes the interview will ideally proceed or her version of the most horrible outcome.

Once members clarify their hopes for a particular outcome, they are in a better position to take specific steps to achieve the future they desire. To return to the case of Jack, he can be asked to carry on the kind of dialogue with Laura that he would ideally like to have a year later. He may even reverse roles and "become" his daughter, saying all those things that he hopes she would say to him. He can also project himself forward and tell her how he has acted differently toward her during the last year. If he gets a clearer sense of the kind of relationship that he would like with her and if he accepts his own responsibility for the quality of this relationship, he can then begin to modify some of the ways in which he approaches his daughter.

Role and Functions of the Director

We have already observed many of the functions that the director of a psychodramatic group must perform. There are other, more general comments that need to be made with regard to these functions. Since psychodrama is a powerful method, it is essential that directors have theoretical, technical, and practical knowledge of its techniques. Beyond simply knowing the techniques, they must have a grasp of the philosophy and theory underlying these techniques. In order to fully appreciate the potential values and risks inherent in these techniques, they need to have experienced them as participants. Inept leadership—manifested, for instance, in forcing people into situations with which they are not ready to deal—can have serious negative consequences for the participants.

Although there is definite value in using members as auxiliary egos, for example, there is also the ever-present risk that they will bring their own distortions to the roles they play, further complicating the protagonist's life. The same situation occurs when members project their own conflicts onto the protagonist and offer quick interpretations and solutions to thorny issues. Another key problem that requires skillful handling by the director is adequate debriefing, so that participants will not be left hanging with unproductive unfinished business. For all these reasons, the sensitivity and expertise of the director are crucial if psychodrama is to be therapeutic.

Evaluation of Psychodrama

Value of Psychodramatic Techniques

I value psychodrama's action-oriented methods and role playing mainly because they lead the participants to the direct experience of real conflicts. I have little patience with endless talk about problems, since it has been my experience that members profit very little from talking about themselves in a detached, storytelling manner. But for the participants to learn about themselves, role playing must be designed to fit a specific situation, and certain role-playing techniques must be used to provide further understanding of actual conflicts in the members' lives. If a psychodrama is set up just to give the members an idea of what it's like, I question the outcomes.

I tend to employ psychodramatic methods when a member is undergoing a conflict situation that can be enacted or dramatized in some form. I see these methods as useful not only for the person who is the focus of the action but for other participants as well. Most of my uses of psychodrama have led to increased participation by other members. This method also binds people together, because it offers opportunities for them to become aware that their own struggles are also the struggles of others.

People often simply don't see other ways of behaving with the significant people in their lives. In psychodrama other group members can demonstrate alternative ways of responding and thus provide the person with different frames of reference. In a role-playing situation, for example, Noreen approaches her husband, Roger, with a litany of all his shortcomings: he's selfish, he doesn't care, and he doesn't show his feelings or truly share his life with her. Another member can show Noreen a different way of relating to Roger that is not accusatory and that won't cause him to close up and ignore her complaints. As a result, she may want to try new approaches, which she may not even have considered before.

Integration of Emotional Work with a Cognitive Perspective

It is not necessary for a group practitioner who wants to develop a psychodrama workshop to adhere to the action-oriented methods that have been described in this chapter. These methods can be integrated into the framework of other group approaches. Despite the value of psychodrama, I have found that some of the workshops I attend as a participant are needlessly restrictive. These techniques are often quite useful and appropriate, yet I am not in favor of converting every interaction into dramatic form. Integrated into other systems, such as some of the cognitive styles of behavior therapy, psychodrama can provide the exploration of emotions that these other systems often play down. The psychodramatic group can be enhanced by more emphasis on the cognitive aspects of the process and by deeper investigation of the meaning of the cathartic experience.

Although there is value in catharsis, my experience with groups has taught me time and again how essential it is to provide a context in which members can come to an understanding of what their bottled-up emotions have done to them, to others, and to their relationships. Yet emotional release and self-understanding alone do not seem sufficient to produce lasting changes in one's way of thinking/feeling/behaving. I am convinced that such deep changes will come about only if members are taught how to transfer what they have learned in their sessions to everyday situations. It is also critical to teach them ways of maintaining these positive emotional and behavioral changes. This can be done by helping them plan ways of coping effectively when they meet with frustration in the world and when they regress by seeming to forget the lessons they have learned. An excellent time for this cognitive work and formulation of action plans is toward the end of the sharing sessions after each psychodrama has been brought to a close. This cognitive work might come after other members and the protagonists have had opportunities to express what they were feeling during the psychodrama. One excellent way to help members achieve closure on some of their emotional issues is to have them begin to think about the meaning of heightened emotional states. They can be encouraged to formulate their own interpretations of their problem situations. Furthermore, they can reflect on how their beliefs and decisions may be contributing to some of the emotional turmoil that they reexperienced in a psychodrama.

Simply encouraging people to "get in touch with their feelings" does not seem potent enough to goad them into *doing* something different when they meet with future difficulties. Thus, rehearsals for future encounters, coupled with constructive and specific feedback, can be of real value to those members who want to develop alternative means of relating to significant people in their lives.

According to Blatner and Blatner (1988), a major contribution of psychodrama is that it supports the growing trend toward eclecticism in psychotherapy. As we have seen, the experiential aspects of psychodrama blend well with cognitive approaches. Many of the psychodramatic techniques can also be adapted to work well within the framework of other contemporary theoretical models, including psychoanalytic therapy and object-relations theory, behavior therapies, multimodal therapy, Gestalt therapy, Adlerian therapy, play therapy, imagination therapy, Jungian therapy, family therapy, and group therapy. (See Blatner and Blatner for a more detailed discussion of integrations with other therapies.)

Ethical Issues in Employing Psychodramatic Techniques

Blatner (1973) emphasizes that psychodrama is not a panacea. He cautions practitioners against the danger of romanticizing a single approach, thus becoming blind to the limits of that approach and to the values of other methods. He encourages his readers to obtain some supervised training in the use of psychodrama before attempting to apply any but its most basic techniques. Recognizing that psychodrama is a powerful form of intervention, he underscores the importance of the practitioner's knowledge and ability to deal therapeutically with what surfaces. Elsewhere, Blatner and Blatner (1988) stress that although the application of psychodramatic methods appears relatively easy, the process of coordinating these methods in an intensive psychodrama requires extensive training. They underscore that sound clinical judgment is needed, along with follow-up procedures. They maintain that psychodrama requires a working through and integration of the insights that flow from an enactment. The clinician's judgment remains the crucial factor, and the methods cannot be used in untrained hands either effectively or therapeutically.

Leveton (1977) warns about the irresponsible use of psychodramatic procedures. Skilled directors, she says, are willing to devote the time necessary to develop their skills, and they have undergone a training program under the supervision of an experienced clinician. She describes some of the "new students" she has encountered, whose "cups may run over with techniques" and who have no fear of using these techniques, no matter what the circumstances.

In agreement with the Blatners and Leveton are J. L. Moreno and Elefthery (1982), who remind us that psychodrama is a potent method and that the potential for harming clients is great when it is practiced by untrained persons. They emphasize how essential it is for leaders to have a thorough knowledge of group dynamics and to know their own limitations as well as the limitations of the method for certain client populations. They write that psychodrama should be used only very carefully, if at all, with acting-out individuals, with a seriously disturbed population, or with a sociopathic population. It is especially important that leaders have the experience and knowledge to deal with underlying psychopathology. In addition, they must have considerable sensitivity so that they do not push disturbed clients past a point that is therapeutic. It is also critical that they exercise good judgment in structuring situations so that members are not likely to open up old wounds without getting some closure to them. In addition to training and supervision in psychodramatic methods, a leader who wants to practice this approach should have considerable experience as a protagonist. If leaders have experienced techniques personally, they have a much better framework for knowing when particular methods are called for and for anticipating their effects.

Both Blatner (1973) and Moreno and Elefthery (1982) discuss the danger of leaders' being attracted to psychodrama to fill their egotistical needs. It is critical that they be aware of how their own personal problems and needs might interfere with their functioning. In this regard, countertransference issues must be worked through before the leader can hope to have a therapeutic impact on the group. If group leaders are not secure in their professional competence, they may easily become impatient with what they perceive as the "slow progress" of clients. Out of their desire to speed up the gains of their clients and to see more immediate results, they may resort to a variety of manipulations designed to stir up emotions for the sake of drama.

Although spontaneity is one of the basic concepts of psychodrama, it can be misused. It is imperative that a group leader's spontaneity, inventiveness, and courage to try new techniques be tempered with a measure of caution, respect for the members, and concern for their welfare. Goldman and Morrison (1984) caution therapists to be aware of both the ease with which individuals can be opened up and the necessity of assisting them to achieve closure. They also suggest that therapists need to have a clear purpose in using specific techniques. The general rule they recommend is "When in doubt, err on the side of caution" (p. 102).

In addition to having been a protagonist in a group many times, directors should have experienced personal psychotherapy. Psychodrama can be a very directive technique and thus lends itself to abuse through countertransference. The dangers of this abuse can be greatly lessened, if not avoided, with the personal awareness gleaned from individual therapy.

Applying Psychodrama in Multicultural Settings

If practitioners take seriously the cautions that have been mentioned in this chapter, psychodrama can make unique contributions in helping ethnically and culturally diverse populations. Rather than having a mother merely talk about her problems in relating to her children, for example, she can take on the role of some of her children during therapeutic sessions. Of course, it is important not to suggest directive techniques that are likely to open up intense emotional experiencing too quickly, for some members will be frightened of these feelings and may withdraw from the group. Rather than pushing members to emote, leaders can look for clues to when an invitation to move into some kind of action or role-playing situation would be most appropriate.

For people who have English as a second language, psychodrama has some interesting applications. My colleagues and I have often asked group members to speak to a significant other in their native language as they are engaged in a role-playing situation (Corey, Corey, Callanan, & Russell, 1988). When they speak in their native language, their emotions quickly come to the surface. I recall a German-born group member who was symbolically speaking in English to her father in a role-playing situation. She did this in a detached manner, and what she said had a rehearsed quality to it. We asked her to continue talking to her father, but to speak in German. She did so and was quickly overcome with emotion. It was difficult for her to keep up her defenses against experiencing her intense feelings when she used her native language. It was not important for the leaders or the other members to understand the exact words spoken. The content was not so important as the process in this case. Even though others in the room may not have understood the verbal exchanges in the psychodrama, they did understand the underlying emotional message through the protagonist's nonverbals and tone of voice. After she finished her psychodrama, we asked her to put some words to what she was experiencing. She said that speaking in German vividly brought back early images, which led to a powerful experience of reliving scenes from her childhood. This helped others who did not understand German to be more tuned into her work, and it also helped her put her emotional work into a cognitive perspective. Questions such as the following are often useful: "What did your father say to you? What were you able to tell him this time that you had not told him before? When did you get stuck as you were talking to him? What emotions did this bring up for you that were familiar? Did you respond to him in different ways today than you did when you were a child?" A few well-timed and appropriate questions can help members sort out their ambivalent feelings and make more sense out of their work.

Consider for a moment another aspect of the scenario just presented. Assume that a member is communicating to her father in her native language and that she gets stuck and does not know what to say. Several possibilities are open here. She can be asked to "make something up," mainly as an attempt to get her unstuck. She can be asked to remain stuck for a time and experience that feeling. Or she can be asked to talk to her father about how this experience now is so typical of what she felt when she was a child. Another direction is to allow other members to get involved and talk about what this psychodrama is bringing up in them. Or other members can eventually offer their interpretations. These hunches and interpretations can then be clarified and confirmed by the member who did the role playing.

If the purpose of the group is to explore intrapersonal and interpersonal problems, the psychodramatic techniques that are aimed at facilitating the expression of feelings are often appropriate for ethnic clients. But if the group has a more didactic, educational, and informational focus, these techniques are more limited. If members demonstrate that they are highly uncomfortable in even talking about personal issues, let alone displaying their emotions in front of others, psychodrama is not the technique of choice. For those members who have grave cultural injunctions against talking about their family in a group context, role playing that would involve "talking to mother or father" would probably be met with resistance. Before attempting such techniques, the leader would have to fully explore the clients' cultural values and any resistance they might have to directly confronting a family member, even through the symbolic process of the role-playing situation. This demands a high level of training and skill on the leader's part. It is easy to see that an untrained and culturally unaware leader could be counterproductive.

Impact of Moreno on the Development of Group Therapy

In closing, I'd like to recognize the profound impact of J. L. Moreno on the field of group therapy. The more I learn about the techniques that he pioneered, the more aware I become of his genius as a practitioner. It is an understatement to say that he was far ahead of his time. With his visionary perspective he created methods for integrating feelings, fantasies, and actions. In spite of his pioneering spirit, as Blatner and Blatner (1988) write, Moreno's work has not been widely accepted in the United States. He was considered a maverick by the majority of professionals in the psychological world, and his mode of therapy was a radical departure from both the analytic and the nonanalytic schools. He clearly defied the intellectual trends of the period. As a person, he is sometimes described as having been narcissistic and grandiose. The Blatners contend that because of the factors of historical unreadiness and his personal idiosyncrasies, his approach has not received the popular or professional recognition that it deserves.

Moreno's enthusiasm was translated into an active leadership role when he was using psychodramatic methods. Even though his own style was flamboyant, he was also intuitive and warm. His wife, Zerka, has demonstrated that it is possible to use a different type of therapeutic style and still be highly effective. Her style includes more refinement and gentleness than did her husband's.

Moreno chose his own epitaph: "Here lies the man who brought laughter back into psychiatry." He approached his death with dignity, creativity, and control. When he was 85, after having led a full and vigorous life, his body failed him, and he elected to die in his own way. He stopped eating and took only water. He showed that even at the time of his death he was the actor and director of his fate, for he died in his own way, at his own pace (Fine, 1979).

As you read about other group-therapeutic approaches, you will see how many of the basic concepts and techniques of psychodrama appear in what are sometimes referred to as "innovative therapies." As I mentioned earlier in this chapter, many of the experiential therapies borrow heavily from psychodrama, and even cognitive, behavior-oriented therapies make frequent use of role-playing procedures. Thus, learning about psychodrama is of value because of the many ways in which it can be integrated with the therapies that you will study in the remainder of this book.

If you are interested in learning more about the practical values and applications of psychodrama, do not limit yourself to reading about the approach in journals and books. Instead, consider seeking out some advanced training and supervision and some reputable workshops where you can experience psychodrama as a group member. You will not only learn how this therapy approach works in a group but also be able to work on some personal concerns and find new ways of dealing with them.

Questions for Reflection and Discussion

1. What are some of the most striking differences, in terms of basic concepts and therapeutic techniques, between psychodramatic and psychoanalytic groups? Do you see some ways of thinking in psychoanalytic terms while working with group members in a psychodramatic format?

2. For what populations do you think psychodramatic techniques would be most appropriate? Can you think of any clients whom you would not recommend for psychodrama?

3. What are your reactions to dealing with both the past and the future as though these events were happening in the present? What are some advantages you can see in this present-centered focus? Do you see any problems with bringing all experiences into the "now" and asking clients to reenact a past event or act out some expected future event?

4. How might you respond to a group member who refused to get involved in any type of role playing on the ground that doing so was artificial? If the person were to say to you: "Why do you want me to go back and relive a painful period in my life? I've tried to forget about those difficult times. What good will it do me to open up that can of worms?" how might you respond?

5. What are some specific psychodramatic techniques that you'd like to include in the groups you are leading or might someday lead? How can you incorporate some basic concepts and practices of psychodrama into the model of group counseling that you favor?

6. If you were to employ role-playing procedures in a group you were leading or if you wanted to create a psychodrama as a way to work with a member's problem, what steps would you take to prepare the members for these techniques? What are some ways you can think of to "warm up" your group so that the members are trusting enough to get involved in the process?

7. In the section of this chapter on ethical issues, a number of the risks involved in practicing psychodrama were mentioned. What are your reactions to these cautions and concerns as they apply to you?
8. What training and experience would you deem essential before you felt confident in employing some of the techniques you have read about in this chapter?
9. How might you go about preparing an agency that you were working for to allow you to organize and lead a psychodramatic group? What concerns or objections might you expect to hear from the administrators of such an agency?
10. If you were a member of a psychodramatic group, how do you imagine that you'd respond to getting involved in the techniques that you've just read about? What kind of member would you be?

Where to Go from Here

The *American Society for Group Psychotherapy and Psychodrama* is geared to the needs of professionals who want to learn about the latest developments in the field. It is an interdisciplinary society, in that its members come from all of the helping professions. The goals of the organization are to establish standards for specialists in group therapy and psychodrama and to support the exploration of new areas of endeavors in research, practice, teaching, and training. If you are interested in further information, contact

Stephen F. Wilson, Executive Director
American Society for Group Psychotherapy and Psychodrama
116 East 27th Street
New York, NY 10016

The *American Board of Examiners in Psychodrama, Sociometry and Group Psychotherapy* was established to serve two basic purposes: (1) to establish, on a national level, professional standards in the fields of psychodrama, sociometry, and group psychotherapy, and (2) to certify qualified professionals on the basis of these standards. Two levels of certification have been established by the American Board of Examiners: (1) Practitioner and (2) Trainer, Educator, Practitioner. Applicants must be certified at the first level before becoming eligible for certification at the second. If you are interested in details about certification or if you want a geographic listing of approved trainers, educators, and practitioners in psychodrama, refer to the *Directory of the American Board of Examiners in Psychodrama, Sociometry and Group Psychotherapy* (1987). Contact

Dale Richard Buchanan, Executive Director
American Board of Examiners
P.O. Box 15572
Washington, DC 20003-0572
Phone: (202) 965-4115

RECOMMENDED SUPPLEMENTARY READINGS

If you are seriously interested in psychodrama, I encourage you to read the works of J. L. Moreno and Zerka Moreno. Also, current and back issues of the *Journal of Group Psychotherapy, Psychodrama and Sociometry* are important readings. This journal is published quarterly, and the annual subscription rate is $40. Write to

Heldref Publications
4000 Albemarle Street, N.W.
Washington, DC 20016

Foundations of psychodrama: History, theory, and practice (Blatner & Blatner, 1988) is an updated and excellent resource dealing with the historical, philosophical, psychological, social, and practical foundations of psychodrama. If you have time to read only one source, this would be my recommendation. The Blatners have a readable style, and they have succeeded in giving a fine overview of psychodrama.

Psychodrama: Experience and process (Goldman & Morrison, 1984) is a concise description of the practice of psychodrama. The authors describe specific techniques for the warm-up, action, and sharing phases. Their book also contains a glossary of terms and techniques in the literature of psychodrama.

Acting-in: Practical applications of psychodramatic methods (Blatner, 1973) is a guide for practitioners interested in using psychodramatic techniques in a group setting. This brief book is written very clearly and contains excellent discussions of the basic elements of psychodrama: its methods, stages, principles, and applications as well as some of its pitfalls. Beginners who want a good overview of psychodrama will find this book extremely valuable.

The psychodramatic method (Haskell, 1973) and *Socioanalysis: Self-direction via sociometry and psychodrama* (Haskell, 1975) are two short books that supply beginning group practitioners with a basic grasp of concepts and techniques of psychodrama, sociodrama, and role playing.

Psychodrama for the timid clinician (Leveton, 1977) offers an excellent and eclectic view of psychodrama. The writing is clear, vivid, and very interesting. A number of psychodramatic techniques are described and illustrated through case examples that attest to the author's skills and creativity in applying these techniques. Group leaders can greatly benefit from reading the book and following the author's encouragement to use experiential techniques in group work.

Psychodrama: Rehearsal for living (Starr, 1977) contains good material on role playing and role training, on setting the stage, and on warm-up and training techniques. Particularly good are chapters dealing with applications of psychodramatic methods to marital therapy, children's groups, work with alcoholics and drug abusers, and psychotics' and outpatient groups.

Psychodrama: Theory and therapy (Greenberg, 1974) is a reader that covers the theory of psychodrama, its history and development, specialized techniques and treatment, and evaluations of the method. This interesting collection of articles gives the reader a good grasp of the various aspects of psychodrama.

If you are interested in an in-depth study of the history and evolution of psychodrama, as well as its applications to many different problems and populations, I suggest that you consult the annotated bibliography prepared by Samuel Cardone in Corsini's (1966) book *Roleplaying in psychotherapy*. This bibliography is the result of a review of the periodical literature up to 1965; these articles deal with both the theoretical and practical dimensions of psychodrama, and the 133 abstracts attempt to capture the language style of the authors of each of these articles.

REFERENCES AND SUGGESTED READINGS*

American Board of Examiners in Psychodrama, Sociometry and Group Psychotherapy. (1987). *Directory*. Washington, DC: Author. (Pamphlet)

American Board of Examiners in Psychodrama, Sociometry and Group Psychotherapy. (Undated). *Examination information pamphlet*. Washington, DC: Author.

American Society of Group Psychotherapy and Psychodrama. (1981). *Code of ethics*. New York: Author. (Pamphlet)

*Blatner, A. (1973). *Acting-in: Practical applications of psychodramatic methods*. New York: Springer.

*Blatner, A. (1989). Psychodrama. In R. J. Corsini & D. Wedding (Eds.), *Current psychotherapies* (4th ed.). Itasca, IL: F. E. Peacock.

*Blatner, A., with Blatner, A. (1988). *Foundations of psychodrama: History, theory, and practice* (3rd ed.). New York: Springer.

Corey, G., Corey, M., Callanan, P., & Russell, J. M. (1988). *Group techniques* (rev. ed.). Pacific Grove, CA: Brooks/Cole.

Corsini, R. J. (1966). *Roleplaying in psychotherapy*. Chicago: Aldine-Atherton.

*Fine, L. J. (1979). Psychodrama. In R. J. Corsini (Ed.), *Current psychotherapies* (2nd ed.). Itasca, IL: F. E. Peacock.

Fox, J. (Ed.). (1987). *The essential Moreno: Writings on psychodrama, group method, and spontaneity*. New York: Springer.

*Goldman, E. E., & Morrison, D. S. (1984). *Psychodrama: Experience and process*. Dubuque, IA: Kendall/Hunt.

*Greenberg, I. A. (1974). *Psychodrama: Theory and therapy*. New York: Behavioral Publications.

*Greenberg, I. A. (1986). Psychodrama. In I. L. Kutash & A. Wolf (Eds.), *Psychotherapist's casebook* (pp. 392–412). San Francisco: Jossey-Bass.

Haskell, M. R. (1973). *The psychodramatic method* (4th ed.). Long Beach: California Institute of Socioanalysis.

Kipper, D. A. (1986). *Psychotherapy through clinical role playing*. New York: Brunner/Mazel.

Leveton, E. (1977). *Psychodrama for the timid clinician*. New York: Springer.

Moreno, J. L. (1947). *Theatre of spontaneity: An introduction to psychodrama*. Beacon, NY: Beacon House.

Moreno, J. L. (1958). *Psychodrama: Vol. 2*. Beacon, NY: Beacon House.

Moreno, J. L. (1964). *Psychodrama: Vol. 1* (3rd ed.). Beacon, NY: Beacon House.

Moreno, J. L. (1969). *Psychodrama: Vol. 3*. Beacon, NY: Beacon House.

Moreno, J. L. (1978). *Who shall survive?* (3rd ed.). Beacon, NY: Beacon House.

Moreno, J. L., & Elefthery, D. G. (1982). An introduction to group psychodrama. In G. M. Gazda (Ed.), *Basic approaches to group psychotherapy and group counseling* (3rd ed.). Springfield, IL: Charles C Thomas.

Moreno, Z. T. (1959). A survey of psychodramatic techniques. *Group Psychotherapy, 12,* 5–14.

Moreno, Z. T. (1965). Psychodramatic rules, techniques, and adjunctive methods. *Group Psychotherapy, 18,* 73–86.

*Moreno, Z. T. (1983). Psychodrama. In H. I. Kaplan & B. J. Sadock (Eds.), *Comprehensive group psychotherapy* (2nd ed.). Baltimore: Williams & Wilkins.

*Moreno, Z. T. (1987). Psychodrama, role theory, and the concept of the social atom. In J. K. Zeig (Ed.), *The evolution of psychotherapy* (pp. 341–366). New York: Brunner/Mazel.

*Books and articles marked with an asterisk are suggested for further study.

Nardi, T. J. (1986). The use of psychodrama in RET. In A. Ellis & R. Grieger (Eds.), *Handbook of rational-emotive therapy: Vol. 2.* New York: Springer.

Nicholas, M. W. (1984). *Change in the context of group therapy.* New York: Brunner/Mazel.

Orcutt, T. L. (1977). Roles and rules: The kinship and territoriality of psychodrama and Gestalt therapy. *Group Psychotherapy, Psychodrama and Sociometry, 30.*

Shaffer, J., & Galinsky, M. D. (1989). *Models of group therapy* (2nd ed.). Englewood Cliffs, NJ: Prentice-Hall.

Starr, A. (1977). *Psychodrama: Rehearsal for living.* Chicago: Nelson-Hall.

Treadwell, T., & Treadwell, J. (1972). The pioneer of the group encounter movement. *Group Psychotherapy and Psychodrama, 25,* 16–26.

Yablonsky, L. (1976). *Psychodrama: Resolving emotional problems through role-playing.* New York: Basic Books.

9

The Existential
Approach to Groups

Introduction

The major approaches to psychotherapy can be grouped into three broad classifications: (1) the psychodynamic approach, which emphasizes insight, unconscious motivation, and personality reconstruction; (2) the various forms of behavioral-oriented therapies, such as transactional analysis, rational-emotive therapy, and reality therapy; and (3) those models that are often referred to as the "third force" and that I find convenient to lump together under the heading "existential-humanistic therapies": existential therapy, person-centered therapy, and Gestalt therapy, to name just a few. These approaches are largely experiential and relationship oriented, and they differ from the other two classifications on philosophical grounds and in their beliefs about the nature of the therapist/client relationship.

In the past the connection between philosophical issues and psychotherapy was rather tenuous. But in recent years, especially because of the prominence achieved by the existential approach, the connection has become much more substantial, and the issues of freedom, responsibility, choice, and the meaning of being fully human have become the focus of much concern.

Departing from the empirical approach that dominated psychology for many years, existentially oriented therapists argue that human behavior cannot be understood only by objective methods—that is, by approaching human beings from an external point of view. These psychologists stress the need to take into consideration the individual's internal frame of reference and subjective experience.

255

Existential therapy can best be considered as an *approach,* or *philosophy,* by which a therapist operates. As such, it is not a separate school or a neatly defined, systematic model with specific therapeutic techniques. Mullan (1979) refers to the existential method as a nonsystem when it is compared with most other group approaches. The group leader cannot assume that he or she alone knows the purpose of the group; rather, it is up to each participant to discover this purpose. I will focus in this chapter on the basic themes, or universal human concerns, of this approach, which have significant implications for the existentially oriented group leader.

It is important to remember that the existential approach developed as a reaction to the two other major models, psychoanalysis and behaviorism. Specifically, it rejects these approaches' deterministic view of human nature. Psychoanalysts see freedom as restricted by unconscious forces, irrational drives, and past events. Behaviorists see freedom as restricted by sociocultural conditioning. Existential psychotherapy, in contrast, is a dynamic approach that focuses on four ultimate concerns that are rooted in human existence: freedom, isolation, death, and meaninglessness (Yalom, 1980). It is grounded on the assumption that we are free and therefore responsible for our choices and actions. We are the author of our life, and we draw up the blueprints for its design. A basic existential premise is that we are not the victim of circumstances, because, to a large extent, we are what we choose to be or not to be. Thus, one of the goals of the therapeutic process is to challenge clients to discover alternatives and choose among them. For many clients, the recognition of the ways in which they have kept themselves in a victimlike stance marks the beginning of change. We can recognize that we do not have to remain the passive victim of our circumstances, and by accepting this, we can consciously become the architect of our life.

The Relationship between Humanistic Psychology and Existential Therapy

In my earlier writings I attempted to blend some key concepts of humanistic psychology with existential therapy, only to find that students had a difficult time separating these two approaches. Indeed, some writers with an existential orientation to therapy speak about an existential-humanistic approach (see Bugental, 1978, 1987; Burton, 1967). In this revised edition I have decided to focus on existential therapy as it applies to groups. But I hope a brief discussion will clarify the distinction between the humanistic approach and the existential approach.

The Focus of Humanistic Psychology.   Synthesizing their theories from many divergent fields and approaches, humanistic psychologists contended that people could not be studied and understood in segmented fashion. Rather, humans must be studied in complete relation to how they interact with others and with the world. Some key figures in the development of humanistic psychology included Carl Rogers, Rollo May, Abraham Maslow, and James Bugental. From its earliest days the humanistic movement was characterized by a focus on the capacities unique to humans—namely, love, choice, creativity, purpose, relatedness, meaning, values, self-actualization, autonomy, responsibility, ego transcendence, humor, and spontaneity. According to humanistic psychologists, any therapy that aims at growth must take these human capacities into account. To a large extent, the encounter-group movement in the 1960s and 1970s grew out of the humanistic force.

Unfortunately, as with many movements, humanistic psychology became associated with anti-intellectualism, living impulsively without consideration for future goals or for others, and a "doing-your-own-thing" approach to life. According to Yalom (1980), some of the key leaders of humanistic psychology became disenchanted with the irrational trends in the movement. Yalom does mention that a hazy relationship links humanistic psychology with existential psychotherapy, since they share many basic tenets and assumptions. Also, many humanistic psychologists have an existential orientation: Maslow, Rogers, May, Fritz Perls, and Bugental.

The Focus of Existential Psychotherapy.   Existentialism is a branch of philosophical thought that began in Europe. The key existential writers, such as Heidegger and Sartre, did not address themselves to psychotherapeutic concerns directly. The existential tradition emphasized the limitations and tragic dimensions of human existence. It grew out of a desire to help people engage the dilemmas of contemporary life, such as isolation, alienation, and meaninglessness. The focus was on being in the world alone and facing the anxiety of this isolation. Rather than trying to develop rules for therapy, it strove to understand these deep human experiences (May & Yalom, 1989).

Existentialism focuses on understanding the person's subjective view of the world and, thus, is a phenomenological approach. Therapy is a journey taken by therapist and client, a journey that delves deeply into the world as perceived and experienced by the client. But this type of quest demands that the therapist also be in contact with his or her own phenomenological world. Bugental (1987) writes about life-changing psychotherapy, which is the effort to help clients examine the manner in which they have answered life's existential questions and to challenge them to revise some of their answers in ways that will result in living authentically.

Existential therapy is best considered as an invitation to clients to recognize the ways in which they are not living fully authentic lives and to make choices that will lead to their becoming what they are capable of being. This approach does not focus on curing sickness or merely applying problem-solving techniques to the complex task of authentic living. In writing about the task of existential psychotherapy, Bugental (1986) centers on the process of bringing out the latent aliveness in the client:

> We do not seek to teach them something so much as to call on them to listen better to what they already know but to which they do not attend, owing to lack of presence. This view contrasts with the perception of therapy as the repair of an ailing or broken being [p. 223].

Perhaps one of the key figures responsible for bringing existentialism from Europe and translating key concepts into psychotherapeutic practice is May. His writings have had a significant impact on existentially oriented practitioners. According to May, becoming a person is not an automatic process, yet people do have a desire to fulfill their potential. It takes courage to be, and our choices determine the kind of person we become. There is a constant struggle within us. Although we want to grow toward maturity and independence, we realize that expansion is often a painful process. Hence, the struggle is between the security of dependence and the delights and pains of growth. Along with May, two other significant contemporary sources of existential theory are Bugental (1987) and Yalom (1980).

The Purpose of an Existential Group.   The existential group represents a microcosm of the world in which its participants live and function. Its members meet for the purpose of discovering themselves as they are by sharing their existential concerns. An existential group can be described as people making a commitment to a lifelong journey of self-exploration. The group provides the encouragement for members to begin listening to themselves and paying attention to their subjective experience. This process of inner searching gives emphasis to what members discover when their own stream of awareness is not directed by the therapist. By being willing to openly share and explore universal personal concerns, members develop a sense of mutuality. The close ties that they feel with one another give them many opportunities for using the group culture differently from other aspects of their existence. In short, an existential group is a place where people can be together in deeply meaningful ways without the superficiality characteristic of so many meetings.

In writing about the goals of an existential group, Mullan (1979) makes it clear that each member must go through a painful process to discover his or her own goals. At the beginning a group experience is painful, because rules and routines are lacking and because members are searching for, but cannot find, roles to play. They find that their pregroup behavior does not work for them in the therapy group. Members often question the role of the leader, as well as the value of the group for themselves. Mullan contends that, in their journey to become more authentic, members typically experience suffering and despair as they face their human condition. Eventually, this depression gives way to periods of calm and joy, but the road is a rough one.

Key Concepts

In this chapter we'll examine some key concepts of the existential approach and their implications for group practice. These concepts are self-awareness, self-determination and responsibility, existential anxiety, death and non-being, the search for meaning, the search for authenticity, and aloneness/

relatedness. Rather than focusing on group techniques, this chapter stresses understanding how these key concepts can be applied in a group.

In keeping with this spirit, this chapter is written from my own perspective on the existential approach. The focus is on concepts that most existential writers and practitioners give attention to. Some of the major themes running through various humanistic writings are summarized and applied to group work.

Self-Awareness

The capacity for self-awareness separates us from other animals and enables us to make free choices. The greater our awareness, the greater our possibilities for freedom. Even though we are subject to the deterministic forces of sociocultural conditioning and to the limitations imposed by our genetic endowment, we are still able to choose based on our awareness of these limiting factors. As May (1961) writes, "No matter how great the forces victimizing the human being, man has the capacity to know that he is being victimized and thus to influence in some way how he will relate to his fate" (pp. 41–42). Furthermore, because of our self-awareness, we come to recognize the responsibility associated with the freedom to choose and to act.

Implications for Group Work.   As mentioned earlier, the basic goal of existential therapy is to expand self-awareness and thus increase the potential for choice. In groups this goal is pursued by helping members discover their unique "being-in-the-world." By asking themselves key questions, participants seek to define themselves and become aware of the central dimensions of their existence: "To what degree am I aware of who I am and where I am going? How do I experience my world? What meanings do I attach to the events I experience? How can I increase my self-awareness? In what concrete ways does expanded consciousness increase my range of alternatives?"

According to May (1983), the task of therapy is to illuminate existence. Clients try to become aware of their existence as fully as possible, which includes realizing their potentialities and learning to act on the basis of them. A central theme of the existential approach is taking existence seriously.

In the group situation participants have the opportunity to express their own unique feelings and their subjective views of the world. They are also explicitly confronted by others, and they learn to deal with the anxiety that arises from having to choose for themselves when they are stripped of the securities of their everyday roles. As we shall see in detail later in the chapter, existentialists view anxiety in positive terms. Anxiety helps "individuate" us, it awakens us to the inauthenticity of merely being who others want us to be, and it reflects the understanding that we are unique and have the potential to move toward our individual possibilities.

But anxiety is uncomfortable. The desire to avoid the anxiety associated with increased self-awareness can lead participants to use their freedom to actually decrease their self-awareness and thus withdraw from life. Kemp (1971) writes that, in order to escape anxiety, clients can relinquish their identity (often unconsciously) by submerging themselves in the group, by meeting life situations without struggle, and by attempting to live by fulfilling the expectations of others. The result is that they also relinquish contact with themselves and give up their individuality.

Thus, I believe that group leaders need to alert the members of their groups to the price they must pay for seeking greater self-awareness. As people become more aware, they find it increasingly difficult to "go back home again." If living in ignorance of the quality of one's existence can lead to staleness, it can also bring a certain degree of contentment or, at least, security. As we open doors that were previously closed, we can expect to encounter more struggle as well as the potential for enhancing the quality of our living. The experience can be exciting and joyful but also frightening and at times depressing. This is an issue that should be mentioned during the early phases of a group, so that members are aware of the need to consider whether they are willing to pay the price that increased self-awareness entails.

What are the options that a higher degree of self-awareness permits us to recognize? Here are some of them:

- We can choose to expand our awareness, or we can choose to limit our vision of ourselves.
- We can determine the direction of our own lives, or we can allow other people and environmental forces to determine it for us.
- We can use our potential for action, or we can choose not to act.
- We can choose to establish meaningful ties with others, or we can choose to isolate ourselves.
- We can search for our own uniqueness, or we can allow our identity to be lost in conformity.
- We can create and find meaning in our life, or we can lead an empty and meaningless existence.
- We can engage in certain risks and experience the anxieties that accompany deciding for ourselves, or we can choose the security of dependence.
- We can make the most of the present by accepting the inevitability of our eventual death, or we can hide from this reality because of the anxiety it generates.
- We can commit ourselves to striving to utilize our full potential, or we can settle for functioning with only a small fraction of our capacity.

Example.   The following example is meant to illustrate how participants in a group can gradually achieve a higher level of awareness. This and the examples that illustrate the other key concepts in this chapter are drawn from my experience with the groups I have led. To protect the identity of the clients, I have changed the names and the specific circumstances, and I have chosen examples that have a universal quality—that is, situations that occur frequently in a group.

When Crystal first entered the group, she could see no value in expressing intense emotions and insisted that she *had* to be rational no matter what. She tried very hard to keep her feelings harnessed at all times, because she was afraid that she'd "go crazy" if she allowed herself to feel intensely. This need to tightly control her feelings manifested itself in several ways. For example, when other group members relived painful emotional events, she panicked and tried to leave the room, and she often attempted to defuse the expression of intense emotions by others in the group. During one session, however, another person's work triggered some very painful memories in Crystal, which she felt fully because, for some reason, she allowed herself to relive a scene from her childhood related to her parents' divorce. Suddenly she became that frightened child again, pleading with her parents to stay together and letting herself "go emotionally out of control."

This unexpected experience made Crystal aware that she had been keeping a lid on her strong feelings and that her defenses against "hurting too much" had resulted in her difficulty in getting close to others, in expressing anger, and in manifesting the love she claimed she felt for her family now. She also learned that she wouldn't "go crazy" by permitting herself to experience the depth of her feelings. After that experience she chose to open herself to feelings and not to run out of the room when she was afraid she couldn't take the intense emotions of other members.

Self-Determination and Personal Responsibility

Another existential theme is that we are self-determining beings, free to choose among alternatives and therefore responsible for directing our lives and shaping our destinies. The existentialists' view is that although we are thrust into the world, how we live and what we become are the result of our choices. As Sartre (1971) puts it, our existence is a given, but we do not have, and cannot have, a fixed, settled "nature," or "essence." We are constantly faced with having to choose the kind of person we want to become, and as long as we live, we must continue to choose. Sartre remarks: "Man being condemned to be free carries the weight of the whole world on his shoulders; he is responsible for the world and for himself as a way of being" (p. 553). For Sartre, we are free in that we are nothing but what we *do,* and what we do is not the result of our past. However, we are much given to making excuses, thus acting in "bad faith."

Russell (1978) notes that, in Sartre's view, nothing in the world has a meaning independent of us, and we are responsible for the world as a significant place. Russell adds: "Each time we act we thereby choose and create ourselves as we want to be, and this is never finished—what we are is never settled—but is created in each of the deeds that constitute us" (p. 262).

We are responsible for the consequences of our actions and for any failure to act: "I author the meaningfulness of my world in giving significance to my situation. . . . It is when I see myself as the *author* of my actions and (relatedly) of the significance I give my world that I get an enlarged sense of my responsibility for this" (p. 261).

Viktor Frankl, an existential psychiatrist, stresses the relationship between freedom and responsibility and insists that freedom can never be taken from us, because we can at least choose our attitude toward any given set of circumstances. To support this statement, Frankl (1963) draws from his own experiences in a German concentration camp, where the prisoners were stripped of every semblance of outward freedom. He contends that, even in a situation of such extreme powerlessness, people can ultimately be their own master, because the attitude they assume toward their suffering is of their own choosing: "Life ultimately means taking responsibility to find the right answer to its problems and to fulfill the tasks which it constantly sets for each individual" (p. 122). In Frankl's brand of existential therapy, *logotherapy,* this means that clients create the distress they experience. They are responsible for (but not to blame for) the symptoms that restrict their ability to live freely and fully. It is not mere chance or the actions of others that are causing them to be miserable, since they are creating their situation. It is essential that clients recognize and accept their part in creating their distress, for until then, they will not change. If they wait around for others to change or for the environment to change, they may well increase their own misery and hopelessness instead of taking action to make something happen differently.

Implications for Group Work.   The members of an existential group are confronted over and over with the fact that they cannot escape from freedom and that they are responsible for their existence. Accepting this freedom and this responsibility generates anxiety, and so do the risk and uncertainty associated with making choices. Another goal of the existential group is to help participants face and deal with these anxieties. The main task of the group leader with regard to the issue of self-determination is to confront members with the reality of their freedom. Group participants often present themselves as victims, talk about their feelings of helplessness and powerlessness, and place the blame for their miseries on others and on external circumstances. In short, clients often are not aware that they do have choices or that they are severely restricting the range of available alternatives. A good place for clients to start on the road to greater self-determination is to become aware of the restrictions they are placing on their freedom and of the roles they have been programmed to play. When people come to *believe* that they can direct their destiny, they ultimately assume control of their life.

Yalom (1980) contends that the group provides the optimal conditions for therapeutic work on personal responsibility. If the group has a here-and-now focus, the members can be encouraged to observe how they are creating victimlike stances for themselves. In Yalom's view members are responsible for the interpersonal position they assume in the group setting, which also gives a glimpse of how they behave in life situations. Members who describe themselves as being victimized by external conditions can be challenged. Through feedback, members learn to see themselves through others' eyes, and they learn the ways in which their behavior affects others. Further, they learn how the group situation represents situations in their everyday life. Building on these discoveries, they also see how their behavior is influencing their perceptions and evaluations of themselves, and they can take responsibility for making changes.

From Yalom's (1980) perspective the existential group leader encourages the members to assume responsibility for their functioning as a group. In this way individual members learn ways to take greater responsibility for their life:

> The interactional therapy group enhances responsibility assumption not only by making members aware of their personal contribution to their unsatisfying life situations but also by accentuating each member's role in the conduct of the group. The underlying principle is that if members assume responsibility for the functioning of the group, then they become aware that they have the ability (and obligation) to assume responsibility in all spheres of life [p. 240].

Examples. Edward had reluctantly joined one of my groups. I say "reluctantly" because he had serious misgivings about the value of participating in a group. At 52, Edward had settled into a dull, predictable, but comfortable and safe lifestyle as a successful business executive. When he joined, he presented himself with this statement: "I don't know if this group will do me any good or not. Frankly, I think that I'm too old to change and that what I have is the most I can hope to get from life. I believe that things will probably stay as they are." In spite of his own statement and in spite of the fact that his life was orderly and safe, he felt that he was "drying up" and that life had lost zest. He was ready for a change, even though he was not sure whether change was possible.

Through his involvement in the group, Edward began to realize that he did have options—many more than he ever thought possible. All along, he had blamed his wife, his three sons, and his daughter for the fact that he couldn't change jobs and live the kind of life he wanted for himself. He was, of course, avoiding the responsibility for his own problems by focusing on what his family expected, often without ever verifying whether they did expect what he thought they did.

The other members and I challenged Edward to begin thinking for himself about how *he* wanted his life to be different. I asked him questions such as "If you were to continue living for the rest of your life as you are now, with no basic changes, how would you feel about it?" "Assume that your family would be willing to make the changes in lifestyle that you want to make. How would your life be different 1 year from now? And 5 years from now?" "What steps can you take today that will help you make some of the changes you want? What is preventing you from taking these steps?"

By the time Edward left the group, he at least saw that he didn't have to live a "life without any seasoning." Although he had not made any major commitments to change, he did feel that if he wanted to change, he could and that if he was willing to take risks, his life would be richer. In my eyes this recognition that he *did* indeed have choices was more important than the specific choices he was going to make. My task as a group leader was not to push him to make choices that I thought were desirable but simply to use the forces within the group to help him recognize that he was both free and responsible for the direction of his own life. The central function of the group leader is to help people accept the fundamental challenge of taking a stand concerning their lives.

In another of my groups, one of the participants refused to take responsibility for her lack of freedom by blaming her parents. When confronted with her dependency, Violet would defend herself by saying: "If I'm afraid of life, it's because *they* didn't care enough when I was a child. I fear men now because my father was a cold fish who never made me feel lovable and worthwhile. If only my mother had pushed me to do more things on my own, instead of doing everything for me, today I would have the confidence of standing on my own two feet." And so it went with Violet. She kept investing her energies in finding reasons for her fear of living and in blaming her parents for her problems rather than in trying to find out what *she* could actually *do now* to take charge of her life.

Basically, my work with Violet in the group consisted of confronting her with the fact that, as long as she continued to cling to her past to justify her unwillingness to make decisions for herself, she would remain helpless. She was challenged to decide whether she wanted to remain the "victim" or whether she wanted to begin to exercise her freedom to design her life so that she could live effectively. Some time after the group terminated, Violet reported:

> Sometimes I wonder what it would be like if I had never been in the group and learned what I did about myself. I felt safer then, because I was faced with fewer choices than I am now. Before, the world was a bleak place—one in which I knew no joy—yet it was safer. There were fewer challenges. Even if I could return to that time of safety and dependency, I know that I would not. I've come too far to go back. There are times, though, when I question if it has been worth it.

Existential Anxiety

From the existential viewpoint anxiety is a basic characteristic of being human. Thus, it is not necessarily pathological but, on the contrary, can be a strong motivational force toward growth. As discussed earlier, anxiety results from having to make choices without clear guidelines and without knowing what the outcome will be and from being aware that we are ultimately responsible for the consequences of our actions. In Kierkegaard's words existential anxiety is "the dizziness of freedom." At some level we know that for new dimensions of ourselves to emerge, old parts of ourselves must die. The knowledge that in order to grow we must exchange familiar and secure ways for new and unknown ones is in itself a source of anxiety. May asserts that "anxiety is the experience of the threat of imminent nonbeing" (1983, p. 109). Although we may not welcome this anxiety, it is the price we must pay for engaging in the process of becoming what we are capable of being.

Anxiety acts as a catalyst for growth by encouraging us to take action for change. It serves as a signal that our activities are growing stale and unexciting and that we are ready for movement and change. Sidney Jourard (1968a) writes that it is at those times when we find our existence dull and boring that we can transcend our limitations by daring to attempt new ways of being. We know that we are ready to make changes when we experience staleness, depression, anxiety, guilt, or even despair. Jourard indicates that we have a choice of how to respond to this anxiety. We can allow ourselves to fully experience the emotions that tell us that "all is not well" and thus become aware of the need to change. Or we can repress them and ignore the signals, so that we continue to live in the security of our stale lives and avoid change. Jourard says "If you help me give up old projects which are no longer satisfying, delightful, or fulfilling and encourage me to dare new ones, you are helping me to grow" (1968b, p. 12). When we blunt existential anxiety, we constrict our lives and limit our choices. Thus, the price we pay is steep indeed.

Implications for Group Work. In a line of thought that is similar to Jourard's, Bugental (1978) describes therapeutic work with existential anxiety as a stripping away of defenses, much like the peeling of an onion. At the core of therapy, clients eventually come to terms with the underlying conditions of being human that are related to the anxiety they experience. These sources of existential anxiety must be faced and worked through in therapy; they involve recognition of our separateness and our need to be with others, of our guilt over not living authentically, of the emptiness in the universe and lack of meaning, of the burden of responsibility associated with choosing for ourselves, and of our fear of death and nonbeing. As therapy progresses and the resistances are peeled away, clients often painfully recognize how much energy they have put into maintaining an idealized image of themselves that is impossible to achieve. They also see that they must let go of old images of themselves that lead to a restricted existence. As clients give up their phony roles, they are able to bring a renewed quality to their living. A death of their old self occurs, which allows room for some kind of breakthrough experience. Yet such a process is typically anxiety provoking, for clients are giving up rigid ways of being that are familiar. As Bugental (1978) says: "In a very real sense, the client must go out of control for at least a brief period because the ways on which control has previously depended have been bound up with old patterns of being. Until they are truly let go of, they cannot be replaced" (p. 79).

Because anxiety is uncomfortable, we sometimes attempt to allay it or escape it altogether. But even if we manage to escape anxiety, the conditions that are producing it do not disappear as if by magic. Therefore, one of the leader's tasks is to encourage participants to accept anxiety as growth-producing and to help them find the courage to face and to fully experience their anxieties. The next step is to encourage members to make a commitment to action. Through the support of the leader and of other participants in the group, the individual can be inspired to explore unknown paths and to investigate new dimensions of self. This search can lead to even greater anxiety, but if the person is in the process of growth, he or she knows that anxiety doesn't have to be devastating and that it is the price one must pay for breaking out of constricting modes of existence.

In my groups I make sure that participants understand the crucial difference between existential and neurotic anxiety. Whereas existential anxiety can be a strong motivational force toward growth, neurotic anxiety "results whenever a person evades existential anxiety by failing to confront it directly and make active choices in spite of it" (Shaffer, 1978, p. 29). Thus, neurotic anxiety, far from being a liberating agent, further constricts the person's life.

Example.   For much of her life Ann had allowed others to make decisions for her. She had uncritically accepted her parents' religious values and had become very dependent on her church to make decisions for her. At this time in her life she was struggling with following the values that she had grown up with. Through her work in a group, Ann came to see more and more clearly that if she wanted to grow, she needed to take more responsibility for her choices. Thus, she decided to look within herself for strength and direction. This decision brought her a great deal of anxiety. She continued to ask herself "Am I doing the right thing?" and "What if the ethical decisions I'm making now on my own are wrong?"

It took Ann some time to begin to trust herself and even longer to let go of the need to lean on some kind of authority for all her answers and for security. A little at a time, however, she began to experience a new sense of power, the exhilarating feeling that *she* was directing her life, even though she kept struggling all along with conflicts and doubts. Surely she would have been more comfortable had she continued to rely on external guidance. Yet when she realized that she had allowed others to make most of her major decisions, she also saw how she had given up control over her life. In choosing for herself, she still felt anxiety over not having a guarantee that she was doing the right thing.

Death and Nonbeing

The existentialist considers the concept of death instrumental to the discovery of meaning and purpose in life. Death in any of its aspects is the fact that makes the present hour of significant value (May, 1983). The realization of our finitude gives meaning to existence because it makes every act count. Life has meaning precisely because it must end. The present is precious because it is all we really have. It is our temporal nature that makes us feel the urgency to do something with our life, to make a choice between affirming life by trying to become the person we are capable of becoming and allowing life to slip by us and eventually realizing that we've never been truly alive. Yalom (1980) summarizes this notion as follows:

> Death and life are interdependent: though the physicality of death destroys us, the *idea* of death saves us. Recognition of death contributes a sense of poignancy to life, provides a radical shift of life perspective, and can transport one from a mode of living characterized by diversions, tranquilization, and petty anxieties to a more authentic mode [p. 40].

Mullan (1979) makes the point that death is an inevitability to be dealt with and accepted in the existential group, since it is always present. For members to face this issue and work with the anxiety it brings, the leader cannot ignore it. According to Mullan:

> The death motif is awakening and challenging and not, as some claim, morbid and nihilistic. Through its use patients are bombarded with the insignificance of their ordinary pursuits. Their usual customs, routines, conventions, and habits all come under fire. Once they have faced the certainty of their death, many persons cease to be victims of the past in which their parents' irrational authority was so pronounced. Suddenly they find that they must act now and with greater intensity than before [p. 173].

Thus, humans, as the only creatures with a strong sense of the future, need to deal with the end of life, which Heidegger calls "cessation of possibility." Because many of us are afraid of facing the reality of our own death and the anxiety that goes with it, we might attempt to escape the awareness of this reality. But the price for trying to flee from the confrontation with nonbeing is awesome. In the words of May (1961): "The price for denying death is undefined anxiety, self-alienation. To completely understand himself, man must confront death, become aware of personal death" (p. 65). Frankl (1963) concurs and adds that it is not *how long* we live but *how* we live that determines the quality and meaningfulness of our life.

Implications for Group Work. Awareness of death and the anxiety it generates has significant implications for the practice of group work. The concern with living life fully, rather than merely existing, is a recurrent theme in many groups. Generally I tackle this theme by encouraging group members to ask themselves honestly how they feel about the quality of their lives. Then I ask them to answer this same question as if they knew that they were about to die. How do the two answers differ? Have they made decisions that were not carried through, or have they ignored opportunities for change? By reflecting on their unfinished business, participants may come to realize that they are not living the kind of life they'd like to live, and they may be able to identify the reasons for this unsatisfactory existence. Sometimes dreams about one's dying may symbolize the coming to a close of one phase of life, of some interest, work, or relationship.

I find it valuable to expand the concept of physical death to other kinds of death. Even though we are physically alive, we may be dead or dying in important areas of life. Perhaps we are numb to our feelings or caught up in deadening roles. We may have lost our intellectual curiosity and wonderment about life. Perhaps our relationships with significant people are characterized by routine and devitalizing acts. What we do may have lost meaning. A group can be a good place to recognize the areas in which we have gone stale and to confront ourselves with what we are willing to do in order to change and flourish again.

The process of change always entails allowing parts of us to die in order to make room for new growth. And growth often demands that we be willing to let go of familiar ways of being. We may need to experience a period of mourning over our losses before we can move forward and establish new patterns. Groups offer a safe place to express this sadness, to explore the ambivalence that generally accompanies change, and to experiment with new ways of being.

Example.   In another book, *I Never Knew I Had a Choice* (Corey & Corey, 1990), I discuss the concept of *freedom in dying*—the notion that even in dying we still have choices concerning how we face and deal with what is happening to us. As I was writing that section of the book, a friend and former group member, Jim Morelock, was dying. He permitted me to use his real name and to share some of the significant moments in his dying.

Jim was 25 years old. He was full of life and seemed to have a bright future when he discovered that he had a rare form of cancer. In the group Jim talked about his fears of dying and expressed his anger about the reality that he wouldn't be able to put to use much of what he had learned about himself, because his time was so limited. As he put it, "I finally learned that I have a lot to offer and that I'm lovable. I'd sure like to hang around and enjoy all those people that love me!"

His own gifts and active interest in life, as well as his counseling and group experience, enabled Jim to face death with courage and to infuse it with meaning. Even after he learned that his illness was terminal, he continued to take a course at the university, because he liked the contact with people there. He decided not to remain in a hospital and not to undergo chemotherapy, primarily because he didn't want to prolong his life if he couldn't live it fully. Jim made a choice to accept God into his life, which gave him peace and serenity. He did many of the things he most wanted to do, maintaining an active interest in life and in the world around him. More than anyone I know, Jim took care of unfinished business. He said everything he wanted to say to his family and close friends and made all the arrangements for his own funeral, including asking my wife, Marianne, to deliver the eulogy.

Jim showed me that his style of dying was no different from his style of living, and through him I have learned much about dying and about living. Shortly before his death, Jim told me that he didn't have regrets about the way he had lived his life, because in those short 25 years he had lived more fully than many older people. He also commented that, although we may not have a choice concerning our losses in dying, we can still choose our attitude toward death.

The Search for Meaning

The struggle for a sense of significance and purpose in life is a distinctively human characteristic. We search for meaning and personal identity, and we raise existential questions—"Who am I? Where am I going and why? Why am I here? What gives my life purpose and meaning?" For the existentialists, life does not have positive meaning in itself; it is up to us to create meaning. As we struggle in a world that often appears meaningless and even absurd, we challenge values we never challenged before, we discover new facets of ourselves, we try to reconcile conflicts and discrepancies, and, in so doing, we create our meaning in the world.

Frankl has devoted his career to developing an existential approach to therapy that is grounded on the role of meaning in life. According to him, the central human concern is to discover meaning that will give one's life direction. On the basis of his clinical work and study, Frankl has concluded that a lack of meaning is the major source of existential stress and anxiety in modern times. He views existential neurosis as the experience of meaninglessness. Many people come to therapy because of an *existential vacuum,* or a feeling of inner void that results from not pursuing meaning. Therefore, according to Frankl, therapy should be designed to help clients find meaning in their life.

Frankl (1963) says that there are many ways of finding meaning— through work, through loving, through suffering, and through doing for others. According to him, the therapist's function is not to tell clients what their particular meaning in life should be but to encourage them to discover meaning for themselves. He believes that even suffering can be a source of growth and that if we have the courage to experience our suffering, we can find meaning in it. Suffering can be turned into achievement by the stand we take in the face of it. By confronting pain, despair, and death and by trying to understand their meaning for us, we turn the negative sides of life into triumph.

Implications for Group Work. Both the issue of finding meaning and the related question of challenging and perhaps discarding values that are no longer meaningful are commonly explored in groups. Discarding old values without finding new and more suitable ones to replace them is a concern that many participants share. Some people live by a value system that they have never challenged and that was handed down to them and merely incorporated. Others have lost their own identity by submitting to group pressure, thus denying their inner reality in order to conform to social mores.

One of the tasks of the therapeutic process is to confront clients with evidence of the fact that they are living by unexamined values that no longer contribute to a meaningful existence. We may not be responsible for having acquired values that don't help our quest for meaning, but we are certainly responsible for clinging to them and for failing to find new ones. Some useful questions that can be explored in a group setting are these:

- "Do you like the direction of your life? If not, what are you doing about it?"
- "What are the aspects of your life that satisfy you most?"
- "What is preventing you from doing what you really want to do?"

With the support of the group, participants can find the strength to question and discard certain values and to create an internally derived value system that is consistent with their way of being. This process is likely to generate anxiety, at least for a time, and they will flounder in the absence of clear-cut values. The leader's job is to remind these people that learning to develop the self-trust necessary to look within, discover one's own values, and live by them is a long and difficult process that requires determination and patience.

Examples. The following examples illustrate the challenges that group members face when they attempt to redefine their lives and develop a value system that is their own.

Priscilla was reared with extremely conventional values, and she had never really examined them. She felt compelled to be a "proper lady" at all times, as if her parents were watching over her shoulder. Whenever she was doing something that she thought her parents wouldn't approve of, she seemed to "hear mother and father speaking," telling her what she *should* do and what she *ought* to feel. In various group exercises, Priscilla "became her parents" and spoke for them by lecturing each of us about how we ought to change our ways.

At one point I urged her to act as if she had no choice but to remain forever the nice and proper lady her parents expected her to be and asked her to exaggerate this ladylike behavior in the group for several sessions. Afterward she reported that doing so "made her sick" and that she would change, no matter how difficult the task was going to be. Although Priscilla still respected some of the core values she had learned at home, she wanted the freedom to retain some of those values and discard others without feeling guilty. Her work in the group and outside of it gave her new freedom to develop her own set of values—values that were meaningful to her and that allowed her to live by her own expectations and not by those of others.

When Herman joined the group, he complained that he felt empty and worthless and that he saw himself as a rock—devoid of life and impossible to penetrate. Since Herman was questioning the meaning of his life—he kept referring to himself as lifeless, empty, and dead—my co-leader and I invited him to give in to what we saw as a death wish. We said: "Since you say that you feel dead and empty most of the time, let yourself die here now. Lie down over there and imagine that you *are* dead. We'll cover you with a sheet, and we'll all talk about you as if you were dead—how we saw you and how we felt about you. We'll even give you a eulogy. Stay underneath the sheet and allow yourself to feel fully the deadness you so often refer to. When you decide that you want to throw off your sheet and begin to live, do so."

Herman stayed there for most of the session, and, when he finally "came to life," he related his experience to the group with deep emotion. As a result he began to see *how* he was cutting himself off from people and how he was contributing to his own numbness. He was then able to explore and identify new ways of relating to others, making contact, and overcoming his psychological and emotional deadness.

I want to emphasize that the technique we used with Herman is very powerful and that it can elicit intense emotions. It is important that the leader possess the therapeutic skills necessary to work sensitively and effectively with whatever may result from the technique. It is also essential that a high level of trust exist between the member and the leader before such a technique is used, since it can be seen as hurtful by the client.

The Search for Authenticity

The theologian Paul Tillich (1952) uses the phrase "the courage to be" to convey the essence of the spirit it takes to affirm ourselves and to live from the inside. Discovering, creating, and maintaining the core deep within our being is a difficult and never-ending struggle.

Being authentic means doing whatever is necessary to define and affirm ourselves. Keen (1970) says that the "authentic being is born of anxiety," the anxiety of never knowing if we are making the "right choices" and yet demonstrating the courage to act. "To choose this or that course, to opt for one value or another under conditions of cognitive ambiguity, is to have control over oneself, to be an agent and to establish oneself as valid" (p. 65).

When we lead an authentic existence, we are constantly becoming the person we are capable of becoming. Living authentically also entails knowing and accepting our limits. The "Serenity Prayer" offers a good example of this knowledge and acceptance: "God grant me the serenity to accept the things I cannot change, courage to change the things I can, and wisdom to know the difference."

A quote with a different twist, one that Frankl is fond of using, is Goethe's admonition: "If we take man as he is, we make him worse; but if we take him as he should be, we help him become what he can be." Frankl sees it as the therapist's task to challenge clients to become their full and authentic selves by getting engaged in life and making commitments. His logotherapy, since it is concerned with people's spiritual dimensions and higher aspirations, provides inspiration to continually seek the meaning that is necessary to live authentically.

We can lead inauthentic lives by giving up the quest for self-definition, by submerging our identity in a group, and by allowing others to determine who and what we will become. Rather than trusting ourselves to search and find the answers within, we sell out by becoming what others expect us to be, and in the process we become strangers to ourselves. The essence of defining oneself is captured in an adage I saw in a church in Hawaii: "Who you are is God's gift to you; what you make of yourself is your gift to God."

Those who typically ignore their inner promptings in a perennial quest for conformity lose themselves in the values and standards of others. One of the most common fears expressed by people in groups is that if they take an honest look at themselves, they will discover that they are just empty shells with no core and no substance. Therefore, they are afraid of shedding masks and pretenses, because, once those are gone, nothing will be left.

A concept related to inauthenticity is guilt. *Existential guilt* grows out of a sense of incompleteness and the realization that we are not utilizing our full potentials—in sum, out of leading an inauthentic existence. According to the existentialists, this neglect of potentiality leads to a narrowing of our lives; although it may help us cope with the unknown, it does hamper our development. Ultimately, the loss of the sense of being becomes psychological sickness. To the extent that we fail to fulfill our potential, we become sick.

At the other end of the spectrum is what Maslow (1968, 1970, 1971) calls the *self-actualizing* person. For Maslow, human beings strive for self-actualization, which is the tendency to become all that we are able to become. Although all people have a natural tendency to develop their uniqueness and fulfill their potentials, the process is not automatic. Because growth entails a struggle between our desire for security and dependence and our desire for self-actualization, we must decide which side of the struggle we want to commit ourselves to.

Maslow has identified the characteristics of self-actualizing people, some of which include the following: inner direction and resistance to being defined by others, the capacity to tolerate and even welcome uncertainty, acceptance of others and of oneself, a fresh perception of the world, spontaneity and naturalness, autonomy, a need for privacy and solitude, deep caring for others and the capacity to form intimate relationships, a sense of humor, and the absence of artificial dichotomies within oneself (such as weakness/strength, love/hate, and work/play).

Implications for Group Work. The struggle for authenticity has deep implications for group work. A group provides a powerful context in which to look at oneself, decide the degree to which one is a fully functioning person as opposed to the reflection of what others expect, and consider what choices might be more authentically one's own. In a group setting members can openly share their fears related to living in unfulfilling ways and come to see how they have compromised their integrity.

Examples. The case of Martha, who at 45 had devoted a major portion of her life to her family, represents a situation characteristic of many women who have been members of my groups and personal-growth workshops. For most of her life Martha had depended almost totally on her roles as wife, mother, and homemaker as sources of identity. As her daughters and sons entered high school and then college and finally left home, Martha kept asking herself more and more frequently: "Is there more to life than what I've done so far? Who am I besides all the roles I've responsibly filled? What do *I* want to do with the rest of my life?"

Martha returned to the university and obtained a degree in human services and psychology, a critical turning point in her life because of the many new doors that her degree opened for her. She engaged in a number of projects that enriched her life, including specialized work with the elderly. Through her program of studies, she joined several intensive personal-growth workshops, which gave her the opportunity to pose and debate questions such as: "Do I have the courage to find out if I can create a new identity for myself? Will I be able to withstand pressures from my family to remain the way they want me to be? Can I give to others and at the same time give to myself?" These questions indicate Martha's growing awareness that she needed to be a person in her own right and that she wanted to live an authentic existence. Her self-questioning also shows that she knew that making choices entails doubts and struggles that one must resolve for oneself.

In one of our workshops Sid loudly exclaimed that he was sick and tired of being a "pleasant phony." He was painfully aware of his need to please everyone and to win approval at all costs, and he was very afraid of losing his own identity by trying to fulfill whatever expectations others had of him. Our work in the group proceeded along these lines:

JERRY (GROUP LEADER)	Sid, I'd like you to take your best shot at pleasing each of us. Since you rehearse internally this pleasing bit much of the time, it shouldn't be too difficult to do out loud. Are you willing to try this experiment?
SID	Sure, but I hate to try to please everyone in here. I want to get away from that!
JERRY	OK. But maybe this will be a beginning. Stand up and go around to each of us and tell us *exactly* what you imagine you'd have to say to please us and get our approval. Start with me.
SID	Well, Jerry, you'd be pleased with me if I were a self-revealing, risk-taking client who decided what he wanted for himself and went after that!

JERRY	Good. Now keep going around.
SID	And, Sue, you'd approve of me if I'd be helpless and let you mother me. Fred, I know you'd like me better if I told you what a great guy I thought you were. And you, Marie, would like me if I came out and said directly what I felt instead of trying to figure out what it was that you might want.

After Sid revealed what he imagined would please each of us, he was given an opportunity to share with us what it was like for him to go through this experiment. He got some valuable feedback from others, which, he said, gave him a clearer picture of how he was losing himself by trying so desperately to win universal approval. I asked Sid to actually *practice* in the group being as pleasing as he could, and I encouraged him to go up to members during breaks and say "Right now, I want you to approve of me, and I think I can get this by . . ." The goal of all of this was to exaggerate Sid's style of seeking others' approval to the point that he would eventually be able to seek approval within himself rather than from others.

Aloneness and Relatedness

The existentialists believe that ultimately we are alone—that only we can give a sense of meaning to our lives, decide how we will live, find our own answers, and decide whether we will be or not be. Because awareness of our ultimate aloneness can be very frightening, some of us try to avoid it by throwing ourselves into casual relationships and frantic activities, trusting that they will numb our fear and anguish.

We also have the choice of experiencing our aloneness and trying to find a center of meaning and direction within ourselves. Only if we make this choice and succeed at establishing our own identity as an individual can we relate genuinely and meaningfully to others. We must stand alone before we can truly stand beside another.

There is a paradox in the proposition that we are existentially both alone and related. Yet, it is this very paradox that describes the human condition. We are social beings, and we depend on interpersonal relationships for our humanness. We have a desire for intimacy, a hope to be significant in another's world, and a desire to feel that another's presence is important in our world. But unless we can stand alone and find our own strength within ourselves, we cannot have nourishing relationships with others, based on fulfillment and not on deprivation.

Implications for Group Work.   In groups, participants have the opportunity to relate to others in meaningful ways, learn to be themselves in the company of other people, and find reward and nourishment in the relationships they establish. They also learn that it is not in others that they can find the answers to questions about significance and purpose in life. If their struggle for self-awareness is successful, they come to realize that, no matter how valuable the relationships, they are ultimately on their own.

The friendships that participants establish within the group are valuable also because they teach people how to relate to others outside of the group. In a group, people recognize their own struggles in others, and this often results in a bond. Even though they may accept that ultimately they are existentially alone, they also come to realize that they are not alone in their struggles and that others, too, are courageously looking at themselves and trying to establish their own identities.

Example.   The case of Zeke shows that a person can be with others and at the same time be very much alone. During a group session Zeke said that he felt cut off from everyone in the group and described himself as a "spectator who seemed out of place." I asked him if he would be willing to experiment with *really* separating himself from the group and observing us from a distance. He agreed to leave the room, sit outside on the balcony, and observe what was going on through the window. I asked him to be aware of what he was thinking and feeling as he sat out there observing. Zeke was told to return to the group when he was ready to talk about what he had experienced sitting on the outside.

When he returned, he said that for the first time he realized how safe it was for him to keep himself in a spectator role, that he was beginning to hate this role, and that he was ready to do something different. I asked Zeke if he would go around to each person in the group and complete these two sentences: "One way I have kept you at a distance is by . . ."; "One way I could be closer to you is by . . ." After he had "made the rounds," he described the circumstances in which he typically felt alone, even when surrounded by many people. Zeke spoke of his desire to achieve intimacy and of his fears of approaching people. His work in the group had intensified his attempts to keep himself separate but finally resulted in a desire to change.

Role and Functions of the Group Leader

Unlike many other group approaches the existential model puts more emphasis on experiencing the client in the present moment than on using a particular set of techniques. May (1983) emphasizes that technique follows understanding. This means that the primary concern of the therapist is to be *with* the client and to understand his or her subjective world. Questions concerning therapeutic technique are subordinate to this quest for understanding. There are no "right" techniques in this approach, because the task is accomplished through the therapeutic encounter between client and therapist.

In the existential view therapy is a partnership and a shared venture between the therapist and the client. To develop this partnership, therapists focus on the human side of the person-to-person relationship. From the existential perspective, therapists must bring their own subjectivity into their work, and it is essential that they demonstrate presence if they are to develop an effective working relationship with members. A central role of existential leaders is to create a therapeutic alliance, for it is assumed that change comes from the relationship itself. This climate for change will not come about if the leader maintains a strictly objective orientation, is psychologically absent from the group, and is merely a skilled but impersonal technician. Bugental (1987) puts this idea beautifully:

> The therapeutic alliance is the powerful joining of forces which energizes and supports the long, difficult, and frequently painful work of life-changing psychotherapy. The conception of the therapist here is not of a disinterested observer-technician but of a fully alive human companion for the client. In this regard my view is in marked contrast to the traditional notion of the therapist as a skilled but objective director of therapeutic processes [p. 49].

In the group context, change is brought about not only by the relationship with the leader but also by relationships with other members. Thus, a primary role of the leader is to foster meaningful relationships among participants. This can be done by having them focus on key existential concerns and providing a climate in which these concerns can be fully explored. A therapeutic community is thus established, based on the commonality of shared struggles. The members make a commitment to confront one another about their unused potentials and inauthentic behaviors and to support one another in the common endeavor to open the door to oneself.

The leader sets the tone for the group, not by introducing techniques and by *doing something* but, rather, by *being* and *becoming somebody*. Mullan (1978) describes how challenges by the group leader bring about personality changes in members (including changes in thinking, feeling, and behaving). The group sessions tend to shake up the conventional ways in which members view the world. When their status quo is jarred, they have a better chance of facing themselves and of changing. Mullan sums up the matter thusly: "This, then, is what the existential group therapist is about. He establishes the conditions for the enhancement of each member's consciousness, directing him to face his *human condition*" (p. 379).

Williams and Fabry (1982) emphasize the leader's function in challenging members to move from where they are to where they want to be, to see the opportunities for learning from failure, to detect the growing edge of a crisis, to be aware of their styles of avoidance and escape from personal responsibility, and to reach out beyond their present limited vision toward a vision that is yet to be realized. Although the leader is a vital force in the group, he or she also encourages each member to accept responsibility for group life. Members are encouraged to participate and initiate and not to wait for the leader to manage conflicts within the group. The leader conveys to the members the value of personal sharing as opposed to diagnostic probing and interpreting. Members learn that the best way to help others is by offering illustrations of how they themselves deal with conflicts and existential concerns.

Evaluation of the Existential Approach

From a conceptual standpoint I value many features of the existential approach and have incorporated them into my practice. I work on the basic assumption that people have the capacity to become increasingly self-aware and that expansion of awareness results in greater freedom to choose their own directions in life. I share the existentialists' view that we are not bundles of instincts or the products of conditioning. Thus, I base my group work on the premises that people are not victims of their past or of the external world and that they have the power to decide for themselves and take action, so that their life is their own and not a reflection of the expectations of others.

I value this approach because it has brought the person back into central focus and because it addresses itself to the central question of what it means to be human. It portrays humans as continually actualizing and fulfilling their potential.

Another contribution of the existential approach is its emphasis on the person-to-person quality of the therapeutic relationship, an emphasis that humanizes psychotherapy and reduces the chances of its becoming a mechanical process in the hands of technicians. I especially value Bugental's (1987) stress on the therapist's being fully present in the therapeutic encounter. This full presence implies having access to one's own feelings and being able to express them appropriately and in a timely way. For Bugental the art of psychotherapy has much to do with what is going on inside the therapist. Through the therapist's concern, sensitivity, and presence, clients are invited to disclose the core life issues they are struggling with. If therapists are not humanly involved in their work, their clients will not be supported as they endure the painful and frightening self-confrontations that are necessary for major life changes to occur.

This approach encourages and challenges me as a group leader to tap and bring to my work my own experiences and my very humanness. It leaves my own modes of existence open to challenge, because I couldn't be genuine with others or help them face their existential concerns without doing the same in my own life. My willingness to remain open to my own struggles determines the degree to which I can be a significant and positive influence for others in a group.

I appreciate the existential view that techniques follow understanding, because it lessens the danger of abusing techniques. Too often leaders use techniques merely to "get things going" in a group. When the focus is on understanding the world of the participant, the leader's first concern is with genuinely grasping the core struggles of others and *then* drawing on certain techniques to help the participants explore these struggles more fully in the group. In my own work I've found that an existential view does provide the framework for understanding universal human concerns. These concerns, which come up over and over again in groups, include wrestling with the problem of personal freedom, dealing with self-alienation and estrangement from others, facing the fear of death and nonbeing, finding the courage to live from within one's center, searching for a meaningful life, discovering a personal set of values, being able to deal constructively with anxiety and guilt, and making self-actualizing choices.

On the other hand, I recognize that the existential approach has its limitations. Many of the existentialist concepts are quite abstract and difficult to apply in practice. Existential theorists such as Kierkegaard, Nietzsche, Heidegger, and Sartre were not writing for group counselors and therapists! As I mentioned at the beginning of this chapter, existentialism began as a formal philosophical movement, and although it eventually led to existential approaches within both psychology and psychiatry, its philosophical nature still dominates the mode. Both beginning and advanced group practitioners who are not of a philosophical turn of mind tend to find many of the existential concepts lofty, abstract, and elusive. Even those group counselors who are sympathetic toward the core ideas of this perspective are often at a loss when they try to apply these concepts to group practice, since very few authors have spelled out existential applications to group work.

Applying the Existential Approach in Multicultural Settings

Many cultures value drawing on the resources within one's own family in times of crisis. In times of need many people are influenced by their cultural injunctions to keep their problems within the family. There is a reluctance to share deeply personal struggles with professionals. Thus, certain ethnic-minority clients approach therapy only after their usual coping strategies have failed. They are usually experiencing psychological pain, and they are often faced with a crisis and feel helpless. Out of this helplessness they often experience their lives as being out of their control. Such clients can begin to recall their personal power by considering their own part in the difficulties they are having. They can be taught about the range of freedom they do possess and the consequences of their behavior.

Although it is true that some ethnic clients may not feel a sense of freedom, their freedom can be increased through their recognition of the environmental limits that they are facing. Such clients may be hindered by institutions or by their family. In fact, it may be difficult to separate individual freedom from the context of the family structure. A client who is struggling with feeling limited by her family situation can be invited to look at her part in this process. For example, a woman who is being abused by her husband may be convincing herself that there are no options and that she must accept whatever harsh treatment comes her way. She may be unwilling to even consider leaving an abusive relationship out of fear of what would happen to her children and herself.

A group experience can be a force in aiding this woman to consider alternatives and to examine the price she is paying for remaining in this relationship and the price she might pay if she were to leave. This illustration shows that there can be a conflict between the woman's values and the values inherent in the group structure. She may believe that no matter how horrible her life is with her husband, she must simply learn to accept this situation. Her values may make the possibility of leaving or getting a divorce seem remote. Yet in the group she is likely to be presented with the value of choosing for herself and of taking action to change her miserable situation. In cases such as this it is useful to explore the client's underlying values and to help her determine if her values are working for her and for her family. Ultimately, it will be up to her to decide in what ways she might change her situation. But the basic clash is still between her feeling that there is almost nothing that she can do to change her situation and the group's invitation to begin to explore what she *can* do to initiate change.

It is essential to keep in mind the client's purpose when she enters a group. What are her goals? What is she seeking from group counseling? If we pay careful attention to what our clients tell us about what they want, we can operate within an existential framework. Our task then becomes encouraging them to weigh the alternatives and to explore the consequences of what they are doing in their lives. Assuming an existential orientation does not mean that we have to preach to group members about the values of self-awareness, choice, and responsibility. Rather, we can help them see that even though oppressive forces may be severely limiting the quality of their lives, they are not merely the victims of circumstances beyond their control. At the same time that these clients are being taught ways in which to change their external environment, they can also be challenged to look within themselves for their own contribution to their plight. Through a group experience they may be able to discover new courses of action that will lead to a change in their situation.

The existential approach has some limitations as it is applied to multicultural populations in group settings. Some clients simply believe that they do not have a choice or that even if they do have some freedom, societal factors are severely restricting their ability to choose for themselves. Existentially oriented group leaders would do well to take into account the sociocultural factors that do restrict choices. In working with minority clients who come from the barrio or ghetto, for example, it is important to deal with their survival issues. Such clients may be motivated primarily by the need for safety and survival and thus be likely to seek help with getting their basic needs met. They may need to know how to best take care of their children, how to cope with a crisis over housing, or how to effectively deal with unemployment. Simply lecturing clients that they have a choice in making their life better will not help, and it is likely to have a negative impact. These very real-life issues provide a good focus for group work, assuming that the leader is willing to deal with them. Another problem of this approach is the lack of direction for clients from the leader. If clients are looking to the leader for concrete solutions to pressing problems, they may not get such answers. The group leader can attempt to deeply understand the world from the client's vantage point and at the same time still help the client take action, even if it is only small steps toward change.

Questions for Reflection and Discussion

1. What are some of the major contrasts between the psychoanalytic approach and the existential approach? Do you see any basis for integrating psychoanalytic and existential concepts as they apply to the practice of group counseling?

2. What are some key concepts of the existential approach that you find personally meaningful? Which of these basic ideas, if any, would you most want to include in your framework in approaching a group?

3. In this chapter the statement is made that anxiety results from having to make choices without clear guidelines and without knowing what the outcome will be. What implications are there for you as a group leader if you accept this view of anxiety? What are your thoughts on the role that anxiety plays in a group?

4. Mullan (1979) makes this statement: "Death as an element to be dealt with, faced, and accepted is always present in the existential group if it is not ignored by the therapist" (p. 173). To what degree do you think that you have faced your own finite nature? Do you have a tendency to avoid reflecting on your own death? How do you think that your answers here will have an influence on your ability to deal with the theme of death as it emerges in your groups?

5. An existential theme is that we are free to choose among alternatives and that we are responsible for directing our life and shaping our destiny. To what extent do you think that you have taken an active stance in shaping the person that you are? What are some critical choices that you have made, and how do these choices affect you now? How do you see your answers to these questions as relevant to how you might deal with the struggles over choices of the members in your groups?

6. According to Frankl, it is not the therapist's job to tell clients what their particular meaning in life should be but rather to encourage them to discover meaning for themselves. Can you think of some ways that you might challenge members to find meaning in their life? How might you deal with the member who continued to look to you for answers and direction?

7. Some existential therapists assume that the driving force behind many interpersonal relationships is existential isolation. If you accept this notion that humans are ultimately alone in the world, what are the implications for group counseling? To what degree

might groups contribute to members' avoidance of their aloneness? How might a group help a person feel less isolated and less alienated?

8. In the existential group it is assumed that intensity is achieved only when the therapist abandons rigid practices for selecting members, fixed rules, routines, and techniques (Mullan, 1979). How comfortable do you feel as a group leader with this orientation? Do you think that groups will become cohesive and engage in productive work without the use of techniques? Do you think you can employ group techniques and still retain an existential outlook on group work? Explain.

9. According to Yalom (1980), there are four ultimate concerns that make up the core of existential therapy—freedom, isolation, death, and meaninglessness. From your vantage point, what meaning do these existential themes have for you personally? How are these human concerns related to your life and your struggles? Based on your experiences in life, what would you hope to be able to teach the people who were in your groups? What meaning do these existential concerns have for the focus you might want to bring to a group you were leading?

10. How might you deal with those group members who spent a great deal of time trying to convince you that they were not responsible for their lives? If they attempted to hold others in their life responsible for their current problems, what might you be inclined to say or do in the group?

Where to Go from Here

If you want to experience existential groups, I'd suggest attending the conferences sponsored by the Association for Humanistic Psychology. At its annual meetings, members can participate in a variety of workshops that are based on existential and humanistic concepts. For information about joining, write

Association for Humanistic Psychology
325 Ninth Street
San Francisco, CA 94103

Membership dues include the quarterly *Journal of Humanistic Psychology,* the *AHP Resource Directory,* a newsletter, priority for attendance at special events, and professional networking services. If you are interested in training and supervision workshops based on existential concepts, I recommend that you look into the resources that I list at the end of the following chapter. I especially suggest that you think about joining the Association for the Development of the Person-Centered Approach (which is a form of the existential approach).

If it is difficult for you to attend these workshops and you would still like to learn more about the existential approach, I highly recommend beginning with the excellent works of Bugental (1987) and Yalom (1980).

RECOMMENDED SUPPLEMENTARY READINGS

I am aware of no books that deal explicitly and exclusively with the application of the existential approach to group counseling. Some of the following sources contain material that group leaders can use to apply this model to their work.

Existential psychotherapy (Yalom, 1980) is a superb treatment of ultimate human concerns of freedom, isolation, death, and meaninglessness as these issues relate to therapy. This book has depth and clarity, and it is rich with clinical examples that illustrate existential themes. If you were to select just one book on existential therapy, this would be my recommendation.

The art of the psychotherapist (Bugental, 1987) is an outstanding book that bridges the art and science of psychotherapy, making places for both. The author is an insightful and sensitive clinician who writes about the psychotherapist's and the client's journey into therapy from an existential perspective.

Psychotherapy and process: The fundamentals of an existential-humanistic approach (Bugental, 1978) is a concise and comprehensive overview. It is highly readable, and the clinical examples add a concrete reality to the discussion of concepts. An excellent source.

Existential psychology (May, 1961) is a reader that examines and evaluates the role of existential psychology. Maslow, May, Rogers, and Allport are among the contributors.

Man's search for himself (May, 1953) is a classic. It deals with key existential themes such as loneliness, anxiety, the experience of becoming a person, the struggle to be, freedom, choice, responsibility, and religion.

The transparent self (Jourard, 1971) is a significant work based on the thesis that our lack of openness results in sickness, maladjustment, and alienation. The chapters on psychotherapy, groups, and the "disclosing therapist" are especially relevant to our discussion.

I never knew I had a choice (Corey & Corey, 1990) is a self-help book written from an existential perspective. It contains many exercises and activities that leaders can use for their group work or suggest as homework assignments between sessions. The topics include our struggle to achieve autonomy; the roles that work, love, sexuality, intimacy, and solitude play in our lives; the meaning of loneliness, death, and loss; and the ways in which we choose our values and philosophies of life. Each chapter is followed by numerous annotated suggestions for further reading.

REFERENCES AND SUGGESTED READINGS*

Bugental, J. F. T. (1978). *Psychotherapy and process: The fundamentals of an existential-humanistic approach.* Reading, MA: Addison-Wesley.

Bugental, J. F. T. (1986). Existential-humanistic psychotherapy. In I. L. Kutash & A. Wolf (Eds.), *Psychotherapist's casebook* (pp. 222–236). San Francisco: Jossey-Bass.

*Bugental, J. F. T. (1987). *The art of the psychotherapist.* New York: Norton.

Burton, A. (1967). *Modern humanistic psychotherapy.* San Francisco: Jossey-Bass.

*Corey, G., & Corey, M. (1990). *I never knew I had a choice* (4th ed.). Pacific Grove, CA: Brooks/Cole.

*Books and articles marked with an asterisk are suggested for further study.

*Frankl, V. (1963). *Man's search for meaning*. New York: Washington Square Press.
Frankl, V. (1965). *The doctor and the soul*. New York: Bantam.
Holt, H. (1986). Existential analysis. In I. L. Kutash & A. Wolf (Eds.), *Psychotherapist's casebook* (pp. 177–194). San Francisco: Jossey-Bass.
Jourard, S. (1968a). *Disclosing man to himself*. New York: Van Nostrand Reinhold.
Jourard, S. (1968b). Growing awareness and the awareness of growth. In H. Otto & J. Mann (Eds.), *Ways of growth: Approaches to expanding awareness*. New York: Viking.
Jourard, S. (1971). *The transparent self* (rev. ed.). New York: Van Nostrand Reinhold.
Keen, E. (1970). *Three faces of being: Toward an existential clinical psychology*. New York: Appleton-Century-Crofts.
Kemp, C. G. (1971). Existential counseling. *The Counseling Psychologist, 2*(3), 2–30.
Maslow, A. (1968). *Toward a psychology of being* (2nd ed.). New York: Van Nostrand Reinhold.
Maslow, A. (1970). *Motivation and personality* (2nd ed.). New York: Harper & Row.
Maslow, A. (1971). *The farther reaches of human nature*. New York: Viking.
May, R. (1953). *Man's search for himself*. New York: Norton.
May, R. (Ed.). (1961). *Existential psychology*. New York: Random House.
May, R. (1967). *Psychology and the human dilemma*. New York: Van Nostrand Reinhold.
*May, R. (1983). *The discovery of being: Writings in existential psychology*. New York: Norton.
*May, R. (1987). Therapy in our day. In J. K. Zeig (Ed.), *The evolution of psychotherapy* (pp. 212–220). New York: Brunner/Mazel.
May, R., & Yalom, I. (1984). Existential psychotherapy. In R. Corsini (Ed.), *Current psychotherapies* (3rd ed.). Itasca, IL: F. E. Peacock.
May, R., & Yalom, I. (1989). Existential psychotherapy. In R. J. Corsini & D. Wedding (Eds.), *Current psychotherapies* (4th ed.). Itasca, IL: F. E. Peacock.
Moustakas, C. (1987). Phenomenology, discovery, and meaning. *Michigan Journal of Counseling and Development, 18*(1), 21–24.
Mullan, H. (1978). Existential group psychotherapy. In H. Mullan & M. Rosenbaum (Eds.), *Group psychotherapy: Theory and practice* (2nd ed.). New York: Free Press.
Mullan, H. (1979). An existential group psychotherapy. *International Journal of Group Psychotherapy, 29*(2), 163–174.
Ohlsen, M. M. (1987). Humanistic group counseling. *Michigan Journal of Counseling and Development, 18*(1), 28–31.
Russell, J. M. (1978). Sartre, therapy, and expanding the concept of responsibility. *The American Journal of Psychoanalysis, 38*, 259–269.
Sartre, J. P. (1971). *Being and nothingness*. New York: Bantam.
Shaffer, J. B. (1978). *Humanistic psychology*. Englewood Cliffs, NJ: Prentice-Hall.
Shaffer, J., & Galinsky, M. D. (1989). *Models of group therapy* (2nd ed.). Englewood Cliffs, NJ: Prentice-Hall.
Tillich, P. (1952). *The courage to be*. New Haven, CT: Yale University Press.
Williams, D. A., & Fabry, J. (1982). The existential approach: Logotherapy. In G. M. Gazda (Ed.), *Basic approaches to group psychotherapy and group counseling* (3rd ed.). Springfield, IL: Charles C Thomas.
*Yalom, I. D. (1980). *Existential psychotherapy*. New York: Basic Books.

10

The Person-Centered Approach to Groups

Introduction

The person-centered approach to group counseling (which was originally known as client-centered therapy) was developed by Carl Rogers. It is grounded on the assumption that human beings tend to move toward wholeness and self-actualization and that individual members, as well as the group as a whole, can find their own direction with a minimal degree of help from the group leader, or "facilitator." The person-centered approach emphasizes the personal qualities of the group leader rather than techniques of leading, because the primary function of the facilitator is to create a fertile and healing climate in the group. This therapy is best considered as a "way of being" rather than a "way of doing." The essence of the approach is captured by Rogers:

> The person-centered approach, then, is primarily a way of being that finds its expression in attitudes and behaviors that create a growth-producing climate. It is a basic philosophy rather than simply a technique or a method. When this philosophy is lived, it helps the person expand the development of his or her own capacities. When it is lived, it also stimulates constructive change in others. It empowers the individual, and when this personal power is sensed, experience shows that it tends to be used for personal and social transformation [1986b, p. 199].

A therapeutic climate is established in the group by the facilitator's creating a relationship based on certain attitudes such as accurate empathic understanding, acceptance, nonpossessive warmth, caring, and genuineness. As the facilitator projects these attitudes and an accepting and caring climate emerges, it is presumed, members will drop their defenses and work toward personally meaningful goals, a process that will eventually lead to appropriate and useful behavioral change.

The contemporary person-centered approach to group counseling is best considered as the result of an evolutionary process that continues to remain open to change and refinement. Certain trends go back about 50 years. In the early 1940s Rogers developed what was known as *nondirective counseling,* in part as a reaction against more directive and interpretive individual therapy. He caused a great furor when he challenged the basic assumption that the counselor was the expert and the client should be in a passive role. He also challenged the validity of such widely used therapeutic procedures as suggestion, giving of advice, direction, teaching, diagnosis, and interpretation. A common theme originating in his early writings and continuing to permeate all of his works is a basic trust in the client's ability to move forward in a constructive manner if the appropriate conditions fostering growth are present. According to him, there is a *formative tendency* in nature, or a central source of energy that seeks fulfillment and actualization, involving both the maintenance and the enhancement of the organism. Although person-centered therapy has changed over the years, this perspective of trust has remained at its foundation.

Beginning in the early 1940s as a method of individual counseling and psychotherapy, the client-centered approach was extended to group therapy by the end of that decade. The principles of client-centered therapy were formulated by Rogers (1951) and later applied to therapy groups by Hobbs (1951) and Gordon (1951). In the 1950s and 1960s these principles were used in groups for physically handicapped children and their parents, parents of retarded children, mothers on public assistance, clients involved in individual counseling, psychiatric inpatients, residents of homes for the elderly, staff-development groups for mental-health professionals, and play-therapy groups (Raskin, 1986a, p. 277). Hobbs (1951) wrote about "group-centered psychotherapy," which was an extension of client-centered individual psychotherapy. He emphasized the importance of the group leader's acceptance and understanding of individuals in groups. He also saw unique advantages for group therapy over individual therapy. From his perspective, being understood and accepted by other members who were also engaging in revealing their feelings in the search of a more fulfilling life was the variable that made a group qualitatively different from individual therapy. Gordon (1951) applied client-centered concepts to leadership and administration. He emphasized group-centered leadership, which called for sharing the facilitation of a group with all the members. The group-centered leader refuses to accept responsibility for the group but encourages members to assume this responsibility by providing the therapeutic conditions of empathy, warmth, positive regard, and acceptance.

In the 1950s Rogers developed a systematic theory of personality and applied this self theory to the practice of counseling individuals, which led him to rename his approach *client-centered therapy* (Rogers, 1951). At this time he was mainly devoted to individual therapy. His 1957 hypothesis on the conditions necessary and sufficient to produce therapeutic change probably stimulated more research on the process and outcome of psychotherapy than any other idea before or since that time (Cain, 1987a). He and his associates continued to test the underlying hypotheses of the client-centered approach by conducting studies of the process and the outcomes of therapy. Most of the research on client-centered therapy was done in the 1950s and the 1960s.

The client-centered approach was broadened to apply to group therapy, teaching, affective/cognitive learning in workshops, and organizational development and leadership. In the 1960s and 1970s Rogers did a great deal to spearhead the development of basic encounter groups and personal-growth groups. As the fields of application grew in number and variety, the name *client-centered therapy* was replaced by *person-centered approach*. It was during this period that Rogers's interest shifted from individual to group therapy. He also broadened his emphasis beyond the therapist's ability to reflect accurately what clients were expressing to include the therapist's congruence and willingness to become increasingly involved in the therapy. His basic encounter groups made it difficult to distinguish between "therapy" and "growth," and they did much to revolutionize the practice of therapy.

Rogers (1980) noted similarities between therapy groups and encounter groups. Whether people came together because they were seeking help for dealing with serious problems (group therapy) or because they were seeking personal growth (encounter group), the process was much the same. The person-centered approach to the facilitation of these groups has been applied to diverse populations such as therapy clients, counselors, staff members of entire school systems, educators, administrators, medical students, groups in conflict, drug users and their helpers, people representing different cultures and languages, and job-training groups. As the group movement developed, the person-centered approach became increasingly concerned with reducing human suffering, with cross-cultural awareness, and with conflict resolution on an international basis (Raskin, 1986a, p. 285).

In 1973 Rogers and some of his colleagues initiated a new form of person-centered group known as the *large community group*. In these groups 50 to 100 or more people (and even up to 2000 for brief periods) worked and lived together for 2 weeks. More recently, Rogers (1987c) focused on learning in large groups and on the implications of such a process for the reduction of social and political tensions. He used many types of groups for various populations in many places in the world. His ideas were also applied to administration, minority groups, community relations, interracial and intercultural groups, and international relationships (Rogers, 1977).

Perhaps Rogers's major recent contribution lies in the person-centered approach to world peace. In the last few years of his life he focused much attention on an alternative to nuclear planetary suicide (Rogers, 1984). He shared his hope of disengaging the world from a precarious entanglement threatening human survival. He sought alternatives that would reduce psychological barriers that impinge on communication between factions (see Rogers, 1987c; Rogers & Malcolm, 1987).

The person-centered approach shares fundamental principles and some basic concepts with the existential approach. As you will recall from the previous chapter, Rogers was one of the key figures in the development of humanistic psychology in the 1950s.

Key Concepts

Trust in the Group Process

Rogers (1986b) makes it clear that the person-centered approach rests on a basic trust in human beings' tendency to realize their full potential. Similarly, person-centered therapy is based on a deep sense of trust in the group's ability to develop its own potential by moving in a constructive direction. For Rogers (1987d) the dissolving of mistrust is essential; learning to develop trust entails risks, for there are no guarantees:

> I think that trust is always a gamble. The more that you take that gamble, the more you find out whether it is rewarded. I do not think it is always rewarded. But in important situations it is rewarded. If you trust people, they respond to trust, and so a willingness to take that kind of gamble is one of the things that I believe builds trust [p. 46].

For a group to move forward, it must develop an accepting and trusting atmosphere in which the members can show aspects of themselves that they usually conceal and move into new behaviors. For example, they move

- from playing roles to expressing themselves more directly
- from being relatively closed to experience and uncertainty to becoming more open to outside reality and tolerant of ambiguity
- from being out of contact with internal and subjective experience to becoming aware of it
- from looking for answers outside of themselves to a willingness to direct their own lives from within
- from lacking trust and being somewhat closed and fearful in interpersonal relationships to being more open and expressive with others

The Therapeutic Conditions for Growth

The basic tenet underlying the person-centered approach to group work is stated briefly by Rogers (1980): "Individuals have within themselves vast resources for self-understanding and for altering their self-concepts, basic attitudes, and self-directed behavior; these resources can be tapped if a definable climate of facilitative psychological attitudes can be provided" (p. 115). According to Rogers (1986b), the necessary climate that releases our formative, or actualizing, tendency is characterized by three primary attitudes of the therapist: genuineness, unconditional positive regard (now called "nonpossessive warmth"), and empathy. These three factors will be introduced here and then taken up in detail later in this section.

The first element is the *genuineness,* realness, or congruence of the therapist (or facilitator of the group). The greater the extent to which facilitators become involved in the group as persons, putting up no professional front, the greater is the likelihood that the members will change and grow. Genuineness implies that leaders are aware of their feelings and attitudes. There is a congruence between what they are experiencing internally and what they are expressing to the members of the group. This means that facilitators may express their persistent feelings even if doing so is risky. It also implies that the process of a group is influenced by the person of the facilitator as much as by the individuality of the group participants.

The second element is the attitude called *unconditional positive regard,* which is an acceptance of and caring for the members. When group facilitators display a positive, nonjudgmental, accepting attitude toward their clients, therapeutic change is more likely (Rogers, 1986b). As we will see later, this caring on the facilitator's part is nonpossessive in that the members are prized fully rather than conditionally.

The third facilitative aspect is an *empathic understanding* of the members' internal and subjective frame of reference. Facilitators show this empathy when they are able to sense accurately the feelings and personal meanings that the members are experiencing. It is also important for facilitators to be able to communicate this understanding to the members.

To the extent that therapists experience genuineness, warm regard, and accurate empathy for their clients and to the extent that the clients perceive these conditions, therapeutic personality change and growth will occur (Bräaten, 1986). Rogers (1987d) maintains that this hypothesis has been put to the test in a wide variety of situations with very divergent groups, different cultures, and different nations. Furthermore, there is a growing body of research evidence, reaching from 1949 to the present, that generally supports this view (Rogers, 1986b).

Rogers (1986b) adds another characteristic of a growth-promoting relationship that he concedes cannot as yet be studied empirically: *presence.* He asserts that when he is at his best as a group facilitator, he is in touch with the unknown in him and that his inner spirit reaches out and touches the inner spirit of the client. The relationship transcends itself and becomes a part of something larger. This presence releases the most profound growth and healing.

Natiello (1987) adds another therapist condition that she believes to be integral to the practice of the person-centered approach: *personal power.* This is a state in which individuals are aware of and can act on their own feelings, needs, and values rather than looking outside of themselves for direction. The greater the degree of autonomy that therapists possess, the less likely they are to attempt to control others and the more they can help their clients tap into their own source of power for self-direction. This power does not rest with the authority and expertise of facilitators; rather, it is a sharing of power by actively trusting individuals to direct their own lives and solve their problems. In training other facilitators of the person-centered approach, Natiello finds that they often experience difficulties in translating the concept of personal power into practice. They struggle with how much of themselves to share, and they fear taking over others' power. This fear sometimes leads them to disown their own power or to deny it. It is a challenge to learn the balance between accepting one's own power as a therapist and sharing power with clients.

Implications for Training Group Leaders. It is a myth that person-centered therapists are self-abnegating, passive, and uninvolved, merely responding to others by mirroring their responses (Natiello, 1987). Rather, they demonstrate behaviorally the core therapeutic attitudes. This involves a willingness to develop a style of facilitating groups that is an extension of who they are. Rogers (1986b) writes that the therapist becomes a companion to clients in their journey toward self-discovery. When the person-centered way of being is lived in therapy, it leads to a process of self-exploration that results in constructive changes in personality and behavior.

It should be clear that group leaders' power rests more in who they are than in their repertoire of intervention strategies. This viewpoint holds important implications for training of group leaders. Although Braaten (1986) agrees with Truax and Carkhuff (1967) that empathy can be learned, to some extent, he thinks that it is doubtful that students can be taught to be truly accepting or genuine. Accepting people as they are, understanding them in their world, and being genuine in human encounters are not techniques but ways of being. Thus, programs would do well to focus on helping students become aware of their attitudes and develop themselves as persons. There might be more emphasis on self-exploration and self-development and less focus on mastery of skills, techniques, and leadership strategies (Bozarth & Brodley, 1986).

Genuineness

According to Rogers, the central characteristic of the therapeutic relationship is *congruence,* a term that implies that the therapist is real, transparent, or genuine. Genuineness means that what the therapist expresses externally is congruent with his or her inner experience, at least during the time of therapy. In other words, genuine therapists don't pretend to be interested when they are not, don't fake attention or understanding, don't say what they don't mean, and don't adopt behaviors designed to win approval. They can perform their professional functions without hiding behind their professional roles.

According to Natiello (1987), in order to maintain genuineness, therapists need a high level of self-awareness, self-acceptance, and self-trust.

Genuineness is the state of authenticity that results from a deep exploration of self and a willingness to accept the truths of this exploration. In her work with helping professionals in a person-centered training program, Natiello finds that congruence is both complex and difficult to achieve and that it is the condition that is most often ignored. She contends that without congruence the other therapeutic conditions are then offered inauthentically and become mere techniques, which are meaningless, manipulative, and controlling.

Implications for Group Leaders.   Genuine therapists, although they are essentially honest in their encounters in the group, are not indiscriminately open, and they know the boundaries of appropriate self-revelation. Although genuineness implies that leaders are internally congruent (which means that they are not self-deceptive), they do not always share all their feelings and thoughts, since that would not be appropriate or therapeutic at certain times. They realize the importance of taking responsibility for any feelings they express in the group and the importance of exploring with clients persistent feelings that may be blocking their ability to be fully present. Through their own authenticity, congruent group leaders offer a model that helps their clients work toward greater realness.

Some group leaders have difficulty with "being themselves." Often that difficulty stems from the misapprehension that genuineness entails expressing *every* immediate thought or feeling or being spontaneous without any restraint or consideration of the appropriateness and timeliness of one's reactions. Another difficulty arises when leaders, in the name of being "authentic," make themselves the focal point of the group by discussing their personal problems in great detail. As Braaten (1986) has noted, not every kind of genuineness is facilitating for clients. Therapist self-disclosure can be overdone in magnitude and kind. Clearly, as indicated above, even the expression of genuineness must be handled with discretion. Leaders need to examine honestly their motivations for discussing their personal issues and ask themselves whether the disclosure serves the clients' needs or their own. If the leader has had an experience similar to that of a client, the sharing of feelings about the experience may be therapeutic for the client. However, it is possible to be an authentic group leader and not be very self-disclosing, especially about matters pertaining to one's personal life. When a group leader does engage in self-disclosure, it is important to focus on the members and not to deter them from exploring their own issues. Leaders who frequently make themselves the focal point of group discussion may be using the group as a platform to air their personal problems.

Unconditional Positive Regard and Warmth

As we have seen, the goal of person-centered groups is to create a climate in which the basic actualizing tendency can freely express itself in each participant and in the group as a whole. For this growth force to be released within individuals and within a group, unconditional positive regard is the second necessary factor.

According to this viewpoint, as mentioned, positive regard involves communicating a caring that is unconditional and that is not contaminated by evaluation or judgment of the client's feelings and thoughts. In other words, group leaders value and accept members without placing stipulations and expectations on this acceptance; they tell the client "I accept you as you are," not "I'll accept you when . . ." Acceptance, however, is not to be confused with approval; therapists can accept and value their clients as separate persons, with a right to their separateness, without necessarily approving of some of their behavior.

Associated with this attitude of positive regard is an attitude of nonpossessive caring and warmth—namely, an attitude that is not dependent on the therapist's own need for approval and appreciation and that can be expressed in subtle ways such as gestures, eye contact, tone of voice, and facial expression. A genuine expression of caring can be sensed by the client and will promote his or her development. Artificial warmth can be as readily perceived and is likely to inhibit the client's change and growth. Obviously, once a client senses that the therapist's expression of warmth is more a technique than a genuine feeling, it becomes difficult for that client to trust the genuineness of other reactions of the therapist.

Braaten (1986) has written about his struggle with the concept of unconditional positive regard, or even the term *positive regard.* He substitutes the phrase *warm regard,* which includes an expression of both positive and negative feelings. He believes that this regard must include a willingness to share one's total self with significant others, including one's anger and possible rejection. Rogers (1987b) does contend that there is room in the person-centered approach for therapists to communicate negative feelings, which are persistently being experienced. This means that boredom and anger, as well as compassion, can be expressed.

Thus, a potential conflict arises between being genuine and maintaining a stance of unconditionality (Lietaer, 1984). It is a rare therapist who can genuinely provide unconditional acceptance for every client on a consistent basis. While unconditionality is not impossible, it is improbable. Unconditional positive regard can best be thought of as an attitude of receptiveness toward the subjective and experiential world of the client. From Lietaer's (1984) perspective, unconditionality means that the therapist values the deeper core of the person. Through the therapist's unconditionality clients sense that the therapist is on their side and that they will not be let down in spite of their current difficulties. In its optimal form unconditionality is not an attitude of indifference; rather, it expresses a deep belief in another person. For a scholarly treatment of the controversial concept of unconditional positive regard, see Lietaer (1984).

Related to the concept of accepting the individual group member with unconditional positive regard, caring, and warmth is the idea of developing an attitude of acceptance of the group as a whole. Just as Rogers believes in

the capacity of the individual to find his or her own direction, so does he
believe in accepting a group where it is, without attempting to impose a
direction on it: "From my experience I know that if I attempt to push a group
to a deeper level, it is not, in the long run, going to work" (1970, p. 48).

It is evident that Rogers has faith in the capacity of a group to move on
its own initiative, although he does note that anxiety and irritation may
result from the lack of external structure. Rogers (1970) gives his groups
permission to determine for themselves how they will spend their time, and
he may open a session with the statement "We can make this group experience whatever we want it to be." Rogers relates an experience with a group
of high-level educational administrators who talked continually about trivi-
al matters in an intellectual and superficial manner. In keeping with his
philosophy and despite his feelings of annoyance and boredom, Rogers
upheld the participants' right to engage in social chatter and his right not to
endure it—he left the group and went to bed.

Certainly Rogers's solution was consonant with his philosophy. However, one can value the person-centered approach to group work without
having to tolerate excessive and nonproductive floundering. Thus, if you
were facilitating the group described by Rogers, you might wish to confront
it with your feelings as a participant/leader. Such a confrontation could take
any one of the following forms:

- "I'd like for each of you to say something regarding what you feel
  about being in this group so far."
- "I'm aware that I've been impatient and bored for some time. It seems
  that we're staying on a very superficial level, unwilling to say much
  that is personal about ourselves."
- "I'm wondering how most of you might feel if the group were to end
  now. I have the uncomfortable feeling that we are avoiding any productive work."

Being a group leader entails encouraging group members to focus on
what they are doing and not doing; being a sincere group leader often
entails expressing one's reactions to what is occurring. Ultimately, group
members have the power to move or not to move to a deeper level, yet the
leader can encourage them to look at their behavior and decide what they
might do differently. It seems to me that a group leader can be a catalyst for
change within a group without violating the principles and the spirit of the
person-centered approach.

Implications for Group Leaders.   It has been my experience that group
leaders in training often struggle with what they feel is the monumental
task of being able to *feel* accepting or being able to demonstrate positive
regard. Some tend to burden themselves with the unrealistic expectation
that they must *always* be accepting and that they must consistently respond
with warmth in all situations. Thus, it is also my experience that group

leaders need to develop an accepting attitude toward themselves as well—an acceptance of the fact that at times they won't feel warmth or unconditional positive regard. It is not necessary to feel a high level of warmth and positive regard all the time in order to be an effective group leader. These attitudes are not an either/or condition; rather, they occur on a continuum of gradations. Being an effective group leader starts by accepting oneself and continues by bearing in mind that the greater the degree of valuing, caring, and accepting of a client, the greater the opportunity to facilitate change in the client.

Empathy and Listening

The third central concept in the person-centered group approach, as we have seen, is accurate empathy, which is basically the ability to enter the subjective world of others and the ability to communicate this understanding. Rogers (1961) defined empathy as the capacity to see the world of another by assuming the internal frame of reference of that person: "To sense the client's private world as if it were your own but without ever losing the 'as if' quality—this is empathy, and it seems essential to therapy" (p. 284). But sensing, even understanding, the client's private world is not enough. The counselor must also be able to effectively communicate this understanding to the client.

Rogers (1975) considers empathy as "an unappreciated way of being" for many group practitioners. He makes a case for regarding empathy as one of the most potent factors in bringing about learning and self-directed change, thus locating power in the person and not in the expert. Rogers summarizes some general research findings concerning empathy as follows:

1. Therapists of many different orientations agree that attempting to sensitively and accurately understand others from their viewpoint is a critical factor in being an effective therapist.

2. One of the main functions of empathy is to foster client self-exploration. Clients come to a deeper self-understanding through a relationship in which they *feel* that they are being understood by others. Research has demonstrated that clients who feel understood by their therapists are encouraged to share more of themselves.

3. Empathy dissolves alienation, for the person who receives empathy feels connected with others. Furthermore, those who receive empathy learn that they are valued, cared for, and accepted as they are. Rogers (1975) makes this point as follows: "Empathy gives that needed confirmation that one does exist as a separate, valued person with an identity" (p. 7).

4. The ability to exhibit empathy depends on the personal development of the therapist. Rogers (1975) has come to the conclusion that "the more psychologically mature and integrated the therapist is as a person, the more helpful is the relationship he provides" (p. 5).

5. Being a skilled diagnostician and making interpretations is not related to empathy, which, at its best, is accepting and nonjudgmental. In

fact, for Rogers "true empathy is always free of any evaluative or diagnostic quality" (1975, p. 7).

Rogers maintains that empathy is possible because there are only a limited number of feelings. Although we may not have encountered the particular situation of another, the chances are that we have experienced similar feelings in different circumstances. Our ability to experience anger, joy, fear, and love is what makes it possible to enter the world of another person, even though this person's circumstances may be different from our own. Rogers makes it clear that empathy is an active process, yet it is often superficially regarded as a passive stance involving sitting back and listening:

> To really let oneself go into the inner world of this other person is one of the most active, difficult, demanding things that I know. And yet, it is worth it because it is one of the most releasing, healing things that I have had any occasion to do. It is one of the reasons why I love doing therapy; it is one of the reasons why I love dealing with very difficult situations like the racial conflict in South Africa [1987d, p. 45].

Accurate empathy is central to the practice of the person-centered approach. It is a way for therapists to hear the meanings expressed by their clients that often lie at the edge of their awareness. Thus, clients expand their awareness when these precognitive meanings are understood and communicated by a facilitator who is able to encourage them to experience what they are feeling more deeply (Natiello, 1987).

A special kind of listening with one's total being is a crucial part of achieving empathy. Sensitive listening involves suspending judgment of others. It is not done to gain personal advantage or with an ulterior motive. Rather, this kind of listening comes from a genuine interest in making significant contact with others by knowing their reality (Barrett-Lennard, 1988). Braaten (1986) finds that his active listening involves grasping the cognitive and affective messages from his clients on a moment-to-moment basis and trying to verify his understanding with his clients. He asserts that person-centered therapists are unique in their careful monitoring to determine whether they have grasped the message of their clients.

Active and sensitive listening is what Rogers *does* when he facilitates a group. "I listen as carefully, accurately, and sensitively as I am able, to each individual who expresses himself. Whether the utterance is superficial or significant, I *listen*" (1970, p. 47). It is apparent that Rogers "listens" to more than the words; he also hears the meaning behind both the verbal and the nonverbal content. In this regard, he is concerned with facilitating the truest expression of the person's subjective experience. According to Cain (1987a), Rogers's most enduring and pervasive contribution is demonstrating the importance of listening, not only in therapy relationships but also in any other relationship. Rogers broadened the meaning of listening and demonstrated the profound healing effect that it has on others. Cain suspects that Rogers will be best remembered as a warm and sensitive therapist who demonstrated for generations of therapists the vital importance of being present and listening. For a scholarly discussion of the role of empathy in the person-centered approach, see Bozarth (1984), and for a thoughtful discussion of listening, see Barrett-Lennard (1988).

Implications for Group Leaders. As suggested earlier, empathic understanding is essential to developing the climate of acceptance and trust necessary for the success of the group. The ability to effectively express empathy rests on an attitude of genuine caring and on the sincere desire to understand the world of another. Presupposing the correct attitude, empathy is a skill that can be developed—and it is a skill that an effective group leader needs to develop. As Carkhuff (1966) has shown, a therapeutic relationship can be "for better or for worse": therapists have the potential to affect their clients either positively or negatively, and empathic understanding is preeminently a skill that influences the degree to which clients become functional in their world.

In working with group counselors, I have found that many mistakenly assume that unless they themselves have directly experienced the same problems voiced by group members, they can't be empathic. Such an assumption can severely limit the leader's potential sphere of influence. Clearly, one need not experience incest to empathize with a group member's anguish over reliving painful sexual experiences. One need not have been abandoned by a parent to feel and experience the sadness of abandonment. It is not necessary to have been divorced to share a client's anger, hurt, and sadness of separation. Such experiences come in many forms and, at one level or another, are common to us all. It is not the specific experience that is essential. What is essential is a willingness on the part of the group leader to face his or her own unique life problems. There are situations in every life that trigger feelings of isolation, rage, resentment, guilt, sadness, loss, or rejection—to name a few of the feelings that will be expressed in groups. By remaining open to their own emotions, by allowing themselves to be touched by the emotions of others, and by reexperiencing certain difficult events, group leaders will increase their capacity to be psychologically present for others.

Barriers to Effective Therapy

In the training workshops that my associates and I conduct, the participants typically lead groups and then receive feedback from the members and ourselves. Many of our students express feelings of inadequacy as group leaders and a sense of frustration and hopelessness; they see little change occurring in the members of their groups, and they perceive that their clients are resistant and don't enjoy coming to groups. In many instances the problems besetting these students can be traced back to the fact that the conditions of active listening, empathy, and positive regard are in some measure lacking in their groups. What follows is a list of specific problems that militate against group progress:

1. *Lack of attending and empathy.* Often these prospective group leaders show that they don't really listen; they are preoccupied with a message that *they* want to impart to their groups and use the group as a vehicle for indoctrination. Or they ask many closed questions and are preoccupied with problem solving rather than with problem understanding. In short, many of our students talk too much and listen too little. At times we observe that leaders are highly judgmental and critical and that they create a dichotomy between "we," the treatment staff, and "they," the clients. Instead of forming an alliance with their clients, they sometimes see the group members as enemies. These counselors often fail to see any of themselves in those they work with.

2. *Absence of counselor self-disclosure.* Some agencies and institutions foster, even require, an aloof and undisclosing leader role. Group counselors are given the messages "Avoid being personal," "Don't get involved," and "Avoid sharing anything about yourself, even if it affects the relationship." Leaders are expected to change the behavior of members, yet they are expected to keep themselves out of their interactions with group members— clearly an unreasonable and self-defeating expectation.

3. *Lack of positive regard, warmth, and acceptance.* Some group counselors are intolerant of the people they are supposedly helping and cling to assumptions that keep their clientele in stereotyped categories. Such prejudice makes client change difficult, if not impossible. Admittedly, it may be hard to maintain positive regard, warmth, and acceptance toward people who are in a treatment program for acts such as wife beating, child abuse, or murder. It is not necessary to condone such actions, and it may not even be possible to avoid feeling negative toward those who have committed such acts. But it is important to try to set aside one's reactions at least during the course of the group. And it *is* possible to see these people as more than "child abusers," "antisocial personalities," "criminals," and so on. Related to a lack of positive regard are impatience, coldness, abruptness, put-downs, sarcasm, and hostility toward clients. Unless counselors recognize these attitudes, there is little chance that they will modify them and a large chance that they will continue to lead unsuccessful groups.

4. *Lack of belief in the therapeutic process.* Underlying the concepts of positive regard and acceptance is the belief that people *can* change and improve their personal condition. In our in-service group-process workshops we have frequently met practitioners who lead groups only because they are required to do so and who do not believe in the effectiveness of group therapy. In a climate in which enthusiasm, motivation, and faith in groups are absent, is it surprising that leaders find that their groups are somewhat less than successful? After all, how can group members be expected to have faith in a process that the group leader does not believe in? No wonder that

little change occurs and that the members are resistant and don't enjoy coming to the group.

Role and Functions of the Group Leader

Rogers (1970) takes a dim view of the use of techniques to get a group moving. If and when techniques are used, he believes, the group needs to be made a party to them:

> I try to avoid using any procedure that is planned; I have a real "thing" about artificiality. If any planned procedure is tried, the group members should be as fully in on it as the facilitator, and should make the choice themselves as to whether they want to use that approach [p. 56].

Rogers also cautions against the facilitator's making interpretive comments. Such comments, he feels, are apt to make the group self-conscious and slow the process down. Thus, he believes that if there are to be group-process observations, they should come from members, a view that is consistent with his philosophy of placing the responsibility for the direction of the group on the members. The term *facilitator* reflects the importance of interactions between group members. The role of the facilitator is to create a climate under which the actualizing tendency will be released. The person-centered group encourages the members to explore the incongruities between their beliefs and behaviors and the urgings of their inner feelings and subjective experiencing. As the members become more aware of these incongruities within themselves, their view of themselves expands. Changes occur in the members' willingness to listen to themselves, to trust their inner promptings, and to rely on them as a basis for their behavior (Meador, 1975).

The person-centered approach assumes that members need the group setting and the time to express what they are ordinarily afraid to express on their own. Given the unstructured approach, along with a facilitator who refuses to do the traditional "leaderly" things, the group members, who are accustomed to following authorities, must eventually rely on themselves to formulate a purpose and a direction. Members are helped to begin listening to themselves and other members by a facilitator who will not act as an expert and save them. They are challenged to struggle and to express themselves, and out of this struggle they have a basis for learning how to trust themselves. Coulson (1970) summarizes this role of the facilitator and its impact on the group:

> The leader of an encounter group errs if he tries to *make* the group happen. He errs in missing the opportunity to find out what people *really* are like when they are not being manipulated. He errs in taking away from the members the rare opportunity to be what *they* want to be, without performance expectations. He errs also because *it simply isn't necessary* to manufacture the events of encounter. I am quite convinced that there is

something in each of us which longs to be personal, even if ordinarily we don't dare it. If this is what we *want,* then it will come out in time if there is a sufficiently uncluttered occasion with other people [p. 10].

In a discussion of the role of the facilitator in the person-centered group, Bozarth (1981) identifies the following major characteristics:

- Facilitators are willing to participate as a member of the group.
- They demonstrate a willingness to attempt to understand and to accept each member of the group.
- They are willing to share their struggles when such personal issues exist, if doing so is appropriate and timely.
- Facilitators are willing to give up the power of control and the image of the expert; instead, they seek ways of having personal influence.
- They trust in the ability of the members to move in positive and healthy directions without their advice.

To help delineate the differences between the person-centered approach and other therapeutic models, I have listed some procedures that are *not* generally considered as part of the facilitator's repertoire:

- advice giving
- catalysts and techniques to initiate action
- diagnosis and evaluation
- structure and directive intervention
- tasks given to members to do outside the session

The person-centered approach emphasizes, instead, certain attitudes and skills as a necessary part of the facilitator's style:

- listening in an active and sensitive way
- reflecting
- clarifying
- summarizing
- sharing of personal experiences
- encountering and engaging others in the group
- demonstrating nonevaluative caring for the members and showing respect for them
- supporting the members
- going with the flow of the group rather than trying to direct the way the group is going
- affirming a client's capacity for self-determination

It might be mentioned that effective person-centered facilitators are not bound by rigid rules, and *at times* they do many of the things that I listed as not being a standard part of the facilitator's repertoire. What is basic to this approach is the focus on the members as being the center of the group, not the leader. Members of the person-centered group are often as facilitative or more so than the group leader. On this point Lieberman, Yalom, and Miles (1973) make the following statement: "Change does not revolve around the solitary sun of the leader; the evidence is strong that psychosocial relations in the group play an exceedingly important role in the process of change" (p. 428). In a similar line of thinking, Wood (1982) captures the essence of the facilitator's role: "Success is not marked by how well the facilitator shines in presenting the cardinal attitudes but in how well the group's creative, growthful wisdom is released and the benefits of growth afforded its members. If the group can create a facilitative climate, the formative tendency will do the rest" (p. 257).

Rogers (1970) sees climate setting as the primary function of the group facilitator. This climate that Rogers wishes to establish is one that promotes psychological safety for the participants (and by "safety" he does *not* imply that members will be spared the pain of new insights). Rogers captures what it means to establish a psychologically safe climate and to "be there for another":

> I would like the individual to feel that whatever happens *to* him or *within* him, I will be psychologically very much *with* him in moments of pain or joy, or the combination of the two, which is such a frequent mark of growth. I think I can usually sense when a participant is frightened or hurting, and it is at those moments that I give him some sign, verbal or nonverbal, that I perceive this and I am a companion to him as he lives in that hurt or fear [1970, p. 48].

In summary, person-centered group leaders use themselves as instruments of change in a group. Their central function is to establish a therapeutic climate in which group members will interact in honest and meaningful ways. Clearly, it is the leader's attitudes and behavior that are the powerful determinants of the accepting group atmosphere conducive to real communication—not the techniques that he or she employs.

The Person-Centered Group Process

Characteristics of the Group

The typical size of the person-centered group is 8 to 12 members. The group might meet weekly for about 2 to 3 hours for an unspecified duration. Another pattern is for a group to meet for a weekend or longer in an intensive format. The residential aspect of small personal-growth groups and encounter groups affords members opportunities to work on personal issues that are troubling them and to become a community as a group. Although these groups often meet from Friday until Sunday, with time out for meals and sleep, they might also meet for a period of 10 days to 2 weeks.

In discussing the mechanics of organizing and conducting a person-centered group, both Meador (1975) and Wood (1982) write that there are no rules for the selection of group members. Because of the personal nature of this approach, each facilitator admits a person if the two can agree that the person could probably benefit from the experience and contribute to the group. There are no stated ground rules that members must abide by. When people meet in a group, they formulate the rules for their own meetings. Wood (1982) notes that groups generally adopt their own rules prohibiting physical violence, setting meeting times, governing the admittance of new members, and adopting a procedure for terminating the group. Also, groups may expect that each member attend each complete meeting of the group.

Stages of the Group

On the basis of his experience with numerous groups, Rogers (1970) has delineated some process patterns that occur in any type of group employing the person-centered approach when most of the conditions that are discussed in this chapter are present. It needs to be emphasized that the following process patterns, or trends, don't occur in a clear-cut sequence and that they may vary considerably from group to group.

1. *Milling around.* The lack of leader direction inevitably results in some initial confusion, frustration, and "milling around"—either actually or verbally. Questions such as "Who is responsible here?" "What are we here for?" or "What are we supposed to be doing?" are characteristic and reflect the concern felt at this stage.

2. *Resistance to personal expression or exploration.* Members initially present a public self—one they think will be acceptable to the group. They are fearful and resistant to revealing their private selves.

3. *Description of past feelings.* Despite doubts about the trustworthiness of the group and the risk of exposing oneself, disclosure of personal feelings does begin—however hesitantly and ambivalently. Generally, this disclosure deals with events outside of the group; members tend to describe feelings in a "there-and-then" fashion.

4. *Expression of negative feelings.* As the group progresses, there is a movement toward the expression of here-and-now feelings. Often these expressions take the form of an attack on the group leader, usually for not providing the needed direction. In general, such expression of negative feelings toward the group leader or others precedes the expression of positive feelings. (A possible reason for this may be that members are testing the group to see whether it is a safe place to express *all* feelings.)

5. *Expression and exploration of personally meaningful material.* If the expression of negative feelings is seen by the members as acceptable to the group, a climate of trust emerges. Because of this feeling of trust, members decide to take the risks involved in disclosing personal material. At this point the participants begin to realize that the group is what they make it, and they begin to experience freedom. Such perceptions make members willing to let others know deeper facets of themselves.

6. *Expression of immediate interpersonal feelings in the group.* Members tend to express both positive and negative feelings toward one another. Usually these feelings are explored at this stage.

7. *Development of a healing capacity in the group.* Next, members begin to spontaneously reach out to one another, expressing care, support,

understanding, and concern. In other words, members become therapeutic for one another by relating in facilitating ways. At this stage, helping relationships are often formed within the group that offer members aid in leading more constructive lives outside of the group.

8. *Self-acceptance and the beginning of change.* Self-acceptance marks the beginning of change in group members. At this stage participants begin to accept aspects of themselves that they formerly denied or distorted; they get closer to their feelings and consequently become less rigid and more open to change. As members accept their strengths and weaknesses, they drop their defenses and welcome change—a process that promotes further change.

9. *Cracking of facades.* Here individual members begin to respond to the group demand that masks and pretenses be dropped. This revealing of deeper selves by some members validates the theory that meaningful encounters can occur when people take the risk of getting beneath surface interaction. At this stage the group strives toward deeper communication.

10. *Feedback.* In the process of receiving both positive and negative feedback, members acquire a lot of data concerning how others experience them and what impact they have on others. This information often leads to new insights that help them decide on aspects of themselves that they want to change.

11. *Confrontation.* Here members confront one another in what is usually an intensely emotional process involving positive and negative feedback. Confrontation can be seen as a stepping up of the interactions described in earlier stages.

12. *The helping relationship outside the group sessions.* By this stage members have begun making contacts outside the group. Here we see an extension of the process described above in number 7.

13. *The basic encounter.* Because in the group the members come into closer and more direct contact with one another than is generally the case in everyday life, genuine person-to-person relationships occur. At this point members begin to experience how meaningful relationships can be when there is a commitment to work toward a common goal and a sense of community.

14. *Expression of positive feelings and closeness.* As the sessions progress, an increasing warmth and closeness develops within the group because of the realness of the participants' expression of feelings about themselves and toward others. This therapeutic feeling of closeness leads to the last and most important process.

15. *Behavior changes in the group.* As members experience increased ease in expressing their feelings, their behaviors, mannerisms, and even their appearance begin to change. They tend to act in an open manner; they express deeper feelings toward others; they achieve an increased understanding of themselves; they develop new insights into their problems; and they work out more effective ways of being with others. If the changes are

effective, the members will carry their new behaviors into their everyday lives.

As noted above, the stages of a person-centered encounter group, as adapted from Rogers (1970), don't necessarily occur in a neat and predictable order. What is important to keep in mind is that each stage describes a *process* and that each process tends to produce the sought-after change within a group and its individual members.

Some Outcomes of the Group Experience

Rogers (1987d) has identified a number of changes that tend to occur within individuals in a successful group experience. Members become more open. As they feel increasingly understood and accepted, they have less need to defend themselves. Because they become more aware of their own feelings and of what is going on around them, they are more realistic and more objective. They tend to be more like the self that they wanted before entering the group experience. They are not as easily threatened, because the safety of the group changes their attitude toward self and others. Within the group there is more understanding and acceptance of who others are. Members become more appreciative of themselves as they are, and they move toward more self-direction. They empower themselves to take charge of their life. They trust themselves to a greater extent, they feel trusted by others, and they are able to trust others in turn. The members become more creative, since they are willing to accept their own uniqueness.

Large Community Workshops

As we have seen, new developments in the theory and practice of client-centered groups took place as the intensive groups became popular in the mid-1960s. The basic encounter groups were relatively small, generally consisting of not more than 12 people and a facilitator. Later, the person-centered approach was applied to working with relatively large groups, often numbering hundreds of people. These large groups, which Rogers and some of his colleagues began in 1973 at the Center for Studies of the Person in La Jolla, California, eventually were offered in many places in the world. These residential groups, lasting anywhere from 4 days to 2 weeks, were designed to build community, to facilitate the self-exploration of members, and to resolve tensions between members, who often represented diverse cultures. The facilitator's goal in these large groups is much like that in small groups—namely, the development of an atmosphere of acceptance and trust that encourages members to discover and accept the range of their feelings and the activation of constructive action leading to significant change in their lives outside of the group (Bozarth, 1981). These groups are characterized by a variety of individuals, with a diversity of languages and cultures. These large community meetings and group workshops provided data for understanding how cross-cultural and international differences can be resolved through the application of conditions advocated by the client-centered approach (Raskin, 1986a).

Evaluation of the Person-Centered Approach

Because the person-centered approach is very much a phenomenological one, based on the subjective world view of the client, I consider it an excellent basis for the initial stages of any type of group. In this approach the emphasis is on truly listening to and deeply understanding the client's world from his or her internal frame of reference. Critical evaluation, analysis, and judgment are suspended, and the focus is on grasping the feelings and thoughts being expressed by the other. I see this form of listening and hearing as a prerequisite to any group approach, particularly during the early stages, when it is essential that members feel free to explore their concerns openly. Unless the participants feel that they are being understood, surely any technique or intervention plan is bound to fail.

Many of the problems I have found among group leaders in training (as I discussed earlier in this chapter) stem from the failure to reach an understanding of the members' subjective world, an understanding that can be achieved only by very careful listening and by restraining the tendency to dive in too quickly to solve members' problems.

Many of the leader attitudes that Rogers sees as essential are a part of the foundations common to all therapeutic models. For example, respect and caring for clients are necessary for any positive movement to occur; without them the group is bound to reach an impasse. I doubt that any approach would question the value of the basic therapeutic conditions stressed by Rogers, although different therapies do place different values on the importance of specific conditions.

Rogers's emphasis on the person of the group leader is something that has much meaning for me. In training and supervising group leaders, I've found an eagerness on their part to acquire techniques that they can use when certain problems arise in a group and a relative lack of interest in learning how the kind of person they are influences the process of the group. Thus, I hear a lot of questions like these:

- "What do I do if nobody wants to work in the group?"
- "How do I handle an aggressive member? a silent member? one who monopolizes? one who won't open up?"
- "What can I do to motivate people who don't want to be in the group?"
- "What do I do when things get too intense in the group?"

I'm suggesting that group leaders would do well to show more interest in questions related to themselves and their attitudes, questions such as these:

- "Am I genuinely interested in people?"
- "What personal needs am I meeting by being a group leader?"
- "Am I authentically myself in a group, or do I hide behind the role of 'leader'?"
- "Am I able to accept people, or do I have a need to direct their lives?"
- "Am I willing to take time to understand others, or do I force them to follow my agenda?"

- "Do I offer a proper model for what I expect the members in my group to become?"
- "What kind of model am I?"

Some people think that in order to practice within the spirit of the person-centered approach one must tolerate excessive floundering and a totally open structure. I myself am not patient with such situations. I have found that I'm most effective, and the group seems to be most productive, when there is a structure that offers some direction yet grants freedom to the members. Thus, I typically provide the most structure at the beginning and ending stages of a group. I generally use techniques to enhance and to highlight the existing material in the group, rather than using them to get things moving. Although I don't like to use techniques to induce emotions, I do use them to help members deepen their experience of certain emotions and to explore their feelings or problems. For example, I am not likely to use a guided fantasy as a catalyst to bring up certain feelings, such as loneliness. When members talk about a lonely time of their life and sadness comes up naturally, however, I am inclined to ask them to do any number of things, a few of which might be looking at another person in the room and talking directly to this person about the sadness, talking to a person as though he or she were a significant other, or reenacting a past event as though it were happening now. When members bring a struggle or some unfinished business with significant people in their lives into the present, whatever they are experiencing is usually intensified. By providing some therapeutic structure, I give such members the encouragement and support they need to stay with their personal pain and make a crucial breakthrough. These techniques or experiments grow out of the existential situation and are designed to facilitate deeper self-exploration, which is quite different from pushing members to feel certain emotions.

Because initiating and directing are part of a leadership style that appears suited to my personality, I find that I am unduly limited by a strict adherence to a model that stresses listening, understanding, reflecting, and clarifying, practices that I see as useful but insufficient. The point here is that whatever techniques one employs or avoids, whatever style one adopts or refrains from, the approach should be adapted to the needs of the group and its members and should, at the same time, fit the personality and style of the leader. Every approach has something of value to offer; the artistry consists of being aware of those aspects of each model that work for us and of those aspects that may work against us. To its credit, the person-centered approach allows considerable room for practitioners to develop their own therapeutic style in applying the concepts that are a basic part of the approach.

Some beginning group leaders have a problem in the way in which they apply the person-centered approach; by remaining passive listeners, they also remain hidden as persons. This unassertive behavior stems partially from a fear of making mistakes. But whatever the reason, an excessively passive approach results in submerging the uniqueness of the leader under a timid stance. It is certainly true that the possibility for harming a person is smaller in less directive approaches than in more directive ones. But a question naturally arises: how much good can leaders do if they become so focused on the group members that they ignore themselves as powerful agents of change? Also, I should add, this misapplication of the person-centered approach runs contrary to Rogers's emphasis on leader authenticity.

In his article "A Lover's Quarrel with the Non-Directive Method," O'Leary (1987, p. 3) points out that the person-centered approach is a rich theory that is not limited to a specific technique or way of being. He adds that the nondirective nature of the approach is subject to criticism. Two of his points are:

- "In groups, this method has given opportunities to the bully, the most disturbed, and the most narcissistic to flourish, and the leader to abdicate."
- "This method can discourage the creativity of therapists who love words, have imagination, and whose challenging spirits could move people into direct, life-affirming action."

Nevertheless, O'Leary summarizes his own experience with the person-centered approach this way:

When I was inexperienced, I was non-directive because I was frightened and didn't know what else to do. With more experience I became more directive as I became confident and eager to be of assistance. With still more experience, I am again becoming non-directive, as I find more people who, though eager to receive thoughtful help, are hungry for understanding attention [p. 3].

My central criticism of the person-centered approach—an approach I see as a good place to begin but not a good place to end—involves not what it includes but, rather, what it omits. Personally, I don't subscribe to the notion that technical skills and knowledge are unimportant. I believe in the value of action; of therapeutic direction, at least at times; of timely interpretations; and of more directive skills than are found in this approach. My rationale is that although I see active support as essential if clients are to experience significant breakthroughs, I think they can also benefit from assistance in translating their insights into action programs. Therefore, I am fond of suggesting homework assignments that are designed to help clients challenge themselves to do difficult things in everyday life. Although I generally ask clients to come up with their own homework, I am not averse to making suggestions and presenting them in an invitational manner. When they say they would like to change how they relate to someone they love, I often suggest that they talk to this person symbolically in the group, in a role-playing exercise. This structure provides a safety, for their loved one is not actually seeing or hearing them in the group, yet these members can benefit by trying on various alternatives, and they also profit from the feedback of others. All of these action-oriented interventions, both in the group and outside of it, are designed to enable members to make decisions about how they want to be different and to gain some practice in thinking, feeling, and behaving differently.

In fairness, it needs to be mentioned that recent developments in the person-centered approach provide more latitude for therapists to share their reactions, to confront clients in a caring way, and to be active in the therapeutic process (Lietaer, 1984). Current formulations of the role of person-centered therapists attach more importance to bringing in their own here-and-now experiences, which can stimulate clients to explore themselves at a deeper level. Although the therapist's receptive attitude is still viewed as being of central importance, this does not exclude the therapist from taking the initiative at times in order to stimulate the client's experiential process. It is important to remain in the experiential frame of reference of the client, yet more room is now given for therapists to provide clients with feedback, to share perceptions and reactions, and to confront clients. Lietaer mentions that even "homework" and other auxiliary techniques can be used in a person-centered manner, if the experience of the client remains as the continuous touchstone.

Applying the Person-Centered Approach in Multicultural Settings

The person-centered approach, more than other models, has been applied to bringing people of diverse cultures together for the purpose of developing mutual understanding. In 1948 Rogers (1987c) began developing a theory of reducing tension among antagonistic groups, and he continued until his death in 1987. In the 1970s he and his associates conducted workshops promoting cross-cultural communication. In 1978, for example, 173 participants from 27 nations attended a 10-day workshop in Spain, which ended with a deep feeling of community. Respect and mutual understanding replaced much of the conflict and hostility that characterized this group at the outset. Rogers conducted similar workshops involving different types of factional differences in Italy, Poland, Brazil, Japan, Mexico, France, the Philippines, South Africa, the Soviet Union, and the United States. An example of an intercultural workshop is the one in Hungary in 1984, which included 300 participants from countries of both the East European and West European blocs as well as citizens of the United States. In 1982 and again in 1986 Rogers and his colleagues held intensive multiracial workshops. The aim was to open communication between the races. The interactions between Blacks and Whites were profound and were characterized by fear, rage, pain, suspicion, and guilt (Rogers, 1987c).

Shortly before his death Rogers conducted 4-day workshops in both Moscow and Tbilisi in the Soviet Union. Rogers maintained that these intensive workshops with Soviet psychologists, educators, and researchers had demonstrated that their concerns differed very little from those felt by a similar professional group in the United States. He found that a psychological climate that had produced certain predictable results in the United States, Latin America, European countries, and South Africa yielded the same results in the Soviet Union (Rogers, 1987a).

Person-centered groups have attained considerable popularity in Japan, and researchers there have conducted numerous studies on these groups. From 1970 to 1986, 165 articles were published in Japan on the behavior of facilitators and cross-cultural studies (Murayama, Nojima, & Abe, 1988). These authors point out that members in these groups commonly experienced feelings of inferiority in expressing their point of view during group meetings. The difficulty Japanese people have in expressing themselves when they feel different from others is largely due to a feeling of shame they attach to expressing their differences. Findings of person-centered groups indicate that Japanese clients prefer to hide their feelings rather than to express them. Because of this tendency to keep their feelings to themselves, group sessions often have intense periods of silence, with members hoping that someone else will begin expressing feelings. Japanese facilitators tend to be more autocratic, partly because members expect them to take the initiative. Murayama and his colleagues conclude: "Person-centered groups have been a great factor in the orientation of persons living in Japanese society. The application of person-centered theory has contributed to the development of a more mature and knowledgeable human being" (1988, p. 490).

As we've seen, a major focus of person-centered therapy lies in active listening, which is a key contribution to effective group work. This approach is grounded on the importance of hearing the deeper messages that clients bring to a group. Empathy, sensitive listening, being present, and respecting the values of clients are particularly important attitudes and skills in groups with ethnic clients. For example, in working with certain Japanese clients the leader might learn of their hesitation in revealing their feelings. Person-centered leaders would respect the cultural norm pertaining to showing one's feelings and not be inclined to push the value of readily displaying feelings. They would help clients work within the framework of their values.

Although the person-centered approach has made significant contributions to working with groups representing diverse social, political, and cultural backgrounds, there are also some limitations to practicing exclusively within this framework in community agency settings and outpatient clinics. Many of the clients who come to a community mental-health clinic or who are involved in some other type of outpatient treatment may need a more structured group experience. This is especially true of short-term groups, open groups with a rapidly changing membership, task-oriented groups, and groups composed of culturally diverse populations. Minority-group clients often seek professional help to deal with some current crisis, to alleviate psychosomatic symptoms, or to learn certain coping skills (such as stress management). When such clients do seek professional help, it is often done as a last resort, and they are looking for expert guidance. Ethnic clients often wait for active probing by the group leader or for an expressed invitation to speak. They expect a directive leader and can be put off by a leader who does not provide some structuring (Chu & Sue, 1984).

There is a high dropout rate for ethnic-minority clients: as many as 52% of them terminate counseling after the first session (Mokuau, 1987). One explanation for this obvious dissatisfaction with professional counseling is that these clients quickly make the assessment that they will not get the help they are looking for from the counseling relationship. This is why it is so crucial that the issue of client expectations and client goals be explored during the first meeting. If leaders simply wait for clients to bring up these issues for themselves, it may be too late, because they may not return for another session. Therefore, more activity and structuring may be called for than is usually the case in a person-centered framework, especially in a group. It is my opinion that groups can benefit from some teaching by the group on what groups are about and how best to participate. Members could profit from a focused discussion of the general goals and procedures of group process and of how the group might be helpful in dealing with their life concerns. Leaders who facilitate a discussion of member expectations are taking steps to increase the retention rate in their group.

Leaders are likely to find that members of some cultural groups expect them to function in an expert role. Individuals with certain cultural backgrounds do not want to solve their problems themselves, and they expect the professional to take an active and directive role in the counseling process (Chu & Sue, 1984). I think that the core therapeutic conditions are a foundation for practice with these groups, but leaders can enhance the group process by making appropriate interventions and by taking an active part in leading (as well as facilitating). They can also design structured groups that are theme-oriented and that have both a therapeutic and an educational focus. A limitation of person-centered therapy is that it is difficult to operationalize the core conditions. For example, consider these questions: How is warmth specifically manifested? How do group leaders demonstrate their realness in behavioral ways? How do they demonstrate unconditional positive regard? How are they to know the degree to which the members are experiencing this unconditional acceptance?

The way that group leaders communicate these core conditions to the members in their group needs to be consistent with the members' cultural framework. Some members may be accustomed to indirect communication and may therefore be uncomfortable with the openness and directness of the group leader. Some group leaders who express their warmth by touching their clients do not realize that some clients may feel offended by touching. Warmth is interpreted differently in different cultural contexts. As Chu and Sue (1984) have observed, physical contact is not taken as casually in Eastern cultures as it is in mainstream America, especially in heterosexual contact. Thus, leaders need to be aware of when and with whom to have such contact, especially in cases of contact with the opposite sex. Chu and Sue provide a useful guideline when they write that practitioners must be sensitive to the cultural values of ethnic clients while at the same time avoiding the stereotyping of individuals. Respect can be shown by recognizing and appreciating the rich diversity that exists within any group of people.

Another problem with applying the person-centered approach to ethnic clients is that it extols the value of an internal locus of evaluation. Yet some ethnic groups place a value on an external locus of evaluation. For example, they may look to family tradition for their answers. They are likely to be highly influenced by familial expectations and not motivated simply by their own personal preference.

Although there are distinct limitations to working exclusively within a person-centered perspective with ethnic minority clients, it should not be concluded that this approach is unsuitable for these clients. There is great diversity among any group of people, and therefore there is room for a variety of therapeutic styles. Although some clients prefer a directive and active style, others respond well to a less directive leader. The literature suggests that the appropriateness and effectiveness of counseling styles depend largely on the cultural values and world view embraced by an individual (Mokuau, 1987). It is a mistake to assume that one style of group leadership will be effective for all ethnic clients. Mokuau has observed that the prescription of a directive counseling style with Asian-American clients is limiting because it is based on a monocultural perspective of Asian world view and values:

> We can no longer suggest that the directive counseling style with a focus on structure, explanations, concrete services, and a nonegalitarian relationship may be more effective than the nondirective counseling style with attention to client self-disclosure and affect, an egalitarian relationship, and more client direction. The conclusion is that the directive counseling style, the nondirective counseling style, and variations of the two may be effective depending on the client's problem and value orientation [1987, p. 335].

I am becoming more convinced that person-centered therapy supplies an ideal foundation for a solid relationship with ethnically diverse clients. Leaders are likely to find it necessary to utilize some structure, while also encouraging self-direction in the members.

Research Efforts

From 1946 to 1952 a significant amount of research was published on client-centered groups (Raskin, 1986b). Using verbatim transcripts as a basic source of data, researchers found that clients changed in the direction of becoming more positive, insightful, and self-congruent and freer in their experiencing (Raskin, 1986b, p. 404).

Early Studies. The following studies, published between 1946 and 1952, were some of the most important to deal with client-centered group therapy:

Hobbs and Pascal (1946), Peres (1947), Telschow (1950), Gorlow (1950), Gorlow, Hoch, and Telschow (1952), and Haimowitz and Haimowitz (1952). These studies, which are summarized below, are noteworthy for a number of reasons (Raskin, 1986b, p. 393):

1. In the area of group therapy, these studies represented a pioneering research effort into the process and outcomes of groups.
2. The analyses of these studies were based mainly on verbatim typescripts of group sessions. They also employed tests of personality adjustment, behavior ratings, and sociometric ratings.
3. They provided supporting evidence for the therapeutic conditions outlined by Rogers during this period.
4. Behavior changes in the group were correlated with changes outside the therapy situation.
5. Attitudes toward the self made up an important aspect of client behavior, lending support to the emerging theory of personality change that emphasized self-concept.
6. There were specific bases that distinguished more successful clients from the less successful ones.

Research on Hospital Patients. As the client-centered approach to group therapy progressed, evidence was advanced that extremely disturbed individuals could be helped. It was also shown that the progress of individuals in these groups was related to group leaders' providing conditions such as empathy, congruence, and warmth (Raskin, 1986b, p. 404). The following studies were conducted to assess specific aspects of the client-centered approach to group work: Baehr (1954), Ends and Page (1957, 1959), Truax (1961), Barrett-Lennard (1962), Truax and Carkhuff (1967), Dies (1973), May and Thompson (1973), Abramowitz, Abramowitz, Roback, and Jackson (1974), Kilmann and Howell (1974), Kilmann, Albert, and Sotile (1975), Strassberg, Roback, Anchor, and Abramowitz (1975), and Braaten (1982). According to Raskin (1986b, p. 400), who reviewed and summarized these studies, they are significant for the following reasons:

1. Client-centered groups can be effective with seriously disturbed populations.
2. Evidence indicates that individual client-centered therapy, group therapy, and a combination of the two are equally effective.
3. Positive outcomes with client-centered group therapy are related to the therapeutic conditions of empathy, genuineness, and warmth. Group atmosphere, related to cohesiveness, shows promise as a correlate of participants' progress.
4. The progress shown by more seriously disturbed populations can be delineated in terms of changes in self-concept and in the quality of experiencing. There is a trend from fixed and rigid behavior to spontaneous and open behavior.

5. There is evidence that a relationship exists between the degree of directiveness in a therapy group and the dimension of locus of control in the participants. It appears that group members with an internal locus of control respond better to less directive groups.
6. Therapists' self-disclosure is related to the perception of the therapist as caring and to a positive outcome of therapy.
7. The locus of control and the self-disclosure findings were based on studies that included encounter groups and the traditional weekly format.

Research Efforts in Perspective.   To his credit, Rogers has consistently demonstrated a willingness to state his formulations as testable hypotheses and to submit his hypotheses to research efforts. This has been especially true of individual therapy and to some extent of the applications of the person-centered approach to groups. His theories of therapy and personality change have had tremendous heuristic effect, and, though much controversy surrounds this approach, even his critics give him credit for conducting extensive research on the process and outcomes of psychotherapy. Wood (1982) points out that studies on person-centered groups have been hampered by the slow development of appropriate methods to examine groups in naturalistic settings. Wood contends, however, that the available research to date supports the theory and practice of the person-centered approach to group therapy.

Rogers and his associates have conducted research to determine the efficacy of the basic encounter groups described in this chapter. Rogers (1970) describes a systematic follow-up study that he conducted to assess the outcomes of small groups led by himself and his associates. The follow-up questionnaire—essentially a self-reporting instrument that identified reactions to group participation as well as the value of applying what was learned in the group to everyday life situations—was sent to 500 group participants. The study was conducted 3 to 6 months after the group experience. The following were some of the general findings of Rogers's study: two individuals felt that the experience had been mostly damaging and had changed their behavior in negative ways; a "moderate number" viewed their group experience as neutral and saw very little behavior change after the group; another "moderate number" felt that the group had only temporarily changed their behavior; most of the participants viewed the experience as deeply meaningful and positive—one that had made a significant and continuing impact and that had produced positive results in their behavior. (The study also contained open-ended questions that were designed to give a sample of the subjective perceptions of the group experience.)

It should be noted that psychologists who favor the empirical approach in evaluating the effects of individual and group counseling criticize the self-report style of Rogers's research as being too subjective. It should also be noted, however, that the self-report approach is consistent with the basic assumption of person-centered theory that only the individual can determine the meaning of a therapeutic experience. For readers interested in further details and in Rogers's able defense of his method of conducting outcome studies of encounter groups, I suggest consulting Rogers (1970, pp. 126–134).

Questions for Reflection and Discussion

1. What specific attitudes would person-centered leaders hold that would assist them in understanding and working with culturally diverse populations?

2. From what you know of yourself, how comfortable do you think you'd be as a leader in an unstructured group situation? How might you function as a leader if there were no plans in advance, no agenda, and no preconceived structure and you refrained from using any techniques to get things moving?

3. What implications do you see in using a person-centered approach in working with a mandatory group? Can you think of ways to apply the key concepts of this approach to counseling reluctant and involuntary clients?

4. What are your thoughts on the matter of selecting members to participate in a group? Can you think of both advantages and disadvantages to the absence of screening and selection procedures?

5. What are the advantages of having group facilitators who are not professional psychotherapists? the disadvantages? What are the qualities you would want in a group facilitator whom your loved one would be working with?

6. What are some key concepts and basic attitudes of the person-centered approach that you think could be effectively integrated into any other theory of groups?

7. Do you think that you can adopt a person-centered philosophy and still incorporate techniques from some of the directive therapies into your group leading? Can you view people from a person-centered perspective yet assume a more active and central role in leadership? Explain.

8. What are your thoughts about the role of the person-centered facilitator of groups? Would you feel comfortable in being a member in a group you were leading or facilitating? In what sense might you be a member, and how might you function differently from the other members?

9. Review the basic attitudes of the person-centered group leader (genuineness, unconditional positive regard, and empathy). Which of these attitudes do you think you'd have the greatest difficulty in living by and in translating from a belief you hold into concrete actions?

10. With what populations, and with what types of group, do you think the person-centered approach would be the most effective? In what cases, if any, do you think this approach would be inappropriate and ineffective?

Where to Go from Here

An organization that you might consider joining is the Association for the Development of the Person-Centered Approach, an interdisciplinary and international organization. Membership includes a subscription to the *Person-Centered Review,* the association's quarterly newsletter, a membership directory, and information about the annual meeting. It also provides continuing education, as well as supervision and training, in the person-centered approach. General membership is $45 a year. Contact

Person-Centered Association
2831 Cedarwood Way
Carlsbad, CA 92008
Phone: (619) 434-6080

Perhaps one of the best ways to evaluate a person-centered group is to participate in one. The La Jolla Programs emphasize the experiential group, the small group, the community meeting, and exchanges between individuals as ways of learning about person-centered therapy. If you have an interest in finding out more about the sort of workshops described in *Carl Rogers on Encounter Groups* (1970), you can contact

Bruce Meador
Center for Studies of the Person
1125 Torrey Pines Road
La Jolla, CA 92037
Phone: (619) 459-3861

If you are interested in obtaining training and supervised experience in the person-centered approach, you might be interested in the Carl Rogers Institute of Psychotherapy Training and Supervision. The institute conducts four training programs each year, including a 1-month intensive program. For more information, contact

Norman E. Chambers
Center for Studies of the Person
1125 Torrey Pines Road
La Jolla, CA 92037
Phone: (619) 459-3861

An In-Depth Training Program in the Person-Centered Approach is designed to bring together person-centered theory and practice in an interactive group process. The format consists of 10 monthly weekends per year. For more information, write to the following address:

Center for Interpersonal Growth
Box 271
Port Jefferson, NY 11777
Phone: (516) 331-2061

RECOMMENDED SUPPLEMENTARY READINGS

One of the best ways to stay current in the area of theory, research, and application of the person-centered approach is by reading the *Person-Centered Review*. This journal is published quarterly by Sage Publications, Inc., 2111 West Hillcrest Drive, Newbury Park, CA 91320. Its aim is to carry forward the work of Carl Rogers and his pioneering spirit as well. This is an excellent journal that features personal reactions from person-centered practitioners, articles on the current state of theory applied to practice, reviews of research, and roundtable discussions.

Carl Rogers on encounter groups (Rogers, 1970) is an excellent introduction to encounter groups. It is a readable account of the process and outcomes of encounter groups, change as a result of these groups, and glimpses of the subjective struggles and experiences of those who participate in such groups.

On becoming a person (Rogers, 1961) is an important work addressing the characteristics of the helping relationship, the philosophy of the person-centered approach, and practical issues related to therapy. I especially recommend reading Chapters 2–9, 16, and 17.

Carl Rogers on personal power: Inner strength and its revolutionary impact (Rogers, 1977) describes the effectiveness of the person-centered approach in dealing with problems encountered in professions, marriage and family life, education, and even politics. A chapter is devoted to the description of a 2-week workshop from the planning stages to its outcome.

A way of being (Rogers, 1980) contains a series of updated writings on Rogers's personal experiences and perspectives, as well as chapters on the foundations and applications of a person-centered approach. Especially useful are the chapters on person-centered communities, large groups, and perspectives on the world and person of tomorrow.

REFERENCES AND SUGGESTED READINGS*

Abramowitz, C. V., Abramowitz, S. I., Roback, H. B., & Jackson, C. (1974). Differential effectiveness of directive and nondirective group therapies as a function of client internal-external control. *Journal of Consulting and Clinical Psychology, 42*, 849–853.

Aspy, D. N., & Roebuck, F. N. (1988). Carl Rogers' contributions to education. *Person-Centered Review, 3*(1), 10–18.

Baehr, G. O. (1954). The comparative effectiveness of individual psychotherapy, group psychotherapy and a combination of these methods. *Journal of Consulting Psychology, 15*, 179–183.

Barrett-Lennard, G. T. (1962). Dimensions of therapist response as causal factors in therapeutic change. *Psychological Monographs, 76*(43, Whole No. 562).

Barrett-Lennard, G. T. (1988). Listening. *Person-Centered Review, 3*(4), 410–425.

*Bozarth, J. D. (1981). The person-centered approach in the large community group. In G. Gazda (Ed.), *Innovations to group psychotherapy* (2nd ed.). Springfield, IL: Charles C Thomas.

*Books and articles marked with an asterisk are suggested for further study.

Bozarth, J. D. (1984). Beyond reflections: Emergent modes of empathy. In R. F. Levant & J. M. Shlien (Eds.), *Client-centered therapy and the person-centered approach: New directions in theory, research, and practice* (pp. 59–75). New York: Praeger.

Bozarth, J. D. (1987). Person-centered workshop. *Person-Centered Review, 2*(3), 311–314.

Bozarth, J. D., & Brodley, B. T. (1986). Client-centered psychotherapy: A statement. *Person-Centered Review, 1*(3), 262–271.

Braaten, L. J. (1982, July). Individually perceived group atmosphere and goal attainment: A methodological pilot study. *Proceedings of the First International Forum on the Person-Centered Approach*, Oaxtepec, Mexico.

*Braaten, L. J. (1986). Thirty years with Rogers' necessary and sufficient conditions of therapeutic personality change: A personal evaluation. *Person-Centered Review, 1*(1), 37–50.

Cain, D. J. (1986). Editor's introduction to the *Person-Centered Review. Person-Centered Review, 1*(1), 3–14.

*Cain, D. J. (1987a). Carl R. Rogers: The man, his vision, his impact. *Person-Centered Review, 2*(3), 283–288.

*Cain, D. J. (1987b). Carl Rogers' life in review. *Person-Centered Review, 2*(4), 476–506.

Carkhuff, R. R. (1966). Toward explaining success or failure in interpersonal learning experiences. *Personnel and Guidance Journal, 44*.

Chu, J., & Sue, S. (1984). Asian/Pacific-Americans and group practice. In L. E. Davis (Ed.), *Ethnicity in social group work practice*. New York: Haworth.

Corsini, R. J. (1970). Issues in encounter groups: Comments on Coulson's article. *The Counseling Psychologist, 2*(2), 28–34.

Coulson, W. R. (1970). Major contribution: Inside a basic encounter group. *The Counseling Psychologist, 2*(2), 1–27.

Coulson, W. R. (1972). *Groups, gimmicks, and instant gurus*. New York: Harper & Row.

Dies, R. R. (1973). Group therapist self-disclosure: An evaluation by clients. *Journal of Counseling Psychology, 20*, 344–348.

Ends, E. J., & Page, C. W. (1957). A study of three types of group psychotherapy with hospitalized male inebriates. *Quarterly Journal of Studies in Alcohol, 18*, 263–277.

Ends, E. J., & Page, C. W. (1959). Group psychotherapy and concomitant psychological change. *Psychological Monographs, 73*(Whole No. 1480).

Evans, R. (1975). *Carl Rogers: The man and his ideas*. New York: Dutton.

Fischer, C. T. (1987). Beyond transference. *Person-Centered Review, 2*(2), 157–164.

Gordon, T. (1951). Group-centered leadership and administration. In C. R. Rogers, *Client-centered therapy*. Boston: Houghton Mifflin.

Gorlow, L. (1950). *Nondirective group psychotherapy: An analysis of the behavior of members as therapists*. Unpublished doctoral dissertation, Columbia University, Teachers College, New York.

Gorlow, L., Hoch, E. L., & Telschow, E. F. (1952). *The nature of non-directive group psychotherapy*. New York: Bureau of Publications, Columbia University, Teachers College.

Haimowitz, N. R., & Haimowitz, M. L. (1952). Personality changes in client-centered therapy. In W. Wolff & J. A. Precker (Eds.), *Success in psychotherapy*. New York: Grune & Stratton.

Hill-Hain, A., & Rogers, C. R. (1988). A dialogue with Carl Rogers: Cross-cultural challenges of facilitating person-centered groups in South Africa. *Journal for Specialists in Group Work, 13*(2), 62–69.

Hobbs, N. (1951). Group-centered psychotherapy. In C. R. Rogers, *Client-centered therapy*. Boston: Houghton Mifflin.

Hobbs, N., & Pascal, G. (1946). A method for the quantitative analysis of group psychotherapy. *American Psychologist, 1,* 297.

Horwitz, L. (1986). An integrated, group centered approach. In I. L. Kutash & A. Wolf (Eds.), *Psychotherapist's casebook* (pp. 353–363). San Francisco: Jossey-Bass.

Howard, G. S. (1987). The person in research. *Person-Centered Review, 2*(1), 50–63.

Kilmann, P. R., Albert, B. M., & Sotile, W. M. (1975). The relationship between locus of control, structure of therapy, and outcome. *Journal of Consulting and Clinical Psychology, 43,* 588.

Kilmann, P. R., & Howell, R. J. (1974). Effects of structure of marathon group therapy and locus of control on therapeutic outcome. *Journal of Consulting and Clinical Psychology, 42,* 912.

Lambert, M. J. (1986). Future directions for research in client-centered psychotherapy. *Person-Centered Review, 1*(2), 185–200.

Levant, R. F. (1984). From person to system: Two perspectives. In R. F. Levant & J. M. Shlien (Eds.), *Client-centered therapy and the person-centered approach: New directions in theory, research, and practice* (pp. 243–260). New York: Praeger.

*Levant, R.F., & Shlien, J.M. (Eds.) (1984). **Client-centered therapy and the person-centered approach: New directions in theory, research, and practice. New York: Praeger.**

Lieberman, M. A., Yalom, I. D., & Miles, B. B. (1973). *Encounter groups: First facts.* New York: Basic Books.

Lietaer, G. (1984). Unconditional positive regard: A controversial basic attitude in client-centered therapy. In R. F. Levant & J. M. Shlien (Eds.), *Client-centered therapy and the person-centered approach: New directions in theory, research, and practice* (pp. 41–58). New York: Praeger.

May, D. P., & Thompson, C. L. (1973). Perceived levels of self-disclosure, mental health, and helpfulness of group leaders. *Journal of Counseling Psychology, 30,* 349–352.

Meador, B. D. (1975). Client-centered group therapy. In G. Gazda (Ed.), *Basic approaches to group psychotherapy and group counseling* (2nd ed.). Springfield, IL: Charles C Thomas.

Mearns, D., & McLeod, J. (1984). A person-centered approach to research. In R. F. Levant & J. M. Shlien (Eds.), *Client-centered therapy and the person-centered approach: New directions in theory, research, and practice* (pp. 370–389). New York: Praeger.

*Mokuau, N. (1987). Social workers' perceptions of counseling effectiveness for Asian American clients. *Journal of the National Association of Social Workers, 32*(4), 331–335.

Murayama, S., Nojima, K., & Abe, T. (1988). Person-centered groups in Japan: A selected review of the literature. *Person-Centered Review, 3*(4), 479–492.

*Natiello, P. (1987). The person-centered approach: From theory to practice. *Person-Centered Review, 2*(2), 203–216.

O'Leary, C. J. (1987). A lover's quarrel with the non-directive method. *Renaissance, 4*(4), 1–3.

Peres, H. (1947). An investigation of nondirective group therapy. *Journal of Consulting Psychology, 11,* 159–172.

*Raskin, N. J. (1986a). Client-centered group psychotherapy, Part 1: Development of client-centered groups. *Person-Centered Review, 1*(3), 272–290.

*Raskin, N. J. (1986b). Client-centered group psychotherapy, Part 2: Research on client-centered groups. *Person-Centered Review, 1*(4), 389–408.

Raskin, N. J., & Rogers, C. R. (1989). Person-centered therapy. In R. J. Corsini & D. Wedding (Eds.), *Current psychotherapies* (4th ed.). Itasca, IL: F. E. Peacock.

Rogers, C. (1951). *Client-centered therapy.* Boston: Houghton Mifflin.

*Rogers, C. (1957). The necessary and sufficient conditions of therapeutic personality change. *Journal of Consulting Psychology, 21,* 95–103.

*Rogers, C. (1961). *On becoming a person*. Boston: Houghton Mifflin.

*Rogers, C. (1970). *Carl Rogers on encounter groups*. New York: Harper & Row.

Rogers, C. (1975). Empathic: An unappreciated way of being. *The Counseling Psychologist, 5*(2), 2–9.

Rogers, C. (1977). *Carl Rogers on personal power: Inner strength and its revolutionary impact*. New York: Delacorte Press.

*Rogers, C. (1980). *A way of being*. Boston: Houghton Mifflin.

Rogers, C. R. (1984). One alternative to nuclear planetary suicide. In R. Levant & J. Shlien (Eds.), *Client-centered therapy and the person-centered approach: New directions in theory, research, and practice* (pp. 400–422). New York: Praeger.

Rogers, C. (1986a). Carl Rogers on the development of the person-centered approach. *Person-Centered Review, 1*(3), 257–259.

*Rogers, C. (1986b). Client-centered therapy. In I. L. Kutash & A. Wolf (Eds.), *Psychotherapist's casebook* (pp. 197–208). San Francisco: Jossey-Bass.

Rogers, C. (1986c). Reflections of feelings. *Person-Centered Review, 1*(4), 375–377.

*Rogers, C. R. (1987a). Inside the world of the Soviet professional. *Counseling and Values, 32*(1), 46–66.

Rogers, C. R. (1987b). Rogers, Kohut, and Erickson: A personal perspective on some similarities and differences. In J. K. Zeig (Ed.), *The evolution of psychotherapy* (pp. 179–187). New York: Brunner/Mazel.

Rogers, C. R. (1987c). Steps toward world peace, 1948–1986: Tension reduction in theory and practice. *Counseling and Values, 32*(1), 12–16.

*Rogers, C. R. (1987d). The underlying theory: Drawn from experience with individuals and groups. *Counseling and Values, 32*(1), 38–45.

Rogers, C. R., & Malcolm, D. (1987). The potential contribution of the behavioral scientist to world peace. *Counseling and Values, 32*(1), 10–11.

Shlien, J. M., & Levant, R. F. (1984). Introduction. In R. F. Levant & J. M. Shlien (Eds.), *Client-centered therapy and the person-centered approach: New directions in theory, research, and practice* (pp. 1–16). New York: Praeger.

Smith, D. (1982). Trends in counseling and psychotherapy. *American Psychologist, 37*(7), 802–809.

Strassberg, D. S., Roback, H. B., Anchor, K. N., & Abramowitz, S. I. (1975). Self-disclosure in group therapy with schizophrenics. *Archives of General Psychiatry, 32*, 1259–1261.

Telschow, E. F. (1950). *The role of the group leader in nondirective group psychotherapy*. Ed.D. project, Columbia University, Teachers College, New York.

Truax, C. B. (1961). The process of group psychotherapy: Relationships between hypothesized therapeutic conditions and intrapersonal exploration. *Psychological Monographs, 75*(14, Whole No. 511).

Truax, C. B., & Carkhuff, R. R. (1967). *Toward effective counseling and psychotherapy*. Chicago: Aldine-Atherton.

Watson, N. (1984). The empirical status of Rogers's hypotheses of the necessary and sufficient conditions for effective psychotherapy. In R. F. Levant & J. M. Shlien (Eds.), *Client-centered therapy and the person-centered approach: New directions in theory, research, and practice* (pp. 17–40). New York: Praeger.

Whiteley, J. M. (1987). The person-centered approach to peace. *Counseling and Values, 32*(1), 5–8.

Wood, J. K. (1982). Person-centered group therapy. In G. Gazda (Ed.), *Basic approaches to group psychotherapy and group counseling* (3rd ed.). Springfield, IL: Charles C Thomas.

Gestalt Therapy

Introduction

Gestalt therapy, a form of existential therapy developed by Fritz Perls, is based on the premise that individuals must find their own way in life and accept personal responsibility. The focus is on what the client experiences in the present moment and on the blocks that the person must overcome to achieve full awareness of the here and now. The basic goal of a Gestalt group is to challenge the participants to become aware of how they are avoiding responsibility for their awareness and to encourage them to look for internal, rather than external, support. Moment-to-moment awareness of one's experiencing, together with the almost immediate awareness of one's blocks to such experiencing, is seen as therapeutic in and of itself.

As clients acquire present-centered awareness and a clearer perception of their blocks and conflicts, significant unfinished business emerges. It is assumed that the way to become an autonomous person is to identify and deal with unfinished business from the past that interferes with current functioning. By reexperiencing past conflicts as if they were occurring in the present, clients expand their level of awareness, sometimes gradually and sometimes explosively, and are able to face and integrate denied and fragmented parts of themselves, thus becoming unified and whole.

The Gestalt view is that we are essentially responsible for our own conflicts and that we have the capacity to deal with our life problems. Therefore, the approach of the Gestalt group is basically noninterpretive. Group members make their own interpretations and statements and discover the meaning of their experiences. Leaders avoid interfering with the

318

clients' interpretations and focus instead on whatever the person seems to be experiencing at the moment. Gestalt leaders tend to be active and use a wide range of action-oriented techniques designed to intensify the members' feelings and experiences.

Gestalt therapy has been described as the integration of phenomenology and behaviorism (Zinker, 1978). On the one hand, it deals with the *subjective* world of the client's perceptions, or here-and-now experiencing. Gestalt therapists attempt to capture the person's way of being in the world, and from this subjective vantage point they try to help the client stretch the boundaries of his or her world. On the other hand, Gestalt therapy is also a behavioral approach, in that the basic methodological tool is the *experiment*. Group members are constantly being urged to try on a new style of behavior, to give expression to certain dimensions of their personality that are dormant, and to test out alternative modes of behavior so as to widen their ability to respond in the world. According to Zinker, Gestalt experiments are anchored in the experiential life of the members as they present themselves in the situation. Prefabricated exercises that are imposed on the group without having experiential roots are not within the province of phenomenology and Gestalt therapy, since they do not grow out of a living context for the group.

Key Concepts

Therapeutic Goals

Gestalt therapy has several important aims. One is to challenge clients to move from "environmental support" to "self-support." According to Perls (1969a), the aim of therapy is "to make the patient *not* dependent upon others, but to make the patient discover from the very first moment that he can do many things, *much* more than he thinks he can do" (p. 29).

The basic aim of Gestalt therapy, as mentioned, is the attaining of awareness. Awareness, by and of itself, is seen as curative. Without awareness, clients don't possess the tools for personality change. With awareness, they have the capacity to recognize the impasses and blockages that they create and find within themselves the resources necessary to solve their problems and discover the conditions that will make change possible. It is awareness that allows clients to recognize and reintegrate parts of themselves that they have disowned and, thus, become unified and whole.

The question of therapeutic goals can be considered from the point of view of personal goals for each member and of group-process goals for the group as a whole. Zinker (1980) describes the following individual goals:

- integrating polarities within oneself
- achieving contact with self and others
- learning to provide self-support instead of looking to others for this support

- becoming aware of what one is sensing, feeling, thinking, fantasizing, and doing in the present
- defining one's boundaries with clarity
- translating insights into action
- being willing to learn about oneself by engaging in creative experiments

Goals for the members to achieve on the group level include these:

- learning how to ask clearly and directly for what they want or need
- learning how to deal with one another in the face of conflict
- learning how to give support and energy to one another
- being able to challenge one another to push beyond the boundaries of safety and what is known
- creating a community that is based on trust, which allows for a level of deep and meaningful work
- learning how to make use of the resources within the group rather than relying on the group leader as the director

The Here and Now

One of Perls's most significant contributions is his emphasis on learning to appreciate and experience fully the present: the present is the only significant tense, for the past is gone, and the future has not yet arrived. He notes, however, that for most people the power of the present is lost because, instead of being in the present, they ruminate about the past or engage in endless plans and resolutions for the future. As they direct their energies toward what might have been or to what might be, their capacity to seize the power of the moment diminishes dramatically.

Perls (1973) makes it clear that Gestalt is an *experiential* therapy, not a verbal or interpretive one, and that it is aimed at helping clients make direct contact with their experience in the immediacy of the moment. In the Gestalt view, if we think and talk about an experience, we interrupt the flow of present-centered experiencing and become detached from ourselves.

This focus on the present doesn't indicate a lack of interest in the past. The past *is* important but only insofar as it is related to our present functioning. In Gestalt groups, participants bring past problem situations into the present by reenacting the situation as if it were occurring now. For example, if a group member begins to talk about the difficulty she had when she was younger and attempted to live with her father, the therapist will typically intervene with a request that she "be here now" with her father and speak directly to him. The therapist might say: "Bring your father into this room now, and let yourself go back to the time when you were a child. Tell him now, as though he were here and you were that child, what you most want to say."

It is not uncommon for group members to question a leader about the purpose and value of bringing a past event into the present by reenacting it. The member might well ask: "I feel foolish talking to my father in that empty chair just like the time when I was 10 years old. Why can't I tell the group what I remember about that time?" (In Gestalt terms this is known as "aboutism" instead of direct experiencing.) Although it is probably unwise for the group leader to engage in a lengthy theoretical explanation of the rationale behind present-centered techniques, the leader should surely have a clear understanding of the reasons for this focus. In some brief way the leader can offer a simple explanation for the technique or can invite the member to discuss more fully her feeling foolish in the group and how this feeling might prevent her from engaging in what could be a powerful experiment.

For group leaders, it is useful to know that many problems that members bring up relate to unfinished situations with significant people in their life. In this example the group member may harbor feelings of resentment and mistrust toward men, based on her convictions that men will simply not be there for her in time of need. She may connect this present feeling to old feelings associated with her alcoholic father, who continually let her down and brought much pain into her life. Based on her early decision not to trust men, she may be projecting her negative feelings toward all men now. Concluding that if her own father could not be counted on for love and protection, then surely other men will not be more trustworthy, she now looks for evidence to support her hypothesis. The Gestalt group leader would invite her to in some way deal with her father symbolically in the here and now. She might have a dialogue with him, becoming both her father and herself. She could now say all the things that she wanted to say to her father as a child but, because of her fear, kept deep inside herself. She might tell her father what she most wanted from him then and what she still wants with him now.

Of course, there are many creative possibilities within the group. She could look at the men in the group, expressing to each some of her resentments. In making contact with each man in the group, she could share her fantasies of all the ways in which they would let her down or of what she would like from them now yet is afraid to ask for. The theoretical rationale for this technique is rooted in the assumption that the emotions that were overwhelming to her as a child were dealt with by some form of distortion or denial. The Gestalt leader encourages her to reexperience these past events by reliving them in the here and now so that the emotions that were repressed can come to the surface. With the support of the leader and the group members, she can allow herself to experience feelings that she has sealed off from awareness, and she can now work through some of these feelings that are keeping her stuck. By challenging her assumptions of how men are, she is able to establish a new basis for relating to men.

The technique of making a situation a present one can be applied to future events. If the above group member is afraid of a future confrontation with her father, she'll be asked to live her expectations in the here and now by speaking directly to her father in the group and by expressing her fears and hopes. Thus, she may say to her father: "I want to tell you how much I'd like to be close to you, but I'm afraid that, if I do so, you won't care. I'm afraid of saying the wrong things and pushing you even further away from me."

Perls (1969a) maintains that we tend to cling to our past in order to justify our unwillingness to assume responsibility for the present direction of our life. By staying in the past, we can play endless games of blaming others for the way we are, and we never really face our own capacity to move in a different direction. We get caught up in the process of making resolutions and rationalizing about our lifeless state. We would rather do anything than become conscious of how we are keeping ourselves from being fully alive.

Since Gestalt therapy focuses on the power of the present, most Gestalt techniques are designed to put clients into closer contact with their ongoing experiencing and increase their awareness of what they are feeling from moment to moment. Just as there are advantages to focusing on the here and now, there are disadvantages to this exclusive focus, if the past and the future are discarded. E. Polster (1987a) observes that too tight a focus, with a highly concentrated emphasis only on the here and now, will foreclose on much that matters, such as continuity of commitment, the implications of one's acts, dependability, and responsiveness to others.

Awareness and Responsibility

Awareness is the process of recognizing what we are thinking about and what we are feeling, sensing, and doing. As an ongoing process, awareness can be directed at our feelings, values, wants, or expectations. Awareness should not be confused with introspection or insight; rather, "at its best, awareness is a continuous means for keeping up to date with one's self. . . . It is always there, like an underground stream, ready to be tapped into when needed, a refreshing and revitalizing experience" (Polster & Polster, 1973, pp. 211–212).

The task of the member of a Gestalt group is to pay attention to the structure of his or her experience and to become aware of the *what* and *how* of such experiencing. Whereas the psychoanalytic approach is interested in why we do what we do and not in how we do it, the Gestalt leader asks "what" and "how" questions but rarely "why" questions. Perls (1969a) says that *why* is a dirty word in Gestalt therapy, because it leads to rationalizations and, at best, to clever explanations but never to understanding. By contrast, Perls adds, focusing on what people experience in the immediate situation and on how they experience it does lead to increased awareness of the present. By attending to the continuum of awareness—that is, by staying with the moment-to-moment flow of experiencing—clients discover how they are functioning in the world.

According to Perls's colorful description, the two legs on which Gestalt therapy walks are the *now* and the *how*. The essence of Gestalt theory hinges on these two words: *now* covers all that exists, and it is the basis of awareness; *how* covers behavior and what is involved in an ongoing process. Perls contends that all else is irrelevant. To help clients get focused on the present and experience more intensely their immediate feelings, the Gestalt leader asks questions that lead to present-centeredness:

- "What are you experiencing now?"
- "What is going on inside you as you are speaking?"
- "How are you experiencing your anxiety in your body?"
- "How are you attempting to withdraw at this moment, and how are you avoiding contact with unpleasant feelings?"
- "What is your feeling at this moment—as you sit there and attempt to talk?"
- "What is happening to your voice as you talk to your father now?"

In order to attain present-centered here-and-now awareness of our existence, Gestalt therapy focuses on the obvious—on the surface of behavior—by concentrating on the client's movements, postures, language patterns, voice, gestures, and interactions with others. Since many people fail to see what is obvious (Perls, 1969a), the Gestalt therapist challenges clients to learn how to use their senses fully, to become aware of how they avoid the obvious, and to become open to what is here now. Polster and Polster (1973), too, point to the value of focusing on the surface of behavior and stress the need to provide a climate in which clients can become more clearly focused on their changing awareness from moment to moment.

The core of Gestalt therapy relates to helping members assume responsibility for whatever they are experiencing and doing, rather than placing blame on others for who and what they are now. For Perls, personal responsibility is *not* the same as meeting obligations. In his view, mature individuals do not try to meet the expectations of others and live by obligations to others; rather, they are concerned with living by their own expectations and being true to themselves.

Briefly then, the crux of assuming responsibility is becoming aware of moment-by-moment experiencing and seeing how we are providing meaning to this experience. It means that we avoid manipulating others by fixing on them the blame for whatever we are feeling and doing. Nobody is *making* us feel any way or take any particular course of action. It also means that we do not keep ourselves helpless by expecting others to support us in a variety of ways when we are able to provide this support to ourselves. One way we can promote an increasing sense of personal responsibility is by becoming aware of the ways in which we give away our power by making others responsible for us. Another way is to separate our own expectations from what we think others expect of us and then to make a conscious decision to live by our own expectations.

Unfinished Business and Avoidance

Unfinished business includes unexpressed feelings—such as resentment, hate, rage, pain, hurt, anxiety, guilt, and grief—and events and memories that linger on in the background and clamor for completion. Unless these unfinished situations and unexpressed emotions are recognized and dealt with, they keep interfering with present-centered awareness and with our effective functioning. In writing about the effects of unfinished business, Polster and Polster (1973) say: "These incomplete directions *do seek* completion and when they get powerful enough, the individual is beset with preoccupation, compulsive behavior, wariness, oppressive energy and much self-defeating behavior" (p. 36).

A concept related to unfinished business is avoidance, which refers to the means people use to keep themselves from facing unfinished business and from experiencing the uncomfortable emotions associated with unfinished situations. Perls (1969a) says that most people would rather avoid experiencing painful emotions than do what is necessary to change. Therefore, they become stuck and are unable to get through the impasse, blocking their possibilities of growth.

Because we have a tendency to avoid confronting and fully experiencing our anxiety, grief, guilt, and other uncomfortable emotions, the emotions become a nagging undercurrent that prevents us from being fully alive. Perls speaks of the catastrophic expectations that we conjure up and that keep us psychologically stuck: "If I express my pain fully, people will be embarrassed, and they won't have anything to do with me"; "If I were to express my anger to the significant people in my life, they would abandon me"; "If I ever allowed myself to mourn over my losses, I might sink so deep into depression that I'd never get out of that hole."

Perls maintains that these fantasies keep us from living, because we use them to avoid taking the necessary risks that growth demands. Thus, the Gestalt therapist encourages expressing in the now of the therapeutic session intense feelings never directly expressed before. If a client says to the group that she is afraid of getting in touch with her feelings of hatred and spite, she may be encouraged by the therapist to become her hateful and spiteful side and express these negative feelings to each group member. By experiencing the side of herself that she works so hard at disowning, this participant begins a process of integration and allows herself to get beyond the impasse that keeps her from growing.

During a group session, a member says that he feels empty and powerless. The therapist is likely to encourage him to stay with these uncomfortable feelings, even to exaggerate them—to "be empty," to "be powerless." The theory is that if this person can endure and truly experience the depth of his feelings, he will probably discover that whatever catastrophic expectations he has with regard to those feelings are more of a fantasy than a reality and that his helplessness and void will not destroy him. Experiencing dreaded emotions leads to integration and growth. By going beyond our avoidances, we make it possible to dispose of unfinished business that interferes with our present life, and we move toward health and integration.

Layers of Neurosis and Modes of Defense

Perls (1970) has likened the unfolding of adult personality to the peeling of an onion. In order for individuals to achieve psychological maturity, they must strip off five layers of neurosis. These superimposed growth disorders are (1) the phony, (2) the phobic, (3) the impasse, (4) the implosive, and (5) the explosive. The first layer we encounter, the *phony layer,* consists of reacting to others in stereotypical and inauthentic ways. This is the level where we play games and get lost in roles. By behaving *as if* we are a person that we are not, we are trying to live up to a fantasy that we or others have created. Once we become aware of the phoniness of game playing and become more honest, we experience unpleasantness and pain.

The next layer we encounter is the *phobic layer.* At this level we attempt to avoid the emotional pain that is associated with seeing aspects of ourselves that we would prefer to deny. At this point our resistances to accepting ourselves the way we actually are pop up. We have catastrophic fears that if we recognize who we really are and present that side of ourselves to others, they will surely reject us.

Beneath the phobic layer is the *impasse,* or the point where we are stuck in our own maturation. This is the point at which we are sure that we will not be able to survive, for we convince ourselves that we do not have the resources within ourselves to move beyond the stuck point without environmental support. Typically, this is the time when we attempt to manipulate the environment to do our seeing, hearing, feeling, thinking, and deciding for us. At the impasse we often feel a sense of deadness and feel that we are nothing. If we hope to feel alive, it is essential that we get through the impasse.

If we allow ourselves to fully experience our deadness, rather than denying it or running away, then the *implosive level* comes into being. Perls (1970) says that it is necessary to go through this implosive layer in order to get to the authentic self. By getting into contact with this layer, or our deadness and inauthentic ways, we expose our defenses and begin to make contact with our genuine self.

Perls contends that peeling back the implosive layer creates an explosive state. When we contact the *explosive layer,* we let go of phony roles and pretenses, and we release a tremendous amount of energy that we have been holding in by pretending to be who we are not. To become alive and authentic, it is necessary to achieve this release, which can be an explosion into pain and into joy, anger, sadness, or sexuality.

A concept related to these layers of personality is that of resistance and ego-defense mechanisms. From a Gestalt perspective resistance refers to defenses we develop that prevent us from experiencing the present in a full and real way. The five layers of neurosis represent a person's style of keeping energy pent up in the service of maintaining pretenses. There are also ego-defense mechanisms that prevent people from being authentic. Five major channels of resistance that are challenged in Gestalt therapy are introjection, projection, retroflection, confluence, and deflection.

Introjection involves the tendency to uncritically accept others' beliefs and standards without assimilating them and making them congruent with who we are. These introjects become alien to us, because we have not analyzed and restructured them. When we introject, we passively incorporate what the environment provides, spending little time on getting clear what we want or need. During the early stages of a group introjection is common, for the members tend to look to the leader to provide structure and direction. At this phase of a group's development members typically do not question the leader's interventions or rules. As the group reaches a working stage, members are less inclined to swallow whole the suggestions of the group leader.

Projection is the reverse of introjection. In projection we disown certain aspects of ourselves by ascribing them to the environment. When we are projecting, we have trouble distinguishing between the inside world and the outside world. Those attributes of our personality that are inconsistent with our self-image are disowned and put onto other people. By seeing in others the very qualities that we refuse to acknowledge in ourselves, we avoid taking responsibility for our own feelings and the person who we are. Of course, projection is the basis of transference. As transference feelings surface early in a group, these dynamics can be fruitfully explored. As members attempt to get a sense of both the leader and other members, they often attribute characteristics to these individuals that really belong to significant others in their lives. During the transition stage, when issues such as the struggle for control and power become central, projection continues to be a primary contacting style. Now participants may disown their own needs to control the group. The conflicts that occur at this phase are difficult to resolve unless those members who are projecting their need to control recognize and own their projections (Frew, 1986).

Retroflection consists of turning back to ourselves what we would like to do to someone else. For example, if we lash out and injure ourselves, we are often directing aggression inward that we are fearful of directing toward others. Typically, these maladaptive styles of functioning are done outside of our awareness; part of the process of Gestalt therapy is to help us discover a self-regulatory system so that we can deal realistically with the world. During the initial phase of a group, retroflection is easily observed in the tendency of some members to "hold back" by saying very little and expressing little emotion.

Confluence involves the blurring of awareness of differentiation between the self and the environment. For people who are confluent, there is no clear demarcation between internal experience and outer reality. Confluence in relationships involves an absence of conflicts, or a belief that all parties experience the same feelings and thoughts. It is a style of contact that is characteristic of group members who have a high need to be accepted and liked. Conflicts can be very anxiety-producing for individuals who rely on confluence as a style of contact (Frew, 1986). Confluence makes it difficult for people to have their own thoughts and to speak for themselves. This condition makes genuine contact next to impossible.

Deflection is the interruption of awareness, so that it is difficult to maintain a sustained sense of contact. People who deflect attempt to diffuse contact through the overuse of humor, abstract generalizations, and questions rather than statements (Frew, 1986). Deflection involves a diminished emotional experience. People who deflect speak through and for others.

Introjection, projection, retroflection, confluence, and deflection represent styles of resisting contact. Terms such as *resistance to contact* or *boundary disturbance* are used to characterize people who attempt to control their environment. The premise in Gestalt therapy is that contact is both normal and healthy. Therefore, a discussion of these styles of resistances to contact focuses on the degree to which these processes are in the individual's awareness. Clients in Gestalt therapy are encouraged to become increasingly aware of their dominant style of blocking contact.

Energy and Blocks to Energy

Because members need energy to work in group sessions, Gestalt leaders pay special attention to where energy is located, how it is used, and how it can be blocked. Blocked energy can be thought of as *resistance,* and there are a number of ways in which it can show up in the body. One member will experience tension in his neck and shoulders, and another member will experience shortness of breath. Another person will typically speak with a restricted voice, by holding back power. A few other ways that these blocks to energy will manifest themselves are keeping one's mouth shut tightly (as though one were afraid what might slip out); slouching; looking at the ground or in the air as a way of avoiding contact with others' eyes, keeping one's body tight and closed; talking in a fast and staccato fashion; being emotionally flat; and experiencing body sensations such as a lump in the throat, a quivering of the mouth, a hot and flushed feeling, shaking movements of the hands and legs, or dizziness.

In commenting on the value of focusing on the client's energy in therapeutic work, Zinker (1978) says that clients may not be aware of their energy or where it is located, and they may experience it in a negative way. From his perspective, therapy at its best is "a lively process of stoking the client's inner fires of awareness and contact" (p. 24). This process involves a therapeutic relationship that awakens and nourishes the client in such a way that the therapist does not become sapped of his or her own energy. Zinker maintains that it is the therapist's job to help clients locate the ways in which they are blocking energy and to help them transform this blocked energy into more adaptive behaviors. This process is best accomplished when resistance is not viewed as a client's refusal to cooperate and as something simply to be gotten around. Instead, therapists can learn to welcome resistance and use it as a way of deepening therapeutic work. Members can be encouraged to recognize how their resistance is being expressed in their body, and, rather than trying to rid themselves of certain bodily symptoms, they can actually delve fully into tension states. By allowing themselves to exaggerate their tight mouth and shaking legs, they are able to discover for themselves how they are diverting energy and keeping themselves powerless.

Although talking can be provocative, the most direct access to feeling involves focusing on bodily experience. With body awareness, clients are asked to report bodily sensations that bespeak areas of diminished aliveness or blocks in the flow of that aliveness (Smith, 1985, p. 103). Using body-awareness work is a way of mobilizing clients and bringing them to take an active responsibility for their therapy. Smith writes about the role of the body in psychotherapy, and many of his ideas have applicability to group work. He describes "soft techniques" in working with the body. For example, if a member sits with a closed posture, the leader can invite him or her to uncross and experience the feeling, and then cross again. By inviting clients to move out of a particular posture and experiment with a new posture, leaders can facilitate awareness. Members who slouch and who also complain about low self-esteem can be invited to stand and walk erect. In a like way, members can be asked to exaggerate a particular gesture or posture as a way of learning more about themselves. In short, paying attention to the body and energy blockages within the body can be a productive way to explore the meaning of a member's experience.

Methods of working with the body can be fruitfully combined with other techniques in a Gestalt group. Reichian body-work concepts and techniques are particularly useful in working with energy and blocks to energy. Wilhelm Reich's (1949, 1967, 1969) central idea was that emotions were an expression of the movement of body energy and that chronic tensions blocked this flow of energy and thus blocked emotions. He associated forms of resistance with specific patterns of "muscular armoring." He emphasized the value of loosening and dissolving this muscular armor, along with dealing with psychological issues in an analytic way. Reich demonstrated that relaxing these patterns of muscular armoring could release bottled-up emotions. In his therapy work he paid attention to nonverbal behaviors such as the client's general appearance, facial expressions, tensions in various parts of the body, and gestures. As a way of helping his clients increase their awareness of their body and character traits, he asked them to exaggerate certain habitual behaviors that were thought to be a part of character armor. Reichian body work included emphasis on breathing in a spontaneous and relaxed way. Methods that deepened the client's breathing led to an opening of the feelings. His approach focused on working with muscular tensions, such as a tight jaw, neck, or mouth, frowns, and so forth. Reichian work is based largely on a reading of the body and proceeds in a systematic way, beginning with the eyes and ending with the pelvis. Reich's therapeutic work increasingly dealt with freeing intense emotions such as pleasure, rage, fear, pain, and anxiety through working with the body. He found that after repressed emotion was expressed, chronic muscular and psychological tension could also be released.

It is interesting to note that Perls was a patient and a student of Reich's, and in his writings Perls credits Reich with having had a significant influence on the concepts and techniques of Gestalt therapy. It is good to add the caution that, before group leaders even consider incorporating some of the Reichian body techniques in a Gestalt group, they should have extensive training and supervision in these techniques. Even though Gestalt leaders might not have had such training, however, they can still make use of some of these concepts by learning how to pay attention to the energy flow and blockage as evidenced by looking at the bodies of the group members. Also, members can be taught how to pay attention to what they are experiencing within their own body, so that they can learn from the messages that their body is sending them.

Role and Functions of the Group Leader

Perhaps the best way to describe the functions of the Gestalt therapist or group leader is to review how Gestalt therapy proceeds. (Note that the following discussion applies to group as well as individual therapy.) According to Perls (1969a), the goal of therapy is the client's maturation and the removal of "blocks that prevent a person from standing on his own feet." In order to achieve this goal, the therapist helps the client make the transition from external to internal support by locating the *impasse*. Perls described the impasse as the place where people get stuck—the point at which they avoid experiencing threatening feelings and attempt to manipulate others by playing the game of being helpless, lost, confused, and stupid. These games permit clients to remain stuck and thus avoid doing what they need to do in order to resolve pressing unfinished business.

One of the therapist's functions is to challenge clients to get through the impasse so that growth is possible. It is a difficult function indeed, because at the point of impasse clients think that they have no chance of survival; they simply don't believe that they can find inside themselves the means for going on. So they give up their own eyes and ears and desperately try to manipulate others into doing their seeing and hearing for them. If therapists are not careful, they can easily get caught up in the manipulations of their clients. If they try to be "helpful," they may foster dependency and helplessness and reinforce the belief of clients that they don't have the ability to cope with life. Then clients can give in to their catastrophic expectations and avoid challenging the fears that are keeping them stuck.

The therapist must confront clients so that they will face what they are doing and decide whether they will develop their potential. This confrontation consists of challenging clients to fully experience whatever blockages and barriers are within them and to make contact with the frustration resulting from the feeling of being stuck.

Although Gestalt leaders encourage members to assume responsibility for raising their own level of consciousness, they can nevertheless take an active role in creating experiments to help the members tap their resources. Zinker (1978) writes that the therapist, functioning much like an artist, invents experiments with clients to augment their range of behaviors. He adds that the group leader is not always the person who invents the experiments. Rather, the leader's function is to create an atmosphere and structure in which the group's own creativity and inventiveness can emerge. For example, a theme of loneliness may come up in a group. Here a central task of the leader is to orchestrate this theme by connecting members with one another and finding ways to involve the group as a whole in exploring loneliness.

Gestalt therapists employ a wide range of techniques to help clients gain awareness and experience their conflicts fully. It should be made clear, however, that, although the skillful and appropriate use of techniques is an important function of the therapist, Gestalt therapy is much more than a collection of techniques. Techniques cannot be separated from the personality of the therapist who uses them, and overuse of techniques may keep the therapist hidden and lead to "phony therapy that *prevents* growth" (Perls, 1969a, p. 1).

Polster and Polster (1973) see the therapist as nothing less than an artist involved in creating new life. Yet in Gestalt, as in most other approaches, the danger exists that the therapist will lose sight of the true meaning of the therapeutic process and become a mere technician. Therapists should use their own experience as an essential ingredient in the therapy process and never forget that they are far more than mere responders, givers of feedback, or catalysts who don't change themselves (Polster & Polster, 1973). Since the client/therapist relationship is the core of the therapeutic process, the use of techniques should never be allowed to interfere with the authenticity of the relationship. Techniques need to be individually tailored to each client, and they need to be the outgrowth of the therapeutic encounter—an encounter grounded in the mutual experiencing of client and therapist.

M. Polster (1987) describes the nature and purpose of experiments in this way: "Experiment is a Gestalt technique aimed at restoring momentum to the stuck points of a person's life. It is one way to recover the connection between deliberation and spontaneity by bringing the possibilities for action right into the therapy room" (p. 318). Through these experiments clients are able to confront the crises of their lives by playing out their troubled relationships in the safety of the therapeutic setting. Polster mentions some of the forms that Gestalt experiments might take: dramatizing a painful memory, imagining a dreaded encounter, playing one's parent, creating a dialogue between two parts within oneself, attending to an overlooked gesture, and exaggerating a certain posture. One of the therapist's functions is to observe whether the experiment appears too safe or too risky.

Therapists have latitude to invent their own techniques (or experiments), which are basically an extension of their personality. Thus, therapists must be grounded and in tune with themselves, as well as being present for their clients. If clients are to become authentic, they need contact with an authentic therapist on a genuine I/Thou basis. Shepherd (1970) emphasizes that the therapist's capacity for I/Thou, here-and-now relationships is a basic requisite for effectively using Gestalt techniques. According to Shepherd, these techniques are developed through therapeutic experiences gained at professional training workshops and through work with competent therapists and supervisors.

For Zinker (1978), creative therapists possess a rich personal background, having opened themselves to a range of life experiences and become able to celebrate life fully. In short, they are able to use themselves as a person as they function as a therapist. In addition to being mature and integrated people, creative therapists also possess certain capacities, abilities, and technical skills. Out of their experimental attitude, they use themselves, other group members, and objects and events in the group environment in the service of inventing novel visions of the members. Some of the specific skills that Zinker mentions as being related to the functioning of creative therapists are the following:

- the capacity to identify energy within the members and to move with this energy
- a sensitivity to introducing experiments in a timely and appropriate fashion
- the ability to be flexible by letting go of some things and moving to other areas that are more lively
- the willingness to push and confront members so that they will get their work done, along with the ability to know when to back off
- the ability to help members express their feelings and summarize what they are learning after they complete an experiment
- the wisdom to know when to let members stay confused so that they can learn to find clarity in their own way

From this discussion of the role and functions of the Gestalt group leader, it should be apparent that skilled leadership entails a great deal more than merely grabbing one technique after another from a Gestalt bag. Who the leader is as a person and how he or she functions in the group, creatively drawing on technical expertise, are the critical factors that determine the potency of leadership.

Applications and Techniques

As was mentioned earlier, Gestalt therapy employs a rich variety of action-oriented techniques designed to intensify what group members are experiencing in the present moment. Gestalt therapy encourages "becoming a conflict" or "being what we are feeling," as opposed to merely talking about conflicts, problems, and feelings. It cannot be overemphasized that these techniques need to be tailored to the individuals within the group and to the unique context of a particular group interaction. Applied mechanically or inappropriately, the techniques become mere gimmicks that can result in increased defensiveness by the members and in even less authentic living on their part. Simkin (1982) discourages the use of stereotyped exercises of any kind and prefers to reinforce natural, creative expressions in his Gestalt groups. However, he acknowledges that some Gestalt therapists use structured exercises. For example, at the beginning of a session, leaders may ask for a go-around in which each participant makes a brief here-and-now statement of what he or she is aware of. Members may be asked to declare if they have any personal issues they are willing to explore or what they want from the session. In this way session time can be maximized by focusing on common themes.

It is useful to differentiate between a group *exercise* and a group *experiment*. With group exercises, leaders prepare some kind of structured technique before the group meets. Members might be asked to pair up and talk, or a catalyst might be introduced into the group to provide a specific focus for work during a session. In contrast, a group *experiment* is a creative happening that grows out of the group experience; as such it cannot be predetermined, and its outcome cannot be predicted (Zinker, 1978). Therefore, it is essential to keep in mind that the techniques described in this chapter are not arbitrarily imposed on a group to *make* something happen. Rather than being used as catalysts for stirring up action in a group, these techniques are best conceived of as experiments that grow out of the ongoing interplay among the members.

To increase the chances that members will benefit from Gestalt techniques, group leaders need to communicate the general purpose of these techniques and to create an experimental climate. "Let's try something on for size and see how it fits" conveys this experimental attitude on the part of the leader. The message also says that the leader is not trying to prove a point and that the members are free to try something new and determine for themselves whether it's going to work. In discussing the need for a brief explanation of the purpose of the technique, Passons (1975) observes that clients may be puzzled by certain Gestalt exercises—for example, by being asked to talk to an empty chair, or to "be their sadness," or to become aware of what they are "saying" with their bodies—and that a brief explanation can dispel this perplexity and lead to greater willingness to experiment. Occasional explanations also foster trust in the leader by making clear that the exercise has a therapeutic purpose and is not an attempt to "trick" someone.

Zinker (1978) views the experiment as a way of modifying a member's behavior in the group context. He asserts, as we have seen, that Gestalt therapy is a combination of phenomenology and behavior modification. He sees therapeutic work as rooted in the subjective perspective of the members; at the same time, experiments are introduced in such a manner that behavior is modified in a timely way. As the cornerstone of experiential learning, the experiment transforms talking about a situation into actual doing and rejects stale theorizing in favor of trying novel behaviors with a sense of excitement and imagination. Zinker emphasizes that each aspect of an experiment is presented at a point of developmental readiness for the client. In this sense experiments can be considered graded activities aimed at specific modifications of behavior.

It is clear that the emphasis is on *inviting* (not commanding) members to examine their behaviors, attitudes, and thoughts. Leaders can encourage members to look at certain incongruities, especially gaps between their verbal and nonverbal expression. Thus, the Gestalt group is characterized by challenge and positive confrontation. This confrontation is aimed at helping the members pay attention to what they are doing and experiencing in the here and now, not in a harsh or critical insistence that they be different than they are. Also, confrontation does not necessarily have to be aimed at weaknesses or negative traits; members can be challenged to recognize the ways in which they are blocking their strengths and ways in which they are not living as fully as they might. In this sense confrontation can be a genuine expression of caring that results in positive changes in a member, not a brutal assault on a defenseless member. Of course, it cannot be overstressed that members must be prepared for taking part in experiments. They need to know that they can choose to go along and that they can also decide to stop when they want. Rather than pushing them into experimenting, the spirit is always one of inviting them to discover something new about themselves.

Keep in mind these introductory comments as you read the following pages, which describe several Gestalt techniques, their rationales, and their applications to group situations. As with all other techniques, here, too, it is up to the individual practitioner to integrate the exercises into his or her own therapeutic style, so that they become expressions of the personality of the leader. My discussion is based on a variety of sources—among them, Levitsky and Perls (1970), Passons (1975), Perls (1969a), Perls, Hefferline, and Goodman (1951), Polster and Polster (1973), Stevens (1971), and Zinker (1978). Note that I have modified some of the techniques to fit the needs of the group situation.

Language Exercises

Gestalt emphasizes the relationship between language patterns and personality. It suggests that our speech patterns are often expressions of our feelings, thoughts, and attitudes and that by focusing on our overt speaking habits, we can increase our self-awareness (Passons, 1975). Words can bring us to ourselves, or they can take us away from ourselves. The following Gestalt interventions, by making us more aware of some of our speech patterns, can enhance our self-awareness and bring us closer to ourselves.

It should be noted that the following language exercises require a great deal of skill on the part of the leader. Unless the members, through the leader's help, are able to see the value of paying attention to the impact of their language style, they will come to feel that everything they say and do is subject to unnecessary scrutiny.

It. "It" talk is a way of depersonalizing language. By using *it* instead of *I*, we keep distant from our experience. When group members say "It's frightening to come to this group," they can be asked to change the sentence to "I'm frightened to come to this group." Substituting personal pronouns for impersonal ones is a way of assuming responsibility for what we say.

You. Often group participants say something like "You feel hurt when someone rejects you." By using "you" talk, people detach themselves from whatever they may be feeling. Therefore, members are asked to pay attention to the differences between the above statement and "I feel hurt when someone rebuffs me." By changing a "you" statement to an "I" statement, we reveal ourselves, and *we* take responsibility for what we are saying. Beginning a sentence with the word *you* tends to put others on the defensive and makes us disown our own experience.

Questions.   In a Gestalt group, members are discouraged from asking questions. Questions direct attention to other people and can easily put others on the defensive. Also, questions often demand that those being questioned reveal themselves while those who ask them are keeping themselves safe behind their interrogation. Group members who tend to ask too many questions are asked to experiment with any of the following:

- Instead of asking a question, make a direct statement to the person, and share your own motivation for your question.
- Avoid "why" questions, because they lead to a chain of "why/because" exchanges. Try instead "how" and "what" questions.
- Practice making "I" statements. By doing so, you take responsibility for your position, your opinions, and your preferences.

Qualifiers and Disclaimers.   By paying attention to the qualifiers they attach to their statements, group members can increase their awareness of how they diminish the power of their messages. A common example is the use of *but:* "I like you, but your mannerisms drive me up the wall"; "I often feel depressed, but I don't know what to do to change the situation"; "I think that this group is helping me, but people outside are so different from those in here." In each of these cases the word *but* essentially discounts the statement that precedes it. Without making group members excessively self-conscious, the leader can encourage them to pay attention to the impact of the use of qualifiers and disclaimers. Also, participants can be asked to substitute the word *and* for the word *but* and experiment with omitting qualifiers such as *maybe, sort of, possibly, I guess,* and *I suppose,* thus changing ambivalent messages into clear and direct statements.

"Can't" Statements.   Group members often say "I can't" when they really mean "I won't." Sally says "I simply can't talk to my father and tell him what I feel; he'd never understand me." It would be more precise and more honest for Sally to say that she *won't* make the attempt to talk with her father. Essentially, Sally is unwilling to (won't) take the risk or sees it as not being worth the effort. If a group leader consistently and gently insists that members substitute *won't* for *can't,* he or she is helping them own and accept their power by taking responsibility for their decisions.

"Shoulds" and "Oughts."   Some group members seem to be ruled by "shoulds" and "oughts": "I should be interested in what others say in this group"; "I ought to care for everyone, and if I don't, I feel terrible"; "I should express only positive feelings"; and so on. The list of "shouldisms," both in daily life and in a group situation, is endless. Members can at least become aware of the frequency of their "should" and "ought" remarks and of the feelings of powerlessness that accompany their use.

One way of increasing one's awareness of the limitations imposed by a "should" standard is to experiment with changing phrases such as "I have to" or "I should" to "I choose to." For example, if Fred says "I hate to stay in school, but I *have to* because my parents expect this of me," he could say instead "I don't like school, and I *choose to* stay in school because I don't want to have a hassle with my parents."

Nonverbal Language

Perls maintains that when we block an aspect of our personality, the denied side finds ways of expressing itself—for example, in our movements, gestures, posture, and voice. Therefore, skilled therapists listen not just to the verbal level of communication but also, and even more keenly, to the message behind the words, which is often conveyed in the voice tone, pitch, and volume, in the speed of delivery, and so forth.

The group setting offers many opportunities to explore the meaning of nonverbal messages. Such explorations are especially useful when participants exhibit nonverbal cues that are incongruent with what they are saying verbally. For example, Frank tells the group leader that he is angry at him for passing him over, but as he utters his angry words, he is smiling. The leader is likely to call to Frank's attention the discrepancy between his angry words and his smile. Frank may then be asked to carry on a dialogue between his words and his smile, or he may be asked to "become his smile" and give this smile a voice: "What is your smile saying?" This procedure gives Frank the opportunity to discover for himself the meaning of the discrepancy. In fact he may be saying "I want to let you know that I'm upset that you passed me by, yet I don't want to risk your disapproval by letting you know how angry I am."

The following are other examples of how the exploration of nonverbal expressions can increase members' awareness of what they are really experiencing in the moment.

• Dan typically carries himself in a slouched posture. The leader says: "Become aware of your posture, go around the group, and tell what your posture says about yourself to each member of the group. Complete the sentence 'I am my posture, and what I am telling you about me is . . .'"
• Marilyn tends to speak in a soft voice and with a very tight mouth. The leader invites her to give a speech to the group and consciously exaggerate these mannerisms. She could "become her tight mouth" and say something like "I'm holding my words and myself back from you. I'm not going to be open, and, if you want something from me, you'll have to pry me open."

• John comes across as though he were always delivering a lecture to an audience. Group members have told him that his voice and his style of speaking create a barrier between him and the others. He could be asked to stand before the group and give a lecture, perhaps on the value of lecturing people.

Examples of how one deals with nonverbal cues are endless. Creative group leaders can invent a wide variety of spontaneous techniques designed to help participants become increasingly aware of what they are communicating through their eye contact, mannerisms, subtle gestures, tone of voice, and hand movements, as well as through their whole bodies. Group leaders would do well to avoid making bold interpretations—for example, that keeping one's arms crossed means that one is closed—and instead encourage members to merely pay attention to the nonverbal cues they emit.

Techniques Related to Assuming Responsibility

The Gestalt approach emphasizes taking full responsibility for ourselves— that is, being aware of our thoughts, feelings, and actions and avoiding making others responsible for what we are experiencing. Assuming responsibility also means recognizing our projections, reidentifying with them, and becoming what we project (Perls, 1969a).

Group members frequently dodge responsibility for their feelings by assigning the blame to others. Thus, they will say that the *group* is boring them or that someone in the group is *making* them angry. A Gestalt exercise designed to help individuals recognize and own their feelings instead of projecting them onto others is known as "I take responsibility for . . ." Pauline says she feels that the group is excluding her and making her feel like an outsider. The leader can suggest to her that she make direct statements to several members such as "I feel left out of the group, and I take responsibility for feeling excluded" or "I feel like an outsider, and I take responsibility for this feeling."

Unwillingness to assume responsibility is a common problem, both in groups and in life. As long as, when we are scared, angry, critical, or confused, we say "You are making me feel this way," we are delegating control to others and refusing to take charge of our own lives. The Gestalt leader keeps confronting participants with their unwillingness to take responsibility, so that they can come to recognize and accept their feelings instead of projecting them onto others.

Experiments with Dialogues

Because a goal of Gestalt therapy is to achieve integrated functioning and the acceptance of aspects of one's personality that have been disowned and denied, therapists pay close attention to splits and polarities in personality function. Fantasy dialogues are meant to promote awareness of internal splits and eventual personality integration. These dialogues can take many forms—for example, dialogues between opposing sides or polarities within oneself (like tender/tough, masculine/feminine, loving/hateful, aggressive/passive) and dialogues with a parent or other significant person, fantasized others, or inanimate objects.

Understanding how polarities are related to inner conflicts is central to Gestalt therapy. A variety of experiments with dialogues can help members increase their awareness of the dichotomies within themselves and help them come to terms with dimensions of their personality that seem to oppose each other. Our self-concept often excludes painful awareness of the polarities within us. We would rather think of ourselves as bright than as dull, as kind than as cruel, as loving than as unloving, and as sensitive than as indifferent. Typically, we may resist "seeing" in ourselves those parts that we don't want to accept as being part of who we are. Although we can recognize the altruistic side of ourselves, we might have trouble coming to terms with our self-centered nature. Ideally, as we move closer to becoming psychologically mature and healthy, we are aware of most of the polarities within ourselves, including those thoughts and feelings that society does not sanction. As we become more tolerant of the complexities and seeming contradictions within us, there is less of a tendency to expend energy on fighting to disown those parts of our nature that we don't want to accept.

Dialogue experiments are a powerful method of contacting parts of our nature that we work hard at keeping secret from both ourselves and others. Learning how to carry on a conversation between our feminine and masculine sides, for instance, is one way of bringing to the surface inner conflicts we might have with these polarities. Alternatively, becoming each side as fully as we can is a way to *experience* both of these facets of our personality.

Dialogue experiments are typically used to heighten awareness of introjections and projections. *Introjection,* as was mentioned earlier, is the process by which we uncritically take in aspects of other people, especially parents, and incorporate them into our personality. The danger of uncritical and wholesale acceptance of another's values as our own is that it can prevent personality integration. Gestalt techniques are aimed at getting these introjections out in the open, so that we can take a good look at what we have been swallowing whole without digesting it.

For example, by experimenting with dialogues, Hal becomes aware of some of the messages that he has bought without question: one must be practical; one ought to cling to security and never launch on a new path unless one has carefully assessed all the odds; only irresponsible people seek fun for the sake of fun—in other words, a long list of "dos," "don'ts," "shoulds," and "shouldn'ts" that keep him from enjoying life. At last, Hal begins to realize that he has listened to these directives from others and given others the power to direct his life. He also becomes aware that he wants to reclaim this power for himself. Some of the fantasy dialogues that help him see his introjections more clearly are dialogues with the different facets of himself.

The dialogues can be carried out with the empty-chair technique or with the two-chair technique. Sitting on one chair, Hal becomes one of his introjects—say, the side of him that doesn't have any fun. Speaking in the present tense, Hal "becomes the serious side" and says: "You can't let yourself go; you may go off the deep end and never accomplish anything. Be serious; be practical; get rid of foolish notions." Then Hal switches chairs and "becomes the fun side." He says to the serious side: "You are dull and demanding. If I listen to you, I'll never feel like I've done enough to earn the right to play. Let me show you how to loosen up and have fun." The dialogue proceeds back and forth, all for the purpose of giving Hal an increased awareness of which side is dominant and of how it feels to be in either role. The goal is not to get rid of either side but to integrate the polarities. If he reaches this goal, Hal will recognize that he can be *both* serious and light and that *he* is the one who can make this happen through awareness.

Projection is the attribution of one's ideas, feelings, or attitudes to others—especially those very ideas, feelings, or attitudes one does not want to see and accept in oneself. In working with projections, participants are asked to identify with and become a particular characteristic that they attribute to others. For example, if Cindy says that she cannot trust the group—she feels that, if she opened up, no one would care or even know what she was talking about—she is asked to play the role of the untrustworthy person. By becoming the other, she may be able to discover the degree to which the distrust is due to an inner conflict between the side that wants to trust and the side that cannot trust. In what is known as "playing the projection," Cindy is asked to go to other members in the group and play the role of the untrustworthy person by completing the sentence "You don't trust me because, if you do, I'll . . ." The exercise may enable her to experience the inner conflict more intensely and see more clearly the two sides of herself.

Making the Rounds

In this exercise a person goes around to each of the group members and says something that he or she usually does not communicate verbally. For example, assume that Larry sees himself as a self-made man who needs nothing from others. Although he may not *say* this about himself, the theme of "I can do it by myself" runs through much of his life. For the purpose of seeing how this theme actually determines what he does, he could be asked to stand before each member in the group and tell that person something about himself, and then add ". . . and [or but] I can do everything by myself." Thus, Larry goes to Sue and says "I never ask for emotional support from others, and at times I feel lonely . . . but I can do everything by myself." He then goes to Marie and says "I make all the decisions in my business . . . and I can do everything by myself." The aim of this experiment is to have him feel fully what it's like for him to do everything by himself. Ultimately, he may decide to continue to do things for himself, but with the awareness of the price he pays for doing so. Or he may come to see that he doesn't have to be totally self-reliant and that he can be independent while letting others do things for him from time to time.

The following are a few more examples of the use of making the rounds:

- Paul says that he is afraid of women. He could make the rounds and say to each woman "I'm afraid of you because . . ."; or "If I were to get close to you, . . ."
- Susan worries about boring people in the group. She might be asked to make the rounds and, for each person, complete the sentence "One way I could bore you is by . . ." or "You would be bored if I . . ."
- Pam says that she feels distant from the rest of the group, even though she would like to have a sense of identification. Pam could make the rounds and experiment with completing the sentence "One way I feel distant from you is . . ." or "The way we are different from each other is . . ."

Fantasy Approaches

Experimenting with a diversity of fantasy situations in a group can lead to significant growth. Fantasy can promote personal awareness in a number of ways, as the following brief list suggests.

• Fantasy can be used when members are too threatened to deal with a problem in concrete terms. For example, members who are afraid to be assertive can imagine themselves in situations in which they *are* assertive. Thus, they can compare what they feel when they are passive with what they feel when they are able to ask for what they want.

• Fantasy approaches are useful in dealing with catastrophic expectations, which often result in a sense of paralysis. Members who are afraid to express what they think and feel to someone they love can be guided through a fantasy situation in which they say everything they want to say but are afraid to express. Essentially the person speaks in the here and now to the loved one (as if he or she were present) in front of the group. The leader may say: "Your mother (or some other significant person) is in this empty chair. Come up to the chair and say what you *most* want her to hear and that you never told her. What are you feeling now? Are you willing to tell how you feel? Tell her now all the terrible things you imagined would happen if you told her what you kept from her." There is a possible psychological value in working through these feelings in the safety of the fantasy approach, because the person may be able to release submerged feelings that have become split off. Note that it is *not* necessary that the person express these feelings in real life; as a matter of fact, to do so could be unwise.

• Fantasy can be used to express and explore feelings of shame and guilt. In the technique known as "I have a secret," the leader asks members to fantasize about a well-guarded secret. They are not asked to reveal the secret in the group but only to imagine themselves disclosing the secret to the others. The leader may ask "What are people thinking about you?" "How do you feel about letting others know your secret?"

• Fantasy is a useful and safe way to explore the members' fears about getting involved in the group. For example, members can be asked to imagine the thing they most fear occurring in the group. If, for example, some members are afraid of being rejected by the group, they can be directed to imagine that everyone is systematically rejecting them and then work with the feelings associated with this fantasy.

There are constructive uses of fantasy that, after having been tried in the group, can be carried outside of it. At times members can be invited to picture themselves as they wish they were in interpersonal situations. They might share their fantasies aloud in the group as they experience themselves in powerful, alive, creative, and dynamic ways. Then they can be asked to try acting in the group *as if* they were the person they imagined themselves to be. If the experiment is successful, members may feel encouraged enough to try the new behavior in real-life situations.

Rehearsal

For Perls much of our thinking is rehearsing. We rehearse for roles we think we are expected to play, and we worry that we may not say the "right" thing and perform "properly." Internal rehearsing consumes much energy and frequently inhibits spontaneity. The rehearsal technique invites members to say *out loud* what they are thinking silently. Rehearsal experiments are especially useful when it is obvious that members are doing a lot of blocking and censoring and when what they say seems carefully measured out for a certain effect. For example, during the initial stages of one of my groups, Joan was quite silent and appeared to be developing an observer's stance. When I asked her if she was indeed saying everything she wanted to say, she shook her head in denial. So I asked her to express aloud some of the random thoughts she had as she was sitting there in silence.

Rehearsal can also be fruitful when a member is anticipating some future confrontation. Assume that Sam wants to tell his boss that he doesn't feel appreciated and that he wants to be recognized for his accomplishments. Sam can, in fantasy, picture himself standing before his boss, ready to tell him what he wants to say. Sam's out-loud rehearsal could go something like: "I'm standing here like a fool. What if I mess up? He won't listen to me, and I don't really have anything to say. How can I let him know what I'm thinking? Right now I feel like running away and apologizing."

In a Gestalt group the participants share their rehearsals with one another in order to become more aware of the many preparations they go through in performing their social roles. By doing so, they become more aware of how they strive to please others, of the degree to which they want to be accepted and approved, and of the extent of their efforts to avoid alienating others. And then they can decide whether this role playing is worth the effort.

Reversal Techniques

Certain symptoms and behaviors often represent reversals of underlying or latent impulses. The reversal technique asks participants to become a side of themselves that they rarely or never express, because they don't want to see it and accept it. The theory underlying the use of this technique is that integration is possible when people allow themselves to plunge into the very thing that produces anxiety and make contact with those parts of themselves that have been submerged and denied. Groups provide plenty of timely opportunities for using reversal techniques.

I remember the case of a young man who was excessively nice, overly polite, and constantly trying to "do things" for other people. I suggested that he experiment with asking other people in the group to do something for him. He had great difficulty carrying out my suggestion, but eventually he succeeded. The exercise made him aware of how uncomfortable he was with accepting something from others. Also, it gave him an increased awareness of the denied side of himself and a chance to integrate it.

Other examples of the reversal method are asking someone who says almost nothing to take on the role of monopolizer and deliberately interrupt the group; inviting someone with inferiority feelings to play the role of being superior; and suggesting to someone who pays compliments to everybody to say something negative to each person in the group. Time and time again, I've found that this and similar techniques truly help people become aware of and reconcile polarities within themselves.

Just as the empty-chair experiment gives members an opportunity to take ownership of opposing forces within themselves, so does experimenting with giving expression to a dimension that is kept hidden often result in a creative integration of polarities. For example, the member who habitually presents a tough exterior may well be afraid of contacting a sensitive side of himself. If he is invited to experiment with being the side that he works so hard at denying, he is likely to find joy in broadening his emotional and behavioral range, and if he does not like the results of the experiment, he can always go back to the "tough-guy" role.

The Exaggeration Exercise

This experiment involves becoming more aware of the subtle signals and cues we send through body language. Movements, postures, and gestures are exaggerated, so that the meanings they communicate become clearer. By exaggerating the movement or gesture repeatedly, the person experiences more intensely the feelings associated with the behavior and becomes more aware of its inner meaning.

For example, if the leader notices that Sandy consistently nods her head in an approving way when people speak, he or she could ask Sandy to go before each group member and really give in to her head nodding while, at the same time, putting words into this action. Other examples of behavior that lends itself to the exaggeration technique are habitually smiling while expressing painful or negative emotions, trembling, clenching one's fists, tapping one's foot, crossing one's arms tightly, and pointing a finger at someone.

A member I'll call Jill said "I feel burdened by listening to everyone's problems in here!" At an earlier session she was confronted by Fred for intervening so quickly and trying to make him feel better when he was working on conflicts he was having with his family. She then revealed that during her childhood years she typically assumed the role of family arbitrator, always doing her best to smooth over the battles in her family. Jill eventually says that she is sick and tired of carrying everyone's burdens, for it weighs her down and gives her a heavy feeling.

A technique for working with the material that Jill is providing involves asking her to pick up some heavy objects and hold them as she looks at each person in the group. She can be invited to allow herself to get into the experience of the heaviness and being burdened. For example, while holding the heavy objects she might make the rounds and complete the sentence "Looking at you I am burdened by . . ." Or she might say something to each member like "Here, let me take on all your burdens; I really enjoy carrying everyone's problems and I just wouldn't know what to do if I didn't have all these burdens weighing me down!" Even though she says that she is sick and tired of carrying around everyone's burdens, we encourage her to allow herself to give in to the part of herself that feels burdened and experiment with telling others all the benefits of being this way. The rationale here is that, if she can fully experience being burdened, there is a good chance that she can allow herself to experience shedding these burdens and being light, at least for a few moments. Again, this experiment is related to the reversal experiment and the empty-chair experiment in that the member is asked to play with polarities. Often the best way to discover the aspect of ourselves that we say we'd like to experience more of is to allow ourselves to stay with that part of us that we want to avoid.

Dream Work

Consistent with its noninterpretive spirit, the Gestalt approach does not interpret and analyze dreams. Instead, the intent is to bring the dream back to life, to re-create it, and to relive it as if it were happening now. For those readers who are interested in a detailed presentation of the Gestalt approach to dream work, good sources are Downing and Marmorstein (1973), Perls (1969a), Rainwater (1979), and Zinker (1978). A brief description of this approach follows.

Group members don't report their dreams in the past tense: they relive them and act them out in the present, transform key elements of the dream into a dialogue, and become a part of the dream. Perls assumes that each part of a dream is a projection of oneself and that all the different parts are expressions of one's own contradictory and inconsistent sides. Therefore dreams contain existential messages. They represent our conflicts, our wishes, and key themes in our lives. By making a list of all the details in a dream—remembering each person, event, and mood—and then acting out ("becoming") each of these parts as fully as possible, one becomes increasingly aware of one's opposing sides and of the range of one's feelings. Eventually the person comes to appreciate and accept his or her inner differences and integrate the conflicting forces, with each piece of work on a dream leading to further assimilation and integration. By avoiding analyzing and interpreting the dream and focusing instead on becoming and experiencing it in all its aspects, the client gets closer to the existential message of the dream. Freud calls the dream "the royal road to the unconscious"; Perls (1969a) calls it "the royal road to integration" (p. 66).

Rainwater (1979) offers some helpful suggestions to dreamers for exploring their dreams:

- Be the landscape or the environment.
- Become all the people in the dream. Are any of them significant people?
- Be any objects that link and join, such as telephone lines and highways.
- Identify with any mysterious object, such as an unopened letter or an unread book.
- Assume the identity of any powerful force, such as a tidal wave.
- Become any two contrasting objects, such as a younger person and an older person.
- Be anything that is missing in the dream. If you don't remember your dreams, then speak to your missing dreams.
- Be alert for any numbers that appear in the dream, become these numbers, and explore associations with them.

Rainwater suggests that in working with a dream you notice how you feel when you wake up. Is your feeling state one of fear, joy, sadness, frustration, surprise, anger? Identifying the feeling tone may be the key to finding the meaning of the dream. In working with dreams in Gestalt style, she suggests, dreamers can focus on questions such as the following:

- What are you doing in the dream?
- What are you feeling?
- What do you want in the dream?
- What are your relationships with other objects and people in the dream?
- What kind of action can you take now? What is your dream telling you?

Group experiments can emerge out of the dream work of individuals in a group. Zinker (1978) has developed an approach he calls *dream work as theater,* which goes beyond working with an individual's dream. After a dream is reported and worked through by a participant, a group experiment is created that allows other members to benefit therapeutically from the original imagery of the dreamer. Based on his assumption that all the members share certain archetypal themes, Zinker suggests that various images within a dream can be used to enhance self-understanding. Each plays out a part of the dream. This offers the group participants many opportunities for enacting certain dimensions of the dream that relate both to the dreamer and to their own life.

For example, assume that one of the members, Joan, has had a dream that contains a broken-down car, a man shooting at people in the car, and a woman trying to save the passengers. One member may choose to take on the identity of the person doing the shooting, another can take on the role of one of the people in the car being shot at, and still another can be the car that doesn't function. Each of the members can play out his or her part, and the dreamer can help them understand the characters or objects in the dream. The group leader can facilitate the production of the dream as a dramatic and therapeutic experience for the entire group. There are many advantages to this approach in increasing group cohesion and linking one member's work with others.

The dreams of group participants may have implications for how they feel in their group (Polster & Polster, 1973). In the example given above, Joan may discover that she feels frightened in the group and would like to escape. She may feel attacked (shot at) by one or more members, with a woman coming to her rescue. In this case she can act out her dream in the group by selecting the person whom she feels most seriously attacked by and talking to that person directly. She can then become the broken-down car—her powerless vehicle of escape—and see what associations this association brings. She can also pick out the woman in the group whom she feels most supported by and have a dialogue with her. She might reverse roles, becoming the person doing the shooting. Working with the dream in this way has rich potential for dealing with unfinished business with others in the group.

Styles of Gestalt Groups

Gestalt therapy can be practiced in a variety of ways, whether it is in an individual or a group setting. In groups, it can be applied in the puristic form that Perls developed, which is characterized by focus on a single member at a time. Basically, this style is individual therapy done in a group setting, in which a member and the leader work together while other members observe the process. When the interaction between leader and member is over, the leader typically asks members to give feedback and to relate their own reactions to what occurred. In this form of Gestalt practice direct and spontaneous interaction within the group is discouraged. A volunteer takes the "hot seat" and focuses as much as possible on the here and now, while the leader applies the Gestalt techniques described earlier to intensify the person's present-centered awareness.

Gestalt-oriented groups can also function in a less puristic fashion. These groups are characterized by more freedom of spontaneous interaction. Latner (1973) points out that there are regional styles of Gestalt practice. Therapists on the West Coast, who have been greatly influenced by Perls, tend to pay attention to the issues of self-awareness, centering, and responsibility. On the East Coast, Gestaltists tend toward a more interactive model, longer-term groups, more attention to the cognitive side of the therapeutic process, and a greater variety of personal styles.

Polster and Polster (1973) describe the "floating hot seat," a technique that encourages other members to get involved in a member's work in a spontaneous way. With this approach there is an understanding that whatever takes place within the group has relevance and potential for interaction among the members. In this way members avoid passively observing one member's work and waiting for their turn. An interactional focus is promoted whereby members can be touched by one another's work and can use this work as a way of getting into an exploration of their own personal issues.

In the kind of group process advocated by the Gestalt Institute of Cleveland, attention is given to the intrapersonal, interpersonal, and group levels of functioning. In Zinker's (1978) view, purist Gestalt à la Fritz Perls does not encourage the building of a community in a group. Although he agrees that people learn vicariously by observing a leader work with one member, he contends that they have little feeling of kinship and interaction with one another. It becomes a matter of doing individual therapy with an audience observing the process. One of the disadvantages of this traditional style, from Zinker's perspective, is that the therapist does all of the work and does not allow the group members to take charge of the unfolding situation. By contrast, the Cleveland style of Gestalt group process operates on several key principles: the primacy of the present group experience, the process of emerging group awareness, the value of active contact between participants, and interactional experiments that are suggested by an actively involved leader. Regardless of what the members are doing, they are encouraged to be aware of themselves as a member of society and of their role in the group as it changes from moment to moment.

Evaluation of the Gestalt Approach

What I Value in Gestalt Therapy

I have incorporated much of the spirit of Gestalt therapy into my own style of group leadership. In working with groups, I make frequent use of Gestalt techniques that facilitate the expression and exploration of intense feelings. These techniques are powerful and often lead to the expression of immediate feelings and the reexperiencing of old feelings. The here-and-now focus does intensify the work of members. Instead of merely talking about their problems, they experience their struggles in the present moment. As is the case with psychodramatic techniques, Gestalt techniques bring a certain vitality both to an individual's work and to the participants of the group.

Another distinct feature of Gestalt therapy is its focus on the body. Without making interpretations for members, leaders can encourage them to pay attention to what they are experiencing bodily. This focus can provide a rich clue to areas that members want to avoid, and it also offers a way for them to come into contact with their anxiety. It is especially important to avoid telling members what their gestures, postures, and body symptoms mean. Instead, a useful point of departure is to ask members to stay with what they are experiencing and eventually find their own meaning.

Since Gestalt therapy is grounded on existential principles, the genuineness of the group leader and the quality of the therapeutic relationships between the leader and members (and among the members themselves) are given primary emphasis. In this respect the Gestalt approach has some common denominators with both the existential and person-centered approaches. I think this is a main strength of Gestalt therapy, for the techniques described in this chapter will be most effective when they are used by group leaders who are real and who have a commitment to the welfare of the members. A number of Gestalt therapists emphasize the importance of the therapeutic relationship and view techniques as secondary to the quality of the relationship (see M. Polster, 1987; Polster & Polster, 1973; Yontef & Simkin, 1989; Zinker, 1978). The therapist's presence and ability to form good contact with clients is certainly as important as being skilled in using the techniques that were described in this chapter. Gestalt therapy is part of the existential approach, and the I/Thou encounter is seen as essential for therapy to succeed. The best experiments grow out of the trusting relationship that the leader creates. This approach encourages genuine experimentation and allows for a great deal of creativity on the part of leaders and members (see Zinker, 1978).

Some Limitations

In my view one of the limitations of traditional Gestalt therapy is its tendency to discount the cognitive side of counseling. To a large extent Perls adopted an anti-intellectual position by derogating the intellectual factors of personality. His statement "Lose your mind and come to your senses" reflects his reaction against the cognitive therapy of the psychoanalytic approach and illustrates his focus on the role of feelings in therapy. With his preoccupation with experiencing feelings and the body, Perls went to the other end of the continuum from the traditional therapies of the time. Following this lead, some Gestalt group leaders have ignored the value of conceptualizing in a group.

The emphasis on feelings and the body at the expense of cognitive factors may not provide the optimum therapeutic balance. To balance out this limitation, I also draw from the cognitive and behavioral approaches (transactional analysis, behavior therapy, rational-emotive therapy, and reality therapy). Helping participants discover the meaning of their emotional experiences is a significant factor in producing personality changes that will extend beyond the group. Although the earlier phase of Gestalt's development did not focus on cognitive processes, there appears to be a current trend to pay more attention to these factors and to integrate the affective and cognitive dimensions of human experiencing (see E. Polster, 1987a; M. Polster, 1987; Yontef & Simkin, 1989).

Another criticism that is directed toward Gestalt therapy concerns the meager research that has been done to assess its effectiveness. On this matter Simkin (1982) writes: "Most Gestalt therapists are busy practicing their art rather than evaluating it. Thus far there has been very little traditional research in the area of Gestalt therapy. This may change in the 1980's" (p. 376). From what I can tell, this situation has not changed in the 1980's.

Some Cautions and Ethical Concerns

As exciting and dynamic as Gestalt methods are, they are not for everyone. The appropriate application of Gestalt techniques hinges on questions of *when, with whom,* and *in what situation* (Shepherd, 1970). According to Simkin (1982): "Gestalt therapy is the treatment of choice for people who are 'up in their head.' It is not for people who act out their impulses. It is most effective in the hands of competent well-trained clinicians" (p. 377). Shepherd (1970) writes that, in general, Gestalt therapy is most effective with overly socialized, restrained, constricted individuals, who are often described as neurotic, phobic, perfectionistic, ineffective, and depressed. On the other hand, Shepherd asserts, work with less organized, more severely disturbed or psychotic individuals is more problematic and requires caution, sensitivity, and patience.

A major concern I have about Gestalt therapy is the potential danger for abusing techniques. Typically, Gestalt therapists are highly active and directive, and if they do not have the characteristics mentioned by Zinker (1978)—sensitivity, timing, inventiveness, empathy, and respect for the client—the experiments can easily boomerang. Also, the members can grow accustomed to the leader's assuming the initiative in creating experiments for them instead of coming up with some of their own experiments.

With an approach that can have powerful effects on members, either constructive or destructive, ethical practice requires adequate training and supervision. The most immediate limitation of Gestalt or any other therapy is the skill, training, experience, and judgment of the therapist. Probably the most effective application of Gestalt techniques comes after personal therapeutic experiences have been gained in professional workshops and in work with competent therapists and supervisors (Shepherd, 1970).

The Gestalt approach can be dangerous because of the therapist's power to manipulate the client with techniques. Inept therapists may use powerful techniques to stir up feelings and open up problems that members have kept from full awareness, only to abandon the members once they have managed to have a dramatic catharsis. Such leaders fail to help members work through what they have experienced and bring some closure to it.

It is easy to see that many of the Gestalt techniques offer a tempting place for group leaders to hide their personal responses and forget about the I/Thou relationship that Perls wrote about. Through the use of confrontive techniques they can direct the pressure primarily toward the members. The therapist's willingness to encounter clients with his or her honest and immediate responses and the ability to challenge clients' manipulative use of their symptoms without rejecting them are crucial (Shepherd, 1970). It is essential for Gestalt practitioners to learn how to confront in a manner that does not entrench the client's resistance. A blend of support and challenge goes a long way in creating the kind of I/Thou relationship that enables clients to explore their defensiveness.

Some Gestalt practitioners make the mistake of becoming too rigid, pushing such injunctions as "Always be in the present" or "Take responsibility for yourself." There are some situations in which stopping what members are doing and asking them to bring something into the here and now is quite counterproductive. Gestalt leaders who have truly integrated their approach are sensitive enough to practice in a flexible way. They strive to help clients experience themselves as fully as possible in the present, yet they are not rigidly bound by dictates, nor do they routinely intervene with a directive whenever members stray from the present. Sensitively staying in contact with a member's flow of experiencing entails the ability to focus on the person and not on the mechanical use of techniques for a certain effect.

Applying Gestalt Therapy in Multicultural Settings

There are many opportunities for Gestalt leaders to exercise their creativity in multicultural settings. Some ethnic clients may express themselves non-verbally to a greater extent than they do with words. For example, group leaders may ask members to focus on their gestures, facial expressions, and the experience within their own body. If a client says that he is feeling threatened, the leader may invite this person to pay attention to his bodily reactions. Some very creative work can emerge from work with people's gestures and body sensations. If this client is having a struggle between two conflicting parts within himself, one hand could represent one side of the conflict, and the other hand, the other side of the conflict. If the client does feel a sense of trust and security with the leader and the other members, he might be willing to engage in some Gestalt experiments as a way of heightening his own present experience and of gaining increased clarity into the nature of his struggle. One of the advantages of drawing on Gestalt experiments is that they can be tailored to fit the unique way in which an individual member perceives and interprets his or her culture.

The use of imagery and fantasy has much potential if clients are well prepared and if there is a high degree of trust within the group. If a client is dealing with unfinished business pertaining to guilt surrounding the death of a loved one, for instance, she can make significant inroads into completing this unfinished business by bringing this dead person symbolically into the room and dealing with her in the present. The importance of the personhood of the group leader cannot be overemphasized. If the group leader is trusted, his or her invitations are much more likely to be accepted by the client.

To a greater extent than is true of most other approaches, there are definite cautions in too quickly utilizing some Gestalt techniques with ethnic clients. As is evident from this chapter, these techniques tend to produce a high level of intense feelings. This focus on affect has some clear limitations with those clients who have been culturally conditioned to be emotionally restricted and reserved. Some ethnic clients have been conditioned to believe that expressing feelings openly is a sign of weakness and a display of one's vulnerability. Leaders who push for catharsis are likely to find certain clients becoming increasingly resistant, and these members may eventually terminate.

Even though there are certain limitations to utilizing Gestalt techniques with ethnically diverse group members, this does not mean that Gestalt has no value in multicultural settings. While the resistance of such clients can be escalated by ill-timed interventions on the leader's part, timely Gestalt interventions can be one approach in helping clients work through some of their deeper resistances and struggles.

Questions for Reflection and Discussion

1. Both Gestalt therapy and person-centered therapy share some features with the existential approach, yet they employ very different methods in a group. Although they have some common philosophical views of human nature, Gestalt relies on therapist direction and techniques, whereas person-centered therapy deemphasizes techniques and therapist direction. Do you see any basis for the typically active/directive Gestalt leader to incorporate some person-centered concepts? Why or why not?

2. Do you see a possibility of thinking in psychoanalytic terms and using Gestalt techniques? What are some ways in which you might integrate psychoanalytic concepts with Gestalt concepts and methods as a part of your leadership style?

3. What are some basic similarities and differences between psychodramatic groups and Gestalt groups? Again, do you see ways of blending some procedures from the two approaches in the groups you might lead?

4. Gestalt therapy focuses on what people are *experiencing* and *feeling* moment to moment. Do you think that this emphasis on feeling precludes thinking and conceptualization in therapy work? Explain.

5. What is your reaction to Perls's dictum "Lose your mind and come to your senses"?

6. What do you consider to be the major ethical considerations that need to be addressed in Gestalt group work? What safeguards can you think of against the most common dangers associated with Gestalt groups?

7. What are some key Gestalt concepts and experiments that you can apply to the process of understanding yourself? How might you use some Gestalt techniques as a way of increasing your awareness and promoting personality change in yourself? What do you think it would be like for you to be in a Gestalt group?

8. If you were to include Gestalt techniques in your group, in what ways might you prepare your members to increase their readiness to get involved in these techniques? What might you say to a member who asked what good it does to relive an event in the here and now, rather than telling about a problem in the past?

9. What are some ways in which you might work with the body in therapy? What kind of training would you want before you introduced body-oriented techniques? What advantages, if any, do you see in incorporating body work, as opposed to limiting the group strictly to verbal methods? What risks, if any, do you see in working with the body?

10. What are your reactions to the Gestalt approach to working with dreams in a group setting?

Where to Go from Here

If you have become excited about including Gestalt techniques in your style of group leadership, I encourage you to attend a workshop led by a competent professional. Just as I have real concerns about practitioners' employing psychodramatic techniques if they have not experienced them personally, I worry about leaders who routinely use Gestalt techniques that they have learned about mainly through reading. Although reading is surely of value, I don't think that it is sufficient to produce skillful clinicians.

Some resources for training in Gestalt therapy are

Gestalt Institute of Cleveland
1588 Hazel Drive
Cleveland, OH 44106
(Joseph Zinker is the director)

Gestalt Training Center
P.O. Box 2189
La Jolla, CA 92038
(Erv and Miriam Polster are the co-directors)

Gestalt Therapy Institute of Los Angeles
620 Venice Boulevard
Venice, CA 90291

Recommended Supplementary Readings

The Gestalt Journal, published twice yearly, offers articles, reviews, and commentaries of interest to the practitioner, theoretician, academician, and student. A 1-year (two-issue) subscription is $25. Contact

The Gestalt Journal
P.O. Box 990
Highland, NY 12528
Phone: (914) 691-7192

In addition to the journal, subscribers receive *The Gestalt Newsletter* free of charge. Issued twice a year, the newsletter includes current programs and workshops of training centers throughout the country, conference notes, and employment opportunities.

Creative process in Gestalt therapy (Zinker, 1978) is a beautifully written book that is a delight to read. Zinker captures the essence of Gestalt therapy as a combination of phenomenology and behavior modification by showing how the therapist functions much like an artist in creating experiments that encourage clients to expand their boundaries. His concepts are fleshed out with rich clinical examples. The book shows how Gestalt can be practiced in a creative, eclectic, and integrative style.

Gestalt therapy verbatim (Perls, 1969a), which consists essentially of transcripts of lectures, workshops, seminars, and demonstrations given by the author, provides a graphic description of his unique and dramatic therapeutic style. It is also an excellent source of information about "affective techniques" based on Gestalt-therapy exercises. The first part of the book deals primarily with the theory of Gestalt.

Gestalt therapy: Excitement and growth in the human personality (Perls, Hefferline, & Goodman, 1951) is one of the most important books in Gestalt therapy. The first half deals with applications of Gestalt principles to group situations. The rest of the book, rather difficult to read, discusses theoretical aspects of Gestalt therapy.

Gestalt therapy now (Fagan & Shepherd, 1970) is a collection of articles that gives a good indication of the diversity among Gestalt-therapy practitioners. The articles deal with the theory, techniques, and applications of Gestalt therapy. I particularly recommend Chapters 7–11 and Chapter 18.

Gestalt approaches in counseling (Passons, 1975) is a clear, concise, and practical account of the application of Gestalt-therapy principles to group counseling. It contains some extremely useful material on group techniques related to present-centeredness, expanding awareness, verbal and nonverbal approaches, the use of fantasy, working with feelings, and dealing with the past and future. The book also offers an excellent, easy-to-read overview of the theoretical components of Gestalt therapy.

Gestalt therapy integrated: Contours of theory and practice (Polster & Polster, 1973) is a scholarly and penetrating treatment of some of the concepts underlying the practice of Gestalt therapy. Theory and practice are successfully integrated in the unique and personal style characteristic of the authors.

Beyond the hot seat: Gestalt approaches to group (Feder & Ronall, 1980) discusses the application of Gestalt theory to group practice. Separate chapters are devoted to Gestalt group process, Gestalt family therapy, training groups, intensive workshops, and other clinical applications.

REFERENCES AND SUGGESTED READINGS*

Downing, J., & Marmorstein, R. (Eds.). (1973). *Dreams and nightmares: A book of Gestalt therapy sessions.* New York: Harper & Row.

Fagan, J., & Shepherd, I. (Eds.). (1970). *Gestalt therapy now.* New York: Harper & Row (Colophon).

Feder, B., & Ronall, R. (Eds.). (1980). *Beyond the hot seat: Gestalt approaches to group.* New York: Brunner/Mazel.

Frew, J. E. (1986). The functions and patterns of occurrence of individual contact styles during the development phase of the Gestalt group. *The Gestalt Journal, 9*(1), 55–70.

Harman, R. L. (1984). Recent developments in Gestalt group therapy. *The International Journal of Group Psychotherapy, 34*(3), 473–483.

James, M., & Jongeward, D. (1971). *Born to win: Transactional analysis with Gestalt experiments.* Reading, MA: Addison-Wesley.

Kempler, W. (1982). Gestalt family therapy. In A. M. Horne & M. M. Ohlsen (Eds.), *Family counseling and therapy.* Itasca, IL: F. E. Peacock.

Kepner, E. (1980). Gestalt group process. In B. Feder & R. Ronall (Eds.), *Beyond the hot seat: Gestalt approaches to group.* New York: Brunner/Mazel.

Latner, J. (1973). *The Gestalt therapy book.* New York: Bantam.

Levitsky, A., & Perls, F. (1970). The rules and games of Gestalt therapy. In J. Fagan & I. Shepherd (Eds.), *Gestalt therapy now.* New York: Harper & Row (Colophon).

Passons, W. R. (1975). *Gestalt approaches in counseling.* New York: Holt, Rinehart & Winston.

*Perls, F. (1969a). *Gestalt therapy verbatim.* New York: Bantam.

Perls, F. (1969b). *In and out of the garbage pail.* New York: Bantam.

Perls, F. (1970). Four lectures. In J. Fagan & I. L. Shepherd (Eds.), *Gestalt therapy now.* New York: Harper & Row (Colophon).

Perls, F. (1973). *The Gestalt approach and eyewitness to therapy.* New York: Bantam.

Perls, F., Hefferline, R., & Goodman, P. (1951). *Gestalt therapy: Excitement and growth in the human personality.* New York: Dell.

Polster, E. (1987a). Escape from the present: Transition and storyline. In J. K. Zeig, (Ed.), *The evolution of psychotherapy* (pp. 326–340). New York: Brunner/Mazel.

*Polster, E. (1987b). *Every person's life is worth a novel.* New York: Norton.

*Polster, E., & Polster, M. (1973). *Gestalt therapy integrated: Contours of theory and practice.* New York: Brunner/Mazel.

Polster, M. (1987). Gestalt therapy: Evolution and application. In J. K. Zeig (Ed.), *The evolution of psychotherapy* (pp. 312–325). New York: Brunner/Mazel.

*Rainwater, J. (1979). *You're in charge! A guide to becoming your own therapist.* Los Angeles: Guild of Tutors Press.

Reich, W. (1949). *Character analysis.* New York: Noonday Press.

Reich, W. (1967). *The function of the orgasm.* New York: Bantam.

Reich, W. (1969). *Selected writings.* New York: Noonday Press.

*Books and articles marked with an asterisk are suggested for further study.

Shaffer, J., & Galinsky, M. D. (1989). *Models of group therapy* (2nd ed.). Englewood Cliffs, NJ: Prentice-Hall.

*Shepherd, I. L. (1970). Limitations and cautions in the Gestalt approach. In J. Fagan & I. L. Shepherd (Eds.), *Gestalt therapy now* (pp. 234–238). New York: Harper & Row (Colophon).

Simkin, J. S. (1982). Gestalt therapy in groups. In G. M. Gazda (Ed.), *Basic approaches to group psychotherapy and group counseling* (2nd ed.). Springfield, IL: Charles C Thomas.

*Simkin, J. S., Simkin, A. N., Brien, L., & Sheldon, C. (1986). Gestalt therapy. In I. L. Kutash and A. Wolf (Eds.), *Psychotherapist's casebook* (pp. 209–221). San Francisco: Jossey-Bass.

*Simkin, J. S., & Yontef, G. M. (1984). Gestalt therapy. In R. Corsini (Ed.), *Current psychotherapies* (3rd ed.). Itasca, IL: F. E. Peacock.

Smith, E. (1976). *The growing edge of Gestalt therapy*. New York: Brunner/Mazel.

Smith, E. (1985). *The body in psychotherapy*. Jefferson, NC: MacFarland & Co.

Stevens, J. O. (1971). *Awareness: Exploring, experimenting, experiencing*. Moab, UT: Real People Press.

*Yontef, G. M., & Simkin, J. S. (1989). Gestalt therapy. In R. J. Corsini & D. Wedding (Eds.), *Current psychotherapies* (4th ed.). Itasca, IL: F. E. Peacock.

*Zinker, J. (1978). *Creative process in Gestalt therapy*. New York: Random House (Vintage).

Zinker, J. (1980). The developmental process of a Gestalt therapy group. In B. Feder & R. Ronall (Eds.), *Beyond the hot seat: Gestalt approaches to group*. New York: Brunner/Mazel.

12

Transactional Analysis

Introduction

Transactional analysis (TA) is an interactional therapy grounded on the assumption that we make current decisions based on past premises—premises that were at one time appropriate to our survival needs but that may no longer be valid. TA emphasizes the cognitive/rational/behavioral aspects of the therapeutic process. More specifically, it stresses the capacity of the person to change decisions and is oriented toward increasing awareness with the goal of enabling people to make new decisions (redecide) and thereby alter the course of their life. To achieve this goal, TA group participants learn how to recognize the three ego states (Parent, Adult, and Child) in which they function. They also learn how their current behavior is being affected by the rules and regulations they received and incorporated as children and how they can identify the "life script" that is determining their actions. Ultimately, they come to realize that they can now redecide and initiate a new direction in life, changing what is not working while retaining what serves them well.

TA provides an interactional and contractual approach to groups—interactional, in that it emphasizes the dynamics of transactions between people, and contractual, in that group members develop clear statements of what they will change and how they will go about making these changes. These contracts establish the goals and direction of the group.

Historical Background

Transactional analysis was originally developed by Eric Berne (1961), who was trained as a Freudian psychoanalyst and psychiatrist. TA evolved out of

Berne's dissatisfaction with the slowness of psychoanalysis in curing people of their problems. Historically, it developed as an extension of psychoanalysis with concepts and techniques especially designed for group treatment. Berne discovered that his clients, by using TA, were making significant improvement. As his theory of personality evolved, he parted ways with psychoanalysis to devote himself full time to the theory and practice of TA (Dusay, 1986).

Berne said he had formulated most of the concepts of TA by paying attention to what his clients were saying. He began to see an ego image that related to the childhood experiences of his patients. He concluded that there was a Child ego state that was different from the "grown-up" ego state. Later, he postulated that there were two "grown-up" states: one, which seemed to be a copy of the person's parents, he called the Parent ego state; the other, which was the rational part of the person, he named the Adult ego state.

One of Berne's contributions was his perspective on how young children develop a personal plan for their life as a strategy for physical and psychological survival. He felt that people were shaped from their first few years by a script that they followed during the rest of their life.

As is true of many theories in this book, there is a parallel between the basic concepts of TA and the personal life of its founder. Claude Steiner (1974) has contended that Berne was himself under the influence of a life script that called for an early death of a broken heart. Apparently, Berne had strong injunctions against loving others and accepting the love that others had for him. His life could be characterized as work oriented, and his driving motivations were to write books on the development of a new theory (TA) and to cure people. In writing about Berne's life script, Steiner comments about his interest in people who had a history of heart disease. Berne died of a coronary occlusion when he was 60 years old, which was the age his mother had died of a coronary. Steiner believes that such a limited-life-expectancy script is by design and that in Berne's situation his heart gave way when he had completed the last two books he wanted to write.

In this chapter two schools of TA are considered. There is the *classical, or Bernian, approach,* which emphasizes transactions in the here and now, views the group as a microcosm of the world, and deals with four kinds of analysis (structural analysis, transactional analysis, game analysis, and life-script analysis). These levels of analysis are further developed later in this chapter. Classical transactional analysis had been largely developed by the late 1960s.

Contemporary TA practitioners have moved in various directions and modified many of the basic concepts that Berne formulated. Because there are different models of TA, it is difficult to discuss practices that apply to all of them. But this chapter will highlight the expansion of Berne's approach by Mary and Robert Goulding (1979), leaders of the *redecisional school* of TA. The Gouldings differ from the classical Bernian approach in a number of ways. They have combined TA with the principles and techniques of Gestalt therapy, family therapy, psychodrama, and behavior therapy. The redecisional approach helps group members experience their impasse, or the point at which they feel stuck. They relive the context in which they made earlier decisions, some of which were not functional, and they make new decisions that are functional. Redecisional therapy is aimed at helping people challenge themselves to discover ways in which they perceive themselves in victimlike roles and to take charge of their lives by deciding for themselves how they will change.

Basic Assumptions

Underlying the practice of TA group work is the premise that awareness is an important first step in the process of changing our ways of thinking/ feeling/behaving. In the early stages of a group, techniques are aimed at increasing the participants' awareness of their problems and their options for making substantive changes in their life.

Another basic assumption of TA is that each of us is in charge of what we do, of the ways in which we think, and of how we feel. Robert Goulding (1987) asserts that others do not *make* us feel in a certain way; rather, we respond to situations largely by our choices. He believes that the therapist's task is to confront clients on the ways they have abdicated personal responsibility and insist that they assume responsibility during the course of therapy:

> All along the way, we help people realize that they are responsible for themselves, for their thinking, their feeling, their behavior, their body. Unless we can get them to claim their own autonomy, there is no way for them to make a valid redecision. So we insist, and we teach, that each of us is autonomous, even though we might feel like a victim [p. 306].

People are capable of transcending their early programming and choices by being able to understand their past decisions and by being able to make new choices in the present that will affect their future. According to Mary Goulding (1987):

> This concept of personal autonomy—the concept that I alone am responsible for my thoughts, beliefs, emotions, and actions—is crucial to change. As long as an individual blames others for her fate and spends her energy attempting to change others, she simply cannot make the desired changes in her own life [p. 287].

Rationale for a Group Approach

The practice of TA is ideally suited for groups. Berne believed that group therapy yielded information about one's personal plan for life much more quickly than individual therapy. Redecisional therapy, as practiced by the Gouldings, is done in a group context in which members can experience their script coming to life by reliving early memories and by interacting with others in the group. From a redecisional perspective, group therapy is the treatment of choice. People change more rapidly than they do in individual therapy, and groups seem to add a humanness to therapy (R. Goulding, 1987). There are many avenues of self-understanding through analyzing transactions within the group. In the same way that Gestalt groups function in the here and now, TA groups bring past issues into the present. The presence of group members facilitates action by having many people representing both family members from the past and contemporaries. Because of the interaction within the group, TA group members are given many opportunities to review and challenge their past decisions and experiment with new ones. For Robert Goulding, one rationale for a group is that it provides a living experience that members can take out to their family, friends, and community.

The TA group emphasizes teaching procedures (didactic methods), and members are expected to master a basic vocabulary of TA concepts, such as *Parent, Adult, Child, strokes, decision, redecision, games,* and *scripts.* To become acquainted with the key concepts of TA and prepare for a group, members are urged to read certain works, including *Changing Lives through Redecision Therapy,* by Mary and Robert Goulding (1979); *Scripts People Live: Transactional Analysis of Life Scripts,* by Steiner (1974); *Games People Play* and *What Do You Say After You Say Hello?* by Berne (1964, 1972); *Born to Win: Transactional Analysis with Gestalt Experiments,* by Muriel James and Dorothy Jongeward (1971); and *Redecision Therapy: Expanded Perspectives,* by Leslie Kadis (1985). Group members are also encouraged to attend introductory TA courses, workshops, and conferences.

Key Concepts

The Ego States

As mentioned, people operate in three dynamic ego states that each encompass important facets of the personality: Parent, Adult, and Child (P-A-C). These ego states are considered to be essential and distinguishing characteristics of TA therapy (Dusay, 1986). According to TA, people are constantly shifting from one of these states to another, and their behavior at any one time is related to the ego state of the moment.

The Parent ego state contains the attitudes and behavior incorporated from external sources, primarily one's parents. Outwardly, this ego state is expressed toward others in critical or nurturing behavior. Inwardly, it is experienced as old parental messages that continue and influence the inner Child. Harris (1967) describes that Parent as "a huge collection of recordings in the brain of unquestioned or imposed external events perceived by a person in his early years, a period which we have designated roughly as the first five years of life" (p. 40). When we are in the Parent ego state, we react to situations as we imagine our parents might have reacted, or we may act toward others the way our parents acted toward us. The Parent contains all the "shoulds" and "oughts" and other rules for living. When we are in that ego state, we may act in ways that are strikingly similar to those of our parents or other significant people in our early life. We may use some of their very phrases, and our posture, gestures, voice, and mannerisms may replicate those that we experienced in our parents. Such behavior occurs when the Parent in us is a positive ego state (a Nurturing Parent) or a negative one (a Critical Parent).

The Adult ego state is the objective and computerlike part of our personality that functions as a data processor: it computes possibilities and makes decisions on the basis of available data. This state is neither emotional nor judgmental but simply works with the facts and with external reality. The Adult is oriented toward current reality, is objective in gathering information, and is not related to chronological age.

The Child ego state consists of feelings, impulses, and spontaneous actions. This state contains all the impulses that come naturally to a child, and it includes "recordings" of early experiences. The Child can be either the Natural Child—that is, the spontaneous, impulsive, open, alive, expressive, often charming but untrained being within each of us—or the Adapted Child—the tamed version of the Natural Child and the part of us that learns to accommodate to the expectations of others in order to gain acceptance and approval. Berne describes the Adapted Child as "the one who modifies his behavior under Parental influence. He behaves as father (or mother) wanted him to behave: compliantly or precociously, for example. Or, he adapts himself by withdrawing or whining" (1964, p. 26). The modifications referred to by Berne result generally from traumatic experiences, demands, training, and decisions about how to get attention or other forms of "strokes."

In a TA group, members are first taught how to recognize which of the three ego states they are functioning in at any given time, with the aim of enabling them to consciously decide whether that state or another state is most appropriate or useful. For example, a member who typically responds to others in a Critical Parent style and who has contracted to become more tolerant toward others must recognize his or her habitual ego state before any steps can be taken to change. Mary and Robert Goulding (1979) describe the value of ego-state awareness as follows:

> As patients learn to be more aware of the ego state they are in, they learn to better handle their feelings, to better recognize their position in their life script, to be more aware that they have been, or are, game playing. They become much more aware of their adaptive behavior, adaptive to their internal Parent and to the outside world. After becoming aware, they can knowingly choose to adapt or not to adapt [p. 26].*

The Need for Strokes

A basic premise of the TA approach is that humans need to receive both physical and psychological strokes in order to develop a sense of trust in the world and a basis for loving themselves. Steiner (1974) writes that "strokes are as necessary to human life as are other primary biological needs such as food, water, and shelter—needs which if not satisfied will lead to death" (p. 132). And, indeed, there is ample evidence that lack of physical contact can

---

*From *Changing Lives through Redecision Therapy,* by M. Goulding and R. Goulding. Copyright 1979 by Brunner/Mazel, Inc. This and all other quotations from this source are reprinted by permission.

not only impair infant growth and development but also, in extreme cases, lead to death. Psychological strokes—verbal and nonverbal signs of acceptance and recognition—are also necessary to people as confirmations of their worth.

Strokes can be either positive or negative. Positive strokes, which express warmth, affection, or appreciation either verbally or with a look or a smile, a touch or a gesture, are seen as necessary for the development of psychologically healthy people. Negative strokes, which leave people feeling discounted and diminished as persons, are seen as impairing healthy psychological development. Interestingly, despite their ill effects, negative strokes are considered preferable to no strokes at all—that is, to being ignored. We are all familiar with cases of children who, feeling ignored and dismissed, act to elicit negative strokes from their parents because such responses are the only form of recognition they can get.

Positive strokes can be given either unconditionally or conditionally. Unconditional strokes—that is, strokes that are not predicated on the receiver's being or acting in a certain way—tend to elicit the feeling that one is significant just because one exists. Conditional positive strokes—strokes that entail a variety of stipulations that must be met before the strokes are given—typically elicit the feeling that one is acceptable only *if* one meets certain expectations.

TA group members are taught how to recognize the strokes that motivate them and to become sensitive to the ways in which they discount themselves. Take, for example, a group member named Sara who continually puts herself down with self-deprecating remarks. She either doesn't hear or soon forgets the positive feedback she gets from others in her group. When paid a sincere compliment, she finds some way to play it down or make a joke of it. If she is the focus of positive attention or receives any display of tenderness, affection, or caring, she becomes extremely uncomfortable, yet she remembers and stores up any critical remarks and feels depressed. As Steiner (1974) would put it, she collects the "cold pricklies" rather than the "warm fuzzies."

In her TA group Sara is confronted with the fact that she discounts her worth and doesn't allow others to give her positive strokes. She is also challenged to decide whether she wants to change this behavior. If she accepts the challenge to change, the group can help her learn how to ask for and accept positive strokes.

The Gouldings' group therapy methods are designed to help people make new decisions, anchor those redecisions in place, and stroke positively for these changes (R. Goulding, 1987, p. 303). Contending that this form of behavior therapy works, Robert Goulding asserts that a major advantage of group therapy is the therapeutic power that results when members receive strokes not only from the therapist but also from the other members. TA groups also teach members how to stroke themselves. The Gouldings begin their marathon groups with a quiet time during which participants are asked to reflect on the question "What do you like about yourself?" The aim is to create a climate in which the clients can become aware of unrecognized strengths, which are deserving of self-generated positive strokes. The Gouldings operate on the premise that clients will meet their therapeutic contracts to a greater extent through self-love than through self-hate (M. Goulding & Goulding, 1979).

Injunctions and Counterinjunctions

The Gouldings' redecision work is grounded in the TA concepts of injunctions and early decisions (M. Goulding, 1987, p. 288). *Injunctions* are parental messages that stem from the parents' Child ego state. Such messages, which are often expressions of disappointment, frustration, anxiety, and unhappiness, establish the "don'ts" by which children learn to live. Out of their own pathology, parents give injunctions such as the following: "Don't," "Don't be," "Don't be close," "Don't be separate from me," "Don't be the sex you are," "Don't want," "Don't need," "Don't think," "Don't feel," "Don't grow up," "Don't be a child," "Don't succeed," "Don't be you," "Don't be sane," "Don't be well," and "Don't belong" (M. Goulding, 1987; M. Goulding & Goulding, 1979).

According to Mary Goulding (1987), children decide either to accept these parental messages or to fight against them. If they do accept them, they decide precisely *how* they will accept them. Based on accepting certain injunctions, children then make decisions that become a basic part of their permanent character structure.

The counterpart of injunctions are parental messages that come from the parents' Parent ego state, which are known as *counterinjunctions*. These messages convey the "shoulds," "oughts," and "dos" of parental expectations. Examples of counterinjunctions are "Be tough," "Be perfect," "Work up to your potential," "Do what I expect of you," "Hurry up," "Try hard," "Please me," "Be careful," and "Be polite." The problem with these counterinjunctions is that it is almost impossible to live up to them; thus, no matter how hard people try to be pleasing, they are bound to feel that they have not done or been enough.

In TA groups, members explore the "shoulds" and "shouldn'ts," the "dos" and "don'ts" that they have been trained to live by. The first step in freeing oneself from behaviors dictated by the often irrational and generally uncritically received parental messages is awareness of the specific injunctions and counterinjunctions that one has accepted as a child. Once group participants have identified and become aware of these internalized "shoulds," "oughts," "dos," "don'ts," and "musts," they are in a better position to critically examine them to determine whether they are willing to continue living by them.

Decisions and Redecisions

As indicated earlier, transactional analysis emphasizes cognitive/rational/ behavioral aspects, especially our ability to become aware of decisions that govern our behavior and of the capacity to make new decisions that will beneficially alter the course of our life. This section focuses on the decisions determined by parental injunctions and counterinjunctions and investigates how TA group members learn to relive these early decisions and make new ones.

Following is an example of decision making that has been dictated by parental injunctions. A TA group member, Bill, apparently received the parental injunction "Don't trust anybody." The decisions about the behavior resulting from this injunction are implicit in many of Bill's characteristic pronouncements: "If you don't let yourself care, you won't be hurt"; "If I keep to myself, I won't need anything from anyone"; "Whenever I've wanted something from another, I've been hurt. It's just not worth getting involved with, or even close to, others." Indeed, it became clear in group sessions that by accepting his parents' injunction against trusting people, Bill consistently made decisions that caused him to avoid others. To support these decisions, Bill was able to find plenty of data—both in the group and in his everyday life—to maintain his view that trust would inevitably lead to hurt. Consequently he continued, often unwittingly, to abide by his parents' injunction.

In the TA group Bill not only had the opportunity to become aware of his decisions and of the injunction behind them but was also helped to investigate whether these decisions were still appropriate. At one time the decisions to avoid people might have been necessary for Bill's physical and psychological safety—a matter of sheer survival. In the group Bill was able to question whether such decisions currently served any purpose and determine whether they were, instead, thwarting his development. He made a new decision to trust people and to approach them as friends, not enemies.

Berne (1964, 1972) takes the position that, to a large degree, people are victims of their injunctions and of the decisions based on them. For Berne, how people are "scripted" by their parents in the long run *determines* their life plans. The Gouldings disagree with Berne's deterministic and victim-like stance and state that people are not passively "scripted," for "injunctions are not placed in people's heads like electrodes. . . . Each child makes decisions in response to real or imagined injunctions, and thereby 'scripts' her/himself" (R. Goulding & Goulding, 1976, p. 42).

Elsewhere, the Gouldings (1978, 1979) also point out that, even though injunctions and counterinjunctions carry the weight of parental authority, the child must *accept* these messages if they are to have an impact on his or her personality. The Gouldings add that many injunctions children live under are not issued by the parents but derive instead from the children's own fantasies and misinterpretations. It is important to note that a single parental injunction may foster a variety of decisions on the part of the child, ranging from reasonable to pathological. For example, the injunction "Don't be stupid" may give rise to decisions ranging from "I'll never do *that* again" to "I'll let others make decisions" to "I *am* stupid, and I always *will be* stupid." Similarly, the injunction "Don't be you" may evoke decisions ranging from "I'll hide who I really am" to "I'll be someone else" to "I'll be a nobody" to "I'll kill myself, and then they will accept me and love me."

Whatever injunctions people have received, and whatever the resulting life decisions were, transactional analysis maintains that people can change by changing their decisions—by learning to redecide. In their groups the Gouldings develop an atmosphere in which members are challenged from the outset to make new decisions for themselves. Early in the course of a group, Robert Goulding (1975) asks: "What did you decide to do to screw up your life, and what are you going to decide now to unscrew it?" (p. 246).

The group work related to making new decisions frequently requires members to return to the childhood scenes in which they arrived at self-limiting decisions. The group leader may facilitate this process with any of the following interventions: "As you are speaking, how old do you feel?" "Is what you are saying reminding you of any times when you were a child?" "What pictures are coming to your mind right now?" "Could you exaggerate that frown on your face? What are you feeling? What scene comes to mind as you experience your frowning?" Mary Goulding (1987) says that there are many ways of assisting a member to return to some critical point in childhood. "Once there," she adds, "the client reexperiences the scene; and then she relives it in fantasy in some new way that allows her to reject old decisions" (p. 288). After members experience a redecision through this fantasy work, they design experiments so that they can practice new behavior to reinforce their redecision.

Consider the following example of a member named Helga, who relives scenes with her parents when she was positively stroked for failing or was negatively stroked for succeeding. It was apparently at those times that she accepted the injunction "Don't succeed." The group challenges her to examine whether the decision, which may have been functional or even necessary in the past, is currently appropriate. She may redecide that "I will make it, and I am successful, even though it is not what you want from me."

Another group member, Gary, is able to see that he responded to his father's injunction "Don't grow" by deciding to remain helpless and immature. He recalls learning that, when he was independent, his dad shouted at him and, when he was helpless, he was given his father's attention. Because he wanted his father's approval, Gary decided "I'll remain a child forever." During a group session Gary goes back to a childhood scene in which he was stroked for his helplessness, and he talks to his father now in a way that he never did as a child: "Dad, even though I still want your approval, I don't *need* it to exist. Your acceptance is not worth the price I'd have to pay. I'm capable of deciding for myself and of standing on my own two feet. I'll be the man that I want to be, not the boy that you want me to be."

In this redecision work Helga and Gary enter the past and create fantasy scenes in which they can safely give up old and currently inappropriate early decisions, because both are armed with an understanding in the present that enables them to relive the scene in a new way. According to the Gouldings, it is possible to give a *new ending* to the scenes in which original decisions were made—a new ending that often results in a *new beginning* that allows clients to feel, think, and act in revitalized ways. Mary Goulding (1987, p. 290) summarizes the essence of how clients are taught to create new endings to old scenarios:

> The client restructures her internal self, by discarding and growing beyond her Child decisions. She eliminates her carping Critical Parent, enhances her own self-nurturing and other-nurturing, decontaminates her thinking from her beliefs, and gives herself permission to be a Free Child when that is appropriate. She frees herself from the self-restricting and self-destructive straitjackets of the past. As she changes, she takes her new self into the world to relate with others in happier and healthier ways.

Games

A game is an ongoing series of attractions that ends with bad feelings for at least one player. By their very nature games are designed to prevent intimacy. Games consist of three basic elements: a series of complementary transactions that on the surface seem plausible; an ulterior transaction that is the hidden agenda; and a negative payoff that concludes the game and is the real purpose of the game. Berne described a variety of common games, including "Yes, but," "Kick me," "Harassed," "If it weren't for you," "Martyr," "Ain't it awful," "I'm only trying to help you," "Uproar," and "Look what you made me do!" Games always have some payoff (or else they wouldn't be perpetuated), and one common payoff is support for the decisions described in the preceding section. For example, people who have decided that they are helpless may play the "Yes, but" game. They ask others for help and then greet any suggestions with a list of reasons why the suggestions won't work; thus they feel free to cling to their helplessness. Addicts of the "Kick me" game are often people who have decided to be rejected; they set themselves up to be mistreated by others so that they can play the role of the victim whom nobody likes.

By engaging in game playing, people receive strokes and also maintain and defend their early decisions. They find evidence to support their view of the world, and they collect bad feelings. These unpleasant feelings that people experience after a game are known as *rackets*. They have much the same quality as feelings the people had as children. These rackets are maintained by actually choosing situations that will support them. Therefore, those who typically feel depressed, angry, or bored may be actively collecting these feelings and feeding them into long-standing feeling patterns that often lead to stereotypical ways of behaving. They also choose the games that they will play to maintain their rackets. When people "feel bad," they often get sympathy from others or control others by their bad moods.

A group situation provides an ideal environment for the participants to become aware of the specific ways in which they choose game-playing strategies as a way of avoiding genuine contact and choose patterns of thinking/feeling/behaving that are ultimately self-defeating. Group members can learn about their own games and rackets by observing the behavior of others in the group, as well as by analyzing how their responses in the group are connected to their responses to life situations in early childhood. Members can begin by using the games they are currently playing in the group to understand that, although games often give the appearance of intimacy, their actual effect is to create distance between people. Later, as members become aware of the more subtle aspects of game playing, they begin to realize that games prevent close human interaction and that it takes at least two to play a game. Consequently, if the members decide that they want to relate more closely to others, they also have to decide not to play games anymore.

Eventually, members are taught to make connections between the games they played as children and the games they play now—for example, how they attempted to get attention in the past and how those past attempts relate to the games they play now in order to get stroked. The aim of this TA group process is to offer members the chance to drop certain games in favor of responding honestly—an opportunity that may lead them to discover ways of changing negative strokes and to learn how to give and receive positive strokes.

Basic Psychological Life Positions and Life Scripts

Decisions about oneself, one's world, and one's relationships to others are crystallized during the first 5 years of life. Such decisions are basic for the formulation of a life position, which develops into the roles of the life script. Generally, once a person has decided on a life position, there is a tendency for it to remain fixed unless there is some intervention, such as therapy, to change the underlying decisions. Games are often used to support and maintain life positions and to play out life scripts. People seek security by maintaining that which is familiar, even though the familiar may be highly unpleasant. As we have seen earlier, games such as "Kick me" may be unpleasant, but they have the virtue of allowing the player to maintain a familiar position in life, even though this position is negative.

Transactional analysis identifies four basic life positions, all of which are based on decisions made as a result of childhood experiences and all of which determine how people feel about themselves and how they relate to others:

1. I'm OK—You're OK.
2. I'm OK—You're not OK.
3. I'm not OK—You're OK.
4. I'm not OK—You're not OK.

The *I'm OK—You're OK* position is generally game free. It is characterized by an attitude of trust and openness, a willingness to give and take, and an acceptance of others as they are. In this position there are no losers, only winners.

I'm OK—You're not OK is the position of people who project their problems onto others and blame them, put them down, and criticize them. The games that reinforce this position involve a self-styled superior (the "I'm OK") who projects anger, disgust, and scorn onto a designated inferior, or scapegoat (the "You're not OK"). Briefly, this position is that of the person who needs an underdog to maintain his or her sense of "OKness."

The *I'm not OK—You're OK* position is that of the depressed person, one who feels powerless in comparison with others. Typically such people serve others' needs instead of their own and generally feel victimized. Games supporting this position include "Kick me" and "Martyr"—games that support the power of others and deny one's own.

The *I'm not OK—You're not OK* position is held by those who have given up all hope, who have lost interest in life, and who see life as totally without promise. This self-destructive stance is characteristic of people who are unable to cope in the real world and may lead to extreme withdrawal, a return to infantile behavior, or to violent behavior resulting in injury or death of themselves or others.

Related to the concept of basic psychological positions is the life script, or plan for life. This script, as we have seen, is developed early in life as a result of parental teaching (such as injunctions and counterinjunctions) and the early decisions we make as children. Among these decisions is selecting the basic psychological position, or dramatic role, that we play in our life script. Indeed, life scripts are comparable to a dramatic stage production, with a cast of characters, a plot, scenes, dialogues, and endless rehearsals. In essence, the life script is a blueprint that tells people where they are going in life and what they will do when they arrive.

According to Berne (1972), through our early interactions with parents and others we receive a pattern of strokes that may be either supporting or disparaging. Based on this stroking pattern, we make a basic existential decision about ourselves; that is, we assume one of the four positions described above. This existential decision is then reinforced by continuing messages (both verbal and nonverbal) that we receive during our lifetime. It is also reinforced by the results of our games, rackets, and interpretations of events. During our childhood years we also make the decision whether people are OK and trustworthy (Berne, 1964; Harris, 1967). Our basic belief system is thus shaped through this process of deciding about ourselves and others. If we hope to change the life course that we are traveling, it helps to understand the components of this script, which to a large extent determines our patterns of thinking/feeling/behaving.

One function of the TA group is to help members, through a process known as *script analysis,* become aware of how they acquired their life script and to see more clearly their life role (basic psychological life position). Script analysis helps members see the ways in which they feel compelled to play out their life script and offers them alternative life choices. Put in another way, this group process helps to relieve participants of the compulsion to play games that justify behavior called for in their life script. It should be mentioned here that Goulding and Goulding (1979) reject the rather passive concept of "scripting." They contend that we write our own script and that we can rewrite it. Consequently, the Gouldings do not deal much with scripts in their group therapy.

In addition to script analysis, the TA group offers opportunities to actually experience oneself in unfamiliar dominant life positions. For example, the members who have cast themselves in the "I'm not OK" role can become aware of how they relate to others in the group through games like "Kick me," whereby they elevate others and keep themselves feeling inferior and depressed. Once they have gained an awareness of how they keep themselves victims, they can use the group situation to experience an "I'm OK" role. Armed with an awareness of their habitual ineffective behavior and the newly acquired experience of functional behavior, participants are in a better position to effect a change in their experiences. Briefly, the aim of the TA group in this instance is to provide a vehicle for members to develop the life position "I'm OK—You're OK."

Role and Functions of the Group Leader

From the perspective of the classical (Bernian) approach, the group leader functions as a teacher. Although TA is designed to develop both emotional and intellectual awareness, the focus is clearly on the cognitive aspects. Harris (1967) says that the therapist is a "teacher, trainer, and resource person with a heavy emphasis on involvement" (p. 239). As a teacher, the TA therapist explains concepts such as structural analysis, script analysis, and game analysis. As noted earlier, TA stresses the importance of equality in the client/therapist relationship, an equality that is manifested through contracts between the group leader and the individual members that make them partners in the therapeutic process. Consequently, the role of the therapist is to apply his or her knowledge to fulfilling the contract that the client initiates.

From the perspective of redecision therapy, the group leader's function is to create a climate in which people can discover for themselves how the games they play are supporting chronic bad feelings and how they hold onto these feelings to support their life script and early decisions. Another function of the TA therapist is challenging group members to discover and experiment with more effective ways of being. In short, the role of the therapist is to help members acquire the tools necessary to effect change.

Robert Goulding (1975, 1987) favors rapid and decisive therapy that is aimed at clients' autonomy; he objects to lengthy group therapy that fosters dependence and strokes sickness. He encourages clients to rely on their own inner resources rather than continuing to look to the therapist for direction. Goulding sees himself as a guide and a mapmaker. It is the client who makes the journey.

The therapist's style in a TA group tends to promote individual work within a group setting, rather than facilitating interaction between group members and thus encouraging therapy *by* the members. In TA groups the leader assumes an active role as the primary agent of change (Kapur & Miller, 1987). The focus tends to be on interactions between the group leader and individual members. The therapist occupies a central position in the group and works with each client in turn. Robert Goulding (1986) writes "Our model for group therapy is that the therapist is a facilitator, bringing about change by asking the patient to work within the group" (pp. 26–27). Woollams and Brown (1978) capture the TA therapist's role thusly: "Our model of working with clients in groups is to focus mostly on one client at a time, helping her to reach her individual contract" (p. 259).

Therapeutic Procedures and Techniques

This section discusses the carrying out of the contract, the first step in the TA therapeutic process, and examines the two main variants of TA group therapy. It should be noted that not all TA therapists conduct their groups according to the order and structuring described here.

Contracts: The Structure of the Therapeutic Relationship

Transactional analysis is largely based on the capacity and willingness of the group participants to understand and design a therapeutic contract that requires them to state their intentions and set personal goals. Contracts are the key to all TA groups. They are specific and measurable and contain a concrete statement of the objectives that the group participant intends to attain and the criteria to determine how and when these goals are to be met. Contracts place the responsibility on members for clearly defining what, how, and when *they* want to change. Thus, from the very beginning, members learn that therapy is a shared responsibility and that they cannot passively wait for the leader to direct the group. In short, the members' contracts establish the departure point for group activity.

Group members agree to work on specific issues within the group. For example, a woman who reacts to others in a highly critical way can design a contract that will lead to changing such behavior. Her contract describes *what* she will do in the group to change her actions and experiences, *when* she will do it, and *how many times*. The contract can then be expanded to include situations outside the group.

Dusay (1983) asserts that a well-stated treatment contract will make it clear whether clients are obtaining what they want from therapy. He says that such a contract is an acceptable answer to the therapist's question

"How will you know and how will I know when you get what you are coming to the group for?" Since everyone in the group knows the other participants' contracts, a productive focus can be developed in the group sessions. The process of TA treatment focuses primarily on change as defined by the contract, and there is an Adult to Adult agreement between the therapist and the client about what the process and the desired goal will be (Dusay & Dusay, 1989).

Contracts are intended to be practical tools for helping people change themselves. As such, they cannot be rigid and should be open to revision. Long-term contracts can be limiting; thus, it is often useful to develop contracts in steps, subject to modification as members penetrate more deeply the areas that they are seeking to change. Furthermore, people sometimes make contracts that later prove unacceptable.

Unacceptable contracts include Parent contracts, contracts to change others, game contracts, "forever" contracts, and ulterior contracts (M. Goulding & Goulding, 1979). Parent contracts are generally based on what clients feel they *should* change rather than on what they themselves *want* to change. Contracts to change others are simply unworkable. We cannot change others; we can change only ourselves. In game contracts clients seek therapist approval for actions that lead to the clients' feeling hurt or unhappy. Ulterior contracts (pacts between therapist and client to prevent the client from reaching his or her goals) are a denial of the client's power. The Gouldings suggest that therapists pay attention to how their language patterns may convey a denial of autonomy. When therapists use words such as *try, can,* and *perhaps,* they reinforce the client's lack of autonomy.

The Classical Bernian Approach

Berne (1961) developed four techniques for conducting therapy groups, as ways of carrying out the contracts formulated between the leader and group participants: (1) structural analysis, (2) transactional analysis, (3) game analysis, and (4) life-script analysis.

Structural Analysis.   Structural analysis is a tool by which group members become aware of the content and functioning of their ego states of Parent, Adult, and Child. The aim of structural analysis is to help members learn how to identify and analyze their own ego states, so that they can change behavioral patterns that they feel stuck with. The process allows participants to discover which ego state their behavior is based on. In turn, this awareness makes it possible for clients to discover what their options may be.

Berne (1961) discusses two types of problems related to the structure of personality that can be considered by structural analysis: (1) exclusion and (2) contamination. The first one, *exclusion,* is manifested by a stereotyped attitude that is rigidly held to in threatening situations. Put in another way, exclusion consists of rigid ego-state boundaries that don't allow free movement; that is, one ego state "blocks out" another ego state. There are three forms of exclusion: the Constant Parent, the Constant Adult, and the Constant Child, in each of which the person relates primarily as Parent, as Adult, or as Child, respectively. The *Constant Parent,* which excludes the Adult and the Child, is typically found in duty-bound people, sometimes known as "workaholics." Such people are generally judgmental and demanding of others and have a difficult time playing. The *Constant Adult,* which excludes the Parent and the Child, is found in people who are highly objective—that is, who tend to be involved in, and concerned with, only facts. Such people often have the emotional appeal and spontaneity of a computer. The *Constant Child,* which excludes the Adult and the Parent, is typically found in people who refuse to grow up and face the demands of reality. Such people are reluctant to make their own decisions, preferring instead to remain dependent on others in order to avoid taking responsibility for their own behavior.

Contamination exists when the boundary of one ego state overlaps that of another one and the contents of the two states intermix. It is possible for either the Parent or the Child, or both, to contaminate the Adult. An example of the Adult's being contaminated by the Parent can be found in statements such as "Keep with your own kind, and never mix with people who are 'different' " or "Look out! People will take advantage of you." An example of the Adult's being contaminated by the Child is seen in statements like "Nobody ever likes me; everybody always picks on me" or "I deserve whatever I want—immediately."

Transactional Analysis. Transactional analysis, which is basically a description of what people do and say to one another, is best done in therapy groups, according to Berne (1961). When people, such as the members of a group, are interacting, they are in effect conducting transactions among their ego states. Berne describes three types of transactions: (1) complementary, (2) crossed, and (3) ulterior.

1. *Complementary transactions* occur when a message sent from a specific ego state gets the predicted response from a specific ego state of another person. For example, a complementary Child/Child transaction takes place when Fred's Child says "Let's dance" and Sharon's Child replies "Oh, yes! That's fun."

2. *Crossed transactions* occur when an unexpected response is made to a message that a person sends out—for example, when Sharon's Parent responds to Fred's invitation to dance (which comes from his Child) with "I'm not going to make a fool of myself on the dance floor!"

3. *Ulterior transactions* are more complex, because they involve more than two ego states and a disguised message. For example, Fred might say "Let's dance—that is, if you don't think we'll make fools of ourselves." Here there is a message from Fred's Child to Sharon's Child (see above) and a

disguised message from Fred's Parent to Sharon's Child suggesting more decorous behavior.

Game Analysis. Berne's (1964) *Games People Play* is an investigation of the defense strategies and "gimmicks" people use to prevent intimacy and manipulate others in order to get what they want. As indicated earlier, games have certain payoffs—generally, a "bad" feeling that the player experiences and reinforcement of script decisions such as "Nobody loves me" or "No matter how hard I try, I can't make it." Berne (1964) stresses the importance of learning to observe and understand why games take place, what their payoffs are, and how they keep people apart.

The classical TA group devotes considerable time to helping members become aware of the games they initiate and participate in, so that they can come to develop intimate and nonmanipulative relationships. James and Jongeward (1971) write of the importance of clients' recognizing games and identifying their roles in these games. With regard to helping clients learn how to interrupt and avoid games, they state simply "The game may be foiled by a refusal to play or a refusal to give a pay-off" (p. 208).

Life-Script Analysis. Recall that life scripts are basically plans, decided on at an early age, for meeting our needs in the world as we see them from the viewpoint of our life position. Briefly, life-script analysis refers to that part of the TA therapeutic process devoted to identifying the life pattern of a person and involves both transactional and game analysis. As an example, Berne (1961) describes a common tragic script, the drama of a woman who marries one alcoholic after another. Generally, this script calls for the heroine/wife to rescue, by means of a magical cure, the alcoholic husband, who, typically, is a victim of circumstances that he cannot control. It takes little imagination to see the endless possibilities for games and Parent, Adult, and Child transactions in such a drama and the collection of many feelings.

Script analysis helps demonstrate the process by which group members acquired a script and the strategies they employ to justify their actions based on it. The aim is to help members open up possibilities for making changes in their early programming. The participants are asked to recall their favorite stories as children, to determine how they fit into these stories or fables, and to see how these stories fit their current life experiences.

The analysis of the life script of a group member is based on the drama of his or her original family. Through the process of acting out portions of their life script in the group sessions, members learn about the injunctions they uncritically accepted as children, the decisions they made in response to these messages, and the games and rackets they now employ to keep these early decisions alive. The group leader can gather information about the family drama by taking a history of the childhood experiences of the members. Members can be asked the kind of drama that would probably result if their family were put on the stage. Other group members can be given a part to play in this family play.

These and other cognitive and emotive techniques often help the group participants recall early events and the feelings associated with them. The group setting provides a supportive place to explore the ways in which these past situations are influencing the participants. By being a part of the process of the self-discovery of other members, each member increases the opportunities for coming to a deeper understanding of his or her own unfinished psychological business.

Didactic procedures such as the Karpman Drama Triangle (see Karpman, 1968) can be employed to help members identify scripts and games. The triangle has a "Persecutor," a "Rescuer," and a "Victim." Persecutors criticize others and invite others to assume the position of Victim. Rescuers depend on helping or "saving" others in order to feel OK. If others do not play the role of Victim, then the Rescuers are not able to play their game of taking care of others. Victims assume a passive and helpless stance, maintaining that they have no power to change unless someone else changes first. It should be noted that the same individual might alternate between all three of these roles at different times in various situations. However, most group members have a favorite position in life, which may become evident in the way they behave in the group sessions. For example, Betty may quickly come to the rescue of any member who experiences sadness. Betty may do her best to provide such members with ready-made solutions for complex problems. In her life outside of the group Betty may well depend on others to need her so that she can save them from pain. Another member, Jim, may assume a victimlike stance by continually complaining about how awful his life is and how he could change if only others would make certain changes first. The group situation allows members to analyze the positions they often take and the games they play, both in the group and in everyday life. As a result, group participants gain the capacity to take some initial steps to break out of self-defeating patterns. As the group members analyze their own life from a TA perspective, they can check the accuracy of their self-interpretations by asking for feedback from the leader and the other members.

Script analysis can be carried out by means of a script checklist. Steiner (1967) developed a life-script questionnaire that can be used as a catalyst in group situations to help members explore significant components of their life script, among them, life positions and games. In completing this script checklist, members provide basic information such as the general direction of their life, the models in their life, the nature of their injunctions, the payoffs they seek in life, and the tragic ending they expect from life.

The Gouldings' Redecisional Approach to Groups

The *redecision model*, developed by the Gouldings, differs from the classical Bernian group model in a number of important respects. The following is a summary of the redecisional approach to TA groups, based on an adaptation of some of the chief works of the Gouldings (1976, 1978, 1979, 1982, 1987). It should be mentioned that the core of the work in this approach consists of helping clients make redecisions while they are in their Child ego state. This is done by having them reexperience an early scene as if the situation were occurring in the present. Merely talking about past events or understanding early feelings and decisions from the Adult ego state is not sufficient to push them beyond the places where they are stuck. The plan that helps members get into their Child ego state and make a new decision from that perspective can best be seen in the stages of redecision group therapy, which follow.

The Initial Stages of the Group.   The first step in the group process consists of establishing good contact. To a large extent, the outcome for group members depends on the quality of the relationship that the group leader is able to establish with the members and the leader's competence. Even though the group leader makes good contact with the members and is competent, Robert Goulding (1982) has found, the members' most important symptom is typically not brought forward initially. He finds that group participants sometimes tell what they *think* is significant but avoid addressing more pertinent issues. Therefore, Goulding attempts to get at the chief complaint of the client. Obviously, the trust factor in the group has a lot to do with the willingness of clients to get to their chief complaint.

The next step in the process consists of making an inquiry into the group member's actual contract for change. A typical question is "What are you going to change about yourself today?" Notice that members are not asked to state what they hope to change or what the therapist will do to bring about change; nor are they asked what changes they want in the future. The emphasis is upon the client's *taking action now* to do something that will bring about change.

The Working Stage of the Group.   After contracts have been formulated, the Goulding group focuses on *rackets*—essentially, collections of bad feelings that people experience when they play games and that they use to justify their life script and, ultimately, their decisions (M. Goulding & Goulding, 1979). The aim is to expose the rackets of group members and have them take responsibility for them. For example, a person with an "anger racket"—one who is chronically angry—may be asked "What do you do to maintain your anger?" Beginning with recent events, the person is led back through his or her life in an attempt to remember early situations involving anger. As in Gestalt, members are asked to *be* in these situations—to recall them not as observers but as participants in the here and now. Members are asked to act out both their own responses and the responses of other significant people in the scene.

As I said earlier, Robert Goulding asserts that people are responsible for their feelings and that they sometimes respond in a stereotyped and predictable way based on their rackets. Thus, from the initial sessions, participants are taught that they are autonomous and responsible for *both* their actions and their feelings (1975, p. 240).

During this stage of group work the Gouldings also focus on games. Games are analyzed, mainly to see how they support and maintain rackets and how they fit with one's life script. In this connection much work is devoted to looking for evidence of the participants' early decisions, discovering the original injunction that lies at the base of these early decisions, and determining the kinds of strokes that the person received to support the original injunction.

A major function of the TA group leader is to alert the members to take responsibility for their thinking/feeling/behaving. Members are challenged when they use "cop-out language," such as *can't, perhaps, if it weren't for, try,* and other words that keep members from claiming their own power. The leader also creates a group climate in which the members rapidly become aware of how they maintain their chronic bad feelings by their behavior and fantasy. It is the therapist's task to challenge them to discover alternate choices.

The Gouldings take the position that clients can change *rapidly,* without years of analysis. Consequently, they stress the redecisional aspects of TA therapy on the assumption that when clients perceive that they are responsible for their early decisions, they also have it in their power to change those decisions (R. Goulding & Goulding, 1976). This approach emphasizes helping participants reexperience early, highly emotional situations in order to generate the energy to break through the places where they are stuck (M. Goulding & Goulding, 1979): "Most good therapy is centered on assisting the patient to break through a series of impasses, which had their origins in childhood, and decisions he made about these messages" (p. 6). Such breakthroughs, according to the Gouldings, usually require that participants remember and relive situations involving real parenting figures. Through the use of fantasy, in which group members reexperience how their parents sounded, acted, and looked, the therapist creates a psychological climate that allows members to feel the same emotional intensity they felt when, as children, they made their original decisions. The Gouldings stress that if participants are to be successful in going beyond an impasse, they must be in the Child ego state, actually reliving psychologically early scenes, rather than in their Adult ego state, merely thinking about new information and insights (R. Goulding, 1987, p. 305).

The Final Stages of the Group. Once a redecision is made from the Child ego state, the changes in one's voice, body, and facial expressions are obvious to everyone in the group. However, Robert Goulding (1982) emphasizes the importance of reinforcement of this redecision by the client and by the others in the group. The group process provides support for members who begin to feel and behave in new ways. Group members are encouraged to tell a new story in the group to replace their old story, and they typically receive verbal and nonverbal stroking to support their new decision. Attention is also given to ways that members might devise other support systems outside the group. It is also important for members to plan specific ways in which they will change their behavior, thinking, feeling, and body. The focus during the final phase of group work is challenging the members to transfer their changes from the therapy situation to their daily life and then supporting them in these changes. Before members set out on their own, it is important that they fantasize about how some of their changes are likely to lead to other changes. It is well for them to prepare themselves for the new situations they will face when they leave the group and to develop support systems that will help them creatively deal with new problem situations and new successes when they arise (for example, old anxiety arising from these successes).

Evaluation of Transactional Analysis

Transactional analysis provides a cognitive basis for group process that is often missing in some experientially oriented groups. The insistence of this approach on having members get out of their victimlike positions and realize that they don't have to be chained to early decisions is, I believe, crucial to effective therapy. In my opinion TA, especially redecision therapy, provides a useful conceptual framework for understanding *how* these early decisions are made, how they are related to present self-defeating life stances, how games perpetuate bad feelings, and how our lives are governed by old programs and scripts. Redecision therapy has been called a "genuine innovation in both theory and method of psychotherapy" (Madison, 1985). Developed by the Gouldings, redecision therapy began with psychoanalysis, included key concepts of Berne's system, incorporated techniques of Perls's Gestalt therapy, and became an integration of all three systems in novel ways (Madison, 1985; McCormick & Pulleyblank, 1985).

I consider the emphasis on becoming aware of outmoded early decisions to be one of the major contributions of TA. Many people are enslaved by these early decisions; they cling to parental messages, live their lives by unexamined injunctions, and frequently are not even aware that they are living in a psychological straitjacket. Conceptually, redecision therapy offers tools that members can use to free themselves from an archaic life script and achieve a successful and meaningful life.

Personally, I favor integrating TA concepts and practices with Gestalt techniques. Of course, this is what the Gouldings have accomplished. Working from a theoretical base provided by TA, they use a combination of therapeutic methods, including psychodrama, fantasy and imagery, Gestalt techniques, behavior therapy, desensitization, family-therapy procedures, and psychosynthesis. For example, the value that the Gouldings find in emotional experiences is evidenced by their stress on having clients reexperience the early scenes in which they made decisions. At the same time, they place considerable emphasis on helping group members reach a cognitive understanding of how outmoded patterns of thinking, feeling, and behaving are interrelated and how such patterns are influencing their current lives. They contend that pure Gestaltists may fail to give such cognitive feedback and that pure TA therapists seldom encourage the intense emotional work that leads to breaking through those impasses that prevent further growth.

This blending of TA concepts with Gestalt techniques lessens, to some extent, certain objections that I have to both therapeutic approaches. As I see it, Gestalt therapy does not sufficiently emphasize the cognitive factors, so that it tends to leave participants with many experiences that have little meaning attached to them. TA, in contrast, tends to overemphasize cognitive factors, so that it can result in therapy that is intellectually stimulating but emotionally arid.

In all fairness, I should mention that some writers are opposed to combining transactional analysis with Gestalt therapy. Simkin (1979) has warned that such a blending can result in ineffective therapy unless this synthesis is carried out by a gifted clinician. From Simkin's perspective, good therapeutic work encourages clients to integrate new behavior through awareness rather than interrupting the experiential process to focus on cognitive explanations. He adds: "Mixing what is essentially a cognitive-rational approach (TA) with what is essentially an experiential-existential approach (Gestalt therapy) is like trying to amalgamate water and oil—they simply do not mix well unless you keep shaking them continuously. The moment you stop, they begin to separate" (p. 277). Simkin and Yontef (1984) maintain that when Gestalt techniques are used in an analytic and cognitive style, these techniques are not Gestalt therapy.

In spite of the criticisms of combining TA theory and Gestalt techniques, some research supports the idea. In an encounter-group study by Lieberman, Yalom, and Miles (1973), positive outcomes of a group experience were traced to a combination of *meaning attribution* (explaining, clarifying, providing a cognitive framework for change, interpreting, and assisting members to make sense of emotional experiences) and *emotional stimulation* (catharsis, confrontation, high self-disclosure, intense emotionality, and reexperiencing of emotional situations). These researchers found that although emotional experiences may be related to learning, such experiences are not, in themselves, sufficient and that affective experiences need to be combined with some form of cognitive learning.

Like most of the other approaches to therapeutic groups that have been discussed so far, TA can be criticized on the ground that its theory and procedures have not been adequately subjected to empirical validation. Indeed, many of the concepts formulated by Berne were stated in such a manner that it would be impossible to design a research study to test them. It appears that most of the claims of success rest on clinical observations and testimonials. Conducting well-designed research studies to evaluate the process and outcome of group therapy has surely not been one of the strengths of TA. This is not to say that no one has attempted to study the outcomes of TA group therapy. Research studies are described in various issues of the *Transactional Analysis Journal.* Some TA therapists contend that the use of specific contracts provides built-in accountability. Measures can be taken to determine the extent to which members have fulfilled their contract and benefited from group therapy. In my opinion TA could benefit by integrating the commitment to research that is characteristic of behavior therapy.

As I mentioned, TA group leaders tend to foster individual work in a group, rather than promoting free interaction among the members. My personal bias is that this style of leadership does not make the optimum use of the interactive qualities inherent in group process. Kapur and Miller (1987) suggest that future research on TA groups could well measure the relative lack of attention paid by TA clinicians to the unique properties of groups. Based on their research, Kapur and Miller would like to see TA therapists encourage processes such as cohesiveness and universality by varying their therapeutic technique. They also suggest a decentralized role for the group leader, with more emphasis on promoting spontaneous interaction among members. According to Kapur and Miller, there is a need for further controlled research designs in order to determine the effects of deliberate variation of therapeutic technique on group processes and on outcome.

A final problem I have with transactional analysis relates to the way in which some practitioners use the structure and vocabulary of this system to avoid genuine contact with their clients or to keep from revealing their reactions. The structure of TA can be used by the therapist to avoid person-to-person interactions and to focus on labeling ego states, devising contracts, and directing traffic between transactions. Also, I have observed some group members who seem to be using TA jargon to deceive themselves into believing that they are becoming self-actualized when, in reality, they are only learning new terms to identify old processes. Some TA clients also tend to slip into the use of jargon as an intellectual front that they can safely hide behind. In fairness, I should emphasize that the dangers of becoming lost in the structure and vocabulary of TA can be lessened by a therapist who confronts members when they are misusing the model. I see value in the TA model, particularly for practitioners who are willing to combine TA theory with the concepts and therapeutic techniques of other models.

Applying TA in Multicultural Settings

The contractual approach to therapy has much to offer in a multicultural context. As we have seen in this chapter, TA clients decide what they are willing to change. Their contracts act as a safeguard against therapists' imposing their cultural values.

TA provides a structured approach that teaches clients about specific ways in which their early decisions have a continuing influence on their present behavior. The structure allows clients to see connections between what they learned in their family and their attitudes toward others. The structure provided by analysis of the life script can be especially useful as a catalyst for exploration in groups. Ethnic clients are likely to find this type of structure useful, for it helps them to understand how their culture has influenced them.

To my way of thinking, two of the major assets of TA groups are the focus on cultural and familial injunctions and the emphasis on early decisions. Consider some of the following injunctions, any of which you are likely to hear if you work with ethnic clients: "Don't cry, or at least don't shed tears in public." "Do not confront your parents." "Live up to the expectations of your parents and your family." "Don't be too concerned about yourself." "Do not show your weaknesses." "Don't talk about your family or about family problems with strangers." "Don't put your own good above the social good." These cultural injunctions provide a good beginning place for exploration in a group setting. It is important for group leaders to respect their clients' cultural injunctions, yet at the same time they can create a climate in which these clients can begin to question the degree to which they have accepted these messages. The clients will then be in a position to decide in what ways they want to be different and how they want to expand their boundaries. Some injunctions, and the decisions based on them, may not be changed if the client determines that change is not necessary. One caution is that therapists should avoid challenging clients too quickly, so that they lessen the chances of having dropouts.

A limitation of applying TA to multicultural group practice is that the terminology may seem foreign to some ethnic clients. Even though TA therapists assert that TA is simple and easy to understand, many clients may have difficulty with the complexity of concepts such as crossed transactions, the structure and dynamics of games, and the subcomponents of the various ego states. Before TA group leaders challenge the life scripts of ethnic group members, it is well for them to make sure that a trusting relationship has been established and that these clients have demonstrated a readiness to question their family traditions. In some cultures it is considered taboo to doubt family traditions, let alone talk about such matters in a nonfamily group.

Questions for Reflection and Discussion

1. To what degree do you think that children are "scripted" and then destined to live out their life in accord with this script? Do you think that children actually make decisions about the messages they receive, or do you think they accept the injunctions uncritically? How does your answer influence the manner in which you would work with a group?

2. What are some of the possibilities you can see in combining TA theory with Gestalt techniques? What are the advantages, if any, of such a merger of theories?

3. What are some of the major injunctions that you were exposed to, either verbally or nonverbally? What injunctions still have an influence on you?

4. What early decisions did you make about yourself and about others during your childhood years? To what extent are these decisions still an influential factor in your life? Are you aware of making any basic changes in your early decisions?

5. If you were to join a TA group, what kind of contract do you think you'd draw up? What are the advantages and disadvantages that you can think of in insisting that all group members formulate a therapeutic contract?

6. Consider the possibility that you might be a leader of a TA group. How do you think that your patterns of games, rackets, and early decisions would affect the way in which you worked with certain members in your group? Using what you know of yourself, are there any types of member that you think you might have particular difficulty working with?

7. TA is generally a didactic model of group therapy. Would you be comfortable in the role of teaching, along with the structuring that would be expected if you were to function within this model? What aspects of this educational model might you incorporate into your style of group leadership, even if you did not adhere to TA theory?

8. TA is direct. As a leader you would be talking with participants about the games they play and the ways they cling to chronic bad feelings. Do you think you would be able to be direct in working with members of your group to recognize their games and help them design contracts for what they would change?

9. Compare and contrast TA with psychoanalytic therapy with respect to the group leader's role and functions. Which role seems more compatible with your leadership style and view of group counseling? Why?

10. As you know, a contract is a basic part of a TA group. How do you think you'd proceed with one or more group members who refused to negotiate a contract with you? What might you do with a member who argued that making a contract seemed rigid?

Where to Go from Here

According to Dusay (1986), TA is recognized as a complete theory of personality and an entire system of psychotherapy. The regulatory body, the International Transactional Analysis Association, certifies the therapists who enroll in its rigorous training program. TA is practiced internationally, by both professionals and paraprofessionals. It is applied to business and organizational development. Prison inmates, schizophrenic patients, and people in drug-rehabilitation programs and outpatient clients from all socioeconomic levels have participated in TA treatment programs.

If you want to learn more about TA group work, I encourage you to participate in a workshop or a group as a member. Experiencing TA as a member could benefit you personally by bringing many of the concepts in this chapter to life in a concrete way. Also, you may want to consider attending a teaching workshop where you can apply TA principles in a group setting.

For further information, contact

International Transactional Analysis Association
1772 Vallejo Street
San Francisco, CA 94123
Phone: (415) 885-5992

This association provides guidelines for becoming a Certified Clinical Member. Before certification is granted, candidates must pass both a written and an oral examination, in which samples of their work are reviewed by a board of examiners to determine their level of clinical competence.

RECOMMENDED SUPPLEMENTARY READINGS

The *Transactional Analysis Journal* is a good source for keeping current with the developments of TA theory, clinical applications, and research. The subscription rate is $25 annually, and the journal is published quarterly. For information concerning dues for various membership classifications and for journal subscriptions, contact the ITAA office, 1772 Vallejo Street, San Francisco, CA 94123.

Redecision therapy: Expanded perspectives (Kadis, 1985) consists of a collection of articles on the theory and technique of redecision therapy as well as the applications of this approach to specific settings.

Changing lives through redecision therapy (M. Goulding & Goulding, 1979) is the work I would recommend to a practitioner who had time to read only one book on the TA approach to group work. The authors describe their successful integration of Gestalt and behavioral techniques into their TA theoretical framework.

Born to win: Transactional analysis with Gestalt experiments (James & Jongeward, 1971) is a valuable source for both laypersons and group leaders. This easy-to-read book presents an overview of the principles of transactional analysis and a description of Gestalt experiments in such diverse areas as stroking, life scripts, parenting, childhood, personal and sexual identity, game playing, adulthood, and autonomy.

Scripts people live: Transactional analysis of life scripts (Steiner, 1974) is a comprehensive discussion of life scripts that can be applied to group work.

Principles of group treatment (Berne, 1966) provides a useful discussion of group structure and process from the TA perspective.

REFERENCES AND SUGGESTED READINGS*

Berne, E. (1961). *Transactional analysis in psychotherapy*. New York: Grove Press.
Berne, E. (1964). *Games people play*. New York: Grove Press.
Berne, E. (1966). *Principles of group treatment*. New York: Oxford University Press.
Berne, E. (1972). *What do you say after you say hello?* New York: Grove Press.

*Books and articles marked with an asterisk are suggested for further study.

Dusay, J. M. (1983). Transactional analysis in groups. In H. I. Kaplan & B. J. Sadock (Eds.), *Comprehensive group psychotherapy* (2nd ed.). Baltimore: Williams & Wilkins.

*Dusay, J. M. (1986). Transactional analysis. In I. L. Kutash & A. Wolf (Eds.), *Psychotherapist's casebook* (pp. 413–423). San Francisco: Jossey-Bass.

Dusay, J. M., & Dusay, K. M. (1989). Transactional analysis. In R. J. Corsini & D. Wedding (Eds.), *Current psychotherapies* (4th ed.). Itasca, IL: F. E. Peacock.

Goulding, M. M. (1985a). The joy of psychotherapy. In L. B. Kadis (Ed.), *Redecision therapy: Expanded perspectives* (pp. 4–8). Watsonville, CA: Western Institute for Group and Family Therapy.

Goulding, M. M. (1985b). A redecision exercise. In L. B. Kadis (Ed.), *Redecision therapy: Expanded perspectives* (pp. 65–67). Watsonville, CA: Western Institute for Group and Family Therapy.

*Goulding, M. M. (1987). Transactional analysis and redecision therapy. In J. K. Zeig (Ed.), *The evolution of psychotherapy* (pp. 285–299). New York: Brunner/Mazel.

*Goulding, M., & Goulding, R. (1979). *Changing lives through redecision therapy.* New York: Brunner/Mazel.

*Goulding, R. (1975). The formation and beginning process of transactional analysis groups. In G. Gazda (Ed.), *Basic approaches to group psychotherapy and group counseling* (2nd ed.). Springfield, IL: Charles C Thomas.

*Goulding, R. (1982). Transactional analysis/Gestalt/redecision therapy. In G. Gazda (Ed.), *Basic approaches to group psychotherapy and group counseling* (3rd ed.). Springfield, IL: Charles C Thomas.

*Goulding, R. (1985). History of redecision therapy. In L. B. Kadis (Ed.), *Redecision therapy: Expanded perspectives* (pp. 9–11). Watsonville, CA: Western Institute for Group and Family Therapy.

Goulding, R. (1986). Discussion of therapist transparency. *International Journal of Group Psychotherapy, 36*(1), 25–27.

*Goulding, R. (1987). Group therapy: Mainline or sideline? In J. K. Zeig (Ed.), *The evolution of psychotherapy* (pp. 300–311). New York: Brunner/Mazel.

Goulding, R., & Goulding, M. (1976). Injunctions, decisions, and redecisions. *Transactional Analysis Journal, 6*(1), 41–48.

*Goulding, R., & Goulding, M. (1978). *The power is in the patient.* San Francisco: TA Press.

Harris, T. (1967). *I'm OK—you're OK.* New York: Avon.

*James, M., & Jongeward, D. (1971). *Born to win: Transactional analysis with Gestalt experiments.* Reading, MA: Addison-Wesley.

*Kadis, L. B. (Ed.). (1985). *Redecision therapy: Expanded perspectives.* Watsonville, CA: Western Institute for Group and Family Therapy.

Kapur, R., & Miller, K. (1987). A comparison between therapeutic factors in TA and psychodynamic therapy groups. *Transactional Analysis Journal, 17*(1), 294–300.

Karpman, S. (1968). Fairy tales and script drama analysis. *Transactional Analysis Bulletin, 7*(26), 39–43.

Lieberman, M. A., Yalom, I., & Miles, M. (1973). *Encounter groups: First facts.* New York: Basic Books.

Madison, P. (1985). Redecision therapy: What it is, how and why it works. In L. B. Kadis (Ed.), *Redecision therapy: Expanded perspectives* (pp. 20–25). Watsonville, CA: Western Institute for Group and Family Therapy.

McCormick, P., & Pulleyblank, E. (1985). The stages of redecision therapy. In L. B. Kadis (Ed.), *Redecision therapy: Expanded perspectives* (pp. 51–59). Watsonville, CA: Western Institute for Group and Family Therapy.

Saper, B. (1987). Humor in psychotherapy: Is it good or bad for the client? *Professional Psychology: Research and Practice, 19*(4), 360–367.

Simkin, J. S. (1979). Gestalt therapy. In R. J. Corsini (Ed.), *Current psychotherapies* (2nd ed.). Itasca, IL: F. E. Peacock.

Simkin, J. S., & Yontef, G. M. (1984). Gestalt therapy. In R. J. Corsini (Ed.), *Current psychotherapies* (3rd ed.). Itasca, IL: F. E. Peacock.

Steiner, C. (1967). A script checklist. *Transactional Analysis Bulletin, 6*(22), 38–39.

Steiner, C. (1974). *Scripts people live: Transactional analysis of life scripts.* New York: Grove Press.

Woollams, S., & Brown, M. (1978). *Transactional analysis.* Dexter, MI: Huron Valley Institute.

Behavioral
Group Therapy

Introduction

Behavioral approaches are becoming increasingly popular in group work. One of the reasons for this popularity is the emphasis these approaches place on teaching clients self-management skills they can use to control their lives, deal effectively with present and future problems, and function well *without* continued therapy. Writers with a behavioral orientation, such as Watson and Tharp (1989), have devoted books to the subject of helping people work toward "self-directed behavior." This goal is achieved through a wide variety of cognitive and behavioral action-oriented techniques. Most of these therapeutic techniques are procedures that clients can use on their own to solve interpersonal, emotional, and decision problems.

The main defining features and the basic procedures of contemporary behavior therapy are discussed by Berkowitz (1982). This approach

- focuses on selecting target behaviors to be changed and specifying the nature of the changes desired
- studies the observable events in the environment that are maintaining the behavior
- clearly specifies both the environmental changes and the intervention strategies that can modify behavior
- insists on data-based assessment and evaluation of treatment
- asks the question "Once a new behavior is established, how can it be maintained and generalized to new situations over a period of time?"

The term *behavior therapy* refers to the application of a diversity of techniques and procedures that are rooted in a variety of learning theories.

Since no single theory undergirds the practice of contemporary behavior therapy, there is no single group model that, strictly speaking, can be called a "behavioral group." Rather, there are various types of groups that operate on behavioral and learning principles. On this matter, Goldfried and Davison (1976) contend that it is undesirable to restrict the label *behavior therapy* to a single "school" of therapy that is defined in terms of a particular set of concepts and procedures. They think that behavior therapy is best conceptualized as a general orientation to clinical practice that is based on the experimental approach to the study of behavior.

A basic assumption of the behavioral perspective is that all problematic behaviors, cognitions, and emotions have been learned and that they can be modified by new learning. Rose (1980) contends that although this modification process is often called "therapy," it is more properly an educational experience in which individuals are involved in a teaching/learning process. It is educational in that people are taught how to view their own learning process, develop a new perspective on ways of learning, and try out more effective ways of changing their behaviors, cognitions, and emotions. Many of the techniques employed by groups of different orientations (such as rational-emotive therapy, reality therapy, and transactional analysis) share this basic assumption of group therapy as an educational process, and they stress the teaching/learning values inherent in a group context.

Another assumption of the behavioral orientation is that the behaviors that clients express *are* the problem (not merely symptoms of the problem). Successful resolution of these problematic behaviors resolves the problem, and a new set of problems does not necessarily arise. This behavioral perspective is in contrast to the relationship-oriented and insight-oriented approaches, which place considerable emphasis on clients' achieving insight into their problems as a prerequisite for change. Whereas the insight-oriented approaches assume that if clients understand the nature and causes of their symptoms, they will be better able to control their life, the behavioral approach assumes that change can take place without insight. Behavior therapists operate on the premise that changes in behavior can occur prior to understanding of oneself and that behavioral changes may well lead to an increased level of self-understanding.

Group leaders who operate from a behavioral perspective draw on a wide variety of interventions that are derived from social-learning theory, such as reinforcement, modeling, shaping, cognitive restructuring, desensitization, relaxation training, coaching, behavioral rehearsal, stimulus control, and discrimination training. However, behavioral group leaders may develop other strategies from diverse theoretical viewpoints, provided their effectiveness in meeting therapeutic goals can be demonstrated. Therefore, these leaders follow the progress of group members through the ongoing collection of data before, during, and after all interventions. Such an approach provides both the group leader and members with continuous feedback about therapeutic progress. In this sense, the behavioral leader is both a clinician and a scientist who is concerned with testing the efficacy of his or her techniques.

Key Concepts

Behavior therapy has some unique characteristics that set it apart from most of the other group approaches discussed in this book. It relies on the principles and procedures of the scientific method. Its experimentally derived principles of learning are systematically applied to help people change maladaptive behaviors. The distinguishing characteristic of behavioral practitioners is their systematic adherence to specification and measurement. In fact, unless problems and goals are specified and recorded, there is no true behavior therapy (Kuehnel & Liberman, 1986). Concepts and procedures are stated explicitly, tested empirically, and revised continually. Assessment and treatment occur simultaneously. Research is considered essential to providing effective treatments and to advancing beyond current therapeutic practices. In summary, the specific unique characteristics of behavior therapy are (1) conducting a behavioral assessment, (2) precisely spelling out treatment goals, (3) formulating a specific treatment procedure appropriate to a particular problem, and (4) objectively evaluating the outcomes of therapy.

Behavioral Assessment

Kuehnel and Liberman (1986) describe the process of pinpointing and specifying a client's behavioral problems as the core of behavior therapy, and they identify six steps in conducting a behavioral assessment. The first step is identifying behaviors that are considered maladaptive or problematic and to assess the frequency, intensity, and duration of such behaviors. The next step in behavioral assessment consists of determining the client's assets and strengths. The third step is putting the information gathered into the context of situations in which the problem behaviors occur. This includes specifying the probable antecedents and consequences of behavioral problems. The fourth step involves setting up a strategy to measure each of the identified problem behaviors. Assessing the frequency of selected target behaviors produces a baseline evaluation, which can be used as a reference point to determine the effectiveness of the interventions. In the fifth step the client's potential reinforcers are surveyed to identify those people, activities, and things that can provide motivation for treatment and for maintaining changes after therapy ends. The sixth and final step of the assessment process involves formulating treatment goals. Cooperatively, the client and the clinician explore alternative behaviors that could lead to effectively dealing with the problem situation.

Kuehnel and Liberman note that this assessment covers a client's functioning in the affective, cognitive, behavioral, and interpersonal domains. They see the therapist's task as applying principles of human learning to facilitate the replacement of maladaptive behaviors with more adaptive ones. Although they are not writing specifically about behavioral group counseling, the steps in the assessment process just described can be easily applied to group work.

Precise Therapeutic Goals

In most behavior-therapy groups the initial stages are devoted to clients' expanding the final step of their assessment by formulating specific statements of the personal goals that they want to achieve. Group members spell out concrete problematic behaviors they want to change and new skills they want to learn. Goals that clients typically set include reducing anxiety in test-taking situations, eliminating phobias that interfere with effective functioning, losing weight, and getting rid of addictions (to smoking, alcohol, or other drugs). New skills that clients typically want to acquire include

- learning to ask clearly and directly for what they want
- acquiring habits that lead to physical and psychological relaxation
- developing specific methods of self-control, such as exercising regularly, controlling eating patterns, and eliminating stress
- learning to be assertive without becoming aggressive
- monitoring their behavior or cognitions as a means to change
- learning to give and receive both positive and negative feedback
- being able to recognize and to challenge self-destructive thought patterns or irrational self-statements
- learning communication and social skills
- developing problem-solving strategies to cope with a variety of situations encountered in daily life

The task of the leader is to help the group members break down broad, general goals into specific, concrete, measurable goals that can be pursued in a systematic fashion. For example, if a group member says that he'd like to feel more adequate in social situations, the leader asks: "In what specific ways do you feel inadequate? What are the conditions under which you feel inadequate? Can you give me some concrete examples of the situations in which you feel inadequate? In what specific ways would you like to change your behavior?" The group can be used to help the members formulate answers to these difficult questions.

Treatment Plan

After members have specified their goals, a treatment plan to achieve these goals is formulated. Behavioral techniques are action oriented; therefore, members are expected to do *things,* not just reflect passively and engage in merely talking about their problems. The most commonly used techniques are those that lend themselves to group interaction, such as modeling, behavioral rehearsal, coaching, homework, feedback, training, and information giving; these are defined and discussed later in this chapter.

Objective Evaluation

Once target behaviors have been clearly identified, treatment goals specified, and therapeutic procedures delineated, the outcomes of therapy can be objectively assessed. Because behavioral groups emphasize the importance of evaluating the effectiveness of the techniques they employ, assessment of clients' progress toward their goals is continual. If a group is going to meet 10 weeks for social-skills training, for example, baseline data on these skills are likely to be taken at the initial session. Then, every subsequent session may include an assessment of behavioral changes, so that members can determine how successfully their objectives are being met. Providing members with ongoing feedback is a vital part of behavioral group therapy.

The decision to use certain techniques is based on their demonstrated effectiveness. The range of these techniques is quite wide, and many behaviorally oriented group counselors are very eclectic in their choices of treatment procedures. Lazarus (1986, p. 65) asserts that lasting change is a function of combined techniques, strategies, and modalities. Although he espouses the virtues of *technical eclecticism,* he adds that it is important to avoid a random melange of techniques based on subjective preferences and impressions. He emphasizes that the aim of behavior therapy is to formulate a consistent conceptual framework that permits (1) specification of goals and problems, (2) specification of treatment techniques to achieve these goals and remedy these problems, and (3) systematic measurement of the relative success of these techniques.

Role and Functions of the Group Leader

Because behavioral group counseling is considered a type of education, group leaders perform teaching functions. They are expected to assume an active, directive role in the group and to apply their knowledge of behavioral principles and skills to the resolution of problems. Thus, they carefully observe behavior to determine the conditions that are related to certain problems and the conditions that will facilitate change.

In discussing the social learning that occurs in therapy through modeling and imitation, Bandura (1969, 1977, 1986) suggests that most of the learning that takes place through direct experience can also be acquired by observing the behavior of others. In Bandura's view one of the fundamental processes by which clients learn new behavior is imitation of the social modeling provided by the therapist. Therefore, group leaders need to be aware of the impact of their values, attitudes, and behaviors on group members. If they are unaware of their power in actually influencing and shaping their clients' ways of behaving, they deny the central importance of their influence as human beings in the therapeutic process.

In addition to these broad functions, the behaviorally oriented group leader is also expected to perform a number of specific functions and tasks:

• Group leaders conduct intake interviews with prospective members, during which the preliminary assessment and orientation to the group takes place.

• Teaching participants about group process and how to get the most from the group is another leader function. The leader explains the purpose of the group, orients members to the activities and structure of the sessions, reviews the expectations of the members, and gives them suggestions on how the group can be personally useful.

• Group leaders conduct an ongoing assessment of member problems. Through procedures such as the initial interview, selected tests and inventories, and group discussion, the leader helps each member identify target behaviors that will give the group sessions some focus. This assessment includes a summary of the major strengths, interests, and achievements of each member, as well as a summary of those behaviors the member wants to change.

• Leaders draw on a wide array of techniques designed to achieve the members' stated goals.

• The leader collects data to determine the effectiveness of treatment for each member.

• A major function of leaders is serving as a model of appropriate behaviors and values. Also, leaders prepare and coach members to model by role-playing for one another how an individual might respond in a particular situation.

• Leaders provide reinforcement to members for their newly developing behavior and skills by making sure that even small achievements are recognized.

• An essential aspect of the leader's role is teaching group members that they are responsible for becoming actively involved in the group and for implementing new behaviors outside therapy. The behavioral approach demands action and a plan for change. Leaders help members understand that verbalizations and insight are not enough to produce change. To broaden their repertoire of adaptive behaviors, members must take action, experiment in the group, and practice homework assignments in real-life situations.

• The leader helps members prepare for termination. Members are reminded well ahead of the group's ending date. Thus, they have adequate time to discuss their reactions, to consolidate what they have learned, and to practice new skills they hope to apply at home and work. Appropriate referrals are made when reasonable goals have not been achieved. Suggestions are given for social activities that can help members generalize their learning in the group.

It is a good practice for leaders to gradually make the group less structured as it progresses. According to Rose and Edleson (1987), members should be given the opportunity to act as discussion leaders and therapeutic partners for others in the group in order to improve their self-management skills. Rose and Edleson suggest delegating many leadership responsibilities to the members.

A basic assumption of behavioral group therapy is that a good working relationship between the leader and members is a necessary, but not a sufficient, condition for change. Although it is unfair to cast behavior therapists in a cold and impersonal role that reduces them to programmed machines, it remains true that most behaviorally oriented group leaders do not assign an all-important role to the therapeutic relationship. In his stress-management programs, Meichenbaum (1985) emphasizes the value of establishing a collaborative working relationship between clients and trainers. He asserts that the degree to which treatment is successful is based in large part on the degree to which clients feel accepted, understood, and liked by the trainer.

Lazarus (1989) writes that it is necessary for therapists to establish a climate of respect and trust so that clients will confide personal and emotionally significant material. He views the client/therapist relationship on a continuum extending from a formal and businesslike approach, on one end, to a close-knit and warm approach, on the other. He suggests that it is appropriate to discuss the client/therapist relationship only when there is reason to think that it is getting in the way of therapeutic progress. Elsewhere, Lazarus (1986) finds certain personality characteristics to be associated with highly successful therapists. Such therapists possess a high and genuine respect for people, flexibility, responsibility, a nonjudgmental perspective, personal warmth, a good sense of humor, the willingness to practice what they preach, and a sense of congruence and authenticity. In short, behavioral group leaders must be skilled technicians who also possess the human qualities that lead to the climate of trust and care necessary for the effective use of these therapeutic techniques.

Stages of a Behavior-Therapy Group

The Multimethod Group Approach

This discussion of stages of a group is especially geared to the "multimethod group approach," which has been developed by Rose and his associates (see Rose & Edleson, 1987; Rose, Tallant, Tolman, & Subramanian, 1986). The multimethod group approach is called that because it uses various coping strategies for dealing with specific problems: training group members in systematic problem solving, cognitive restructuring, assertion training, relaxation training, behavioral rehearsal, and other strategies that are appropriate for specific problems. This approach involves gradually increasing members' participation and involvement in setting specific goals, planning, decision making, and mutual helping of others. The process progresses from a high degree of leader structure to a low degree of structure. Each client is helped to establish individualized goals and coping skills. Groups often have a common theme, such as stress management, anger control, or pain management. The goal goes beyond demonstrating change within the group setting. The ultimate goal is the transfer of change into the real world. Later group sessions are structured to make this generalization of learning more likely.

Finally, the approach is characterized by the use of data throughout the entire history of the group. These data are relied on in assessing the specific focus of treatment, in making clinical decisions, in identifying group-process concerns, and in evaluating outcomes. The multimethod approach also uses data to identify problems within the therapy group. These data are interpreted by the group leader and the group members, who may not always reach the same conclusions (Rose, 1986). A major source of these group data is a questionnaire administered at the end of each session. This questionnaire can pinpoint a number of problems within the group (Rose, 1984). Questions deal with self-disclosure, the interrelations of the members, and the perceived level of group cohesion. Participants are asked to describe their moods in the group. When there is a pattern of persistent negative attitudes, this problem can be discussed within the group. Members are also asked to evaluate their degree of satisfaction with the group. The evaluation instrument contains a number of open-ended questions that tap what members find useful, what they want more of or less of, and what direction the group should take. This instrument, which takes about 3 minutes to complete, is a useful way to detect group problems and provides a guide for needed changes in the structure of the group. (Copies of both the member's postsession questionnaire and a similar questionnaire for leaders are reproduced in the student manual of this text.)

The phases in the multimethod group approach are outlined by Rose and Edleson (1987). These phases, which are somewhat overlapping in time and in content, are guided by the group leader. Each phase focuses on different tasks for the leader.

1. In planning for group treatment, the leader establishes the group's purposes, assesses potential membership, recruits members, and decides on the structure of the group.

2. Orientation of the client and significant others to the possibilities and limitations of group therapy is done early in treatment. This process is essential if groups are to develop cohesion. Inadequate orientation often leads to a high dropout rate.

3. Assessment of the presenting problems and client resources is a basic part of behavioral groups. Data must be systematically collected before treatment, during treatment, immediately following treatment, and at some point after the termination of the group.

4. Interventions are designed to achieve change in a wide range of action-oriented methods. Problem situations are analyzed, and possible solutions are generated. Cognitive and behavioral procedures are typically used in working out plans for change. Homework is assigned to require clients to practice new solutions to problem situations in the real world. These assignments are monitored at subsequent sessions.

5. Strategies are developed that will enable members to transfer what they have learned in the group to everyday situations. Members are prepared for termination, and other sources for continued growth are presented. "Booster sessions" a few months after the termination of a group provide an opportunity for members to discuss what they have learned and how to deal with any new problems that might have arisen.

The following material on the stages of a behaviorally oriented group is based largely on the works of Sheldon Rose (1977, 1980, 1982, 1983, 1986) and Rose and Edleson (1987).

Initial Stage

Since prospective clients usually know very little about behavioral programs, before they join the group they are given all the pertinent information about group process. Pregroup individual interviews and the first group session are devoted to exploring the prospective members' expectations and to helping them decide whether they will join the group. Those who decide to join negotiate a treatment contract, spelling out what the group leader expects from the member over the course of the group, as well as what the client can expect from the leader.

During the early stages of the group the focus is on building cohesiveness, on becoming familiar with the structure of group therapy, and on identifying problematic behaviors that need to be corrected. Since the building of cohesion is the foundation for effective work during each stage of a group's development, the leader has a central role in the establishment of trust. According to Rose (1980), the leader must initially strive to make the group attractive to its members; create group situations that require social competence on the part of the members; create many functional roles that members can play in the group; delegate the leadership responsibility to the members in a gradual and appropriate manner; present situations in which the members function as therapeutic partners for each other; control excessive group conflict; and find ways of involving all members in the group interactions. Assessment is a vital component of these early sessions, because before treatment can begin, problems must be stated in specific behavioral terms. Complex problems are not avoided but are broken down into smaller components.

After the goals have been identified, the group leader begins to select therapeutic strategies to meet these goals. Cormier and Cormier (1985) suggest that counselors obtain a commitment from clients to do the work necessary to reach their goals, preferably in the form of a written contract. This contract specifies the procedure to select goals and the strategy to achieve these goals. There are several reasons for having a written contract. According to Gottman and Leiblum (1974), ethical practice suggests that in any form of treatment clients have a right to know in advance what they are committing themselves to. An unambiguous contract promotes trust and thus helps forge the therapeutic alliance. Also, a contract sharpens the clients' awareness of their roles as active participants in the therapeutic process. Finally, it serves to link specific therapeutic procedures to specific goals.

Working Stage: Treatment Plan and Application of Techniques

Treatment planning involves choosing the most appropriate set of procedures from among specific strategies that have been demonstrated to be effective in achieving behavioral change. It should be emphasized that *assessment* and *evaluation* continue throughout the working stage. Group leaders must go beyond the data they initially get at the pregroup interviews and initial group sessions. They must continually evaluate the degree of effectiveness of the sessions and how well treatment goals are being attained. To make this evaluation during the working stage, they continue to collect data on matters such as participation, member satisfaction, attendance, and completion of agreed-on assignments between sessions. These assessments also include gathering data to determine whether problems exist within the group and the degree to which group goals are being attained. Throughout the course of a group, individuals monitor their behaviors and the situations in which they occur. In this way they can quickly determine those strategies that are effective or ineffective. By means of this continuing evaluation process, both the members and the leader have a basis for looking at alternative and more effective strategies. We now turn to a description of some of these strategies that are typically used during the working stage: reinforcement, contingency contracts, modeling, behavior rehearsal, coaching, feedback, cognitive restructuring, problem solving, stress inoculation, coping-skills techniques, and the buddy system.

Reinforcement.   Reinforcement is a key intervention procedure in behavioral groups. In addition to the reinforcement provided by the group leader, other members reinforce one another through praise, approval, support, and attention. It is a good idea to begin each session with members reporting their successes, rather than their failures. This sets a positive tone in the group, provides reinforcement to those who did well in everyday life, and reminds the group that change is possible. Reports of success, no matter how modest the successful attempt was, are especially important when the members are improving but are still falling short of their expectations and when their changing behavior is being met with disapproval in their everyday environments. In these cases the reinforcement and support of the group are critical if members are to maintain their gains.

  If social reinforcement is a powerful method of shaping desired behaviors, so is self-reinforcement. Participants are taught how to reinforce themselves for their progress in order to increase their self-control and become less dependent on others.

Contingency Contracts.   Contingency contracts spell out the behaviors to be performed, changed, or discontinued; the rewards associated with the achievement of these goals; and the conditions under which rewards are to be received. Whenever possible, contracts also specify a time period for performing the desired behaviors. Effective contingency contracts should have the following features: (1) a clear description of the specific behaviors to be performed in the assignments; (2) a specification of the immediate reinforcement to be received as well as the group reinforcement; and (3) a description of the means by which the assignment is to be observed, measured, and recorded (Rose & Edleson, 1987). Contingency contracts are often used with children, but some adults find them patronizing.

Modeling.   Role modeling is one of the most powerful teaching tools available to the group leader. As we have seen with other approaches, an advantage of group counseling over individual counseling is that it offers members a variety of social and role models to imitate. The modeling is performed by both the leader and the participants.

What are the characteristics of effective models? Reviews of research (Bandura, 1969) indicate that a model who is similar to the observer in age, sex, race, and attitudes is more likely to be imitated than a model who is unlike the observer. Models who have a degree of prestige and status are more likely to be imitated than those who have a low level of prestige. If the client is too different from the model in many of these characteristics, the client tends to perceive the model's behavior as unrealistic. Also, models who are competent in their performance and who exhibit warmth tend to increase modeling effects. As much as possible, models should be reinforced in the presence of the observer, and observers should be reinforced for their imitation of the behavior that is modeled. Modeling of specific behavior is carried out in role playing during the sessions and practiced *in vivo*. For example, Henry has difficulty in initiating contacts with women and would like to feel freer in approaching them in his classes. He can observe another member modeling at least one way of effectively starting conversations with women. He can then practice in the sessions, using skills he has learned from the model. Then, Henry may make a contract to initiate several conversations in real life in his classes. Modeling is especially useful in assertion-training groups and in teaching clients how to make more constructive self-statements and change cognitive structures. The effect of modeling is enhanced by three other procedures: behavior rehearsal, coaching, and group feedback (Rose, 1982).

Behavior Rehearsal.   The aim of behavior rehearsal is to prepare members to perform the desired behaviors outside the group, when modeling cues will not be available. New behaviors are practiced in a safe context that simulates the real world. Not only are members protected from adverse consequences while they are learning, but they can also benefit from positive reinforcement, which is likely to increase their willingness to experiment with the new behavior in their daily life (Rose, 1977). Cormier and Cormier (1985) point out that the actual practicing of desirable behaviors should take place under conditions that are as similar as possible to the situations that occur in the client's environment, so that maximum generalization from the group to the real world will take place.

Behavior rehearsal, which can be thought of as a gradual shaping process, is a useful technique in teaching social skills. As Goldfried and Davison (1976) indicate, effective social interaction includes many behavioral components besides simply knowing *what* to say in a particular social situation. Specific factors such as vocal quality, rate of speech, gestures, body posture, eye contact, and other mannerisms are significant aspects. Goldfried and Davison suggest that it is wise to select only a few of these specific behaviors at a given time during a behavior rehearsal. They add that feedback is a useful mechanism of change during behavior rehearsals. This feedback can include the member's own subjective evaluation (which can be aided by either audio or videotaped replays of the rehearsal), the leader's commentary, and the reactions of other group members. As much as possible, Goldfried and Davison would like to see clients evaluate the adequacy of their own behavioral rehearsals, for this can help them learn to become more sensitive to their behavior and take corrective actions between sessions. Once members achieve successful performance in the group situation, they need to be made aware that application in real life is a basic part of behavior rehearsal. This can be accomplished by reminding members of the importance of completing homework assignments, by devoting some time in each session to deciding on appropriate assignments, and by routinely beginning each group session by checking on the assignments of each member.

Coaching.   In addition to modeling and behavior rehearsal, group members sometimes require *coaching*. This process consists of providing the members with general principles for performing the desired behavior effectively. Coaching seems to work best when the coach sits behind the client who is rehearsing. When a member gets stuck and does not know how to proceed, another group member can whisper suggestions. It is important, however, that coaching be reduced in subsequent role playing and that the member rehearse independently before trying out a new role in the real world.

Feedback.   After members practice a new behavior in a group session, as mentioned, others provide them with verbal reactions to their performances. These impressions can be given by fellow group members or the group leader. There are typically two aspects to feedback: praise and encouragement for the behavior and specific suggestions for correcting or modifying errors. Feedback is a useful part of learning new behaviors, especially if it is constructive, specific, and positive. Rose and Edleson (1987) provide the following guidelines for offering feedback on a group member's rehearsal performance:

- Positive feedback is given first, so that the member can be reinforced immediately.
- In criticizing a performance the observer says what could have been done differently.
- Useful feedback is specific and focuses on behaviors.
- In the early sessions observers are provided with specific criteria for giving feedback.
- Either the group leader or a group member reviews the feedback.

Cognitive Restructuring.   An individual's cognitive processes are likely to have implications for behavior change. Indeed, group members often reveal self-defeating thoughts and irrational self-talk when they find themselves in stressful situations. *Cognitive restructuring* is the process of identifying and evaluating one's cognitions, understanding the negative behavioral impact of certain thoughts, and learning to replace these cognitions with more realistic and appropriate thoughts. Ellis (1962) and Ellis and Harper (1975) have described in detail ways in which to identify self-defeating thinking, methods of sabotaging and undermining such irrational thinking, and methods of learning how to substitute rational thoughts in the place of irrational ones.

Rose (1986) describes several forms of cognitive restructuring used in groups. Some clients suffer from acute anxiety because they lack correct information, because they have difficulty in controlling thoughts, because they cling to irrational and self-defeating beliefs, or because they have assigned self-deprecating labels to themselves. To manage such anxiety, they can use certain strategies to change their cognitive processes. These procedures include acquiring corrective information, learning to control their thoughts, dispelling irrational beliefs, and relabeling themselves. Cognitive restructuring has been used to help anxious clients cope with test anxiety, speech anxiety, social anxiety, depression, and stress (Rose, 1986).

Elsewhere, Rose (1983) describes the process of cognitive restructuring as applied to group work. Initially, members may be taught through group exercises how to differentiate between self-defeating and self-enhancing statements. Typically, they provide one another with feedback and various models of a cognitive analysis. A further step is to encourage participants to devise self-enhancing statements that promote problem solving or effective actions. After clients decide on a set of realistic cognitive statements, cognitive modeling is used, in which the members imagine themselves in stressful situations and substitute self-enhancing statements for self-defeating remarks. The rationale for the use of cognitive restructuring is that a client's "self-talk" influences performance. Self-defeating thoughts can cause emotional distress and can interfere with performance. Constructive self-statements can lead to improved performance. In cognitive rehearsal members imitate the model and get feedback from others in the group. After several trials in the group they are given the assignment to practice a new set of statements at home before they try out a new style in the real world. In the final step of cognitive restructuring, homework is assigned at the end of each session and then monitored at the beginning of the following session. As members make progress, assignments can be developed at successive levels of difficulty.

Problem Solving.   Problem solving is a cognitive-behavioral approach that enables clients to develop a pattern of behavior to deal with various difficulties. The main goal is to identify the most effective solution to the problem and to provide systematic training in cognitive and behavioral skills that will help the client deal independently with it in the real world. The stages in the problem-solving process are described by Goldfried and Davison (1976):

1. Training begins with a general orientation to the problem. At this time clients are helped to understand why certain problem situations are likely to occur and are given the expectation that they can learn ways of effectively coping with these problems.
2. The next step consists of teaching clients to be specific in describing the *external* events leading to the problem situation as well as the *internal* events (thoughts and feelings). Clients define the problem situation, and then they identify the aspects that make the situation problematic for them and formulate their goals.
3. The suggestion of alternatives follows the formulation of the problem. Clients are instructed to brainstorm possible solutions and come up with diverse ways of coping with the situation. They are discouraged from evaluating any of the possible solutions until after all the suggestions have been presented.
4. The group helps the member evaluate the list of suggestions in light of their relative risk, appropriateness, and probable effectiveness. It is the client's task to predict which of the possible alternatives would be the best to follow and to decide on the strategy to be selected. In making this decision, the client can consider the possible consequences of carrying out a particular course of action.
5. Following the decision-making phase, clients should be encouraged to take action on their decision and then to *verify* the degree of effectiveness of their course of action. This verification phase consists of having clients observe and evaluate the consequences of their actions in the real world.

Procedures such as modeling, coaching, and reinforcement are used during problem-solving training. Throughout the therapy process, clients are taught self-control techniques, and they are encouraged to reinforce their own successful performance. Further, once clients have had an opportunity to observe the therapist (or other models) demonstrating effective problem-solving procedures, they are expected to assume a more active role. At this time the therapist functions largely as a consultant, providing guidance, giving feedback, and encouraging and evaluating real-life applications (Rose, 1986).

Stress Inoculation. Designed primarily by Meichenbaum (1977, 1985, 1986), stress inoculation provides members with a set of skills to deal effectively with future stressful situations. This procedure involves three phases: First is the conceptionalization phase, which is designed to give clients a conceptual framework for understanding their stressful reactions. This phase lays the foundation for later interventions by developing a collaborative working relationship between the members and the trainer.

Various methods are used during this phase, including the interview, imagery recall, self-monitoring, behavioral assessments, and psychological testing to collect information about the nature of the client's stress. This information is used to reconceptualize the client's stress reactions. In the second phase clients practice specific cognitive and behavioral coping techniques and rehearse new skills. The main aim of this phase is to help them develop and consolidate a variety of interpersonal coping skills. Some interventions at this phase include relaxation training, cognitive-restructuring procedures, problem solving, and self-instructional training. In the final phase members are helped to apply the training and the new cognitive and behavioral skills they have acquired to varied stressful situations they encounter in everyday living. Trainers employ a variety of techniques, including imagery rehearsal, behavioral rehearsal, role playing, modeling, graduated *in vivo* exposure, relapse prevention, and follow-through. Stress-inoculation training can be extended into the future by the use of booster sessions and follow-up interventions.

Coping-Skills Techniques. A number of other, more general behavioral strategies have been found effective in coping with both specific and general stress. An example of a coping-skill strategy is relaxation training. Meichenbaum (1977) developed a treatment procedure that is used in teaching coping skills. First, clients are exposed to anxiety-provoking cognitions they experience in the situation. The next step consists of a rational reevaluation of their cognitions or self-statements. Finally, clients note their level of anxiety after the rational reevaluation.

The Buddy System. Rose (1977, 1986) makes reference to the "buddy system" as a form of therapeutic alliance between members. Typically, a client is assigned or chooses another as a monitor and coach throughout the group-treatment process. Thus, the members monitor each other's behavior in the group, remind each other between meetings to stick to their commitments and practice their assignments, and play a supportive role both in and out of the group. The buddy system is useful in developing a supportive network in the natural environment. Buddies are trained in giving reinforcement for achievements and in giving and receiving criticism. The most important part of treatment occurs outside of the group with the practice of homework assignments. This arrangement offers members opportunities to be helpful to others and to practice their newly learned leadership skills. The buddy system becomes a self-help network that functions after the group terminates (Rose & Edleson, 1987).

Final Stage

During the final stage of the behavioral group the leader is primarily concerned with having members transfer the changes they have exhibited in the group to their everyday environment. Practice sessions involving simulations of the real world are used to promote this transfer. Members rehearse what they want to say to significant people in their life and practice alternative behaviors. Feedback from others in the group, along with coaching, can be of the utmost value at this final stage. Sessions are systematically designed so that new behaviors are gradually carried into daily life. Although preparation for generalization and maintenance of change is given a special focus in the final stage, it is a characteristic of all phases of the group.

Transferring changes from the therapy group to daily life is accomplished largely by the following actions taken by the group leader (Rose & Edleson, 1987):

- encouraging members to assume an increasing share of responsibility for their own treatment
- providing many varied practice situations for the members
- simulating the real world in the training context
- preparing members for facing a nonaccepting environment and for dealing with possible regressions
- overtraining members in the desired target behaviors
- instructing members in practicing generalization

Self-responsibility is emphasized throughout the life of the group, but it is especially critical in planning for termination. Rose (1986) maintains that the leader changes from a direct therapist to a consultant in the final stage. Members are typically encouraged to join various nontherapeutic groups where they can practice and develop their newly acquired skills under less controlled conditions than those offered in the group. In addition, they are taught self-help cognitive skills such as self-reinforcement and problem solving as a way of preparing them for situations they have not encountered in the group. This move toward member independence from the group is essential if clients are to gain confidence in their ability to cope effectively with new problems. As the time of termination approaches, many of the initial assessment instruments are repeated as a way of evaluating the effectiveness of the group program.

Termination and follow-up are issues of special concern to behaviorally oriented group leaders. Therefore, short- and long-term follow-up interviews are scheduled for a number of purposes: to compare the clients' performance before and after counseling, to determine the extent to which they can use their newly acquired behaviors in their environment without relying on counseling, and to determine the extent to which they have maintained desired behaviors and avoided undesired ones (Cormier & Cormier, 1985).

Rose and Edleson (1987) assert that follow-up interviews and group sessions serve as "booster shots" for maintaining the changed behaviors and continuing to engage in self-directed change. Follow-up sessions, which are often held 2 months after the group terminates and then again 4 to 6 months later, are finding modest but growing support in the research literature. These sessions provide rich opportunities for members to review what they have learned, to update the group on how they are doing, and to encourage them to be accountable for their changes or lack of them. Knowing that they will be accountable, members feel some pressure to maintain and use the discipline they learned in the group. They are encouraged to make use of their buddies and to discover alternative resources (which may include other groups or other forms of counseling) for continuing their progress.

Applications and Techniques

As mentioned earlier, the behavioral group therapist systematically uses a variety of specific techniques whose results can be objectively evaluated. Thus, the techniques can be continually refined for therapeutic effectiveness. The use of techniques varies with the group's clients or the problems that the group is dealing with. There are behavioral groups for managing anxiety and stress; for dealing with depression; for controlling specific behaviors such as excessive drinking, eating, and smoking; for teaching people how to be more effective in interpersonal relating; and for treating specific fears—to mention a few. Behavior therapy in groups can be applied to a variety of settings, such as schools, mental hospitals, day-treatment centers, community clinics, and prisons.

In this section I describe some common behavioral techniques that are applicable to group work. For the purpose of this discussion the techniques have been grouped under five general types of behavioral groups: (1) social-skills groups, (2) assertiveness groups, (3) stress-management groups, (4) groups for self-directed behavior change, and (5) multimodal group therapy as developed by Lazarus.

Social-Skills-Training Groups

Social-skills training is a broad category that deals with one's ability to interact effectively with others in a variety of social situations. Social-skills training in groups involves the application of many of the behavioral techniques discussed earlier in this chapter. According to Rose (1986), the group offers unique advantages over individual counseling for the development of new social skills. What follows is a summary of the process he uses in structuring social-skills training.

Before beginning the social-skills-training process, the group leader discusses with the members the general purposes of the group and the main procedures that are likely to be used. The members are given a variety of examples and are encouraged to ask questions. The group leader attempts to draw on the experiences of those members who have used these procedures themselves. If the members have had no prior experience with role playing, the leader generally provides them with some training. Then situations are given to the group, and experienced members from previous groups are asked to demonstrate how to role-play. Once members learn role-playing skills, they are then trained to develop situations that lend themselves to social-skills training. After the group is trained in the development of problem situations, the members are asked to keep a diary of situations as they occur during the course of the week. Each week at least one situation of each member is handled by the group. In presenting a situation, the mem- · ber states his or her goals or is given help in developing goals for the situation. After the goals are established and agreed on, other members are asked to propose the specific things that the client could do or say to achieve his or her goals. After all the suggestions have been presented, the group helps the client evaluate the suggestions with reference to the risks involved in a given course of action, appropriateness, compatibility with one's personality, and likelihood of effective outcomes. Even though other members contribute suggestions, it is the client who ultimately decides on an overall strategy.

Either the therapist or some group member models the desired verbal and nonverbal behaviors in a brief demonstration. Clients then practice their roles in the situation by using the agreed-on behaviors. If clients have trouble using a strategy during the rehearsal, they can be coached by the group leader or other members. When coaching is used, it is generally eliminated in later rehearsals. After each rehearsal clients receive feedback from the group pertaining to their strengths and weaknesses. Clients assign themselves homework to carry out in the real world. As they complete these assignments, they are asked to observe themselves in new situations and to keep a diary of problems. Behavioral procedures such as modeling, rehearsal, and homework are used to restructure cognitions.

Assertiveness-Training Groups

A behavioral approach that has gained increasing popularity is teaching people how to be assertive in a variety of social situations. Alberti and Emmons (1986a) provide the following working definition of assertive behavior: "Assertive behavior promotes equality in human relationships, enabling us to act in our own best interests, to stand up for ourselves without undue anxiety, to express honest feelings comfortably, [and] to exercise personal rights without denying the rights of others" (p. 7).

The basic assumption underlying the practice of assertion training is that people have the right—but not the obligation—to express their feelings, thoughts, beliefs, and attitudes. The goal of assertion training is to increase the group members' behavioral repertoire so that they can make the *choice* of being assertive or not. Another goal of assertion training is teaching people how to express themselves in a way that reflects sensitivity to the feelings and rights of others. Truly assertive individuals do not rigidly stand up for their rights at all costs, riding roughshod over the feelings and opinions of others.

The Purpose of Assertiveness-Training Groups. Assertiveness training can be helpful for people who cannot ask others for what they want; who are unable to resist inappropriate demands; who have difficulty expressing feelings of love, gratitude, and approval as well as feelings of irritation, anger, and disagreement; and who feel that they don't have a right to have their own feelings and thoughts. Alberti and Emmons (1986a) identify three particularly difficult barriers to self-expression: (1) people may not believe that they have the right to be assertive or to express their thoughts or feelings, (2) people may be highly anxious or fearful about being assertive, and (3) people sometimes lack the skills for effectively expressing to others what they think and feel. Assertion training attempts to equip clients with the skills and attitudes necessary to deal effectively with a wide range of interpersonal situations. The specific outcome goals of the training include

- recognizing and changing self-defeating or irrational beliefs concerning one's right to be assertive
- developing an attitude that places value on one's right to express oneself and on the respect for the rights of others
- learning how to identify and discriminate among assertive, aggressive, and nonassertive behaviors
- increasing one's self-esteem to the point of becoming capable of taking the initiative
- being able to apply newly learned assertive skills to specific interpersonal situations

Guidelines for Conducting Assertion-Training Groups.   What follows is a description of group-training procedures that are typically used in assertion-training groups. There are various methods of structuring such groups; the following description is an adaptation of the procedures described by Alberti and Emmons (1986b) in their manual for assertiveness trainers. They use assertiveness/social-skills-training groups in a variety of settings, such as private practice, university counseling centers, and outpatient mental-health clinics.

In the first session of an assertiveness-training group, members hear brief introductory comments about the nature of the training, participate in an exercise to get to know one another, observe a brief demonstration of behavior rehearsal, listen to a presentation on how our thinking affects our behavior, receive a homework assignment, and participate in a relaxation exercise. The behavior-rehearsal demonstration is the core of the initial session. The group leader presents a short common scene and then role-plays a brief segment to demonstrate the differences between nonassertive, aggressive, and assertive behavioral styles. As members watch the demonstration, they are asked to identify specific components of the behavior and to provide feedback on the trainer's effectiveness in each style.

During this first session there is also a brief lecture on the cognitive-restructuring process and how a change in thinking can frequently lead to a change in one's attitude about acting assertively. Members are assigned to keep a log of progress that includes specific and detailed examples. They are asked to keep track of the sources of anxiety in their personal logs between the sessions. Members participate in a relaxation exercise as a way to conclude the first session.

In subsequent meetings the general format is the same, although the focus is more on behavioral rehearsal and practicing newly acquired skills in the sessions. The sessions are divided in the following way:

- There is follow-up on the homework completed by each of the members.
- There is a didactic presentation that deals with some cognitive issue or technique for each session.
- There are many opportunities to practice skills in specific situations.
- Members are taught to use exercises in coping with anxiety and stress.
- Homework to complete between the sessions is assigned.

As assertion training has gained in popularity in the last few years, responsible practitioners have expressed concern about the possible misuse of this counseling technique. Some of the areas of concern are unqualified trainers, illegitimate purposes, and application in inappropriate circumstances. A statement of "principles for ethical practice of assertive-behavior training," developed by a group of nationally recognized assertion-training professionals, is presented by Alberti and Emmons (1986b). A summary list of these guidelines is given in the student manual for this text.

For those who are interested in learning the specifics of planning, setting up, conducting, and evaluating assertion-training groups, a number of excellent sources are available and are listed in the reference section of this chapter (see especially Alberti & Emmons, 1986a, 1986b).

Stress-Management Training in Groups

Assumptions Underlying Stress-Management Programs. Stress is a basic part of contemporary life. Since it is not realistic to assume that stress can be eliminated, it is a good idea to devise strategies for helping people effectively cope with the multiple stresses they experience in daily life. As Meichenbaum (1985) has observed, the goal of stress-management programs is not to eliminate stress but to educate clients about its nature and effects and to teach them a variety of intrapersonal and interpersonal skills to cope with it constructively. A basic assumption of stress-management programs is that we are not simply victims of stress; rather, what we *do* and *think* actively contribute to how we experience stress. In other words, how we appraise events in life (including how we think, feel, and act) determines whether stress will affect us positively or negatively. If this assumption is correct, people can be taught concepts and skills to constructively cope with the many demands and stresses they encounter in various situations.

A Coping-Skills Approach to Stress-Management Training. The following discussion is based largely on a stress-management-training program in groups designed by Rose, Tolman, and Tallant (1985) and by the stress-inoculation-training program developed by Meichenbaum (1985). Since many sources of stress originate in a social context, it makes sense to use a group setting to train people how to manage stress.

Rose and his colleagues have developed a multimethod group program for stress management that has been used in a wide variety of agencies. The program typically consists of eight weekly 2-hour sessions, with a pre- and postassessment individual conference and a follow-up group session. Assessment consists of an initial interview to identify the sources and degree of stress, the use of some paper-and-pencil measures, and daily self-monitoring by clients of their reactions to stressful situations.

Stress is experienced as physiological arousal, with cognitive and behavioral correlates. The experience of stress is influenced by one's thoughts as well as by environmental situations. Training, therefore, should include the social-psychological dimensions. The training program proposed by Rose, Tolman, and Tallant includes teaching clients relaxation procedures for dealing with stress-induced physiological arousal. Cognitive distortions in the appraisal of environmental events are treated through a variety of cognitive-restructuring techniques. Clients are assisted in dealing with social-environmental stressors through social-skills training. The cognitive program of the stress-management groups developed by Rose and his associates draws heavily on principles and procedures from three sources: Albert Ellis's rational-emotive therapy (which is the subject of the following chapter), Aaron Beck's (1976) cognitive therapy, and Meichenbaum's cognitive-behavioral approach (which is described next).

Meichenbaum's Stress-Inoculation Training. Meichenbaum (1985, 1986) is concerned with more than merely teaching people specific coping skills. His program is designed to prepare clients for intervention and motivate them to change, and it deals with issues such as resistance and relapse. Stress-inoculation training (SIT) consists of a combination of elements of information giving, Socratic discussion, cognitive restructuring, problem solving, relaxation training, behavioral and imaginal rehearsals, self-monitoring, self-instruction, self-reinforcement, and modifying environmental situations. This approach is designed to teach coping skills that can be applied to both present problems and future difficulties. The following are some clinical guidelines for developing stress-reduction and prevention programs as suggested by Meichenbaum:

- Conduct an assessment to determine what intrapersonal and interpersonal factors might be inhibiting a client's capacity to cope with stress.
- Enlist the client's cooperation and participation; develop a collaborative approach to assessment, intervention, and evaluation of the program.
- Train the client in a range of coping skills, taking into account individual and cultural differences; foster a flexible coping repertoire.

- Take into account the cognitive and affective dimensions of the coping process.
- Select training tasks carefully.
- Train for transfer and generalization of learning.
- Training should be future-oriented, in that it anticipates possible setbacks and stressful life situations. It should include measures to prevent relapses.
- Training is most effective when it is multilevel and multifaceted. Train in varied settings, if possible.
- Arrange for feedback on the client's performance.
- If possible, arrange for booster sessions, follow-up assessments, and follow-through programs.

Meichenbaum (1985) has designed a three-stage model for SIT: (1) the conceptual phase, (2) the skills-acquisition and rehearsal phase, and (3) the application and follow-through phase.

During the initial stage of SIT (the *conceptual phase*) the primary focus is on creating a working relationship with clients by helping them gain a better understanding of the nature of stress and reconceptualize it in social-interactive terms. During this phase clients are educated about the transactional nature of stress and coping. They learn about the role that cognitions and emotions play in creating and maintaining stress. After an assessment process in which they take an active role, they determine short-, intermediate-, and long-term goals that will guide treatment. Self-monitoring, which begins at this time, continues throughout all the phases. Clients typically keep an open-ended diary in which they systematically record their specific thoughts, feelings, and behaviors. Many clients begin treatment feeling that they have been victimized by external circumstances, thoughts, feelings, and behaviors that they are powerless to control. Training includes teaching them to become aware of their own role in creating their stress. This provides them with a basis for learning ways to reduce the negative effects of stress.

The second phase of SIT, or *skills acquisition and rehearsal,* focuses on helping clients develop and consolidate a variety of intrapersonal and interpersonal coping skills. Some of these specific techniques include relaxation training, cognitive restructuring, problem solving, social-skills training, time management, self-instructional training, and lifestyle changes such as reevaluating priorities, developing support systems, and taking direct action to alter stressful situations. Clients are introduced to a variety of methods of relaxation and are taught to use these skills to decrease arousal due to stress. Through teaching, demonstration, and guided practice, they learn the skills of progressive relaxation. They are expected to practice these skills regularly. Clients need to learn that it is not a waste of time to relax, and they need to grant themselves permission to participate in activities that are relaxing to them. These activities may include meditation, yoga, tensing and relaxing muscle groups, and breath-control techniques. They can also include walking, jogging, gardening, knitting, or other physical activities. Meichenbaum stresses that it is essential that both clients and trainers understand that relaxation is as much a state of mind as a physical state.

Teaching clients a number of cognitive strategies is a basic part of the second phase of SIT. These interventions include cognitive restructuring, problem-solving strategies, and guided self-dialogue. In cognitive restructuring, clients become aware of the role that their cognitions and emotions play in creating and maintaining stress. The cognitive-restructuring approach used in SIT is based on the work of Beck (1976). The goal of his cognitive therapy is to identify clients' unrealistic, maladaptive thought patterns and to replace them with rational and adaptive modes of thinking. He places emphasis on the client's capacity and responsibility for discovering these maladaptive thought patterns. He systematically uses strategies such as modeling, behavioral rehearsal, and graded task assignments in teaching constructive cognitive and coping skills. In treating stress-related problems, SIT uses three core techniques (which are described in detail by Beck, Rush, Shaw, and Emery, 1979): (1) eliciting the client's thoughts, feelings, and interpretations of events; (2) gathering evidence with the client to either support or disprove these interpretations; and (3) designing homework assignments to test the validity of the interpretations and to gather more data for discussion. Through cognitive-therapy techniques clients learn to detect negative and stress-engendering thoughts. They also learn to challenge their "automatic thoughts" and their absolutistic thinking, which compounds their stress. Clients are also given self-instructional training, in which they learn guided self-dialogue techniques to replace negativistic self-statements. Through training, clients develop a new set of coping self-statements that they can apply when they encounter stressors. It is assumed that if the thinking of clients can make them worse, they can adopt a different set of self-statements to reduce, avoid, or constructively use stress.

In the third phase of SIT *(application and follow-through)* the focus is on carefully arranging for transfer and maintenance of change from the therapeutic situation to the real world. The assumption is that coping skills that are practiced in the clinic will not automatically generalize to everyday life situations. To consolidate the lessons learned in the training sessions, clients participate in a variety of activities, including imagery and behavioral rehearsal, role playing, modeling, and graduated *in vivo* practice. Clients are asked to write down the homework assignments, or personal experiments, that they are willing to complete. The outcomes of these assignments are carefully checked at subsequent meetings, and if clients do not follow through with them, the trainer and the members collaboratively consider the reasons for these failures. Follow-up and booster sessions typically take place at 3-, 6-, and 12-month periods as an incentive for clients to continue practicing and refining their coping skills. Instead of being considered a limited intervention, SIT can be part of an ongoing stress-management program that extends the benefits of training into the future. For a more detailed discussion of the techniques typically used during this phase of treatment, review the earlier discussion of the techniques described in the final stage of a behavioral group.

Implications for Practice.   Stress-management training has potentially useful applications for a wide variety of problems and client populations, both for remediation of stress disorders and for prevention. Meichenbaum (1985) summarizes the literature identifying the use of SIT and related procedures with selected populations. Target problems and the populations that have received stress-management training include

- *problems with anger:* adults and adolescents with anger-control problems, abusive parents
- *problems with anxiety:* test anxiety, interpersonal anxiety, performance anxiety, anxiety of adults reentering school
- *problems with phobias:* animal phobias, fear of flying
- *general stress reactions:* Type A individuals, medical outpatients, clients in community mental-health centers
- *medical problems:* preparing patients for surgery, preparing children for dental examinations, pain management, helping cancer patients deal with fear
- *victim populations:* rape victims, victims of terrorist attacks
- *professional groups:* nurses, teachers, school psychologists, probation officers, police officers, parachutists, drill instructors, scuba divers

Based on their experience in conducting stress-management-training groups, Rose and his associates (1985) contend that the training approach is widely applicable. They have conducted stress-management groups with foster parents, abusive spouses, students, patients in a cardiac-rehabilitation program, and clients recruited from the population at large. They have helped social workers manage their stress, as well as teaching them techniques they could use with their clients. Coping-skills training does not have to be done in isolation, for these programs can be integrated with other treatment approaches.

For a detailed description of ways to organize stress-management groups, see the manual by Rose, Tolman, and Tallant (1985); for pain-management groups, see the manual by Rose and Subramanian (1986), both of which are described in the Recommended Supplementary Readings section of this chapter.

Groups for Self-Directed Behavior Change

There is a trend toward "giving psychology away"—that is, a tendency to teach people how to apply interpersonal skills to their everyday life. This trend implies that psychologists will share their knowledge with consumers so that people can lead increasingly self-directed lives and not be dependent on the experts for the effective management of the problems they encounter.

Psychologists who share this perspective are concerned primarily with teaching people the skills they will need for self-direction.

Behaviorally oriented groups offer great promise for those who want to learn the skills necessary for self-management. Areas in which one can learn to control behavior and bring about self-directed change are excessive eating, drinking, and smoking and inadequate self-discipline at work or in school. Some people cannot accomplish certain goals in their work because their efforts are hindered by lack of organization; they don't know where to begin with a project, how to sustain their efforts, and how to avoid the crippling discouragement they experience when they fail to attain their goals. It is in these and similar areas that behavioral groups for self-directed change can provide the guidelines and planning necessary to bring about change.

There are some excellent books on self-directed behavior and its implications for group work. One of the best is *Self-Directed Behavior: Self-Modification for Personal Adjustment,* by Watson and Tharp (1989). Another excellent source is the chapter on "Self-Management Methods," by Kanfer and Gaelick (1986).

Multimodal Group Therapy

The previously described models of behavioral group therapy tend to be short term (6 to 12 sessions) and tend to deal with a homogeneous population. Assertion-training groups are short term, for example, and the members are alike in wanting to learn ways of being assertive. Stress-management training consists of 8 sessions. Pain-management training is done in 10 sessions. Likewise, many of the self-directed groups are homogeneous in nature, and the treatment program is relatively brief. Members are taught skills that they can apply in a program once they complete these specific training groups. In contrast, the multimodal group approach tends to be of longer duration and organizationally more like other forms of long-term group therapy.

A major premise of the broad-spectrum orientation known as multimodal therapy is that the more coping responses a person learns in therapy, the less are the chances for a relapse (Lazarus, 1987a). Although most of the writing about multimodal therapy has been from the perspective of individual psychotherapy, Lazarus's formulation can be applied to group counseling and therapy (see Lazarus, 1982). This approach is included in this chapter because of its potential to include all the major areas of personality functioning in group treatment. Multimodal group therapy takes into consideration the *whole person.* Lazarus stresses that since each client is unique, treatment has to be individually tailored. Care must be taken to avoid fitting clients to a preconceived treatment mode. Instead, in multimodal therapy a careful attempt is made to determine precisely what type of relationship and what treatment strategies would work best with each particular client and under which particular circumstances. The basic question is Who or what is best for this particular client? Therapeutic flexibility and versatility are valued highly in the multimodal orientation (Lazarus, 1986, 1987b, 1989).

The essence of the multimodal approach is the premise that human beings are complex in that they move, feel, sense, imagine, think, and relate. According to Lazarus (1986), there are seven major areas of personality functioning: behavior, affective responses, sensations, images, cognitions, interpersonal relationships, and biological functioning. Although these modalities are interactive, they can be considered discrete functions and defended as useful divisions (Roberts, Jackson, & Phelps, 1980).

The multimodal therapist takes the view that a complete assessment and treatment program must account for each modality of the BASIC ID, which stands for behavior, affect, sensations, imagery, cognition, interpersonal, and drugs/biology. Thus, the BASIC ID is the cognitive map that ensures that each aspect of personality receives explicit and systematic attention (Lazarus, 1981). Further, comprehensive therapy entails the correction of irrational beliefs, deviant behaviors, unpleasant feelings, bothersome images, stressful relationships, negative sensations, and possible biochemical imbalances. It is assumed that since clients are troubled by a number of specific problems, it is best to employ a number of specific treatments. If the therapist fails to tune in to a client's presenting modality, the client often feels misunderstood. It is axiomatic that therapy should start where the client is and then move into more productive areas of discourse (Lazarus, 1989). Enduring change is seen as a function of combined techniques, strategies, and modalities.

There are some other basic assumptions underlying multimodal therapy. First, therapists must be effective as people. Second, they need a range of skills and techniques to deal with the range of problems posed by their clients. Third, they must have "technical eclecticism"; that is, they should be able to employ any techniques that have been demonstrated to be effective in dealing with specific problems (Roberts et al., 1980).

According to Lazarus (1986, 1987b), there are some basic problems in being *theoretically* eclectic, because there are contradictory notions among therapeutic systems. In calling for technical eclecticism, Lazarus endorses using a variety of techniques within a theoretical structure that is open to verification and disproof. He adds that useful techniques can be derived from many sources, which could be divorced from their origins. In espousing technical (or systematic) eclecticism, he is not arguing in favor of a theoretical eclecticism. Multimodal therapy rests primarily upon principles of Bandura's (1969, 1977, 1986) *social-learning theory* (Lazarus, 1986). The kind of technical eclecticism that Lazarus (1987b) believes is needed is scientific and has three other qualities: breadth, depth, and specificity.

In multimodal group therapy the process begins with a comprehensive assessment of all the modalities of human functioning. The BASIC ID assessment allows therapists to utilize interventions that are most likely to be helpful to clients in particular circumstances. Ideally, multimodal therapists are broadly trained so that they can work with individuals, couples, families, and groups; they are also skilled in specific behavioral, affective, sensory, imagery, cognitive, interpersonal, and somatic techniques (see Lazarus, 1981, for a glossary of the 39 most frequently used techniques). An adaptation of Lazarus's (1982, 1986) description of this first phase of group therapy is given below. Members are asked questions pertaining to the BASIC ID:

• *Behavior*. This modality refers primarily to overt behaviors, including acts, habits, and reactions that are observable and measurable. Some questions asked are "What would you like to change? What behaviors would you like to decrease or eliminate? What behaviors would you like to increase or acquire? What are your chief strengths? What specific behaviors are keeping you from getting what you want?"

• *Affect*. This modality refers to emotions, moods, and strong feelings. Questions sometimes asked include "What emotions do you experience most often? What makes you laugh? What makes you sad? What are some emotions that are problematic for you?"

• *Sensations*. This item refers to the five basic senses of touch, taste, smell, sight, and hearing. Examples of questions asked are "Do you suffer from unpleasant sensations, such as pains, aches, dizziness, and so forth? What do you particularly like or dislike in the way of seeing, smelling, hearing, touching, and tasting?"

• *Imagery*. This modality pertains to ways in which we picture ourselves, and it includes memories and dreams. Some questions asked are "What are some bothersome recurring dreams and vivid memories? How do you view your body? How do you see yourself now? How would you like to be able to see yourself in the future? What are some past, present, or future mental pictures that are troubling you?"

• *Cognition*. This item refers to insights, philosophies, ideas, and judgments that constitute one's fundamental values, attitudes, and beliefs. Questions include "What values are most significant in your life? What are some ways in which you meet your intellectual needs? What are some negative things that you say to yourself? What are some of your central irrational beliefs? What are the main 'shoulds,' 'oughts,' and 'musts' in your life? Do they get in the way of effective living for you? How does your thinking influence what you are doing and how you are feeling?"

• *Interpersonal*. This item refers to interactions with other people. Examples of questions include "What do you expect from the significant others in your life? What do they expect of you? What do you give to these people, and what do you get from them? Are there any relationships with others that you would hope to change? If so, what changes would you like to see?"

• *Drugs/Biology*. This modality includes more than drugs; it takes into consideration one's nutritional habits and exercise patterns. Some questions asked are "What is the state of your health? Do you have any medical concerns? Do you take any prescribed drugs? What are your diet and exercise habits?"

It should not be thought that the above list is a complete representation of the BASIC ID, but a preliminary investigation into a client's BASIC ID brings out some central and significant themes that can be productively explored in a group. The preliminary questioning is followed by a detailed life-history questionnaire. Once the main profile of a person's BASIC ID has been established, the next step consists of an examination of the interactions among the different modalities. This second phase of work intensifies specific facets of the person's problem areas and permits the group therapist to understand the person more fully as well as devise effective coping and treatment strategies.

Lazarus (1982) believes that it is best to form groups that are relatively homogeneous with respect to problem areas and goals. Examples include people who are interested in learning to become more assertive, people who are concerned with weight loss, couples who are interested in improving the communication in their relationship, and individuals who want to quit smoking. Group therapy is seen as particularly appropriate (and the treatment of choice) when there is some reason to believe that other people will enhance the processes of learning, unlearning, and relearning. If the BASIC ID assessment reveals that the client has a negative self-image and feelings of inadequacy, then multimodal group therapy can be useful. Likewise, for clients whose assessment reveals interpersonal difficulties, group therapy would offer some distinct advantages over individual treatment.

It is Lazarus's (1982) position that a time-limited group (of approximately 20 sessions) appears to be the most effective format. When the group ends, members might become involved in individual therapy or become a member of another group. Lazarus has found that this format encourages the most active learning, unlearning, and relearning, the basis of multimodal methods. In terms of the methods that are used in the group sessions, Lazarus endorses an eclectic position. Thus, discussion, role playing, relaxation exercises, behavior rehearsal, cognitive restructuring, modeling, assertion-training exercises, and identifying feelings are but a few of the techniques employed. Lazarus emphasizes, however, that most substantial changes occur outside of the group; therefore, he relies heavily on homework assignments and other performance-based methods, rather than exclusively using verbal and cognitive procedures. (For a more detailed discussion of these procedures, see Lazarus, 1981.)

The multimodal therapist tends to be very active during group sessions. Leaders function as trainers, educators, consultants, facilitators, and role models. They provide information, instruction, and feedback. Leaders also serve an important function by modeling assertive behaviors in the group, challenging self-defeating beliefs, offering constructive criticism and suggestions, offering positive reinforcements, and being appropriately self-disclosing. The multimodal approach to group work requires that the leader be flexible in using various methods and in conducting the group.

Brunell (1978) has discussed the multimodal treatment model as the basis for designing programs to meet specific problems in a mental hospital.

According to Brunell, its major advantage in the hospital setting is that it provides a systematic framework for conceptualizing the presenting problems of the patients. The model encompasses specific goals, specifies treatment techniques to meet these goals, and provides a basis for systematic evaluation of the relative effectiveness of these therapeutic procedures. Another advantage of the multimodal approach is that the large pool of therapeutic resources available in a mental hospital can be used to meet the diverse needs of the population.

There are also applications of Lazarus's multimodal therapy model for an entire clinical service-delivery unit (Roberts et al., 1980). The whole therapy program of a day-treatment program was subjected to a multimodal evaluation. Only those therapeutic interventions that passed muster with regard to multimodal analysis were kept in the program. The overall therapy program included group therapy, family therapy, a women's group, a communication group, couples therapy, dance therapy, assertion training, relaxation training, and other forms of traditional treatment. It was found that, from an administrative and organizational perspective, the multimodal model was very useful in generating critical analysis and research as it applied to their service-delivery system.

In summary, one of the values of the multimodal approach to group work is that it does provide a comprehensive view of assessment and treatment. It allows for the incorporation of diverse techniques. If a technique is proved effective for a given problem, it can become part of the multimodal therapist's approach. Thus, this model appears to foster an openness on the part of practitioners.

Evaluation of Behavioral Group Therapy

Contributions of the Approach

More than any of the other therapies discussed in this book, behavior therapy is to be credited with conducting research to determine the efficacy of its techniques. Those approaches that do not work are eliminated, and new techniques are continually being improved. Rose (1983) sums this virtue up well: "Behavior therapy draws upon the best available empirical research to determine what kind of intervention is best suited to what kind of problem" (p. 102).

Two other contributions of behavioral group therapy are discussed by Rose. First, treatment strategies are tailored to each group member, based on an assessment of the individual in the group setting. This makes the approach highly versatile and flexible. Second, a behavioral group is a concrete example of a humanistic approach in action. The individuals and the group contract for mutually determined goals. The members are involved in the selection of both goals and treatment strategies. In many groups, leaders help members move toward independence by delegating leadership functions to the members; the group leader assumes the role of an active consultant to the members to help them most efficiently attain their stated goals. Therapy then becomes a place where members learn how to learn and are encouraged to develop the skills necessary to deal effectively with solving any future problems they will face once they leave the group.

When many factors are taken into consideration, the behavioral approach stands up well in comparison with many other therapies, and it allows for the evolution of intervention methods. With the focus on research, these techniques can become more precise so that they can be implemented with specific clients with a variety of specific problems. Regardless of which models influence our style of group leadership, the spirit of behavior therapy can encourage us to strive for accountability, rather than simply relying on faith and intuition that our practices are working.

The cognitive-behavioral model of group counseling and group therapy makes use of the combined methods of cognitive restructuring, problem solving, social-skills training, coping-skills training, modeling, behavior rehearsal, group feedback, reinforcement, and other tools for changing behavior. There is empirical support for each of these dimensions of group work, and preliminary data suggest that the cognitive-behavioral group model offers a promising set of treatment strategies with various types of clients (Rose, 1983).

Advantages of a Group Approach

Rose (1977, 1986) and Rose and Edleson (1987) have pointed out that almost all of the problems that are amenable to individual therapy can also be dealt with in a group context, provided that they have social and interpersonal dimensions. The most fundamental assumption is that the presence of other clients provides a unique opportunity for practicing new social-interactional skills with peers in a protected setting (Rose, 1986).

The kind of population that is suited to behavioral group therapy includes clients with one or more of the following problems: social-skills deficits, depression, phobias, anxiety, stress, sexual disorders, pain management, stress management, anger control, weight control, substance abuse, and child management (Rose, 1986). To this list Lazarus (1986) adds conflicting feelings, misinformation, missing information, maladaptive habits, interpersonal disturbances, low self-esteem, and biological dysfunctions. Many problems appear to be more amenable to group therapy, and groups offer some distinct advantages over individual treatment. What follows is a summary of some of these advantages, based on the writings of Rose (1977, 1982, 1983, 1986) and Rose and Edleson (1987).

- The group provides members with an intermediate step between performing newly acquired behavior in therapy and transferring this performance to everyday life. The group is a natural laboratory for learning leadership skills that are essential in developing good social relationships.

- The group setting offers powerful norms to control the behavior of individuals. Examples of some positive therapeutic norms are regular attendance, willingness to self-disclose, commitment to evaluating and working on one's problems, and encouragement by others to stick to a plan leading to behavioral and cognitive change.
- Group work provides a setting for accurate assessment, because members can learn how their behavior affects others through the feedback they continually receive from both the other members and the leader. Group members can provide powerful feedback to one another about specific behavior, which is often more readily accepted from peers than it is from the group leader.
- A unique characteristic of group therapy is the opportunity for peer reinforcement.
- There is growing empirical support for the utility of various components of a behavioral and cognitive-behavioral group therapy. Group therapy appears to be at least as effective and more efficient in terms of therapist cost than individual therapy (Rose, 1986).

Disadvantages of a Group Approach

Groups do have their disadvantages. Antitherapeutic norms can develop, which could work against effective treatment. Group contagion and aggression can be more of a problem in groups than in individual counseling. When groups are too highly structured, as behavioral groups can often become, individual clients can be prevented from meeting their personal needs. Even minimal effectiveness with groups requires that leaders have training and supervision and that they develop an extensive repertoire of skills (Rose, 1986; Rose & Edleson, 1987).

A Critique of the Approach

Critics of behavior therapy often tend to focus on the deterministic views inherent in the psychology of B. F. Skinner. Although it is true that traditional behaviorism has rejected the notion of human freedom, it is clear that contemporary behavior therapy clearly emphasizes the role of cognitive factors and the self-control, or independence, of the client (Bandura, 1986; Goldfried & Davison, 1976; Kanfer & Goldstein, 1986; Lazarus, 1971, 1981; London, 1985; Mahoney & Thoresen, 1974; Meichenbaum, 1977, 1985, 1986; Rose, 1977, 1980, 1982, 1983, 1986; Thoresen & Mahoney, 1974). There is a trend toward broadening the scope of behavior therapy while retaining its essential features. For example, behavior therapists are reformulating their techniques in cognitive and social-learning terms instead of the traditional conditioning terms. There have been numerous examples in this chapter of groups designed primarily to increase the client's degree of control and freedom in specific aspects of daily life.

Other critics of the behavioral approach to group work argue that this model ignores the historical causes of present behavior and does not work with the past in the therapeutic process. There is some truth to this criticism. For example, consider this statement by Rose (1977): "By concentrating on specific behaviors as the targets of change, the behavior therapist de-emphasizes the relevance of early life histories. The therapist places less emphasis on subjective experience, insight, and general attitude than does the psychotherapist, and gives no attention to dreams" (p. 3). It seems clear that the behavior therapist opposes the traditional psychoanalytic approach, which assumes that early traumatic events are at the root of present dysfunction. As we have seen, the psychoanalytic theory holds that it is essential to discover the original causes, induce insight in the client, and work through past traumas. Behavior therapists may acknowledge that the deviant responses have historical origins, but they maintain that the responses are still in effect because they are being maintained by reinforcing stimuli. They assume that past events seldom maintain current problems. Therefore, they place most of their emphasis on providing the client with new learning experiences. It is clear that the focus is on learning new responses and changing environmental conditions as a necessary prerequisite for behavior change.

Although I think it is unfair to accuse behavior therapists of ignoring the past or considering it unimportant, I do believe that they fail to work with the past sufficiently. In my own work I have found that most of the contemporary struggles of participants appear to be firmly rooted in their childhood experiences. Although I do not advocate getting bogged down in the past, I have found that it seems necessary for members to relive certain past experiences and resolve some basic conflicts that have lingered since childhood before new learning can proceed. In addition to giving more attention to the past than most behavior therapists, I also value focusing on subjective experiences (such as feelings and dreams) to a much greater extent than they do.

One of the limitations of the behavioral model is that if it is too rigidly applied, it can lead the therapist to lose sight of the people in the group by focusing exclusively on techniques and on the details of the members' specific problems. In my opinion this focus on problems and symptoms can result in a failure to understand the meaning behind an individual's behavior. This is not to say that group therapy should focus on dealing with "underlying causes" of behavior. However, I prefer to deal with factors in one's *external* situation that may be eliciting behavioral problems and with one's *internal* reactions to these environmental variables. For example, in working with a male client who has great anxiety over relating to women, I would be interested in knowing what particular situations in his environment lead to this anxiety, and I would be concerned about his reactions to these situations. How does he feel when he is in the presence of women? What are some things he tells himself when he meets women? How does he perceive women in various situations? What are some historical roots of his fear? Therefore, my aim would not be to simply employ techniques to eliminate his anxiety; rather, I would want to explore with him the *meaning* of this anxiety. I might also encourage him to relive some earlier painful experiences dealing with women and facilitate deeper expression of feelings and self-exploration. In fairness, most behavior therapists now look at the situation and the response. They are interested in exploring cognitions and, to some extent, the affective elements in the context of the client's problem. In other words, behavior therapists are interested in more than merely eliminating symptoms of problem behaviors.

Using Behavioral Methods with Other Approaches

A therapist need not subscribe totally to behavior therapy in order to derive practical benefits from the use of specific behavioral techniques. As a matter of fact, I believe that certain experiential and humanistic models can be enhanced by systematically incorporating some of the behavioral and cognitive techniques into their relationship-oriented frameworks. I am convinced that an understanding of the learning principles that operate within a group is critical for effective group leadership, regardless of one's orientation.

For example, behavioral principles operate behind such therapeutic procedures as modeling and reinforcement, which are used in almost any kind of group. Members are supported (reinforced) in their attempts to be honest, to take risks, to experiment with new behavior, to be active, to take the initiative, and to participate fully in the group. Also, the specificity of the approach helps group members translate fuzzy goals into concrete plans of action, and it helps the group leader keep these plans clearly in focus. Another contribution of the behavioral model is the wide range of techniques that participants can use to specify their goals and to develop the skills needed to achieve these goals. Techniques such as role playing, coaching, guided practice, modeling, feedback, learning by successive approximations, and homework assignments can be included in any group leader's repertoire, regardless of his or her theoretical orientation.

Applying Behavior Therapy in Multicultural Settings

Behavioral group therapy has some clear advantages in working with multicultural populations. Clients from certain cultural and ethnic backgrounds hold values that are contrary to the free expression of feelings and sharing of personal concerns about family matters. Since behavioral groups do not place emphasis on experiencing intense feelings and catharsis, clients who might find this sharing of feelings distasteful are not immediately put off by being expected to emote.

Behavioral groups are often short term and highly structured, and thus clients have a good chance of knowing what they are getting into when they agree to participate. Behavioral practitioners typically spend time in preparing members to participate in the group experience. Members are taught what they can do to work toward their specific goals. The group process is not mysterious, for norms are made clear.

Behavioral groups typically have a specific focus, as we have seen. Other factors that contribute to the usefulness of the behavioral approach to group work include its specificity, task-orientation, focus on objectivity, focus on cognition and behavior, and problem-solving orientation. Clients learn coping strategies and acquire survival techniques. Since minorities are generally not in a position to afford a lengthy introspective therapy, this problem-solving approach appeals to them. Because behavior therapy fits into a short-term format, it is applicable to a variety of practical problems that ethnic clients face, and the time frame makes it possible to deal with day-to-day concerns that clients bring to therapy.

However, it is important for group leaders to help their clients assess the possible consequences of some of their newly acquired social skills. For example, some clients will find that their life becomes even more complicated as they exhibit more assertive behaviors. Their culture may place a premium on compliance with tradition, and being assertive can lead to problems if one decides to stay within his or her culture. Therefore, group leaders need to be mindful of how cultural values can influence the behaviors of clients, and they will do well to also help these members assess the advantages and disadvantages of developing a more assertive style. It is important also that members have opportunities to talk about the problems they encounter as they become different in their home and work settings.

Questions for Reflection and Discussion

1. What are some of the distinguishing features of a behavioral group that separate it from many of the other models covered in this book? To what extent do you think you could incorporate some behavioral concepts and techniques into the relationship-oriented and experiential therapies?

2. What role does assessment play in a behavioral group? Explain how assessment is an ongoing process and talk about the values of this process. Again, how could you include the focus on assessment in other therapeutic models?

3. What are some behavioral techniques that you would most want to include in your groups? How might you broaden the base of your style of leadership by including cognitive and behavioral methods?

4. What are some practical advantages of pregroup interviews and follow-up individual interviews and group sessions? In what ways might you build these into the design of a group?

5. Select a particular kind of group that you would be interested in organizing. Thinking from a behavioral perspective, what are some of the factors you would consider from the time you announced the group to the final group session? How would you design this group at each of its stages? Consider discussing your proposal with others in your class.

6. Mention some ethical considerations involved in behavioral group therapy. Which one issue do you consider to be the most significant?

7. What are your reactions to the focuses of behavior therapy—its emphasis on behavior rather than feelings and insight, interest in current problems rather than exploration of the past, concern with objective factors as opposed to subjective factors, and reliance on empirical validation of results rather than on clinical intuition?
8. Identify as many elements as you can from the behavioral perspective that will be operative in any group. For example, discuss the role of modeling, social reinforcement, and feedback in a group. How can systematically paying attention to some of these factors enhance a group?
9. What are the major shortcomings and limitations of the behavioral model? What is your major criticism of this theory as it is applied to group work?
10. What do you consider to be some of the most important contributions of the behavioral model?

Where to Go from Here

If you have an interest in further training in behavior therapy, sources to contact are

Behavior Therapy Unit
Temple University Medical School
Eastern Pennsylvania Psychiatric Institute
3300 Henry Avenue
Philadelphia, PA 19129

Dr. Sheldon D. Rose
School of Social Work
425 Henry Mall
University of Wisconsin
Madison, WI 53706

Association for the Advancement of Behavior Therapy
15 West 36th Street
New York, NY 10018

The Association for the Advancement of Behavior Therapy has also published a *Directory of Graduate Study in Behavior Therapy,* which gives complete and up-to-date information on nearly 300 programs in clinical/ counseling psychology, psychology internship, psychiatry residency, and social work.

RECOMMENDED SUPPLEMENTARY READINGS

Working with children and adolescents in groups: A multimodal approach (Rose & Edleson, 1987), *Treating children in groups* (Rose, 1972), and *Group therapy: A behavioral approach* (Rose, 1977) are three outstanding books on behavior therapy in groups. In the first one, the authors present a concrete, step-by-step guide for effectively treating problem behavior in children and adolescents using small groups. Based on empirical research and their own work with groups, they show how various approaches can be effectively combined to help children resolve a variety of problem behaviors. Chapters deal with treatment planning, assessment of problems, setting of goals and choosing problem-solving strategies, devising intervention methods to change behavior, practicing new behavior in daily life, and generalizing and maintaining new behavior. In the second book Rose describes different therapy groups for children and some specific techniques for special populations. In the third one he presents an exhaustive account of the principles and procedures of behaviorally oriented groups from their inception to their termination and follow-up stages. Special chapters are devoted to applications of behavioral strategies to a variety of groups.

Also by Rose (1980), *A casebook in group therapy: A behavioral-cognitive approach* is a reader containing contributions by 15 practicing group therapists. Among the topics covered are assertion training in groups, working with the elderly, prevention of obesity, working with elementary school children, communication and problem-solving training for couples, and group in-service training for paraprofessionals in group homes.

Cognitive behavior modification: An integrative approach (Meichenbaum, 1977) reflects a research orientation and is representative of the trend emphasizing the cognitive aspects of behavior therapy.

Interviewing strategies for helpers: A guide to assessment, treatment, and evaluation (Cormier & Cormier, 1985) is a comprehensive and clearly written textbook dealing with training experiences and skill development. Its excellent documentation offers group practitioners a wealth of material on a variety of topics, such as assessment procedures, definition and selection of goals, development of appropriate treatment programs, and methods of evaluating outcomes.

The practice of multimodal therapy (Lazarus, 1981) is an excellent source of techniques and procedures that can be applied to behavioral group therapy. It represents an attempt to deal with the *whole person* by developing assessments and treatment interventions for all the modalities of human experience.

Clinical behavior therapy (Goldfried & Davison, 1976) is one of my favorite books on this perspective. It clearly and simply describes the essence of behavior therapy, the role of assessment, and the therapeutic relationship. It contains highly readable chapters on six major current behavior-therapy techniques, and it is rich with clinical examples to illustrate concepts. Although it is not specifically written for group therapy, most of the material can be usefully applied to group work.

Helping people change (Kanfer & Goldstein, 1986) is an excellent resource for a comprehensive overview of behavioral methods, including cognitive procedures, modeling, simulation and role playing, operant approaches, fear-reduction techniques, self-management strategies, cognitive-behavior modification, and group methods. Although this handbook is not specifically written for group practitioners, almost all of the chapters can be useful for group workers.

Social-skills training and assertion training are particularly well-suited for group work. The two sources that I consider to be excellent in this area are *Your perfect right: A guide to assertive living* by Alberti and Emmons (1986a) and their companion professional edition of *Your perfect right: A manual for assertiveness trainers* (1986b). The latter book contains many helpful guidelines for trainers of these groups.

There are several excellent self-help instruction books that clearly describe a variety of techniques aimed at developing self-control and self-direction. These books can serve as useful supplements to any group counseling program, for members can use these procedures to practice new behaviors outside the group. The books I most recommend are *Self-directed behavior: Self-modification for personal adjust-*

ment, by Watson and Tharp (1989); and *Toward a self-managed life style,* by Williams and Long (1983).

The Behavior Therapist is a journal published by the Association for the Advancement of Behavior Therapy. Articles include reports on topical research and innovative treatment programs, commentaries that discuss controversial issues in behavior therapy, special features on important topics, reviews of the latest important books in the field, and news of the association. You can subscribe to the journal by writing to the AABT, 15 West 36th Street, New York, NY 10018.

The Cognitive Behaviorist is another valuable source for keeping current in this field. For information on getting this newsletter, contact Dr. E. Thomas Dowd, Counseling Psychology Program, 130 Bancroft Hall, University of Nebraska, Lincoln, NE 68588.

If you are interested in subscribing to the newsletter *Empirical Group Work and Group Therapy* (formerly *Behavior Group Therapy*), send $5 to Dr. Sheldon D. Rose, Editor, School of Social Work, 425 Henry Mall, University of Wisconsin, Madison, WI 53706. This newsletter is sponsored by the Interpersonal Skill Training and Research Project of the University of Wisconsin; the Group Therapy Special Interest Group of the Association for the Advancement of Behavior Therapy; and the Symposium for the Study of Empirical Foundations of Group Work. The newsletter presents ideas, abstracts, brief articles, and group exercises used in behavioral group therapy.

A group leader's guide to stress management training is a 75-page manual prepared by Sheldon D. Rose, Richard M. Tolman, and Steven H. Tallant (1985) that describes specific agendas for an eight-session stress-management group. It provides minilectures and exercises for use in group sessions. Also included is a stress diary sheet, a relaxation sheet, an overview of stress-management groups, and a bibliography. *A group leader's guide to pain management training* is a 106-page manual prepared by Rose and Karen Subramanian (1986) that gives an introduction to pain management in groups. It describes a variety of group exercises, contains case studies and sample forms, and provides a review of relevant research in the field. If you are interested in getting a copy of either or both of these manuals, contact Dr. Sheldon D. Rose, Editor, School of Social Work, 425 Henry Mall, University of Wisconsin, Madison, WI 53706.

References and Suggested Readings*

*Alberti, R. E., & Emmons, M. L. (1986a). *Your perfect right: A guide to assertive living* (5th ed.). San Luis Obispo, CA: Impact.

*Alberti, R. E., & Emmons, M. L. (1986b). *Your perfect right: A manual for assertiveness trainers.* San Luis Obispo, CA: Impact.

Bandura, A. (1969). *Principles of behavior modification.* New York: Holt, Rinehart & Winston.

Bandura, A. (1977). *Social learning theory.* Englewood Cliffs, NJ: Prentice-Hall.

Bandura, A. (1986). *Social foundations of thought and action: A social cognitive theory.* Englewood Cliffs, NJ: Prentice-Hall.

*Beck, A. T. (1976). *Cognitive therapy and the emotional disorders.* New York: New American Library.

Beck, A. T., Rush, A. J., Shaw, B. F., & Emery, G. (1979). *Cognitive therapy of depression.* New York: Guilford Press.

Berkowitz, S. (1982). Behavior therapy. In L. E. Abt & I. R. Stuart (Eds.), *The newer therapies: A sourcebook.* New York: Van Nostrand Reinhold.

*Books and articles marked with an asterisk are suggested for further study.

Brunell, L. F. (1978). A multimodal treatment model for a mental hospital: Designing specific treatments for specific populations. *Professional Psychology, 9*(4), 570–579.

Brunell, L. F., & Young, W. T. (Eds.). (1982). *Multimodal handbook for a mental hospital: Designing specific treatments for specific problems.* New York: Springer.

*Burns, D. (1981). *Feeling good.* New York: New American Library.

*Comas-Diaz, L. (1981). Effects of cognitive and behavioral group treatment on the depressive symptomatology of Puerto Rican women. *Journal of Counseling and Clinical Psychology, 49*(5), 627–632.

*Cormier, W. H., & Cormier, L. S. (1985). *Interviewing strategies for helpers: A guide to assessment, treatment, and evaluation* (2nd ed.). Pacific Grove, CA: Brooks/ Cole.

Ellis, A. (1962). *Reason and emotion in psychotherapy.* New York: Lyle Stuart.

Ellis, A., & Harper, R. (1975). *A new guide to rational living.* Englewood Cliffs, NJ: Prentice-Hall.

*Emery, G. (1981). *A new beginning: How you can change your life through cognitive therapy.* New York: Simon & Schuster (Touchstone).

Emery, G., Hollon, S. D., & Bedrosian, R. C. (1981). *New directions in cognitive therapy.* New York: Guilford Press.

*Goldfried, M. R., & Davison, G. C. (1976). *Clinical behavior therapy.* New York: Holt, Rinehart & Winston.

Gottman, J. M., & Leiblum, S. (1974). *How to do psychotherapy and how to evaluate it.* New York: Holt, Rinehart & Winston.

Haaga, D. A., & Davison, G. C. (1986). Cognitive change methods. In F. H. Kanfer & A. P. Goldstein (Eds.), *Helping people change: A textbook of methods* (3rd ed.). New York: Pergamon Press.

*Hall, J. A., & Rose, S. D. (1980). Assertion training in a group. In S. D. Rose (Ed.), *A casebook in group therapy: A behavioral-cognitive approach.* Englewood Cliffs, NJ: Prentice-Hall.

*Kanfer, F. H., & Gaelick, L. (1986). Self-management methods. In F. H. Kanfer & A. P. Goldstein (Eds.), *Helping people change: A textbook of methods* (3rd ed.). New York: Pergamon Press.

*Kanfer, F. H., & Goldstein, A. P. (Eds.). (1986). *Helping people change: A textbook of methods* (3rd ed.). New York: Pergamon Press.

Kindy, P., & Patterson, P. M. (1980). Behavioral-cognitive therapy in a group for the prevention of obesity. In S. D. Rose (Ed.), *A casebook in group therapy: A behavioral-cognitive approach.* Englewood Cliffs, NJ: Prentice-Hall.

Kuehnel, J. M., & Liberman, R. P. (1986). Behavior modification. In I. L. Kutash & A. Wolf (Eds.), *Psychotherapist's casebook* (pp. 240–262). San Francisco: Jossey-Bass.

Lazarus, A. A. (1971). *Behavior therapy and beyond.* New York: McGraw-Hill.

*Lazarus, A. A. (1981). *The practice of multimodal therapy.* New York: McGraw-Hill.

*Lazarus, A. A. (1982). Multimodal group therapy. In G. M. Gazda (Ed.), *Basic approaches to group psychotherapy and group counseling* (3rd ed.). Springfield, IL: Charles C Thomas.

*Lazarus, A. A. (1986). Multimodal therapy. In J. C. Norcross (Ed.), *Handbook of eclectic psychotherapy* (pp. 65–93). New York: Brunner/Mazel.

Lazarus, A. A. (1987a). The multimodal approach with adult outpatients. In N. S. Jacobson (Ed.), *Psychotherapists in clinical practice.* New York: Guilford Press.

Lazarus, A. A. (1987b). The need for technical eclecticism: Science, breadth, depth, and specificity. In J. K. Zeig (Ed.), *The evolution of psychotherapy* (pp. 164–178). New York: Brunner/Mazel.

Lazarus, A. A. (1989). Multimodal therapy. In R. J. Corsini & D. Wedding (Eds.), *Current psychotherapies* (4th ed.). Itasca, IL: F. E. Peacock.

Lazarus, A. A., & Fay, A. (1984). Behavior therapy. In T. B. Karasu (Ed.), *The psychiatric therapies* (pp. 483–538). Washington, DC: American Psychiatric Association.

London, P. (1985). *The modes and morals of psychotherapy* (2nd ed.). New York: Hemisphere.

Mahoney, M. J., & Lyddon, W. J. (1988). Recent developments in cognitive approaches to counseling and psychotherapy. *The Counseling Psychologist, 16*(2), 190–234.

Mahoney, M. J., & Thoresen, C. E. (1974). *Self-control: Power to the person.* Pacific Grove, CA: Brooks/Cole.

Masters, J. C., Burish, T. G., Hollon, S. D., & Rimm, D. C. (1987). *Behavior therapy: Techniques and empirical findings* (3rd ed.). New York: Harcourt Brace Jovanovich.

McMullin, R. E. (1986). *Handbook of cognitive therapy techniques.* New York: Norton.

Meichenbaum, D. (1977). *Cognitive behavior modification: An integrative approach.* New York: Plenum.

Meichenbaum, D. (1985). *Stress inoculation training.* New York: Pergamon Press.

Meichenbaum, D. (1986). Cognitive behavior modification. In F. H. Kanfer & A. P. Goldstein (Eds.), *Helping people change: A textbook of methods* (3rd ed.). New York: Pergamon Press.

Perry, M. A., & Furukawa, M. J. (1986). Modeling methods. In F. H. Kanfer & A. P. Goldstein (Eds.), *Helping people change: A textbook of methods* (3rd ed.). New York: Pergamon Press.

*Rios, J. D., & Gutierrez, J. M. (1985/86). Parent training with non-traditional families: An unresolved issue. *Child and Family Behavior Therapy, 7*(4), 33–45.

Roberts, T. K., Jackson, L. J., & Phelps, R. (1980). Lazarus' multimodal therapy model applied in an institutional setting. *Professional Psychology, 11*(1), 150–156.

Rose, S. D. (1972). *Treating children in groups.* San Francisco: Jossey-Bass.

*Rose, S. D. (1977). *Group therapy: A behavioral approach.* Englewood Cliffs, NJ: Prentice-Hall.

Rose, S. D. (Ed.). (1980). *A casebook in group therapy: A behavioral-cognitive approach.* Englewood Cliffs, NJ: Prentice-Hall.

Rose, S. D. (1982). Group counseling with children: A behavioral and cognitive approach. In G. M. Gazda (Ed.), *Basic approaches to group psychotherapy and group counseling* (3rd ed.). Springfield, IL: Charles C Thomas.

Rose, S. D. (1983). Behavior therapy in groups. In H. I. Kaplan & B. J. Sadock (Eds.), *Comprehensive group psychotherapy* (2nd ed.). Baltimore: Williams & Wilkins.

Rose, S. D. (1984). The use of data in resolving group problems. *Social Work with Groups, 7,* 119–130.

*Rose, S. D. (1986). Group methods. In F. H. Kanfer & A. P. Goldstein (Eds.), *Helping people change: A textbook of methods* (3rd ed.) (pp. 437–469). New York: Pergamon Press.

*Rose, S. D., & Edleson, J. (1987). *Working with children and adolescents in groups: A multimodal approach.* San Francisco: Jossey-Bass.

Rose, S. D., & Feldman, R. (Eds.). (1986). *Research on groups.* New York: Haworth Press.

Rose, S. D., & Subramanian, K. (1986). *A group leader's guide to pain management training.* Madison, WI: Interpersonal Skill Training and Research Project.

*Rose, S. D., Tallant, S. H., Tolman, R., & Subramanian, K. (1986). A multimethod group approach: Program development research. In S. D. Rose & R. Feldman (Eds.), *Research on groups.* New York: Haworth Press.

*Rose, S. D., Tolman, R., & Tallant, S. H. (1985). *A group leader's guide to stress management training*. Madison, WI: Interpersonal Skill Training and Research Project.

Rose, S. R. (1987). Social skills training in middle childhood: A structured group approach. *Journal for Specialists in Group Work, 12*(4), 144–149.

Shaffer, J., & Galinsky, M. D. (1989). *Models of group therapy* (2nd ed.). Englewood Cliffs, NJ: Prentice-Hall.

Thoresen, C. E., & Coates, T. J. (1978). What does it mean to be a behavior therapist? *The Counseling Psychologist, 7*(3), 3–21.

Thoresen, C. E., & Mahoney, M. J. (1974). *Behavioral self-control*. New York: Holt, Rinehart & Winston.

*Turner, S. M., Beidel, D. C., Hersen, M., & Bellack, A. S. (1984). Effects of race on ratings of social skills. *Journal of Consulting and Clinical Psychology, 54*(3), 474–475.

Upper, D., & Ross, S. M. (Eds.). (1979). *Behavioral group therapy 1979: An annual review*. Champaign, IL: Research Press.

Upper, D., & Ross, S. M. (Eds.). (1980). *Behavioral group therapy 1980: An annual review*. Champaign, IL: Research Press.

Upper, D., & Ross, S. M. (Eds.). (1981). *Behavioral group therapy 1981: An annual review*. Champaign, IL: Research Press.

*Watson, D. L., & Tharp, R. G. (1989). *Self-directed behavior: Self-modification for personal adjustment* (5th ed.). Pacific Grove, CA: Brooks/Cole.

Williams, R., & Long, J. (1983). *Toward a self-managed life style* (3rd ed.). Boston: Houghton Mifflin.

Wilson, G. T., Franks, C. M., Kendall, P. C., & Foreyt, J. P. (1987). *Review of behavior therapy: Theory and practice*. New York: Guilford Press.

Wolpe, J. (1958). *Psychotherapy by reciprocal inhibition*. Stanford, CA: Stanford University Press.

Wolpe, J. (1969). *The practice of behavior therapy*. New York: Pergamon Press.

14

Rational-Emotive
Group Therapy

Introduction

Albert Ellis, who founded rational-emotive therapy (RET) in the mid-1950s, is one of the pioneers in emphasizing the influential role of cognition in behavior. He is also a most energetic and productive individual. In his busy professional life, Ellis conducts about 80 individual and 5 group-therapy sessions weekly, along with about 200 talks and workshops for the public and psychological professionals yearly. He has published more than 50 books and 600 articles, mainly on the topic of RET. There is no doubt that he has played a central role in the recent interest in cognitive-behavioral therapy.

Ellis (1979c) has described his emotional problems and consequent inhibited behavior during his youth. One of his problems was his fear of speaking in public. As a way of overcoming his anxieties, Ellis developed a cognitive-philosophical approach combined with an *in vivo* desensitization approach and homework assignments that involved speaking in public regardless of how uncomfortable he might initially be. With these cognitive-behavioral methods, Ellis states, he has virtually conquered some of his worst blocks.

As a part of his own psychoanalytic training, Ellis underwent 3 years of analysis. When he began his practice of psychotherapy, he routinely put his patients on the sofa and proceeded with them in a decidedly orthodox psychoanalytic way. Despite getting generally good results, he reports, he was dissatisfied with this approach. In accordance with classical technique, he would endure long and unhelpful silences and sit idly by with a limply held pencil (Ellis, 1962). He then began deviating from classical psychoanalysis and becoming more of a neo-Freudian therapist. Yet he was still not satisfied with what he observed. Therefore, he began to persuade and impel his clients to *do* the very things they were most afraid of doing, such as risking the rejection of significant others. Gradually Ellis became much more eclectic and more active and directive as a therapist. He acknowledges his debt to the ancient Greeks, especially to the Stoics. According to Ellis, one of the philosophical bases for RET is *phenomenological*. He quotes Epictetus as having said "It's never the things that happen to you that upset you; it's your view of them" (Weinrach, 1980). Thus, Ellis began to find the basis for his clients' emotional and behavioral difficulties in the way they subjectively responded to and interpreted reality.

In his early formulations he stressed *rational* therapy, or the cognitive element in counseling, because this perspective was so radically different from other therapies in the mid-1950s. Later, RET was broadened to include both a cognitive and a behavioral dimension, as can be seen from his classic work, *Reason and Emotion in Psychotherapy* (Ellis, 1962). Recent modifications of RET include the addition of other behavioral techniques like relaxation, imagery methods, *in vivo* desensitization, flooding, and shame-attacking exercises (see Ellis, 1986a; Ellis & Grieger, 1986; Ellis & Harper, 1975). Thus, RET can be viewed as a form of cognitively oriented behavioral therapy. It has evolved into a comprehensive and eclectic approach that emphasizes thinking, judging, deciding, and doing. But the approach still retains Ellis's highly didactic and directive quality, and RET is more concerned with the dimensions of thinking than with those of feeling.

RET holds that thinking and feeling are not experienced in a pure state but involve each other (Ellis, 1962). Thus, a cool thought, "I failed at this task," leads to no emotion or mild emotion; a warm or evaluative thought, "I don't like failing," leads to greater feeling; and a hot thought, "I must not fail, and it's terrible if I do," leads to disturbed feeling. RET therefore emphasizes changing one's thoughts, and changing them strongly or vigorously, especially when "intellectually" or "coolly" seeing one's irrational thinking does not work. Under these conditions, it advocates powerful disputations and strong repetitions of coping statements to change one's irrational beliefs. While stressing cognitive methods, RET also uses a number of powerful, dramatic emotive methods and is more "emotional" in this respect than are most other models of cognitive-behavioral therapy.

RET is based on the assumption that we are born with a potential for both rational, straight thinking and irrational, crooked thinking. The irrational beliefs that are the cause of our emotional disturbance may have been originally incorporated from external sources, but we persist in these self-defeating beliefs by a process of self-indoctrination. In order to overcome the indoctrination that has resulted in irrational thinking, RET therapists employ active/directive techniques such as teaching, suggestion, persuasion, and homework assignments, and they challenge clients to substitute a rational belief system for an irrational one.

The rational-emotive approach does not consider the nature of the relationship between therapist and client as vitally important to the therapeutic process. What is given primary emphasis is the therapist's skill and willingness to challenge, confront, probe, and convince the client to practice activities (both in and outside of therapy) that will lead to constructive changes in the client's thinking and behaving. The approach stresses action—doing something about the insights one gains in therapy. Change, it is assumed, will come about mainly by a commitment to consistently practice new behaviors that challenge old and ineffective ones.

RET lends itself to group-oriented procedures, and frequently RET practitioners use group processes as a method of choice. The group is seen as offering the participants excellent opportunities for challenging self-destructive thinking and for practicing different behaviors.

Key Concepts

Some Hypotheses and Assumptions of RET

A number of the basic assumptions of RET can be categorized under the following main postulates (Ellis, 1986a, 1987a, 1987b):

- Feeling, thinking, and behaving continually interact with and influence one another.
- Emotional disturbances are caused or contributed to by a complex of biological and environmental factors.
- Humans are affected by the people and the things around them, and they also intentionally affect the people around them. People significantly decide, or choose, to disturb themselves—or not disturb themselves—in response to the influences of the system in which they live.
- People disturb themselves emotionally, cognitively, and behaviorally. They often think in a manner that defeats their own best interests as well as those of the others in their social group.
- When unfortunate events occur, people tend to create irrational beliefs about these events that are characterized by absolutist and dogmatic thinking. Typically, these irrational beliefs are centered on competence and success, love and approval, being treated fairly, and safety and comfort.
- It is not unfortunate events by themselves that cause emotional disturbance; rather, irrational beliefs lead to personality problems.
- Most humans have a prodigious tendency to make and keep themselves emotionally disturbed. Thus, they find it virtually impossible to maintain good mental health. Unless they clearly and tough-mindedly acknowledge this reality, they are likely to sabotage their best efforts at changing (Ellis, 1987b).
- When people behave in self-defeating ways, they do have the ability to look at events in their lives and to become aware of ways in which

their beliefs are negatively affecting them. With this awareness they also have the capacity to dispute their irrational thoughts and change them into rational beliefs. By changing these beliefs about certain events, people also change their inappropriate feelings and self-defeating behaviors.

• Once irrational beliefs are discovered, they can be counteracted by using a combination of cognitive, emotive, and behavioral methods. RET has various techniques of showing people how to minimize their self-sabotaging thoughts, feelings, and behaviors.

• RET clients must be willing to (1) acknowledge that they are mainly responsible for their own disturbed thoughts, emotions, and actions; (2) look at how they are thinking, feeling, and behaving when they needlessly disturb themselves; and (3) commit themselves to the hard work that it will take to change.

Origins of Emotional Disturbance

According to Ellis, feelings of anxiety, depression, rejection, rage, guilt, and alienation are initiated and perpetuated by a self-defeating belief system based on irrational ideas that were uncritically embraced during early childhood. These self-defeating beliefs are supported and maintained by negative, absolutist, and illogical statements that people make to themselves over and over. Below are a few examples of self-verbalizations and unconsciously held philosophies identified by Ellis (1987b):

• "Because I strongly desire to perform important tasks competently and successfully, I *absolutely must* perform them *perfectly well!*"

• "Because I strongly desire to be approved by people I find significant, I *absolutely must* have their *outstanding* approval!"

• "Because I strongly desire people to treat me considerately and fairly, they *absolutely must at all times and under all conditions* do so!"

As Ellis indicates, other factors also perpetuate emotional disturbance. Some of these factors are human ignorance, stupidity, unperceptiveness, rigidity, defensiveness, pollyannaism, and focusing on changing the situation rather than on changing oneself.

The A-B-C Theory

The so-called A-B-C theory of personality and emotional disturbance is central to RET theory and practice. According to Ellis (1979c), we "construct our emotions and behaviors in accordance with the premises and philosophies . . . that we have invented" (p. 35). These premises are shaped by our social environment, but, Ellis continues, "it is largely the way we react to the conditions around us, rather than the conditions themselves, that leads to our 'personality traits' and to our disturbances" (p. 35). The A-B-C theory maintains that when people have an emotional reaction at point C (the so-called emotional Consequence), after some Activating event that occurred at point A, it is not the event itself (A) that causes the emotional state (C), although it may contribute to it. It is the Belief system (B), or the beliefs that people have about the event, that mainly creates C. For example, if you feel rejected and hurt (C) over the event of not getting a promotion at work (A), it is not the fact that you weren't promoted that causes your hurt; it is your *belief* (B) about the event. By believing that not receiving a promotion means that you are a failure and that your efforts have not been appreciated and that they *should* be, you "construct" the emotional consequence of feeling rejected and hurt. Thus, human beings are largely responsible for creating their own emotional disturbances through the beliefs they associate with the events of their lives.

Ellis (1986a) maintains that people have the capacity to significantly change their cognitions, behaviors, and emotions. If they exert the choice they have as human beings to think and act differently, they can quickly change disturbance-creating patterns into constructive ways of living. According to Ellis, people can best accomplish this goal by avoiding preoccupying themselves with A and by acknowledging and yet resisting the temptation to dwell endlessly on emotional consequences at C. They can choose to examine, challenge, modify, and uproot B—the irrational beliefs they hold about the activating events at A. Ellis emphasizes that, because humans can think, they can also train themselves to change or eliminate their self-sabotaging beliefs by exercising self-discipline, by seeking the help of objective and rational-thinking people, by undergoing individual therapy or some form of workshop or group-therapy experience, and by reading RET books or listening to tapes.

Confronting and Attacking Irrational Beliefs

The RET therapeutic process begins by teaching clients the A-B-C theory. When they have come to see how their irrational beliefs and values are causally linked to their emotional and behavioral disturbances, they are ready to Dispute these beliefs and values at point D. D is the application of scientific principles to challenge self-defeating philosophies and dispose of unrealistic and unverifiable hypotheses.

Ellis (1988) says that most of our irrational ideas can be reduced to three main forms of what he calls *must*urbation:

1. "I *must* do well and be approved by *significant* others, and if I don't do as well as I *should* or *must,* there's something really rotten about me."
2. "Others *must, ought,* and *should* treat me considerately and fairly and even *specially*. If they don't, it is *horrible,* and they deserve to roast in hell for eternity!"
3. "Conditions under which I live *must* be arranged so that I easily and immediately, with no real effort, will get what I command."

A key concept of RET is that when people seriously disturb themselves, they almost always implicitly or explicitly accept or invent such absolutist and *mus*turbatory irrational beliefs. One of the most effective methods of helping people reduce their emotional disturbances is to show them how to actively and forcefully *dispute* these irrational beliefs until they surrender them. This process of disputation involves three other D's: (1) *detecting* irrational beliefs and seeing that they are illogical and unrealistic, (2) *debating* these irrational beliefs and showing oneself how they are un- supported by evidence, and (3) *discriminating* between irrational thinking and rational thinking (Ellis & Bernard, 1986).

After D comes E, or the Effect of disputing—the relinquishing of self- destructive ideologies, the acquisition of a more rational and realistic philosophy of life, and a greater acceptance of oneself, of others, and of the inevitable frustrations of everyday life. This new philosophy of life has, of course, a practical side—a concrete E, if you wish. In the example I gave above, E would translate into a rational and empirically based conclusion: "Well, it's too bad that I didn't get that promotion. But it's not the end of the world. There may be other opportunities. Besides, not getting the promotion does not mean that I am a failure. So I don't need to keep telling myself all that nonsense." Or a person might make a rational statement such as the following: "I'd like to have gotten the job, but I didn't. I regret that, but it's not awful, terrible, and horrible. It's bad enough that I lost it; I don't have to make myself miserable as well. I'm disappointed, but it's not awful unless I make it awful." And, according to RET theory, the ultimate result is the elimination of feelings of depression and rejection.

Self-Rating

According to Ellis (1979b), we have a strong tendency not only to rate our acts and behaviors as "good" or "bad" but also to rate *ourselves as a total person* as "good" or "bad" on the basis of our performance. Our self-ratings influence our feelings and actions, because this self-rating process con- stitutes one of the main sources of our emotional disturbances. Therefore, the RET therapist teaches clients how to separate the evaluation of their behaviors from the evaluation of their *self*—their *essence* and their *totality*— and how to accept themselves in spite of their imperfections. Some examples of self-rating are:

- "The fact that I make mistakes means that I'm incompetent and worthless."
- "I have committed 'wrong' acts; thus, I am bad, evil, and shameful."
- "If everyone doesn't accept me and approve of me, I'm a terrible person."

Ellis contends that this kind of self-rating inevitably leads to a lot of problems—among them, self-centeredness and self-consciousness; a tenden- cy to damn oneself and others; the feeling that no matter what one accom- plishes, it is never enough; attempts to manipulate others; and the sabotag- ing of one's goals.

Rational-Emotive Therapy in Groups

RET as an Educational Model

As I said earlier, rational-emotive therapy emphasizes cognitive restructuring and relies heavily on the didactic side of the therapeutic process. Therapy is viewed largely as a matter of emotional and intellectual reeducation. Like most forms of teaching, RET is often done in a group setting, and many RET practitioners use group techniques as a method of choice. Rational-emotive group therapy avails itself of audiovisual presentations, bibliotherapy, films and television tapes, programmed instruction, and other teaching methods.

Ellis (1977c) expresses his view of RET in groups as follows: "I stoutly hypothesize that this kind of group intervention is more likely to lead to a quicker, deeper, and more elegant solution to the ubiquitous human condition of childish demandingness and perennial disturbability than any other contemporary form of psychotherapy" (p. 280).* To reach such a "solution," group members learn to separate their rational beliefs from their irrational beliefs and to understand the origins of their emotional disturbances as well as those of other members. Participants are taught the many ways in which they can (1) free themselves of their irrational life philosophy so that they can function more effectively as an individual and as a relational being and (2) learn more appropriate ways of responding so that they won't needlessly feel upset about the realities of living. The group members help and support one another in these learning endeavors.

Goals

The goals in an RET group are to teach clients how to change their dysfunctional emotions and behaviors into appropriate ones and to cope with almost any unfortunate events that may arise in their lives (Wessler, 1986). Ideally, RET develops the following characteristics of a mentally and emotionally healthy individual: self-interest, social interest, self-direction, tolerance, acceptance of ambiguity and uncertainty, flexibility, scientific thinking, commitment, risk taking, self-acceptance, long-range hedonism, the willingness to be imperfect, and responsibility for one's own emotional disturbance (Ellis, 1987a).

RET aims at providing group members with tools for reducing or eliminating inappropriate emotions (such as depression and anxiety), so that they can live a richer and more satisfying life. To accomplish this basic objective, RET offers clients practical ways to identify their underlying faulty beliefs and to exchange them for constructive beliefs.

Ellis contends that rational-emotive therapy can work well with large groups (of 50, 100, and more), utilizing a workshop format, or can be applied

*From *Handbook of Rational-Emotive Therapy*, by A. Ellis and R. Grieger. Copyright 1977 by Springer Publishing Company, New York. This and all other quotations from this source are reprinted by permission.

to small groups with 10 to 13 members. Small groups, Ellis (1982b) writes, have the following aims:

- Members are helped to understand the roots of their emotional and behavioral problems and to put these insights to use in overcoming their symptoms and learning more elegant ways of functioning both intrapersonally and interpersonally.
- Group participants develop an understanding of the problems of others, and they learn how to be of some therapeutic help to fellow group members.
- Members learn ways of minimizing life circumstances and their irrational reactions to them, so that they manage to disturb themselves less often than when they first joined the group.
- The participants learn to achieve both behavioral changes and basic cognitive changes, including learning how to cope with unpleasant realities; surrendering self-defeating thinking and replacing it with rational thinking; and stopping the practice of self-rating, instead learning to accept themselves as fallible humans.

Basically, group members are taught that they are responsible for their own emotional reactions, that they can change their emotional disturbances by paying attention to their self-verbalizations and by changing their beliefs and values, and that if they acquire a new and more realistic philosophy of life, they can cope effectively with most of the unfortunate events in their lives. Although the therapeutic goals of RET are essentially the same for both individual and group therapy, the two differ in some of the specific methods and techniques employed, as you will see in the pages that follow.

Rationale

More than 30 years of experience in conducting and leading RET groups has confirmed Ellis's belief that a group is particularly effective in helping participants make constructive personality and behavior changes. Ellis (1977c) discusses many of the advantages of RET in groups, some of which are briefly summarized below:

1. Group members can remind one another of the desirability of accepting reality and work together to bring about positive changes.
2. Since RET emphasizes a vigorous attack on self-defeating thinking, other members can play a powerful role in challenging the individual's crooked thinking.
3. Group members can contribute suggestions, comments, and hypotheses and reinforce some of the points made by the leader.
4. The activity-oriented homework assignments that are a vital component of RET are more effectively carried out in the group context than in one-to-one therapy.

5. The group offers an effective milieu for several active/directive procedures such as role playing, assertion training, behavior rehearsal, modeling, and risk-taking exercises.

6. The group serves as a laboratory in which behavior can be directly observed in action.

7. RET clients are often asked to complete homework report forms, which require going over the A-B-C's of upsetting situations and then learning how to correct faulty thinking and behaving. By hearing other members' reports and learning how they have dealt with the situations in question, participants can better deal with their own issues. Although these homework assignments can be done in individual therapy, a group format is more effective because the members can then practice together the behaviors they would like to increase or decrease in the real world.

8. Group members discover that, since their problems are far from unique, they don't need to condemn themselves for having these problems.

9. Through feedback from others in the group, participants begin to see themselves as others see them and notice quite clearly the behaviors that might be changed. They also gain social skills during the sessions and in the socializing that takes place after the sessions.

10. When the statements that members make indicate faulty thinking, the other members and the leader can immediately bring these mistakes to the person's attention so that the faulty thinking can be corrected.

11. By watching other members, participants are able to see that treatment can be effective, that people can change, that they can take steps to help themselves, and that successful therapy is the product of hard and persistent work.

12. In groups, clients have the opportunity to consider a wider range of alternatives to solving their problems than is possible in one-to-one therapy.

13. Disclosing intimate problems, some of which the person considers shameful, is therapeutic in itself. Self-disclosure enables participants to realize that taking risks pays off: their "revelations" generally don't have the dire consequences they feared so much, and even if someone does criticize them, it is certainly not catastrophic.

14. Since RET is highly educational and didactic, it typically includes information giving and discussion of problem-solving strategies. Economically and practically, this is better done in a group than in an individual setting. The group also provides a format for teaching/learning/discussing/practicing, which encourages participants to become actively involved in their treatment.

15. The average duration of the RET group session (2¼ hours with the leader and another hour of postgroup work with an assistant leader)

provides enough time to effectively challenge rigidly held self-defeating beliefs.

16. Group procedures are especially useful for people who are rigidly bound by old patterns of dysfunctional behavior, because the group setting provides the challenge necessary to reevaluate these patterns and adopt healthier ones.

Even though Ellis uses this long list of reasons to support his view that RET is especially suitable for group work, these same reasons can be adduced to support the group application of most of the other therapeutic models covered in this book. Therefore, the points discussed by Ellis can be usefully considered by any group practitioner who is in the process of developing a rationale for a group-counseling program, even if he or she has an orientation other than RET.

Role and Functions of the Group Leader

The therapeutic activities of an RET group are carried out with one central purpose: helping the participants internalize a rational philosophy of life, just as they internalized a set of dogmatic and false beliefs derived from their sociocultural environment and from their own invention. In working toward this ultimate aim, the group leader has several specific functions and tasks. The first task is to show the group members *how* they have created their own misery. This is done by clarifying the connection between their emotional/behavioral disturbances and their values, beliefs, and attitudes. With the therapist's help, members come to see how they have uncritically accepted and invented a series of "shoulds," "musts," and "oughts." The leader confronts them with the propaganda they originally accepted without questioning, demonstrates how they are continuing to indoctrinate themselves with unexamined assumptions, and persuades them to engage in counterpropaganda activities.

In describing his personal style of conducting a group during the initial session, Ellis is likely to make a statement such as this (cited in Donigian & Malnati, 1987, p. 88):

> In terms of the form of psychotherapy and group therapy that I am going to employ with you in our subsequent sessions, all of you, like virtually all the rest of the human race, strongly tend to be intense *mus*turbators. You mistakenly—and quite self-defeatingly—often think that you absolutely *must* do well and be approved by others; second, that you *should* and *must* be dealt with considerately and fairly by the other people with whom you closely associate; and third, that the world *ought to* and *must* provide you with conditions that give you, fairly easily and quickly, whatever you dearly want and refrain from giving you the things and situations that you consider highly obnoxious.

To help members move beyond the mere recognition that they originally incorporated irrational thoughts and that they now keep themselves emotionally upset by continuing to think illogically, the therapist strives to modify their thinking. RET assumes that people's illogical beliefs are so deeply ingrained that they will not change easily. Thus, it is the role of the leader to teach members how to challenge their assumptions and how to stop the vicious circle of the self-rating and self-blaming process.

But getting rid of symptoms of disturbances is not enough. If only specific problems or symptoms are dealt with, other illogical fears are likely to appear. Thus, the final step in the therapeutic process is to teach members how to avoid becoming victims of future irrational beliefs. The therapist attacks the core of clients' irrational thinking and teaches them how to apply logical thinking when coping with future problems.

Although RET employs many cognitive and emotive/dramatic techniques, Ellis (1987a) writes that these techniques are best carried out in a directive manner, with the therapist playing the role of a teacher and not that of an intensely relating partner. Although Ellis does not give primacy to the personal nature of the therapeutic relationship, it is true that the RET therapist demonstrates respect for the client. Clients learn that the therapist is not thinking disapprovingly and that they can trust him or her to work actively to help them. RET especially emphasizes the therapist's unconditional acceptance of clients, even when they act badly in and out of therapy. According to Wessler (1986), the RET group leader does not try to create a climate of support in which people are reinforced for a neurotic "need" for love and approval. Instead, group members are encouraged to express full acceptance of one another.

A study conducted by Warren and McLellarn (1987) suggests that RET therapists generally tend to be direct and confrontive rather than subtle and gentle in their interactions with clients. The vast majority of them feel comfortable with behavioral teaching and with forcefully persuading clients to act on this teaching in their daily lives. Personally, they tend to be philosophical, intellectual, hard-hitting, confrontive, instructive, directive, persuasive, risk-taking, tolerant, pragmatic, scientific, unmystical, and eclectic.

Therapeutic Techniques and Procedures

Ellis (1974, 1986a) stresses that rational-emotional therapy lends itself to a wide range of behavioral and cognitive methods to induce behavior change. In keeping with RET's didactic nature, these methods are directive, confrontational, philosophical, and action oriented. RET focuses on specific techniques for changing a client's specific thoughts in concrete situations in such a way that other group members can apply these skills to their own concerns. Thus, an RET group fosters the transfer to other members' personal issues better than many other approaches do. Even though one person may be working at a time, everyone else can be learning how to work on his or her own changes at the same time.

Problems Treated in RET

A wide range of disorders can be treated in RET groups. The following are common clinical problems dealt with by RET therapists: anxiety, depression, anger, marital problems, poor interpersonal skills, parenting skills, character disorders, obsessive/compulsive disorders, eating disorders, psychosomatic disorders, addictions, and psychotic disorders (Warren & McLellarn, 1987). In the case of clients who are involuntarily referred, it is necessary to find ways of motivating them by showing them that they can benefit in some way by taking RET seriously (Wessler, 1986).

Types of Intervention Used in RET

RET therapists believe that because people have a strong tendency to get emotionally upset and to behave dysfunctionally, because they think, feel, and behave in self-defeating ways, and because they keep harboring self-sabotaging thoughts even after some positive change has occurred, they will benefit from a highly active and directive therapy (Ellis, 1979b). RET is truly eclectic, in that it uses a wide range of cognitive, emotive, and behavioral interventions, both during group sessions and outside of them.

An international survey of RET therapists found that the most frequently used techniques were humor, didactic presentations of RET theory, cognitive rehearsal of desired behaviors, and unconditional acceptance (Warren & McLellarn, 1987). This same study found the following in-session techniques also being used by RET therapists: strong and forceful language, disputing methods, assertiveness training, social-skills training, role playing, behavioral rehearsal, teaching rational coping self-statements, rational-emotive imagery, modeling, relaxation training, rational role reversal, problem-solving training, imaginal desensitization, contingency contracting, operant methods, Beck's cognitive therapy, *in vivo* desensitization, and information giving.

Cognitive Methods of RET

From a cognitive perspective RET demonstrates to clients that their beliefs and self-talk are keeping them disturbed. RET has various techniques for dispelling these self-defeating cognitions and teaching people how to acquire a rational approach to living. In an RET group there is a heavy emphasis on thinking, disputing, debating, challenging, persuading, interpreting, explaining, and teaching. Some of the cognitive techniques that are often used in an RET group are described next.

Teaching the A-B-C's of RET. The A-B-C theory of RET, mentioned earlier, is taught to clients undergoing individual or group therapy. Members are taught that no matter how and where they originally acquired their irrational "shoulds," "oughts," and "musts," they have the power now to begin to surrender these dysfunctional beliefs. They are shown ways to apply the A-B-C theory to practical problems they encounter in everyday life.

Disputing Irrational Beliefs. As mentioned earlier, D stands for *disputing,* which can be further subdivided into three others D's: *detecting* irrational beliefs and clearly seeing how they are illogical and unrealistic, *debating* these illogical beliefs by showing that they do not make sense, and *discriminating* them from rational beliefs (Ellis & Bernard, 1986).

RET teaches clients to use logico-empirical methods to check and modify their values and attitudes about themselves and others. Rational-emotive therapists show clients how to detect their absolutistic "shoulds" and "musts," their "awfulizing," and their "self-downing." In their didactic role RET leaders function as teacher and therapist, and they focus on disputing the irrational, logically inconsistent, absolutist, catastrophic, and rationalized ideas of clients. They demonstrate how such ideas bring about unnecessary disturbances and persuade clients to change or surrender these dysfunctional behaviors. They also teach group participants to empirically contradict the disturbance-creating thinking of other group members.

Coping Self-Statements. Group members are taught how irrational beliefs can be countered by sensible coping statements. They are expected to monitor their manner of speaking by writing down and analyzing the quality of their language. For example, a member might tell herself: "I *must* perform well, which means being perfect. If I make any mistakes, it would be *horrible.* I simply *cannot stand it* when I don't attain perfection immediately. People will give me approval and love only when I am perfect, and I *absolutely need* this acceptance from others to feel worthwhile." By becoming aware of the absolutist and demanding quality of her internal and external speech, she can learn how what she tells herself is setting her up for failure. She can replace these self-destructive statements with coping statements such as "I can still accept myself in spite of my imperfections. Although I like doing my best, I don't have to drive myself to unrealistically high performances. Besides, even if I were to fail, I could still accept myself. I don't have to have universal approval to feel that I am a valuable person."

Psychoeducational Methods. Members of RET groups are encouraged to read books and make use of audio tapes. Two of the most popular of these books are *A New Guide to Rational Living* (Ellis & Harper, 1975) and *How to Stubbornly Refuse to Make Yourself Miserable about Anything—Yes, Anything!* (Ellis, 1988). Ellis has made many tapes, a few of which cover ways of stubbornly refusing to be ashamed of anything, ways to stop worrying, conquering the dire need for love, and conquering low frustration tolerance. Members are encouraged to practice and work hard outside of the therapy sessions as a pathway to personal change.

Cognitive Homework. Clients participating in RET groups are given cognitive homework assignments, which consist of ways of applying the A-B-C theory of RET to problems in daily life. Members may be given the "RET Self-Help Form" (which is reproduced in the student manual of this text). They write down activating events, consequences such as disturbed feelings or self-defeating behavior, and irrational beliefs. In an adjoining column they write down a disputing statement for each irrational belief. In another column they record an effective rational belief to replace the irrational belief. Finally, they record the feelings and behaviors they experienced after arriving at an effective rational belief. For example, the statement "I *must* be approved of and accepted by all the significant people in my life" can be disputed with statements such as "Where is it written that I *must* have this approval?" "Why *must* I have their total approval in order to feel like a worthwhile individual?" Replacing an effective rational belief might include the statement "There is no evidence that I *absolutely must* have approval from others, though I would like to be approved of by those I respect." During the week, group members make the time to record and think about how their beliefs are contributing to their personal problems, and they work hard at uprooting these self-defeating cognitions. When they return to the group, they can bring up specific situations in which they did well or in which they experienced difficulty. Group members often teach one another ways of disputing beliefs, based on material that grows out of the "RET Self-Help Form."

RET group therapy is particularly effective with many resistant clients, because in a group other members typically challenge their rigid thinking. Clients are more likely to surrender their ineffective ways of thinking when they are confronted by both the group leader and their peers. They observe others in the group effectively using RET cognitive methods, and they are consequently encouraged to apply these methods to themselves. Furthermore, when other group members give an individual a homework assignment, he or she is more likely to perform it than if it is given by a therapist (Ellis, 1984c).

Use of Humor.   Of the many techniques used by rational-emotive therapists, humor has been ranked as the most popular (Warren & McLellarn, 1987). Ellis (1986a) believes that people take themselves far too seriously. As one of its main techniques to combat the kind of exaggerated thinking that leads people into trouble, RET employs a good deal of humor. It reduces certain ideas that clients tenaciously hold to absurdity by showing them how contradictory and ridiculous these views really are. One example of employing humor is getting group members to sing from the songbook *A Garland of Rational Songs* (Ellis, 1977b). Some clients find benefit in singing to themselves some of these light-hearted songs when they are anxious or depressed.

Emotive Methods in RET Groups

RET is almost always a multimodal approach to change, in that it rarely treats clients without using several emotive and behavioral, as well as cognitive, methods (Ellis, 1986a). Some of these emotive techniques are unconditional acceptance, rational-emotive role playing, rational-emotive imagery, and shame-attacking exercises.

Unconditional Acceptance.   RET gives full and unconditional acceptance to clients, no matter how badly they behave inside and outside of therapy. The therapist can strongly show group members that even though their behavior may be *immoral* or *foolish*, they are never *rotten people* or *total fools*. This kind of RET-flavored unconditional acceptance creates the atmosphere within a group that allows members to feel personally accepted, even though some of their beliefs and behaviors are most likely to be challenged vigorously (Ellis, 1984c).

Rational-Emotive Imagery.   RET shows clients how to imagine some of the worst things they can think of and then trains them to develop appropriate emotions in place of negative emotions. Clients are asked to intensely imagine themselves in specific situations in which they feel habitual and inappropriate feelings. They then actively work on changing these feelings to appropriate ones and, consequently, changing their behavior in the situation. For example, therapists can persuade even resistant clients to imagine vividly that they keep failing and keep getting criticized and thereby induce in them extreme feelings of inadequacy. Then, these clients are encouraged to change their feelings to regret and disappointment instead of worthlessness. Members practice this process for at least 30 days in a row until they have trained themselves to automatically feel regretful and disappointed when they fail instead of feeling inadequate (Ellis, 1984c).

Shame-Attacking Exercises.   Members in RET groups are often encouraged to take risks as a way of challenging their neurotic fears of looking foolish. RET practitioners employ shame-attacking exercises as a way of teaching clients to accept themselves in spite of reactions from others. These exercises are aimed at increasing self-acceptance and mature responsibility, not simply at achieving comfort while doing a specific zany activity (Wessler, 1986). The main thing that clients learn from shame-attacking exercises is that they are no different while they are experiencing disapproval than when they are not. In other words, disapproval does not have to affect their worth or change them, nor does the fear of disapproval have to prevent them from doing things they consider right.

Group members frequently admit that they are inhibiting themselves from doing many things they would like to do because of their fear of what others might think. In a group situation other members may exert therapeutic pressure and also provide support for them to experiment with risky behaviors, first in the group and then in daily situations. Ellis (1984c) describes a few exercises that clients might be induced to perform in public. These include wearing outlandish clothes, borrowing money from a stranger, and shouting out the stops in the train or bus. Ellis contends that if clients will do these acts over and over and also work on their feelings so that they don't feel ashamed or humiliated, they will then be able to conquer some of the powerful feelings that keep them paralyzed from doing many things they would like to do. He suggests that it is better to combine cognitive homework with these *in vivo* shame-attacking exercises. A few other examples of possible shame-attacking exercises follow:

- Walk through a park and sing at the top of your voice.
- In a crowded elevator tell people that you are glad they could attend this important meeting you have called.
- Talk to animals, and pretend that they are talking back to you.
- Ride in a crowded elevator facing the rear.
- Tie a ribbon around a banana and "walk it" down a street.
- In public, shout out the exact time by saying "The time is 11:11 and 20 seconds."
- Go to a drugstore and in a loud voice say to the pharmacist "I want a gross of condoms, and since I use so many of them, you should give me a special discount!" (This is one of Ellis's favorites.)
- After finishing a meal in a restaurant say "Ah, I feel a fart coming on." (This is one of my favorites.)

Role Playing. There are both emotional and behavioral components in role playing. One way of helping clients experience and cope with fear is to ask them to reverse roles. If a member is feeling anxiety over an upcoming job interview, for example, he can assume the role of the interviewer. He can also play himself both in a fearful stance and in a confident manner. In such role-playing situations, of course, there is a combination of working with the client's feelings, thoughts, and behaviors.

Behavioral Methods in RET Groups

Homework Assignments. Earlier, cognitive homework assignments were described, which involve reading, listening to audio tapes, and doing a written A-B-C-D-E analysis. Rational-emotive therapists also frequently use activity-oriented homework assignments to help people think, feel, and behave more rationally. A major tenet in RET is that unless clients put their philosophical restructuring to the test of practice, the effects will not be meaningful or durable. An RET maxim is "There's little gain without pain." RET is not merely a "talk therapy"; rather, it emphasizes that meaningful cognitive change is unlikely unless clients are willing to behave differently (Walen, DiGiuseppe, & Wessler, 1980). Behaviorally oriented homework assignments can include bibliotherapy, risk-taking exercises, relaxation practice, written A-B-C-D-E analyses, shame-attacking exercises, rational-emotive imagery, self-administered rewards and penalties, and listening to tapes of therapy sessions (Warren & McLellarn, 1987). These assignments, which are given by the leader as well as other group members, may be carried out in the group itself or outside of it, in which case the person is supposed to report the results to the group. Here are some examples of in-group exercises:

• A man who is very shy with women is encouraged to approach female group members and systematically challenge his fears and expectations in graduated steps.

• A woman who tends to say very little in the group because she thinks that she has nothing to contribute is asked to make a contract to participate in the discussion at least once each session. She may also be advised to work on changing her irrational ideas about her inability to contribute something of value.

• Members who tend to view the group leader as a superbeing who should be believed without question are invited to challenge the leader in the group and to deal with their attitudes toward authority figures. This assignment allows clients to see how, by maintaining a helpless attitude in the presence of such figures, they keep themselves from growing up or being powerful.

Reinforcement and Penalties.   RET often makes use of both reinforcers and penalties to help clients change. Reinforcements can involve reading a novel, watching a movie, going to a concert, or eating a favorite food. Clients can be taught to reinforce themselves with something they like, but only after they have carried out a specific homework assignment that they have promised themselves to do but that they tend to avoid doing. RET practitioners also show their clients how to use methods of operant conditioning to accomplish something that they consider very difficult or frightening. One of RET's goals is to teach clients better methods of self-management. Members' ultimate success depends on how effectively they can take charge of their life beyond the group sessions. Using principles of reinforcement often helps them develop consistency in applying rational principles to the new problems they encounter. In this sense they become their own therapists and continually teach themselves how to manage their life.

RET uses penalties as well as reinforcers for clients who do not do their homework (Ellis & Grieger, 1977; Ellis & Whiteley, 1979). In cases involving resistant clients, the penalties are often stiff. The goal is to get resistant clients to agree to penalize themselves severely every time they promise themselves to do some homework assignment but then do not follow through. Such penalties may include burning a $20 bill, contributing to a cause they loathe, cleaning a toilet for an hour, visiting a boring relative, or doing unpleasant routine work (Ellis, 1984c).

Role Playing and Modeling.   The group setting is especially suited to many cognitive-behavioral methods such as assertion training, behavior rehearsal, and risk-taking procedures. Some members may hesitate to reveal themselves for fear that if they open up, everyone in the group will reject them. The group provides these members with an opportunity to risk self-disclosure and see what the consequences are. Other members may have trouble being direct with significant people in their life. In the group they can role-play being direct and assertive with significant others and use the group situation to try out and rehearse these new ways.

In an RET group, role playing also involves a cognitive evaluation of the feelings and beliefs that are experienced. Thus, if a member is trying to deal more effectively with a rejecting father who demands perfection, he can adopt a role quite different from his usual one, a role in which he no longer feels victimized by his father's lack of approval. Afterward, this person undertakes a cognitive analysis of the feelings experienced during the role enactment. To that effect, he may try to answer questions such as the following:

- "Do I need my father's approval to survive?"
- "Will I ever be able to attain the level of perfection that my father demands?"
- "Can I accept myself although I'll never be perfect? Can I avoid destructive self-rating and self-blaming because of my imperfection?"
- "Do I *need* my father's approval, or do I simply *want* it?"
- "If I don't have his approval, is it awful, terrible, and horrible?"
- "Do I really have to be perfect before I can accept myself?"

Ellis (1977c) strongly believes that role playing is more effective if it entails a cognitive restructuring of the attitudes revealed by the experience.

The learning that occurs through modeling and imitation is similar to that achieved through role playing. Bandura (1969) has pioneered the theory and practice of social modeling and imitative learning as it relates to behavioral change. By patterning our behavior after those people we perceive as models, we can bring about changes in our thinking, feeling, and behaving.

According to Ellis, effective therapy frequently includes imitating and modeling. In groups, both the leader and other members can serve as models. For instance, if a group member has found a way to identify and change self-destructive modes of thinking, feeling, and behaving, she can be an effective model for the other participants by demonstrating that constructive change *is* possible and by modeling the actual ways in which she has achieved these desirable changes.

In an RET group, modeling, too, involves a cognitive component. Ellis (1979b) says that "when people explicitly perceive how they can use modeling, they can more easily and intensively help themselves than when they have little or no awareness of using imitation" (p. 131).

Skill Training. Related to self-management training is the training RET clients receive in specific skills (such as assertion, socializing, and studying) they would like to have. The assumption is that by acquiring skills they formerly lacked, clients will feel more confident about themselves and will experience significant changes in the way they think, feel, and behave. Ellis (1979b) says "These changes arise not merely from their increased skills but also from their perceptions of their abilities and their self-ratings about their newly acquired competencies" (p. 133). He concludes, "Just as skill training enables clients to change their perceptions of their abilities, so does helping them to perceive themselves differently enable them to acquire better skills" (p. 133). For example, if clients believe that they can make effective contact with others, there is a good chance that they actually will, or at least that they will be less negative if they don't succeed on a particular occasion.

Feedback.   Feedback is very much a part of any group process, and RET groups are no exception. Members get feedback from the group with regard to their ineffective performances, irrational thinking, and self-sabotaging ideas, statements, and behaviors. Using this feedback, they can then practice new behaviors based on fresh or revised assumptions.

Although feedback can greatly contribute to the group process, it can also bog it down in numerous ways, as Ellis (1982b) observes:

> The best-intentioned members can waste time in irrelevancies; lead the problem-presenter up the garden path; sidetrack and diffuse some of the therapist's main points; hold back because they inordinately look for the approval of other group members; bring out their own and others' minor instead of major difficulties; and otherwise get off on various non-therapeutic limbs [p. 394].

It is therefore the role of the therapist to keep the process on track.

A Special Form of RET Group: The RET Marathon

Ellis (1969) has developed a special form of group therapy that he calls "A Weekend of Rational Encounter." Because this type of marathon utilizes the same cognitive-behavioral principles characteristic of other forms of RET, it has very little in common with the encounter marathons that emphasize here-and-now feelings and play down thinking. The RET marathon is divided into two parts. The first part consists of 14 hours of continuous rational-encounter therapy followed by 8 hours of rest. The second part includes 10 more hours of therapy.

The initial stage consists of directed verbal and nonverbal activities designed to help participants get to know one another. During this early stage members are expected to engage in risk-taking procedures and shame-attacking exercises, such as sharing their most shameful experiences with the group. At this stage procedures designed to tap emotional expression are used, and no problem solving and decision making are attempted. As the marathon progresses, the same cognitive and behavioral methods used in the other forms of RET are employed.

During the later stages of the marathon deep personal problems are explored within a highly cognitive framework. In the closing hours of the marathon group members and the leader usually "smoke out anyone who has not as yet brought up any problem for detailed discussion" (Ellis, 1969, p. 212). These participants are asked why they have said little about themselves, and they are encouraged to look for a major problem to bring out into the open. Several questions are generally asked in the closing hours of the marathon. For example:

- What were the most significant experiences you had during this marathon?
- What did you learn about yourself?
- Are there some things that you did not say to the group or to some members of the group that you are willing to say now?

Before leaving the marathon, participants are given specific homework assignments. A postsession is held 6 to 8 weeks later to check on the progress the participants have made with their assignments and to evaluate how well the members are functioning.

Ellis (1969) writes enthusiastically about the value of the marathon format. He says that the marathon is "specifically designed to show group members what their fundamental self-defeating philosophies are and to indicate how they can work at changing these philosophies, in the here-and-now and thereafter" (pp. 126–127).

Evaluation of Rational-Emotive Group Therapy

What I Value in RET

There are several aspects of RET that I consider valuable enough to use in my own approach to group practice. Although I do believe that events and significant others in our past play a critical role in shaping our present beliefs about ourselves, I agree with Ellis that we are the ones who are responsible for maintaining self-destructive and irrational convictions about ourselves. True, we may have learned that unless we were everything that others expected us to be, we could never hope to be loved and accepted. But the fact that at one time we uncritically accepted certain premises doesn't exempt us now from the responsibility of scrutinizing these and other irrational assumptions and replacing them with more rational ones, which will lead to different and more effective behavior.

I often ask group members to express the beliefs or assumptions that underlie the problems they are experiencing. One of the most common answers is that making mistakes is a terrible, unforgivable thing and that we should arrange our lives in such a way that we won't make mistakes. After probing to find out how the person came to accept such a belief, I generally pursue the issue with other questions—for example: "Does this belief really make sense to you now? What would your life be like if you continued to live by these assumptions? Do you think that you'd be different if you could change some of these basic beliefs? If so, in what ways? What actions can you take now, in this group and in your everyday life, that will help you change some of the beliefs you hold?"

In short, I value RET's emphasis on thinking and conceptualizing, and I am critical of some group approaches that denigrate the role of thinking as "detached analyzation" and "abstract head-tripping." In some groups the focus is exclusively on "gut feelings," "here-and-now reactions," and emotional experiences; thinking, or any attempt to make sense of an emotional experience, is generally seen as an obstacle to "getting in touch with feelings." Although I do find considerable value in experiencing a catharsis and expressing pent-up feelings, I've found that for an emotional experience to have significant and lasting effects, it is necessary to attempt to understand the meaning of the experience. And RET does indeed provide the framework for this vital cognitive dimension.

Like any action-oriented approach, RET insists that newly acquired insights be put into action. The homework method is an excellent avenue for translating insights into concrete action programs. In my own groups I often suggest assignments that can be carried out in the group and that allow clients to practice new behaviors and experiment with a different style of being. I recall, for example, Donald, an older man who avoided women in his group because he was sure that they wouldn't want to waste their time talking with him. I asked Donald whether he wanted to change this pattern, and he said yes, that he wanted very much to initiate contact. So I suggested that during the afternoon he seek out the three women in our group he most wanted to talk with and to start a conversation with them. The behavior I suggested was experimental and new and was meant to allow him to see what would happen and to decide whether he wanted to continue with this different style of behavior. Note that these assignments don't have to be "given" by the leader; members can be encouraged to set tasks for themselves that will enable them to practice new assumptions and the resulting new behaviors.

RET is most easily used with clients who are willing to accept their own responsibility for creating their difficulties. As an approach to therapy, it easily incorporates specific techniques developed in other systems (such as behavior therapy, cognitive therapy, and Adlerian therapy) into its practice applied to group work. The versatility and applicability to a wide range of neurotic problems of living are the major strengths of RET (Wessler, 1986).

Ellis (1987a) admits that RET has its limitations, but his discussion of this topic points more to limitations within the client (such as resistance) rather than any limitations in the theory and practice of RET. He mentions some benefits and strengths of RET:

- It is an intrinsically brief therapy, for in a few sessions clients who are willing to work typically experience significant gains.
- It aims not only for effectiveness but also for efficiency. There are many cognitive, emotive, and behavioral techniques that may be uniquely effective for difficult clients.

• RET has been incorporated into education, business, and communications. Its techniques can be used in nontherapy settings. Ellis sees the future of RET evolving from individual and group therapy into the general field of educational and mass-media therapy. He contends that the principles of RET are ideally suited for applications in homes, schools, colleges, social institutions, community centers, and hospitals.

Applying Rational-Emotive Therapy in Multicultural Settings

RET has certain advantages in cross-cultural group situations. If members are not challenged too quickly, they can be effectively invited to examine the premises on which they behave. Consider a group composed of members from a particular culture. This culture stresses doing one's best, cooperation, interdependence, respect for the family, and working hard. Some members of this group may be struggling with feelings of shame and guilt if they perceive that they are not living up to the expectations set for them by their parents and families. Students may feel that they are bringing shame to their family if they get a "B" in a course. Leaders who confront the cultural values of such clients too quickly are likely to see counterproductive results. In fact, these clients may "prematurely terminate," based largely on feeling misunderstood. A sensitive RET group practitioner can, however, encourage such clients to begin to question how they may have uncritically accepted as truth all of the messages from their culture. Without encouraging them to abandon respect for their cultural heritage, the group leader can still challenge them to examine their beliefs and understand their consequences.

Just as is true of behavioral group leaders, the RET group leader functions in the role of a teacher. This image would seem ideal for some ethnic groups, because it detracts from the stigma of being mentally ill and focuses on problems of living. Life can be more fulfilling if clients learn better ways to think about the issues that confront them. The group leader, using the A-B-C model, teaches the client how she became disturbed. One of the leader's functions is to teach her how to dispute her irrational thinking and how to change her self-defeating style of life. With the help of the therapist and other group members, the client learns new ways of thinking and behaving, which result in new feelings.

It needs to be emphasized that, since RET is a forceful and directive approach, the therapist must exert caution in challenging clients about their beliefs and behaviors. What may seem like an irrational belief to a therapist may be a long-cherished value that influences the individual. The client may say: "All my life I've been taught to respect my father. Although I do have respect and love for him, I'm thinking that I want to make some choices about my life that aren't in line with his choice for me. I've always told myself that I simply can't disappoint my father, so I've suppressed my wishes and followed his will." A group leader who would insensitively hammer away at the irrational quality of this woman's beliefs would not be respecting her values. Even though it might be therapeutic for her to question some of her beliefs, the therapist must not err by imposing his or her standards on this person.

A key limitation of RET group therapy for ethnic-minority clients is that they could become dependent on the group leader to make decisions about what constitutes rationality. It would be easy for a group leader who is not well qualified to assume a highly directive stance that would keep the client passive. If therapists do most of the talking, the members do most of the listening. Therefore, although RET leaders are active and directive, it seems important that they teach their clients to question and to assume an active role in the therapeutic process.

Some Personal Concerns about RET

A major reservation I have with regard to RET concerns the dangers inherent in the therapist's confrontive and directive stance. Because the therapist has a large degree of power by virtue of persuasion and directiveness, brainwashing or other forms of psychological harm are more possible in RET than in other, less directive approaches. In RET groups there is a real possibility that, having decided that someone's beliefs are irrational, the group leader will work hard at converting that member to "sound thinking." Aside from the very relevant issue of what constitutes rational thinking and who is the judge of it, I question the value of getting rid of one system of irrational beliefs only to adopt a new set of questionable beliefs, particularly if these values are "pushed" by the group leader or, in some instances, by other group members. Therefore, it is essential that RET practitioners be highly aware of themselves and their own motivations and that they avoid imposing their value system on clients. This implies that the therapist's level of training, knowledge and skill, perceptiveness, and accuracy of judgment are particularly important in RET. Perhaps one ethical safeguard is for group leaders using RET procedures to openly discuss the issue of values and caution members to beware of pressure to change in a definite direction, one that might be alien to their value system.

Another danger I see in RET groups is the possibility of group pressure against members who resist certain changes. As I said earlier, feedback is potentially of great value, but ultimately it should be up to the person getting the feedback to decide what to do about it. If members cajole, push, demand, persuade, and attempt to do the thinking for other members, the results are at least questionable, since the very integrity of the individual members is at stake.

However, if RET is done in the manner prescribed by Ellis, these dangers are considerably lessened. Ellis rarely questions his clients' desires, preferences, values, or morality. What he does question is their "musts," "shoulds," and irrational demands. Thus, if someone says "I want romantic love" or "I prefer to be sexually abstinent," Ellis would rarely disagree. However, if the person said instead "I *must* be loved romantically" or "I *have* to be abstinent under all conditions," he would challenge such *must*urbatory views and encourage the client to change them to strong preferences. It is Ellis's belief that his brand of RET, by showing clients that even rationality is *desirable* but not *necessary,* minimizes bigotry, absolutism, and emotional disturbance—including the potential absolutism of members and leader.

The issue of RET's authoritarian and dogmatic approach has been addressed by other writers. Kleiner (1979), for example, asserts that the degree of authoritarianism of RET is determined by the degree of authoritarianism present in the RET therapist. Claiming that he has become a much less dogmatic and authoritarian therapist after becoming more aware of his own beliefs and prejudices, Kleiner says that therapists should encourage their clients to trust themselves and to question, challenge, and even reject the therapist's notions if they don't ring true. Kleiner also notes that the best safeguard against dogmatism and authoritarianism is the therapist's continuing examination of his or her own basic beliefs and values.

It is well to underscore that RET can be done by many people in a manner different from Albert Ellis's style. Since Ellis has so much visibility, it is worth distinguishing between the principles and techniques of RET and Ellis's very confrontational way of using them. A therapist can be soft-spoken and gentle and still use RET concepts and methods.

Research Efforts in RET

RET and cognitive-behavioral therapy have been studied experimentally, although there were methodological shortcomings in many of these studies. Some studies had inadequate control groups, and others failed to make comparisons with other forms of therapy (DiGiuseppe, Miller, & Trexler, 1979). Many studies focused either on the cognitive dimension as a key factor in emotional disturbance or on therapeutic outcomes. As Wessler (1986) notes, however, very few studies investigated group therapy per se.

One of the problems in conducting research on the practice of RET, whether group or individual, is that RET does not rely on employing a single technique. Therapists typically use a combination of cognitive, behavioral, and emotive methods within a single session with a given client. If a particular technique does not seem to be producing results, the therapist is likely to quickly switch to another. This technical eclecticism and therapeutic flexibility make it difficult to do controlled research (Wessler, 1986).

In a review of outcome studies of RET from 1977 to 1982, McGovern and Silverman (1986) report general findings that support the efficacy of RET. Of the 47 studies reviewed, 31 had significant findings in favor of the RET position. In the remaining studies the RET treatment groups showed improvement, and in no study was another treatment technique significantly superior to RET.

Ellis and Whiteley (1979) have collected several interesting articles dealing with various and often controversial aspects of RET. A discussion of these issues would exceed the scope of this text, but you might well enjoy the lively debates presented in their book.

Questions for Reflection and Discussion

1. In your own experiences as a group member or a group leader, what are some of the common irrational beliefs that you have most frequently heard? What opportunities does a group offer to challenge such ideas?

2. RET urges clients to examine and attack illogical assumptions about life. Do you believe that people will make changes on an emotional and behavioral level if the focus is on attacking cognitive structures?

3. As an educational model, RET stresses teaching, learning, practicing new skills, logical thinking, carrying out homework assignments, and reading. As a group leader, to what degree would you be comfortable with such an educational focus? What aspects of RET would you want to include in your approach to groups, regardless of your theoretical orientation?

4. Compare and contrast RET with Gestalt therapy. What do you see as some of the major differences? Do you see any room to integrate the differing dimensions of these two therapies? If so, what factors might you combine in a group you were leading?

5. What criteria would you employ to determine whether a group member's ideas were rational? How would you determine if certain assumptions were self-defeating or constructive?

6. To what degree do you think the group leader's values become a central part of RET group therapy? How do you think the values held by the leader and by the members influence the group process?

7. Some might criticize RET group therapy on the ground that a participant is subjected to undue group pressure, both from the leader and the other members. This pressure could take the form of persuasion, giving advice, and expecting members to do certain outside assignments. What are your reactions to this criticism?

8. RET calls for an active/directive group leader. Compare this role with that of the person-centered group leader, who gives as much leadership as possible to the members. Which leader role are you more comfortable with, and how do you think these contrasting leadership styles will change a group?

9. Like any action-oriented approach, RET insists that newly acquired insights be put into action, largely through homework assignments. What do you think of a model that is based on action outside of the sessions?

10. To what extent do you think that a personal and warm relationship between the members and the leader is a critical factor in RET group therapy?

Where to Go from Here

The Institute for Rational-Emotive Therapy in New York City offers a variety of professional training involving a primary certificate, an intermediate certificate, an associate fellowship, and a fellowship program. Each of these programs has different requirements, including clinical experience, supervision, and personal therapy experience. Several affiliated branches of RET around the world offer official programs of study. For more specific information, see Appendixes A, B, and C in Ellis and Grieger (1986) or contact

> Institute for Rational-Emotive Therapy
> 45 East 65th Street
> New York, NY 10021-6593
> Phone: (212) 535-0822

RECOMMENDED SUPPLEMENTARY READINGS

Handbook of rational-emotive therapy: Vol. 2 (Ellis & Grieger, 1986) is a comprehensive and updated work that deals with the theoretical and conceptual foundations of RET, the dynamics of emotional disturbance, specific techniques to promote change, and applications of RET.

Handbook of rational-emotive therapy: Vol. 1 (Ellis & Grieger, 1977) discusses both theoretical and applied aspects of RET and contains an excellent section on techniques. I especially recommend Chapter 1 ("An Overview of the Clinical Theory of RET"), Chapter 18 ("RET in Groups"), and Chapter 29 ("The Present and Future of RET"). If you want to read further on research data on RET, Chapters 2 and 3 are quite comprehensive.

Humanistic psychotherapy: The rational-emotive approach (Ellis, 1973) is a clear and up-to-date presentation of the key concepts of RET, especially its humanistic and active/directive aspects. It is a very useful book that I recommend you read in its entirety.

A new guide to rational living (Ellis & Harper, 1975) is a self-help book that presents a straightforward approach to RET, based on homework assignments and self-questioning. It is easy reading, and many of the principles discussed can be applied to group work.

Theoretical and empirical foundations of rational-emotive therapy (Ellis & Whiteley, 1979) is the book I referred to at the end of my evaluation of RET. It represents a comprehensive treatment of the theoretical and practical aspects of RET and offers an interesting range of opinions by a number of professionals on a variety of issues, many of which were covered in this chapter. The book also contains several articles by Ellis.

The Institute for Rational-Emotive Therapy distributes books and other educational material from its headquarters in New York. A complete catalog of books, cassettes, pamphlets, and RET materials can be obtained by writing the institute at 45 East 65th Street, New York, NY 10021-6593.

The *Journal of Rational-Emotive and Cognitive-Behavior Therapy* is published by Human Sciences Press, Inc., 72 Fifth Avenue, New York, NY 10011-8004. This journal is an excellent way to keep informed of the developments in RET. It is published quarterly; subscriptions are $34 a year.

REFERENCES AND SUGGESTED READINGS*

Bandura, A. (1969). *Principles of behavior modification.* New York: Holt, Rinehart & Winston.

Beck, A. T. (1976). *Cognitive therapy and the emotional disorders.* New York: New American Library.

Beck, A. T. (1987). Cognitive therapy. In J. K. Zeig (Ed.), *The evolution of psychotherapy* (pp. 149–178). New York: Brunner/Mazel.

Beck, A. T., & Weishaar, M. E. (1989). Cognitive therapy. In R. J. Corsini & D. Wedding (Eds.), *Current psychotherapies* (4th ed.). Itasca, IL: F. E. Peacock.

DiGiuseppe, R. A., Miller, N. J., & Trexler, L. D. (1979). A review of rational-emotive psychotherapy outcome studies. In A. Ellis & J. M. Whiteley (Eds.), *Theoretical and empirical foundations of rational-emotive therapy.* Pacific Grove, CA: Brooks/Cole.

Donigian, J., & Malnati, R. (1987). *Critical incidents in group therapy.* Pacific Grove, CA: Brooks/Cole.

Ellis, A. (1962). *Reason and emotion in psychotherapy.* New York: Lyle Stuart.

Ellis, A. (1969). A weekend of rational encounter. In A. Burton (Ed.), *Encounter: The theory and practice of encounter groups.* San Francisco: Jossey-Bass.

*Ellis, A. (1973). *Humanistic psychotherapy: The rational-emotive approach.* New York: McGraw-Hill.

Ellis, A. (1974). The group as agent in facilitating change toward rational thinking and appropriate emoting. In A. Jacobs & W. W. Spradlin (Eds.), *The group as agent of change.* New York: Behavioral Publications.

Ellis, A. (1977a). The basic clinical theory of rational-emotive therapy. In A. Ellis & R. Grieger (Eds.), *Handbook of rational-emotive therapy: Vol. 1.* New York: Springer.

Ellis, A. (1977b). *A garland of rational songs.* New York: Institute for Rational-Emotive Therapy.

*Ellis, A. (1977c). Rational-emotive therapy in groups. In A. Ellis & R. Grieger (Eds.), *Handbook of rational emotive therapy: Vol. 1.* New York: Springer.

Ellis, A. (1979a). Rational-emotive therapy. In A. Ellis & J. M. Whiteley (Eds.), *Theoretical and empirical foundations of rational-emotive therapy.* Pacific Grove, CA: Brooks/Cole.

Ellis, A. (1979b). Rational-emotive therapy: Research data that support the clinical and personality hypotheses of RET and other modes of cognitive-behavior therapy. In A. Ellis & J. M. Whiteley (Eds.), *Theoretical and empirical foundations of rational-emotive therapy.* Pacific Grove, CA: Brooks/Cole.

*Ellis, A. (1979c). The theory of rational-emotive therapy. In A. Ellis & J. M. Whiteley (Eds.), *Theoretical and empirical foundations of rational-emotive therapy.* Pacific Grove, CA: Brooks/Cole.

Ellis, A. (1982a). Rational-emotive family therapy. In A. M. Horne & M. M. Ohlsen (Eds.), *Family counseling and therapy.* Itasca, IL: F. E. Peacock.

*Ellis, A. (1982b). Rational-emotive group therapy. In G. Gazda (Ed.), *Basic approaches to group psychotherapy and group counseling* (3rd ed.). Springfield, IL: Charles C Thomas.

Ellis, A. (1984a). Is the unified-interaction approach to cognitive-behavior modification a reinvention of the wheel? *Clinical Psychology Review, 4,* 215–218.

Ellis, A. (1984b). Maintenance and generalization in rational-emotive therapy. *The Cognitive Behaviorist, 6*(1), 2–4.

Ellis, A. (1984c). Rational-emotive therapy (RET) approaches to overcoming resistance, III: Using emotive and behavioral techniques of overcoming resistance. *British Journal of Cognitive Psychotherapy, 2*(1), 11–26.

*Books and articles marked with an asterisk are suggested for further study.

*Ellis, A. (1985). *Overcoming resistance: Rational-emotive therapy with difficult clients.* New York: Springer.

Ellis, A. (1986a). Rational-emotive therapy. In I. L. Kutash & A. Wolf (Eds.), *Psychotherapist's casebook* (pp. 277–287). San Francisco: Jossey-Bass.

Ellis, A. (1986b). Rational-emotive therapy and cognitive behavior therapy: Similarities and differences. In A. Ellis & R. Grieger (Eds.), *Handbook of rational-emotive therapy: Vol. 2.* New York: Springer.

Ellis, A. (1987a). The evolution of rational-emotive therapy (RET) and cognitive behavior therapy (CBT). In J. K. Zeig (Ed.), *The evolution of psychotherapy* (pp. 107–132). New York: Brunner/Mazel.

*Ellis, A. (1987b). The impossibility of achieving consistently good mental health. *American Psychologist, 42*(4), 364–375.

*Ellis, A. (1988). *How to stubbornly refuse to make yourself miserable about anything—Yes, anything!* Secaucus, NJ: Lyle Stuart.

Ellis, A. (1989). Rational-emotive therapy. In R. J. Corsini & D. Wedding (Eds.), *Current psychotherapies* (4th ed.). Itasca, IL: F. E. Peacock.

*Ellis, A., & Bernard, M. E. (1986). What is rational-emotive therapy (RET)? In A. Ellis & R. Grieger (Eds.), *Handbook of rational-emotive therapy: Vol. 2.* New York: Springer.

*Ellis, A., & Dryden, W. (1987). *The practice of rational-emotive therapy.* Secaucus, NJ: Lyle Stuart.

Ellis, A., & Grieger, R. (Eds.). (1977). *Handbook of rational-emotive therapy: Vol. 1.* New York: Springer.

*Ellis, A., & Grieger, R. (Eds.). (1986). *Handbook of rational-emotive therapy: Vol. 2.* New York: Springer.

*Ellis, A., & Harper, R. A. (1975). *A new guide to rational living.* Englewood Cliffs, NJ: Prentice-Hall.

Ellis, A., & Whiteley, J. M. (Eds.). (1979). *Theoretical and empirical foundations of rational-emotive therapy.* Pacific Grove, CA: Brooks/Cole.

*Grieger, R. M. (1986). The process of rational-emotive therapy. In A. Ellis & R. Grieger (Eds.), *Handbook of rational-emotive therapy: Vol. 2.* New York: Springer.

Haaga, D. A., & Davison, G. (in press). Outcome studies of rational-emotive therapy. In M. E. Bernard & R. DiGiuseppe (Eds.), *Inside rational-emotive therapy.* Orlando, FL: Academic Press.

Harrell, T. H., Beiman, I., & Lapointe, K. (1986). Didactic persuasion techniques in cognitive restructuring. In A. Ellis & R. Grieger (Eds.), *Handbook of rational-emotive therapy: Vol 2.* New York: Springer.

Kleiner, F. B. (1979). Commentary on Albert Ellis' article. In A. Ellis & J. M. Whiteley (Eds.), *Theoretical and empirical foundations of rational-emotive therapy.* Pacific Grove, CA: Brooks/Cole.

Lange, A., & Jakubowski, P. (1976). *Responsible assertive behavior: Cognitive-behavioral procedures for trainers.* Champaign, IL: Research Press.

Mahoney, M. J., & Lyddon, W. J. (1988). Recent developments in cognitive approaches to counseling and psychotherapy. *The Counseling Psychologist, 16*(2), 190–234.

Maultsby, M. C. (1981). Rational behavior therapy in groups. In G. Gazda (Ed.), *Innovations to group psychotherapy* (2nd ed.). Springfield, IL: Charles C Thomas.

McGovern, T. E., & Silverman, M. (1986). A review of outcome studies of rational-emotive therapy from 1977 to 1982. In A. Ellis & R. Grieger (Eds.), *Handbook of rational-emotive therapy: Vol. 2.* New York: Springer.

McMullin, R. E. (1986). *Handbook of cognitive therapy techniques.* New York: Norton.

Nardi, T. J. (1986). The use of psychodrama in RET. In A. Ellis & R. Grieger (Eds.), *Handbook of rational-emotive therapy: Vol. 2.* New York: Springer.

*Walen, S., DiGiuseppe, R., & Wessler, R. L. (1980). *A practitioner's guide to rational-emotive therapy.* New York: Oxford University Press.

Warren, R., & McLellarn, R. W. (1987). What do RET therapists think they are doing? An international survey. *Journal of Rational-Emotive Therapy, 5*(2), 71–91.

Warren, R., McLellarn, R. W., & Ellis, A. (1987). Albert Ellis' personal responses to the survey of rational-emotive therapists. *Journal of Rational-Emotive Therapy, 5*(2), 92–107.

Weinrach, S. G. (1980). Unconventional therapist: Albert Ellis. *Personnel and Guidance Journal, 59*(3), 152–160.

*Wessler, R. A., & Wessler, R. L. (1980). *The principles and practice of rational-emotive therapy.* San Francisco: Jossey-Bass.

*Wessler, R. L. (1986). Rational-emotive therapy in groups. In A. Ellis & R. Grieger (Eds.), *Handbook of rational-emotive therapy: Vol. 2.* New York: Springer.

15

Reality Therapy in Groups

Introduction

Like many of the other founders of therapeutic approaches described in this book, William Glasser was psychoanalytically trained. He quickly became disenchanted with this approach, however, and began to experiment with innovative methods, which later came to be called reality therapy.

Glasser's early work focused on asking clients to recognize and take responsibility for what they were doing in the present, rather than dwelling on what they had done, thought, or felt in the past. As an example of this here-and-now focus, Glasser describes his work with a young woman who wanted to talk about having grown up without her parents (Evans, 1982). She attributed all of her problems to the fact that her parents had been absent and that she had been raised by her grandfather. Finally, Glasser told her that he was no longer interested in hearing stories about her past and that if they were to work together, he wanted her to talk about her plans for life.

Reality therapy focuses on solving problems and on coping with the demands of reality in society. Thus, practitioners concentrate on what clients can do practically to change the behavior they use to fulfill needs. People can improve the quality of their life through a process of honest self-examination. Clients are asked to identify their wants and needs. Additionally, they are challenged to evaluate their behavior, formulate a plan for change, commit themselves to such a plan, and follow through with their commitment. By avoiding making excuses and blaming others and by evaluating what they are doing to get what they want, they are able to achieve increasing control over their life.

A basic assumption of Glasser's approach is that everyone has a "growth force"; this force impels one to develop a "success identity" (viewing oneself as being worthy of love and as being a significant person). A further assumption is that any change in one's identity is contingent on behavioral change. Like behavior therapy, transactional analysis, and rational-emotive therapy, reality therapy is an active, directive, and didactic model; it stresses present behavior, not attitudes, insight, one's past, or unconscious motivations.

Until recently, Glasser was more interested in practice than in developing a theory. His work has been aimed at putting a few basic concepts of reality therapy to work in a variety of settings, such as correctional institutions, schools, and community clinics, as well as in private practice, marital and family therapy, and group work. Lately, Glasser (1985) has developed what is known as *control theory*. The use of the principles of control theory need not be restricted to psychotherapists; rather, these ideas can be applied by parents, ministers, doctors, and couples working on interpersonal relationships.

Wubbolding (1988b) provides a concise description of reality therapy:

> Reality therapy is a method of helping people take better control of their lives. It helps people to identify and to clarify what they want and need, and then evaluate whether they can realistically attain what they want. It helps them to examine their own behaviors and to evaluate them with clear criteria. This is followed by positive planning designed to help them control their own lives as well as fulfill their realistic wants and their needs. The result is added strength, more self-confidence, better human relations, and a personal plan for a more effective life. It, thus, provides people with a self-help tool to use daily in coping with adversity, growing personally, and getting more effective control of their lives [p. 173].

Key Concepts

Human Needs and Purposeful Behavior

Reality therapy is built on the notion that human behavior is purposeful and originates from within the individual rather than from external forces. William Glasser (1980) identifies four essential psychological needs—*belonging, power, freedom,* and *fun*—and the physiological need for *survival.* Control theory explains how we attempt to satisfy these basic needs, which are the powerful forces that drive us (Glasser, 1985).

Although all humans have these needs, they fulfill them in various ways. People develop an inner "picture album" of specific wants that contains precise snapshots of how they wish to fulfill their needs. A major goal of current reality therapy is to teach people better ways of fulfilling their needs and to help them effectively get what they want from life. In Glasser's words, "I want to teach people how the control system works and use the concepts of reality therapy not only to teach better behaviors but also to evaluate and improve their perceptions and their internal world" (1981,

p. 267). Responsibility consists of learning how to realistically meet these basic psychological needs, and the essence of therapy consists of teaching people to accept that responsibility. People behave for a purpose: to mold their environment as a sculptor molds clay, matching their own inner pictures of what they want. These goals are achievable only through hard work (Wubbolding, 1988b).

Existential/Phenomenological Orientation

In many ways Glasser's approach is grounded on phenomenological and existential premises. He maintains that we perceive the world in the context of our own needs, not as it really is. It is important for therapists to understand that clients live both in the external world and in their own internal world.

In addition to this focus on the subjective world, contemporary reality therapy continues to have a strong existential orientation. We are viewed as choosing our own goals and as responsible for the kind of world we create for ourselves. We are not helpless victims, and we can create a better life. Glasser (1985) does not accept the notion that misery simply happens to us; rather, it is something that we often choose. He observes that clients are typically quick to complain that they are upset because people in their life are not behaving as they would like them to. It is a powerful lesson for us to recognize that we choose all of our behaviors, including feeling miserable and thinking that we are victims. We choose misery in the attempt to reduce our frustration (which is the gap, or discrepancy, between what we want and what we have at a specific moment). When people do choose misery by developing a range of "paining" behaviors, it is because these are the best behaviors that they are able to generate at the time. But why does it make sense to choose misery? Glasser (1985) answers this question by discussing these four reasons: (1) to keep anger under control, (2) to get others to help us, (3) to excuse our unwillingness to do something more effective, and (4) to gain powerful control. Glasser speaks of people *depressing* or *angering* themselves, rather than being depressed or being angry. With this perspective, depression can be explained as an active choice that we make rather than the result of being a passive victim. This process of "depressing" keeps anger in check, and it also allows us to ask for help. Glasser contends that as long as we cling to the notion that we are victims of depression and that misery is something that happens to us, we will not change for the better. We can change only when we recognize and act on the reality that what we are doing is the result of our choices.

Total Behavior

According to Glasser's latest formulation of control theory (1985), we always have control over what we do. This basic premise is clarified in the context of understanding our total behavior, which always includes four components: *doing* (or active behaviors such as talking or jogging); *thinking* (voluntary thoughts and self-statements); *feeling* (such as anger, joy, depression, anxiety); and *physiology* (such as sweating, "headaching," or developing other psychosomatic symptoms). Although these behaviors are interrelated, one of them is often more prominent than the others. Wubbolding (1988b) uses the "suitcase" analogy to describe the concept of total behavior. In lifting a suitcase you grab it by the easiest part, the handle. Total behavior is like a suitcase. The handle is the *doing* part. Lift the handle and total behavior follows. The sequence is doing, thinking, feeling, and physiology. It is typically easier to force ourselves to *do* something different than it is to feel or think something different.

Control theory is grounded on the assumption that it is impossible to choose a total behavior and not choose all its components. If we hope to change a total behavior (such as experiencing the emotional and physiological consequences of depressing ourselves), it is necessary to change what we are doing and what we are thinking. For example, we might feel upset and then depress ourselves if we fail to get a job that we applied for. We do not have the ability to directly change how we are feeling, independently of what we are doing or thinking. But we have an almost complete ability to change what we are doing and some ability to change what we are thinking, in spite of how we might be feeling. Therefore, the key to changing a total behavior lies in choosing to change what we are *doing*. If we markedly change the doing component, we cannot avoid changing the thinking, feeling, and physiological components as well (Glasser, 1985, pp. 50–52).

Success Identity and Positive Addiction

A primary goal of reality therapy, as mentioned, is to help people achieve a success identity. Those who possess a success identity see themselves as able to give and accept love, to feel that they are significant to others, to experience a sense of self-worth, to become involved with others in a caring way, and to meet their needs in ways that are not at the expense of others.

Those who seek therapy are often people who have a "failure identity": they see themselves as unloved, rejected, and unwanted, unable to become intimately involved with others, incompetent to make and stick with commitments, and generally helpless. People seek therapy because they are in psychological pain and because they are not getting what they want from life. Typically, individuals with a failure identity meet challenges with a despairing "I can't," a self-fulfilling prophecy that leads to further lack of success, which in turn supports a negative self-view and eventually makes these people see themselves as hopeless failures in life. Because reality therapy assumes that we are ultimately self-determining beings who become what we decide to become, the system is designed to teach people how they can change behavior that fosters a failure identity and develop behavior that leads to a success identity.

The Essence of Control Theory

Control theory is based on the premise that *behavior* is the *control* of our *perceptions*. Although we may not be able to control what is actually in the real world, we do attempt to control what we perceive. Behavior is best understood in the light of our attempt to control our perceptions to meet our own needs. In this process we create our internal world. We are not locked into any one mode of behavior, although we must behave in some way.

Glasser (1985) contends that everything that we do, think, and feel is generated by what happens inside of us. In other words, how we feel is not controlled by others or events. We are not psychological slaves to others, unless we choose to be. Regardless of our circumstances, what we do, think, and feel is always our best attempt at the time to satisfy internal forces. This is true whether our behavior is effective or ineffective, for our behavior is an attempt to match what Glasser refers to as "the pictures in our heads":

> Your picture album—in which you find love, worth, success, fun, and free-dom—is the world you would like to live in, where somehow or other all your desires, even conflicting ones, are satisfied. None of us has a picture in his album of himself doing badly. We may at times choose to do what those around us say is self-destructive, but we don't do these things to destroy ourselves [1985, p. 30].

As mentioned previously, reality therapy focuses on changing what we are doing. In group counseling, leaders can help members recognize that what they are doing is not working for them, help them accept themselves as a person, and guide them in making realistic plans to do better. Reality therapists provide help through a process of skillful questioning that is aimed at getting members to assess what they want. Such questions include "Do you want to change? How would you most like to change your life? What do you want in your life that you are not getting? If you were to change, how might your life be different? If you changed, how would you feel better? What would you have in your life if you were to change? What do you have to do now to make the changes happen?" Members can more easily choose better behavior if they come to realize that what they are doing, thinking, and feeling is not simply happening to them but that they are, indeed, making choices.

Role and Functions of the Group Leader

The central task of reality-therapy group practitioners is to become involved with the individual members and then to help them face reality. According to Glasser (1986c), people are most able to create a success identity when they recognize and accept accountability for their own chosen behaviors:

> The role of the reality therapy counselor is to maintain a counseling en-vironment which does the following: (1) helps clients to avoid excuses and accept this responsibility, (2) fosters their clients' psychological strengths and (3) provides the opportunity for clients to learn and test new and more effective behavioral choices [p. 20].

This role requires the leader to perform the following functions:

- providing a model of responsible behavior and of a life based on a success identity
- establishing with each member a therapeutic relationship based on care and respect, one that encourages and demands responsible and effective behavior
- actively promoting discussion of members' current behavior and actively discouraging excuses for irresponsible or ineffective behavior
- introducing and fostering the process of evaluating which of the client's wants are realistically attainable
- teaching members to formulate and carry out plans to change their behaviors
- establishing a structure and limits for the sessions
- being open to challenge and to exploring one's own values with the group
- encouraging members to get involved with one another, to share common experiences, and to help one another deal with problems in a responsible manner
- assisting members in setting practical limits to the duration and scope of their therapy
- teaching members how to apply to everyday life what they have learned in the group

Reality-therapy group leaders assume a verbally active and directive role. They focus on the strengths and potentials of the members rather than on their failures. They assume that dwelling on limitations, problems, and failures tends to reinforce the clients' basic failure identity and ineffective control. Therefore, they challenge members to look at their unused potential and to discover how to work toward creating a success identity and more effective control.

It is important for group leaders to develop their own individual therapeutic style. Sincerity and being comfortable with their style are crucial traits in being able to carry out therapeutic functions. Glasser puts it in this way:

> Whatever this style may be, counselors must be able to show that they are sincere in their desire to help and comfortable in the way that they counsel. Clients are very sensitive either to a lack of sincerity or a lack of comfort on the part of the counselor. If the counselor is not perceived as being sincere, the client will not experience the immediate sense of belonging that is an essential part of the need-fulfilling approach which is basic to reality therapy. If the counselor is not perceived as being comfortable, the client will see this as a lack of skill and have little confidence in the counseling process [1986c, p. 19].

The Practice of Reality Therapy in Groups

The practice of reality therapy, known as the "cycle of counseling," consists of two major components: (1) the counseling environment and (2) specific procedures that lead to changes in behavior. The art of counseling is to weave these components together in ways that lead clients to evaluate their lives and decide to move in more effective directions.

Several points are important to keep in mind. First, although the concepts discussed in this section may seem clear and simple as they are presented in written form, they are difficult to translate into actual therapeutic practice, and it takes considerable skill and creativity to successfully apply them in group work. Although the principles will be the same when used by any certified reality therapist, the manner in which they are applied does vary depending on the therapist's style and personal characteristics. Finally, although the principles are applied in a progressive manner, they should not be thought of as discrete and rigid categories. There is a considerable degree of interdependence among these principles, and taken together they contribute to the total process of reality therapy.

Glasser (1986c) has developed principles and procedures that form the core of reality therapy. He stresses that the practice of reality therapy is a process and that it is a mistake to apply its therapeutic principles and procedures in a rigid step-by-step, or "cookbook," fashion. He adds that the practice of reality therapy is an art. The discussion that follows should be considered as an aid for teaching reality therapy, but it should not be thought of as a replacement for the extensive training that is needed to counsel effectively.

To provide an understanding of how the basic concepts of reality therapy are applied to the group process, this section takes as an example a group of male adolescents who are in a detention facility for some type of criminal offense. Participation in the group constitutes one aspect of these youths' treatment program, and sessions are held several times a week for at least an hour. The evolution and development of this group will be briefly described to demonstrate how reality-therapy principles actually work. For purposes of the example, assume that most of the youths in the group have a failure identity.

The discussion of the practice of reality therapy is an integrated summary and adaptation of material from various sources (Evans, 1982; Ford, 1982; W. Glasser, 1965, 1969, 1976b, 1980, 1981, 1984a, 1984b, 1985, 1986a, 1986b, 1986c; Wubbolding, 1988b).

The Counseling Environment

Personal Involvement with the Client. The practice of reality therapy begins with the counselor's efforts to create a supportive environment within which clients can begin to make changes in their life. To create this therapeutic climate, it is essential for counselors to make friends with clients, getting involved in their lives and creating the rapport that will be the foundation of the therapeutic relationship. It is essential for the counselor to see the world as the clients see it. Yet as Wubbolding (1988b) mentions, this high level of empathy is shown less by reflective listening than by skillful questioning. In a sense this is the most important and demanding phase of therapy, for in the absence of personal involvement there can be no effective therapy. When reality therapy is ineffective, it is usually because such involvement has not been established. The genuine caring on the part of the therapist can go a long way toward building the bonds of trust that will be needed for clients to commit themselves to the challenges of making positive changes.

For real involvement to take place, the leader must have certain personal qualities, including warmth, understanding, acceptance, concern, respect for the client, openness, and the willingness to be challenged by others. One of the best ways to develop this goodwill and therapeutic friendship is simply by listening to clients. Involvement is also promoted by talking about a wide range of topics that have relevance for group members, topics that relate to their everyday behaviors and experiences and that play down misery and past failures. Once involvement has been established, the leader confronts the group members with the reality and consequences of their *current* behavior. This ongoing confrontation constitutes the essence of the group.

Because of the opportunity to form relationships with several other people besides the therapist, there is a definite advantage in practicing reality therapy in groups. The group milieu can do a lot to deepen caring and involvement. Fellow members provide both support and an honest challenge to look at one's life. The nonpunitive atmosphere of the group can promote self-acceptance and the desire to make specific plans for better behavior (Glasser, 1976b). Group interaction is seen as especially important in helping individual members break the vicious circle of failure experiences, because people cannot gain a success identity and more effective control by isolating themselves. In order to achieve success, individuals must fulfill the need for belonging. Indeed, self-help implies being involved with others (Glasser, 1976a).

How does this principle of involvement apply to the case illustration described earlier? To begin with, we should note that many of the youths in the detention facility who are being required to attend group-therapy sessions have never had any meaningful and positive involvements with others. Under such circumstances, how is it possible for a leader to establish a personal friendship with the youths and to facilitate involvement among the group members? First of all, the leader must establish his or her credibility by demonstrating a genuine concern and caring for the youths, seeing them not as they see themselves but as the successful and responsible persons they are capable of becoming. With that caring the foundation for involvement is laid. Lacking this positive view of the participants' possibilities—or, even worse, believing that they cannot change—the leader will foster the youths' sense of hopelessness and their inevitable resistance to seeing themselves in a more positive light.

It should be noted that one effective way to create a therapeutic climate for participants in involuntary groups is for the leader to explain to the members some specific ways in which the group process can be of personal value to them. For example, if participants see the group as a place where they can learn to escape their particular pattern of repeated failures, they may take the first step toward involvement in the group. It should also be noted that involvement is controlled by the reality therapist, who actively defines the nature and purpose of the group as well as the limits of its activities.

Counselor Attitudes and Behaviors That Promote Change. Group leaders with a reality-therapy orientation consistently attempt to focus clients on what they are *doing now*. They try not to allow clients to talk about events in the past unless these events can be easily related to present situations. They also avoid discussing clients' feelings or physiology as though these were separate from their total behavior. Counselors relate what clients are feeling or their physical symptoms to their concurrent actions and thoughts, over which the clients have more direct control. Although reality therapists focus on doing, they consider it quite legitimate to talk about feelings and cognitions. Their assumption is that in changing the doing component, one also changes the feeling component, because behavior is total.

Counselors hope to teach their clients to value the attitude of accepting responsibility for their total behavior. Thus, they accept no excuses for irresponsible behavior, such as not doing what they said they would do. If clients do not follow through with their plans for change, counselors do not ask fruitless questions about why the plan failed. Instead, they teach members that excuses are a form of self-deception that may offer temporary relief but ultimately lead to failure and to the cementing of a failure identity. As Wubbolding (1988b) has pointed out, accepting excuses gives a message to clients: "Your behavior can be excused, because you are weak and not in control of your behavior. It is not really possible for you to change your life." On the other hand, by refusing to accept excuses, the therapist conveys a different attitude: "You are strong and in control of your behavior. You can make a better plan, and you can change your life."

Reality therapy holds that punishment is not a useful means of changing behavior. Instead, the therapist challenges clients to see and to accept *reasonable consequences* that flow from their actions. Consequences that are reasonable are related to the offense and are imposed for the benefit of the person breaking the rule. Consequences that are administered calmly and consistently allow less latitude for anger and recrimination. Such consequences are educational and tend to result in responsibility and rehabilitation (Wubbolding, 1988b). Taking the example of the youths in the detention facility, the therapist would avoid deprecating a group member for, say, having failed to attend a meeting. The therapist might, however, lead him to see that his failure to attend meetings could affect his chances for eventual release. By avoiding the use of critical statements, by not accepting any excuses, and by remaining nonjudgmental, therapists can ask clients if they *really* want to change. Clients can be asked to reevaluate to determine if they still want to stick by their commitments.

It is important for the counselor to try to maintain a belief in the client's ability to find a more responsible life, even if the client makes little effort to follow through on plans. If the counselor gives up, it tends to confirm the client's belief that no one cares enough to help (Glasser, 1986a, 1986c). Those with a failure identity expect others to give up on them. It is a real challenge to refuse to give up easily on clients who are resistant, passive/aggressive, uncooperative, hostile, and apathetic. Regardless of what clients say or do, it is therapeutically helpful for the therapist not to give up. It is unhelpful for a therapist to assume that another person will never change or that a person is hopeless. The group leader must retain faith that the person has the capacity to change.

The concept of not giving up applies well to the example of the group of adolescent delinquents. A leading factor contributing to their delinquent behavior may well be the fact that many people have given up on them and have showed little faith in their ability to succeed. The group leader who adopts a stance of refusing to give up and a commitment to keep trying to reach these adolescents challenges them to find ways to believe in themselves. Once the members believe that the leader and other members will not give up on them, the sense of belongingness is solidified, which allows for work to proceed. The members can then develop faith in themselves, for they know that they are no longer alone. Although it is up to them to make decisions about how they will live in the world, they also realize that they do have the capacity to resolve their problems and make some significant changes in what they are thinking, feeling, and doing.

In addition to the counselor's attitudes mentioned above that create an environment conducive to client change, Wubbolding (1988b) emphasizes the importance of practitioners' being willing to seek consultation with someone who is trained in reality therapy. Regardless of how well a person practices reality therapy, Wubbolding contends, there is room for improvement, which can take place both by consultation and by developing an ongoing plan for professional development.

Procedures That Lead to Change

Exploring Wants, Needs, and Perceptions. Reality therapists ask, "What do you want?" Through the therapist's skillful questioning, clients are encouraged to recognize, define, and refine how they wish to meet their needs. Part of counseling consists of the exploration of their "picture album" and the ways in which their behavior is aimed at moving the external world closer to their inner world of wants. Clients are given the opportunity to explore every facet of their lives, including what they want from their family, friends, and work. Furthermore, it is useful for clients to define what they expect and want from the counselor and from themselves (Wubbolding, 1988b). Even though this exploration of wants, needs, and perceptions occurs early in the therapeutic relationship, it should continue throughout the entire counseling process, because the client's pictures change.

In a group, members explore what they want, what they have, and what they are not getting. This type of assessment provides a basis for making specific changes that will enable them to reduce their frustrations. Useful questions can help them pinpoint what they want: "What kind of person do you wish you were?" "If you had what you wanted, what would you have?" "What would your family be like if your wants and their wants matched?" "What would you be doing if you were living the way that you wish?" This line of questioning sets the stage for the application of other procedures in reality therapy. After clients explore their picture album (wants) and needs, they are later asked to look at their behavior to determine if what they are doing is getting them what they want. As counseling progresses, they will be asked if their present course is satisfactory to them.

Focus on Current Behavior.   Reality therapy stresses current behavior, as we have seen, and it is concerned with past events only insofar as they influence how the client is behaving now. It should be noted that the past may be discussed if doing so will help the client's plan for a better tomorrow. Clients need to be helped to accept that they are contributing to their own problems. The focus on the present is characterized by the question so often asked by the reality therapist: "What are you doing?"

Early during the counseling process it is essential to discuss with clients the overall direction they are taking. This exploration is preliminary to the subsequent evaluation of whether it is a desirable direction. The therapist functions by holding a mirror before the client and asking "What do you see for yourself now and in the future?" Some time is necessary for this reflection to become clear to clients and for them to be able to express their perceptions (Wubbolding, 1988b).

Reality therapy concentrates on changing total behavior, not merely attitudes and feelings. That doesn't imply that attitudes are dismissed as unimportant; rather, the approach is that behavioral change is easier than attitudinal change and of greater value in the therapeutic process. For that reason a client who expressed feelings of helplessness would not be questioned about the reasons for the feelings or encouraged to explore them. Although the reality therapist might encourage the client to discuss feelings, the focus would clearly be on urging the person to identify those behaviors that were causing or supporting the feelings. The aim is to help clients understand *their* responsibilities for their own feelings. As a way of encouraging clients to look at what they are actually doing to contribute to their feelings, questions such as the following are likely to be asked:

- "What are you doing now?"
- "What did you actually do this past week?"
- "What did you want to do differently this past week?"
- "What stopped you from doing what you say you want to do?"
- "What will you do tomorrow?"

According to Glasser (1980, 1981, 1985), what we are doing is easy to see and thus serves as the proper focus in therapy. So feelings and thoughts are explored in reality therapy, but discussing them without strongly relating them to what people are doing is counterproductive (W. Glasser, 1980).

Getting members to focus on what they are doing has the aim of teaching them that they can gain conscious control over their behavior, can make choices, and can change their life. In this process they need to be helped to accept their part in contributing to their own problems. Although they may want to talk in detail about how others are not living up to their expectations and how, if only the world would change, they could be happy, such a tack will only solidify their victimlike position. Briefly, then, the focus of the reality-therapy group is on gaining awareness of current total behavior, because this process contributes to helping a person develop a positive self-image.

Thus, the leader in our example would discourage the group of juvenile offenders from dwelling on their crimes and on the reasons underlying their current feelings and attitudes about themselves and others. Rather, the leader would encourage them to discuss the behavior that led to their sentence and would challenge them to trace and face the practical consequences of their behavior—in short, to evaluate their behavior and accept responsibility for it.

In connection with our example, it is of some interest to note how Glasser sees the behaviors that lead to criminal activity. In his recent formulation he has developed the notion of "not being in effective control of behavior." He asserts that the first choice of people faced with a painful situation is simply to give up. The second choice involves selecting from a variety of behaviors, including acting out (delinquency and sociopathic behavior) and developing psychosomatic symptoms (migraines, ulcers, and bodily aches). A third choice, which emerges as a consequence of being frustrated in the search for love, self-worth, and success, is described as a form of negative addiction (drugs or alcohol). According to Glasser, if people come to understand that their present behavior is based on negative choices leading to increasing loss of self-worth and self-esteem, they are in a position to develop positive choices that can lead to a success identity.

Getting Clients to Evaluate Their Behavior. According to Glasser (1986a, 1986c), the core of reality therapy is to ask clients to make the following evaluation: "Does your present behavior have a reasonable chance of getting you what you want now, and will it take you in the direction you want to go?" It is the therapist's task to confront clients with the consequences of their behavior and to get *them* to judge the quality of their actions. Indeed, unless clients eventually judge their own behavior, they will not change. After clients make value judgments about the quality of their behavior, they can determine what may be contributing to their failures and what changes they can undertake to promote success.

It is important that therapists remain nonjudgmental about clients' behavior and do not assume the responsibility for the client in making these value judgments. Instead, they best serve clients when they challenge them to stop, look, and listen. If therapists can stimulate client self-questioning— "What am I doing now?" "Is it getting me where I want to go?" "Is my behavior working for me?" "Am I making constructive choices?"—the client will be more likely to begin to make changes. Asking clients to evaluate each component of their total behavior is a major task in reality therapy. When therapists ask a "depressing" client if this behavior is helping in the long run, they introduce the idea of choice to the client. The evaluation of doing, thinking, feeling, and physiological behaviors is within the scope of the client's scope of responsibility. Throughout the entire process of reality therapy, the therapist is careful not to take on the responsibility for the answers (Thatcher, 1987).

From the reality therapist's perspective, it is acceptable to be directive with certain clients in the beginning of treatment. By this I mean that reality therapists sometimes express what they think will be helpful. In treating children of alcoholics and even alcoholics themselves, for example, it is necessary to say straightforwardly what will work and what will not work. Certain clients do not have the thinking behaviors in their control system to be able to make consistent evaluations. These clients are likely to have blurred pictures and may not always be aware of what they want or whether their wants are realistic. As clients grow and continually interact with the counselor, they learn to make evaluations with less help (R. E. Wubbolding, personal communication, April 8, 1988).

Some clients insist that they do not have a problem and that their behavior is not getting them into trouble. It is essential to recognize that clients behave according to the perceptions in their internal world and that the counselor must accept that what the client perceives may be far different from what those close to the client perceive (Glasser, 1986a, 1986c). In such cases, Glasser suggests, counselors should continue to focus on the client's present behaviors and keep repeating the core question in a variety of ways. He says that patience is important, for in working with difficult clients, it may take considerable time for them to realize that certain behavior patterns are not getting them what they want.

The evaluation process focuses not only on clients' behaviors but also on their wants. They are helped to clarify what they want, to reflect on the degree to which their behavior is leading to satisfying their wants, and to evaluate the degree to which their wants are realistic. Reality therapists often ask, "Is what you want realistic?" Glasser (1986c, p. 21) writes that clients will not change their behavior until these two prerequisites are met: (1) Using their own evaluation, clients must first decide that their current behavior either will not get them what they want or will not take them in the direction they want to go. (2) Clients must believe that they have available another behavior that will still allow them to satisfy their needs reasonably well.

Returning to the example of the youths in the detention facility, the group leader might ask them: "Does your behavior get you what you want? Where has your behavior led you? Does your behavior hurt you or others? Is your behavior fulfilling your needs?" More specifically, an adolescent who has been sentenced for robbing a liquor store to support a drug habit is asked to evaluate the consequences of continuing his acts and to confront the probable consequences of being caught and jailed. Further, he is directed to face the consequences of taking drugs. It is the task of the youth—with the therapist's help—to determine and evaluate the consequences of his actions and then decide whether he wants to change his behavior. It is not the task of the therapist to do his changing for him, nor can the therapist *make* him want to give up drugs and stealing and lead a more constructive life. In short, the therapist helps the client determine *what* needs to be changed, and the client determines *why,* or if, the change is needed.

Planning and Action.   Much of the work in reality therapy consists of helping members identify specific ways to change their failure behavior into success behavior. Once a client has made a value judgment about his or her behavior and decided to change it, the therapist assists the client in developing a plan for behavioral changes. The art of such planning is to establish practical short-term goals that have a high probability of being successfully attained, because such successes will positively reinforce the client's efforts to achieve long-range goals.

Planning for responsible behavior is the core of the helping process. This is clearly a teaching phase of therapy. Therefore, therapy is best directed toward providing clients with new information and helping them discover more effective ways of getting what they want (Glasser, 1981). A large portion of the therapy time consists of making plans and then checking to determine how these plans are working. In a group context members learn how to plan realistically and responsibly through contact with both the other members and the leader. The members are encouraged to experiment with new behaviors, to try out different ways of obtaining their goals, and to carry out an action program. It is important that these plans not be too ambitious, for people need to experience success. The purpose of the plan is to arrange for successful experiences. Once a plan works, feelings of self-esteem will increase. It is clear that helpful plans are modest in the beginning and specify what is to be done, when it will be done, and how often. In short, plans are meant to encourage clients to translate their talk and intentions into actions.

A plan that fulfills wants and needs is central to effective group counseling. The process of creating and carrying out plans enables people to gain effective control over their lives. Wubbolding (1988b) devotes an entire chapter to the characteristics of effective planning, which are summarized below:

• The plan should be tied as closely as possible to the client's need in counseling. Skillful group leaders help members identify which of their plans involve greater need-fulfilling payoffs and help members assess what their plans will do for them.

• Good plans are simple and easy to understand. Although plans need to be specific, concrete, and measurable, they should be flexible and open to modification as clients gain a deeper understanding of the specific behaviors that they want to change. In short, it is vital that clients run their plans, not vice versa.

• Plans should be realistic and attainable. Leaders can help members recognize that even small plans can help them in taking significant steps toward their desired changes. This idea is captured nicely by my daughter Heidi in paraphrasing a Chinese proverb: "A journey of a thousand miles begins with the first step. So start walking!"

• An effective plan involves doing something, rather than not doing something. That is, the plan should involve a positive plan of action, and it should be stated in terms of what will be done.

• The group leader encourages members to develop plans that they can carry out independently of what others do. Therefore, the leader's task is to focus on the members, rather than on the world external to them, which is often beyond their control. Group members can learn that they have control only over their own world of wants and their behavioral and perceptual systems. If members wait for others to change, then whether they change is contingent on others. Good plans are specific and concrete. Group leaders can help members develop specificity through their skillful questioning. Leaders often ask members questions such as "What?" "Where?" "With whom?" "When?" and "How often?"

• Effective plans are repetitive; that is, they are performed regularly, if not daily. In order for group members to overcome their negative symptoms such as "depressing," "anxietying," negative thinking, and psychosomatic complaints, it is essential to replace them with positive symptoms. These symptoms include feelings of joy and trust, rational thinking, healthful activities, diet and exercise, and other positive qualities that are a part of one's personal growth program. People do not change by practicing new behaviors only when the spirit moves them but, rather, by continuously repeating the positive elements of their program.

• Plans should have a sense of immediacy; that is, they should be put into action as soon as possible. Leaders may ask their members questions such as "What are you willing to do today to begin to change your life?" "You say that you would like to have more fun. So, what are you going to do now to enjoy yourself?" The message behind these questions is that members do have the capacity to control their lives by making immediate changes.

   • Effective planning involves process-centered activities. For example, members may say that they can do any of the following: pay their child three compliments, jog 30 minutes a day, substitute nutritious food for junk food, devote 2 hours a week to volunteer work, and take a vacation that they have been wanting.

   • Before members carry out their plan, it is a good idea to evaluate the plan in the group and get feedback from other members and the leader. They should ask if their plan is realistic and attainable and if it relates to what they need and want. After the plan has been carried out in real life, it is useful to evaluate it again. Members can return to the group and talk about the degree to which their plan has been successful. With input from the group, they can figure out what the plan might be lacking, how it needs to be more specific, or how it might need to be modified in some other way.

   • In order for clients to commit themselves to their plan, it is useful for them to firm it up—for example, by writing it down. Furthermore, both the group leader and other members can help by providing reinforcement for an effective plan.

Most members do not formulate an ideal plan like the one just described. The better the plan, however, the better are the chances that members will attain their wants. Toward this end, it is essential that they commit themselves to following through with their plans.

Although the burden of responsibility for formulating and carrying out plans for change rests with the group members, it is the task of the leader to create an accepting and nourishing atmosphere for planning. It should be emphasized that throughout this planning phase the group leader continually urges members to assume responsibility for their own choices and actions by reminding them that no one in the world will do things for them or live their life for them. Challenging members to make responsible plans calls for considerable skill and inventiveness.

Commitment.   Typically, people with a failure identity have trouble making and keeping commitments. Clearly, formulating even the most reasonable and practical plan is a waste of time if the client lacks the willingness to implement it. Plans can be put in the form of a contract that will assist group members in holding themselves and others accountable for the carrying out of the plans.

Here one can readily see the value of a group, such as the one in our example. Once individual members make plans and announce them to the group, the group is in a position to help them evaluate and review these plans and to offer support and encouragement when needed. If individual members fall short of their commitments or in any way fail to implement their plans, that fact cannot be hidden from others and, more importantly, from themselves. If some members are able to follow through with their plans, they serve as models for the rest of the group. Others may realize that if their peers can do what they have set out to do, so can they.

It is essential that members who are reluctant to make a commitment be helped to express and explore their fears of failing. Members may have many resistances and fear rejection. Therefore, the support of the group is especially critical during this phase. Members can be encouraged to begin each group session by reporting on the activities of the week, including the difficulties they encountered in sticking with their plans as well as the successes they had in trying out new behavior in the real world. Just as in behavioral groups, where the buddy system is used, reality therapy can encourage members to make contacts with each other during the week if they have trouble in sticking by their commitments.

Of course, there are always those who are unwilling to make *any* commitments. As was mentioned earlier, therapists cannot force change. But they can help such people look at what is stopping them from making a commitment to change. Sometimes people are convinced that they cannot change, that they cannot stick to any decision, and that they are destined to remain a failure. In such cases it is important that the client be helped to see clearly the consequences of not changing and then be guided to formulate very short-range, limited plans having goals that are easy to reach. Clients need to achieve some degree of success, and they need to believe that they do have the power to change. As far as this basic principle of reality therapy is concerned, the nature and scope of the plan are not as important as the commitment to some plan for change, however limited.

Commitment places the responsibility for changing directly on the clients. If members say over and over that they want to change and hope to change, they can be asked the question "Will you do it, and when will you do it?" The danger, of course, is that the member's plan may not be carried out, which leads to an increase of frustrations and adds to the person's failures. Reality therapy tries to avoid this problem by not asking for any commitment that is not reasonable and possible (Glasser, 1981).

Special Procedures in Reality Group Therapy

This section describes four special procedures that can be appropriately applied to the practice of reality therapy in group settings: (1) the skillful use of questioning, (2) self-help procedures for a personal growth plan, (3) the use of humor, and (4) paradoxical techniques. In his book *Using Reality Therapy* Wubbolding (1988b) has extended reality therapy by adding these special procedures to the more conventionally used methods. Of course, reality therapists do not have a patent on these procedures, and all of them can be used in many of the other therapeutic approaches that we have discussed. These special procedures can enhance the group process and can also assist members in attaining their personal goals. In addition to the potential value of these techniques, there are also caveats. As useful as these procedures may be, all of them have the potential for misuse by poorly trained leaders or by leaders who are more concerned with gratifying their own power needs than they are with the welfare of the members of their group.

The Art of Skillful Questioning. Because reality therapy makes use of questioning to a greater degree than many other counseling approaches, it is important for group leaders to develop extensive questioning skills. There are four main purposes for questioning: (1) to enter the inner world of group members, (2) to gather information, (3) to give information, and (4) to help members take more effective control of their lives (Wubbolding, 1988b). The art of group counseling implies that leaders know *what* questions to ask, *how* to ask them, and *when* to ask them.

Questioning is often misused by group leaders. Some leaders' questions appear to have no point other than to keep the members talking. Those leaders use the question-and-answer technique mainly because they don't know what else to do. Such questioning can certainly be overdone and can result in client defensiveness and resistance. However, well-timed and strategic questions can get members to think about what they want and to evaluate whether their behavior is leading them in the direction they want to go. In the next section examples of skillful questions are given. (For more information on questioning, see Long, Paradise, and Long, 1981.)

Self-Help Procedures for a Personal Growth Program. One of the contributions of reality group therapy is that members can learn a variety of self-help tools. As was discussed in a previous section, members make plans to carry newly acquired behaviors from the group setting into their daily lives. Wubbolding (1988b) describes his version of an approach to personal growth in his *replacement program*. This program defines categories of pictures to be used in the client's inner world of wants and behaviors, which are specific and unique for each person. According to Wubbolding, "replacements" include "do-it behaviors" in place of "give-up behaviors" and "positive-symptom behaviors" instead of "negative-symptom behaviors." This replacement program helps members to identify specific behaviors that fulfill both wants and needs and to target specific behaviors for change. Used in the context of group counseling, this self-improvement program is a developmental process.

Earlier, the concept of failure identity was described. Members with failure identities can be characterized by a range of give-up behaviors. For example, they may be acting out, violating the rights of others, or experiencing a range of paining symptoms, such as depression and anxiety. Such people may have an addiction to drugs, food, or gambling. The replacement program helps group members acquire do-it behaviors as well as positive-symptom behaviors. Group leaders often ask questions such as the following to help members evaluate their wants: "Do you really want to change your life?" "If right now you had what you want, how do you imagine your life would be different?" "If you were to change, how might your life be better?" "What is it you want that you don't seem to be getting from life?" "What do you think stops you from making the changes you would like?" Some of the following questions can help members think about what they are doing: "Describe a time that you felt a sense of accomplishment. Specifically, what were you doing?" "Describe a time in your life when you felt that you were in charge. What were you doing?" "What are some of the things that you are doing that you would like to stop doing?" "In what ways would you most like your life to be different a year from now?" "If you had only a year to live, what would you be doing differently?" "What are some of the things you do that bring you the greatest satisfaction?"

Groups are instrumental in aiding members to develop positive-symptom behaviors to replace negative-symptom behaviors. Questioning can be a good catalyst for members' exploration of their current behavior. All of the following questions relate in some way to incorporating positive-symptom behaviors: "You say you would like to be more active in your classes. How many times did you participate in discussions this past week?" "You say you would like to have more fun in your life. What have you done in the past few days that you consider to be fun?" "Describe a time when you felt self-confidence. What were you doing?" "What might you do differently that could improve your family life?" "How does it affect you to tell people how depressed you are?" "Describe the last time that you didn't avoid situations that were risky for you. What were you doing?" "What are some of the best things [or worst things] that might happen if you were to change?" "Imagine that right now you had made all the changes you say you want. What kind of person would you be? What steps can you take now to move in this direction?"

Such skillfully executed questions help members focus on what they are doing, what they are thinking, and how they are feeling. Strategic questions can have the effect of getting members to identify specific ways in which they can replace a failure identity with a success identity. Instead of being cemented to negative addictions, members can develop positive addictions. (For a more detailed discussion of positive addictions see Glasser, 1976a; for a discussion of the replacement program see Wubbolding, 1988b.)

The Use of Humor.   A number of other approaches integrate humor as an intervention to promote constructive change (Adlerian therapy, psychodrama, existential therapy, Gestalt therapy, TA, RET). Many times group members feel so "heavy" that they fail to see any humor in their life situation. In dwelling on their negative symptoms, they make little room for levity. Several practitioners have written about the role that fun and humor have in psychotherapy (see Ellis, 1977; and Greenwald, 1975). Of course, the use of humor must be timed appropriately. Group leaders can make mistakes by poking fun at clients before a therapeutic relationship has been developed. There must be a trusting climate within the group that allows members to become spontaneous and to laugh at themselves and with one another. Once a group has achieved a working level of cohesion, it is far more likely that humor will result in positive outcomes. Humor that is therapeutic is not sarcastic, does not ridicule clients, and does not show a lack of respect. Therapeutic humor has an educative, corrective message, and it helps clients put situations in perspective. Once members have worked through a place where they were stuck or some source of emotional pain, they may be able to see things in perspective and even laugh at the very issues they previously cried about in the group.

O'Connell's (1981) "natural high therapy" focuses directly on a sense of humor as the essential criterion of the actualization process. According to O'Connell, a sense of humor is the end result of expanding one's sense of worth and feelings of universal belonging, plus developing an appreciation for the basic paradoxes of the human condition. Both in individual and in group therapy, techniques of inner and outer change are used in natural high therapy to encourage individuals to become active agents in their actualization through training and practice of self-esteem and social interest.

But there are negative dimensions to humor in therapy that need to be considered. According to Saper (1987), harmful humor exacerbates clients' problems, undermines their personal worth, and leaves them feeling resentful. This type of humor consists of making a member a scapegoat, and it often involves discounting a person by laughing at him or her. It goes without saying that joking that undermines the self-esteem of members by deprecating and humiliating them is never appropriate in group counseling, and such behavior should be blocked by the group leader.

Bloch, Browning, and McGrath (1983) describe some of the misuses of humor in a group. Leaders sometimes use humor as a defense against their own anxiety. When they are confused about the purpose of a group, humor can mask their uncertainty. Group members often misuse humor as a way of deflecting the source of their anxiety, use self-mockery as a way to avoid issues, or clown around to get attention and to keep their anxiety in check. The group itself may collude and misuse humor as a way to avoid focusing on serious issues or as a way to deny conflict.

These potential dangers and misuses should not obscure the clear advantages of the use of therapeutic humor in a group (Bloch et al., 1983). The group therapist can model spontaneous and good-hearted humor, can be transparently real and human, and can use humor to present an interpretation to group members. From the standpoint of group members, the use of humor has the potential to open them to new ways of self-expression and to provide the flexibility to look at themselves from a fresh perspective. A solemn and grave attitude characterizes some members, and humor can go a long way in helping them overcome their exaggerated earnestness. Furthermore, being able to smile and laugh and to appreciate the absurdity of the human condition promotes interpersonal skills. As members are able to fully participate in shared humor, a sense of catharsis occurs, and self-disclosure frequently follows. And finally, Bloch and his colleagues make the point that humor can play a key role in the life of the group as a whole by serving as a cohesive force.

If you wish to read more about the role of fun and humor in the therapeutic process, several sources are available. Saper (1987) discusses both sides of the issue of whether humor is good for the client. The role of humor in group therapy is insightfully presented in the article by Bloch and his colleagues (1983). Other interesting sources on the place of humor in therapy include Ellis (1977), Greenwald (1975), Mindess (1976), and O'Connell (1981).

Using Paradoxical Techniques.   Clients in reality therapy are generally encouraged to change by direct and straightforward procedures. Yet there are times when certain clients seem especially resistant to making plans, or if they do make plans, they may resist carrying them out. Some of these group members may return to a session and inform others in their group that they tried their plan, but it didn't work. In response, reality therapists sometimes do the unexpected. Wubbolding (1988b) contends that there are paradoxes in the theory of reality therapy and that in order to perceive this approach, it is necessary to think paradoxically. At times the best way to make desired changes is to do so indirectly, by dealing with the problem in an unexpected way. This involves looking at a client's behavior in an inverse way, seeing the cause as the effect and the effect as the cause.

In one of our weeklong residential groups, Alex seemed intent on winning everyone's approval in the group. One of his concerns in his everyday life was his worry over being inadequate. He disliked working so hard for the approval and acceptance of his family and friends. Alex was indirect about seeking the approval of the members and the co-leaders, yet it was clear that he very much wanted it. As an exercise, I suggested that he try even harder to win the approval of each of us. Of course, he said that he did not want to ask others for their approval, nor did he want to so desperately need this approval. My co-leaders and I asked him to do the very thing that he said he wanted to do less of. We suggested that he might even start a conversation with "I very much want you to like me, and I need your acceptance to feel worthwhile." He was to be as open and direct as possible in soliciting approval, even to the extent of asking us what he could do that would please us. He soon grew very tired of working so hard for our approval. He vividly saw how he was indirectly doing so many things to get others to like him. By the end of the day he began to laugh at himself for being so intent on being accepted by everyone at any price. At least he was much more aware of messages he was sending to others, as well as his own internal dialogue when he sensed he was not totally approved of. Interestingly, as he became much less focused on getting everyone in the group to approve of him, he increasingly said and did things that were pleasing to him. He began the process of valuing his approval of himself more than the approval of others. Although this strategy was effective in Alex's case, it might have been counterproductive in other cases. The leaders had established a good working relationship with him, and the trust level was increasing in the group. Although he was unsure whether he had the approval of everyone in the group, he did feel that the leaders and the members cared for him. He went along with our exercise because he did not sense that we were laughing at him, and eventually he was able to appreciate the humor in his situation.

Paradoxical procedures are powerful interventions, and thus they should be used only by practitioners who have been adequately trained in this technique or are under close supervision. Research findings on the use of paradoxical techniques reveal that they have been successfully applied in dealing with depression, insomnia, phobias, and anxiety disorders. They also appear to be especially well suited for resistant clients with specific behaviorally defined problems (Huddleston & Engels, 1986).

Paradoxical procedures are usually not used until the more conventional procedures of reality therapy have been tried. Furthermore, there are ethical and clinical issues involved in using paradoxical interventions. Ethical practice demands that group leaders know when paradoxical procedures should be avoided. These procedures are not advisable in dealing with crisis situations, suicide, homicide, violence, abuse, or excessive drinking. Paradox in these situations is likely to be counterproductive and irresponsible (Weeks & L'Abate, 1982).

In summary, the value of paradoxical procedures depends largely on the training and experience of the group practitioner. There is potential for misuse when group leaders use them for shock value or as a gimmick because everything else has failed (Weeks & L'Abate, 1982). When these procedures are used at the right time for the client and at the right stage of a group's development, however, they can be powerful therapeutic tools that promote group cohesion and lead to positive change in group members.

Used properly, paradox can have an impact similar to that of humor in helping members cast their problems in a new light. As in the case of Alex, they may actually learn how to laugh at their foibles, which can make change a much easier matter. Dowd and Milne (1986, p. 278) suggest that the appropriate use of paradoxical interventions requires that this question be raised: "What technique used by what counselor causes what change with what type of client in what situation?" In addition to this standard question, other questions a practitioner can raise to determine when the use of paradox is appropriate include these: "As a group leader, have I established a high level of trust between myself and the members?" "What is the degree of cohesion of the group?" "Might the use of paradox have a boomerang effect, with members feeling tricked and thus becoming increasingly resistant?" "How have the members responded to the use of other techniques?" "How effective have the conventional procedures been in promoting client change?" "Do I know why I might introduce a paradoxical procedure?" "Am I clear about what I hope to accomplish, and do I have an educated sense of how a member might react to this procedure?"

If you would like to pursue the topic of the use of paradox, see Wubbolding (1988b), Weeks and L'Abate (1982), Dowd and Milne (1986), Huddleston and Engels (1986), and Frankl (1960).

Evaluation of Reality Therapy

Contributions of the Approach

A characteristic of reality therapy that I especially favor is its stress on accountability. When a group participant indicates a desire to change certain behaviors, for example, the leader confronts the member with a question about what is keeping the person from doing so. I appreciate the fact that it is the members, not the leader, who evaluate their behavior and decide whether they want to change.

Once the decision to change behavior has been made, reality therapy provides the structure for members to make specific plans, to formulate contracts for action, and to evaluate their level of success. In most of my groups I have found it useful to employ these action-oriented procedures as a device to help members carry what they are learning in the group into their everyday life. I also ask members to state the terms of their contract clearly in the group and to report to the group the outcome of their efforts to fulfill it. Other aspects of reality therapy that I endorse include the idea of not accepting excuses for failure to follow through with contracts and the avoidance of any form of punishment and blaming. As I see it, if people don't carry out a plan, it is important to discuss with them what got in their way. Perhaps they set their goals unrealistically high, or perhaps there is a discrepancy between what they say they want to change and what they actually want to change. (One can generally believe behavior; one cannot always believe words.)

I also like reality therapy's insistence that change will not come by insight alone; rather, members will have to begin doing something different once they determine that their behavior is not working for them. I have become increasingly skeptical about the value of catharsis as a therapeutic vehicle unless the release of pent-up emotions is eventually followed up with some kind of action plan. My colleagues and I have worked in groups with people who seem to have immobilized themselves by dwelling excessively on their negative feelings and by being unwilling to take action to change. Therefore, we continue to challenge such members to look at the futility of waiting for others to change. Increasingly, we have asked the members of our groups to assume that the significant people in their life may never change, which means that these members will have to take a more active stance in shaping their own destiny.

Group members must look inward and search for alternatives. Since other members and the group leader will not entertain rationalizations for their failing behavior, the members are forced to choose for themselves whether to change. Applied to the example used in this chapter of the adolescents in a detention facility, we can readily see that the leader will not allow these youths to endlessly complain about their parents' rejection, about their bad breaks in life, and about their many failures. Whatever the reasons are for their being in an institution now, they will have to make a decision about where their behavior is leading them. I consider the challenging and skillful questioning of reality therapists to be a major strength of this approach. Of course, it is important for leaders to ask open-ended questions that get members to search inwardly and to avoid the "district attorney" style of questioning in which they feel grilled and bombarded with intimidating questions.

Reality therapy encourages clients to look at the range of freedom they do possess, along with the responsibilities of this freedom. In this sense reality therapy is a form of existential therapy. As it is currently practiced, the emphasis is on the inner needs, wants, and choices made by clients (Wubbolding, 1988b). Because of this focus on the perceptual and behavioral systems, reality therapy can also be considered as a cognitive-behavioral approach. A strength of the approach is its emphasis on understanding the subjective inner world of clients. This phenomenological view helps the therapist understand more fully how clients perceive their world, and such a perspective is an excellent means of establishing the rapport needed for creating an effective client/therapist relationship. Understanding the personal world of the client does not mean that therapists have to adopt a "soft" approach; on the contrary, they can demonstrate their caring by refusing to give up on the client. A therapist who consistently maintains a sense of hope that clients can change can be the catalyst that instills a sense of optimism.

Reality therapy has the advantage of being a straightforward and clear approach. Although its key principles are simple, basic, and very practical, it should not be concluded that the method is necessarily simple to apply in group-counseling situations. There are skills that need to be mastered and practiced. To use the methods effectively in groups, training and supervision are required.

In my opinion these emphases of reality therapy are well suited to brief interventions in crisis-counseling situations and to working with youths who are in institutions for criminal behavior. They also have value in work with clients who see themselves as the victims of the abusive actions of others. For example, family members who live with an alcoholic often feel that they are victims. Assume that you were working with a group of husbands who lived with alcoholic wives. These men might have a tendency to complain endlessly about all the ways in which they had tried to help their wife, they might feel helpless to change her, and they might see the source of most of their unhappiness in their wife's drinking behavior. In a reality-therapy group these men would be challenged to look at their part in this situation. They might eventually realize that they could not directly change their wife, but they could change the effects they experienced in such situations. Instead of focusing so much on what their wife was doing and not doing, they could begin to focus more on their own options for changing themselves.

Reality therapy's advantages can also be seen in a group of parents with "incorrigible" children. These parents may have a common bond because of their feeling that their life is being destroyed by the acting-out behavior of their adolescent daughters and sons. A therapist can teach these parents how to consistently apply the principles of reality therapy in their dealings with their children. The parents can also be taught how to focus more on their options for changing their behavior, rather than on the problems they are having in trying to "straighten out" their children. Reality therapy, it seems, has much to offer groups of parents, groups composed of children and adolescents who are having behavioral problems and who continually get in trouble at school, groups of teachers who work with a variety of students, groups of people who recognize that their lifestyle is not working for them, and groups of people in institutions for criminal behavior. It is also widely used in addiction counseling and in groups with substance abusers. In many of these situations with these populations, it would be inappropriate to embark on long-term therapy that delves into unconscious dynamics and an intensive exploration of one's past.

Applying Reality Therapy in Multicultural Settings

The core principle of reality therapy is to help a wide range of clients with diverse backgrounds evaluate for themselves whether their wants are realistic and whether their behavior is helping them. Once they have made this assessment, they can make realistic plans that are consistent with their cultural values. This focus clearly empowers clients. It is a sign of respect that the group leader refrains from deciding what behavior should be changed. The reality-therapy leader assumes the role of getting members to think for themselves about how well their current behavior is getting them what they want. Through skillful questioning, the leader can help ethnic clients determine the degree to which they have acculturated into the dominant society. They can then make a personal assessment of the degree to which their wants and needs are being satisfied by having made this decision. It is possible for them to find their own balance of retaining their ethnic identity and at the same time integrating some of the values and practices of the dominant group. Again, the group leader does not determine this for these clients but challenges them to arrive at their own answers.

Practitioners who lead groups composed of culturally diverse members may find such clients reluctant to share their feelings during the early phase of the group. Ethnic clients are likely to react more positively and to cooperate to a greater degree if the focus is on what they are doing and wanting, rather than on what they are feeling. For example, some clients may be experiencing depression and anxiety, and they may hope to gain relief from these symptoms by being in a group. Thinking of these symptoms from a reality-therapy perspective, the leader could guide the members to look at what they are doing (or not doing) that is contributing to their emotional state. There is no pressure to experience a catharsis and to do emotional work within the group. Yet members eventually realize that they are "depressing" and "anxietying," rather than having these things simply happen to them. Once they realize that certain behaviors are not functional for their purposes, they can make changes that will lead to different outcomes.

As is true for the cognitive-behavioral approaches, reality therapy often works with contracts. In this way the group members eventually specify particular problems that are causing them difficulty and that they would like to explore in the group. Thus group counseling is typically cast in the framework of a teaching/learning process, which appeals to many ethnic clients. There is a specific focus—namely, a certain behavioral pattern that becomes the target for intervention. The reality-therapy leader is interested in helping members discover better ways to meet their needs. To its credit, this approach provides group members with tools for making the desired changes. This is especially true during the planning phase that is so central to the process of a reality-therapy group. With the support and help of other members and the group leader, clients can develop specific and workable plans for action. Within this context, minority clients can be assisted in taking specific steps to move the external world closer to the inner world of their wants. If their plans do not always meet with success in everyday reality, these members can then bring concrete situations back to the group sessions. This type of specificity, and the direction that is provided by an effective plan, are certainly assets in working with minority clients in groups.

One of the limitations of using reality-therapy principles with ethnic or minority clients is that such clients might not feel that this approach takes into account some very real environmental forces that are operating against them in their everyday lives. For example, discrimination and racism are unfortunate realities, and these forces do limit many minority clients in getting what they want from life. If the group leader does not accept these environmental restrictions, members are likely to feel misunderstood. There is a danger that some reality therapists might overstress the ability of these clients to take charge of their lives. Such clients might interpret the group leader's line of questioning as "If you try hard enough, you can pull yourself up by your bootstraps and become anything you choose to." Group members who get such messages may prematurely leave the group in the belief that the leader and other members are not fully appreciating their everyday struggles. Rather than being a fault of the reality-therapy approach, this is more a limitation of some who practice it.

Another problem is that some ethnic clients are very reluctant to say what they want. Their culture has not reinforced them for assertively asking for what they want, and in fact, they may be socialized to think more of what is good for the social group and not to be so concerned with their individualistic wants. In working with people with this cultural background, reality therapy must be "softened" somewhat, and such clients should not be pushed to assertively declare their wants. If this method is not softened, these clients are likely to terminate.

Limitations of the Approach

Some critics object to reality therapy as being simplistic and superficial. I have to admit that I, too, have been critical of reality therapy on these grounds; however, I no longer think it is accurate to criticize reality therapy as being simplistic. As I've said, Glasser agrees that the therapeutic procedures of reality therapy are simple and clear-cut to talk about but that actually putting them into practice is not a simple matter. A concern I have about this approach is the danger that group practitioners will resort to a simplistic way of applying the principles in their work. There is the danger of the group leader's assuming the role of a "preacher," of a moral expert, and of one who judges for the members how they should change. Clearly, if group members accept the leader's standards of behavior instead of questioning and struggling, they don't have to look within themselves to discover their own values. From my perspective this is a very undesirable outcome. (Let me add here that Glasser would contend that if therapists assume the role of moral experts and attempt to impose their values on clients, they are not practicing within the spirit of reality therapy.) Neither is it therapeutic for participants to mimic other members or the group leader in an unthinking manner. Certainly with the group's help, they may arrive at a useful standard to evaluate their own behavior, but ultimately it is up to each individual to make this assessment. William Glasser (1980) puts this issue very clearly: "In the end everyone has to be responsible for his or her own life and for living in a world much larger than the limited world of therapy" (p. 53). Therefore, it is clearly a misconception when people are critical of reality therapists for assuming the role of judging the lifestyle and behavior of their clients. Glasser (1980, 1981) forcefully makes the point that clients must make their own value judgments.

In spite of the fact that I agree that an action program is essential for changes in behavior, my personal preference is to give more attention to the realm of expressing and exploring feelings than reality therapy calls for. Once involvement is attained in a group, my inclination is to give members many opportunities to express *feelings* that they may have kept buried for years. Therapeutic work is deepened by paying attention to the realm of feelings. Therefore, I draw heavily on techniques from Gestalt therapy and psychodrama as a way of helping the members *experience* their feelings, rather than simply talking about their feelings or about situations. Further, I go along with transactional analysis, rational-emotive therapy, and the cognitive-behavioral therapies in placing emphasis upon the role of *thinking* as a key determinant of behavior. Many problems that show up behaviorally have a connection to the self-defeating statements that we often repeat to ourselves. So in addition to encouraging members to come into full contact with the range of their feelings, I also try to get them to look at the thoughts and beliefs that are contributing to their emotional and behavioral problems.

Another limitation I see is the tendency to carry valid points to an invalid extreme. For example, although it is true that focusing on the past can constitute avoidance of present responsibility, discounting the role of the past can easily lead to a superficial view and treatment of certain problems. However, some reality therapists do make it a practice to talk about the past if it is tied to the present (Wubbolding, 1988b). For example, they are likely to help an adult who was abused as a child to talk about it, for this is not really purely a past event, even though it happened many years ago; it is a present source of pain. Similarly, although there are advantages to focusing on conscious aspects of behavior, carried to an extreme this emphasis denies the powerful place of the unconscious in human experience.

A criticism of reality therapy from a behavior therapist's perspective would be that empirical research is lacking to justify the claims that its procedures actually work. As Ford (1982) asserts, empirical evaluation and research have not been major activities in reality therapy to date. He explains this by observing that reality therapy is most popular with practitioners (especially in the fields of education, substance abuse, and corrections), not with research centers and universities. Thus, those who are looking for empirical data rather than advocacy data will probably be critical of reality therapy for its lack of attention to research.

In summary, although I think that there are some limitations in restricting the practice of group work to the reality perspective alone, I do see some unique values and contributions for group leaders. I accept the value of the principles and concepts of reality therapy, most of which can be fruitfully integrated into several of the other systems that have been discussed in this book. Furthermore, as I've indicated, reality therapy appears to work effectively for a variety of practitioners in a diversity of groups, and it has been successfully used in educational settings, in correctional institutions, in various mental-health agencies, and in private practice. Its principles can be used by parents, social-welfare workers, counselors, marriage and family therapists, school administrators, the clergy, and youth workers. As is true of all models, the practitioner must examine the principles and concepts of reality therapy to determine what elements can be effectively incorporated into his or her individual therapeutic style.

Questions for Reflection and Discussion

1. Control theory is based on the premise that we can control what we do and think and that if we change what we are doing and thinking, it is highly likely that we will also change how we are feeling. Do you agree with this assumption? What are the implications of this viewpoint in working with clients who are depressed? How does this assumption fit for you personally?

2. Control theory rests on the assumption that everything we think, do, and feel is generated by what happens inside of us. Thus, the proper focus for therapy is not to discuss the external world but to deal with the internal world of the client. What are the implications of this perspective for your group practice? How would this view influence the interventions that you made in a group?

3. What is the importance of defining and clarifying wants, or "pictures"? What are the implications of having clear, unblurred, and realistic wants?

4. In many respects, reality therapy is at the opposite end of the therapeutic spectrum from psychoanalytic therapy. What contrasts do you see between these two models? Do you agree or disagree with Glasser's objections to the psychoanalytic perspective?
5. What are some of the unique advantages of practicing reality therapy in groups as opposed to individual counseling? How can others in the group help a member make a behavioral evaluation, form a realistic plan, and commit to an action program?
6. Compare and contrast reality therapy with the experiential therapies (such as person-centered therapy, Gestalt therapy, psychodrama, and the existential therapies). To what extent do you think reality therapy incorporates or fails to incorporate elements of these approaches into practice?
7. Some of the more cognitively oriented therapies (such as TA, rational-emotive therapy, and cognitive-behavioral therapy) emphasize the role of one's thoughts, values, beliefs, and attitudes as crucial determinants of behavior. On the other hand, reality therapy focuses on behavior, not the cognitive realm. What are your thoughts on this matter?
8. What are your reactions to those who criticize reality therapy on the ground that it is simplistic? To what extent do you agree with Glasser's contention that although the procedures are simple to discuss, putting them into practice requires considerable therapeutic skill and creativity?
9. Reality therapy requires members to make an honest assessment of their current behavior to determine whether it is working for them. In considering some of the groups that you want to organize, what problems might you anticipate with respect to actually getting the members to make such a value judgment?
10. From what you know about yourself, do you think you might be inclined to make value judgments for the members in your group? Might you be judgmental? To what degree do you think that your own values would affect the way you'd work with your group?

Where to Go from Here

The programs offered by the Institute for Reality Therapy are designed to teach the concepts of control theory and the practice of reality therapy. The institute offers a certification process, which starts with a 1-week intensive seminar in which participants become involved in discussions, demonstrations, and role playing. For those who then wish to pursue certification in reality therapy, a supervised practicum is arranged to best meet the needs of each trainee. There are also a second intensive week and a second practicum. The basic and advanced practicums each entail a minimum of 30 hours over at least a 6-month period. For further information about these training programs, contact either of the following two organizations:

Institute for Reality Therapy
7301 Medical Center Drive, Suite 407
Canoga Park, CA 91307
Phone: (818) 888-0688

or

Center for Reality Therapy
7777 Montgomery Road
Cincinnati, OH 45236
Phone: (513) 561-1911

RECOMMENDED SUPPLEMENTARY READINGS

Glasser has written little on group counseling; however, the principles and concepts discussed in the following books easily translate to group work.

Control theory: A new explanation of how we control our lives (Glasser, 1985) is the one book that I would recommend most highly. In this popular and easy-to-read book, Glasser discusses how we can choose to change our actions and thus gain better control of our feelings and thoughts and live healthier and more productive lives. Other interesting topics that are explored include choosing misery, craziness and responsibility, psychosomatic illness as a creative process, addicting drugs, taking control of our health, and how to start using control theory.

Using reality therapy (Wubbolding, 1988b) extends the principles of reality therapy by presenting case studies that can be applied to group and family counseling as well as individual counseling. This book is very clearly written, with many practical guidelines for using the principles of reality therapy in practice. There are many excellent questions and brief examples. The author has expanded the scope of reality therapy to include marriage counseling, the use of paradoxical techniques, supervision, and self-help. He presents reality therapy as a philosophy of life rather than a doctrinaire theory or set of prescriptions.

The *Journal of Reality Therapy* began semiannual publication in September 1981. It publishes manuscripts concerning research, theory development, and specific descriptions of the successful application of reality-therapy principles in field settings. Subscriptions are $6 a year. If you are interested in subscribing, contact

Dr. Lawrence Litwack, Editor
Journal of Reality Therapy
203 Lake Hall, Boston-Bouve College
Northeastern University
360 Huntington Avenue
Boston, MA 02115

REFERENCES AND SUGGESTED READINGS*

Bloch, S., Browning, S., & McGrath, G. (1983). Humour in group psychotherapy. *British Journal of Medical Psychology, 56,* 89–97.

Donigian, J., & Malnati, R. (1987). *Critical incidents in group therapy.* Pacific Grove, CA: Brooks/Cole.

*Dowd, E. T., & Milne, C. R. (1986). Paradoxical interventions in counseling psychology. *The Counseling Psychologist, 14*(2), 237–282.

*Books and articles marked with an asterisk are suggested for further study.

Ellis, A. (1977). Fun as psychotherapy. *Rational Living, 12,* 2–6.

Evans, D. B. (1982). What are you doing? An interview with William Glasser. *Personnel and Guidance Journal, 60*(8), 460–465.

Ford, E. E. (1982). Reality therapy in family therapy. In A. M. Horne & M. M. Ohlsen (Eds.), *Family counseling and therapy.* Itasca, IL: F. E. Peacock.

Frankl, V. E. (1960). Paradoxical intention: A logotherapeutic technique. *American Journal of Psychotherapy, 14,* 520–535.

Geronilla, L. (1985a). Handling patient non-compliance using reality therapy. *Journal of Reality Therapy, 5*(1), 2–13.

Geronilla, L. (1985b). Helping clients assess and evaluate their needs. *Journal of Reality Therapy, 5*(1), 31–36.

*Glasser, N. (Ed.). (1980). *What are you doing? How people are helped through reality therapy.* New York: Harper & Row.

*Glasser, W. (1965). *Reality therapy: A new approach to psychiatry.* New York: Harper & Row.

Glasser, W. (1969). *Schools without failure.* New York: Harper & Row.

Glasser, W. (1976a). *Positive addiction.* New York: Harper & Row.

Glasser, W. (1976b). Reality therapy. In V. Binder, A. Binder, & B. Rimland (Eds.), *Modern therapies.* Englewood Cliffs, NJ: Prentice-Hall.

*Glasser, W. (1980). Reality therapy: An explanation of the steps of reality therapy. In N. Glasser (Ed.), *What are you doing? How people are helped through reality therapy.* New York: Harper & Row.

Glasser, W. (1981). *Stations of the mind.* New York: Harper & Row.

Glasser, W. (1984a). Reality therapy. In R. Corsini (Ed.), *Current psychotherapies* (3rd ed.). Itasca, IL: F. E. Peacock.

Glasser, W. (1984b). *Take effective control of your life.* New York: Harper & Row.

*Glasser, W. (1985). *Control theory: A new explanation of how we control our lives.* New York: Harper & Row (Perennial paperback).

*Glasser, W. (1986a). *The basic concepts of reality therapy* (chart). Canoga Park, CA: Institute for Reality Therapy.

Glasser, W. (1986b). *Control theory in the classroom.* New York: Harper & Row (Perennial paperback).

*Glasser, W. (1986c). *The control theory–reality therapy workbook.* Canoga Park, CA: Institute for Reality Therapy.

Glasser, W. (1988). CHOICE: A new drug education program. *Journal of Reality Therapy, 7*(2), 33–34.

Greenwald, H. (1975). Humor in psychotherapy. *Journal of Contemporary Psychotherapy, 7,* 113–116.

*Huddleston, J. E., & Engels, D. W. (1986). Issues related to the use of paradoxical techniques in counseling. *Journal of Counseling and Human Service Professions, 1*(1), 127–133.

Kaltenbach, R. F., & Glasser, W. (1982). Reality therapy in groups. In G. M. Gazda (Ed.), *Basic approaches to group psychotherapy and group counseling* (3rd ed.) (pp. 276–318). Springfield, IL: Charles C Thomas.

Long, L., Paradise, L. V., & Long, T. J. (1981). *Questioning: Skills for the helping process.* Pacific Grove, CA: Brooks/Cole.

Mindess, H. (1976). The use and abuse of humour in psychotherapy. In A. J. Chapman & H. C. Foot (Eds.), *Humour and laughter: Theory, research, and applications* (pp. 331–341). London: Wiley.

Nishio, K., & Bilmes, M. (1987). Psychotherapy with Southeast Asian American clients. *Professional Psychology: Research and Practice, 18*(4), 342–346.

O'Connell, W. E. (1981). Natural high therapy. In R. Corsini (Ed.), *Innovative psychotherapies* (pp. 554–568). New York: Wiley.

O'Donnell, D. J. (1987). History of the growth of the Institute for Reality Therapy. *Journal of Reality Therapy, 7*(1), 2–8.

Parish, T. S. (1988). Why reality therapy works. *Journal of Reality Therapy, 7*(2), 31–32.

Saper, B. (1987). Humor in psychotherapy: Is it good or bad for the client? *Professional Psychology: Research and Practice, 18*(4), 360–367.

*Thatcher, J. A. (1987). Value judgments: A significant aspect of reality therapy. *Journal of Reality Therapy, 7*(1), 23–25.

Weeks, G. R., & L'Abate, L. (1982). *Paradoxical psychotherapy: Theory and practice with individuals, couples, and families.* New York: Brunner/Mazel.

Whipple, V. (1985). The use of reality therapy with battered women in domestic violence shelters. *Journal of Reality Therapy, 5*(1), 22–27.

Wubbolding, R. E. (1981). Balancing the chart: "Do it person" and "positive symptom person." *Journal of Reality Therapy, 1*(1), 4–7.

Wubbolding, R. E. (1984). Using paradox in reality therapy—Part 1. *Journal of Reality Therapy, 4*(1), 3–9.

Wubbolding, R. E. (1985a). *Changing your life for the better.* Johnson City, TX: Institute of Social Sciences and Arts.

*Wubbolding, R. E. (1985b). Characteristics of the inner picture album. *Journal of Reality Therapy, 5*(1), 28–30.

Wubbolding, R. E. (1985c). Legal, ethical, and professional issues in reality therapy. *Journal of Reality Therapy, 5*(1), 14–15.

*Wubbolding, R. E. (1985d). Paradoxical techniques in reality therapy—Part 2. *Journal of Reality Therapy, 4*(2), 3–7.

Wubbolding, R. E. (1985e). Reality therapy: Principles and steps. *The West Virginia School Counselors Newsletter.*

Wubbolding, R. E. (1986a). Cycle of counseling (chart). Adapted from W. Glasser, *Basic concepts of reality therapy.* Canoga Park, CA: Institute for Reality Therapy.

Wubbolding, R. E. (1986b). Professional ethics, informed consent and professional disclosure in reality therapy. *Journal of Reality Therapy, 6*(1), 30–35.

Wubbolding, R. E. (1987a). A model for group activities related to teaching reality therapy. *Journal of Reality Therapy, 6*(2), 23–28.

Wubbolding, R. E. (1987b). Professional ethics: Handling suicidal threats in the counseling session. *Journal of Reality Therapy, 7*(1), 12–15.

Wubbolding, R. E. (1988a). Professional ethics: Intervention in suiciding behaviors. *Journal of Reality Therapy, 7*(2), 13–17.

*Wubbolding, R. E. (1988b). *Using reality therapy.* New York: Harper & Row (Perennial Library).

PART

III

APPLICATION AND INTEGRATION

16

Illustration of a Group in Action: Various Perspectives

To give you a better picture of how the various approaches just discussed actually work, this chapter describes a model group in action. It explores the different ways in which practitioners of various orientations would deal with some specific issues and aspects of group work. To adequately describe how all the orientations might be used in a group of ten people and two co-leaders would prove cumbersome. Thus, in order to simplify this project, I give a brief description of the group's members and their problems and then demonstrate how several therapeutic approaches might be functional for each case. For this purpose I have selected what I consider to be typical themes that emerge in many groups. I present each theme and then show how some of the group approaches might deal with it. It needs to be stressed that this chapter reflects my own biases and experiences with respect to the group themes I've selected, as well as my personal interpretation of how the various leaders would work with their groups. The actual implementation of any specific model, as well as the techniques and style of the group leader, would naturally vary from my description.

The Model Group

Our model group is a closed and time-limited group with ten members (five women and five men) and two co-leaders. The setting is a community mental-health center, and our group is a part of the group-therapy program that the center offers to adults who have problems coping effectively with the demands of everyday living. These adults might be termed "normal neurotics"; although none of them is seriously disturbed, they all experience

485

enough anxiety to seek therapy as a way of dealing more successfully with their personal problems.

All the group members have had some individual counseling, they are joining the group voluntarily, and they have agreed to come to all of the sessions, which take place once a week for 2 hours for the duration of the group. The group will meet for 20 weeks, during the course of which no new members will be admitted. Before making the decision to join the group and attend all its sessions, the members participated in a presession in which they met with the co-leaders to get acquainted and determine whether they wanted to have this type of group experience.

The Emerging Themes

The themes I've selected from among the many that typically emerge during the life of a group are the following:

1. clarifying personal goals
2. creating and maintaining trust
3. dealing with fears and resistances
4. coping with loneliness and isolation
5. resolving dependence/independence conflicts
6. overcoming the fear of intimacy
7. dealing with depression
8. searching for meaning in life
9. challenging and clarifying values
10. dealing with the termination of the group

I approach these themes by describing how they apply in concrete ways to various members of our model group. For each theme, I present the *essence* of what these members explore at different sessions. Then, I show how the co-leaders of the group, using the various theoretical approaches, could deal with these themes, the individual members, and the group as a whole. I conclude by describing how I would use concepts and techniques from these various approaches to deal with some issues characteristic of the ending stages of a group.

Theme: Clarifying Personal Goals

As you know, in most groups the initial sessions are devoted to exploring group goals and clarifying the members' personal goals. Following is the essence of what each member of our model group hopes to get from partici-pating in the group:

EMILY   (age 23, single, lives at home with her parents and attends col-lege): I hope to get up enough courage to finally attempt to make it on my own. Though I don't like living with my parents because it limits me, I must admit that it's a comfortable arrangement.

ED   (age 60, an engineer, twice divorced and now living alone, has had drinking problems for years): I'm afraid of being isolated, but I'm also afraid that people will reject me. I want to learn to deal with these fears and with my depression and anxiety without having to resort to drinking.

BETH   (age 55, a widow with two teenage sons living at home, has devoted most of her life to taking care of her sons and others): Maybe I could learn how to ask for something for myself without feeling so terribly guilty.

ROBERT   (age 28, single, a social worker, has difficulty forming close interpersonal relationships, is afraid of women, and tends to "use" them): Sometimes I feel dead and numb, and I wonder if I'll ever change. I expect to work on my fears of getting close to women.

JOANNE   (age 35, three children and a miserable marriage, has recently returned to college): I decided to stay with my husband until I finish college and get a good job and until my kids go to high school. I want to reexamine this decision and determine if the price is too high.

SAM   (age 34, married, hates his work in maintenance and wants to change it but is not confident enough to do so): Besides making some vocational decisions, I hope to leave this group feeling better about myself and my possibilities.

SHARON   (age 25, an executive secretary, lives with a man despite her parents' objections): I'm confused about what I really hope to get from this group. I know I feel guilty for letting my parents down, but I don't know if a group will help me or not.

RANDY   (age 47, a high school teacher, has been abandoned by his wife, who took the children with her): I can't concentrate. I keep thinking of her and our kids. I want to be able to deal with the anger and the pain I feel much of the time.

JUDY   (age 38, single, a university professor, is struggling to find new meaning for her life): I keep asking myself "Is this all there is to life?" I think I have a lot to be thankful for, yet I often feel empty. I want to take another look at my values and see if they still fit.

BOYD   (age 22, a college student, lately has experienced moments of panic, anxiety, and some bouts of depression): There have been times that I wanted to commit suicide, and it scares me. I hope to understand some of my feelings. Also, I hope to find out that I'm not the only one who feels like this.

Some Therapeutic Approaches

Co-leaders with a *behavioral, TA,* or *reality-therapy* orientation will probably begin by having each member state his or her goals as clearly and concretely as possible. They will help the members formulate specific contracts for their own work, contracts that will provide a direction for the group. For example, in working with Robert, leaders with these orientations will have him clarify what it is that he fears about women and how he sees himself as keeping distant. This effort may lead him to formulate a working contract as follows: "I agree to work with the women in this group by openly exploring my reactions to them. By dealing with the feelings I have toward women in the group, I may get a clearer understanding of the impact I have on women in general." As another example, Beth—the person who has trouble asking for what she wants—may be helped to develop a list of her specific wants and to formulate a contract to explore her feelings about trying to satisfy these wants.

One form of a behavioral group is the *multimodal* approach to therapy, which takes the whole person into consideration. Comprehensive group therapy entails the correction of irrational beliefs, deviant behaviors, unpleasant feelings, bothersome images, stressful relationships, negative sensations, and possible biochemical imbalances. The group process is characterized, from this perspective, by a broad assessment that may include questions such as the following: "What are your major strengths? What keeps you from getting what you want? What behaviors would you like to acquire, and what ones do you want to eliminate? What are some emotions that are a problem for you? How do you see yourself now? What are the values that give your life the most meaning? What are some ways in which you satisfy your intellectual needs? What is the quality of your relationships with others? What do you give to others, and what do you get from them? What is the state of your health?" This process of initial assessment brings out some central and significant themes that can be productively explored in a group. It gets clients to think about what is going on in their life and encourages them to formulate personal goals that will give the group some direction.

From the *reality-therapy* perspective, the group leader may help members recognize that what they are doing is not working for them and encourage them to make a value judgment about the quality of their behavior. Members will be given hope that they are capable of making realistic plans for changing the aspects of their behavior that they decide to change. This goal of enabling members to choose better behavior is likely to come about if they realize that what they are doing, thinking, and feeling is not simply happening to them but that they are, indeed, making choices. Initially, the members may be asked to think about the questions "What are you doing now? What do you want to do differently? Is what you are doing actually working for you? What do you want to get from this group?"

In an *Adlerian group* there will be emphasis on the alignment of the group members' goals and the leader's goals. Cooperation and focus on a common therapeutic task are essential if change is to occur. Attention will be devoted to the beliefs and mistaken perceptions that interfere with the members' progress in dealing with the challenges of life. The assumption of an Adlerian group is that the group process can be effective only if it deals with things that the members recognize as important and want to explore and change. Thus, during the initial stage of a group, contracts will be established with the members that clearly state why they are attending the group and what they expect from their participation in it.

Theme: Creating and Maintaining Trust

Trust soon becomes an issue as the group gets under way. Members will often question their ability to trust the group leaders, the other members, and even themselves.

Judy, the professor, says: "I'm concerned that what I say to the group will not remain in the group. I have no reason to distrust anybody in here; still, I know that I have some reservations about revealing myself to the group."

Sharon expresses her lack of trust in herself: "I've never been in a group before, and I don't know if I'll fit in here or what is appropriate. I mean, I don't even know how to let others know what is going on within me, and I'm afraid that if I do let people know, I'll just bore everybody."

Boyd doubts whether the leaders are competent to deal with what he calls his "heavy" feelings, such as suicidal impulses. "I'm afraid you guys will just try to cheer me up or maybe tell me I'm really crazy. Also, I'm worried about what the other people here will think about me."

Typically, groups focus on issues of trust, such as those illustrated by the examples just given, during the early stages of group process. It is clear that if members are to drop their defenses and reveal themselves—as indeed they must if the group is to be effective—they need assurance that the group is a safe place to do this. More importantly, they need a *reason* to reveal themselves. Thus, members must see that by being open and taking risks, they will understand themselves more fully.

Helping to build trust in the group is a vital task for group leaders, and the way in which they approach the group is of crucial importance. In the following section I summarize some comments that might be made by practitioners of the various orientations during the early stages of a group. Note that the leaders try to promote trust by specifying what the group is designed to do and by indicating how the group process will work. Also note how their comments clearly reveal their different orientations.

Some Therapeutic Approaches

The following are summaries of what the leaders of the various group models might say to the group as they seek to establish a climate of trust at the opening session:

Psychoanalytic Group. "This group is a place where you can safely explore feelings, events, and experiences that you've buried. We're here to help you work through unfinished business from your past, which will show itself through the interactions in the group. It's our job to create an accepting and tolerant climate that will promote your active participation."

Adlerian Group.   "In this group we'll be focusing on your style of life as it becomes evident through your behavior in here. We'll also be giving attention to some of your early recollections, your memories of what it was like for you to be in your family, and how your position in your family might be still affecting you. A group is an ideal place to make changes in your life, for the group is a microcosm of your social world. In here we'll encourage you to try on new behaviors and to put your insights into action by testing them in this group and in your encounters in daily life."

Psychodrama Group.   "In this group you'll act out—not just talk about—your conflicts, and you'll reenact emotionally significant scenes. By releasing pent-up feelings, you'll gain more insight, and you'll experiment with more spontaneous ways of behaving."

Existential Group.   "Here each of you can discover how you've restricted your freedom. Our main task is challenging you to assume the responsibility for your own choices and to search for a more real existence. We hope to share ourselves with you in the process."

Person-Centered Group.   "Our job is to facilitate, not direct, this group. In part this means helping to make it an accepting and caring group. Since we assume that each of you has the capacity to know what you want, we also assume that once you see this as a safe place, you'll drop your pretenses and show your real selves. We believe that you'll eventually learn to trust yourselves and to rely on your own judgments."

Gestalt Group.   "We'll stay as much as possible in the here and now and deal with whatever prevents you from maintaining a present-centered awareness. Our focus will be on the *what* and *how,* rather than the *why,* of behavior. With this focus, which will help you to express parts of yourselves that you've denied, we expect that you'll eventually become more integrated and whole. Above all, we're here to assist you in identifying the unfinished business from your past that's impeding your present functioning."

Transactional-Analysis Group.   "Each of you is our colleague in your own therapy. We don't presume the right to special knowledge about you; rather, we assume that *you* will decide on the course of your work in here, largely by developing clear contracts that will specify what you want to change and how you want to do it."

Behavior-Therapy Group.   "We assume that if you've learned ineffective behavior, you can learn new, constructive behavior. The group will offer a context for this learning. Our task is to teach you new coping skills; your task is to practice these skills, both within and outside the group. The group will give you the support needed to reinforce any changes you make, so that they become an integral part of you."

Rational-Emotive Group.   "Although others may be largely responsible for indoctrinating you with self-defeating beliefs, we hold you responsible for maintaining such beliefs. Accordingly, we'll be active in getting you to critically evaluate your processes of self-indoctrination. Group work will be directed toward replacing your current irrational belief systems with a rational philosophy of life."

Reality-Therapy Group.   "Since we believe that each of you is seeking a success identity, our main goal in this group is to assist you in determining whether your current behavior promotes success. If you discover that it doesn't and if you decide to change, it will be your responsibility to formulate a plan of action designed to promote change. The group will offer you a place to practice this plan for change, and outside homework assignments will help you carry these changes into your everyday behavior."

Theme: Dealing with Fears and Resistances

During the early stages of the group, members typically express fears about getting involved and display resistance toward any attempt at delving into deeply personal concerns. Some members keep their fears about becoming involved in the group to themselves, whereas others seem eager to express their fears and put them to rest so that they can begin to work. Whether or not the fears are expressed, they tend to give rise to some ambivalence: the desire to reveal oneself is balanced by the reluctance to expose oneself. Following are some typical expressions of the ambivalence:

- Why do I have to reveal my private feelings in this group? What good will it do anyhow?
- I'm afraid to get involved, because I may make a fool of myself.
- I'm afraid that if I say what I really think and feel, the group will reject me.
- If I see myself as I really am, I may find that there is nothing inside me.
- I'm afraid that by becoming too involved in this group, I may make my problems bigger than they really are.
- If I get too involved in the group, I'm afraid I'll become too dependent on it for solving problems that I have to handle alone.
- Right now my life is rather confortable; if I become too involved in the group, I may open up a can of worms that I can't handle.
- I'm afraid that the group will strip away my defenses and leave me vulnerable.
- I'm somewhat afraid of disclosing myself to others, not only because of what *they* may think but also because of what *I* might find out about myself.
- I want to protect myself by not letting myself care. If I get too close to people in the group, I'll feel a real loss when it ends.

Some Therapeutic Approaches

Psychodrama Group. Using a psychodramatic framework, the co-leaders may direct members to express and share their fears, with the aim of showing participants that they are not alone in these fears. The resulting sense of commonality helps the group develop cohesiveness.

Psychoanalytic Group. Psychoanalytically oriented leaders see resistance as a basic part of the group process. Since in this model resistance to self-knowledge often presents itself in the form of resistance to others, dealing with resistance to the group is an essential aspect of therapy. At appropriate times the leaders may interpret the individual members' resistance to the group. The aim is to help members learn about themselves by exploring their reactions to other group members, who serve as catalysts to evoke early memories.

Gestalt Group. Gestalt leaders tend to deal with resistance by rehearsing the associated fears. For example, Ed, who holds back because of his fear of being rejected by the group, may be asked to stand in front of each group member and complete the sentence "You could reject me by . . ." Next, he may be asked to make the rounds again, this time to finish the sentence "You would reject me if you knew . . ." By completing the sentence in a different way with each member, Ed can express the full spectrum of the fears of rejection that he normally keeps inside of himself. The goal is to render the fears less compelling and to take some steps toward dealing with them.

Rational-Emotive Group. Taking the example of Ed again, leaders of this orientation may confront him with questions such as "What would be so terrible if everyone in here *did* reject you? Would you fall apart? Why do you tell yourself that rejection is such an awful thing?" The attempt here is to show Ed that he has uncritically bought the irrational idea that he will not survive if he gets rejected. The leaders may then invite other members to express similar irrational fears and then proceed to teach the group members that they are responsible for making themselves emotionally disturbed by unquestioningly accepting such irrational notions.

Existential Group. During the early stages of a group, members may express their fears that if they take a look at themselves, they may find that they are empty or that they are not the person they have convinced themselves they are. This confrontation with oneself can be terrifying for some, and in an existential group these fears are openly acknowledged and worked with. The group leaders may ask the members to close their eyes and imagine that these fears of theirs are actually occurring in this group. For example, Robert, who is afraid of women and closeness with them, can imagine his worst fears happening in the group. Judy may confront her fears that she is living without any values of her own. And Boyd can allow himself to imagine his panic over the times he has feared he might want to kill himself. This is the first step in making a commitment to themselves and the group to face and deal with their fears.

Theme: *Coping with Loneliness and Isolation*

Randy, the high school teacher who has been abandoned by his wife and children, is the exponent of this theme. He keeps asking himself: "Why did she leave me? Am I to blame for what happened? Will I ever be able to trust anyone again? Will I be able to get over the pain of this breakup?"

Some Therapeutic Approaches

Person-Centered Group. The person-centered co-leaders may invite Randy to tell his story in detail. While he does so, the leaders pay full attention not only to what Randy is saying but also to his nonverbal expressions of pain over his losses and his feelings of being utterly alone and abandoned. The leaders' attention and the support of the group stimulate Randy to fully experience and share the intensity of his feelings.

The group leaders may notice that Ed, who has had similar experiences, appears deeply moved, and they will ask Ed to express what he is feeling. Ed may reveal that he is identifying with Randy and that he still feels torn up over his second divorce—a revelation that may cause Ed and Randy to spontaneously talk with each other, which in turn may provoke other members to share what they are feeling and demonstrate that they care about the two men. The support of the leaders and of the group as a whole would tend to encourage a full and open expression of both men's feelings, which previously may have been bottled up.

Psychodrama Group. The leaders using a psychodramatic approach are likely to ask Randy what he would like to understand more fully about the breakup of his marriage. Randy replies "There are a lot of things that have gone unsaid—things that I feel stuck with, things that I'm afraid I won't ever say." Randy is then asked to go to the stage area and say what he fears he'll never be able to say. When he has done so, he is asked to "become his wife" and, in this role, to say all the things he imagines that she would say. This exchange of roles is continued until the group can get a feeling of how Randy sees his wife.

Next, Randy is asked to select a member to play his wife's role. He picks Joanne and begins by expressing his hurt—his feelings of loneliness and loss. Joanne (as his symbolic wife) responds. Eventually Randy's pain turns to anger; he begins to release the bottled-up anger yet keeps blocking it with self-deprecating remarks. At this point Robert, the member who has difficulty with women, is selected as Randy's double and steps next to Randy, shouting many of the things that Randy seems to be cutting off with his guilt. By having someone speak in his behalf, Randy may be able to eventually release his most intense, deepest rage.

When this scene has finally served its purpose, the leader may ask Randy to fantasize a future as he would wish it, say, 5 years from now. In this fantasy Randy sees his wife and children reunited with him. He is then asked to act out a scene from this future as he would wish it to be, playing his wife's role as well as his own. During the course of this psychodrama Randy recalls how his wife's departure vividly reminded him of the scene when his mother left him after she divorced his father. The importance of this connection would be underscored by the leader, who might suggest to Randy that he could deal with his childhood experience later within the group.

Rational-Emotive Group.   The approach of RET leaders to Randy's problems will focus on getting him to stop his vicious self-blaming. Members of an RET group are quickly taught what is called the A-B-C of therapy. In Randy's case, the Activating event (A—that is, his wife's leaving) is not the cause of Randy's misery now. Rather, the cause is Randy's response to the Activating event—namely, his irrational Beliefs (B). Specifically, his response is to keep telling himself that because his wife left him, he is rotten; that if his wife does not love him, nobody will or can; that, if he had not been basically worthless and *if only* he had been different, his wife would still be with him. Thus, the emotional Consequence (C) of his emotional pain is due not to his wife's departure but to his faulty and illogical thinking. In the RET group other members will confront Randy with his self-destructive style and persuade him to consider changing his thinking.

In the course of this work it is discovered that Randy has been avoiding making contacts with other women because he has convinced himself that no woman could *ever* want anything to do with him. Thus, the leaders challenge him to attack this self-defeating notion of basic unworthiness. Randy is asked to role-play asking a woman in the group for a date, and the male co-therapist coaches him in this play by showing him how to be assertive. Randy is given an opportunity to discuss his fears of getting involved again, which can lead him to begin differentiating between realistic and unrealistic fears. He receives a homework assignment, such as the task of initiating and maintaining a conversation with some women at his place of work. He is asked to keep a written record of his reactions to these encounters and to report the results to the group at its next session.

Adlerian Group.   In working with the theme of loneliness and isolation, the Adlerian group leaders may pay attention to Randy's family constellation and his early recollections. From this perspective it is assumed that he wants to belong, to fit in with others, and to have a place of prominence in his family of origin. Randy may be asked to describe each sibling as he remembers him or her. He may also be asked for specific information on the social groupings of the siblings, along with some rating of how he sees himself in relation to his brothers and sisters. He may say something like the following: "I can remember how alone I felt at home as a kid. My bigger brother got all the attention, and I was sure I'd never measure up to him. I often felt that I didn't belong in our family. Especially when he was around. I just couldn't seem to get any of the attention no matter what I did! Just saying all this brings back the feelings of loneliness that I so often felt as a child."

Randy can be encouraged to look for some themes in his life and identify some key characteristics that distinguish him. He may very well see connections between his childhood experiences and the feelings of isolation he now feels.

Theme: Resolving Dependence/Independence Conflicts

Emily, the group member who is living with her parents and going to college, discusses the resentment she feels toward her parents. According to Emily, her parents control her life, are responsible for her insecurity, and make it difficult for her to break away and live on her own. She has admitted that she finds living at home comfortable. As she begins delving further, she sees that she is frightened of taking increased responsibility for her own life and that her parents are scapegoats for her own inability to become independent. In the group she struggles with conflicting desires—a desire to remain secure by clinging to what is known and a desire to assume more responsibility for directing her own life. She is torn between wanting to become her own parent (doing for herself what she now expects her parents to do for her) and fearing the added responsibility of increased maturity.

Some Therapeutic Approaches

Reality-Therapy Group. If Emily discusses her problem in a reality-therapy group, the leaders may confront her tendency to blame her parents as follows: "You seem to be getting a lot of mileage from making your parents responsible for your dependency. Also, you seem to dwell on the past too much, almost as if you were clinging to it as an excuse for not being the free person you say you want to be. Using your past to justify your current 'inability' to make decisions keeps you from getting in touch with your power. As long as you hold onto your past and blame your parents, you never really have to take an honest look at yourself."

The aim of this approach is to get Emily to evaluate her current behavior and to accept the role she is playing now; exploring her feelings or discussing her changing attitudes is of little interest here. The pivotal question for her is "Do I want to continue my dependent behavior, or do I want to change it?" If she decides that she does want to change, she will then be asked to develop a plan of action, which will include definite steps toward behaving more independently, and a contract to change, which will include a commitment to try new behavior outside the group.

Existential Group. Assume now that Emily brings up her dependence/independence conflicts in an existentially oriented group. It is probable that one of the co-leaders will ask other group members if they can identify with her. In our model group Joanne, who has a desire to leave her secure but boring marriage, Sharon, who feels guilty for not living up to her parents' expectations, and Beth, who may see herself in the parental role with respect to Emily's conflict, can all identify with Emily. In the existential group Emily, Joanne, Sharon, and Beth may be asked to form an inner circle and sit in the center of the group. The leader may instruct this subgroup to "discuss all the ways that you are unfree now, talk about how it feels to not be in charge of your own lives, express your fears of giving up your security in order to gain independence, and examine the advantages of remaining dependent."

The purpose behind this exercise is to provide these four participants with an opportunity to fully explore how they feel and think about their practice of giving up their power to others. The aim is to assist them to clearly see what keeps them secure (and unfree) and to honestly determine the cost of this security.

Transactional-Analysis Group. If Emily's problems are raised in a TA group, the leaders may take one or more of several exploratory paths—for example:

- identifying and analyzing the games that Emily is playing
- working on her life script to determine how she is following a plan for life drawn up by her parents
- assisting her in seeing the typical ego state in which she functions (probably the Child ego state, at least with respect to her parents)
- exploring the injunctions that she has lived by, as well as her early decisions

The exploration of Emily's injunctions can involve many group members who share similar injunctions, such as "Don't grow up"; "Don't disappoint your parents"; "Don't think for yourself"; "Don't trust yourself"; "Do what is expected of you." The sharing of Emily's injunctions can provide other members with a valuable catalyst for examining the ways in which they have incorporated parental messages without thinking about them. Similarly, the sharing of an early decision that she has apparently made—"Let your parents take care of you, because you are not able to take care of yourself"—will be used by the group to explore other instances of early decisions.

Behavior-Therapy Group. In a group with a behavioral orientation Emily will probably be asked to specify ways in which she would like to change her relationship with her parents. Next, she may be invited to role-play herself with the co-leaders, who act as her parents. In this role play she is directed to tell her parents what she would like to change in their relationship.

Later, other members may be invited to give Emily feedback answers to questions such as "Was she assertive? Is her style effective for the purpose of having her parents listen to her?" If the feedback indicates that Emily comes across as a whining apologizer, the female co-leader may step in to demonstrate a direct style for clearly stating desires without apologies. Emily may then be asked to replay her role with the symbolic parents, using the information that she has just received. If appropriate, the group may then offer positive feedback, pointing out and supporting assertive behavior on her part.

Theme: Overcoming the Fear of Intimacy

Another theme is exemplified by Robert's difficulties in forming close relationships of any kind, particularly intimate relationships with women. As Robert describes his struggles, he mentions several times that often he feels numb and emotionally dead. He worries that something is basically wrong with him, because he finds it hard to care for fellow group members who express psychological pain. As he puts it: "As some of you go through 'heavy' stuff, I feel detached, sort of cold and isolated. I'm not letting myself identify with anybody in here, and that makes me wonder if I'd ever be able to care and if I have the capacity to get intimately involved with anyone. I feel sort of dead inside." The themes that are evoked and explored in the group include the fear of intimacy (and the need for intimacy), feelings of isolation and deadness, and, to some extent, feelings of hopelessness.

Some Therapeutic Approaches

Gestalt Group. The Gestalt leaders will focus on Robert's ambivalence toward intimacy. First, he is asked to face each of the women in the group and state his worst fear about getting close to her. Next, he is asked to concentrate on his here-and-now fears toward the women in the group. Then, he is asked to conduct a dialogue between the two sides of himself from two chairs.

As he sits in one chair and plays the side of him that wants to care and get involved, he says: "It feels lonely and cold behind the walls that I build around myself. I work so hard to keep people out. I want to get out of the walls, but I'm afraid of what is out there." As he sits in the other chair and plays the side that wants to remain behind those walls, he says: "Stay behind those walls that you've worked so hard to build. You're isolated, but at least you're safe. You know what happens whenever you let yourself really care: you always get burned, and that pain isn't worth the effort of getting involved." This dialogue, which may continue for about 5 minutes, helps Robert become more aware of the polarities within him, without forcing him to choose between his two sides yet.

Behavior-Therapy Group.   The behavior therapists will use relaxation and desensitization techniques to approach Robert's fear of intimacy. Relaxation techniques, which are taught to the entire group, consist essentially of systematically tensing and relaxing all the muscles in the body. They are practiced daily at home.

A practical application of relaxation techniques to Robert's difficulties may proceed as follows. He is instructed to construct an imaginary hierarchy of interpersonal situations ranging from those that would produce the least amount of anxiety to those that would produce the most. He is then asked to use the techniques that he has learned to become extremely relaxed. Next, he is guided through a fantasy about an interpersonal situation that, according to his hierarchy, generates the least degree of anxiety—say, merely seeing a woman that he is attracted to. This is followed by fantasies of situations involving greater and greater anxiety. As soon as Robert experiences anxiety, he is instructed to "switch off" that scene and relax. In this manner he may manage to work himself up to sustaining fantasies about a high-anxiety-producing situation—for example, approaching a woman and initiating a conversation with her.

At another session Robert may practice behavioral rehearsal, putting himself into a real-life situation in the group. For example, after inviting him to assume that Sharon is a woman that he would like to date, the group leader may ask him: "How would you let Sharon know that you are interested in her? Assume that you and Sharon are actually on a date. What might your conversation be like? Pretend that you are saying good-bye. What would you tell her about your feelings concerning her and your evening with her? What is it that you hope you could say?" After this rehearsal, the leader asks Robert to select a woman in his everyday life that he would actually like to make contact with and, with the help of other group members, to develop a homework assignment relating to making that contact—an assignment that he is to practice during the week and to report on during the following session.

The action-oriented behavior-therapy approach has Robert challenge his fears of intimacy, not analyze their cause. He begins in the relative safety of his fantasies as guided in the group situation, progresses to dealing with his feelings toward a female member of his group (Sharon) by role playing (behavior rehearsal), and finally applies his newly acquired skills to his everyday life.

Rational-Emotive Group.   The description of the behavioral group could easily fit the RET group. The RET leaders, however, are more likely to challenge Robert's perceptions about the catastrophic consequences of becoming intimate. The emphasis here is on teaching him that he is stopping himself by his fears, many of which are unfounded or based on irrational beliefs. The aim is to have him put himself in situations where he has to critically appraise his beliefs regarding emotional closeness. As in the behavioral approach, he is expected to carry out homework assignments.

Transactional-Analysis Group.   The TA leaders may well focus on exposing and working with an early decision that Robert made—for example: "If you open yourself to being loved by others, or if you let yourself care about others, you are bound to be hurt. Thus, it's best to seal off your feelings and become emotionally numb, because then you won't feel the pain." After some initial probing, the leaders may have him reconstruct a specific, relevant scene with his parents when he was 10 years old. With the help of the leaders, who would probably use a Gestalt technique (combined with some psychodrama), he attempts to experience the scene as completely as possible, including the feelings of helplessness that he felt as a child. In that manner, he may be led to see that a decision concerning closeness that he made as a helpless child served his survival needs *then* but is no longer an appropriate basis for his actions *now*.

Following this reconstruction, wherein Robert can experience the intensity of his fear of closeness, the leaders have him engage his cognitive faculties by asking him to consider *when* and *why* he made his early decision and to think about how that decision impedes his relationships in the present. Finally, some of his injunctions—for example, "Don't get close"; "Never let people know what you're feeling"; "Don't trust women"; "Don't feel"—may be challenged.

Psychoanalytic Group.   The psychoanalytic leaders may use Robert's response to them as a therapeutic device, and the following scenes may ensue: the male leader points out that Robert typically avoids, and appears uncomfortable with, the female leader. Robert admits his discomfort, explaining that he sees her as a dynamic and insightful woman who, he feels, could use her power to hurt him. While maintaining the focus on Robert's feelings toward the woman leader, the therapists draw parallels between his responses in the group and his relationships with his mother and sisters.

Assuming that the interpretations are apt and timely, Robert may make some fruitful associations between how he behaved in his mother's presence and how he behaves in the group. He may begin to see how he is transferring some of his childhood feelings for his mother to the female leader. (This transference is encouraged, because it provides useful material that will eventually allow him to work through some of his attitudes toward women.) At the same time he may become aware of the ways in which he is competing with the women in the group for the therapists' attention—a behavior that may relate to his childhood behavior of competing with his sisters for their parents' attention. Whatever the insights, they are merely the beginning of significant work in a psychoanalytic group. In Robert's case, awareness of a connection between his childhood experiences and his current fear of closeness would be followed by an effort to use the transferences that have occurred with respect to women in the group to work through his fears of closeness.

Theme: Dealing with Depression

One common theme that emerges is exemplified by Ed (the oldest person in the group), who is chronically depressed and, like Robert, feels isolated and incapable of breaking out of his isolation. After two divorces, he sees himself as a failure in maintaining relationships; thus, he lives alone rather than risk further failure. Ed, an admitted alcoholic, describes how his drinking has ruined his personal and professional life and how all these failures have left him feeling hopeless, helpless, and in great need of alcohol for comfort. After some limited success with Alcoholics Anonymous, he clearly sees that booze doesn't solve his problems and that he is guilt ridden by his failures in life and weakness for alcohol. Now he wants to probe deeper into the reasons that compel him to seek refuge in drinking—reasons that he realizes are merely symptomatic of personality problems. He also realizes the importance of coming to grips with his bouts of depression.

Some Therapeutic Approaches

Person-Centered Group.   Leaders of a person-centered group will work to develop a climate of acceptance and trust in which Ed can express his feelings. By providing an example of accepting attentiveness, the leaders let him know that he has permission to feel what he feels and share these feelings with the group. In this manner someone like Ed, who punishes himself with disapproval and rejection and expects the same treatment from others, may for the first time feel that he is accepted and acceptable. Armed with this new view of himself, he is in a far better position to probe the reasons behind his drinking.

Psychoanalytic Group.   The psychoanalytic leaders will focus on any dependencies that Ed may develop with respect to the group—for example, dependence on the leaders for decision making and dependence on other members for support and approval. The leaders may direct him toward exploring how he views each therapist, what he wants from them, and how he uses them (as he used his parents) to get confirmation as a person. By examining his need for approval from the group leaders, he may become aware, for instance, that he never really felt loved by his parents and that he grew up believing that not achieving perfection meant that he was a failure.

By exploring his reactions within the group, particularly with respect to the group leaders, and with the help of some interpretations by them, Ed begins to draw parallels between his interactions with his parents and family and his interactions with the group leaders and other members. For several sessions this association is explored in greater depth, and he begins working through his feelings toward each therapist. Eventually he may find that in many ways he is making the leaders his symbolic parents (expecting them to respond to him as his parents did and keeping himself a helpless child waiting for their approval) and, more generally, that he is reliving his past in the group.

In future sessions Ed may work on his inordinate need for approval and love, on his extreme dependence on others to direct him, and on his taking refuge in drinking to blunt the anxiety of not feeling loved. Thus, he could fruitfully explore the roots of his excessive drinking and come to understand that it is both an escape from anxiety and an attempt to create the illusion of being the powerful person he would like to be.

Reality-Therapy Group. A way of describing the reality-therapy approach to Ed's problem is to contrast it with the approach of the psychoanalytic group:

• Since reality therapy focuses on future success, not on past failure, Ed is not allowed to dwell on his past.

• Whatever reactions he has toward the leaders, they are assumed to be generated by the present therapeutic relationship and not to be the result of transference or distortions from his past.

• The co-therapists actively work at having him look at his current behavior and decide whether this behavior is getting him what he wants. If he decides that his behavior is dysfunctional, he is challenged to develop a plan for change.

• The reality-therapy leaders discourage Ed from focusing on his *feelings* of hopelessness, despair, isolation, and dependence; rather, he is encouraged and directed to examine what it is that he is doing now that contributes to these feelings. To direct this examination of how his actions are contributing to his feelings, the leaders ask questions such as "What exactly did you do today from the time you woke up to now? You say that you feel despair and isolation; taking the last week, could you tell us specifically *what* you did whenever you had such feelings? How did your behavior contribute to your feelings? What do you see that you *can* do before our next session to begin to change your pattern? Are you willing to take specific steps that involve behaving differently? What are some constructive things that you can do when you feel a need to drink?"

• Regarding Ed's stated desire to penetrate the reasons underlying his drinking problem, the reality therapists will probably say: "We don't go looking for causes from the past to explain what we view as current ineffective behavior. Insight into the unconscious reasons for your behavior is not our concern. Instead, we want to talk about your options for beginning to actually decide on a course of action that will lead to responsible and effective behavior and, ultimately, a success identity."

Transactional-Analysis Group.   The TA approach to Ed's "theme" will probably include the following elements:

• Work focuses on Ed's life script, which in his case may be captured succinctly in the phrase "drinking myself to death" and his supporting injunctions such as "Don't think!" "Don't succeed!" "Don't be competent!" In the group he may work on his process of developing his life course, so that he can come to see that his current script, "drinking myself to death," may be a self-fulfilling prophecy.

• The therapists may also point out the ways in which Ed is slowly killing himself psychologically by keeping himself isolated. In the group, time is devoted to examining the games he plays, along with the payoffs for these games. Eventually, he is led to see that his games are related to a purposeful plan. (That is, if he plays his games long enough, he will eventually collect enough bad feelings to justify the final ending of his script, which could be suicide. This would fulfill his basic injunction "Don't be!")

• Ed would also be led to examine the connection between the games he plays and his basic life position "I'm not OK—you're OK." Eventually, he may come to see that his game is to put the responsibility for his self-worth on others.

The aim of the work in the TA group is to help Ed understand *how* and under *what conditions* he formulated his original decision—for example: "Don't trust yourself, because you'll always fail. Instead, expect others to decide for you, because you're incapable of directing your own life." Once Ed sees how he made his decision, and once he becomes aware of the games he plays—even in his group—he can be led to see that he doesn't have to continue being the victim of an early decision and that he is now in a position to make a new decision.

Theme: Searching for Meaning in Life

Boyd, the 22-year-old college student who experiences much anxiety and entertains occasional suicidal thoughts, shares with the group the acute panic he feels because of his fantasies of killing himself. He says that even though he has a large quantity of life left, he cannot see that it will have much quality, and he wonders why he should go on. Like Ed, Boyd feels anxiety about making choices, and, like Ed—who is taking the slower route of alcohol—he wants to "end it all." When Boyd reveals the emptiness of his life, Judy says that she identifies with his problem. Despite her success as a professor, she is concerned over the emptiness of her life and is struggling to find meaning.

After making an assessment of suicidal risk, and determining that there is no present danger, various practitioners may proceed as follows.

Some Therapeutic Approaches

Existential Group. In an existential group the leaders may well use the fact that Judy identifies with Boyd's problems. They will ask both of them to sit in the center of the group to discuss their perceptions of how their life has lost meaning and to explore their sense of emptiness in greater depth. When this dialogue has run its course, the leaders invite other members to talk about aspects of their own life that have grown stale. Using these discussions as a basis, the leaders may then work with Judy, Boyd, or any of the other members on a variety of themes:

- Life doesn't have meaning by itself; it is up to us to create meaning in our life.
- Feelings of emptiness and a sense that life has lost its meaning may signal the need to begin building new meanings. The sense of purposelessness can be a sign that we are ready for a change.
- If we don't like the direction in which we are moving, we need to ask what we can do to change the direction and what we are doing to prevent change.
- We must accept responsibility for our own capacities and limitations and for what we are becoming.

In working with Judy, existential group leaders may focus on some of the paths she is taking to find meaning in her life—for example, her work, her relationships with others, and her leisure-time activities. In the existential view the anxiety that she is feeling over what she terms "emptiness" is not seen in negative terms; rather, it is viewed positively as a potential growth force. The fact that she is questioning her values to determine the extent to which they still hold meaning for her indicates that she is ready for change. Her anxiety is seen as a natural response to the contemplation of change.

In working with Boyd, the existential group leaders may look beyond the obvious implications of his suicidal thoughts to discover how alive or how dead he is feeling with respect to the life that he still has. Here again his anxiety over his death impulses may be seen as a positive sign, as though he were actually saying: "I want more from life than I am receiving. No longer am I content with merely existing; I want to be *alive!*" In short, his anxiety will probably be viewed as an impetus for changing his life in such a way that he will *want* to live.

Behavior-Therapy Group. Behaviorally oriented leaders approaching the themes exemplified by Boyd and Judy will first help the two members define in concrete and specific terms what they want to explore. General goals, such as trying to find meaning in life, coping with emptiness, or experiencing existential anxiety over outworn projects, are far too vague for these leaders. Their focus will be on specifics, as seen in the following dialogue between Judy and one of the co-leaders, who is helping Judy define a specific area to focus on in the group.

JUDY   I have a vague feeling of hollowness, as if my life didn't have any unifying purpose. I question the meaning of life.

CO-LEADER   You're not being specific about this lack of meaning. Could you pinpoint what it is that you'd like to change?

JUDY   What I'd like to change is the emptiness I often feel. I want to feel that what I'm doing matters, that my life has meaning.

CO-LEADER   Perhaps we can make this goal more concrete by identifying what it is you do that makes you question your meaning.

JUDY   I feel that when I'm needed and appreciated, there's meaning in my life. When I'm unrecognized, I feel that my life is empty.

CO-LEADER   Right now, could you list some of your activities that make you feel meaningful and also list specific things that lead you to feel unappreciated?

JUDY   I think I could, but not right now. Maybe before our next group meeting.

CO-LEADER   Fine. Let me make a suggestion. Before we meet again, try to pay attention to the conditions that tend to be associated with either a feeling of purpose or the sense of emptiness you describe. Carry a notebook, and jot down a few notes concerning what you actually *do* in situations attached to these feelings. In this way we'll have a better sense of what you're doing, and we can work on specific areas of change.

As can be seen, the behavior therapist is attempting to break down the task into manageable parts—to identify specific behaviors that can be observed and to develop specific goals that can be measured. Rather than working on broad existential concerns such as the meaning of life, the leader focuses on behaviors that contribute to Judy's feelings of emptiness and teaches her how to observe such behaviors. One can readily see how a similar approach would be taken to Boyd's case.

Adlerian Group.   In the cases of Ed, Boyd, and Judy—all of whom are searching for meaning—Adlerian procedures are quite appropriate. Adlerians assume that people are motivated by goals; the function of a group is to help members identify their life goals. This is done by asking them to look at what they are striving toward. Questions that can be asked are "What are you after? Where are you going? What is your image of the central goal that gives your life meaning?" For members such as Boyd, Judy, and Ed, attention is given to their life plan, including their fictional goals. For example, Ed probably developed in early childhood a fictional image of what he would like to be in order to be safe and to feel that he belonged. His assessment of his early experiences might well be inaccurate, and his lifestyle today could be based on his striving for goals that he had as a child. Ed may have learned that drinking was a way for him to escape from painful reality. When he drank, he felt strong and superior, and eventually his whole life became centered on drinking. With alcohol he could convince himself that he was all that he wanted to be. However, this style of life is now proving to be ineffective, and Ed is seeing how empty his life is. With the encouragement of the group, he begins to challenge his mistaken beliefs, gains more awareness of how he has deceived himself by living in fantasy, and starts talking about ways to find new goals that will provide him with meaning in life.

Gestalt Group.   In her Gestalt group Judy's declaration that she feels empty will probably be met by a question about how she experiences this emptiness. Let's postulate that Judy answers such a question as follows: "Sometimes I feel like I'm alone and lost in a desert. In fact, last night I had a dream about just that, about being lost in a desert. I was dying for lack of water—all I could see was rocks, sand, and one cactus bush with thorns on it. Then I stumbled across a well, but when I dipped into it, the well was bone dry. I began to cry, but there were no tears."

The Gestalt leaders will probably focus on Judy's dream as a way of helping her experience her emptiness more fully. They don't interpret her dream; rather, they help her discover the meaning of her dream for herself by asking her to *become* selected parts of her dream, giving them a voice and speaking in the present. What follows is a sample of this dream work:

CO-LEADER	Judy, I'd like you to become the cactus with thorns and speak as if you were the cactus bush.
JUDY	Nobody better get close to me; if you do, I'll stick you. I'm all alone here, and that's the way I want to be. It's taken me a long time to grow these thorns, so stay away!
CO-LEADER	Now let yourself become the rocks.
JUDY	I'm hard; nothing can get to me. I'll last forever. Nothing can get inside me.
CO-LEADER	What are you experiencing now?
JUDY	In many ways I'm like that rock and thorny bush. People can't really get to me. I'm hard and protected.
CO-LEADER	And how does it feel to be hard and protected?
JUDY	Safe. Yet, at the same time I'm lonely out here on this empty desert.
CO-LEADER	Now I'd like you to become the well. Try to speak as if you were the well in your dream.

JUDY   I look as if I could keep you from dying of thirst—as if I could nourish you. Yet, when you dip inside me, you'll find that I'm all dried up. There's really no water deep inside me—I'm just a bottomless pit, dried and empty.

This process of becoming various parts of her dream can enable Judy to make connections between the different parts of her dream and her own life. She apparently fears that although people see her as a bright and talented person with much to offer (a full well), she actually has nothing of value to offer (an empty well). Although the Gestalt technique of dream interpretation doesn't solve her problem of emptiness or end her quest for meaning, it does help her move closer to experiencing her emptiness and becoming aware of her fear that she is the one who is keeping people out of her life.

Theme: Challenging and Clarifying Values

Sharon, the 25-year-old executive secretary who is living with a man over her parents' objections, feels comfortable with her lifestyle yet is uncomfortable about her parents' strong disapproval. According to Sharon, her parents feel that she is letting them down and that unless she gets married, she is not worthy of their respect. She is in pain over the loss of their esteem: "I don't really expect them to agree with me, and I can accept their right to think as they do. What troubles me, though, is that I'm really hung up on their refusal to let me live my life as I see fit. In order to live life as I want to, I have to decide to be disowned by them."

Some Therapeutic Approaches

Psychodrama Group. Psychodrama directors will probably want to know whether Sharon remembers any time as a child when she wanted parental approval and didn't receive it. Let's say that she recalls a time when she decided not to go to church anymore—a decision her parents could not accept, although they had no way of forcing her to continue attending church. The directors help her reenact this childhood scene with the help of two group members who play her parents. The following are a few possibilities for a psychodrama format:

- Playing herself as a child, Sharon says all the things now that she thought and felt but never said when her parents withdrew their affection.
- She asks her parents (still as the child) to respect her and allow her to have her own life.
- The symbolic parents play their roles either as rejecting parents or as accepting parents.
- Other group members stand in for Sharon and say things that she finds difficult to express.

- Sharon projects a scene with her parents in the present that incorporates an interaction with them as she would wish it to be. In this case she coaches others to be the parents she would want.

Following the psychodrama there is an effort to connect Sharon's present problem with the feelings she had as a child. The ways in which she now pleads with her parents for approval could be much like her dynamics as a child. The experience of the psychodrama could at least help her see how to deal with her parents in a more direct and mature way than she typically does.

Person-Centered Group. The leaders of a person-centered group will give Sharon the freedom to express and explore her feelings about the pain she feels over the loss of her parents' esteem. If the members and facilitator can really understand her struggle between wanting to live her own life and wanting parental acceptance, she is likely to gain more clarity on this issue. The facilitator probably does not introduce any techniques; rather, Sharon is invited to talk about her feelings, values, and thoughts. The goal is not to get the group's validation, for this would be the same as her striving for her mother's and father's validation. Instead, it is hoped that as she explores her conflicts, she will come to trust her ability to find a direction in life that is acceptable to her. The primary goal in this type of group is to foster a climate in which the actualizing tendency can freely express itself. If the members and the facilitator can show Sharon respect and positive regard, if they can understand her struggle as she experiences it, and if they can show her warmth and caring, it is likely that she will profit from the group experience and move forward in a constructive manner. With the support of the group, she will find within herself the answers she is searching for, and she will probably rely less on others to confirm her worth as a person.

Psychoanalytic Group. From an analytic perspective, Sharon can be viewed as having a passive, dependent attitude toward her parents. In some ways she is keeping herself infantile by looking at them to feed her and nourish her as a person. She has not given up the fantasy of being the type of young girl that her parents wanted; this frustration of her need to be seen as the "ideal daughter" by her parents may bring about feelings of insecurity, disillusionment, and anxiety. The analytic leaders, and other members as well, can interpret her behavior as seeking the parents she has always wanted. She may now be treating others in the group as she treated her parents. She may look to the leaders and some members to tell her how she should live her life and how she could win their unconditional love.

At the working stage Sharon may regress and reexperience some old and familiar patterns, which will be seen as material to be worked through in the group. How she behaves in the group sessions provides some clues to the historical determinants of her present behavior. The group therapists make timely interpretations so that some of her past can be brought to the surface. Another focus will be guiding her in working through her transferences with the leaders and other members. In the group situation it is probable that she has re-created her original family; this transference interferes with her accurate appraisal of reality, since she is now projecting onto others in the group feelings she had for her parents.

Adlerian Group.   As in the psychoanalytic group, interpretation will probably be a central therapeutic technique in the Adlerian group. However, Adlerian interpretation is different from psychoanalytic interpretation in that it is done in relation to Sharon's lifestyle. No time is devoted to exploring the possible causes of her struggle to win her parents' approval. Instead, the focus is the here-and-now behavior that she displays, on her expectations that arise from her goals, and on ways in which she can begin to challenge her thinking and thus make changes in her behavior. In the Adlerian group she is invited to consider the leaders' interpretations of her striving for parental approval. She explores her style of life to see how searching for approval may be a theme. The interpretation is focused on her goals, purposes, and intentions, as well as on her private logic and how it works. As she gains insight, through referring to her basic premises and to the ways these beliefs are mistaken, she can begin the process of modifying these cognitions and thus find ways of leading a more satisfying life. The focus of the work is typically of a *cognitive* nature, for it is assumed that if she changes her beliefs, her actions will also change.

Gestalt Group.   The Gestalt leaders will probably focus on a specific behavior related to Sharon's problems—say, the fact that she speaks in a soft and pleading voice. To help her get in touch with what she is doing, the leaders can ask her to exaggerate her mannerism—for example: "Go around to each group member, and be as apologetic as you can be. Keep your eyes fixed to the ground, and tell everyone how much you need them to approve of you; then apologize for being a bother to them."

Through this exercise Sharon may gain an awareness of how her general style expresses tentativeness and how her demeanor invites people to feel sorry for her. Since, as suggested by her statement above, she would like to deny her apologetic aspect, this exercise is aimed at exposing this aspect by exaggerating it. The leaders may then ask her to bring her parents into the room and speak to them openly and candidly, in the way she would like to. Next, she is asked to switch places and "become her parents," in order to answer what she has just told them and to disclose what they may be thinking of her yet not saying. This shifting in and out of roles—Sharon playing herself and then "becoming her parents"—continues until she can identify unfinished business from her past that is getting in her way now. In the process she may work on her feelings of resentment, anger, and fear toward her parents.

Theme: Dealing with the Termination of the Group

Up to this point I've given examples of how the various approaches to group therapy might be practiced with respect to the themes that have emerged in the model group. Although it is valuable to practice working within the framework of each theory as you learn about it, there is no need to limit yourself to practicing any one model exclusively. Instead, you can integrate various components from all these models and begin to develop your own leadership style—a style that suits your personality and the kind of group you may lead. To assist you in thinking about ways to integrate these different group models into your personal style, I will now describe how I would use concepts and techniques from the various approaches in dealing with some typical issues that I observe in most groups during the last few sessions: wrapping up, saying good-bye, consolidating learning, closing out personal issues, applying group learning to daily life, and evaluating outcomes.

Feelings of Separation and Loss

The final stage of a group is a very difficult time. The members are aware that their community is about to dissolve, and they are beginning to mourn their impending separation. Some of them are pulling back; they are becoming less intense and are no longer contributing much new material to work on. Others wonder whether they'll be able to maintain the openness they have learned in the group once they can't count any longer on the group's encouragement and support. They fear that in their everyday lives they won't find people who give them the kind of support they need to keep experimenting with change and, as a consequence, that they may regress to old ways.

If I were leading our model group, I would want to give its members an opportunity to fully express their feelings about the termination of the group. The *person-centered* approach, which stresses listening actively and giving permission to explore whatever feelings are present, offers a useful model for this phase of group work. Here members don't need much direction; rather, they need to be encouraged to face the reality that after sharing in an intense experience, they will soon be going their separate ways. It is necessary to allow members to talk about any unfinished business they may have concerning their own problems or other members. If participants can fully express their feelings about separation, the transition period between leaving the group and carrying what they've learned in the group into their day-to-day life will be made easier.

I have often observed what I consider to be an irrational conviction on the part of many group participants that they won't be able to create in their everyday life that which they have experienced within the group. Here I apply the concepts of the *rational-emotive* approach and encourage participants to substitute rational ideas for what appear to be unfounded beliefs about separation from the group. The following examples may shed light on this process:

- *Irrational belief No. 1:* In this group I can be open and trusting, but I don't think that this is possible in my everyday life.
  Rational belief No. 1: I can be open with selected others, and I am largely responsible for initiating trust in my relationships.
- *Irrational belief No. 2:* I don't see any way I can do all of the things I learned in the group in my everyday life.
  Rational belief No. 2: If I choose to, I can create in my daily life the kind of relationships I valued in this group; that will enable me to be the kind of person I want to be wherever I am.
- *Irrational belief No. 3:* In the group I received support for the changes I made and valued; in my everyday life most people won't like many of my changes, and they won't give me the support I need to maintain them.
  Rational belief No. 3: I probably won't receive support or even approval for the changes I have made and will make, but I am no longer in desperate need of support from everyone.

The process of helping members challenge their beliefs about separation and about incorporating what they've acquired in the group can be most valuable. My goal is to help participants see that their group has been a place where they could learn *how* to form meaningful interpersonal relationships, a process that is not restricted to the group but that can be applied in any setting.

In this regard there is some value in helping participants understand any connections that might exist between their past and their family, on the one side, and the relationships they have developed within the group, on the other. For that purpose the *psychoanalytic* approach is useful. In some ways the group represents a new family for its members, and by relating their behaviors in the group "family" to their behaviors in their actual families, members can learn much about themselves. To assist participants in their process of making connections among behaviors, I ask them to consider the following questions:

- To whom was I drawn in this group?
- With whom did I have the most conflict?
- In what ways did my feelings and actions in this group resemble the ways in which I felt and acted as a child in my family?
- Were my reactions to the group leaders in any way similar to my reactions to my parents?
- What did I want from them?
- How did I react toward them?
- Did I experience feelings of competitiveness or jealousy within the group?

Looking Ahead

Another tool I use as the group is drawing to a close is the development of fantasies. I find that too often group members don't allow themselves to creatively imagine how they would like to experience their life. To assist them in their endeavor, I ask members to picture themselves and their life in some ideal future circumstance, a technique that is used by both the *Gestalt* and the *psychodrama* approaches. Applying the fantasy technique to the case in point, I might suggest to members the following:

- Imagine that you are attending a reunion of the group 5 years from now and that we are meeting to discuss how our life has changed. What do you *most* want to be able to say to us at this reunion?
- Let yourself fantasize about all the ways in which you want to be different in your everyday life once you leave this group. Close your eyes, and carry on a silent dialogue between yourself and the people who are most special in your life. What are you telling them? What are they replying?
- Imagine that a year has passed since we ended the group. Also imagine that nothing has changed in your life—that you have continued the way you have always been. Try to picture how you would feel.

I have found that some members and the group in general might benefit by sharing fantasies. For this purpose a brief Gestalt exercise that has members be themselves in the future and carry on a dialogue with significant people is useful. (In this exercise the members themselves play all parts in the dialogue.) Role-playing exercises are also helpful. For example, I sometimes ask participants to select a member of the group to role-play a person in their life. The role play begins by having the participant briefly tell the person selected what it is that he or she would like to change in their relationship and *how* he or she intends to make those changes.

Also during the final stages of the group, I ask the members to review what they have learned about their early decisions as a result of participating in this group, an approach characteristic of both *transactional analysis* and *rational-emotive therapy*. To stimulate this review, I typically question the members as follows:

- Do you want to revise any of these early decisions?
- Are these decisions still appropriate for you now?
- What new decisions do you want to make?

In addition, I ask members to review what they've learned concerning the games they play, as well as the payoffs from these games, and to think about specific ways in which they might experiment with game-free behavior outside of the group. Further, I ask members to identify, even write down, the self-defeating statements that they continue to indoctrinate themselves with, to share them, and to offer one another feedback concerning the validity of these self-statements, as well as suggestions on how to combat self-destructive thinking.

Toward the final stages of the group I rely heavily on the cognitive and action-oriented approaches characteristic of the *behavior therapies, reality therapy, rational-emotive therapy,* and *transactional analysis.* I see the group as a learning laboratory in which the members have identified the specific changes that they are willing to make and have experimented with new behaviors. Assuming that this has indeed occurred, it becomes extremely important that the members carry out their own action-oriented programs outside the group. During the last session I have members work in small groups to formulate a *specific* contract—a brief statement of the plans they have concerning behavioral changes once the group ends. The aim of this small-group work is to have members clearly define what they now want to do and how they specifically intend to do it. The results of the efforts are then shared with the entire group. Finally, I try to schedule a follow-up session—usually several months after the termination of the group—for the purpose of allowing members to discuss, from that perspective, what the group meant to each of them as well as to report on the extent to which they have fulfilled their contract.

My experience has taught me that members tend to forget some of what they learned and to discount the actual value of what they did in the group. To help prevent this from occurring and to help members retain whatever they have learned—about others, about human struggling, about life, and about themselves—I ask them at the final session to review specific insights they had throughout the course of the group. It is my contention that unless one articulates and shares with others the specifics of what one has learned in the group, one's group experience may soon become an indistinct blur.

Here, again, I find the principles of the *behavioral* approaches useful during the final session—specifically, the application of feedback principles to help members strengthen the perceptions that they gained during the course of the group. For example, I often ask members to complete feedback sentences for every member in the group such as:

- "One of the things I like best about you is . . ."
- "One way I see you blocking your strengths is . . ."
- "My hope for you is . . ."
- "My greatest concern or fear for you is . . ."
- "The way I'll remember you in this group is . . ."
- "A few things that I hope you'll remember are . . ."

Focused feedback, whether verbal or written, can give the participants a good sense of the impact they had on others in the group.

As the final session draws to a close, I give members a message to take with them—a message grounded in the *existential* approach: "I hope that you have become aware of your role and of the responsibility you bear for who you are now and for who you are becoming, that you will no longer blame others for your problems, and that you will no longer see yourself as a victim of circumstances outside of yourself. Many of you have become aware of the choices that are open to you; thus, you can now reflect fruitfully on the decisions you will make. Even if you decide to remain largely as you are, you now are aware that you *can* choose, that you don't need to have others design your life for you. Although choosing for yourself can provoke anxiety, it does give you a sense that your life is yours and that you have the power to shape your own future."

Finally, and as mentioned earlier, I feel it is important to schedule a follow-up group meeting several months after the end of the group to allow members to evaluate the outcomes of the group experience for themselves and to evaluate the group as a whole. In this connection I offer members some guidelines for evaluating themselves and their group experience, as well as topics to discuss at the follow-up group meeting.

Behavioral approaches stress developing clear goals, working on these goals during the sessions, and then evaluating the degree to which these goals were met. I see that what members do after the group ends is as important as the group sessions. Therefore, I tend to devote ample time to suggesting ways in which members might consolidate their learning and carry it into daily living. Specifically, I encourage members to develop the habit of keeping a journal—writing down the problems they are encountering, describing how they feel about themselves in specific situations, and listing their successes and difficulties in following through with their contracts. Because I feel that an appropriate book read at an appropriate time can be a powerful catalyst in helping people make the changes they want to make, I encourage members to read as a way of continuing to work on themselves and to grow.

Comparisons, Contrasts, and Integration

The purpose of this chapter is fourfold: (1) to compare and contrast the various models as they apply to issues special to group work; (2) to raise some basic questions that you'll need to answer now and throughout the course of your practice; (3) to challenge you to attempt an integration of the various perspectives that is consistent with your personality; and (4) to stimulate your thinking about ways of developing and refining group techniques that reflect your leadership style. The questions that this chapter will help you answer include these:

- Is it possible to achieve some integration of the diverse group models by focusing on their commonalities?
- How would an integrated view of the various perspectives actually help you define your own goals of group counseling?
- How do you go about blending concepts and techniques from several approaches to achieve your own definition of the leader's role and your own unique leadership style?
- How can you achieve an optimum balance between responsible leadership and responsible membership, whereby you accept your rightful share of responsibility for the direction of the group without usurping the members' responsibility?
- How much structure does a group need?
- How do you develop techniques that are consonant with your personality and style and are also appropriate for the kinds of group you lead?
- What are some of the possible abuses and misuses of group techniques?

- What are the advantages and the dangers of an eclectic approach to group practice?
- How can the techniques of the theoretical approaches be modified to fit the cultural backgrounds of various clients?

The Goals of Group Counseling: Various Perspectives

In order to impart meaningful direction to their groups, leaders need to address themselves to the issue of goals. What should be the specific goals of a given group, and who should determine them? How can the leader help group members develop meaningful goals for themselves? How does the leader's theoretical orientation influence the process of goal setting? Is it possible to set group goals based on a variety of theoretical orientations?

Beginning group leaders would have great difficulty in giving a positive answer to the last question above; the differences among theoretical approaches with regard to goals seem irreconcilable. For example, behaviorally oriented groups stress specific, concrete goals such as becoming more assertive, losing weight, or eliminating phobias. On the other hand, the relationship-oriented and existential groups focus on lofty, often unmeasurable, goals such as achieving self-actualization or becoming an autonomous person.

Extreme as these differences may appear, they shouldn't stand in your way as you attempt your own theoretical integration. Each group model stresses certain facets of the human experience, and what seems a conflict can actually be reinterpreted in unifying terms.

To help you find common denominators among the goals stressed by the various theoretical models and to guide you in your attempt to integrate these models, I've brought together in Table 17-1 the essential therapeutic goals of each of the group approaches discussed in the preceding chapters. As you read the table, keep in mind that the diversity of goals can be simplified by seeing the goals as existing on a continuum from general, global, and long-term objectives to specific, concrete, and short-term objectives. Existential and relationship-oriented group approaches tend to deal with broad goals, and behavioral and cognitively oriented systems focus on short-term, observable, and precise goals. The goals at opposite ends of the continuum are not necessarily contradictory; it is just a matter of how specifically the goals are defined. Thus, a convergence is possible if practitioners view concrete short-term goals as components of broad, long-range goals.

Most theoretical perspectives agree on the importance of group members' formulating their own specific goals. When leaders decide that they know what is best for the participants and force their own goals on them, they typically encounter resistance. To be sure, leaders need to have some overall goals for the group, but such goals should in no way infringe on the members' freedom to select personal goals that will give direction to their work in the group. The individual goal setting is an ongoing process that

Table 17-1 Comparative Overview of Group Goals

MODEL	GOALS
Psychoanalytic	To provide a climate that helps clients reexperience early family relationships. To uncover buried feelings associated with past events that carry over into current behavior. To facilitate insight into the origins of faulty psychological development and stimulate a corrective emotional experience.
Adlerian	To create a therapeutic relationship that encourages participants to explore their basic life assumptions and to achieve a broader understanding of lifestyles. To help clients recognize their strengths and their power to change. To encourage them to accept full responsibility for their chosen lifestyle and for any changes they want to make.
Psychodrama	To facilitate the release of pent-up feelings, to provide insight, and to help clients develop new and more effective behaviors. To open up unexplored possibilities for solving conflicts and for experiencing dominant sides of oneself.
Existential	To provide conditions that maximize self-awareness and reduce blocks to growth. To help clients discover and use freedom of choice and assume responsibility for their own choices.
Person-centered	To provide a safe climate wherein members can explore the full range of their feelings. To help members become increasingly open to new experiences and develop confidence in themselves and their own judgments. To encourage clients to live in the present. To develop openness, honesty, and spontaneity. To make it possible for clients to encounter others in the here and now and to use the group as a place to overcome feelings of alienation.
Gestalt	To enable members to pay close attention to their moment-to-moment experiencing, so they can recognize and integrate disowned aspects of themselves.
Transactional analysis	To assist clients in becoming free of scripts and games in their interactions. To challenge members to reexamine early decisions and make new ones based on awareness.
Behavior therapy	To help group members eliminate maladaptive behaviors and learn new and more effective behavioral patterns. (Broad goals are broken down into precise subgoals.)
Rational-emotive therapy	To teach group members that they are responsible for their own disturbances and to help them identify and abandon the process of self-indoctrination by which they keep their disturbances alive. To eliminate the clients' irrational and self-defeating outlook on life and replace it with a more tolerant and rational one.
Reality therapy	To guide members toward learning realistic and responsible behavior and developing a "success identity." To assist group members in making value judgments about their behaviors and in deciding on a plan of action for change.

needs to be constantly reevaluated. The leader can be of invaluable assistance in this regard by encouraging members to formulate clear and specific goals for themselves and by helping them to determine how they can work toward achieving these goals.

Role and Functions of the Group Leader: Various Perspectives

Should the leader be a facilitator? a therapist? a teacher? a catalyst? just another, albeit more experienced, group member? a technician? a director? an evaluator? some or all of these?

How you answer these questions will depend in part on your theoretical perspective, but ultimately your answers will be based on your own definition of the leader's role and on your own assessment of what the most significant functions of the leader are. There are also certain criteria that cut across all the theoretical approaches—for example, the type of group and its goals, the setting, the nature of the participants, and the demands of your job.

Before discussing the various perspectives on the group leader's role and functions, let's briefly review some of the tasks that I consider essential to successful group leadership:

1. Group leaders initiate and promote interaction by the way they structure the group and model behaviors. Thus, they demonstrate how to share, take risks, relate honestly, and involve others in interactions. They can also share their leadership functions so that group members are able to become increasingly independent and don't need to lean on the leader to initiate and direct every action in the group.

2. Group leaders have the task of orienting members to group process, teaching them how to get the most from their group, and helping them become aware of the group dynamics. These goals are achieved by encouraging members to look at the direction their group is taking, to determine whether there are barriers that prevent them from working effectively, and to become aware of any hidden agenda that could obstruct the flow of the group.

3. Group leaders must be capable of sensitive, active listening. Only by paying full attention to the members' verbal and nonverbal communication can they help participants move toward a deeper level of self-exploration and self-understanding. If attending skills are lacking, genuine empathy and understanding between group leader and participants are not possible.

4. Group leaders are responsible for creating a climate conducive to exploring personally significant issues. Trust needs to be established early in a group, and the leader has a crucial role in building an atmosphere in which people can reveal themselves, behave in new ways, and question their basic beliefs and assumptions.

5. Group leaders are responsible for setting limits, helping establish group rules, and protecting members. Although leaders don't have to pre-

Table 17-2 Comparative Overview of Leader's Role and Functions

MODEL	LEADER'S ROLE
Psychoanalytic	Facilitates group interaction by helping create an accepting and tolerant climate. Remains relatively anonymous and objective, so that members will develop projections toward him or her. Signals indications of resistance and transference and interprets their meanings. Helps members work through unfinished business. Sets limits for the group.
Adlerian	Uses procedures such as confrontation, self-disclosure, interpretation, and analysis of prevailing patterns to challenge beliefs and goals. Observes social context of behavior. Models attentive caring. Helps members accept and utilize their assets. Encourages members to develop the courage needed to translate what is learned in the group to behavior outside of the group.
Psychodrama	Functions as both facilitator and director. Has the job of warming up the group, helping set up a psychodrama, directing the enactment, and then processing the outcomes with the participants. Specific tasks include facilitating, observing, directing, producing, and summarizing.
Existential	Has the central role of being fully present and available to individuals in the group and of grasping their subjective being-in-the-world. Functions by creating a person-to-person relationship, by disclosing himself or herself, and by confronting members in a caring way.
Person-centered	Facilitates the group (as opposed to directing it)—deals with barriers to communication, establishes a climate of trust, and assists the group in functioning effectively. Central task is to be real in the sessions and demonstrate caring, respect, and understanding. Has the primary role of creating a climate of tolerance and experimentation. Often becomes directly involved by sharing personal feelings and impressions about what is happening in the group.

pare a lengthy list of "dos" and "don'ts," they do need to establish certain ground rules. They need to inform members of their rights and responsibilities, stress the importance of the issue of confidentiality throughout the group's life, and take the necessary steps to ensure the physical and psychological safety of the group members.

6. Finally, group leaders need to direct attention to ways in which people can profit as much as possible from the group experience. They can do this by clarifying, summarizing, and integrating what has gone on and what has been learned, by helping members crystallize their feelings and new insights, and by encouraging them to decide on action programs that will facilitate applying what they have learned in the group to their outside lives.

As we have seen, each therapeutic approach stresses different functions for the group leader. For example, the person-centered approach emphasizes

Table 17-2 *(continued)*

MODEL	LEADER'S ROLE
Gestalt groups	Suggests techniques designed to help participants intensify their experience and be alert to their body messages. Assists clients in identifying and working through unfinished business from the past that interferes with current functioning. Focuses on members' behaviors and feelings.
Transactional analysis	Has a didactic role. Teaches clients how to recognize the games they play to avoid intimacy, the ego state in which they are functioning in a given transaction, and the self-defeating aspects of early decisions and adopted life plans.
Behavior therapy	Functions as an expert in behavior modification; thus, must be directive and often functions as teacher or trainer. Imparts information and teaches coping skills and methods of modifying behavior, so that members can practice outside group sessions.
Rational-emotive therapy	Functions didactically: explains, teaches, and reeducates. Helps members see and rigorously confront their illogical thinking and identify its connection with self-defeating behavior. Teaches them to change their patterns of thinking and behaving.
Reality therapy	Encourages members to evaluate their behavior and make choices that will allow them to fulfill their needs in socially acceptable ways. Helps members by establishing a personal relationship with them, by firmly expecting that they will formulate and implement a plan for change.

the role of facilitator. Since in this model the group is seen as having the resources to direct itself, the leader is supposed to facilitate rather than direct group process. Other approaches see the leader as a teacher. Rational-emotive therapy, reality therapy, Adlerian therapy, behavior therapy, and transactional analysis are all based on the assumption that group counseling or therapy is essentially an educational and learning process, and consequently the leader's key function is that of teaching skills and providing a cognitive framework that will lead to reeducation and behavioral changes.

Other models, such as the psychoanalytic approach, focus on the role of the group leader as a technical expert who interprets intrapsychic and interpersonal processes as they manifest themselves in a group. Still other models, such as the existential, the person-centered, and the Gestalt approaches, stress the leader's role in helping members gain an experiential awareness of their conflicts through meaningful relationships with the leader and others in the group. As we have seen, your roles and functions as a group leader are many; which of them you choose to emphasize is partly determined by your theoretical orientation. As you review the different perspectives summarized in Table 17-2, consider what elements you want to incorporate from each of them in defining your own role as group leader.

Degree of Structuring and Division of Responsibility: Various Perspectives

Group leaders often struggle with the question of what constitutes the optimum degree of structure in a group. It should be clear that all groups have a structure. Even the least directive group leaders, who avoid imposing a format on the group, do make the choice of having an open structure and letting the participants determine the course of the group.

Group structuring exists on a continuum, from extremely nondirective to highly directive. On the nondirective end of the continuum are psychoanalytic groups, person-centered groups, and some existential groups. In these groups the leaders tend to assume a passive stance and encourage group members to give direction to the group. One aspect of the learning value of these groups is that the members assume much of the responsibility.

At the opposite end of the continuum are those leaders who provide a high degree of structure for the group. They often use structured exercises to open the group sessions; also, they employ techniques to focus members on specific themes or problem areas and to intensify certain emotions and conflicts. Many behavior-modification groups are characterized by a very directive group leadership. Typically, there is a progression from session to session, the meetings are organized in accordance with a predetermined agenda, and certain procedures are used to direct the group toward exploration and resolution of specific problem areas.

Like structuring, division of responsibility can be conceptualized in terms of a continuum. At one end are those group leaders who see themselves as experts and who believe that they should actively intervene to keep the group moving in ways that they deem productive. The group's outcomes are seen as very dependent on the leader's skills. Thus, explaining members' failures in terms of their insufficient motivation or lack of ego strength is considered a rationalization on the part of the leader, who, being the expert, is the one who has failed and is the one responsible for the failure of the treatment plan. Behaviorally oriented group leaders embrace this view in full.

The rational-emotive group approach, too, places a large share of responsibility on the group leader. Since therapy is considered an educative process, the group leader is seen mainly as a teacher in charge of the reeducation of the group members. For effective results, group therapists are expected to employ a rapid-fire, didactic, persuasive methodology aimed at cognitive restructuring. However, despite the highly directive role RET assigns to the leader, it also places a considerable share of responsibility for directing the group on the members, who are expected to be active, work hard, and practice between group sessions.

At the other end of the continuum are group leaders who expressly announce at the beginning of a group that the members are responsible for themselves and that what they get (or fail to get) from a group depends on them and on them alone. This type of leadership is characteristic of some encounter-group leaders, who refuse to hold themselves responsible for what members choose to do or not do in the group.

Another group approach that emphasizes the responsibility of the group participants is the person-centered model, which sees the participants as the ones who truly know what is best for them. The leader does not assume responsibility for actively directing the group process; he or she functions as a facilitator by attempting to create a trusting climate wherein members can safely explore deeply personal issues and search for the necessary resources within themselves.

Somewhat in the middle of the continuum are Gestalt group leaders. They are typically active, in that they intervene with techniques that provide the group with structure, but they also insist that group members are responsible for whatever they experience. The group process is seen as a way of helping the participants become aware of how they are denying personal responsibility and learn how to rely on themselves for their own support. Group leaders are responsible for being aware of their own experience throughout the group process and for introducing appropriate techniques to intensify group work. Members are responsible for bringing up issues that they want to investigate in group and for making their own interpretations. Table 17-3 gives you an idea of the variety of theoretical positions on structuring and division of responsibility.

My view is that group leaders need to achieve a balance between assuming too much responsibility for the direction of the group and assuming too little. On the one hand, leaders who assume too much responsibility rob members of the responsibility that is rightfully theirs. If clients are perceived by the leader as not having the capacity to take care of themselves, they soon begin to live up to this expectation. Besides undermining members' independence, leaders who assume an inordinate amount of responsibility burden themselves greatly. They tend to blame themselves for whatever failures or setbacks the group suffers. If members do little productive work, these leaders see it as their fault. If the group remains fragmented, they view this as a reflection of their lack of skill. In short, this style of leadership is draining, and the leaders who use it may soon lose the energy required to lead groups.

On the other hand, leaders who place all the responsibility for the direction and outcomes of a group on the participants may simply be trying to avoid their own role in the success or failure of their groups. Thus, if a group seems to go nowhere, these leaders avoid asking themselves whether their leadership or lack of it is a contributing factor.

The Use of Techniques: Various Perspectives

Techniques are quite useful both as catalysts for group action and as devices to keep the group moving. But techniques are just tools, and like all tools they can be used properly or misused. When leaders fall into a pattern of

Table 17-3 Comparative Overview of Degree of Structuring and Division of Responsibility

MODEL	STRUCTURING AND RESPONSIBILITY
Psychoanalytic	*Leader:* shies away from directive leadership and allows the group to determine its own course; interprets the meaning of certain behavioral patterns. *Members:* raise issues and produce material from the unconscious; assume increasing responsibility for interacting spontaneously, making interpretations, and sharing insights about others; become auxiliary therapists for one another.
Adlerian	*Leader:* at the outset, works toward goal alignment; takes active steps to establish and maintain a therapeutic relationship, to explore and analyze the individual's dynamics, and to communicate a basic attitude of concern and hope. *Members:* develop insight about themselves; assume the responsibility for taking positive measures to make changes; consider alternative beliefs, goals, and behaviors.
Psychodrama	*Director/leader:* suggests specific techniques designed to intensify feelings, re-create past situations, and provide increased awareness of conflicts; makes sure that the protagonist is not left hanging and that other members of the group have a chance to share what they experienced during the psychodrama. *Members:* produce the material for psychodramas and, when in the role of protagonist, direct their own psychodramas.
Existential	*Leader:* may structure the group along the lines of certain existential themes such as freedom, responsibility, anxiety, and guilt; shares here-and-now feelings with the group. *Members:* are responsible for deciding the issues they want to explore, thus determining the direction of the group.
Person-centered	*Leader:* provides very little structuring or direction. *Members:* are seen as having the capacity to find a meaningful direction, of being able to help one another, and of moving toward constructive outcomes.

employing techniques mechanically, they become technicians and are not responding to the needs of the particular group they are leading. Also, indiscriminate use of techniques tends to increase the resistance level of the group instead of facilitating deeper communication. Some leaders, overly eager to use new techniques, treat them as if they were a bag of tricks. Others, out of anxiety over not knowing how to deal with certain problems that arise in a group, try technique after technique in helter-skelter fashion. In general, group leaders should have sound reasons for using particular methods of intervention, and an overreliance on technique is, in my view, questionable.

Table 17-3 *(continued)*

MODEL	STRUCTURING AND RESPONSIBILITY
Gestalt	*Leader:* is responsible for being aware of his/her present-centered experience and for using it in the context of the group; brings structure to the group by introducing appropriate techniques to intensify emotions. *Members:* must be active and make their own interpretations.
Transactional analysis	Because of the stress on an equal relationship between leader and members, responsibility is shared, as specified in a contract. *Members* and *leader* spell out in the contract what changes members want to make and what issues they want to explore in the group.
Behavior therapy	*Leader:* is responsible for active teaching and for having the group proceed according to a predetermined set of activities. *Members:* are expected to be active, to apply what they learn to everyday life situations, and to practice new behaviors outside the group.
Rational-emotive therapy	*Leader:* is responsible for hammering away at any signs of member behavior based on faulty thinking; structures the group experience so that members stay with the task of making constructive changes. *Members:* are responsible for attacking their own self-defeating thinking and that of fellow group members; are expected to carry out self-confrontation outside the group and work hard at changing illogical thoughts.
Reality therapy	*Leader:* teaches members to assume responsibility for how they live their life; structures the group by focusing on present behavior and ways of making specific behavioral changes; influences members by modeling success-oriented behavior; confronts clients who are not living realistically. *Members:* decide on specific changes they want to make; make value judgments regarding present behavior; are held responsible for implementing desired changes.

Techniques need to be an extension of who the leader is as a person, and group leaders should not force themselves to use techniques that don't suit their personality and their unique leadership style. Techniques need to be employed sensitively, appropriately, and skillfully. In observing group leaders in action, I have often noticed that many of them rely too much on techniques. I've seen, for example, the leader of a group that had become stale and seemed to be going nowhere intervene with technique after technique to merely get activity going or to keep the members talking, even though the talk was of a nonproductive nature. Instead of dealing openly and directly with what was going on in the group and with his own reactions, this leader (probably out of anxiety) tried to solve the problem by relying on gimmicks. The countless techniques I saw him use one after the other may have given this leader the false impression that the group was moving, but in reality they reaffirmed the group's immobility.

My basic assumption is that techniques should facilitate group process, not artificially create action in a group. I also assume that they are most effective when the group leader learns how to pay attention to the obvious. They can deepen feelings that are already present, and they should grow out of what is going on in the group at the time. There is always something going on in a group, and this material can suggest appropriate techniques. Although my colleagues and I sometimes use techniques to introduce material at the initial stage of a group and often use them to integrate what members have learned at the final stage, we generally do not have a preset agenda. We take our cues from what is occurring within the group and flow with that, rather than attempting to direct the group to pursue a specific theme. For example, if I notice that there is little energy in the room and that nobody appears willing to do significant work, I don't introduce an exercise designed to stir up feelings or promote interaction. Instead, I may let the group know that I am feeling strained from taking too much responsibility for keeping the group alive, and I try to get some assessment of what each person is experiencing.

In conducting a training workshop for group leaders, I typically stress the importance of maintaining flexibility in the use of techniques. It is essential to pay attention to what the group members are experiencing and take your cues from them on where to go next. In other words, it is helpful to let them provide the lead and at the same time suggest ways for them to keep the issue they are exploring in focus.

In choosing techniques to facilitate group process, you must consider several factors. Your theory, of course, will influence what techniques you employ. If it focuses on cognitive aspects, then your techniques are likely to encourage clients to look for the connection between their thought patterns and their actions. If you have a Gestalt orientation, your techniques will tend to promote an awareness of present feelings and an intensification of these feelings. If you are behaviorally oriented, many of your techniques will be geared to getting members to monitor their actions and experiment with specific behaviors. Your style of leadership also has much to do with what techniques you will use. Finally, the population with whom you are working, the purpose of your group, and the stage of development of the group are all factors to consider in the selection of techniques.

To avoid using techniques routinely, leaders must understand the relationship between techniques and theoretical concepts and be fully aware of why they are using certain methods; that is, they must have an idea of what they expect to occur. In addition to having a rationale for using group techniques, leaders need to continually assess their effects.

As illustrated by Table 17-4 (pp. 526–527), the various group models offer a variety of strategies for initiating and maintaining group interaction. There is no reason why group practitioners should restrict themselves to the techniques of a single approach simply because that's the approach they favor. For example, group leaders with an existential orientation can comfortably draw on techniques from the behavioral and cognitively oriented models. There are imaginative ways of blending Gestalt and transactional analysis, both conceptually and technically. The point I'm making here is that leaders need to use their imagination to discover ways of adapting techniques from various theoretical models to the specific type of group they lead and of modifying them to suit their leadership style.

Group Work in a Multicultural Context: Various Perspectives

Each of the theories presented in this book has been briefly examined for its relevance to culturally diverse populations. As can be seen in Table 17-5 (pp. 528–529), each perspective has certain concepts or techniques that can contribute to effective multicultural group counseling. Yet they all have some limitations, and caution is needed in using certain techniques that flow from a given theory (see Table 17-6, pp. 530–531). Technical eclecticism seems especially necessary in working with a diverse range of cultural backgrounds. Harm can come to group participants who are expected to fit all the specifications of a given theory, whether or not the values espoused by the theory are consistent with their own cultural values. Rather than stretch the client to fit the dimensions of a single theory, the leader's theory and practice must be made to fit the unique needs of the client. This requirement calls for group leaders who possess knowledge of various cultures, awareness of their own cultural baggage, and skills to help diverse clients meet their needs within the realities of their culture.

It is essential for leaders to be able to assess the special needs of clients. Depending on the group member's ethnicity and culture and also on the individual concerns that bring a member to a group, the leader will need to show flexibility in utilizing diverse therapeutic strategies. At times, some clients will need more direction, and even advice. Others will be very hesitant in talking about themselves in personal ways, especially during the early phase of a group. Leaders need to be patient and to avoid quickly pushing members to "open up and be real." Furthermore, leaders need to recognize that what may appear to be resistance is very likely to be the client's response to years of cultural conditioning and respect for certain values and traditions. What the matter comes down to is the familiarity of group leaders with a variety of theoretical approaches and the ability to employ and adapt their techniques to fit the person-in-the-environment. It is not enough to merely assist members in gaining insight, expressing suppressed emotions, or making certain behavioral changes. The challenge

Table 17-4   Comparative Overview of Group Techniques

MODEL	TECHNIQUES
Psychoanalytic	Interpretation, dream analysis, free association, analysis of resistance, and analysis of transference—all designed to make the unconscious conscious and bring about insight.
Adlerian	Analysis and assessment, exploration of family constellation, reporting of earliest recollections, confrontation, interpretation, cognitive restructuring, challenging of one's belief system, and exploration of social dynamics and of one's unique style of life.
Psychodrama	Self-presentation, presentation of the other, interview in the role of the other and interview in the role of the self, soliloquy, role reversal, double technique and auxiliary egos, mirroring, multiple doubles, future projection, and life rehearsal.
Existential	Since this approach stresses understanding first and techniques second, no specific set of techniques is prescribed. However, leaders can borrow techniques from other therapies to better understand the world of clients and to deepen the level of therapeutic work.
Person-centered	The stress is on the facilitator's attitudes and behavior, and few structured or planned techniques are used. Basic techniques include active listening, reflection of feelings, clarification, support, and "being there" for the client.
Gestalt	Many action-oriented techniques are available to the leader, all of which intensify immediate experiencing and awareness of current feelings. Techniques include confrontation, empty chair, game of dialogue, making the rounds, fantasy approaches, reversal procedures, rehearsal techniques, exaggerating a behavior, staying with feelings, dialogues with self or significant others in the present, and dream work. Exercises are designed to enable participants to become increasingly aware of bodily tensions and of the fear of getting physically and emotionally close, to give members a chance to experiment with new behavior, and to release feelings. Guided fantasy, imagery, and other techniques designed to stimulate the imagination are used.

for leaders is to find practical strategies for adapting the techniques they have developed to enable clients to question the impact their culture continues to have on their lives and to make decisions about what facets of their lives they want to change.

You can readily see that the other core issues we have just explored—group goals, leader roles and functions, degree of structuring and division of responsibility, and use of group techniques—all take on special meaning when considered in the context of multicultural group counseling. Being an

Table 17-4 *(continued)*

MODEL	TECHNIQUES
Transactional analysis	Techniques include the use of a script-analysis checklist or questionnaire to detect early injunctions and decisions, games, and life positions; family modeling; role playing; and structural analysis.
Behavior therapy	The main techniques, which are based on behavioral and learning principles and are aimed at behavioral changes and cognitive restructuring, include systematic desensitization, implosive therapy, assertion training, aversive techniques, operant-conditioning methods, self-help techniques, reinforcement and supportive measures, behavioral research, coaching, modeling, feedback, and procedures for challenging and changing cognitions.
Rational-emotive therapy	The essential technique is active teaching. Leaders probe, confront, challenge, and forcefully direct. They model and teach rational thinking, and they explain, persuade, and lecture clients. They use a rapid-fire style that requires members to constantly use their cognitive skills. RET uses a wide range of behavioral techniques such as deconditioning, role playing, behavioral research, homework assignments, and assertion training.
Reality therapy	A wide range of techniques is used, such as role playing, confrontation, modeling, use of humor, contracts, and formulation or specific plans for action.

effective group leader involves reflecting on how your own culture influences you and your interventions in your groups. This awareness will be a critical factor in your becoming more sensitive to the cultural backgrounds of the members in your groups.

Applications of the Integrated Eclectic Model

The term *integrated eclectic model* refers to a perspective based on concepts and techniques from the various theoretical approaches. It is the model I use in my own practice of group work. This section describes how I apply my synthesis at each stage of a group's development. This model is designed to address the three factors of thinking, feeling, and doing. As you've seen, some of the ten theories discussed in this book focus on cognition, others on the experiencing of feelings, and others on behavior. My goal is to blend the unique contributions of these approaches so that all three dimensions of human experiencing are given attention at each phase of a group. At the same time, it is important to avoid the trap of emerging with a hodgepodge of unamalgamated theories thrown hastily together. Your goal should be a consistent conceptual framework that you can use as a basis for selecting from the multiple techniques that you've studied.

Table 17-5   Comparative Overview of Contributions to Multicultural Counseling

Model	Contribution
Psychoanalytic	Focus on family dynamics is appropriate for working with many minority groups. Therapist formality appeals to those clients who expect professional distance. Notion of defense is helpful in understanding inner dynamics and dealing with environmental stresses.
Adlerian	Focus on social interest, doing good for society, importance of family, goal orientation, and striving for belonging is congruent with Eastern cultures. Focus on person-in-environment allows for cultural factors to be explored.
Psychodrama	For reserved clients, this approach invites self-expression in the present. Director can create scenes that are culturally sensitive and assist members in understanding the impact of their culture on them. Through enactment, nonverbal clients have other means of communication. Opportunities for developing spontaneity and creativity within the framework of one's culture.
Existential	A core value is the emphasis on understanding the member's phenomenological world, including cultural background. This approach leads to empowerment in an oppressive society. It can help members examine their options for change within the context of their cultural realities.
Person-centered	Rogers made significant contributions to breaking cultural barriers and facilitating open dialogue among diverse cultural populations. Main strengths are respect for client's values, active listening, welcoming of differences, nonjudgmental attitude, understanding, willingness to allow clients to determine what will be explored in sessions, and prizing of cultural pluralism.

Theories Applied to the Pregroup Stage

The preparatory period in the formation of a group may be the most critical of all. If the group's foundation is weak, the group may never get off the ground. Effective groups do not simply "happen." The hard work and careful organization that go into planning a group are bound to have payoffs once the group gets under way. At this point it would be a good idea for you to review the major considerations in forming groups, found in Chapter 4.

The behavioral theories are particularly relevant at the pregroup stage, for they emphasize assessing both the need for a particular kind of group and the participant's readiness and appropriateness for a group. As a group leader, you must have clear expectations, a rationale for why and how a group is an effective approach, and a sense of how to design a specific group tailored to the unique needs and interests of the members. If you are clear about how a group can benefit prospective members, you'll be better able to

Table 17-5 *(continued)*

MODEL	CONTRIBUTION
Gestalt	Focus on expressing oneself nonverbally is congruent with those cultures that look beyond words for messages. Provides many techniques in working with clients who have cultural injunctions against freely expressing feelings. The focus on bodily expressions is a subtle way to help clients recognize their conflicts.
Transactional analysis	Contractual method acts as a safeguard against therapist imposition of values that may not be congruent with a client's culture. This approach offers a basis for understanding the impact of cultural and familial injunctions. It provides a structure that many clients will value.
Behavior therapy	Focus on behavior, rather than on feelings, is compatible with many cultures. Strengths include preparation of members by teaching them purposes of group; assisting members in learning practical skills; educational focus of groups; and stress on self-management strategies.
Rational-emotive therapy	This approach provides ways of questioning one's beliefs and identifying values that may no longer be functional. Its focus on thinking and rationality (as opposed to expressing feelings) is likely to be acceptable to many clients. Focus on teaching/learning process tends to avoid the stigma of mental illness. Many clients may value the leader directiveness and stress on homework.
Reality therapy	Focus is on members' making own evaluation of behavior (including how they respond to their culture). Through personal assessment they can determine the degree to which their needs and wants are being satisfied; they can find a balance between retaining their own ethnic identity and integrating some of the values and practices of the dominant society.

help them decide whether to join. If members know what they are getting into, the chances are increased that they will become active and committed participants. In this regard the therapeutic approaches that structure a group on a contractual basis have much to offer. A contract can help demystify the group process, can increase the members' sense of responsibility to become active agents in their own change, and can structure the course a group takes. Contracts set forth the division of responsibility between the members and the leader, and they are a useful departure point for productive work. As you will remember, the cognitively and behaviorally oriented therapies stress contracts as a way of beginning the process. TA groups, Adlerian groups, behavioral group therapy, and, sometimes, rational-emotive and reality-therapy groups work on a contractual basis. Whatever your theoretical orientation, open-ended and flexible contracts can be drawn up before the group actually meets as a whole.

**Table 17-6   Comparative Overview of Limitations
in Multicultural Counseling**

MODEL	LIMITATIONS
Psychoanalytic	Focus on insight, intrapsychic dynamics, and long-term treatment is often not valued by clients who prefer to learn coping skills in dealing with pressing environmental concerns. Internal focus is often in conflict with cultural values that stress an interpersonal and environmental focus.
Adlerian	This approach's detailed interview about one's family background can conflict with cultures that have injunctions against disclosing family matters. Leader needs to make certain that the goals of members are respected and that these goals are congruent with the goals of a given group.
Psychodrama	Emphasis on experiencing and expressing feelings, on catharsis, and on enacting past problems in the present can be highly threatening for some clients. Caution needed in encouraging clients to display their intense emotions in presence of others.
Existential	Its values of individuality, freedom, autonomy, and self-realization often conflict with cultural values of collectivism, respect for tradition, deference to authority, and interdependence. Some may be deterred by absence of specific techniques. Others will expect more focus on surviving in their world.
Person-centered	Some of the core values of this approach may not be congruent with the client's culture. Lack of leader direction and structure are unacceptable for many clients who are seeking help and immediate answers from knowledgeable leader.

The functions of the leader that are especially important at the pregroup phase are developing a clear proposal for a specific group; recruiting, screening, and selecting members; providing orientation to the members so that they can derive the maximum gains from the experience; and, ideally, arranging for a preliminary group session to help members get acquainted and provide some teaching about the nature and functioning of groups.

Theories Applied to the Initial Stage

Basic Characteristics.   The early phase of a group is a time for orientation and exploration. Some of the distinguishing characteristics at this time are the following: Members are attempting to find a place in the group. They are trying to get acquainted and learn what a group is all about. They are gradually learning the norms and expectations. Interactions tend to be of a socially acceptable nature and somewhat on the surface, and there is a certain tentativeness within the group. Perhaps the most basic issue per-

Table 17-6 *(continued)*

MODEL	LIMITATIONS
Gestalt	Clients who have been culturally conditioned to be emotionally reserved may not embrace Gestalt techniques. It is important not to quickly push for expressing feelings until relationship is established. Some may not see how "being aware of present experiencing" will lead to solving their problems.
Transactional analysis	Terminology of TA may distract clients from some cultures with a different perspective. Leader must establish clear contract of what client wants before challenging client's life scripts, cultural and familial injunctions, and decisions. Caution required in probing into family patterns.
Behavior therapy	Leaders need to help members assess the possible consequences of making behavioral changes. Family members may not value clients' newly acquired assertive style, so clients must be taught how to cope with resistance by others.
Rational-emotive therapy	If leader has a forceful and directive leadership style, members may retreat. It is necessary to understand client's world before forcefully attacking beliefs perceived as irrational by leader.
Reality therapy	This approach stresses taking charge of one's own life, yet some members hope to change their external environment. Leader needs to appreciate the role of discrimination and racism and help clients deal with social and political realities.

tains to creating and maintaining trust. The attitudes and behaviors of the group leader are directly related to the creation of a level of trust that will promote significant interaction.

Drawing on Theories. The relationship-oriented approaches, especially person-centered therapy and existential therapy, provide an excellent foundation for building a community characterized by trust and the willingness to take the risks that are necessary for change. The leader's modeling is especially important, for it is my belief that members learn more from what the leader does than from what he or she says. Here is where enthusiasm about groups can be communicated to the members by a dedicated, competent, and caring group leader. A basic sense of respect for what the members are experiencing as they approach a new group can best be demonstrated by a leader's willingness to allow members to express what they are thinking and feeling in the here and now. Typically, members do have some initial anxieties. They may fear an unfamiliar situation, rejection, or closeness. Some may fear opening up more than they will be able to manage, disrupting their life outside the group, or incurring the disapproval of others in the group. A genuine interest in listening to these feelings sets the tone for caring, attentiveness, and compassion and goes a long way toward creating a climate in which members can be free to share what they feel and think.

Besides encouraging members to express their feelings, I draw on the cognitive therapies. Thus, members come to a group with certain expectations of themselves and of what they think a group can do for them. Some may expect others to provide them with answers to their problems, some may expect to get from the group what they see themselves as missing in their relationships at home and work, and some may be convinced that a group will not really help them. Such expectations need to be stated and addressed at the early sessions.

Defining Personal Goals.   It is during the initial stage that the *behavioral* approaches and the *cognitive* therapies have special relevance. I like the behavioral emphasis on helping members identify concrete aspects of their behavior that they most want to change. From there the leader may do some teaching to show members how involvement in the group can be instrumental in attaining their goals. I see it as counterproductive for leaders to impose on members specific goals that they should work toward, for unless the members really want to change, there is little hope that change can be forced on them. For this reason I value the Adlerian concept of goal alignment. Adlerians make special efforts to negotiate a congruence of goals between the client and the therapist. TA groups are also characterized by mutually agreed-on therapeutic goals. In reality-therapy groups there is emphasis on asking members to evaluate their wants and to determine whether these desires are realistic. Reality therapy also challenges members to look at their behavior and decide whether it is working for them. If members make the value judgment that their current behavior is not working, the process of making specific behavioral changes can begin. If members are not aided in making an evaluation of their wants, needs, and current behavior, they find it very difficult to know where to begin. Careful consideration of this personal evaluation is a way to engage the group members and to motivate them to do something different. Of course, the skill in group leading involves showing members how a group can help them get what they say they want. I cannot overstress the importance of inducing the members to decide if they really want to change some of their feelings, thoughts, and behaviors.

Although I am very sympathetic toward the existential goal of learning how to live more creatively by accepting freedom and responsibility, I think such broad goals need to be narrowed down so that members have a clear idea of what feelings, thoughts, and actions they are willing to change and can learn how to make such changes. A way to help members specify their goals is to ask them to write them down. Questions such as the following can be useful: "What do I want to change about myself? Do any of my thoughts lead to unwanted feelings? What would I like more of or less of? What am I willing to do to make the specific changes that I say I want to make? What are some short-range goals that I want to attain in this group?"

Theories Applied to the Transition Stage

Learning to Deal with Conflict and Resistance. One of the most challenging and often frustrating periods in the life of a group is the transition phase. Before a group can progress to the working stage, it typically must learn to recognize and deal with anxiety, defensiveness, resistance, conflict, the struggle for control, challenges to the leader, and various other problematic behaviors. Some groups reach the transitional period only to remain stuck there. This impasse can be traced either to an earlier failure to establish norms or to inept handling of resistance and conflict within the group. It is essential that conflict be both recognized and then dealt with therapeutically if the group is to move forward. One way to recognize resistance is to regularly assess the group members' level of satisfaction with their participation in the group. This can be done in a brief written evaluation, which can then be tabulated and brought back to the group. It is useful to get members used to regular assessments, for in this way problems within the group can be detected and then worked on in the sessions. Specific questions can be asked about each member's level of investment, satisfaction with the sessions, trust level, and willingness to take risks. You might refer to the student manual of this text for ideas about inventories that can be used to assess group process. Of course, this type of assessment is consistent with behavioral approaches that stress specificity of behavior, outcomes, and regular feedback about the process as a way to determine whether the group interventions are effective.

Again, the role of leader modeling is critical when it comes to accepting and dealing with resistance. At times, leaders create resistance or make it worse by what they say or do. If leaders take too personally any problems that occur within the group, they burden themselves and tend to become defensive. It is essential to give members some room to maneuver, to avoid responding sharply or defensively, and, most certainly, to avoid sarcasm. The manner in which the group leader deals with the inevitable resistance that manifests itself in various avoidances and defensive maneuvers will determine how well the group meets the developmental tasks at the transition phase. I hope you will learn how to respect resistance by seeing it as a normal and healthy sign of a group's movement toward autonomy. Rather than viewing resistance as a nuisance to be gotten around, you can help members deal with the sources of their resistance in a therapeutic way.

Ways of Conceptualizing Resistance. Several theoretical perspectives shed some light on the dynamics of resistance and suggest methods of dealing with it constructively. From a psychoanalytic perspective, resistance is seen as anything that prevents members from dealing with unconscious material. It is the unconscious attempt to defend oneself from the anxiety that would arise if the unconscious were uncovered. It helps me to remember that members have to struggle with intrapsychic conflicts as well as interpersonal conflicts. A leader who is sensitive to the ambivalence that members experience in both wanting to be a part of the process of self-discovery and fearing self-knowledge can help participants begin to look at their fears and defenses.

I see ways of combining the psychoanalytic and Adlerian views of resistance. Group members typically reexperience some of the old feelings they had in their original family. Sibling rivalry, position in the group, acceptance/rejection feelings, strivings for attention and success, authority issues, managing of negative feelings, and childhood traumas all surface in the group experience. People are often stuck in a developmental sense because of these unfinished situations that now intrude on their ability to function effectively. In many ways the group resembles one's family of origin. By working with their projections, transferences, attractions, and other feelings toward others in the group, the members can experiment with new ways of thinking about themselves and others.

A Thinking/Feeling/Behaving Perspective.   When a group is in transition, I appreciate the freedom given by the person-centered approach to express any feelings and have this expression accepted. My hope is that members will allow themselves to *feel* the ways in which they are resisting and to intensify those feelings. Here is where I draw on some of the action-oriented techniques of Gestalt therapy and psychodrama so that clients will have a way to experience as fully as possible whatever they feel. It is important to assess what clients need, however, and to work within the framework of their cultural background. Some members, because of their cultural injunctions, would have a difficult time getting involved in the emotional aspects of Gestalt experiments or emotionally intense psychodramas. It is certainly not therapeutically productive to push clients to experience emotions, but it could be helpful to explore with them their reluctance to share their emotions.

At some point I would also want to work with the belief systems and self-talk of the members. Here is where I find transactional analysis, rational-emotive therapy, and the cognitive therapies of value. For example, a member might participate very little in a group because she is following certain parental injunctions, such as "Don't show other people what you feel." "Don't talk in public about your family and personal problems." "Don't trust others." "Be strong, and don't give in to feelings of self-pity." I think TA provides a useful framework within which members can gain awareness of these parental messages and their early decisions. Although a group experience can help these clients eventually challenge the validity of certain messages, it is important to avoid confronting some of these values too quickly. Patience and respect are extremely important at this time.

RET is also of value in helping members challenge some of the self-defeating beliefs that lead to an entrenchment of their defensiveness in the group. A member may say very little because of his fear of disapproval or because he has convinced himself that he must say things "perfectly" so that others will understand him. Once members allow themselves to experience their resistance on a feeling level, they are better able to genuinely challenge their cognitions. Here is where writing helps again. If members can be encouraged to keep a journal of their thoughts (and how these thoughts lead to some unwanted behaviors and feelings), they can then do some in-depth exploration of certain self-talk that is not productive. They can learn new and more functional cognitions, and they can practice them both in and out of group. Related to this is their willingness to begin to behave in different ways. I like the emphasis of reality therapy on paying attention to what one is *doing* and RET's emphasis on the need to practice new behaviors as the basis for making lasting changes. Reality therapy provides some particularly useful questions that can lead members to make plans for change. This planning can be one way for members to actually begin to act differently.

Theories Applied to the Working Stage

During the working stage there is a commitment by members to explore the significant problems that they bring to the sessions and to express their reactions to what is taking place within the group. I find that this stage requires the least degree of structuring. In part this is because members bring up issues they want to work on, freely interact with one another, have the feeling of being a group rather than a bunch of strangers, and assume responsibility to keep the sessions moving.

Concepts and Techniques.   My preference is to let the members raise the issues they are willing to seriously pursue rather than taking the responsibility for calling on them, drawing them out, or telling them what they should talk about. I still find it helpful to ask members to create their own agenda for each meeting, and I like to begin a group session by asking each person to declare in a clear sentence what he or she wants for the session. This does not imply a passive stance, however, for during the working stage I am very willing to suggest experiments and to invite members to take part in a technique that is designed to heighten whatever it is that they are experiencing. Again, my concern is with the thinking, feeling, and doing dimensions, and the techniques I suggest reflect this type of integration. Once members declare that they do want to work and we decide what it is they want to accomplish, I typically ask them if they are willing to participate in an experiment.

Generally, I prefer to begin with helping members get into contact with what they are feeling in the here and now. Gestalt techniques are most useful in focusing on present-centered awareness and bringing any unfinished business from the past to the surface. I favor the approach that asks members to bring any past issue into the present, as is true of both psychodrama and Gestalt. There is a lively quality to the work, and members rather quickly begin to experience what they feel rather than talking abstractly about feelings and thoughts. For example, if a woman becomes aware that she is afraid that she is growing up to be just like the mother she resents, a good place to begin is to ask her to "bring your mother into the group" symbolically. Again, Gestalt and psychodrama offer a rich range of techniques to help her get into focus and intensify her experience. She might experiment with assuming her mother's identity and actually speaking to others in the group "as her mother." Although I value the contact with feelings, I think it is pseudowork to stop with catharsis or the mere expression of her feelings. I am likely to suggest that she identify some of the beliefs that she has picked up from her mother. Perhaps she has uncritically accepted some irrational ideas that she is stubbornly clinging to and is keeping herself upset by living by untested assumptions.

Coupled with her emotional work, some exploration of her cognitions is likely to reveal how her daily behavior is limiting her. Therefore, I see debates as productive in a group. Especially valuable are debates that members can learn to have with themselves. They can challenge untested assumptions, argue the pros and cons of a given issue, and think about how they sometimes set themselves up for defeat. Working at a *behavioral* level is an excellent way to correct faulty thinking and emotional disturbances. For example, Luigi says that he has a low estimation of his worth, that he feels depressed and anxious much of the time, and that he is afraid to ask for what he wants. Rather than waiting around until he feels better and begins to think differently about himself, I suggest ways that he might begin to behave differently. My assumption is that if he begins to behave more assertively, he may like himself better and eventually change his view of the person he is. Role playing, behavioral rehearsals, and other behaviorally oriented techniques can teach him some of the social skills he needs to function effectively. Of course, during the working and final phase I encourage him to practice new behaviors in a variety of social settings and bring the results back to the group.

My particular emphasis during the working phase is to focus on what members are doing outside of the sessions. Therefore, I like to allow time toward the end of each session to ask every member to respond to questions such as "What did you learn about yourself in today's session? What kind of behaviors can you practice during the week? What is one specific homework assignment that you are willing to give yourself and carry out?" This approach reinforces in-group learning, and it helps members continually think about how to apply new ways of thinking and behaving in everyday situations.

Theories Applied to the Final Stage

Review of Tasks.   The final stage of the group's evolution is critical, for members have an opportunity to clarify the meaning of their experiences in the group, to consolidate the gains they have made, and to revise their decisions about what newly acquired behaviors they want to transfer to their daily life. The major task facing members during this consolidation stage is to learn ways of maintaining these changed behaviors in the outside world. My focus is on getting the members to review the nature of any changes on a thinking/feeling/behaving level. Have they learned the value of expressing negative feelings rather than swallowing them? Have they learned that repressing their feelings results in some indirect expression of them? What cognitions have they modified? Have they let go of some dysfunctional cognitions that lead to emotional upsets? Have they challenged their beliefs and values and made them their own? What concrete behavioral changes have they made that they value? How did they make these changes? How can they continue to behave in ways that are productive? What plan for action can they devise now that the group is coming to an end so that they can continue to make progress?

Theoretical Perspectives.   I tend to use the most structure during the beginning and ending phases of a group. It is not my style to hope that members will automatically transfer specific emotional, cognitive, and behavioral changes from the group to the outside world. Therefore, I provide a structure that I hope will promote this transfer of learning. I have mentioned that in ongoing groups I do whatever I can to promote action on the part of the members by getting them to create their own homework assignments and then to report of their progress at the next group meeting. This is a way of continually using the group as a place to learn how to be different and then of carrying this new behavior into life. The group is a means to an end and should never become an end in itself.

Whereas I tend to use experiential therapies and exploration of feelings during the working phase, I lean during the final stage toward the cognitive-behavioral therapies and toward putting one's learning into some type of conceptual framework. From the behavioral therapies I draw techniques such as practice and rehearsal for leaving a group, self-monitoring procedures, building a support system beyond the group, and learning methods of self-reinforcement. Since I see therapy as a teaching/learning process, I try to help members devise a conceptual framework that will ensure that they make sense of what they have experienced. Therefore, at the final stage I tend to ask over and over: "What did you learn in this group that you valued, and how did you learn it?" I don't want members attributing their changes to the magic of the group but, rather, to specific actions that they took to change. Both RET and reality therapy are relevant models at this point in a group's history, since they stress the importance of developing specific plans for change, making a commitment to do what is needed to bring about change, and evaluating the outcomes of the therapeutic process. Although members are urged to try out a plan of action during the working phase, it is during the final stage that such a plan is essential. It is also important to help members find ways to continue to build on their newly acquired skills. Members can promote their change by deciding toward the end of the group on other paths for growth. They can make decisions about specific activities that will keep challenging them. They can make contracts to behave in certain ways once the group ends.

It should not be assumed, because of the emphasis I am placing on cognitive work and behavioral plans for action during the final stage, that feelings are unimportant at this time. I see it as critical that members deal with their feelings about separation and termination, that they express any fears or reservations they may have about making it in the world without the support of the group, and that they learn how to say good-bye. Also, the opportunity to complete any unfinished business is paramount at this time.

During the ending stage the leader needs to watch for certain dangers. Members may avoid reviewing their experience and fail to put it into some cognitive framework, thus limiting the generalization of their learning. And because of their anxiety over separation, some members may distance themselves and thus get less benefit from the group. Toward the end of a group's history there is a place for the role of the leader as a teacher. Leaders can caution members and provide them with practical strategies for dealing with setbacks once they leave a group. Members need to learn that the path toward growth is bumpy and uneven. At this time they can be taught how to evaluate the impact of the group on them as well as assess the progress they have made as a group.

Theories Applied to Postgroup Issues

After the group comes to an end, the members' main task is applying their in-group learning to an action program in their daily life so that they can function in self-directed ways. I value setting aside time for individual interviews with each member, if possible, along with arranging for a follow-up group session. Such procedures build in accountability, for both the members and the leader can more accurately assess the impact of the group. Again, the behavioral approaches stress this accountability and evaluation, which enable the leader to make modifications in future groups based on what seemed to work. Follow-up procedures also provide a safety valve, for if members left the group with unresolved or negative feelings, they can at least discuss them with the group leader.

I hope you will see that groups can be effective if there is careful planning to bring about change. It should by now be obvious that changes in one's thinking, feeling, and behaving come about as a result of conscious strategies. Once such changes have been achieved, one cannot assume that they will automatically be permanent; this is why I devote attention to designing ways of extending such changes beyond the life of the group.

The Pros and Cons of an Eclectic Model

As I've said many times, I am convinced that each practitioner must find a style that fits him or her as a person; the model I've described is the result of my own search for an approach to groups that fits me both professionally and personally. It is a model that reflects my view of groups as entities that express in an integrated fashion the feeling, thinking, and doing dimensions of individual members. It also combines the didactic with the experiential, since I believe that what we experience in a group needs to be supported by a conceptual framework. Without such a framework, it would be impossible for us to make sense of the experience and to understand its implications for our daily existence. Finally, it is a model that brings together the action-oriented, the insight-oriented, and the experientially oriented approaches—that is, the affective, cognitive, and behavioral dimensions—to pursue more effectively the basic goal of any therapeutic group: change.

There are many limitations in subscribing totally to the tenets of a single model. If you become a rigid follower of any one approach, you may overlook valuable dimensions of human behavior and unduly limit your effectiveness with different clients by trying to force them to fit into the confines of your theory. Yet I want to encourage you to give each of the theories that you have studied a fair chance. You'll need to do much more reading about those theories that you found especially valuable. In addition, attending workshops where you can experience these approaches is vital in helping you decide which techniques you might want to incorporate in your personal style of leadership. Effective leaders are continually defining and refining a personalized group theory that guides them in their practice and allows them to make sense of what occurs in groups. Of course, the specific type of group that you are leading and the makeup of its clients are critical variables in deciding what strategies are most appropriate. Be open to modifying your techniques so that they fit the needs of the members of the group, including their social and cultural background.

Having said all that, I wish to add that there are some dangers in encouraging an eclectic approach. At its worst, eclecticism can be an excuse for sloppy practice, a practice that lacks a systematic rationale for what you actually do in your work. If you pick and choose according to whims, it is likely that what you select is merely the reflection of your biases and preconceived ideas. At its best, however, eclecticism can be a creative synthesis and a selective blending of the unique contributions of diverse theories, a dynamic integration of those concepts and techniques that fit the group leader's unique personality and style.

Concluding Comments

It has been my experience that between the first and the last day of an introductory course in group counseling, students find that what seemed at first to be an overwhelming mass of knowledge and a bewildering array of theories eventually becomes a manageable store of understanding about the basis of counseling. Although, as most students recognize, a survey course does not turn prospective counselors into accomplished group leaders, the survey course on the theory and practice of group counseling does give students a basis for selecting from the many models to which they are exposed those therapeutic procedures that may be most useful and practical for them.

It is my hope that this will be your experience and that, at this point in the course, you will begin putting the theories together for yourself. Be patient enough to recognize that much of the theoretical foundation you have received in this book will take on new meanings as you gain more practical experience in leading various groups. The same is true for the many professional and ethical issues that were discussed in the book. I think it's essential that you reflect on these basic issues, that you begin to formulate your own position on them, and that you discuss them with fellow students and instructors. Keep in mind, though, that these issues will also assume different meanings and dimensions once you confront them in your own practice. I am convinced, however, that, even though experience will teach you many new lessons, you will be far better equipped to deal with these and related issues when you meet them if you have reflected on them now.

I hope that this book and the manual that accompanies it have stimulated you to think productively about group process, to read more and learn more about the topics we have explored together, and to seek group experience both as a member and as a leader. I am sincerely interested in getting feedback from you regarding this textbook and the accompanying manual as well as your experience in your own training program. I'll welcome and value any suggestions for making this book more useful in future revisions. You can use the tear-out evaluation at the end of this book or write to me in care of Brooks/Cole Publishing Company, Pacific Grove, California 93950-5098.

Name Index

Subject Index

545

To the owner of this book:

I hope that you have enjoyed *Theory and Practice of Group Counseling* (3rd Edition) as much as I enjoyed writing it. I'd like to know as much about your experiences with the book as you care to offer. Only through your comments and the comments of others can I learn how to make this a better book for future readers.

School: _____

Address of school (city, state, and zip code): _____

_____

Your instructor's name: _____

1. What did you like *most* about *Theory and Practice of Group Counseling?* _____

_____

_____

2. What did you like *least* about the book? _____

_____

3. Were all the chapters of the book assigned for you to read? _____

(If not, which ones weren't?) _____

4. How interesting and informative was the last chapter (Chapter 17)? _____

_____

_____

5. What material do you think could be omitted in future editions? _____

_____

_____

_____

6. If you used the student manual, how helpful was it as an aid in understanding concepts and theoretical approaches? _____

_____

_____

7. In the space below or in a separate letter, please let me know what other comments about the book you'd like to make. (For example, were any chapters *or* concepts particularly difficult?) Please recommend specific changes you'd like to see in future editions. I'd be delighted to hear from you!

Optional:

Your name: _____ Date: _____

May Brooks/Cole quote you, either in promotion for *Theory and Practice of Group Counseling* or in future publishing ventures?

Yes _____ No _____

Sincerely,

Gerald Corey

FOLD HERE

- -

||| |||

BUSINESS REPLY MAIL

FIRST CLASS   PERMIT NO. 358   PACIFIC GROVE, CA

POSTAGE WILL BE PAID BY ADDRESSEE

ATT: **Dr. Gerald Corey**
Brooks/Cole Publishing Company
511 Forest Lodge Road
Pacific Grove, California 93950-9968

||.|....||.|.|....|.|.||....|.|....|.|....||..|..|....|.||

FOLD HERE